Visions of Antiquity

Visions *of* Antiquity

Neoclassical Figure Drawings

Richard J. Campbell and Victor Carlson

with contributions by

Sylvain Bellenger

Edgar Peters Bowron

Bjarne Jørnæs

Lisa Dickinson Michaux

Stig Miss

Marsha Morton

Los Angeles County Museum of Art The Minneapolis Institute of Arts

COPUBLISHED BY
Los Angeles County Museum of Art
5905 Wilshire Boulevard
Los Angeles, California 90036
and
The Minneapolis Institute of Arts
2400 Third Avenue South
Minneapolis, Minnesota 55404

This book was published in conjunction with the exhibition *Visions of Antiquity: Neoclassical Figure Drawings*, which was jointly organized by the Los Angeles County Museum of Art and the Minneapolis Institute of Arts and was made possible by a grant from the National Endowment for the Arts.

EXHIBITION ITINERARY
Los Angeles County Museum of Art
July 22–September 19, 1993

Philadelphia Museum of Art
October 30, 1993–January 2, 1994

The Minneapolis Institute of Arts
February 6–April 3, 1994

The essay and entries by Sylvain Bellenger were translated by Garrett White.

Edited by Susan L. Caroselli and Chris Keledjian
Designed by Jim Drobka
Production assistance by Eileen Delson
Typeset in Bodoni, Bembo, and Meridian typefaces by Andresen Graphic Services, Tucson, Arizona
Printed by Typecraft, Inc., Pasadena, California
Bound by Roswell Bookbinding, Phoenix, Arizona

COVER
Pierre-Paul Prud'hon, *Venus*, c. 1810–12, CATALOGUE NO. 44

TITLE PAGE
John Flaxman, *Leucothea Preserving Ulysses*, 1792, CATALOGUE NO. 8

LIBRARY OF CONGRESS
CATALOGING-IN-PUBLICATION DATA

Visions of antiquity: neoclassical figure drawings / Richard J. Campbell and Victor Carlson ; with contributions by Sylvain Bellenger . . . [et al.].
p. cm.
"Exhibition itinerary, Los Angeles County Museum of Art, July 22–September 19, 1993; Philadelphia Museum of Art, October 30, 1993–January 2, 1994; the Minneapolis Institute of Arts, February 6–April 3, 1994"—T.p. verso.
Includes bibliographical references and index.
ISBN 0-295-97309-9
1. Human figure in art—Exhibitions. 2. Neoclassicism (Art)—Exhibitions. 3. Drawing—18th century—Exhibitions. 4. Drawing—19th century—Exhibitions. I. Campbell, Richard J. (Richard James), 1948– . II. Carlson, Victor I. III. Bellenger, Sylvain. IV. Los Angeles County Museum of Art. V. Minneapolis Institute of Arts.
NC87.5.N46V57 1993
741.94'09'03307473—dc20
93-15097
CIP

NOTE TO THE READER
Throughout the text the reader will find references (for example, "New York 1962") to publications that are fully cited in the Bibliography, which begins on page 331.

PHOTO CREDITS
Photographs are reproduced courtesy of the owners of the works, except in the following instances:

Jörg P. Anders, Berlin: figs. 39–40
Art Resource, New York: cat. no. 90, fig. 3
Scott Bowron Photography, New York: cat. no. 59
Will Brown: cat. no. 79
Richard Caspole, Yale Center for British Art: cat. nos. 6, 10; fig. 4
© 1985 Founders Society, Detroit Institute of Arts: cat. nos. 15, 23
Norman Jones Fine Art Photography: cat. no. 77
The Minneapolis Institute of Arts: cat. no. 53
The Trustees of the Pierpont Morgan Library: cat. nos. 9, 17, 36
© 1992 Trustees of Princeton University: cat. nos. 1, 50; fig. 19
© Rijksmuseum-Stichting Amsterdam: fig. 42
Service de Documentation Photographique, Réunion des Musées Nationaux, Paris: figs. 5, 8–9, 13, 43–44, 46–50
Statens Konstmuseer, Stockholm: figs. 21, 36
Jim Strong, Hempstead, New York: cat. no. 72
Ole Woldbye, copyright Thorvaldsens Museum, Copenhagen: fig. 15
Horst Ziegenfusz, Frankfurt am Main: fig. 25

Contents

Foreword

The period encompassed by this exhibition and catalogue lasted roughly eight decades, from about 1760 until 1830. The political, social, and artistic innovations of this revolutionary epoch have had repercussions that are felt even today. Philosophers, scientists, writers, and artists shared a belief that human nature could be perfected through education, that the relations between the individual and government could be reordered to create a more equitable social structure, and that scientific investigation of the world could provide resources to build a more prosperous society. This epoch has been called the Age of Reason or the Enlightenment in recognition of the belief in the perfectibility of humans and their world.

During this time the visual arts throughout Europe underwent a profound revolution or, some would say, a reinvigoration that countered the baroque and rococo traditions that came before. To effect this visual and cultural revolution artists and critics turned to the past, to the distant glories of Greek and Roman civilization, aided in their search by the new discipline of archaeology and the flood of publications that spread a renewed interest in and knowledge of the classical past throughout Europe. No artist working at this time, whether painter, sculptor, or architect, could entirely escape the influence of the classical tradition. This neoclassical style has never been easy to define in simple, convenient generalizations. Individual temperaments as well as the conditions under which artists worked varied greatly. It is the goal of this exhibition to investigate one facet of this visual phenomenon, that of figure drawing. A command of the human form has always been the most basic aspect of an artist's education in Western civilizations. Figure drawings are at once the most essential and the most spontaneous evidence of artists' knowledge of the classical past.

The development and execution of this exhibition proved to be a lengthy and complex undertaking, ably carried out by Richard Campbell, curator of Prints and Drawings at the Minneapolis Institute of Arts, and Victor Carlson, senior curator of Prints and Drawings at the Los Angeles County Museum of Art. It is a pleasure to acknowledge the successful realization of this project by them and their able coworkers in both institutions. We are grateful to the National Endowment for the Arts for generous subventions essential to the planning and fulfillment of this exhibition and catalogue and to our many lenders, whose generosity has made it all possible.

MICHAEL E. SHAPIRO
Director
Los Angeles County Museum of Art

EVAN M. MAURER
Director
The Minneapolis Institute of Arts

Acknowledgments

When this exhibition was conceived, we expected that most of the drawings to be borrowed could be located in private and public collections in the United States. Neoclassical drawings have long been an interest of American collectors, a situation that in no small part is due to the enthusiasm and scholarship of the late Tony Clark, one of the foremost scholars of eighteenth-century Roman art and director of the Minneapolis Institute of Arts from 1963 until 1973. In the course of planning the exhibition, however, several exceptional opportunities arose to borrow from European collections extraordinary drawings by artists not well represented in America. In many respects the selection of Italian drawings in this exhibition reflects the interests of Clark; in fact, he once owned a number of these sheets. American collections are lacking in important drawings by Italy's greatest neoclassical artist, the sculptor Antonio Canova, and we are most grateful to Paola Marini of the Museo Civico, Bassano, and Giandomenico Romanelli of the Biblioteca Correr, Venice, for allowing the important sheets in their collections to be shown here. We would like sincerely to thank Sylvain Bellenger, who made it possible for us to represent Anne-Louis Girodet de Roussy-Trioson by some of his most brilliant works on paper, never before shown in the United States; Bellenger, former director of the Musée Girodet, Montargis, also contributed an essay on Girodet's draftsmanship and wrote the relevant catalogue entries. The representation of Girodet in the exhibition is further enhanced by the exceptional loan of his wonderful pastel, for which we wish to acknowledge Catherine Buret, curator of the Musée de l'Avallonnais, Avallon. Drawings by Scandinavia's major neoclassical artists are virtually absent from American collections, thus we gratefully welcome the exceptional loan of some of the finest known drawings by Nikolai Abraham Abildgaard, Asmus Jacob Carstens, Christoffer Wilhelm Eckersberg, and Johan Tobias Sergel, which are being shown for the first time in the United States through the kindness of Chris Fischer, head of the Königlichen Kupferstichsammlung at the Statens Museum, Copenhagen. The loan of a brilliant selection of drawings by one of Denmark's greatest neoclassical artists, the sculptor Bertel Thorvaldsen, never before lent to America, has been made possible because of the generosity of Stig Miss, director, and Bjarne Jørnæs, curator, of the Thorvaldsens Museum, both of whom also contributed catalogue entries.

We wish also to acknowledge the warm support of our other institutional lenders: Harry S. Parker III, director, Robert Johnson, curator in charge, and Karin Breuer, associate curator, at the Achenbach Foundation for the Graphic Arts; Charles W. Millard III, director, and Timothy Riggs, assistant director, at the Ackland Art Museum; Arnold L. Lehman, director, and Jay M. Fisher, curator of Prints, Drawings, and Photographs, at the Baltimore Museum of Art; James N. Wood, director, Douglas Druick, Prince Trust curator of Prints and Drawings and Searle curator of European Painting, and Suzanne McCullagh, curator of Earlier Prints and Drawings, at the Art Institute of Chicago; Evan H. Turner, director, Jane Glaubinger, curator of Prints and Drawings, and Michael J. Miller, assistant curator of Prints and Drawings, at the Cleveland Museum of Art; Dianne Pilgrim, director, and Marilyn Symmes, curator of Drawings and Prints, at the Cooper-Hewitt Museum; Barbara K. Gibbs, director, and Peter J. Flagg, associate curator, at the Crocker Art Museum; Samuel Sachs II, director, and Ellen Sharp, curator of Graphic Arts, at the Detroit Institute of Arts; James Cuno, director, William Robinson, Ian Woodner curator of Drawings, and Miriam Stewart, assistant curator of Drawings, at the Fogg Art Museum; John Walsh, director, and George R. Goldner, curator of Paintings and Drawings, at the J. Paul Getty Museum; Timothy Rub, director of the Hood Museum of Art; Philippe de Montebello, director, the late Jacob Bean, formerly curator of Drawings, and Helen B. Mules, associate curator of Drawings, at the Metropolitan Museum of Art; Charles E. Pierce, Jr., director, Peter Dreyer, curator and head of the Prints and Drawings

Department, and Cara D. Denison, curator of Prints and Drawings, at the Pierpont Morgan Library; J. Carter Brown, former director, Andrew Robison, curator of Prints and Drawings, and Margaret Morgan Grasselli, curator of Old Master Drawings, at the National Gallery of Art; Shirley L. Thomson, director, and Mimi Cazort, curator of Prints and Drawings, at the National Gallery of Canada; Allen Rosenbaum, director, and Barbara T. Ross, associate curator of Prints and Drawings, at the Art Museum, Princeton University; Franklin W. Robinson, director, and Maureen C. O'Brien, curator of Prints, Drawings, and Photographs, at the Museum of Art, Rhode Island School of Design; Villads Villadsen, director of the Statens Museum, Copenhagen; James D. Burke, director, and Barbara Butts, curator of Prints, Drawings, and Photographs, at the Saint Louis Art Museum; Suzannah Fabing, director, and Ann H. Sievers, associate curator of Prints, Drawings, and Photographs, at the Smith College Museum of Art; Wanda Corn, acting director, and Betsy Fryberger, curator of Prints and Drawings, at the Stanford University Museum and Art Gallery; and Duncan Robinson, director, and Patrick Noon, curator of Prints, Drawings, and Rare Books, at the Yale Center for British Art.

Collectors who live with their works of art feel their absence most vividly; we consequently appreciate the generous loans from Robert A. Tuggle, M. and Mme. Hubert Prouté, the late Martin L. H. Reymert, Ivan and Neil Phillips, Louis-Antoine Prat, Mr. and Mrs. Steven Broidy, Stevan Baloga, and Dr. and Mrs. John Weber, and several anonymous collectors. The assistance of Joseph Baillio, Mark Brady, David Daniels, Annamaria Edelstein, Neal Fiertag, Phyllis Hattis, Steven Mazoh, Marianne Roland Michel, and Wheelock Whitney was essential in securing the loan of several major drawings.

We would like to thank the many colleagues and friends whose aid was invaluable during the research and organization of our project. From the outset the directors of the sponsoring institutions and their boards of trustees supported the project. It is a pleasure to thank Earl A. Powell III, former director of the Los Angeles County Museum of Art and now director of the National Gallery, Washington, D.C., and Evan M. Maurer, director of the Minneapolis Institute of Arts, for their interest and practical help.

At the Los Angeles County Museum of Art Bruce Davis, curator of Prints and Drawings, ably assisted Victor Carlson at all times and cheerfully assumed numerous administrative burdens that permitted Carlson to concentrate on the exhibition. The secretary to the Department of Prints and Drawings, Catherine Sturgeon, typed much of the manuscript and attended to the many, and often vexing, details with her customary expertise and command of administrative tasks. In the museum's Department of Exhibitions Elizabeth Algermissen and John Passi were most helpful, especially in arranging that the exhibition would be shared with the Philadelphia Museum of Art. In the Registrar's Office Renée Montgomery, Tamra Yost, and Mikal Sebens capably handled shipping arrangements for some of the foreign loans. Research on the catalogue went more smoothly thanks to the Research Library's staff, in particular Eleanor Hartman and Anne Diederick, who were always available. The publication of the exhibition catalogue was supervised by the museum's capable editor in chief, Mitch Tuchman. The content of the catalogue was edited by Susan Caroselli, whose thoroughness and professionalism has placed all of the contributors in her debt. Chris Keledjian served as the production editor. Jim Drobka is responsible for the catalogue's attractive design.

At the Minneapolis Institute of Arts Timothy Fiske, associate director, reviewed the grant applications and participated in the negotiations of the exhibition contracts. Michael P. Conforti, chief curator, provided advice and encouragement from the outset to the completion of the project. Beth Desnick, former exhibitions coordinator, collaborated in drafting our successful applications for preliminary and implementation grants from the National Endowment for the Arts; she also oversaw the myriad details of organizing the show with the able assistance of Thea Nelson, exhibitions associate. Mary Cummings, exhibitions administrator, continued the work of Desnick and Nelson with budget development and exhibition coordination. Marcia Riopelle, administrative assistant, efficiently coordinated the loan letters and forms in the Office of the Director. Catherine Ricciardelli, registrar, and Peggy Tolbert, associate registrar, handled the complicated logistics of the exhibition, including loan forms and insurance, and arranged and supervised the transportation of the drawings. Harold Peterson, librarian, Michael K. Boe, assistant librarian, and Brian Mulhern, assistant librarian, rendered invaluable aid in purchasing reference materials, arranging interlibrary loans, and providing bibliographic information. Dennis Michael Jon, curatorial assistant, attended to the countless, day-to-day responsibilities that allowed Richard Campbell to pursue his research and complete the writing of his catalogue essay and entries. Lisa Dickinson Michaux, curatorial intern, wrote the artists' biographies and engaged in bibliographic research. Mave Lawler, department secretary, typed initial letters of inquiry, loan requests, much of the manuscript, and follow-up correspondence related to the show. Jane Satkowski, curatorial assistant in the Paintings Department, generously assisted in the translation of Italian loan agreements and correspondence.

During the lengthy research necessary for the realization of the exhibition the curators depended on the kindness of many people. Although it is not possible to name each individual, we would like to acknowledge certain persons and institutions who were unfailing in answering our requests. At the Los Angeles County Museum of Art Nancy Thomas, associate curator of Ancient and Islamic Art, gave valuable suggestions concerning the antiquities that artists might have known. The curators, librarians, and photography archivists at the J. Paul Getty Center for the Visual Arts, Malibu, the New York Public Library, Rare Book Department, the Yale Center for British Art, New Haven, the Frick Art Reference Library, New York, the Metropolitan Museum of Art, New York, and the Wilson Library, University of Minnesota, responded to our many queries. At various stages of work on the exhibition the following offered valuable advice and assistance: Gwen Bitz, Anselmo Carini, Elaine Evans Dee, James David Draper, Elizabeth Fairman, Nancy Finlay, Renzo Grandi, William McAllister Johnson, Fred Licht, Robert H. Luck, Austin J. McLean, Phyllis Dearborn Massar, Pierre Rosenberg, Robert Rosenblum, Charles Ryskamp, and Henrietta Susser. Much of the research took place in Paris; at the Musée du Louvre, the Service de Documentation, Département des Peintures, and the Service de Documentation, Département des Arts Graphiques, allowed us access to their incomparable archives of research materials. At the Département des Arts Graphiques, it is a pleasure to thank Arlette Serullaz and Régis Michel for their courteous assistance. We also wish to thank Laure Beaumont-Maillet, conservateur-en-chef at the Cabinet des Estampes, Bibliothèque Nationale, for making available certain restricted research materials.

The content of the exhibition catalogue has benefited immeasurably from the contributions of our three essayists: we are pleased to thank Marsha Morton for her ground-breaking contribution to our knowledge of neoclassicism as it evolved in Germany; Sylvain Bellenger for his writing on Girodet, which should make this major artist better known to an American audience; and Edgar Peters Bowron, an internationally recognized authority on the art of eighteenth-century Rome.

We were gratified when our colleagues at the Philadelphia Museum of Art immediately expressed their interest in hosting the exhibition on the East Coast; our thanks go to Anne d'Harnoncourt, director, Innis H. Shoemaker, senior curator of Prints, Drawings, and Photographs, and Ann Percy, curator of Drawings. Their participation was especially welcome since that institution received through the bequest of Tony Clark an enviable collection of drawings from that period.

It is with profound sadness that the undersigned dedicate this catalogue to the memory of Martin L. H. Reymert (1936–92). His interest, as a dealer, in many of the artists represented here was far in advance of the time, and a number of the drawings chosen for this exhibition were at one time in his possession. Mr. Reymert looked forward to seeing the exhibition, hence this dedication is an inadequate expression of our regret.

VICTOR CARLSON
Senior Curator
Prints and Drawings
Los Angeles County
Museum of Art

RICHARD J. CAMPBELL
Curator
Prints and Drawings
The Minneapolis
Institute of Arts

Lenders to the Exhibition

Ackland Art Museum, University of North Carolina
at Chapel Hill
The Art Institute of Chicago
The Art Museum, Princeton University
The Baltimore Museum of Art
Biblioteca Correr, Venice
The Cleveland Museum of Art
Cooper-Hewitt Museum, New York
Crocker Art Museum, Sacramento
The Detroit Institute of Arts
The Fine Art Museums of San Francisco,
Achenbach Foundation for Graphic Arts
The Fogg Art Museum, Harvard University
Hood Museum of Art, Dartmouth College
The J. Paul Getty Museum, Malibu
Los Angeles County Museum of Art
Lutheran Brotherhood, Minneapolis
The Metropolitan Museum of Art, New York
The Minneapolis Institute of Arts
Musée de l'Avallonnais, Avallon
Musée Girodet, Montargis
Museo Civico di Bassano del Grappa
Museum of Art, Rhode Island School of Design
National Gallery of Art, Washington, D.C.
National Gallery of Canada, Ottawa
Philadelphia Museum of Art
The Pierpont Morgan Library, New York
The Royal Museum of Fine Arts, Copenhagen
The Saint Louis Art Museum
Smith College Museum of Art
Stanford University Museum of Art
Thorvaldsens Museum, Copenhagen
Yale Center for British Art

Stevan Baloga
Caron and Steven Broidy
The Phillips Family Collection
Prat collection, Paris
Private collection, Memphis, Tennessee
Private collection, New York
Private collection, Paris
Private collection, courtesy Phyllis Hattis Fine Arts
Private collection, courtesy Stephen Mazoh & Co., Inc.
Private collection, courtesy Wildenstein & Co., Inc.
Estate of Martin L. H. Reymert
Robert Tuggle

OVERLEAF
Benjamin West
Antiochus and Stratonice
1777
(CATALOGUE NO. 3, detail)

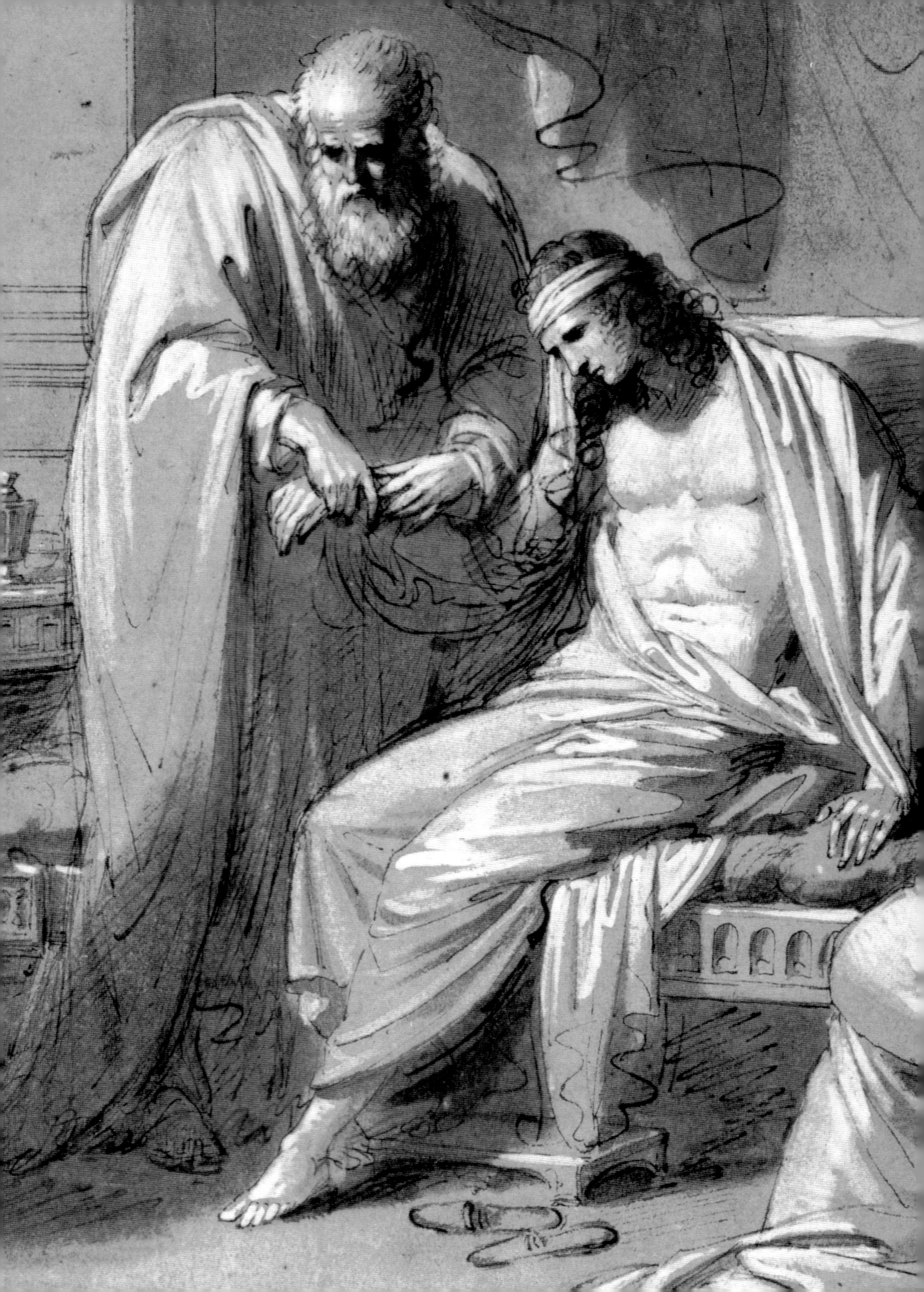

Visions of Antiquity from Mengs to Ingres

RICHARD J. CAMPBELL

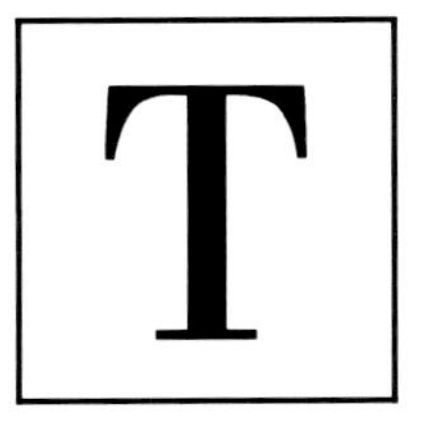

he arts of Graeco-Roman antiquity have served cyclically as a source of inspiration and catalyst for aesthetic reform in the history of western European art from the late thirteenth through the early twentieth centuries.[1] *Visions of Antiquity: Neoclassical Figure Drawings* is focused upon the extraordinary regeneration of the visual arts that transpired in Europe between the years 1760 and 1830. The reasons for this international phenomenon are multiple, diverse, and complex, with roots in Enlightenment philosophy and the sociopolitical upheavals of the French Revolution, the Napoleonic Empire, and the Bourbon Restoration. The exhibition addresses the issue of the influence of Graeco-Roman antiquity on three generations of European artists, from Anton Raphael Mengs in the mid-eighteenth century to Jean-Auguste-Dominique Ingres in the mid-nineteenth, specifically examining how they expressed their respective visions of antiquity in their figure drawings. This essay considers the artistic and historical issues that motivated the drawings.

The multifaceted stylistic trends of this epoch have traditionally been lumped under the catchall label "neoclassical," which came into use in the 1880s.[2] Interestingly, the term was applied in 1881 to Nicolas Poussin's *Landscape with Saint John at Patmos* (The Art Institute of Chicago), 1644–45, in a relatively negative discussion of the painting, then on exhibition at the Royal Academy, London.[3] While artists and critics of the late eighteenth and early nineteenth centuries referred to the then-current revitalization of the arts as the "true style" or "correct style," the Victorian label has prevailed into the twentieth century.

In the course of the past twenty-five years the stylistic manifestations of "neoclassicism" versus "romanticism" have been analyzed and redefined by scholars including Frederick Antal, Walter Friedlaender, Hugh Honour, Mario Praz, and Robert Rosenblum, to name a few. Most recently Régis Michel, in his insightful exhibition catalogue *Le Beau Idéal, ou l'Art du concept*, which focuses primarily on the evolution of figure drawing in France in 1760–1810, proscribes the term *neoclassicism* as the pejorative implication of a vulgar stylistic pastiche of Poussin. Michel speaks instead of a "new classicism," an "art of concept," characterized by a stylistic relationship to phases of aesthetic theory from Johann Joachim Winckelmann to Georg Wilhelm Friedrich Hegel.[4] In our subtitle, *Neoclassical Figure Drawings*, the word has been retained simply as a convenient art-historical point of reference.

The Classical and Baroque Polemic in Rome

To gauge the magnitude of the aesthetic transformations that transpired between 1760 and 1830, it is pertinent to examine the artistic legacy of the previous century. In the first three decades of the seventeenth century Annibale Carracci, his followers Domenichino and Guido Reni, and the expatriate Poussin revived the classical tradition of the high Renaissance in Rome. In his ceiling frescoes for the Palazzo Farnese, 1597–1600, which depict the adventures of Hercules as well as Ovidian themes, Carracci evoked the art of Raphael and his school (specifically the Farnesina and the Vatican Logge decorations) and demonstrated his knowledge of Roman bacchic sarcophagi.[5] For two centuries the Farnese frescoes were praised by critics as paragons of classical art.

Through the influence of his patron Cassiano dal Pozzo, the art of Poussin reflected the most current archaeological research on Graeco-Roman antiquity. Dal Pozzo made available to the artist his collections of statuary and medals, his library, and his celebrated volumes of drawings commissioned from contemporary artists recording the venerated monuments of antiquity and illustrating the modes and mores of life in the ancient world.[6] Nurtured in dal Pozzo's elite circle of intellectuals, Poussin painted his first epic masterpiece, *The Death of Germanicus* (FIGURE 1), 1627, based on the *Annals* of Tacitus, which became a major source of inspiration for generations of artists from 1760 to 1830.[7]

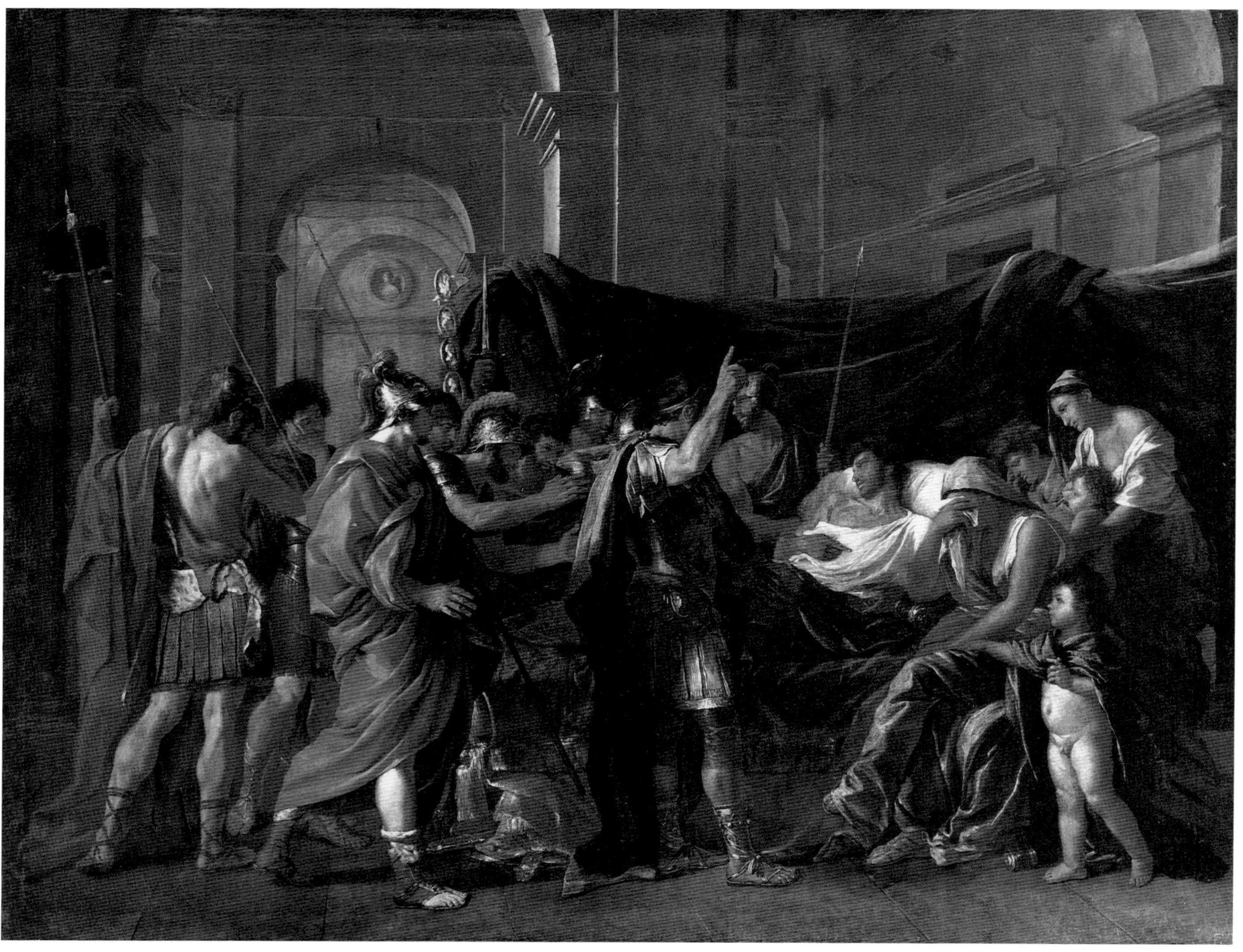

FIGURE I
Nicolas Poussin
France, 1594–1665

The Death of Germanicus
1627, oil on canvas, 148 x 198.1 cm (58 1/4 x 78 in.),
the Minneapolis Institute of Arts, William Hood Dunwoody Fund (inv. no. 58.28)

Rome remained a vital artistic center despite a decline of patronage beginning in the mid-seventeenth century. Stylistic currents were varied, complex, and controversial due to the confluence of the baroque, naturalistic, and classical that had begun early in the century. In 1599, when Carracci was at work on the Farnese ceiling, Michelangelo Merisi, called Caravaggio, was painting his Saint Matthew cycle for the Capella Contarelli in the church San Luigi dei Francesi, a series of intensely mystical, highly individual religious paintings characterized by realism (that is, unembellished nature) and dramatic chiaroscuro. Caravaggio's paintings constituted the antithesis of the classicism of Carracci and his followers, and they incurred the wrath of all but a few connoisseurs for their apparent lack of decorum. While Caravaggio did not establish a school, he inspired many followers, "the Caravaggeschi"—Italians, French, and Flemish—who emulated the master's realism and tenebrism in their genre paintings. Caravaggio's work was to exert an extraordinary influence on the artistic development of a maverick, antiacademic pensioner of the Académie de France, Jacques-Louis David, when he first came to Rome.[8]

The classicizing school of the Carracci was also challenged by the supreme artistic genius of the epoch, Gianlorenzo Bernini. Intellectually, Bernini venerated the art of antiquity and respected principles of classical composition. In practice, however, he espoused a completely different aesthetic. While the Borghese Warrior served as the point of departure for Bernini's famous statue of David, 1623, the latter's dynamic pose, psychological tension, visual dialogue with the spectator, and amalgamation of actual and implied space defy the canons of classical taste.[9] Bernini's rupture with classicism is complete in his grandiose and exuberant decorative ensembles for San Pietro and Santa Maria della Vittoria, with their masterfully orchestrated integration of architecture, sculpture, and painting, replete with illusionism and theatrical lighting effects. Bernini imposed the indelible imprint of the high baroque on the face of Rome from the Vatican to the Piazza Navona.

Toward 1636 a polemic concerning classical values versus baroque values erupted at the Accademia di San Luca at Rome. The opponents were Andrea Sacchi, who had recently completed a classicizing fresco, *Divine Wisdom*, for the Palazzo Barberini, and Pietro da Cortona, who was then engaged in painting his baroque masterpiece, *The Glorification of the Reign of Urban VIII*, for the ceiling of the grand salon in the same palace.

Sacchi upheld the traditional values of the classical school: akin to ancient tragedy, painting should appeal to the intellect and convey a moralizing narrative; compositions should be simple and unified; expression, gesture, and movement were to be communicated through a limited number of figures. Cortona, however, advocated that painting should appeal to the senses; he compared a painting to an epic poem with a dominant theme and subordinate episodes. He championed vast, complex compositions populated with groups of figures, an ensemble to be achieved with light and shade.[10]

The stylistic stratification of the baroque and classical camps persisted into the early decades of the eighteenth century. The high baroque tradition was perpetuated by Giovanni Battista Gaulli, Bernini's protégé and the painter of the nave ceiling of the church of Il Gesù, although the taste for such bombastic illusionism was on the wane in Rome.[11] The wave of the future appeared in the oeuvre of the influential virtuoso painter Luca Giordano, who modified and fused elements of the Roman baroque and Venetian colorism in a manner that anticipated the rococo.

In Venice painters such as Antonio Pellegrini, Giovanni Battista Pittoni, Sebastiano Ricci, and Giambattista Tiepolo received widespread recognition and commissions for their eclectic "Venetian rococo" style. Until recent decades Italian painting of the eighteenth century was virtually synonymous with the Venetian School.[12] In Rome the rococo surfaced and evolved through the 1760s in works by the painters Sebastiano Conca, Corrado Giaquinto, Benedetto Luti, Michelle Rocca, and Francesco Trevisani.

Carlo Maratta, Italy's most famous master of the era, upheld, at least in theory, the principles of the classical school of painting. This tradition was sustained to varying degrees through the mid-century in the paintings of Marco Benefial, Giuseppe Chiari, Placido Costanzi, and Agostino Masucci. By the 1750s the stage was set for the "neoclassical" revival in Rome under the auspices of Winckelmann, his disciple Mengs, and Pompeo Batoni.[13]

Académie Royale de Peinture et de Sculpture

By the mid-seventeenth century Rome had been eclipsed by Paris as a center of political power and artistic patronage. In 1641 Poussin had been summoned by Louis XIII and Cardinal Richelieu from his beloved Rome to paint a series of commissions, including the decorations for the Grande Galerie of the Palais du Louvre. During his eighteen-month sojourn in Paris Poussin created a vogue for his classical paintings among influential Parisian patrons. Meanwhile, Poussin's contemporary and friend, Jacques Stella, introduced to France a classical mode of painting that remarkably anticipated elements of style to emerge about 1790–1800.[14] A younger generation of painters—Laurent de La Hyre, Eustache Le Sueur, and Charles Lebrun—responding to Poussin and Stella, embraced a modified classicizing manner of painting, which has been cogently dubbed "Atticism."[15]

In 1648 the Académie Royale de Peinture et de Sculpture was created in Paris by a group of painters. Lebrun, a founder and eventual chancellor of the Académie, codified and promoted principles of classical art in his lectures and treatises, advocating that painting should be governed by reason and should appeal to the intellect rather than to the eye. Drawing took precedence over color. The observation of nature was subjected to rigid rules of proportion, perspective, and composition. The models for imitation were to be Graeco-Roman art and the work of Raphael and Poussin; the colorism of the Venetian school and the unrefined naturalism of the Flemish and Dutch Schools were proscribed. Only noble and intellectually edifying themes were to be depicted; even the portrayal of various states of emotion was emphatically prescribed.

By 1664, three years after the ascendance of Louis XIV to the throne, Lebrun was appointed to first painter to the king, director of the Gobelins factory, and supervisor of painting commissions for the royal residences, as well as chancellor of the Academy for life. Consequently, Lebrun reigned as a veritable artistic dictator and for two decades impressed the stamp of classicism on the major decorative projects of the epoch—the Louvre, Saint-Germaine, Sceaux, and, above all, Versailles. His classical paintings became synonymous with the reign of Louis XIV, who was portrayed in the guise of an emperor or a bewigged Apollo.

In 1666 Louis XIV decreed the establishment of a branch of the Académie in Rome. Thus, the most promising French students could reside in Rome at royal expense and experience firsthand and copy the marvels of antiquity, putting them on an equal footing with their Italian confreres. The Académie pensioners molded vast quantities of casts after Graeco-Roman statuary to be sent to France both as models for study and to populate the gardens of Versailles and the other royal domains. For two centuries the Académie de France à Rome continued to exert significant influence on the artistic life of the Eternal City with its doctrinaire promulgation of classicism.[16]

The director of the Roman Académie was ever watchful for outstanding examples of original sculpture that might become available for acquisition by the French crown. By the early 1680s Paris came to be regarded as a "New Rome," due to the accumulation of statuary and the power of patronage.[17]

Ironically, Lebrun's Académie provided the forum for the great debates between the "Poussinists" and "Rubenists" over the relative merits of drawing and color, a quarrel that led ultimately to the decline of classical painting in France. As early as 1671 academic orthodoxy was challenged by proponents of Venetian colorism and the art of Rubens; they were in effect promoting an art that appealed to the senses. Despite Lebrun's intervention and proclamation in favor of drawing, the polemic persisted, and within a decade the art of Rubens and the Venetians came to be accepted at the Académie, largely through the influential publications of Roger de Piles, an ardent Rubenist amateur and later an academician.

The triumph of color is manifest in the works of members of the subsequent generation of artists, painters such as Charles de la Fosse and Antoine Coypel, friends of de Piles, for whom Venice was as powerful a mecca as Rome for artistic instruction. The careers of La Fosse and Coypel extended into the Regency period, and their paintings prepared the way for the art of Jean-Antoine Watteau, François Boucher, Charles André Van Loo, and Charles-Joseph Natoire, and the rococo style that prevailed in Europe through the 1750s. In France one can cite history painters who paid lip service to Lebrun's classical tenets despite the encroachment of Rubenism. Like their Italian counterparts, however, academicians Nicolas Bertin, Bon de Boullogne, Louis de Boullogne, Nicolas Colombel, Henri de Favanne, Louis de Galloche, René-Antoine Houasse, and François Verdier painted in an eclectic manner that fluctuated between Roman or Bolognese classicism and Venetian colorism.

History painting was by now in a state of decline in France. Major royal commissions were lacking due to the political and military reversals sustained by Louis XIV toward the end of his reign. The new patrons demanded *fêtes galantes*, genre subjects, and frivolous mythological scenes on the intimate scale of easel paintings. In 1727 Louis XV's arts minister, the duc d'Antin, sponsored an academic competition to stimulate history painting. His plan proved to be ineffectual, as evidenced by the prize-winning but uninspired entries of Charles-Antoine Coypel, Noël-Nicolas Coypel, François Lemoyne, and Jean-François de Troy.[18] A second competition, organized in 1747 by the *directeur des bâtiments*, Charles-François-Paul de Le Normand de Tournehem, yielded the same feeble results.[19] The traditional classical formulas had failed to produce history painters capable of attaining the exalted standards expected of them.

Appeals for Artistic Reform

Appeals for the reform of the arts came early in the century. In 1711 Lord Shaftesbury dictated to the Neapolitan painter Paolo de Matteis the program for his commission *Hercules at the Crossroads between Vice and Virtue*:

> *The merely natural must pay homage to the historical or moral. . . . nothing is more fatal, either to painting, architecture or the other arts, than this false relish, which is governed rather by what immediately strikes the sense, than by what consequentially and by reflection pleases the mind and satisfies the thought and reason.*[20]

In 1747 the Salon critic La Font de Saint-Yenne, in his influential treatise *Réflexions sur quelques causes de l'état présent de la peinture en France* (Thoughts on some of the reasons for the current state of painting in France), declared: "Of all the genres of painting, the premier, easily, is history painting. The painter-historian alone is the painter of the soul; the others paint solely for the eyes."[21] Seven years later, in his *Sentiments sur quelques ouvrages du Salon du 1753* (Thoughts on some works in the Salon of 1753), La Font de Saint-Yenne demanded from artists a "school of morality" and urged them to depict "the virtuous and heroic actions of great men, examples of humanity, generosity, magnanimity, courage, contempt for danger and even life, a passionate zeal for the honor and the welfare of the nation, and especially the defense of its religion." He went on to recite a litany of heroes and heroines worthy of an artist's attention.[22]

Through the efforts of La Font de Saint-Yenne, Charles-Antoine Coypel, director of the Académie, and the comte de Caylus, that indefatigable amateur, collector, and associate of the Académie, the École Royale des Élèves Protégés program was established in Paris in 1749. Here the winners of the Prix de Rome would be instructed in history, literature, and geography as well as geometry, perspective, and anatomy; the students would also copy antique statuary and old-master paintings and would draw from the live model each evening. The students were immersed in the works of Homer and Virgil and the ancient historians Plutarch, Herodotus, Thucydides, Xenophon, Tacitus, and Livy. Through this course of instruction the aspiring artists would receive the rudiments of a liberal arts education and be better prepared for their sojourn at the French Académie in Rome.

Caylus himself took a lively interest in the education of these artists. He instituted competitions and prizes for work showing excellence in expression of emotions, anatomy, and perspective. He encouraged the students to draw after Greek and Roman statuary and casts at the Académie and in his private collection. He lectured on the art of drawing and on the lives of celebrated artists. Most important, Caylus advocated a balance between the study of antiquity, of the great masters of the sixteenth and seventeenth centuries, and of nature itself. In this way the young artist would avoid developing a "routine or manner."[23]

The attitude toward nature was the underlying problem in the education of the history painter. Earlier in the eighteenth century the Rubenists had restored the fleeting, accidental effects of nature as a model for artists, which led to the proliferation of portraiture, still life, and genre painting—all straightforward transcriptions of natural phenomena. Pure nature was, however, deemed by orthodox academicians to be imperfect and riddled with accidental deformities. With the attempts to revive the genre of history painting, it became the mission of the Académie to train the artist to render nature in an idealized form (*la belle nature*). In the second half of the eighteenth century the prospective history painter was encouraged to view nature through the eyes of the ancients. The anecdote of the ancient painter Zeuxis, who based his image of Helen of Troy on five different models, was often cited.[24]

Antiquomania

Traditionally, the revival of interest in the arts of antiquity has been ascribed to the archaeological excavations at Herculaneum (1737) and Pompeii (1748), which revealed the "domestic" aspects of ancient life, with the discovery of homes, furnishings, and personal artifacts. The incipient science of archaeology, however, was being fostered in Rome. The international demand for antiquities—originals and composites—on the part of monarchs and aristocratic connoisseurs and collectors had been threatening to denude Rome of its ancient artistic patrimony. In response to this "antiquomania" Pope Clement XI reaffirmed in edicts of 1701 and 1704 a ban on the exportation of ancient art. In addition, what are now the Vatican and Capitoline museums were created under the auspices of popes Clement XI, Clement XII, and Benedict XIV to house and display the papal collections of ancient statuary, gems, medallions, and vases. In 1725 the French Académie installed its important collection of casts after antique statuary in the Palazzo Mancini, including casts of the most celebrated masterpieces in Rome as well as casts of those works that had been taken from the city. In effect, the Académie served as a major center of research for scholars and collectors.

Eighteenth-century Rome has been described most aptly as "the Academy of Europe."[25] The city was an international mecca for gentlemen on the Grand Tour, who, under the tutelage of a *cicerone* (guide), came to round out their educations by viewing the marvels of antiquity. One of the more notable visitors was Abel Poisson, the marquis de Marigny, the brother of madame de Pompadour and the influential future arts minister of Louis XV, who came to Rome in 1749 with the art theorists abbé Le Blanc and Charles-Nicolas Cochin and the architect Germain Soufflot. The Roman experience was critical to Marigny's efforts to reform history painting in France during the 1760s.[26] In addition, the tastes of celebrated English amateurs such as Thomas Coke, William Weddell, and Charles Townley (whose collection of antiquities was acquired by the British Museum) were cultivated in Rome.

Rome was also the center of a competitive international art market stimulated by the presence of the grand tourists, who commissioned paintings (especially portraits), sculptures, and drawings. Collector-dealers like Cardinal Albani, Thomas Jenkins, Gavin Hamilton, and Philipp von Stosch scurried to supply antiquities for export to the affluent and eager dilettanti.

A vast corpus of literature devoted to the arts of antiquity was published in response to eighteenth-century "antiquomania"; acknowledged masterpieces of ancient art and newly excavated works were illustrated and discussed in lavishly engraved portfolios. In 1704 the Roman publisher Domenico de' Rossi produced the volume *Raccolte di statue antiche e moderne* (Collection of ancient and modern statuary), by Paolo Alessandro Maffei, which featured the most famous sculptures in the Vatican and Capitoline collections; this was followed in 1707 by Maffei's *Gemme antiche figurate* (Antique carved gems). A seminal work was Bernard de Montfaucon's *L'Antiquité expliquée et representée en figures* (Antiquity explained and represented in [engraved] plates), published between 1719 and 1724, which reproduced ancient statues, reliefs, and gems in ten volumes. It was the most sizeable compilation of reproductions of iconographical types of ancient art ever produced and remained a standard source of reference for more than a century. Between 1752 and 1767 the comte de Caylus published in seven volumes *Recueil d'antiquités égyptiennes, étrusques, grecques et romaines* (Selection of Egyptian, Etruscan, Greek, and Roman antiquities), which reproduced his own vast collection and works in other private collections. Interestingly, Caylus, a dedicated archaeologist who had traveled to Greece and Italy, attempted to reconstruct in his *Recueil* a complete history of ancient art. He also encouraged his fellow antiquarians to publish their own collections to advance the contemporary knowledge of antiquity to a wider public.[27]

In 1757, under the auspices of Charles VII, king of the Two Sicilies, and the Royal Academy of Herculaneum, the first of the nine volumes of *Le antichità di Ercolano* (The antiquities of Herculaneum) was published. For the first time examples of Roman mural painting were engraved and revealed to European amateurs. The bronzes uncovered in the excavations were illustrated in subsequent volumes published in 1767 and 1771. Until 1773, however, the volumes were unavailable for sale; they were retained by the crown as diplomatic gifts.

In 1764 the diplomat and later dealer Sir William Hamilton assumed his post as British envoy to the court of Ferdinand IV, son of Charles VII. Hamilton assembled a major collection of Greek and Etruscan vases, bronzes, terra-cottas, and other material in Naples. In 1766–67 he published with Pierre-François Hugues d'Hancarville four volumes illustrating his collection, *Collection of Etruscan, Greek and Roman Antiquities, from the Cabinet of the Honourable William Hamilton*. As was the intent of the authors, the publication was to exert an extraordinary influence on contemporary artists and designers, who "quoted" figures and incorporated images of ancient artifacts in their own productions.

Johann Joachim Winckelmann

A radically new and subjective vision of antiquity was proffered in the literary works of the German antiquarian Johann Joachim Winckelmann, based on his romanticized perceptions of Greek civilization. In Dresden in 1755 Winckelmann published a tract entitled *Gedanken über die Nachahmung der griechischen Werke in der Malerei und Bildhauerkunst* (Thoughts on the imitation of Greek art in painting and sculpture), in which he exhorted contemporary artists to emulate the ancient Greeks in their artistic production. Specifically, Winckelmann advocated the imitation of Greek statuary to achieve the ideal human form rather than a slavish copy of nature: "To those who know and study the works of the Greeks, their masterpieces reveal not only nature in its greatest beauty, but sometimes more than that; namely, certain ideal beauties of nature which exist only in the intellect."[28] Winckelmann's attitude toward antiquity departed from that of his antiquarian predecessors, whose publications reflect a more "clinical" historical or archaeological bias. Winckelmann extolled the beauty of Greek art in effusive prose and ardently maintained that it remained a vital, relevant source of instruction for the modern school. For Winckelmann, the perfection of the art of Greece stemmed from its superior civilization, where

> *The school of the artist was the gymnasium, where the youths, ordinarily clothed because of modesty, exercised quite naked. It was the gathering place of philosophers as well as artists. . . . There one learned the movement of muscles, and studied the contours of the body, or the impressions the young wrestlers had made in the sand. The most beautiful aspects of the nude revealed themselves here in many varied and noble poses unattainable by hired models such as are used in our academies.*[29]

Systematically, Winckelmann elucidated the characteristics of Greek art to be emulated by artists: contour, drapery, expression. Of the latter element Winckelmann made the now-famous declaration: "The last and most characteristic of the Greek works is a noble simplicity and sedate grandeur in Gesture and Expression. As the bottom of the sea lies peaceful beneath a foaming surface, a great soul lies sedate beneath the strife of passions in Greek figures."[30]

A stipend from August III of Saxony (to whom *Gedanken* was dedicated) enabled Winckelmann to make the longed-for journey to Rome, where he arrived in 1755 to take up the position of librarian to the former papal nuncio to Dresden. Three years later he was engaged as librarian and keeper of antiquities by Cardinal Alessandro Albani, the most important collector-dealer of the epoch. Winckelmann thus gained access to the most elite international circles of antiquarians and artists in Rome, where his unconventional perceptions of antiquity would wield enormous influence.

Between 1759 and 1767 the prolific Winckelmann published extensively on topics including the Torso Belvedere and the Apollo Belvedere, the concept of grace in artworks, the antique gem collection of Baron von Stosch, the excavations at Herculaneum, ancient architecture, allegory, and a compendium of unpublished or inadequately treated antiquities (*Monumenti antichi inediti*). His acknowledged magnum opus of the period was *Geschichte der Kunst des Alterthums* (History of ancient art) of 1764. For the first time Winckelmann applied art-historical stylistic criteria to the analysis of the evolution and decline of Greek art, which he classified in four epochs: archaic (pre-Phidias), grand style (Phidias), beautiful style (Praxiteles), and imitators (decline of Rome).[31] It was in his *Geschichte* that Winckelmann published a homoerotic reverie on the Apollo Belvedere that heralded a new era of art criticism.

In 1763 Winckelmann's renown as an archaeologist was acknowledged with his appointment by Pope Clement XIII as prefect of the Vatican antiquities. He was courted unsuccessfully by Frederick the Great of Prussia, who offered him a position as his librarian and curator, and he was honored by the London Society of Antiquaries and the Roman Accademia degli Inscrizioni. In 1768 he made a brief visit to Germany and Austria, where Empress Maria Theresa presented him with gold and silver medallions. Shortly thereafter, Winckelmann was murdered in Trieste en route back to his beloved Rome.

Winckelmann's achievement was recognized by his contemporaries. Goethe later observed that "it was Winckelmann who first urged on us the need of distinguishing between various epochs and tracing the history of styles in their gradual growth and decadence. Any true art lover will recognize the justice and importance of this demand."[32]

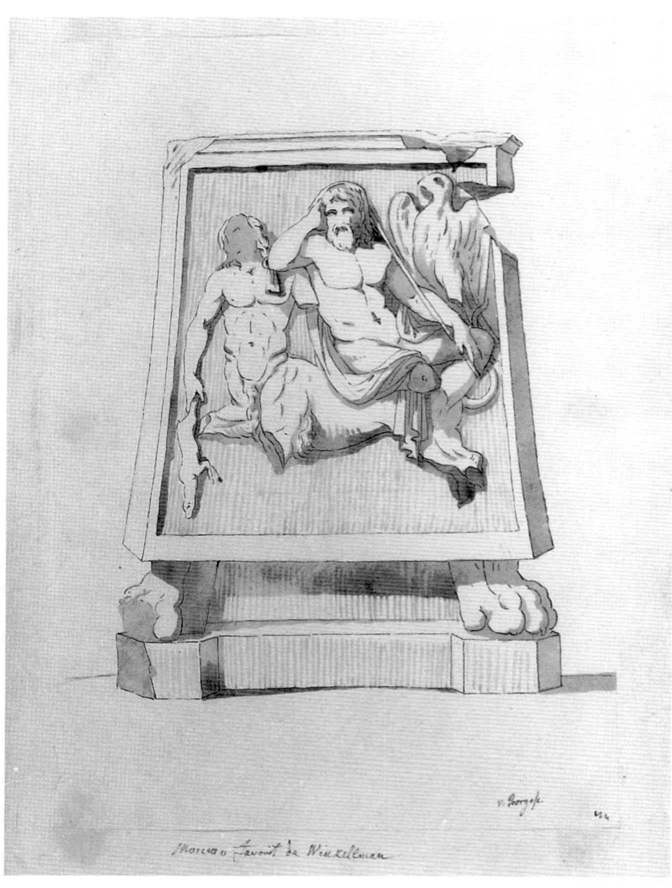

FIGURE 2
Johannes Wiedewelt
Denmark, 1731–1802

Jupiter and the Sign of Sagittarius
From the artist's Roman sketchbook, 1758, pen and black ink, gray wash on white laid paper, 22.9 x 15.2 cm (9 x 6 in.), Kunstakademiets Bibliotek, Copenhagen (inv. no. Ltr. c. Nr. 6, 129)

Antiquity: The Ideal of Beauty

Winckelmann's theories on Greek art had a major impact on European art. His writings were translated widely even in his own lifetime. His message was disseminated through the international channel of fine-art academies, which increased five-fold between 1720 and 1790 from Venice to Saint Petersburg.[33] In 1763 the Copenhagen Kunstakademiet commissioned a Danish translation of Winckelmann's *Gedanken*. The Kunstakademiet retains a Roman sketchbook produced in 1758 by the precocious Danish sculptor Johannes Wiedewelt, who was a disciple of Winckelmann. A typical sheet is Wiedewelt's study of the so-called Jupiter and the Sign of Sagittarius relief at the Villa Borghese (FIGURE 2), which bears the inscription *morceau favorit de Winkelman* (Winckelmann's favorite piece).[34] Similarly, in 1769 the Belgian painter André Corneille Lens reported to the Antwerp Academy on the Roman art milieu and the ideas of Winckelmann in his own treatise *Du bon goût* (Concerning good taste).[35]

In his *Gedanken* Winckelmann exhorted, "Let the artist's pencil, like the pen of Aristotle, be impregnated with reason, that after having satiated the eye, he may nourish the mind."[36] However, the critical issue of the practical application of Winckelmann's theories by contemporary artists remains problematic. It has been traditionally accepted that Winckelmann guided the hand of his German compatriot Anton Raphael Mengs when the latter painted the *Parnassus* ceiling (FIGURE 3) for the Villa Albani in 1761. Mengs had assiduously copied the work of his namesake Raphael from his earliest youth. Through the influence of Winckelmann, Mengs came to perceive that Raphael's masterpieces lacked the "ideal" beauty that distinguished the art of the Greeks. By emulating the latter, Mengs strove to perfect his own art. His "test case" would be the *Parnassus* ceiling, commissioned in 1760 by Cardinal Albani for his splendid villa on the outskirts of Rome, which housed his fabled collection of antiquities (and served as the residence of both Winckelmann and Mengs). The composition, inspired by Raphael's *Parnassus* fresco in the Sala della Segnatura at the Vatican and based on ancient sculpture and Roman wall painting, depicts Apollo and the nine Muses with their mother, Mnemosyne, on Mount Parnassus. Mengs's decision to include Mnemosyne, who does not appear in the original preparatory drawing, was probably influenced by the more erudite Winckelmann.[37] The composition is fundamentally an apotheosis of Albani as a patron of the arts. Apollo and his retinue have been identified as idealized portraits of the cardinal, his

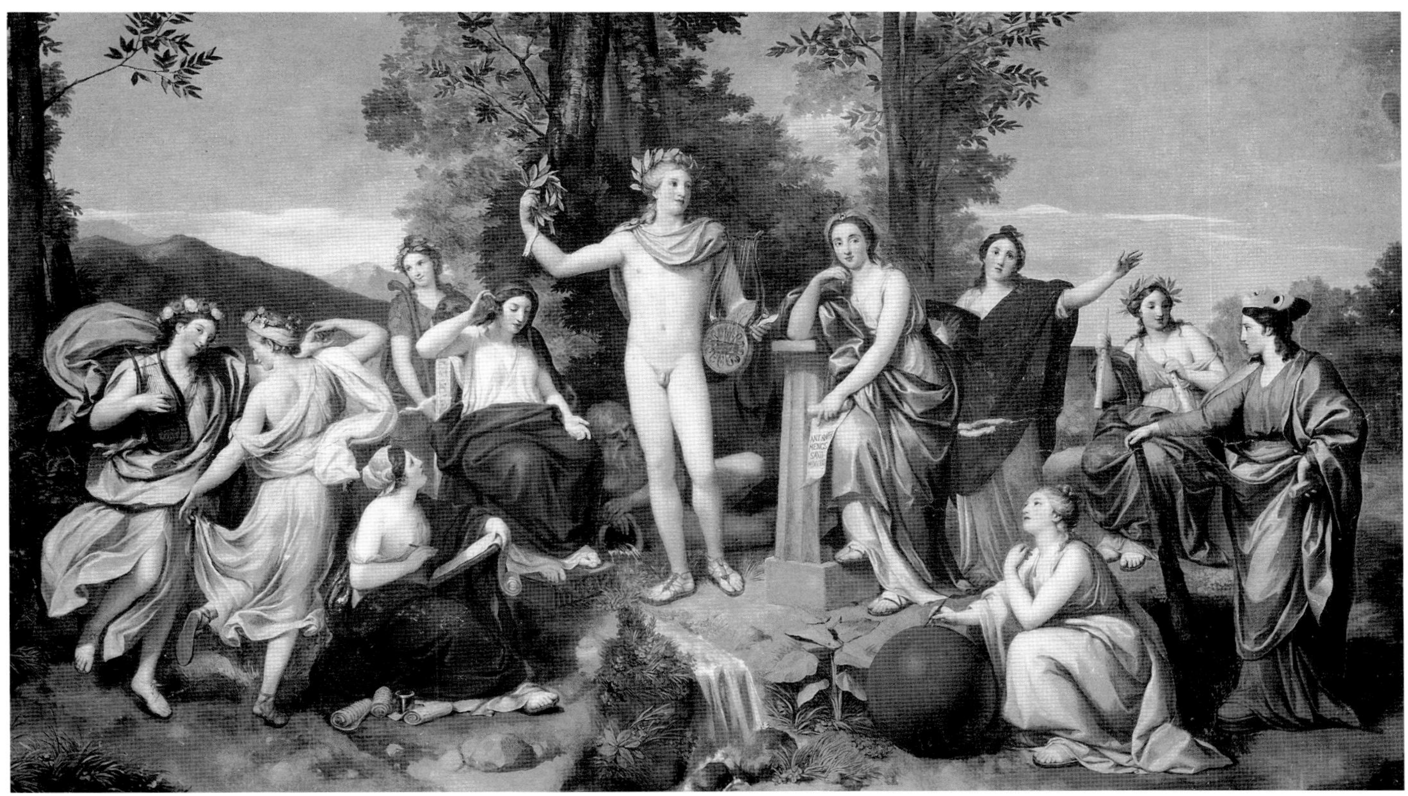

FIGURE 3
Anton Raphael Mengs
Germany, active Italy and Spain, 1728–79

Parnassus
1761, oil on canvas, 300 x 600 cm (118 x 236 in.),
Villa Albani (now Torlonia), Rome

mother, sister, and mistresses, even Mengs's wife. Formally, the figures were adroitly adapted from the Apollo Belvedere, the Sarcophagus of the Muses, and mural paintings from Herculaneum depicting Theseus in Crete and female dancers.[38]

From the perspective of Mengs's stylistic evolution the *Parnassus* does represent a break with the past. He discarded baroque illusionism in the composition. The modeling of the figures and the rendering of the drapery impart the effect of sculpture and reflect Winckelmann's obsession with contour. Subsequently, Winckelmann described the *Parnassus* ceiling in his *Geschichte der Kunst des Alterthums* and hailed Mengs, to whom the book is dedicated, as the "German Raphael."[39]

Winckelmann's evaluation of Mengs and his *Parnassus* has not withstood the judgment of posterity. For all its borrowings from "Greek" art, the porcelain countenances of the figures and the curvilinear conception of the design betray the underlying taste for the rococo. And the enthusiasm that it generated among connoisseurs in eighteenth-century Rome can now only be understood by comparing it to the contemporary illusionistic confections by Tiepolo and Boucher.

Between 1756 and 1760 Mengs executed a fascinating series of drawings that evoke a more heroic vision of antiquity than his contemporary paintings. The drawings—*Joseph in Prison*, about 1756–58; *The Death of Virginia*, about 1757–60; and *The Testament of Eudamidas* (see FIGURE 20), about 1758—have been analyzed in detail by Thomas Pelzel.[40] Importantly, these works on paper situate Mengs's development more logically within the stylistic and iconographical mainstream of the neoclassical innovators in Rome in the 1760s. The composition of the *Joseph* creates an austere, stagelike prison interior composed of masonry vaults and iron grills that herald the severe architectural settings prevalent in the 1780s, most notably in Jacques-Louis David's *Death of Socrates*, 1787.[41] *The Death of Virginia*, based on Livy, depicts a terrifying *exemplum virtutis* totally removed from the pseudo-classicism of the *Parnassus* and Mengs's other early mythologies. Unfortunately, these heroic drawings represent a path not taken by the artist in his paintings. Mengs departed for Madrid in 1761 to assume his post as court painter to Carlos III, who did not encourage his neoclassical aspirations. By comparing this series of drawings with his contemporary paintings, one may surmise that Mengs heeded unwisely Winckelmann's axiom "Sketch with fire, and execute with phlegm."[42]

Antiquity Revived: Gavin Hamilton

Throughout the 1760s the reaction of artists to Winckelmann varied greatly. In Rome the ideal of antiquity was expressed consummately in the pioneering paintings of the Scottish expatriate Gavin Hamilton, who came to Rome in 1748. A unique combination of artist, archaeologist, and dealer, Hamilton encapsulated in his oeuvre the ideals of the first phase of the neoclassical movement, from Homer and antiquomania to neo-Poussinism.[43] He first studied at Rome's Accademia di San Luca with the classicizing painter Agostino Masucci. An intrepid archaeologist, Hamilton's explorations drew him to Herculaneum, Pompeii, Spalato, Tor Colombaro, Monte Cagnolo, Ostia, Castel del Guido, and Gabii. He was actively engaged in the excavation of various sites, and his significant discoveries, which included a fifth-century B.C. Wounded Amazon and two fourth-century B.C. works, an Apollo Sauroktonos and a Hermes, placed him on the "cutting edge" of contemporary antiquarians. As a dealer in antiquities, Hamilton instilled the taste for ancient art in some of the leading English patrons of the era, including Charles Townley and Lord Shelburne.[44]

Hamilton's paintings mirrored his passion for antiquity and stylistically constituted the avant-garde of neoclassical currents in eighteenth-century Rome. His first series of paintings, executed in 1761–66 for various English patrons, was a Homeric cycle—*Andromache Mourning the Death of Hector*, *Achilles Mourning the Death of Patroclus*, and *Achilles Dragging Hector's Body around the Walls of Troy*. These paintings were engraved by Domenico Cunego (FIGURE 4) and became widely known throughout Europe. Hamilton's Homeric themes conform to the appeals of the early reformers Caylus and La Font de Saint-Yenne. The figures are derived from antique statuary and are disposed in planar compositions inspired by ancient friezes; his "Greek forms" were even acknowledged by Winckelmann. Details of architecture, furniture, decoration, and costume reflect Hamilton's archaeological studies. His compositions, with their shallow, stagelike spaces and the inclusion of massive curtains to define interior planes, are also evocative of Poussin. Winckelmann's influence is perceptible in the restraint of expression. And, although the individual paintings were acquired for and dispersed into private English collections, the impact of the ensemble was recorded and disseminated internationally through Cunego's reproductive engravings, which would influence artists of the stature of Jacques-Louis David and Antonio Canova.[45]

In recent literature Hamilton's artistic activities have been linked inextricably to his commercial interests as a successful dealer in antiquities and old-master paintings,[46] but regardless of his motives, his critical influence on the subsequent evolution of neoclassicism is undeniable. In 1762 he sowed the seeds of neoclassicism in England when his *Andromache* was exhibited at the Society of Artists in London.[47] In his immediate circle in Rome, Hamilton would exert a decisive influence on the artistic formation of the American Benjamin West's *Agrippina with the Ashes of Germanicus*, 1768, and the Swiss Angelica Kauffmann's *Last Interview of Hector and Andromache*, 1769.

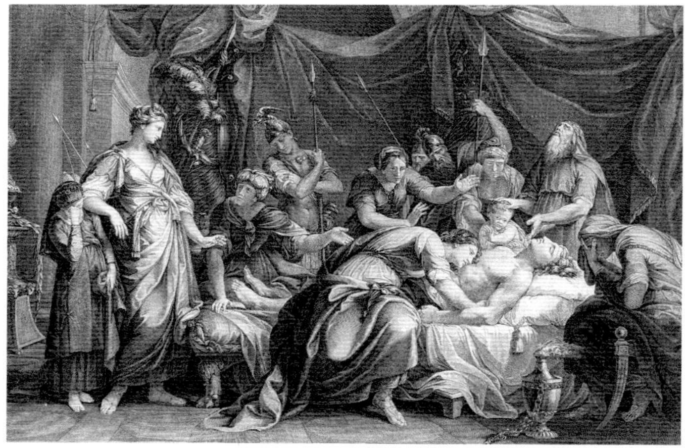

FIGURE 4
Domenico Cunego
Italy, 1727–94

Andromache Bewailing the Death of Hector
1764, after Gavin Hamilton, Scotland, active Italy, 1723–98, engraving, 40.1 x 61.4 cm (15 3/4 x 24 1/8 in.), Yale Center for British Art, New Haven, gift of David Bindman (inv. no. B1980.21)

The *Goût Grec* in Paris

In Paris Joseph-Marie Vien executed between 1761 and 1763 a series of paintings—*Young Greek Girl Decorating a Bronze Vase with a Garland of Flowers* (*Une Jeune Grecque, qui orne un vase de bronze, avec une guirlande de fleurs*); *Priestess Burning Incense in a Tripod* (*Une Prêtresse brûle de l'encens sur un trépied*); and *The Merchant of Cupids* (*La Marchande d'amours*)—that incorporated ancient artifacts, architectural elements, decorative motifs, and figurative compositions gleaned from Caylus's own *Recueil d'antiquités* and his personal copy of *Le antichità di Ercolano*. Vien's notion of imitation was more indebted to his protector Caylus than to Winckelmann, who eschewed Roman wall painting.[48] The first two paintings, subsequently retitled *The Young Corinthian Maiden* (*La Jeune Corinthienne*) and *The Virtuous Athenian Woman* (*La Virtueuse Athénienne*) in the engraved versions, reflect the moralizing tenor that characterized French art of the 1760s. *The Merchant of Cupids* is blatantly erotic in theme. In essence, Vien merely imposed the trappings of antiquity upon a fundamentally rococo vision. In this sense his paintings are akin to the contemporary classicizing exercises of Mengs.[49] Nevertheless, Vien's paintings galvanized the vogue for the *goût grec* in Paris, a trend heartily encouraged by Caylus and his circle.

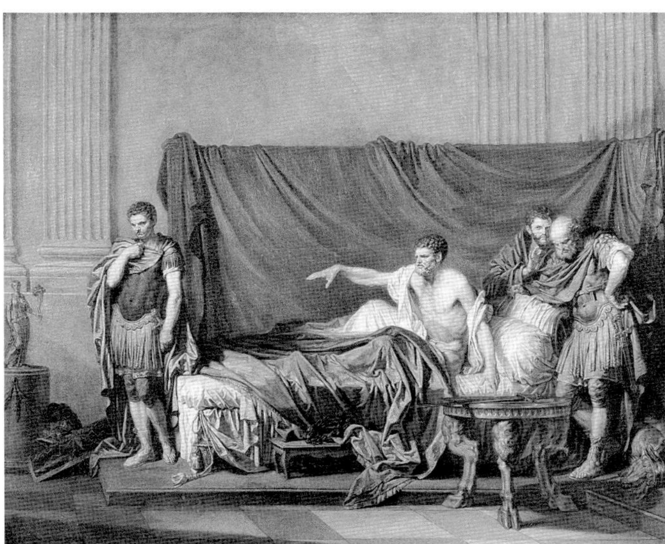

FIGURE 5
Jean-Baptiste Greuze
France, 1725–1805

Septimius Severus Reproaching Caracalla
1769, oil on canvas, 124 x 160 cm (48 13/16 x 63 1/16 in.),
Musée du Louvre, Paris (inv. no. 5031)

In the course of the 1760s Jean-Baptiste Greuze was riding the crest of critical and popular acclaim for his realistic, moralizing genre paintings that celebrated the simple, rustic life of dignified peasants. At the Salon of 1769 Greuze exhibited his long-overdue academic reception piece, *Septimius Severus Reproaching Caracalla* (FIGURE 5), originally titled *L'Empereur Sévère reproche à Caracalla son fils, d'avoir voulu l'assassiner dans les défilés d'Écosse, & lui dit: "Si tu désires ma mort, ordonne à Papinien de ma la donner avec cette épée"* (The emperor Severus reproaches his son Caracalla for wanting to have him assassinated in the glens of Scotland, and tells him: "If you desire my death, order Papinian to dispatch me with this sword").[50] It may be inferred that with this painting the entrepreneurial Greuze was finally reacting to the neoclassical developments in Rome and to the *goût grec* in Paris. The artist, who was regarded as a master of genre, aspired to the exalted and privileged status of a history painter. At any rate, he temporarily abandoned the modern genre to explore the realm of antiquity. *The Roman History* of Dion Cassius was the thematic source for his ambitious composition.[51] Importantly, the painting is a prime example of the early Poussin revival in eighteenth-century France. Greuze's disposition of his figures in a friezelike setting flanked by stark architecture and massive drapery harks back to Poussin's *Germanicus*, then in the Palazzo Barberini in Rome. Greuze himself was in Italy from 1755 to 1757 and would have known the *Germanicus* as well as the masterpieces of antiquity. The pose of Caracalla is based upon the Belvedere Antinoüs, while that of Papinian derives from the Capitoline Faun.[52]

Greuze's neoclassical experiment, however, proved to be an unmitigated failure. His contemporaries perceived *Septimius Severus Reproaching Caracalla* as a genre painting in classical guise.[53] Of Greuze's borrowing from the antique, the critic Diderot caustically observed:

> *But tell me, if the Caracalla is made after the Antinoüs, it ought to be a beautiful figure. Answer. Make Raphael draw the Antinoüs and you will have a masterpiece; make an ignoramus copy the Antinoüs behind a veil and you will have a cold and miserable drawing. But Greuze is not an ignoramus. The most skillful man in the world is an ignoramus when he attempts something that he's never done. Greuze has abandoned his métier. A scrupulous imitator of nature, he did not know how to raise himself to the level of exaggeration that history painting demands.*[54]

The critics were virtually unanimous in their condemnation of Greuze's picture, assailing the subject matter, the drawing, the anatomy, the archaeological details, the composition, and the drapery. The Académie deigned to accept Greuze only as a genre painter and in recognition for his efforts prior to the *Septimius Severus Reproaching Caracalla*. The humiliated Greuze severed his ties with the Académie and resumed an independent career as a genre painter, thus abruptly catapulted back to modernity. Nevertheless, Greuze still acknowledged Poussin as "the most learned painter" of the French school and continued to emulate him in his subsequent genre works, for example, the painting *The Father's Curse*, 1778,[55] and the drawing *The Return of the Young Hunter* (CATALOGUE NO. 16), about 1775.

The contemporary assessment of Greuze's *Septimius Severus Reproaching Caracalla* has since been mitigated. As asserted by Edgar Munhall, "In his attempt to revive Poussin's sober manner Greuze had passed beyond the level of the very history painters who judged his first history painting and found it merely awkward and peculiar. It is David's paintings of the 1780s that make obvious the originality of Greuze's accomplishment."[56]

The Antique Ideal Reinterpreted

In London Benjamin West began to execute his seminal neoclassical paintings: *The Judgment of Hercules*, 1764, *Pylades and Orestes*, 1766, *Agrippina with the Ashes of Germanicus*, 1768, and *The Departure of Regulus*, 1769. In the field of sculpture the precocious Thomas Banks exhibited a bas-relief of *The Death of Epaminondas* at the Society of Arts in 1763. The Swiss expatriate Henry Fuseli established his residence in London in 1764. Through his father, the painter Johann Casper Fuseli, an admirer of Mengs and Winckelmann, he had developed an appreciation for the arts of antiquity. He provided the first English translation of Winckelmann's *Gedanken*, which was published in London in 1765 and 1767. Finally, in 1768 the Royal Academy was established to promote history painting in Great Britain. Its first president, Sir Joshua Reynolds, fostered principles of classical art in his famous *Discourses*, delivered at the Academy between 1769 and 1790.[57]

However, there coexisted in London in the 1760s artistic subcurrents that challenged Winckelmann's concepts of noble simplicity and sedate grandeur. In 1757 Edmund Burke had published his *Philosophical Enquiry into the Origin of Our Ideas of the Sublime and Beautiful*, in which he proposed the aesthetic of terror as the ultimate emotional manifestation of the sublime.[58] John Hamilton Mortimer's painting *Sextus the Son of Pompey Applying to Erictho to Know the Fate of the Battle of Pharsalia*, exhibited in 1771 at the Society of Artists, conjured an irrational, "neo-classical horrific" vision of antiquity.[59] Based on Lucan's *Pharsalia*, Mortimer depicted the witch Erictho revivifying a withered corpse to prophesy the outcome of the fatal showdown between Julius Caesar and Pompey the Great. British artists sought inspiration not only from ancient authors but also from the native bards—Shakespeare, Milton, and Spenser—for equally "terrifying" thematic sources. In a further salute to nationalism the Society of Artists encouraged its exhibitors through its system of prizes to depict scenes from English medieval history.[60]

In 1771, however, Benjamin West revolutionized the genre of history painting with his *Death of General Wolfe*, which he exhibited at the Royal Academy.[61] West rendered a somewhat fictionalized account of the last moments of the British general on the Plains of Abraham in Quebec, attended by officers and observed by a crouching Native American, none of whom had actually been present at the event.[62] Although he idealized the portrait of Wolfe, who lies in the traditional pose of the dead Christ in scenes of lamentation, the general is depicted in a contemporary military uniform. West's conception of the death of a contemporary hero scandalized upholders of the grand manner like Joshua Reynolds, who protested the use of modern dress as opposed to classicizing drapery.[63] West defended his composition and maintained that "the event had taken place in the eighteenth century, in a country unknown to either Greeks and Romans at a period in time when no such nations, nor heroes in their costumes, any longer existed."[64] Moreover, *The Death of General Wolfe* was engraved by William Woollett in 1776 and distributed to a wide and immensely enthusiastic audience. Yet, the polemic concerning the proper representation of a modern historical event would persist into the Napoleonic Era.

The stylistic eclecticism inherent in the art of the 1760s from Vien to West would augur the more extreme developments of the 1770s. Already in 1762 Anton Raphael Mengs had published his own treatise, *Betrachtungen über die Schönheit und den guten Geschmack in der Malerei* (Thoughts on beauty and good taste in painting), in which he advocated that artists adopt an eclectic style to achieve perfection. As a practicing modern artist, Mengs would not accede to the superiority of the ancients. He observed:

Beauty in itself is nothing other than the perfection of every concept, for which reason the most perfect things, invisible as well as visible, are called beautiful. This should guide us in looking at the works of the ancients: their beauty does not always consist of the same part, but lies in the fact that that part which the Idea has chosen has been represented most beautifully. The most beautiful works of the first class are the Laocoön and the [Belvedere] Torso, the highest of the second class the Apollo [Belvedere] and the Borghese Gladiator, those of the third class are numberless, and of the inferior works I shall not speak at all.[65]

Mengs thus reevaluated Winckelmann's models. Concerning imitation, Mengs concluded:

The painter who wants to discover the good, that is to say, the best taste, must learn about taste from these four: from the ancients the taste for beauty; from Raphael the taste for significance or expression; from Correggio the taste for the graceful or harmonious; from Titian the taste for truth (i.e., nature) or color. . . . These exemplars have often been imitated by other great men, but none has surpassed them, which confirms the truth that the great masters who I have named above took the proper road to perfection. This is why I have used them as models and shown the way of understanding and truly imitating them.[66]

Like Winckelmann, Mengs acknowledged that "the ancient Greeks, too, had one main aim, . . . the mean between high perfection and humanity, namely beauty, and took only the significant from truth [nature]. For this reason, there is beauty in all their works, and even significance [expression] is never so much emphasized as to extinguish beauty."[67] Significantly, the issue of expression would spark the next controversy concerning Winckelmann and would have an impact on the next generation of neoclassical artists from Fuseli to David. The question of expression was focused upon the famous Hellenistic sculptural group, the Laocoön, which represented the strangulation of the Trojan priest and his two sons by the serpents of Athena. In his *Gedanken* Winckelmann lauded the Laocoön as the embodiment of "noble simplicity" and "sedate grandeur" in gesture and expression. Despite his physical and mental anguish, the physiognomy of Laocoön reflected a sedate soul:

He pierces not heaven, like the Laocoön of Virgil; his mouth is rather opened to discharge an anxious overloaded groan. . . . Laocoön suffers, but suffers like the Philoctetes of Sophocles: we weeping feel his pains, but wish for the hero's strength to support his misery. . . . The Expression of so great a soul is beyond the force of mere nature.

Winckelmann went on to claim, "This noble simplicity and sedate grandeur is also the true characteristic mark of the best and maturest Greek writings, of the epoch and school of Socrates."[68] In 1766 Gotthold Ephraim Lessing took issue with Winckelmann's indiscriminate comparison of the aims of the visual arts and poetry in his provocative treatise *Laokoon oder, Über die Grenzen der Malerei und Poesie* (Laocoön, or on the limits of painting and poetry). Lessing agreed that the sculptor did not express in Laocoön's face the intensity of the suffering that the violence of his death would provoke. Lessing maintained that the sculptor of the Laocoön strove to elicit the highest ideal of beauty in a body subject to the conditions of bodily pain. He asserted that pain, "in its disfigurative extreme," was incompatible with beauty and that the sculptor amended Laocoön's screams to sighs "not because the screams betrayed weakness but because they deform the countenance to a repulsive degree."[69] He infers that works of art are not created to be glanced at but are created for long and often contemplation and the artist must depict "the most fruitful moment and the most fruitful aspect of that moment."[70]

Lessing objected to Winckelmann's comparison of the suffering of Laocoön to that of Sophocles's *Philoctetes* and to his "deprecatory allusion" to Virgil's less than stoic description of Laocoön in the *Aeneid*.[71] He distinguished the aims and means of the visual artist and the poet, noting that the poet is not subject to the same limitations as the visual artist: "When Virgil's Laocoön screams, who stops to think that a scream necessitates an open mouth and that an open mouth is ugly? . . . Whoever requires a beautiful picture has missed the whole intention of the poet."[72]

In an exhortation to the modern school, Lessing remarked:

The realm of art has in modern times been greatly enlarged. Its imitations are allowed to extend over all visible nature, of which beauty constitutes but a small part. Truth and expression are taken as its first law. As nature always sacrifices beauty to higher ends, so should the artist subordinate it to his general purpose, and not pursue it further than truth and expression allow. Enough that truth and expression convert what is unsightly in nature into a beauty of art.[73]

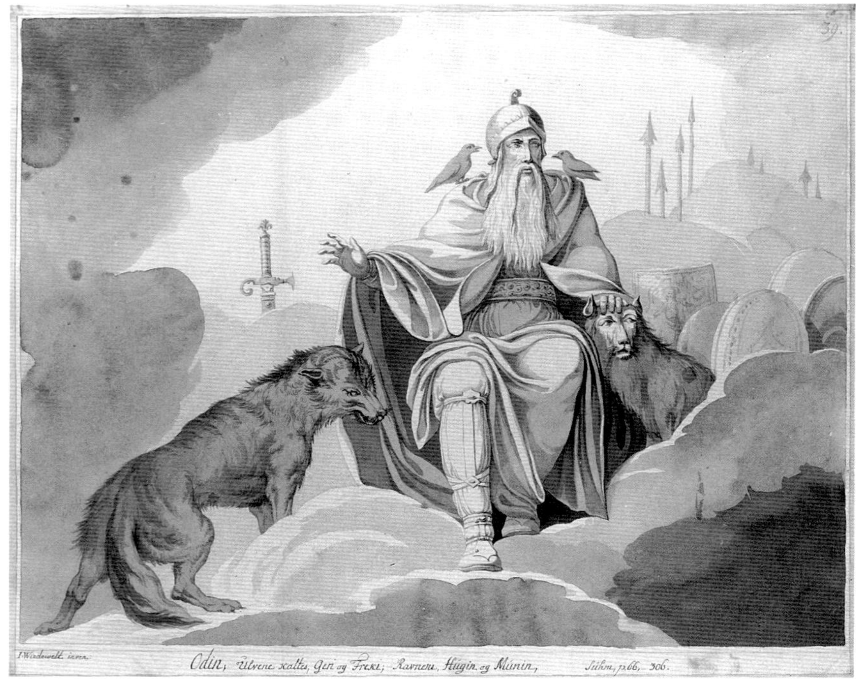

FIGURE 6
Johannes Wiedewelt
Denmark, 1731–1802

Odin, His Wolves Geri and Freki, His Ravens Hügin and Münin
c. 1771, pen and black ink, gray wash on off-white laid paper, 17.2 x 21.7 cm (6¾ x 8 9/16 in.),
Kunstakademiets Bibliothek, Copenhagen (inv. no. Ltr. c. 20, 39)

Antiquity Romanticized

There existed in Rome in the 1770s a colony of avant-garde artists, dominated by the British and Scandinavians, who conjured up a more "romantic" vision of antiquity. Ironically, the firebrand who ignited this aesthetic rebellion was Henry Fuseli, Winckelmann's first English translator. Encouraged by Joshua Reynolds, Fuseli embarked on a career as a professional artist in 1768 and settled in Rome from 1770 until 1778. A resolute classicist, Fuseli was welcomed into the coterie of Cardinal Albani. He toured the ancient monuments, filled his sketchbooks with the obligatory copies after the antique, and consulted engraved repertories of collections like Sir William Hamilton's *Etruscan, Greek and Roman Antiquities*. Although Fuseli devoted relatively little time to drawing from the model, he attended the evening life classes at the French Académie with the Swedish sculptor Johan Tobias Sergel.[74] Early on, however, Fuseli became disenchanted with the Roman neoclassical "establishment," in particular Mengs, who had returned from Madrid in 1771. In a letter to his mentor, the Swiss scientist Johann Kaspar Lavater, Fuseli attacked Mengs as a mediocre artist and criticized Winckelmann for ranking him with Phidias and Apelles.[75] By 1771 Fuseli had been seduced by the art of Michelangelo and the sixteenth-century mannerists Parmigianino, Rosso, Bandinelli, and Cambiaso. The Sistine Chapel and the *Battle of Cascina* rivaled monuments of antiquity as worthy models for imitation. Formally, in his drawings and paintings, Fuseli emulated the muscular, contoured, titanic nudes of Michelangelo. Violently contorted figures, as seen in his drawings *Psychostasy* (CATALOGUE NO. 98), c. 1800–1802, and *Hercules Killing the Flesh-Eating Mares of Diomedes* (CATALOGUE NO. 99), c. 1800–1805, constitute the quintessence of Fuseli's art. Similar stylistic tendencies are discernible in the drawings of Fuseli's fellow artists, for example, *Chiron Teaching Achilles to Throw a Javelin*, by Sergel (CATALOGUE NO. 96), c. 1770–71, *Claudius Discovered by a Soldier*, by Nikolai Abraham Abildgaard (CATALOGUE NO. 100), c. 1780, and *The Origin of Painting*, by George Romney (CATALOGUE NO. 1), c. 1775–80.

Fuseli's erudition and natural literary bent drove him to depict themes from Dante, Shakespeare, Milton, and Spenser, as well as Homer, Apuleius, and Plutarch. In 1771 he explored a novel literary source in a drawing entitled *Odin's Departure from the Gates of Hell*, which illustrates an episode in Thomas Gray's poem *The Descent of Odin*. In response, artists in Fuseli's circle, such as Abildgaard, Romney, and Alexander Runciman turned to northern sagas as a thematic source for their paintings.[76] The universal fascination with northern myths had been generated in 1765 with the publication in London of James Macpherson's purported translation of *The Works of Ossian, the Son of Fingal*. Macpherson had fabricated an epic based on fragments of verse collected in the Scottish Highlands, allegedly composed by the third-century bard Ossian, celebrating the exploits of his father, the warrior-king Fingal. Despite a persistent controversy concerning the authenticity of the Ossian fragments and their literary refinement, Macpherson's ruse proved to be an international success. Ossian, "the northern Homer," was emulated by German *Sturm und Drang* poets, such as Friedrich Gottlieb Klopstock in his *Hermannschlacht*, and inspired a corpus of literature based on Norse mythology, including Gray's *Descent of Odin*. In the eyes of numerous contemporary artists, Winckelmann's vision of antiquity, suffused with sunlight and populated with nude ephebes exercising in gymnasia, yielded to an equally romanticized view of ghostly warriors battling on a cloudy, moonlit moor. Even a disciple of Winckelmann, the Danish neoclassical sculptor Johannes Wiedewelt, executed drawings depicting scenes from Peter Friedrich Sühm's *Odin* (FIGURE 6) in 1771. Themes from Norse mythology had become popular in Denmark as early as the mid-1750s, although Copenhagen was the seat of the most resolutely neoclassical fine arts academy in Europe. Ossian and the Nordic epics cast a spell on generations of artists, including Abildgaard, Canova, Eckersberg, Girodet (CATALOGUE NOS. 57–58), Ingres, Koch, Romney, Runciman, and Westall (CATALOGUE NO. 12).

For Fuseli and his friends in Rome in the 1770s, the art of drawing afforded the opportunity to give full reign to their violently expressive imaginations without the encumbrance of a patron's demands. Upon return to their more artistically conservative homelands of Britain, Denmark, and Sweden, they had to apply their efforts to the more mundane tasks of portrait painting and tomb sculpture in the service of patrons indifferent to historical subjects. By and large, their romantic visions of antiquity, Homeric and Ossianic, dissolved into wistful memories of their Roman sojourns.[77]

The Triumph of Jacques-Louis David

In the 1770s the royal pensioners who came to the French Académie at Rome included the future luminaries of the school—Jean-François-Pierre Peyron, François-André Vincent, and Jacques-Louis David. The students had received sound instruction in drawing at the Académie in Paris and were well versed in literature and history through the École Royale des Élevès Protégés. In general, their response to antiquity was more solemn than that of their northern counterparts. Ironically, David had expressed his grave reservations about the impact of antiquity prior to his departure from France: "The antique isn't going to seduce me, it leaves you cold."[78] Nevertheless, under the guidance of his master Vien, then director at Rome, David assiduously applied himself to rendering the prescribed copies after the antique and eventually filled a dozen sketchbooks (see CATALOGUE NO. 41). He traveled to Naples and inspected the excavations at Herculaneum and Pompeii in 1779, becoming acquainted with the antiquarian Dominique Vivant-Denon and the archaeologist Antoine-Chrysôstome Quatremère de Quincy, who expounded for him the theories of Winckelmann. In Rome he met the pioneers of neoclassicism, Mengs, Batoni, and Gavin Hamilton, as well as a new talent, Antonio Canova.[79]

David's assimilation of ancient art is expressed consummately in a magnificent drawing, executed about 1778–80, titled *Frieze in the Antique Manner: Funeral of a Warrior* (FIGURE 7). The drawing reveals David's diligent study of not only antique reliefs and statuary at sites around Rome but also the engraved plates in the portfolios published by Montfaucon, Caylus, Winckelmann, d'Hancarville, and Piranesi. It likewise documents the artist's attentiveness to the correct archaeological rendering of ancient artifacts that he would resurrect in future compositions.[80]

By no means was David's Italian experience restricted exclusively to the emulation of Graeco-Roman antiquity. Like Mengs, his taste was eclectic and he professed an admiration for the Renaissance masters Raphael, Michelangelo, and Correggio. More importantly, however, David turned to the Caravaggeschi, especially Moïse Valentin, for an appreciation of bolder chiaroscuro, more resonant color, and a keener observation of nature.[81] In his paintings *Saint Jerome* and *Saint Roch Interceding with the Virgin for the Plague Victims*, both 1780, and the *Equestrian Portrait of Count Potocki*, 1781, David disclosed his indebtedness to the seventeenth-century masters. This would be the key to his artistic revolution of the 1780s.

In the summer of 1780 David returned to Paris, where he painted his preliminary academic reception piece *Belisarius*, originally titled *Bélisaire reconnu par un soldat qui avait servi sous lui, au moment qu'une femme lui fait l'aumone* (Belisarius recognized by a soldier who had served under him, just as he is receiving alms from a woman), which he exhibited at the Salon of 1781. The composition depicts the unjust disgrace of a victorious general in the service of the emperor Justinian who became a victim of intrigue, was blinded, reduced to poverty, and forced to beg for his subsistence. David's painting was acclaimed by Diderot in his ultimate Salon review for its "grand manner, soul, expression without affectation, and drapery."[82] Antoine Schnapper called the *Belisarius* "the first truly neo-classical painting in France . . . which miraculously reconciled the sensibility of the eighteenth century with the dream of antique grandeur."[83] In this painting David incorporated aesthetic ideals expressive of his own generation, which launched the first phase of a "new classicism," a concept expounded by Régis Michel in 1989.[84] In 1784 David painted a second, reduced version for Louis XVI's arts minister, the comte d'Angiviller, which is now at the Louvre (FIGURE 8).

In 1785 David completed *The Oath of the Horatii* (*Le Serment des Horaces*; FIGURE 9, Paris, Musée du Louvre), which is regarded as Europe's first masterpiece of neoclassical painting. Appropriately, David returned to Rome to paint this canvas, which created a sensation among artists, connoisseurs, and critics when it was first exhibited at his Casa Costanzi studio in August of 1785. The painting was next shown as an intentionally late entry in the Paris Salon of that year. The adulation for the picture in Rome had fueled the fires of anticipation in Paris, where equally enthusiastic crowds thronged to view it at the Louvre.

The painting had been commissioned for the crown in about 1781 by the comte d'Angiviller. Since the mid-1770s d'Angiviller had attempted to revive the grand genre in France by offering royal commissions for large-scale paintings and sculptures that treated heroic themes from antiquity and French history.[85] Livy, Plutarch, and Dionysius of Halicarnassus had each chronicled the story of the combat between two groups of brothers, the Roman Horatii and the Alban Curiatii, to resolve a dispute between the rival states over cattle theft. The Horatii prevailed, but only one son emerged alive from the battle. David's choice of theme was most likely motivated not so much by the accounts of the ancient authors as by Charles Rollin's *Histoire romaine* (Roman history) and a 1782 production in Paris of Pierre Corneille's tragedy *Horace*, written in 1639.

The artist was intrigued with this subject throughout his lifetime. There is no specific literary source for his theme; David drew his inspiration for the scene from two paintings depicting *The Oath of Brutus*, one, about 1763, by Gavin Hamilton (Drury Lane Theater, London) and another by Jacques-Antoine Beaufort (Musée des Beaux-Arts, Nevers), 1771.[86] Benjamin West's *Hamilcar Making His Son Hannibal Swear Implacable Enmity against the Romans* (Kensington Palace, London), 1770, and Henry Fuseli's *Oath on the Rüttli* (Rathaus, Zurich), 1780, may also be cited as precedents.[87] In David's final composition the elder Horatius presents swords to his three sons, who vow to defeat their Alban opponents for Rome or to die in its defense. With the inclusion of the grieving women in the middleground David created a powerful allegory of supreme loyalty to the state despite family ties.

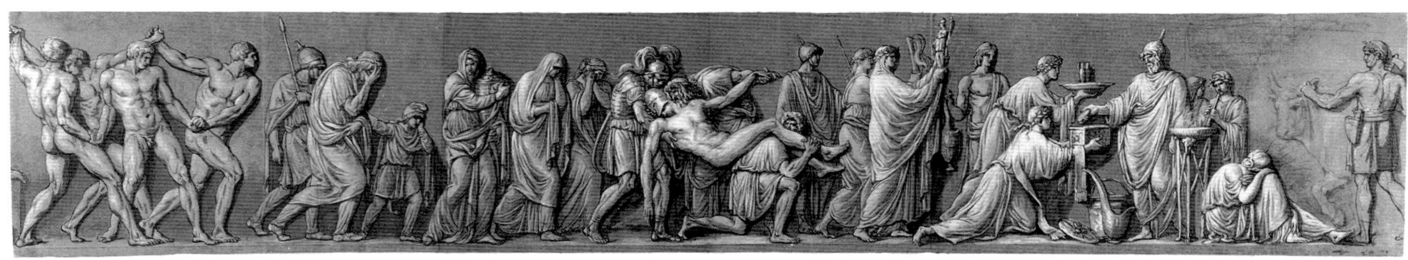

FIGURE 7
Jacques-Louis David
France, 1748–1825

Frieze in the Antique Manner: Funeral of a Warrior
c. 1778–80, black chalk, pen and black ink, gray wash,
heightened in white on gray-blue laid paper, 26 x 152.4 cm (10 7/16 x 60 in.),
Crocker Art Museum, Sacramento (inv. no. 1871.408)

Apart from the theme, *The Oath of the Horatii* serves as a veritable and radically new aesthetic manifesto, recently and provocatively referred to as "Painting's Constitution."[88] The pictorial means employed express a unique, vital, and personal evocation of antiquity. The stylistic transformation was perceived by the Salon critics, who were aware that David was intentionally breaking the traditional rules of contemporary art. First of all, he had abandoned the standard ten-foot-square format required for royal commissions and painted on a canvas ten by thirteen feet. Although David's debt to Poussin's *Germanicus*, *Eudamidas*, and *The Rape of the Sabines* is evident, the seventeenth-century master's classicizing principles are pushed to abstraction.[89] Above all, David reduced the composition to extremes of simplicity that heighten the emotional impact of the painting. The three friezelike groupings—of the brothers, the grieving women, and the nurse with two children—are unified by the central image of the elder Horatius and integrated by the massive, shadowy arches that flank them. David's restricted palette, bold chiaroscuro, and inflated musculature recall the lessons of the Caravaggists. The exaggerated gestures and strident poses of the men, all seen in profile, convey a rigidity of expression that dramatically contrasts with the limpid configuration of the women. David was willing to subordinate archaeological accuracy—as in the scimitar and details of costume and architectural elements—for the sake of compositional unity. The academic taste for complex and varied expression, refined coloration, complex highlighting, and anecdote is sacrificed to achieve a severe, brutal, sublime image, which could appeal simultaneously to the general public, progressive critics, and aristocratic connoisseurs.[90] David would continue to paint in this severe and heroic mode throughout the decade and produced his masterpieces *The Death of Socrates* (*La Mort de Socrate*), 1787, and *The Lictors Returning to Brutus the Bodies of His Sons* (*Les Licteurs rapportent à Brutus les corps de ses fils*), 1789, which truly elicit the ethos of ancient civilization. David thus secured his position as the most influential painter in Europe.

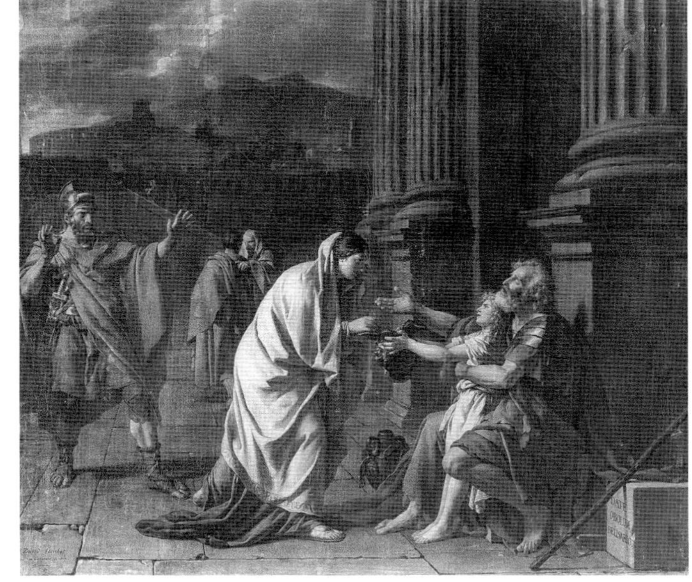

FIGURE 8
Jacques-Louis David
France, 1748–1825

Belisarius
1784, oil on canvas, 288 x 312 cm (113 3/8 x 122 13/16 in.),
Musée du Louvre, Paris (inv. no. 3694)

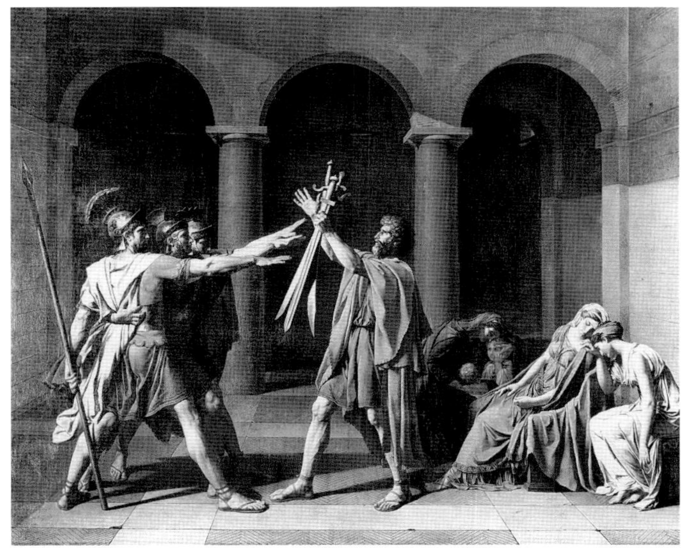

FIGURE 9
Jacques-Louis David
France, 1748–1825

The Oath of the Horatii
1785, oil on canvas, 330 x 425 cm (129 15/16 x 167 5/16 in.),
Musée du Louvre, Paris (inv. no. 3692)

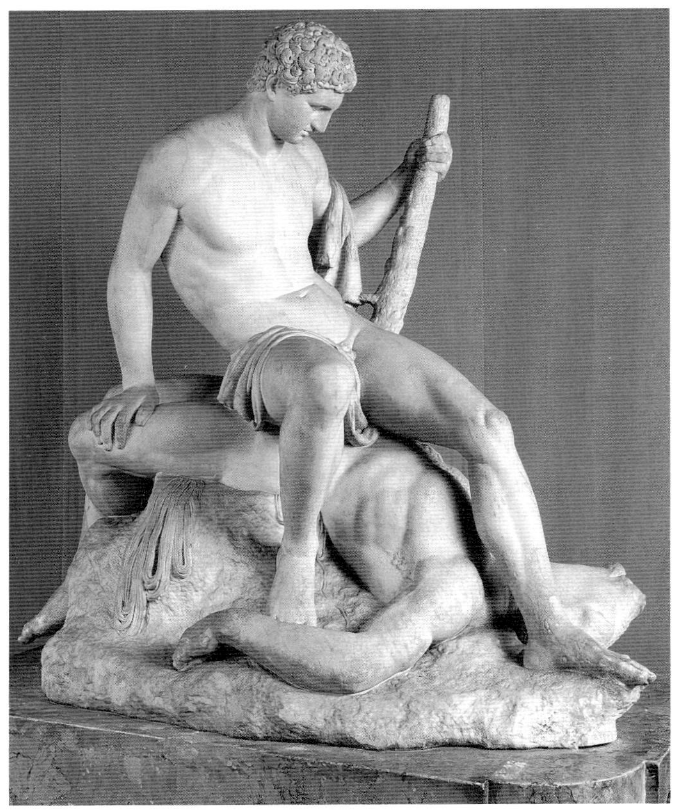

FIGURE 10
Antonio Canova
Italy, 1757–1822

Theseus and the Minotaur
1781–83, marble, 144.5 x 587 x 914 cm (56⅞ x 231⅛ x 359⅞ in.),
Victoria and Albert Museum, London (inv. no. A.5–1962)

Antiquity Politicized: The School of Virtue

During the past two decades French art of the 1780s has been interpreted in relation to the wide-ranging political events that led to the Revolution of 1789.[91] In more general terms, social historians have cited the disruptive socioeconomic effects of the Seven Years' War (1756–63) and the emergence of the Industrial Revolution in the generation of neoclassicism, which is identified as the aesthetic idiom of the French Revolution.[92]

For example, between 1767 and 1791 the painters Nicolas-René Jollain, Louis-Jacques Durameau, François-André Vincent, Jean-François-Pierre Peyron, as well as David and the sculptor Jean-Antoine Houdon, rendered versions of the history of Belisarius. While the theme was ancient, having been recounted in the *Secret History* of Procopius, it became notorious in 1767 with the publication of the novel *Belisaire* by Jean-François Marmontel, with its unflattering parallel of the France of Louis XV and the declining Roman empire and its veiled attacks on unjust taxation and state religion. In particular, the tragic Belisarius is linked to a contemporary French general, Thomas-Arthur Lally-Tolendal, hero of the Battle of Fontenoy (1745), who subsequently suffered a decisive defeat at the hands of the British in India in 1758, early in the Seven Years' War. Upon his return to France after imprisonment in London, Lally-Tolendal was charged with sedition and extortion and was executed in 1766. Through the efforts of Voltaire and the general's son, Lally-Tolendal was posthumously exonerated in 1786.[93] The contemporary depictions of the Belisarius theme are deemed to be indictments of royal injustice. By way of contrast, the proliferation of themes such as Roman matrons offering their jewelry to the public coffers, Curiatus Dentatus refusing the gifts of the Samnite ambassadors, the courage of the Spartan women, Horace slaying his sister Camilla, the deaths of Virginia and Lucretia, and Manlius Torquatus condemning his son to death (see CATALOGUE NO. 71) constitutes the ancient *exemplum virtutis* and self-sacrifice as an alternative to tyranny.[94]

In recent literature David's *The Oath of the Horatii* and *The Lictors Returning to Brutus the Bodies of His Sons* have been analyzed in depth as "protorevolutionary" works, indicative of his post-1789 Jacobin sentiments and disenchantment with the *ancien régime*. Even his painting of 1788, *Paris and Helen* (*Les Amours de Paris and Hélène*; see CATALOGUE NO. 39), has been scrutinized iconographically as a castigation of the illicit amorous relationship between Queen Marie Antoinette and the comte d'Artois, and even as a harbinger of revolution itself.[95] It is clear that the controversy concerning the relationship of David's art and politics and the nature of his appropriation of ancient themes will persist in art-historical literature.

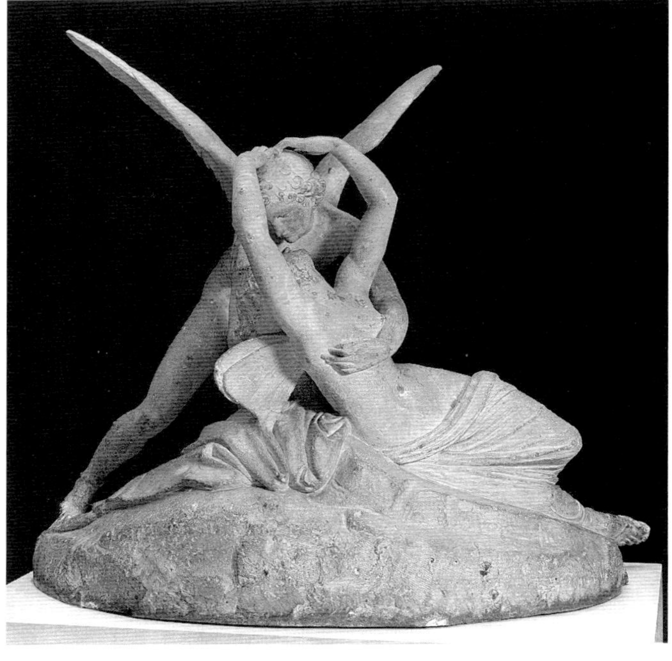

FIGURE 11
Antonio Canova
Italy, 1757–1822

Cupid and Psyche
1794, plaster, 134.6 x 151.1 x 81.3 cm (53 x 59½ x 32 in.),
the Metropolitan Museum of Art, New York,
gift of Isidor Strauss, 1905 (inv. no. 05.46)

Antiquity Rejuvenated: Antonio Canova

In Rome in the 1780s the sculptor Antonio Canova achieved a reform in the art of sculpture of the same magnitude as David's reform of painting in Paris during the same epoch. Trained in Venice in the rococo tradition, Canova settled in Rome in 1780. He was appalled that contemporary Italian sculptors channeled so much of their energy into the restoration or slavish copying of ancient statuary for export. Canova frequented the English community at Rome, which included the sculptor Christopher Hewetson and the painter Gavin Hamilton, both of whom took a lively interest in his career, and the young sculptor fortunately enjoyed the protection of the Venetian ambassador, Girolamo Zulian, who provided him with a block of marble and permitted him to carve a subject of his own choosing.[96] The result was his first classicizing masterpiece, *Theseus and the Minotaur* (FIGURE 10), 1781–83. At Hamilton's suggestion, Canova represented the victorious Theseus seated calmly atop the corpse of the Minotaur instead of their mortal combat. As H. W. Janson observed, "The work is created in the spirit of the antique without in any sense being a copy, and the lack of action consciously emphasizes its 'timelessness,' its claim to being a new classic with the classics of old."[97] Because the statue was a commission from the Venetian ambassador, political motives have also been read into the theme: Theseus is construed as the liberator of his country from foreign oppression and, more specifically, as an allegory of the prolonged hostilities between Venice and the Ottoman Empire and the political aspirations of the reform-minded, aristocratic Venetian Barnabotti party.[98]

In 1783 Canova, at the age of twenty-six, received his first papal commission, the tomb of Clement XIV, which he completed in 1787. His reductivist neoclassical design purified the traditional baroque concept of a papal tomb as established by Gianlorenzo Bernini nearly a century and a half earlier. Canova purged the tomb of polychrome marble, convulsively expressive allegorical figures, swelling drapery, extraneous symmetry, architectural embellishments, and any hint of illusionism. Instead, simplicity and tranquility reign in the autonomous ensemble of white and gray marble. Clement XIV is enthroned atop the sarcophagus with his right arm extended grandly; he is attended by allegorical figures of the virtues Meekness and Temperance framing the sarcophagus yet disposed asymmetrically on different levels of the socle. Classicizing drapery models the figures, who gravely mourn the death of the pontiff.[99] The tomb imparts an air of stoicism worthy of the ancients—a quality extolled by Canova's most progressive critics.[100] As asserted by Fred Licht, the tomb of Clement XIV evinced "a new style, full of moral and even political connotations, [that] had stormed the citadel of the Vatican and had conquered the very birthplace of the baroque tradition."[101]

Canova's *Cupid and Psyche*, a private commission from Lord Cawdor, an English resident in Rome, boldly reveals the distinctly carnal aspect of his complex, artistic personality.[102] Conceived and executed between 1787 and 1793, the sculpture represents the amorous adolescents gracefully interlocked in a languorous embrace, about to kiss (Canova's plaster model is conserved at the Metropolitan Museum of Art, New York; FIGURE 11). The sensuous pose, articulated by the exquisite carving and polishing of the translucent marble, elicits from the viewer a frisson. This passionate image is frozen in time, universal and independent of either an ancient model or text. As observed by Honour, Canova "established the notion of 'modern' sculpture. By concentrating on form rather than literary context, by insisting on the importance of multiple view-points, and by investigating the problem of precarious balance, he seems to have looked far beyond the preoccupations of most of his contemporaries."[103] The *Cupid and Psyche* was later acquired by Joachim Murat and ultimately entered the collection of the Louvre. Its quixotic eroticism presents a fascinating comparison with David's exactly contemporary painting *Paris and Helen*; it enhanced Canova's reputation in France and heralded artistic developments during the Napoleonic Empire.

With yet another papal commission, the marble *Perseus with the Head of Medusa* (FIGURE 12), 1804–6, Canova established his reputation as the preeminent sculptor in Europe. In its sensual male nudity Canova succeeded in creating a modern counterpart to Winckelmann's ancient idol, the Apollo Belvedere. With his aggressive pose counterbalanced by his outstretched arms, the *Perseus* offers a harmonious alternative to the traditional contrapposto format.[104] (Ironically, Canova's *Perseus* actually occupied the Belvedere niche from 1798 until 1816 while the Apollo was on display at the Louvre, having been seized by the French under the terms of the Treaty of Tolentino.)

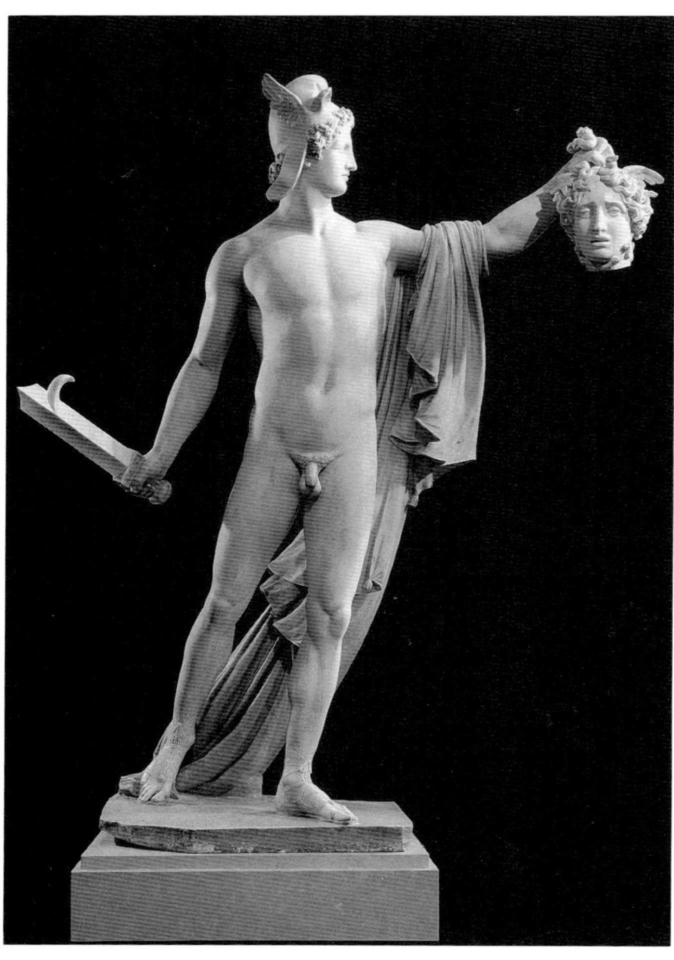

FIGURE 12
Antonio Canova
Italy, 1757–1822

Perseus with the Head of Medusa
1804–6, marble, height 217 cm (86⅝ in.), the Metropolitan Museum of Art, New York, purchase, Fletcher Fund, 1967 (inv. no. 67.110.1)

John Flaxman and the Linear Style

Winckelmann had discussed extensively the element of contour in Greek art in his *Gedanken über die Nachahmung der griechischen Werke in der Malerei und Bildhauerkunst*:

> *But even supposing that the imitation of nature could supply all the artist wants, she could never bestow the precision of contour, that characteristic distinction of the ancients. . . . The noblest contour unites or circumscribes every part of the most perfect nature, and the ideal beauties in the figures of the Greeks. . . . This contour reigns in Greek figures, even when covered with drapery, as the chief aim of the artist; the beautiful frame pierces the marble like a transparent . . . skin.*[105]

Winckelmann's advocacy of contour seems to have influenced the elliptical composition and conception of the figures in the *Parnassus* ceiling at the Villa Albani by his protégé, Mengs.[106] The ultimate expression of the concept emerged three decades later in what has been termed the international linear style of 1800,[107] whose roots can be traced to the English art colony in Rome and Naples in the 1790s. Between 1791 and 1795 the collector and British envoy to Naples, Sir William Hamilton, published his collection of ancient vases in three illustrated folio volumes. To execute the engravings, Hamilton had engaged the German Johann Heinrich Wilhelm Tischbein. For the project Tischbein adopted a sparse, linear style of engraving, devoid of shading, which stressed the contours of the vase paintings. It was a highly cost-effective means to reproduce a vast body of material. His reductivist engravings, determined equally by economic and aesthetic factors, succinctly conveyed the flat, abstract character of the models. Between 1791 and 1814 Hamilton's publications appeared in multiple editions and reprints in English and French.[108] The volumes stimulated an international vogue for "Greek primitivism."

As a corollary to this phenomenon, the striving for simplicity of design, abstraction, and universality led to the rediscovery of the art of the Italian "primitive" painters such as Cimabue and Giotto. Between 1770 and 1774 the painter Thomas Patch had published biographies of Masaccio, Fra Bartolommeo, Giotto, and Ghiberti with engravings after their works.[109] In the 1790s the scholars Humbert de Superville, William Young Ottley, Seroux d'Agincourt, and Paillot de Montabert came to Italy to study the works of the primitives. This new stylistic orientation toward abstraction and archaism is revealed in William Blake's *A Breach in a City, the Morning after the Battle* (CATALOGUE NO. 11), the composition of which was conceived as early as 1784, and John Flaxman's *Adoration of the Magi* (CATALOGUE NO. 10), c. 1796. In the course of the 1790s

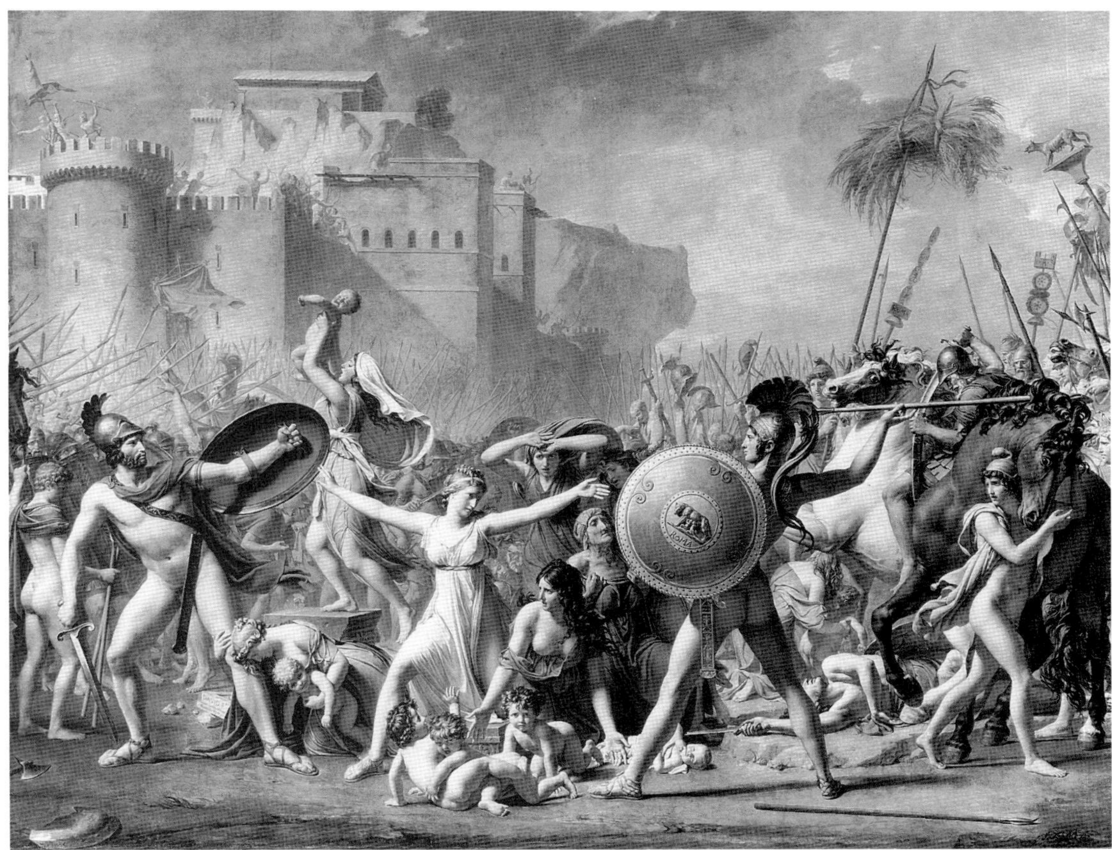

FIGURE 13
Jacques-Louis David
France, 1748–1825

The Sabine Women
1799, oil on canvas, 385 x 522 cm (151 9/16 x 205 1/2 in.),
Musée du Louvre, Paris (inv. no. 3691)

portfolios of outline engravings proliferated in Rome. The earliest, *Dix-huit estampes au trait* (Eighteen outline prints), was executed in 1792 by the precocious Burgundian painter Bénigne Gagneraux. The etchings vary in subject from Gagneraux's own paintings to allegories of Venus and Cupid and genre scenes *à l'antique*.[110]

It was the English sculptor Flaxman who provided the drawings for the most influential portfolios of outline engravings in Europe, executed by Tommaso Piroli and based on episodes from Homer's *Odyssey* and *Iliad* and Dante's *Divine Comedy*, all published in 1793. These commissions came from private English patrons residing in Rome: Georgina Hare-Naylor and Mr. Udney for Homer (CATALOGUE NO. 8) and Thomas Hope for Dante. Simultaneously, Flaxman provided the dowager Countess Spencer with drawings for the tragedies of Aeschylus (CATALOGUE NO. 9), also engraved by Piroli but not published until 1795. Although the drawings and engravings were executed for private collectors, Flaxman's designs soon became known to a wider public and were greeted with unabashed enthusiasm by artists and connoisseurs alike. Eventually the copyrights were acquired by commercial publishers, and the engravings were issued in more than nineteen editions and formats in London, Paris, Rome, Hamburg, Leipzig, Amsterdam, Berlin, Milan, Florence, Karlsruhe, Saint Petersburg, and New York through the mid-1840s.[111] In the eyes of his contemporaries, Flaxman's "primitive" designs equaled or even surpassed the ancients in simplicity, purity, and expression.[112] Much to Flaxman's chagrin, the popularity of his outline engravings overshadowed his renown as a monumental sculptor. Nevertheless, Flaxman's engravings would influence the conception of such diverse masterpieces as *Caprices* (*Los Caprichos*), 1797–98, by Francisco de Goya, and *The Sabine Women* (*Les Sabines*; FIGURE 13), 1799, by David, who considered this painting his first exercise in the "pure Greek" style.[113] Within the context of this exhibition, Flaxman's outline manner is reflected in the work of Anne-Louis Girodet de Roussy-Trioson (CATALOGUE NO. 60), Asmus Jacob Carstens (CATALOGUE NO. 105), and Bertel Thorvaldsen (CATALOGUE NO. 110).

The Evocation of Imperial Rome: The Empire Style

The heroic genre celebrating republican virtue, instigated by David's generation in the 1780s, prevailed through the turn of the century. This mode was transformed stylistically, however, by the quest for "primitivism" and thematically by the rapidly changing political climate from 1789 to 1804, encompassing the Federation, the Terror, Thermidor, the Directory, and the Consulate. The cult of antiquity persisted, with Marius, Cicero, Gaius Gracchus, Timoleon, and Marcus Sextus—to name a few—joining the ranks of Belisarius and Brutus in the iconographical repertory.[114] In his role as a member of the Committee of Public Instruction, David employed the trappings of antiquity—tripods, candelabra, chariots, military standards, and Roman costumes—in his elaborate program for public festivals celebrating Fraternity (1793), Martyrs of the Revolution Le Pelletier de Saint-Fargeau and Marat (1793), and the Supreme Being (1794).[115] Neoclassicism clearly embodied the political aspirations of the French Revolution.

The political changes effected by the ascendancy of Napoleon Bonaparte as first consul (1799) and emperor (1804) left an indelible imprint on the neoclassical style. Strident republicanism was no longer tolerated, and the heroic character of revolutionary neoclassicism was muted. The emperor viewed the arts as a means to promote his legend and so propagandize the benefits of his rule. Pierre-Henri Révoil's *Bonaparte Relieving the City of Lyons* (CATALOGUE NO. 67), a preparatory study for a painting exhibited at the Salon of 1804, is indicative of the new impulse. Révoil depicts Napoleon in the guise of a Roman emperor, raising a female personification of Lyons from the ruins. The painting commemorated Napoleon's visit to Lyons in 1800 to lay the cornerstone for the reconstruction of the city, which had been devastated by a ferocious siege in 1793.

Révoil's painting conformed to imperial decorum, as opposed to Canova's marble statue of a heroically nude Napoleon as Mars bearing a Winged Victory, which the emperor banished to a storage area in the Louvre in 1811.[116] Napoleon seems in fact to have been opposed to the form and content of neoclassical art, as evidenced by his brusque dismissal of David's *Sabine Women* and *Leonidas at Thermopylae*. He also ordered David to remove a Winged Victory from *The Distribution of the Eagles*, 1810, an updated and propagandistic version of *The Oath of the Horatii*.[117] Napoleon was an emphatically nineteenth-century emperor, and his taste is best reflected in the veristic and protoromantic paintings of Antoine-Jean Gros. In Gros's *The Plague at Jaffa*, 1802, and *Napoleon on the Battlefield of Eylau*, 1808, the emperor is represented as a modern savior, calm amid the disease and carnage.

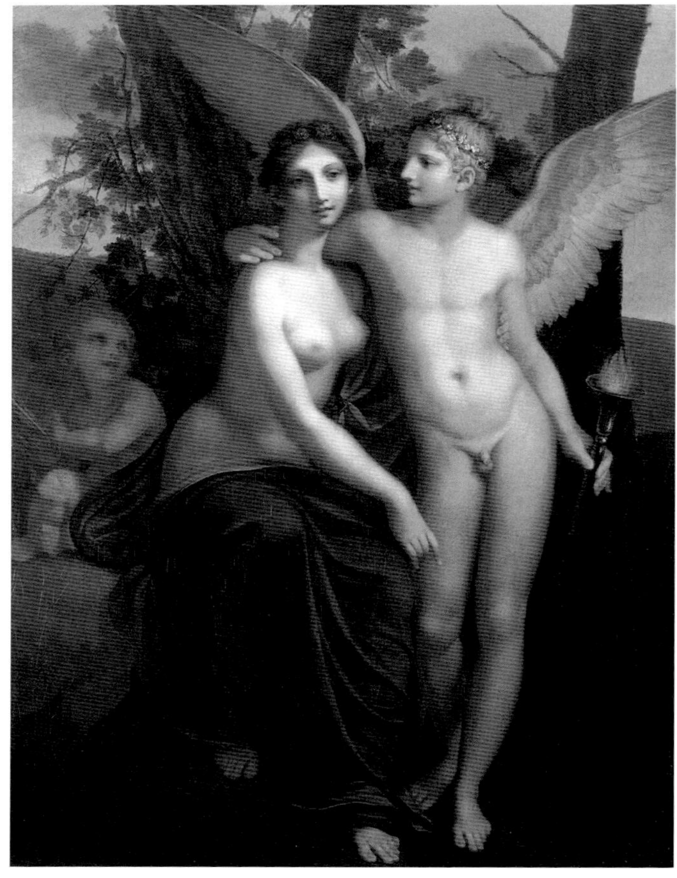

FIGURE 14
Pierre-Paul Prud'hon
France, 1758–1823

The Union of Love and Friendship
c. 1793, oil on canvas, 146.1 x 114.3 cm (57 1/2 x 45 in.),
the Minneapolis Institute of Arts,
William Hood Dunwoody Fund
and the John R. Van Derlip Fund (inv. no. 64.50)

Despite the inroads of "modernism," neoclassicism did persist during the Empire, although new characteristics emerged. Superficially, ancient models permeated architecture and the decorative arts of the epoch in the fashionable empire style with its revival of interest in late Roman ornament. As codified by Charles Percier and Pierre-François-Léonard Fontaine, it was sanctioned by Napoleon as the official court style of France and its satellite states.[118] The precise relationship of the empire style to neoclassicism remains problematic, however.

In his classic 1968 study Hugh Honour interpreted the empire style as the degeneration of neoclassicism: "The Empire marks its rapid decline and transformation back once more into a mere antique revival, drained of all the high-minded ideas and force of conviction that had inspired its masterpieces. It became a purely decorative style comparable with the *goût grec* of fifty years earlier though now evocative of Imperial luxury and grandeur."[119]

Mario Praz viewed the style as the logical and ultimate phase of neoclassicism, characterizing it as "the final flowering of the neo-classical tendency," which was in fact a curious hybrid of three distinct elements—the *Encyclopédiste* scientific rationalism, Jean-Jacques Rousseau's cult of nature, and Winckelmann's myth of a golden age of Greek civilization. Consequently, he viewed the protoromantic characteristics that surfaced in the empire style as new and original. Praz firmly challenged the notion that the style was the hardening into formula of a once dynamic and vital movement.[120]

At the heart of the matter lies the deviation of the art of the Empire from the classical ideal articulated by Winckelmann in the mid-1750s. It is from this perspective that Régis Michel examined post-1800 "new classicism" as a decadent corruption of the *beau idéal*.[121] Like Honour, Michel regards the empire aesthetic as the eclipse of neoclassical heroism and virtue. He identifies the traits of the style that diverged from the classical ideal: grace, *morbidezza* (softness of modeling), and quasi-eroticism. These elements are encapsulated in the art of Pierre-Paul Prud'hon (CATALOGUE NOS. 43, 46, 48), making their debut as early as 1793 in his canvas *The Union of Love and Friendship* (FIGURE 14). Its figural types reflect Prud'hon's study of the antique in Italy (Apollo Sauroctonus, Capuan Venus) as well as the influence of his acquaintance Antonio Canova. The predominant source of inspiration, however, is Leonardo da Vinci and, even more pertinently, Correggio—the idol of Mengs—for sfumatesque modeling, effusively graceful pose and expression, and ambiguous eroticism.[122]

The lyricism that pervades aspects of the empire style (or "suave style," as Michel has described it) reflects the eclipse of Homer as a main source of themes for artists. Between 1795 and 1802 the famous publisher Pierre Didot issued lavishly illustrated editions of the works of Virgil, Horace, and Longus.[123] The new themes drastically altered the vision of antiquity during the empire and would have broader ramifications for the future of classicism. Significantly, toward 1800 Virgil's *Aeneid* was preferred to Homer's *Iliad* and *Odyssey* as a source of inspiration for artists. In 1798 Didot published an edition of Virgil's works with illustrations by Gérard and Girodet (CATALOGUE NO. 60). Winckelmann's distaste for Virgil had been clearly expressed in his *Gedanken*: "A statue by a Roman master compares with its Greek prototype as Virgil's Dido compares with the Nausicaa of Homer on whom she is modeled."[124] He also assailed Virgil's account of the suffering of Laocoön in the *Aeneid*.[125] Yet, as indicated by Michel, Homer's pure Greek epic poetry was eclipsed by Virgil's Roman "epic melodrama," and this change of allegiance would sound the death knell of classicism.[126]

Just as Virgil was regarded as Homer's equal, Jean Racine came to be revered as the modern Euripides, and his dramas of tragic heroes and heroines rivaled the works of the authors of antiquity as a prime thematic source.[127] In 1801 Didot issued a luxurious edition of Racine dedicated to Napoleon, with engravings designed by Chaudet, Gérard, Girodet, Moitte, Peyron, Prud'hon, Serangeli, and Taunay, all of whom were recommended to the publisher by David. The edition coincided with a veritable cult of Racine in the theaters of Paris.[128] The painters were, in turn, inspired by the rhetorical gestures and emotional verse in the performances of Racine's tragedies.[129] Girodet's illustrations for Racine's *Andromache* reveal the impact of theatrical productions (CATALOGUE NO. 55), but the influence of the stage is felt most profoundly in the histrionic compositions of Pierre-Narcisse Guérin (CATALOGUE NO. 65), especially his paintings *Phaedra*, 1802, *Andromache and Pyrrhus*, 1810, and *Clytemnestra*, 1817. The forced expressions and exaggerated postures developed in the theater of course violated the fundamental tenets of Winckelmann's classical ideal. And, after 1800, as cogently observed by Michel, "classicism dissolved into theatricality: a rhetoric of [engraved] plates."[130]

Antiquity Revealed: The Impact of Archaeology

While Winckelmann is credited for his chronological survey and differentiation of the phases of the evolution of Greek art, it is conceded that his aesthetic reveries on "Greek" sculpture were spurious, being based on his assessment of Roman copies (he himself never made a voyage to Greece, although he did have the opportunity to do so).[131] Even Mengs recognized that the works so lovingly extolled, such as the Apollo Belvedere, the Laocoön, and the Niobe group, were in fact Roman copies.[132] At the turn of the nineteenth century, however, the incipient science of archaeology was coming into its own, and new discoveries were being made at a hitherto unparalleled rate. From this new perspective scholars like Quatremère de Quincy recognized that Winckelmann lacked sufficient archaeological evidence to expound his theories.[133]

In 1808 Lord Elgin brought the Parthenon marbles from Athens to London, and the majesty and purity of fifth-century Greek sculpture were revealed to artists and connoisseurs. The unrestored marbles provided a striking contrast to the composite, over-restored, and even fabricated Roman sculptures that British collectors such as Charles Townley had been importing since the mid-1760s. The "realism" of the Elgin Marbles sparked a controversy in that it contradicted the false classical ideal of Roman copies. Richard Payne Knight and members of London's Dilettanti Society even challenged the authenticity of the marbles and proposed that they were Roman copies from the age of Hadrian (A.D. 117–138).

The artists Benjamin West, Henry Fuseli, Joseph Nollekens, and John Flaxman rallied in defense of the marbles and lauded their originality and expressive power.[134] Through their efforts the Elgin Marbles were finally purchased for the British nation in 1816 and were spared from obtrusive restoration.[135]

In the previous year Canova had come to London to view the sculptures and was struck not only by their grandeur and purity of style but especially by the "living" quality of the marble, which imitated flesh.[136] The impact of the Parthenon sculptures on Canova is reflected in the sensuously carved surfaces of the marble in subsequent masterpieces like the *Three Graces* (1815–17).

After Canova's death in 1822 the Dane Bertel Thorvaldsen reigned as Europe's preeminent sculptor. He had already achieved renown in Rome in the early 1800s and for two decades he and Canova were rivals. The two sculptors were responsive to highly distinct ancient sources.[137] About 1802–3 Thorvaldsen executed the model for his first masterpiece, the over life-sized *Jason with the Golden Fleece* (FIGURE 15); the marble (completed

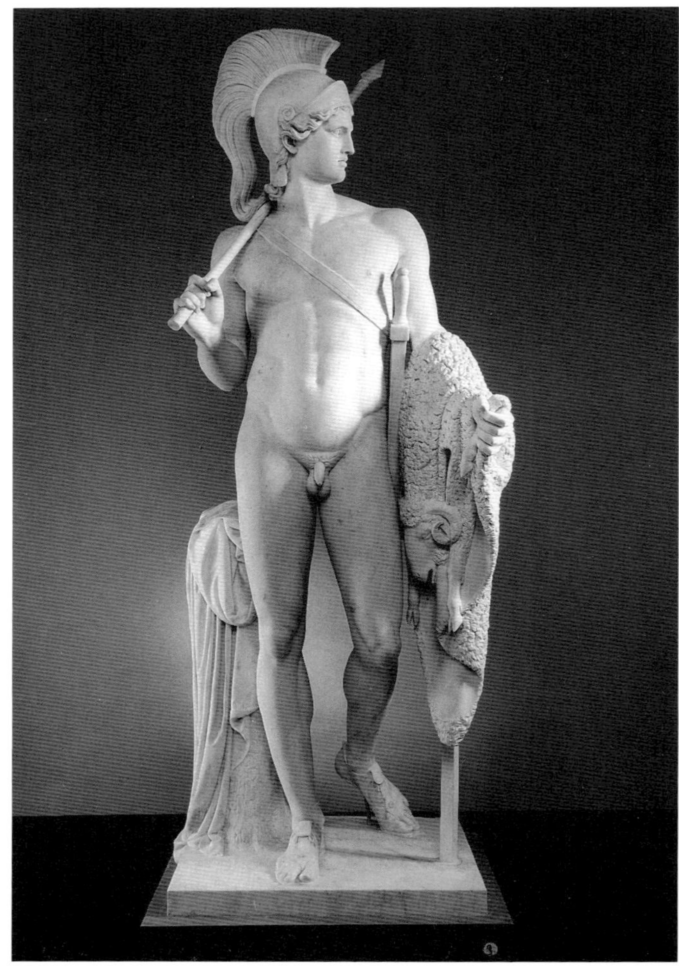

FIGURE 15
Bertel Thorvaldsen
Denmark, active Italy, 1770–1844

Jason with the Golden Fleece
1802–3, completed 1828, marble, height 242 cm (95 ¼ in.), Thorvaldsens Museum, Copenhagen (inv. no. A 822)

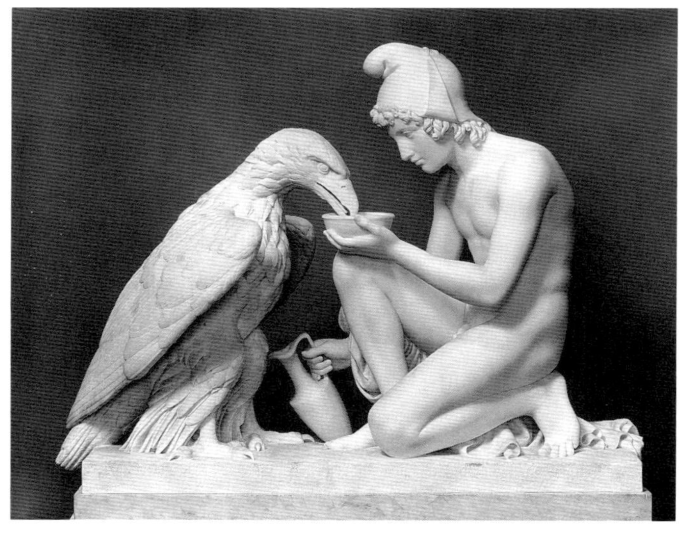

FIGURE 16
Bertel Thorvaldsen
Denmark, active Italy, 1770–1844

Ganymede with the Eagle of Jupiter
1817–29, marble, height 93.3 cm (34 ¾ in.), the Minneapolis Institute of Arts, gift of the Morse Foundation (inv. no. 66.9)

only in 1828) was commissioned by the English collector Thomas Hope. In conception Thorvaldsen's *Jason* derives from a mid-fifth-century bronze, the *Spear Bearer,* by the celebrated Greek sculptor Polyclitus. This athletic canon of the so-called Severe style had not yet been codified by contemporary archaeologists, although the image was familiar from Roman marble copies.[138] The firm contrapposto and overall naturalism that distinguish Thorvaldsen's *Jason* were greatly appreciated by contemporary connoisseurs, including Canova, who recognized in it "a new and grand style."[139]

Thorvaldsen's striving for simplicity of design and purity of contour is expressed in his marble *Ganymede with the Eagle of Jupiter,* commissioned in 1817 by the English collector Lord Cawdor (FIGURE 16). The formal stylization and rigid, frozen pose of the kneeling youth provides a startling contrast to Canova's contemporary *Three Graces,* inspired by the Parthenon marbles. In 1816 Thorvaldsen had encountered the primitive phase of Greek art, the late Archaic style, when he was engaged to restore the pediment sculpture from the Temple of Aphaia at Aegina, the fragments of which his patron, Crown Prince Ludwig of Bavaria, had acquired in 1812. Thorvaldsen did not emulate the Archaic style of the Aegina marbles in his subsequent production; however, his *Ganymede with the Eagle of Jupiter* evokes the kneeling archers of the pediment in its stark symmetry and chaste profile.

Significantly, also in 1817, Thorvaldsen executed a model for an allegorical figure of *Hope* that he conceived in a superficially "Archaic" mode. Its coiffure with long braids, the disposition of the drapery, and the rigid stance hark back to *kore* dating to 530–500 B.C.[140] He did not proceed beyond the stage of the model, however; the extant marble was carved after his death by Herman Wilibald Bissen. Greek Archaism must have haunted Thorvaldsen, since he incorporated the image of *Hope* in *Self-Portrait: Leaning on the Statue of Hope* (FIGURE 17), which he modeled in plaster in 1839 (it also was later carved in marble by Bissen). In his self-portrait Thorvaldsen in effect includes a reference to antiquity as an accessory and reflects the new fascination of the neoclassical artist with archaeology.

The "archaeological" appreciation of antiquity is revealed to the ultimate degree in the art of Jean-Auguste-Dominique Ingres, in terms of his own stylistic evolution and attitude toward the ancients. Ingres had absorbed the basic tenets of the first generation of Roman neoclassicists as a student at the Toulouse Académie. There exists a corpus of his drawings after casts of the Ares Borghese, the Laocoön, the Richelieu Bacchus,

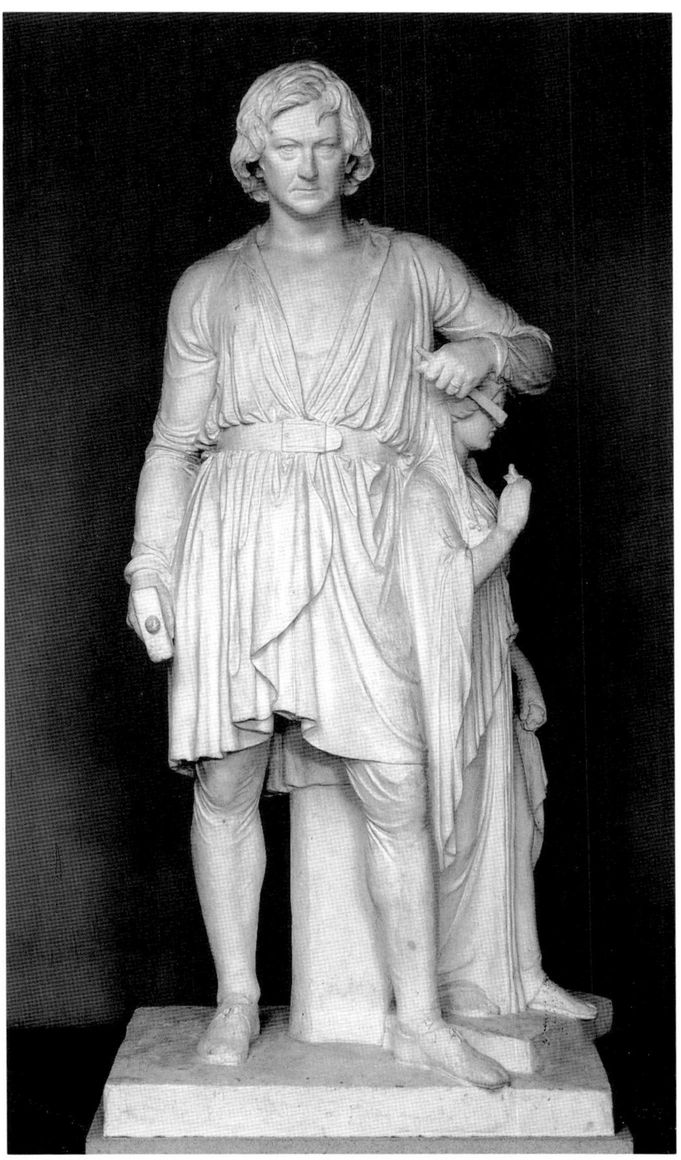

FIGURE 17
Bertel Thorvaldsen
Denmark, active Italy, 1770–1844

Self-Portrait: Leaning on the Statue of Hope
1839, plaster, height 198 cm (77 15/16 in.),
Thorvaldsen Collection, Nysø (inv. no. A 162)

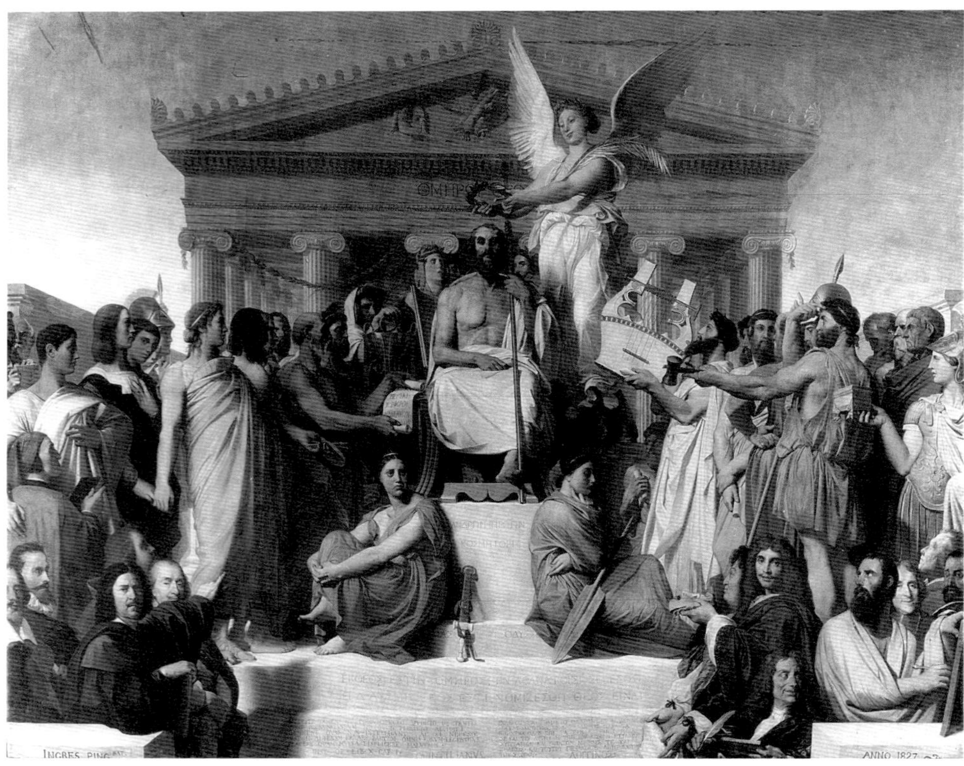

FIGURE 18
Jean-Auguste-Dominique Ingres
France, 1780–1867

The Apotheosis of Homer
1827, oil on canvas, 386 x 512 cm (152 x 201 ½ in.), Musée du Louvre, Paris (inv. no. 5417)

and the Apollo Belvedere.[141] In Paris, in the atelier of David, Ingres witnessed the execution of *The Sabine Women*, his mentor's masterpiece in the pure Greek style. Archaism would influence his own first major paintings executed in Rome, *Jupiter and Thetis*, 1811, and *Romulus Victorious over Acron* (see CATALOGUE NO. 73), 1812.[142] The latter was an imperial commission for the decoration of the Palazzo del Quirinale in anticipation of Napoleon's expected visit to Rome (Thorvaldsen also modeled his *Alexander* frieze for the edifice in 1812[143]). Ingres's composition is clearly indebted to David, Flaxman, and Thorvaldsen in its friezelike disposition of the figures. The painting was executed in muted tones of tempera to heighten the effect of Archaism.[144] Contemporary theorists attributed the harmony of ancient painting to the restricted palettes of the Greeks, as opposed to the brilliant and seductive confections of color espoused by the modern school.[145]

In 1815 the archaeologist Quatremère de Quincy, a close friend of Ingres, presented a radically new vision of antiquity in his treatise *Le Jupiter olympien* (Olympian Jupiter), which undermined traditional assumptions of neoclassicism. In his imaginative reconstructions of Phidias's colossi, the Olympian Jupiter and the Athena Parthenos, he described statuary wrought in gold, ivory, and polychrome marble. Winckelmann and his generation of scholars had chosen to ignore the role of color in ancient art. Pompeiian wall painting was dismissed as a corruption of taste. The extant traces of color on the Parthenon and other monuments of Athens had been conveniently ignored.[146]

Quatremère de Quincy's reconstructions undoubtedly influenced Ingres's early works such as *Jupiter and Thetis*. However, the "archaeological style" is most consummately represented in Ingres's *Antiochus and Stratonice* of 1840 (see CATALOGUE NO. 75). The composition reconstructs an opulent Roman interior, decorated in the Pompeiian Third style, with red painted columns, mural paintings illustrating the Labors of Hercules, a bronze statue of Alexander, and a magnificent bed adorned with Ionic columns and metopes. Ingres's masterful narration of the dramatic discovery of the cause of Antiochus's malady (see CATALOGUE NO. 3 for a discussion of the iconography) tends to be overpowered by the profusion of archaeological detail, painted with the assistance of his pupils Paul and Raymond Balze.[147] According to Rosenblum, the painting "resembles a dollhouse crammed with so much archaeological information that it might serve as a museum display or as a classical handbook for students at the École des Beaux-Arts."[148]

With this painting, Ingres had set the stage for nineteenth-century academicism,[149] which he himself promoted when, as director of the Académie de France in Rome, he instituted a course in archaeology for the pensioners.[150] From the archaeological perspective antiquity ceased to be a vital source of artistic inspiration. Instead, it became a visual resource of accessories for an "art of pastiche."[151] The conception of imitation was supplanted by that of the sterile copy.

Epilogue

At the Salon of 1827 Ingres exhibited his *The Apotheosis of Homer* (FIGURE 18). Appropriately, the painting had been commissioned as a ceiling decoration for the Salle des Antiquités at the Louvre[152] (see also CATALOGUE NO. 62). The composition constitutes the artist's manifesto of Hellenism, which reaffirms the superiority of the ancients over the moderns. Homer, enthroned before a temple dedicated to his memory, is crowned with laurel by Renown. At his feet sit female allegories of the *Iliad* and the *Odyssey*. Luminaries of the ancient world—Aeschylus, Pindar, Apelles, Phidias, Aristotle, Aristarchus, and Virgil—are represented immediately below. Raphael is the sole "modern" to be depicted among the elite. One step below, literally, appear Ingres's modern *Homérides*—Dante, Poussin, Corneille, La Fontaine, Boileau, Molière, Racine, Shakespeare, Tasso, and Michelangelo, among others.[153] In essence, Ingres was regurgitating in 1827 the hierarchical canons of Winckelmann—without credibility, however. As noted by Régis Michel, Ingres's credo had devolved into an empty fetishism for all things Greek, devoid of the ethos of the ancients.[154] By 1827 Ingres had already strayed from the classical ideal, as demonstrated by paintings such as *King Philip of Spain Investing the Marshal of Berwick with the Order of the Golden Fleece after the Battle of Almanza*, 1818, and *The Dauphin, Later Charles v, Entering Paris*, 1821, which encompass the nascent romantic impulses of historicism and medievalism.[155]

In the same Salon of 1827 Eugène Delacroix exhibited his controversial painting *The Death of Sardanapalus*, which may be interpreted as a "manifesto" of romanticism. The purist vision of antiquity as it had evolved from Winckelmann's Grecian fantasies to Quatremère de Quincy's pseudo-scientific reconstructions was diffracted after 1800 into varied stylistic spectra reflecting the pervasive influence of romanticism. This new direction had been signaled in such stylistically adventurous works as Pelagio Palagi's *Medea Killing Jason's Children* (CATALOGUE NO. 92), c. 1810–15, which invites comparison with Delacroix's own *Medea* (Musée des Beaux-Arts, Lille) of 1838.[156]

Julius Schnorr von Carolsfeld's *Life Study of a Female Nude* (CATALOGUE NO. 116), 1825–26, a figure that appears in his Villa Massimo fresco, *The Army of Charlemagne in Paris*, reveals both the Nazarenes' formal and thematic preoccupation with the Italian Renaissance and their quasi-religious esteem of the figure drawing as an expression of the soul.

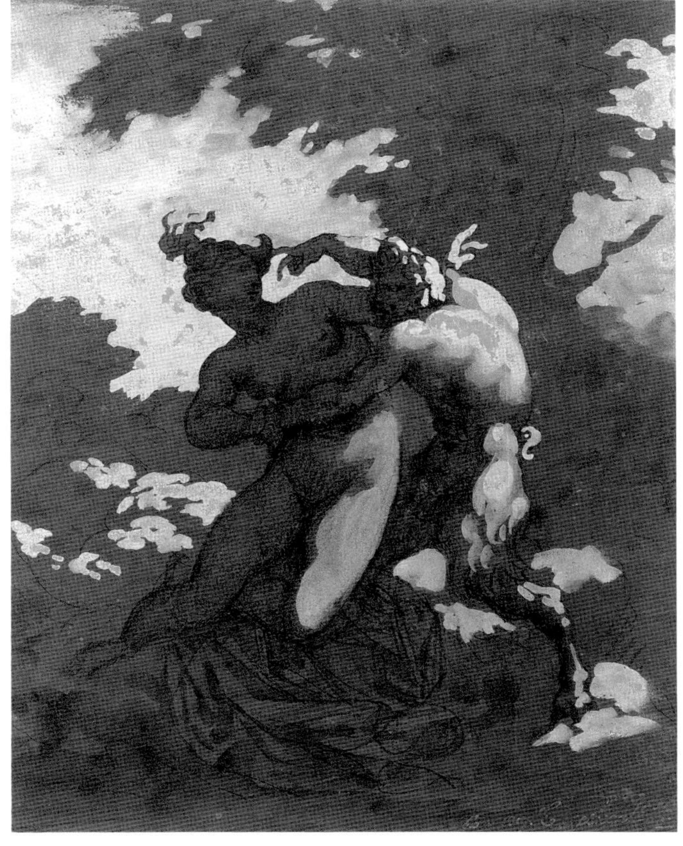

FIGURE 19
Théodore Géricault
France, 1791–1824

Satyr and Nymph
1817, black chalk, brown wash, and white gouache on brown prepared paper, 22.2 x 18.2 cm (8 3/4 x 7 3/16 in.), the Art Museum, Princeton University, museum purchase, gift of Mrs. George L. Craig, Jr., in memory of her husband (inv. no. x1986-19)

The sentimental aspects of the *style troubadour*, here in the guise of antiquity, are echoed in the tender exchange between a druidess and a Gallic warrior in Révoil's watercolor *Woman Painting Designs on the Body of a Warrior* (CATALOGUE NO. 68), after 1809.

The subversion of the ancient ideal, however, comes to the forefront in works such as Théodore Géricault's violently animated *Studies of Hercules Casting Off the Cloak of Nessus* (CATALOGUE NO. 77). It culminates in a series of bold brown-ink-wash and white-gouache drawings executed by Géricault in Rome in 1817, typified by his *Satyr and Nymph* (FIGURE 19). The drawing conjures up a dark vision of antiquity in which a malevolent eroticism mocks Winckelmann's concepts of calm grandeur and noble simplicity.[157] The drawings by Palagi, Schnorr, Révoil, and Géricault document the complex stylistic diffusion and digression from the antique ideal of beauty that had inspired the generation of the 1760s. By 1830 the vital neoclassical spark ignited by Winckelmann had been extinguished; artists were now beckoned by the new muse of romanticism.

NOTES

1 Cornelius C. Vermeule, *European Art and the Classical Past* (Cambridge: Harvard University Press, 1964); Michael Greenhalgh, *The Classical Tradition in Art* (London: Gerald Duckworth and Company, 1978); Francis Haskell and Nicholas Penny, *Taste and the Antique: The Lure of Classical Sculpture 1500–1900* (New Haven: Yale University Press, 1981); Elizabeth Cowling and Jennifer Mundy, *On Classic Ground* (exh. cat., London: Tate Gallery, 1990).

2 James A. H. Murray, ed., *A New English Dictionary of Historical Principles* (Oxford: Clarendon Press, 1908), vol. 6, 88.

3 "Royal Academy of Art, The Exhibition of Works by the Old Masters," *The Athenaeum*, no. 2782 (February 19, 1881): 270.

4 Régis Michel, *Le Beau Idéal, ou l'Art du concept* (exh. cat., Paris: Musée du Louvre, 1989), 7.

5 Rudolf Wittkower, *Art and Architecture in Italy 1600–1750*, 3d ed. (Harmondsworth, Middlesex: Penguin Books, 1973), 67.

6 Anthony Blunt, *Nicolas Poussin* (New York: Bollingen Foundation, 1967), vol. 1, 100–102; Haskell/Penny, *Taste* (NOTE 1), 43–44.

7 Blunt, *Poussin* (NOTE 6), vol. 1, 77; Pierre Rosenberg, *La Mort de Germanicus de Poussin du Musée de Minneapolis* (exh. cat., Paris: Musée du Louvre, 1973); Ekkehard Mai and Anke Repp-Eckert, *Triumph und Tod des Helden* (exh. cat., Cologne: Wallraf-Richartz-Museum, 1987–88), 179–81; *Poussin: The Early Years in Rome* (exh. cat., Fort Worth: Kimbell Art Museum, 1988), 129–72.

8 Antoine Schnapper, *David* (New York: Alpine Fine Arts Collection, 1982), 42.

9 Howard Hibbard, *Bernini* (Baltimore: Penguin Books, 1968), 57; Wittkower, *Art and Architecture* (NOTE 5), 145.

10 Ellis K. Waterhouse, *Italian Baroque Painting* (London: Phaidon, 1969), 55–62; Wittkower, *Art and Architecture* (NOTE 5), 263–66.

11 Ellis K. Waterhouse, "Painting in Rome in the Eighteenth Century," *Museum Studies*, no. 6 (1971): 9–10.

12 Wittkower, *Art and Architecture* (NOTE 5), 461.

13 Catherine Legrand and Domitilla d'Ormesson-Peugeot, *La Rome baroque de Maratti à Piranèse* (exh. cat., Paris: Musée du Louvre, 1990).

14 Jacques Thuillier and Albert Châtelet, *French Painting from Le Nain to Fragonard* (Geneva: Skira, 1964), 66–68; Pierre Rosenberg, *France in the Golden Age* (exh. cat., New York: The Metropolitan Museum of Art, 1982), 318.

15 Thuillier/Châtelet, *French Painting* (NOTE 14), 63.

16 Georges Brunel et al., *Piranèse et les français, 1740–1790* (exh. cat., Rome: Académie de France, 1976); Wittkower, *Art and Architecture* (NOTE 5), 363.

17 Haskell/Penny, *Taste* (NOTE 1), 37–42; Wittkower, *Art and Architecture* (NOTE 5), 163.

18 Pierre Rosenberg, *Le Siècle de Louis XV* (exh. cat., Ottawa: Galerie Nationale du Canada, 1976), 14; Philip Conisbee, *Painting in Eighteenth-Century France* (Ithaca: Cornell University Press, 1981), 77–80; Donald A. Rosenthal, *La Grande Manière: Historical and Religious Painting in France, 1700–1800* (exh. cat., Rochester: Memorial Art Gallery, University of Rochester, 1987), 12–13.

19 Conisbee, *Painting in Eighteenth-Century France* (NOTE 18), 92–93.

20 Lord Shaftesbury, letter to Paolo de Matteis, June 3, 1711; cited in Francis Haskell, *Patrons and Painters: A Study in the Relations between Italian Art and Society in the Age of the Baroque* (New Haven: Yale University Press, 1980), 198–99.

21 La Font de Saint-Yenne, *Réflexions sur quelques causes de l'état présent de la peinture en France* (La Haye: Jean Neaulme, 1747; reprint Geneva: Slatkine Reprints, 1970), 18.

22 La Font de Saint-Yenne, *Sentiments sur quelques ouvrages du Salon du 1753* (1754), 51.

23 Jean Locquin, *La Peinture d'histoire en France de 1747 à 1785* (Paris: Henri Laurens, 1912), 92–93.

24 Hugh Honour, *Neo-Classicism* (Harmondsworth, Middlesex: Penguin Books, 1968), 105.

25 Frederick den Broeder, *The Academy of Europe: Rome in the 18th Century* (exh. cat., Storrs: William Benton Museum of Art, University of Connecticut, 1973).

26 Albert Boime, *Art in an Age of Revolution, 1750–1800* (Chicago: University of Chicago Press, 1987), 150–51.

27 Ibid., 146–50.

28 Johann Joachim Winckelmann, *Gedanken über die Nachahmung der griechischen Werke in der Malerei und Bildhauerkunst* (1755); cited in Elizabeth G. Holt, ed., *A Documentary History of Art* (Garden City, New York: Doubleday Anchor Books, 1958), vol. 2, 338.

29 Holt, *Documentary History* (NOTE 28), vol. 2, 340.

30 Ibid., 345–49.

31 David Irwin, ed., *Winckelmann: Writings on Art* (London: Phaidon, 1972), 4–9; Édouard Pommier, ed., *Winckelmann: La Naissance de l'histoire de l'art à l'epoque des lumières* (Paris: La Documentation française, 1991).

32 Johann Wolfgang Goethe, *Italian Journey, 1786–1788*, trans. W. H. Auden and Elizabeth Mayer (London: Collins, 1962), 155–56.

33 Honour, *Neo-Classicism* (NOTE 24), 85; Anton W. A. Boschloo et al., ed., *Academies of Art between Renaissance and Romanticism* (*Leids Kunsthistorisch Jaarboek* 5–6, 1986–87; published 1989).

34 Kunstakademiets Bibliothek, Copenhagen, Ltr. C. Nr. 6, 129; Winckelmann himself published an engraving of the relief in his *Monumenti antichi inediti* (pl. 11).

35 Denis Coekelberghs and Pierre Loze, *Autour du Néo-Classicisme en Belgique, 1770–1830* (exh. cat., Brussels: Musée Communal des Beaux-Arts d'Ixelles, 1985–86), 21.

36 Irwin, *Winckelmann* (NOTE 31), 85.

37 Thomas Pelzel, *Anton Raphael Mengs and Neoclassicism* (New York: Garland Publishing, 1979), 113.

38 Ibid., 109–16.

39 Ibid., 126.

40 Ibid., 85–91.

41 Ibid., 304–5 n. 210.

42 Irwin, *Winckelmann* (NOTE 31), 48.

43 David Irwin, "Gavin Hamilton: Archaeologist, Painter, and Dealer," *The Art Bulletin* 44, no. 2 (1962): 87–102; id., *English Neoclassical Art* (London: Faber and Faber, 1966), 31–38.

44 Irwin, *English Neoclassical Art* (NOTE 43), 34–35.

45 Ibid., 36; Schnapper, *David* (NOTE 8), 36–37; Locquin, *La Peinture d'histoire* (NOTE 23), 153.

46 Boime, *Age of Revolution* (NOTE 26), 78–79.

47 Irwin, *English Neoclassical Art* (NOTE 43), 36.

48 Boime, *Age of Revolution* (NOTE 26), 153–55; Thomas Gaehtgens, "Archaeology and Enlightenment," in Colin B. Bailey, ed., *The First Painters to the King* (exh. cat., New York: Stair Sainty Matthiesen, 1985), 37–45.

49 Mengs had executed in 1754 a pair of pseudoclassical pastels, *Vanity* and *Wisdom*, for the marquis de Croismare that were greatly admired in Paris; see Pelzel, *Mengs* (NOTE 37), 73–76, 210; see also Steffi Röttgen, "L'Interprétation idéaliste du bonheur: Une commission romaine du marquis de Croismare," in Pommier, *Winckelmann* (NOTE 31), 161–94.

50 Anita Brookner, *Greuze: The Rise and Fall of an Eighteenth-Century Phenomenon* (Greenwich: New York Graphic Society, 1972), 67–70; Edgar Munhall, *Jean-Baptiste Greuze, 1725–1805* (exh. cat., Hartford: Wadsworth Atheneum, 1976–77), no. 70; *Diderot & l'art de Boucher à David: Les Salons 1759–1781* (exh. cat., Paris: Hôtel de la Monnaie, 1984–85).

51 Munhall, *Greuze* (NOTE 50), 146.

52 Ibid., 148; Michel, *Le Beau Idéal* (NOTE 4), 35–36.

53 Michel, *Le Beau Idéal* (NOTE 4), 35.

54 Denis Diderot, *Salons*, ed. Jean Seznec and Jean Adhémar (Oxford: Clarendon Press, 1957–67), vol. 4, 103–6.

55 Munhall, *Greuze* (NOTE 50), 178–80.

56 Ibid., 148.

57 Joshua Reynolds, *Discourses on Art* (London: Collier-Macmillan, 1966), v.

58 Edmund Burke, *Works* (Boston: Charles C. Little and James Brown, 1839), vol. 1, 98–99.

59 Robert Rosenblum, *Transformations in Late Eighteenth-Century Art* (Princeton: Princeton University Press, 1970), 11.

60 Irwin, *English Neoclassical Art* (NOTE 43), 94–99.

61 Edgar Wind, "The Revolution of History Painting," *Journal of the Warburg Institute* 2 (1938–39): 116–27.

62 Boime, *Age of Revolution* (NOTE 26), 131–32.

63 Irwin, *English Neoclassical Art* (NOTE 43), 148–49; see also Reynolds, *Discourses* (NOTE 57), no. 10, 164–65.

64 John Galt, *The Life, Studies, and Works of Benjamin West, Esq.* (London, 1820), vol. 2, 47–49.

65 Lorenz Eitner, ed., *Neoclassicism and Romanticism 1750–1850: Sources and Documents* (Englewood Cliffs, N.J.: Prentice-Hall, 1970), vol. 1, 32–33.

66 Ibid., 33–34. Mengs's conception is rooted in seventeenth-century academic theory; see Pelzel, *Mengs* (NOTE 37), 174–80, for Mengs's pedagogic activities.

67 Eitner, *Neoclassicism and Romanticism* (NOTE 65), 33.

68 Holt, *Documentary History* (NOTE 28), vol. 2, 349–51.

69 Gotthold Ephraim Lessing, *Laocoön, or On the Limits of Painting and Poetry*, trans. Ellen Frothingham (New York: Noonday Press, 1968), 13.

70 Ibid., 16.

71 Ibid., 2–3.

72 Ibid., 20–22.

73 Ibid., 16.

74 Irwin, *English Neoclassical Art* (NOTE 43), 46–47; Gert Schiff, "Fuseli, Lucifer, and the Medusa," in *Henry Fuseli, 1741–1825* (exh. cat., London: Tate Gallery, 1975), 10; Nancy L. Pressly, *The Fuseli Circle in Rome: Early Romantic Art of the 1770s* (exh. cat., New Haven: Yale Center for British Art, 1979), viii, 28.

75 Fuseli, letter to Lavater, July 30, 1770; cited in Schiff, "Fuseli" (NOTE 74), 40.

76 Pressly, *The Fuseli Circle* (NOTE 74), xviii, 38, no. 39.

77 Ibid., xi–xii.

78 Schnapper, *David* (NOTE 8), 37.

79 Pelzel, *Mengs* (NOTE 37), 214–16; Schnapper, *David* (NOTE 8), 34–45; Jean Leymarie, Giulio Carlo Argan, et al., *David e Roma* (exh. cat., Rome: Académie de France, 1981–82).

80 Seymour Howard, *Sacrifice of the Hero, the Roman Years: A Classical Frieze by Jacques-Louis David* (Sacramento: E. B. Crocker Art Gallery, 1975); Schnapper, *David* (NOTE 8), 52–53; Antoine Schnapper and Arlette Sérullaz, *Jacques-Louis David, 1748–1825* (exh. cat., Paris: Musée du Louvre/Versailles: Musée National du Château, 1989), nos. 38–39.

81 Schnapper, *David* (NOTE 8), 42, 50–51.

82 Diderot, *Salons* (NOTE 54), vol. 4, 377.

83 Schnapper, *David* (NOTE 8), 61–63.

84 Michel, *Le Beau Idéal* (NOTE 4), 7–8, 82.

85 Wend Graf Kalnein and Michael Levey, *Art and Architecture of the Eighteenth Century in France* (Harmondsworth, Middlesex: Penguin Books, 1972), 155–56.

86 Schnapper, *David* (NOTE 8), 73; Rosenblum, *Transformations* (NOTE 59), 68–74.

87 Warren Roberts, *Jacques-Louis David, Revolutionary Artist* (Chapel Hill: University of North Carolina Press, 1989), 18.

88 Carter Ratcliff, "Painting's Constitution," *Art in America* 78, no. 5 (May 1990): 211–14, 263.

89 Anita Brookner, *Jacques-Louis David* (New York: Icon Editions/Harper and Row, 1980), 79.

90 Thomas E. Crow, *Painters and Public Life in Eighteenth-Century Paris* (New Haven: Yale University Press, 1985), 211–20; Robert Rosenblum, "Reconstructing David," *Art in America* 78, no. 5 (May 1990): 192.

91 Thomas E. Crow, "*The Oath of the Horatii* in 1785: Painting and Pre-Revolutionary Radicalism in France," *Art History* 1, no. 4 (December 1978): 424–71; id., *Painters and Public Life* (NOTE 90), 211–58; Boime, *Age of Revolution* (NOTE 26), 162–83, 391–424; Régis Michel, *David: L'Art et le politique* (Paris: Gallimard, 1988); Roberts, *David* (NOTE 87); Schnapper/Sérullaz, *David* (NOTE 80), 14, 167; Rosenblum, "Reconstructing David" (NOTE 90), 191–92.

92 Boime, *Age of Revolution* (NOTE 26), 55–183, 391.

93 Ibid., 168–80; Crow, *Painters and Public Life* (NOTE 90), 198–209.

94 Crow, *Painters and Public Life* (NOTE 90), 200–203.

95 Yvonne Korshak, "*Paris and Helen* by Jacques-Louis David: Choice and Judgment on the Eve of the French Revolution," *The Art Bulletin* 69, no. 1 (March 1987): 102–16; id. and Francis Dowley, "An Exchange on Jacques-Louis David," *The Art Bulletin* 70, no. 3 (September 1988): 504–20. See also Régis Michel, "*Pâris et Hélène* (Salon de 1789)," in Leymarie/Argan, *David e Roma* (NOTE 79), 144–53.

96 H. W. Janson, *19th-Century Sculpture* (New York: Abrams, 1985), 48–49.

97 Ibid., 49.

98 Boime, *Age of Revolution* (NOTE 26), 140–42.

99 Hugh Honour speculates that Canova's figures influenced those of Camilla and Sabina in *The Oath of the Horatii*; see Honour, "Canova and David," *Apollo* 96, no. 128 (October 1972): 313.

100 Honour, *Neo-Classicism* (NOTE 24), 39–40.

101 Fred Licht, *Canova* (New York: Abbeville Press, 1983), 21.

102 Ibid.

103 Hugh Honour, "Neo-Classicism," in *The Age of Neo-Classicism* (exh. cat., London: Royal Academy/Victoria and Albert Museum, 1972), 195.

104 Licht, *Canova* (NOTE 101), 186.

105 Holt, *Documentary History* (NOTE 28), vol. 2, 345–46.

106 Pelzel, *Mengs* (NOTE 37), 123–25.

107 Rosenblum, *Transformations* (NOTE 59), 146–91.

108 Ibid., 164.

109 Ibid., 164–66; Irwin, *English Neoclassical Art* (NOTE 43), 89, 108.

110 Sylvain Laveissière et al., *Bénigne Gagneraux (1756–1795): Un pittore francese nella Roma di Pio VI* (exh. cat., Rome: Galleria Borghese, 1983), 148–58, nos. 70–87; Rosenblum, *Transformations* (NOTE 59), 179–80; Michel, *Le Beau Idéal* (NOTE 4), 91.

111 Detlef W. Dorrbecker, "Survey of Engravings after Flaxman's Outline Compositions, 1793–1845," in *John Flaxman R.A.* (exh. cat., London: Royal Academy, 1979), 184–85.

112 Rosenblum, *Transformations* (NOTE 59), 172–73.

113 Sarah Symmons, "Flaxman and the Continent," in *Flaxman* (NOTE 111), 156–62.

114 Michel, *Le Beau Idéal* (NOTE 4), 105–20; Georges Vigne and Florence Vigulier, *La Révolution française à l'école de la virtu antique, 1775–1796* (exh. cat., Montauban: Musée Ingres, 1989); Philippe Bordes and Régis Michel, *Aux armes & aux arts: Les Arts de la révolution, 1789–1799* (Paris: A. Biro, 1988).

115 David Lloyd Dowd, *Pageant Master of the Republic: Jacques-Louis David and the French Revolution* (Lincoln: University of Nebraska Press, 1948); Schnapper, *David* (NOTE 8), 136–57; Stephanie Carroll, "Reciprocal Representations: David and Theater," *Art in America* 78, no. 5 (May 1990): 203–4.

116 Licht, *Canova* (NOTE 101), 101–3; Janson, *19th-Century Sculpture* (NOTE 96), 54–56.

117 Brookner, *David* (NOTE 89), 145–48; Schnapper, *David* (NOTE 8), 253.

118 Charles Percier and Pierre-François-Léonard Fontaine, *Recueil de décorations intérieures comprenant tout ce qui rapport à l'ameublement* (Paris, 1801).

119 Honour, *Neo-Classicism* (NOTE 24), 171.

120 Mario Praz, "The Meaning and Diffusion of the Empire Style," in *Age of Neo-Classicism* (NOTE 103), lxxxviii–xci.

121 Michel, *Le Beau Idéal* (NOTE 4), 126–27.

122 Anne-Louis Girodet de Roussy-Trioson's *The Sleeping Endymion* (see FIGURE 43), 1791, and François Gérard's *Cupid and Psyche*, 1798, reveal the same sources.

123 Michel, *Le Beau Idéal* (NOTE 4), 132; Gordon N. Ray, *The Art of the French Illustrated Book, 1700–1914* (New York: Dover, 1986), 120–33.

124 Holt, *Documentary History* (NOTE 28), vol. 2, 337.

125 Ibid., 349.

126 Michel, *Le Beau Idéal* (NOTE 4), 67–72.

127 James Henry Rubin, "Guérin's Painting of Phèdre and the Post-Revolutionary Revival of Racine," *The Art Bulletin* 59, no. 4 (December 1977): 610–11.

128 C. M. Osborne, "Pierre Didot the Elder and French Book Illustration 1789–1822" (Ph.D. diss., Stanford University, 1979).

129 Rubin, "Guérin's Painting" (NOTE 127), 606–10.

130 Michel, *Le Beau Idéal* (NOTE 4), 72, 93–94.

131 Irwin, *Winckelmann* (NOTE 31), 8–9.

132 Pelzel, *Mengs* (NOTE 37), 259; Haskell/Penny, *Taste* (NOTE 1), 106.

133 Michael Greenhalgh, "Quatremère de Quincy as a Popular Archaeologist," *Gazette des Beaux-Arts* 6, no. 71 (April 1968): 249.

134 Irwin, *English Neoclassical Art* (NOTE 43), 72–75; Boime, *Age of Revolution* (NOTE 26), 144–45.

135 Vermeule, *European Art* (NOTE 1), 13.

136 Antoine-Chrysostôme Quatremère de Quincy, *Canova et ses ouvrages* (Paris: Adrien Le Clere et Cie., 1834), 260.

137 Emma Salling, "Canova and Thorvaldsen: A Study in Contrasts," *Apollo* 96, no. 127 (September 1972): 214–19; see also Dyveke Helsted, Eva Henschen, and Bjarne Jørnæs, *Thorvaldsen* (Copenhagen: Thorvaldsens Museum, 1990), 19–20.

138 Janson, *19th-Century Sculpture* (NOTE 96), 57.

139 Salling, "Canova and Thorvaldsen" (NOTE 137), 217.

140 Gisela M. Richter, *Archaic Greek Art* (New York: Oxford University Press, 1949), 138–39.

141 Phyllis Hattis, *Ingres' Sculptural Style: A Group of Unknown Drawings* (exh. cat., Cambridge: Fogg Art Museum, Harvard University, 1973), 42–64.

142 George Wildenstein, *Ingres* (New York: Phaidon, 1954), nos. 72, 92; Robert Rosenblum, *Jean-Auguste-Dominique Ingres* (New York: Abrams, 1967), 84–94.

143 Siegfried Gohr, "Der Alexander Fries," in *Bertel Thorvaldsen* (exh. cat., Cologne: Museen der Stadt, 1977), 81–87.

144 For a different point of view see Michel, "L'Hérésie de la couleur," in *Le Beau Idéal* (NOTE 4), 142–44.

145 Brunel de Varennes, *L'Art du dessin chez les grecs* (Paris: Colas, 1816).

146 Greenhalgh, "Quatremère de Quincy" (NOTE 133), 251; Haskell/Penny, *Taste* (NOTE 1), 107.

147 Rosenblum, *Ingres* (NOTE 142), 146.

148 Ibid.

149 Greenhalgh, *The Classical Tradition* (NOTE 1), 231.

150 Rosenblum, *Ingres* (NOTE 142), 51.

151 Michel, *Le Beau Idéal* (NOTE 4), 144–47.

152 Wildenstein, *Ingres* (NOTE 142), no. 168.

153 Rosenblum, *Ingres* (NOTE 142), 130–31; Patricia Condon, Marjorie B. Cohn, and Agnes Morgan, *In Pursuit of Perfection: The Art of J.-A.-D. Ingres* (exh. cat., Louisville: J. B. Speed Art Museum, 1984), 110–13.

154 Michel, *Le Beau Idéal* (NOTE 4), 144.

155 Wildenstein, *Ingres* (NOTE 142), nos. 87, 89, 114, 119, 120–21, 146; see also Greenhalgh, *The Classical Tradition* (NOTE 1), 230–33; Robert Rosenblum, "La Peinture sous la Restauration," in *De David à Delacroix: La Peinture française de 1774–1830* (exh. cat., Paris: Grand Palais, 1974), 233–47; Albert Boime, *Thomas Couture and the Eclectic Vision* (New Haven: Yale University Press, 1980); Robert Rosenblum and H. W. Janson, *19th-Century Art* (New York: Abrams, 1984).

156 Lee Johnson, *The Paintings of Eugène Delacroix* (Oxford: Clarendon Press, 1986), vol. 2, pl. 79; vol. 3, 78, no. 261.

157 *Géricault* (exh. cat., Paris: Grand Palais, 1991–92), 72, 75, fig. 13.

OVERLEAF
Bertel Thorvaldsen
Sheet of Studies
c. 1823
(CATALOGUE NO. 112, detail)

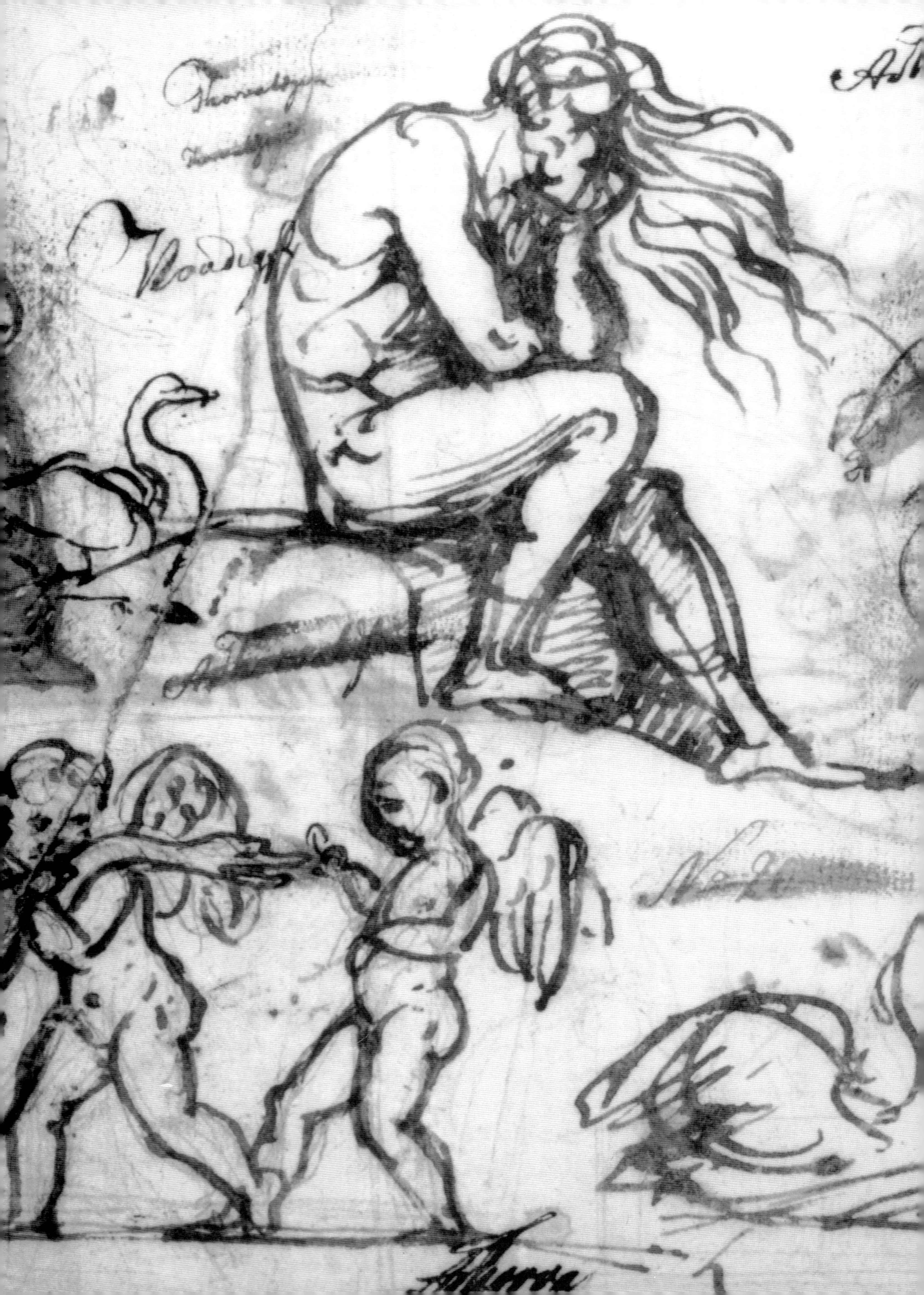

"Imitating the Ancients": The Revival of Art in Northern Europe

Marsha Morton

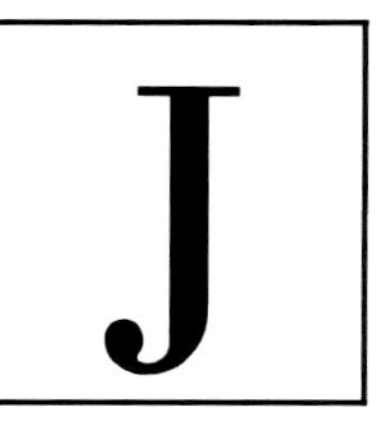

ohann Wolfgang Goethe wrote that "in Germany, more than in France, neoclassicism has been founded on drawing."[1] This situation arose from a variety of circumstances, some common to neoclassicism in other countries. As elsewhere, writers provided theoretical justification for the importance of a linear-plastic art, while academic instruction was based on drawing. Throughout the north artists were even more indebted to philosophical doctrines that usually preceded and influenced their work. Practices in patronage also served inadvertently to foster the growth of drawing. For some artists, especially sculptors, local rulers exercised strict control over their client's commissions, so that drawings offered the only means of free expression. To a great extent, themes from classical history remained unpopular, and most artists supported themselves through portraiture. Finished drawings offered the only economically feasible opportunity for depicting historical subjects. Increasingly in the early nineteenth century these drawings were sold to and printed by publishers such as Johann Friedrich Cotta and Johann Friedrich Frauenholz.[2]

The flourishing of drawings during this period is evident in the variety of styles and purposes—academies (studies, usually in chalk, of academic models), copies, preparatory studies—employed by each artist. Overall, a growing preference was shown for finished independent drawings, especially among painters, and for the mediums of pen and pencil, which facilitated the desired precision of contour. Among nearly all sculptors, drawings were a personal mode of expression separate from their sculptural oeuvre, for which they preferred to "sketch" in clay.

The development of neoclassicism in the Germanic countries was shaped by the constraints of political fragmentation and lack of economic competitiveness. The Holy Roman Empire of the German Nation consisted of more than eighteen hundred separate territories, with what is now Germany comprising more than three hundred states. Intellectuals and artists were denied the benefits of a cosmopolitan center or a cultural heritage viewed with respect internationally. This situation began changing during the late eighteenth century through the promotion of nationalism by writers and historians. While patriots frequently viewed neoclassicism suspiciously as yet another imported movement, many artists embraced the antique as a means to reinvigorate German art, and some used classical forms and themes as social and political criticism. The emergence of a new generation of Enlightenment rulers who modeled themselves on the example of the Prussian king Frederick the Great was a mixed blessing. Increased financial support for the arts was frequently contingent upon conformity to imposed aesthetic tastes. To these rulers, however, was owed the establishment and growth of nearly one hundred academies during this period, a number far exceeding that in other countries.[3]

The main academic centers of neoclassicism were in Copenhagen, Vienna, and Stuttgart (the Berlin Akademie remained more important for classical architecture and sculpture than for painting). Despite regional differences, common patterns characterized each institution. During these decades a transition occurred in the academic leadership from French rococo artists imported by the provincial aristocracy to native talent trained locally and in Rome in a neoclassical style. The parallel emergence of neoclassicism and nationalism was most extreme in Denmark, where it resulted in the banishment of most foreign artists in the early 1770s, when Danish, rather than German, was established as the official language of the country. The resulting interest in Nordic legends, promoted through the writings of Johannes Ewald, Friedrich Gottlieb Klopstock, and Elias Schlegel, was reflected in the popularity of these themes among Danish neoclassical artists.

Curricula were generally standardized and based on the model of the seventeenth-century French Académie. Training was incremental, beginning with drawing after engravings and drawings, followed by plaster casts and live models. The finest collections of casts were found in Berlin, Dresden, Düsseldorf, Leipzig, and Mannheim, the last celebrated in Goethe's memoirs.[4] Neoclassical theory was emphasized, and professors frequently published scholarly texts, as, for example, in Copenhagen (Johannes Wiedewelt's *Tanker om Smagen udi Konsterne i Almindelighed* [Thoughts on taste in the arts], 1762) and in Stuttgart (Nicolas Guibal's *Traité sur les proportions du corps humain* [Treatise on the proportions of the human body], c. 1774). At the same time, drawings by teachers and students remained in a baroque style, with broken lines and wash used for shading and movement.

Academic neoclassicism developed through the promotional efforts of artists who had been pupils or friends of Johann Joachim Winckelmann and Anton Raphael Mengs in Rome. In 1762 Mengs's student Guibal designed the curriculum for the Stuttgart Hohe Karlsschule, where he taught and was later director. His pupils included Johann Heinrich Dannecker, Ferdinand Hartmann, Philipp Friedrich Hetsch, and Eberhard Wächter. Winckelmann's friend Wiedewelt returned to Denmark in 1758, where his students at the Copenhagen Kunstakademiet included Nikolai Abraham Abildgaard, Asmus Jacob Carstens, Alexander Trippel, and Bertel Thorvaldsen. In Vienna, Mengs's brother-in-law, Anton Maron, implemented academic reforms in 1772. The influence of Winckelmann and Mengs was also felt at smaller academies, including those in Dresden, Karlsruhe, Kassel, and Leipzig.

The training of most northern artists was completed in Rome, usually through royal travel grants administered by the local academy. In Italy artists studied in the Vatican and Capitoline museums and at private villas. Life drawing from male models was available at the Académie de France à Rome, the Accademia del Nudo, or one of the private academies that were preferred because rules of silence were not imposed. More adventuresome spirits, such as Johan Tobias Sergel and Henry Fuseli, sketched in fencing halls and in the streets. Northern artists considered their Italian experience as training in draftsmanship—Wilhelm Tischbein remarked, "Rome is the place where one learns to draw"[5]—and invariably their neoclassical style first emerged in Rome. Drawing and the absorption of the antique were inextricably linked. Rome also played an extremely important role for German artists by providing them with a center for cultural exchange lacking in the north and access to wealthy international patrons. Many never returned home, and those who did often failed to maintain their creative momentum. The critic and historian Carl Ludwig Fernow spoke for his generation when he wrote, "Germany produces great artists, but provides no supportive environment for them. In Italy German artists live, struggle, and create."[6]

Neoclassical doctrine was established by Winckelmann, whose writings cast a spell on the century with their vision of a pagan, Hellenistic utopia. The core of his philosophy was contained in his first publication, *Gedanken über die Nachahmung der griechischen Werke in der Malerei und Bildhauerkunst* (Thoughts on the imitation of Greek art in painting and sculpture), 1755.[7] Winckelmann formulated principles adhered to by future generations of neoclassicists: the essential content of art was humanity; art depicted idealized beauty; form took precedence over color; canonical works of good taste included the Apollo Belvedere, the Laocoön, and the Belvedere Torso; Homer was the supreme source for subject matter; and Raphael was the most revered of Renaissance artists. Greek sculpture was presented as offering a model of idealized beauty transcribed from an idea in the artist's mind of perfected nature, which contemporaries should imitate—that is, create in the same spirit—rather than copy. As Winckelmann observed, Greek artists formed "concepts that were meant to rise above nature, being taken from a spiritual realm that exists only in the mind."[8]

These Platonic notions resulted in a vision of nearly incorporeal beauty characterized by reduction and absence, which Winckelmann compared to clear water, and best captured by the delineation of form. According to Winckelmann, outlines traced from the silhouettes of shadows represented "not the manner in which a man appears to us, but what he is."[9] Winckelmann established drawing as the most appropriate medium for imaging the invisible and essential. Humanity was to be shown godlike, with "noble simplicity and quiet grandeur," purged of violent emotion, exaggerated movement, and individual imperfection. Repose was necessary in order to convey the true, noble character of the soul and to maintain beauty, the latter view also espoused by the Hellenist Gotthold Ephraim Lessing in his treatise *Laokoon* of 1766.[10]

The sources of Winckelmann's originality and popularity were not to be found in these ideas, most of which derived from the baroque academic theory of writers such as Giovanni Pietro Bellori, Nicolas Boileau-Despreaux, and Lord Shaftesbury, but in a new presentation of the ideas shaped by his sexual preferences and his reaction against rococo culture.[11] Remarkably, Winckelmann's Apollonian view of Hellenism was founded upon his attraction to the sensual appeal of classical sculpture. As the more pious Klopstock was quick to observe, Winckelmann was often led astray by his "not always chaste" imagination.[12] Winckelmann found no inconsistency in using fervidly passionate prose to describe art "that exists only in the mind," nor did he hesitate to locate beauty in both the purity of water and in the undulating curves of slim, adolescent male youths.

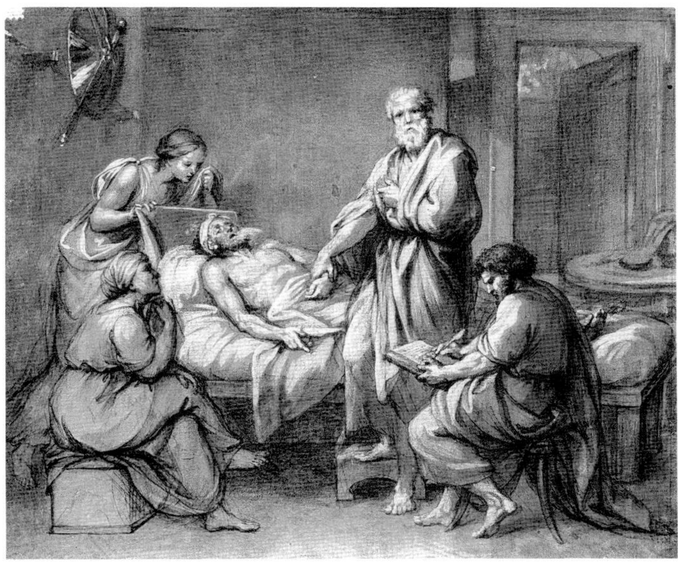

FIGURE 20
Anton Raphael Mengs
Germany, 1728–79

The Testament of Eudamidas
1758, pen and ink, wash, white heightening over chalk,
21 x 25.6 cm (8 1/4 x 10 1/16 in.),
Museum der bildenden Künste, Leipzig (inv. no. NI.124)

Greek culture was presented by Winckelmann as a paradigm to be emulated by modern society. The Greeks were a race of superior beauty and intellect whose social and political structure was based on freedom. Art thrived because of this liberal attitude, which was reflected in their democratic government as well as in the practice of exercising and dancing in the nude. Winckelmann's celebration of the values of simplicity and naturalness can best be understood in the context of rococo culture, in which artifice, affectation, and tyranny were perceived to prevail.[13] To future generations of German neoclassicists Winckelmann bequeathed a legacy in which the representation of male nudes was politicized as a symbol of liberty and truth.

Among modern painters Winckelmann most admired his good friend Mengs, whom he met in Rome in 1755. Mengs, a celebrated portraitist, is regarded as the first German neoclassicist, although his history paintings are transitional in style and seem undeserving of Winckelmann's high praise. He earned the appellation the "German Raphael" through a facility for duplication demonstrated by his copy of *The School of Athens* in 1752 for the duke of Northumberland. As preparation for the commission he completed fifty-two drawings of heads, which were later engraved and published in 1785.

Most of Mengs's drawings were copies, academies, and preparatory studies in ink or chalk that retained the broken contours and fluid lines of the rococo. Significantly, however, his most advanced neoclassical style appeared in drawings from the late 1750s, rather than in the more renowned paintings from the next decade, such as the *Parnassus* ceiling in the Villa Albani, Rome (see FIGURE 3), and *Augustus and Cleopatra* (two versions, both 1760, are in the Galerie Czernin, Vienna, and Stourhead, Wiltshire). All of these works paralleled a new interest in antiquity, reflected in his acquisitions of ancient art, and were stimulated by the artistic exchange with Winckelmann.[14]

Joseph in Prison (*Josef als Traumdeuter im Gefängnis*; Graphische Sammlung Albertina, Vienna), 1756–58, and *The Testament of Eudamidas* (*Das Testament des Eudamidas*; FIGURE 20), 1758, both preparatory drawings for paintings, display austere, shallow, stagelike spatial settings with rectilinear compositions reminiscent of classical friezes. Figures are reduced in number and restrained in pose. *The Testament of Eudamidas* was based on the painting of this subject by Nicolas Poussin, known to Mengs through an engraving of the later seventeenth century by Jean Pesne (sources for other drawings included the work of Hubert Gravelot and Gavin Hamilton). This drawing is precocious in its use of a theme from Greek literature as well as in its style, anticipating by a decade Denis Diderot's admiration for Poussin's painting and the exemplary morality of Eudamidas. Mengs's only depiction of a subject from Homer was the neoclassical drawing *The Sacrifice of the Achaians* (*Das Opfer der Achaier*; Graphische Sammlung Albertina), also from the late 1750s. Stylistically, these remained an anomaly, and it was only in his academies, as, for example, his studies of male nudes (CATALOGUE NO. 95; see FIGURE 41), that he continued to work in a more severe, polished manner.

Mengs's theoretical writings, *Betrachtungen über die Schönheit und den guten Geschmack in der Malerei* (Thoughts on beauty and good taste in painting), 1762, and *Lezioni pratiche di pittura* (Practical lessons in painting), 1780, modified Winckelmann's doctrine to include Correggio and Titian as exemplars of ideal beauty, while excluding even further the "coarse" forms of Michelangelo. Unlike Winckelmann, Mengs believed that modern artists had the potential to surpass antiquity through a judicious combination of techniques learned from Renaissance and

Greek art. More crucial to their success, however, would be their ability to conceive and create like the ancients.[15] This concept derived from Winckelmann's own distinction between imitating and copying and reflected Mengs's earlier study of Raphael under the guidance of his martinet father, for whom he had to provide explanations of the ideas motivating Raphael as well as drawn copies. Mengs's rigorously disciplined education shaped his conception of the creative process as an intellectual exercise and resulted in his reputation as a pedant. He maintained that artistic success was guaranteed if the student was attentive, patient, and "free of too much fire and vitality," which was frequently mistaken for genius.[16]

The theories of Winckelmann and Mengs did not go unopposed, and it is ironic that northern neoclassicism was critically antithetical to Winckelmann's Apollonian Hellenism. Drawings by Abildgaard, Fuseli, and Sergel from the 1770s expressed a passionate and demonic vision of the classical world that was indebted to beliefs of "Counter-Enlightenment" philosophers.[17] These writers, who became known as the *Sturm und Drang* (Storm and stress) movement, contributed substantially to the unique character of northern neoclassicism, which merged proto-romantic attitudes with selected precepts of Winckelmann. The early critics who took issue with Winckelmann were not opposed to Hellenism but to the dogmatic assertion of normative standards of taste and to the advisability of imitation as the correct path to modern excellence. Individuality, originality, and genius were celebrated in place of rational order, standardization, and imposed systems based on rules. Universalism, it was believed, would lead to mediocrity and uniformity. These convictions arose in response to the French Enlightenment and were accompanied in Germany by a rising tide of cultural nationalism manifested in a new interest in the German artistic heritage.[18]

Opposition to the Enlightenment and to Winckelmann appeared during the early 1760s in writings by Johann Georg Hamann, who championed intuition and feeling in the creative process and who opposed classical culture as an exclusive artistic model. Klopstock was one of the first to attack Winckelmann, in his article "Eine Beurtheilung der Winckelmannischen *Gedanken über die Nachahmung der griechischen Werke in den schönen Kunsten*" (A review of Winckelmann's "Thoughts Concerning the Imitation of Greek Works in the Fine Arts"), published in *Der nordische Aufseher* in 1760.[19] Klopstock objected to the cult of imitation and to the German tendency toward excessive admiration of foreign culture. While acknowledging the Greek achievement, he urged artists to consider religious themes and events from their national history. His own poetry was based on medieval bardic literature, an enthusiasm shared by the Swiss scholar Johann Jakob Bodmer, who published works on the *Niebelungenlied* as well as studies of Dante, Homer, Milton, and Shakespeare.[20]

Johann Gottfried Herder was the philosopher most closely identified with the *Sturm und Drang* movement, although he had begun his career as a great admirer of Winckelmann, having read *Geschichte der Kunst des Alterthums* (History of ancient art) seven times during his youth.[21] He viewed the art and language of different nations as unique cultural expressions resulting from varied geographical, temporal, and historical circumstances.[22] Accordingly, artists could only create great art when it was derived from their own common heritage rather than adopted from another tradition. Herder's writings awakened an appreciation for Nordic medieval literature, Ossian, and Shakespeare as well as Homer, since he did believe, unlike Winckelmann, that differences of artistic expression should not be judged according to fixed aesthetic norms.

Herder disparaged academic standards and rational discipline, believing that art should be the original expression of inner inspiration. In his perceptive tribute to Winckelmann, written in 1778, he observed that "what is divine in us is born within us: learning, books and marble cannot plant it where it is not from nature."[23]

During the 1770s enthusiasm for Winckelmann waned as Herder's influence dominated. The *Teutscher Merkur*, founded by Christoph Martin Wieland in 1773, became a center of opposition, with articles by Wieland and Johann Heinrich Merck. The Swiss scientist Johann Kaspar Lavater, a friend of Bodmer and Fuseli, published *Physiognomische Fragmente* (Physiognomical fragments) in 1775–78. Although the book expressed uncritical admiration for Greek art and society buttressed with numerous quotations from Winckelmann and Mengs, Lavater's basic tenet—that human character could be interpreted through physiognomical appearance—undermined Winckelmann's advocacy of generalized forms in favor of the individual and characteristic. Indeed, Lavater rejected any conceptual notions of the ideal in his belief that Greek artists were realists who faithfully transcribed the beauty of their contemporaries. Yet he reinforced certain precepts of Winckelmann's neoclassicism, stating unequivocally that man was the central subject of art, and he "proved" the correlation between outer appearance and inner essence that had only been intimated by Winckelmann. In his praise for the silhouette as the most accurate representation of form, Lavater echoed Winckelmann's appreciation of contour and contributed to the emergence of outline drawing in the 1790s. His work was widely read by many eighteenth-century artists.[24]

The writings of Wilhelm Heinse contained a complete rejection of Enlightenment principles. His "Über einige Gemählde der Düsseldorfer Gallerie" (Description of several paintings in the Düsseldorf Gallery), published in the *Teutscher Merkur* in 1776–77, and his novel *Ardinghello*, 1787, presented a Dionysian view of art that championed the carnal, amoral, and violent. Painting and color took precedence over drawing, and Rubens was extolled as the finest artist. Heinse was a confirmed voluptuary whose art criticism yielded lengthy comparative analyses of the female breast and who found beauty in Rubens's portrayal of "lust . . . sweat and danger" and "wild, cruel" girls.[25] Not surprisingly, Winckelmann and his friends were denounced as "that sterile crowd" who drew "in the midst of plaster phantoms."[26] Heinse deplored the German penchant for abstract aesthetic speculation and defined beauty as the expression of life in form and movement. Art resulted from original creation rather than academic exercises and imitation: "All art is human, not Greek."[27]

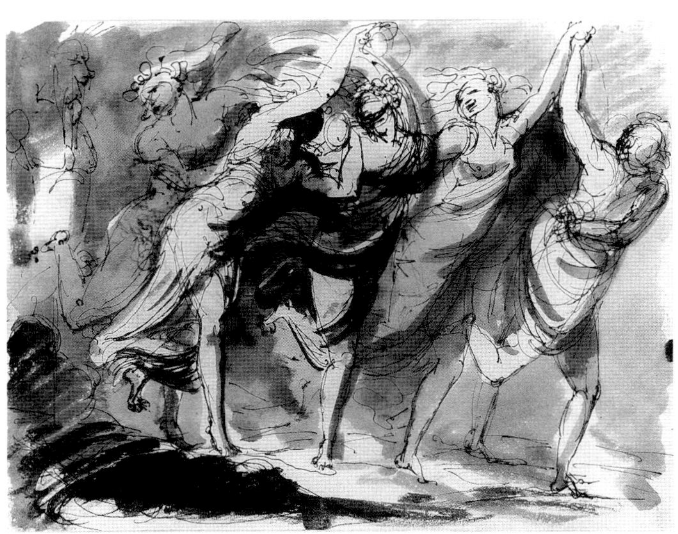

FIGURE 21
Johan Tobias Sergel
Sweden, 1740–1814

Bacchanalian Dance
Pen and black ink, wash, over black chalk,
18 x 24.2 cm (7 1/16 x 9 1/2 in.),
Nationalmuseum, Stockholm (inv. no. NMH-Z 23/1954)

In *Ardinghello* Heinse identified the most difficult and essential task of the artist as the rendering of life in its full intensity: storms in nature, murder, loneliness, and separation.[28] By the time he wrote this a group of artists working in Rome during the 1770s had already produced a body of work dedicated to this *Sturm und Drang* endeavor. Abildgaard, Fuseli, and Sergel, together with English artists Thomas Banks, James Barry, John Brown (CATALOGUE NO. 7), James Northcote, George Romney (CATALOGUE NOS. 1–2), and Alexander Runciman, had evolved a common style of drawing based on dramatic chiaroscuro, bold washes, and fluid contours to convey a content of passion and violence. A proto-Nietzschean, pagan vision of classicism emerged that temporarily overthrew Winckelmann's lofty, cerebral restraint and exposed his sublimated sensuality. Ancient art was now studied as a source for the dramatic, erotic, and mystical.

Sergel's mature style is exemplified in *Bacchanalian Dance* (*Bacchanalisk dans*; FIGURE 21), with its Dionysian content of passionate abandon conveyed through delicate, agitated lines and abstract stains of ink wash whose darker shadows suggest troubled psychological depths. The emotional extremes implicit in this drawing are autobiographical, reflecting the artist's hedonistic Roman life of wild parties at the Villa Madama (which inspired scenes in Heinse's novel) alternating with periods of severe depression. Sergel's central themes during his Roman period were relationships between the sexes, with women in seductive or submissive roles that anticipated Ingres, as in *Achilles Consoled by a Young Woman* (*Achilles med trøstende terne*; Nationalmuseum, Stockholm), 1775–76, whose tone of introspection and despair reveals the influence of Fuseli and Michelangelo.[29] In contrast to his more restrained, idealized sculptures, Sergel's drawings are frequently distinguished by their painterliness and emphasis on movement and psychological drama, indicating that they provided him with an alternative means of artistic expression (many of them are unrelated to his work in sculpture). The artist also completed detailed illusionistic chalk academies and copies, especially after antique sculptures and after paintings by Annibale Carracci and Raphael.

Preparatory drawings were important in the early evolution of Sergel's sculptural ideas but were discontinued once he began work on clay *bozzetti*. Even the early sketches for sculptures, such as his *Mars and Venus* (*Mars och Venus*; Nationalmuseum, Stockholm), c. 1771, bear little relation to the finished work. This drawing is a remarkable expressionist vision in which the frenzied scratchings of his pen create an image of nearly disembodied energy and anger. In style and psychological content Sergel created an eighteenth-century version of surrealist automatic drawing. His graphic manner evolved in Rome but was based on his earliest training in Stockholm with the Edmé Bouchardon student and Swedish court sculptor Pierre-Hubert L'Archevêque.[30] Sergel's interest in Homeric themes also dates from his early familiarity in the 1750s with the writings of the comte de Caylus.

Sergel returned to Sweden in 1778 as court sculptor for the young King Gustavus III. Nearly all of his Swedish commissions were portrait busts and medallions, which provided no outlet for antique subject matter. After the murder of his beloved patron in 1792 even this activity ceased, and drawing increasingly became his sole means of artistic expression. He maintained a close circle of friends with similar interests, including the architect Carl August Ehrensvärd. Sergel's later drawings, such as the *Allegory of the Death of Gustavus III* (*Allegori över Gustav IIIs död*; Nationalmuseum, Stockholm), about 1792, frequently present contemporary events in a neoclassical manner. The depiction of the king's assassination paraphrases classical tragedy and is similar in style to his drawing *Achilles Mourning over the Body of Patroclus* (*Akilles vid Patroklos' likbål*; private collection, Dömestorp, Denmark) from 1796. His later thematic range broadened to include theatrical scenes from Schiller and Shakespeare that are stylistically reminiscent of Fuseli. Sergel never ceased to yearn for a return to Italy, and he expressed the views of many northern artists when he later wrote, "The air of Rome is unique. . . . all the Nordic countries are graves to artistic genius."[31]

Fuseli arrived in Rome from Switzerland in 1770, where he remained for eight years, his artistic perspective shaped by the contradictory influences of Winckelmann, whose *Gedanken über die Nachahmung der griechischen Werke in der Malerei und Bildhauerkunst* he translated into English in 1765, and his Swiss *Sturm und Drang* literary colleagues Bodmer, Lavater, and Johann Jacob Breitinger. His complex assimilation of these sources is reflected in his drawing *Seated Youth* (*Sitzender Jüngling*; FIGURE 22) from 1774, in which a figure meditates on a vision of Winckelmann's Apollonian male beauty. The compelling nature of this model, as well as its inaccessibility, are conveyed through the precise clarity of the drawing, which is contrasted to the shadowy rendering of forms in the real world. Winckelmann's classicism, however, is subverted through the irrational, dreamlike setting, the mood of brooding despair, and the bizarre attenuation of the figure, whose pose is derived from Michelangelo and the drawings of the Italian mannerists.[32] This drawing

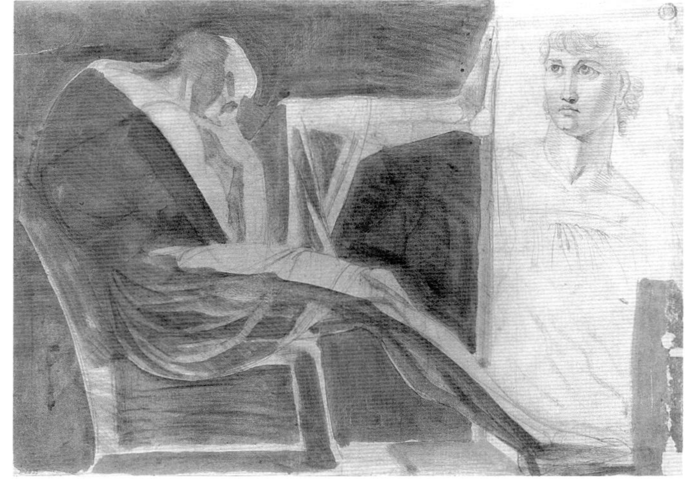

FIGURE 22
Henry Fuseli
Switzerland, active England, 1741–1825

Seated Youth
c. 1774, graphite, sepia wash, shades of gray,
37.3 x 52.8 cm (14 11/16 x 20 13/16 in.),
Museum der bildenden Künste, Leipzig (inv. no. 2699 verso)

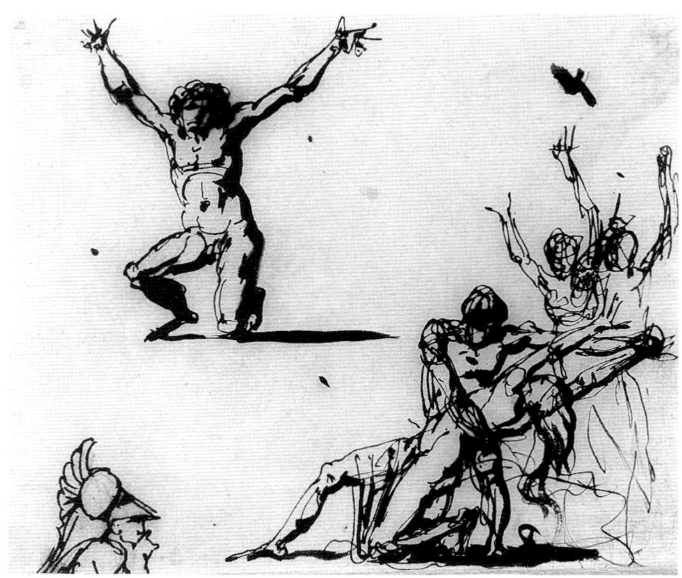

FIGURE 23
Nikolai Abraham Abildgaard
Denmark, 1743–1809

Achilles and the Handmaidens Mourning the Death of Patroclus
c. 1775, pen and brown ink and wash, 14 x 16.8 cm (5 1/2 x 6 5/8 in.),
Kongelige Kobberstiksamling, Statens Museum for Kunst,
Copenhagen (inv. no. TD.540.23)

exemplifies Fuseli's simplified style formulated in Rome, in which a wash is applied along contours in a broad and abstract manner. Figures customarily determine the space, which is shallow and undefined. Fuseli's desire to create universal images of poetic timelessness resulted in the elimination of historical detail in settings as well as costumes.

Disregarding the advice of Winckelmann, Fuseli introduced his friends to the art of Michelangelo, which inspired their expressive depictions of the human body in contorted poses. Similar discoveries had been made earlier by Sergel through his copies of figures by the Carracci.[33] Fuseli's "five-point drawings" from the 1770s reflect his study of the Sistine Chapel ceiling. They evolved as an artistic game with the British sculptor Thomas Banks in which five arbitrarily placed points determined the position of a man's hands, feet, and head. Fuseli often shackled the figures with chains, augmenting the sense of physical and psychological anguish.[34] Grimacing faces flaunt standards of serene beauty, which Lessing and Winckelmann held to be the essence of art. Similar compressed forms appear in the paintings of Abildgaard, as in *Philoctetes* (*Filoktet*; Statens Museum for Kunst, Copenhagen), 1774–75, and in the early drawings of his student Carstens. The prominent muscles and tendons reflect Fuseli's study of *écorchés* (flayed figures), which he preferred to life drawing.

Although Fuseli copied antique art less frequently than other neoclassicists, he continually utilized his studies in drawings that ranged thematically over a broad spectrum of literature, from classical mythology to Nordic sagas and medieval poetry. His disparate sources were united by themes chosen according to his taste for the macabre and bizarre. Drawings such as *Teiresias Drinks the Sacrificial Blood* (British Museum, London), about 1774–79, reveal Fuseli's appropriation of Homer's *Odyssey* as a source for the supernatural. Here, Odysseus, modeled on the Borghese Warrior, is shown in Hades holding back the spirits of the dead while the prophet Teiresias greedily gulps the blood of sacrificial animals. Fuseli's preoccupation with hellish scenes is reflected in his many drawings of subjects from Dante's *Divina Commedia*, in which figures were frequently based on classical sculpture and the art of Michelangelo.[35] While many of Fuseli's drawings served as sketches for paintings completed later in London, they were finished works, large in size and eagerly collected by his *Sturm und Drang* friends.[36]

The Danish painter Abildgaard arrived in Rome on a travel grant in 1772 after many years of study at the Copenhagen Kunstakademiet, where he had acquired a foundation in neoclassical theory and a preference for subject matter that included both classical and Nordic literature. His tastes reflected those of Wiedewelt, who was among the first to depict scenes from the writings of Johannes Ewald and whose drawings reveal a restrained, early neoclassical style generally absent from his baroque sculpture.[37] Abildgaard's graphic manner developed in Rome through the influence of Fuseli and Sergel. His drawings feature expressive poses and dramatic themes, often involving the supernatural, executed in brown ink and wash with bold chiaroscuro. His figural types were inspired by Fuseli and vary from elongated, nearly wraithlike forms to powerful, muscular anatomies in compressed poses, as in *Philoctetes*, his masterpiece from this period, or in *The Rage of Achilles* (ex-collection S. Ramström, Västerås, Denmark), 1775, influenced by the Belvedere Torso, Abildgaard's favorite sculpture.[38]

The theme of Achilles's rage in Abildgaard's work was related to the sculpture of that subject by Sergel, to whom Abildgaard gave his painting as a gift. Abildgaard's preoccupation with Achilles is also evidenced in his drawings such as *Achilles and the Handmaidens Mourning the Death of Patroclus* (*Achilleus og ternerne klagende over Patrokles' død*; FIGURE 23), about 1775, and may have been motivated by his own poverty and depression during this period. The figures in these rapid ink sketches are condensed images of extreme grief, barely materialized, which anticipate his future symbolic use of classical figures and which define poses frequently repeated. *Achilles and the Handmaidens* is typical of the tentative quality of Abildgaard's work in Rome, where he rarely produced finished drawings.

Abildgaard matured as an artist after his return to the north. He was named a professor at the Copenhagen Kunstakademiet in 1778 and served as its director in 1789–91 and 1801–9. His subsequent drawings and paintings depicted an extensive range of subjects, encompassing classical literature and history, Ossianic themes, Northern sagas and history, contemporary Danish literature, Shakespeare, and the Old Testament.[39] Like Fuseli, whose literary tastes were comparable, he was an intellectual and linguist with a library containing more than 3,700 volumes. He remained a prolific draftsman, completing drawings as preparatory studies for paintings and published illustrations. Recent scholarship has also shown that Abildgaard alone among the northern neoclassicists created a body of work that was strongly politicized and reflected his egalitarian beliefs. During the 1780s, when the Danish monarchy was more reform-minded, Abildgaard was outspoken in his Enlightenment opposition to the clergy, nobility, army, and police.[40]

Artistically, his critical viewpoint was conveyed through allegory and symbol. References to social injustice appear in his illustrations to the collected writings of Ewald, engraved in 1780, and to Ludwig Holberg's satirical novel *Niles Kim*, published in a new edition in 1789.[41] During the 1780s Abildgaard evolved a private iconography to express his Enlightenment antireligious beliefs: images of bondage, darkness, sacrificial smoke, and Medusa's head were attributes of theology, while Minerva, protector of the arts and sciences, symbolized liberty.[42] His admiration for antiquity was intensified by his contempt for the Judeo-Christian tradition, in contrast to which he (like Winckelmann) perceived pagan classicism as a culture embracing sensual freedom and democratic beliefs.[43]

Abildgaard's opposition to political monarchies in the years before the French Revolution was also reflected in the many drawings and paintings he did of ruthless rulers, as in *Caracalla Sacrificing* (*Caracalla ofrer dolken*; Statens Museum for Kunst, Copenhagen) and *Claudius Discovered by a Soldier* (CATALOGUE NO. 100), from the 1780s. His art continued to be politically motivated during the more repressive years in Denmark following the execution of Louis XVI in France. In 1799 he completed allegorical drawings of classical figures, including *Light in Darkness* (*Lys i mørket*; Statens Museum for Kunst, Copenhagen), in response to government censorship of the press, which led to the exile of his friend Peter Andreas Heiberg.[44] The melancholy mood of these drawings occurs in many of his later works, such as *Narcissus* (CATALOGUE NO. 101), c. 1790–1800, reflecting his own misanthropic spirit and recalling the troubled introspection of figures in drawings by Fuseli and Sergel.

The *Sturm und Drang* movement declined in the 1780s, and the fluid, mannered style of Abildgaard, Fuseli, and Sergel was not continued by later neoclassicists. Their influence prevailed, however, with Carstens, the most celebrated German classicist, and his followers. Affinities are evident in their attitudes toward creativity and artistic genius and, stylistically, in an expressive use of Michelangelesque forms in works that resonate with a depth of inner feeling. Abildgaard in particular provided a crucial link between generations of neoclassicists. Although he extended little encouragement to his students, with the exception of Thorvaldsen, he was the teacher of Carstens, Philipp Otto Runge, and Christoffer Wilhelm Eckersberg.[45]

An austere neoclassical style embodying the vision of Winckelmann did not flourish until the last decade of the century and was primarily associated with Carstens. Its foundation was laid during the 1780s through a convergence of diverse circumstances, including a revival of interest in Winckelmann by Goethe and other theorists, a new appreciation of more "primitive" art, and the influence of Jacques-Louis David and Antonio Canova on German artists studying in Italy. These artists—including the history painters Wilhelm Tischbein, Friedrich Heinrich Füger, and Philipp Friedrich Hetsch and the sculptors Johann Heinrich Dannecker, Johann Gottfried Schadow, and Franz Anton Zauner—returned home by the early 1790s to create works representative of the first mature generation of northern neoclassicists.

The center for German artists in Rome was the private academy of the sculptor Alexander Trippel. A Swiss artist who had studied in Copenhagen with Wiedewelt and in Paris with Augustin Pajou and Jean-Baptiste Pigalle, Trippel arrived in Rome in 1776 and replaced Mengs, who died in 1779, as the principal disseminator of classical theory. He was a purist who advised his students—including Füger, Goethe, Schadow, Tischbein, and Zauner—to copy Greek sculpture exclusively, after which Raphael could be studied for his expressive physiognomies and group compositions, and Michelangelo for his well-drawn figures.[46] Trippel was renowned for his teaching of proportion, a subject much debated at this time and discussed by Winckelmann in his *Geschichte der Kunst des Alterthums*; he and his students measured antique statues and studied the proportions of the works of Polyclitus in order to scientifically determine an anatomical formula for ideal beauty.[47]

Surprisingly, Trippel also urged his students to sketch in the streets, where, he maintained, they would quickly discover the sources for Raphael and Michelangelo. This advice anticipated the future direction of northern neoclassicists such as Eckersberg, Johann Peter Krafft, and Gottlieb Schick, who incorporated increasing amounts of realism into their work.[48] Few Germans at this time mingled with the local population, but an unexpected glimpse into their social life, and a rare moment of humor, is provided by Tischbein's drawing *Carnival Scene* (*Maskenszene*; FIGURE 24), 1787. A figure in costume for the Roman carnival poses as the Apollo Belvedere for his admiring friends. The popularity of this event is also evidenced in an essay on the carnival written by Tischbein's close friend Goethe in 1788.[49]

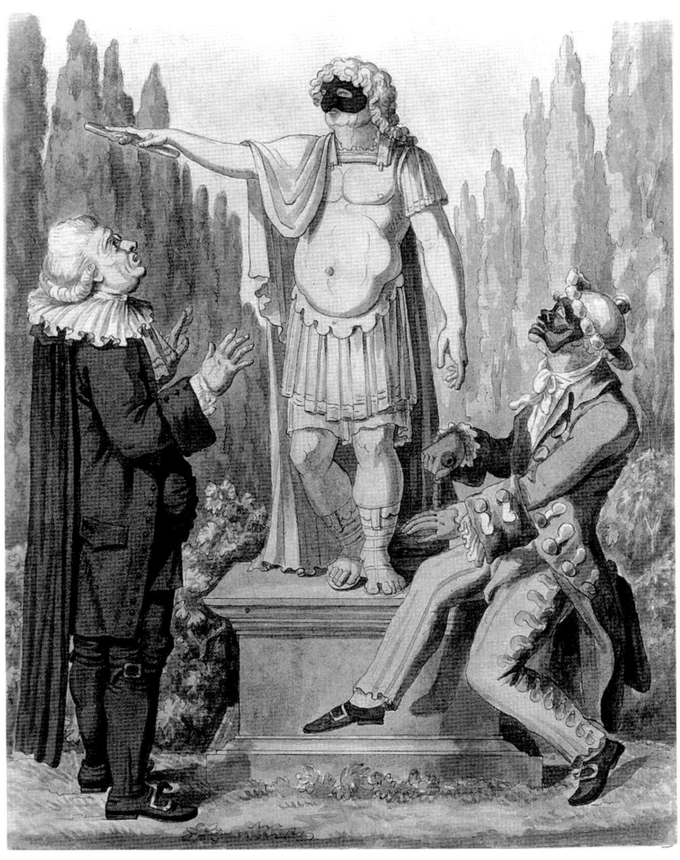

FIGURE 24
Johann Heinrich Wilhelm Tischbein
Germany, 1751–1829

Carnival Scene
1787, pen and brush with gray and brown ink and watercolor,
23.5 x 18.8 cm (9 1/4 x 7 3/8 in.),
Nationale Forschungs- und Gedenkstätte, Weimar (inv. no. 694)

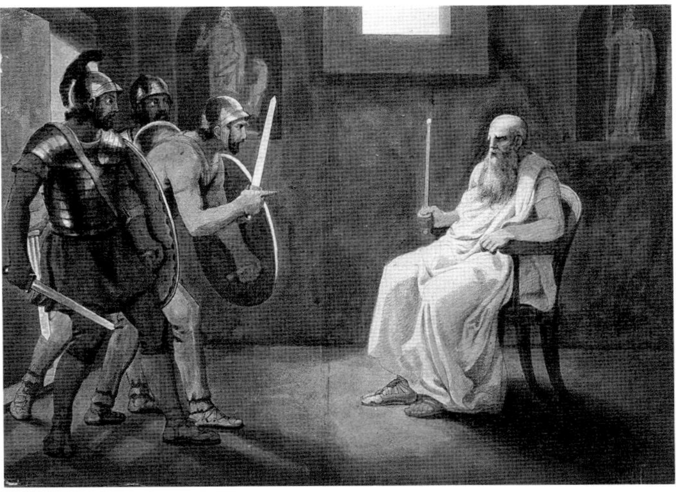

FIGURE 25
Johann Heinrich Wilhelm Tischbein
Germany, 1751–1829

The Death of Cicero
1785, pen and watercolor, 51.5 x 75 cm (20 1/4 x 29 1/2 in.),
Freies Deutsches Hochstift, Frankfurt am Main
(inv. no. XIa-gr-13 913/1)

Tischbein, best known for his painting *Goethe in the Roman Campagna* (Städelsches Kunstinstitut, Frankfurt), 1787, was an artist whose oeuvre incorporated a range of currents, beginning with Dutch baroque realism and medieval themes inspired by his *Sturm und Drang* friends Bodmer and Goethe (for example, *Götz von Berlichingen* [Goethe-Nationalmuseum, Weimar], 1782, and *Konradin von Schwaben in Prison* [*Konradin von Schwaben in Gefängnis*; Staatliche Kunstsammlungen, Dresden], 1784). Tischbein's enthusiasm for his national artistic heritage peaked in the early 1780s in letters extolling the virtues of Germanic subject matter as equivalent in nobility to classical themes.[50]

In 1782 Tischbein returned to Rome for a second time, in order to study antiquity and "learn how to draw the human body" (his previous training with his uncles had been in painting). Tischbein's memoirs, *Aus meinen Leben* (From my life), provide detailed accounts of his strategy, exhaustively copying and measuring statues in the Cortile Belvedere at the Vatican and correcting the drawings at night. He vividly describes the crowded conditions in the Vatican Stanze, where artists jockeyed for a favorable vantage point from which to sketch the compositions of Raphael. Tischbein's interest in facial expression, developed through his friendship with Lavater, also motivated him to copy paintings by Leonardo da Vinci. He drew from models at Trippel's academy, and his progress can be measured in black-chalk academies skillfully executed in the finished, detailed manner of Mengs and Pompeo Batoni. These drawings are often distinguished by a physiognomical individualism and an expressive moodiness created through dramatic pose and lighting.[51]

From the mid-1780s Tischbein's style was increasingly influenced by his admiration for David and "primitive" early Greek and Renaissance art. *The Death of Cicero* (*Der Tod des Cicero*; FIGURE 25), 1785, reveals a new austerity and linearity, based on David's *The Oath of the Horatii* (*Le Serment des Horaces*; see FIGURE 9), 1785, not seen before in German neoclassicism. Tischbein knew David personally and proudly recounted the French artist's visit to his studio, where he praised *Konradin von Schwaben in Prison*.[52] This enthusiasm for David and his pupil Jean-Germain Drouais was widespread, shared by Goethe and many other northerners. Tischbein's work was admired for an innovative, primitive ruggedness, evident in *The Death of Cicero* in the bulging eyes and postures of soldiers derived from fifth-century B.C. Greek reliefs known to him through illustrations in archaeological treatises such as in Winckelmann's *Monumenti antichi inediti* (Unpublished ancient monuments) of 1767.

Tischbein's interest in earlier Greek art resulted in his decision to execute line engravings of the vases owned by Sir William Hamilton, published in 1791–1803.[53] These influenced John Flaxman and contributed to the emerging international linear style of the 1790s. The engravings illustrated scenes and figures from the vases in outline against a white ground. Their new simplicity and clarity derived partly from pedagogical goals, according to Tischbein, providing his students with models of pure Greek contour. At the time of their preparation Tischbein was director of the Accademia di Belle Arti in Naples, where he lived from 1787 until 1797. He admired archaic art for its directness and honesty, qualities he also perceived in early Renaissance art. He was among the first of a growing number of artists who expressed enthusiasm for the work of Dürer and Trecento and Quattrocento painters such as Giotto, Masaccio, Mantegna, Perugino, and Giovanni Bellini.[54]

Friedrich Heinrich Füger, the leading Austrian neoclassical painter, also profited by his exposure to an international circle of artists in Rome, where he studied from 1776 until 1783. He and the sculptor Zauner were among the first recipients of the Vienna Akademie's Rome prize.[55] Füger's early training in Stuttgart with Guibal and in Leipzig and Dresden with Adam Friedrich Oeser exposed him to advanced neoclassical theory taught by baroque painters. His own graphic style prior to his departure for Rome emphasized a painterly application of wash, broken contours, and elongated figures with tapering limbs. In Rome he participated in the Akademie's new program of study, which targeted the improvement of drawing skills and was supervised by Anton Maron. For the first time in his career Füger, already an accomplished miniaturist, focused exclusively on drawing, producing red-chalk academies in the style of Mengs and meticulously finished copies after Raphael's paintings in the Vatican.[56] Among contemporaries he was most influenced by the art of Gavin Hamilton, Benjamin West, and the neo-Poussinist style of French artists during the 1770s. Many of his later classical themes from Roman and Greek history had first been painted by David, whom Füger may have known in Rome.[57]

Following his return to Vienna, Füger reverted to a looser, baroque graphic manner, and his mature, neoclassical drawings were not created until the 1790s. Greater austerity was first evident in paintings such as his celebrated reception piece for entry into the Akademie der bildenden Künste, *The Death of Germanicus* (*Der Tod des Germanikus*; Österreichische Galerie, Vienna), from 1790. A more heroic, sober neoclassicism appears in *The Blind Homer Reciting His Verses* (*Der blinde Homer, seine*

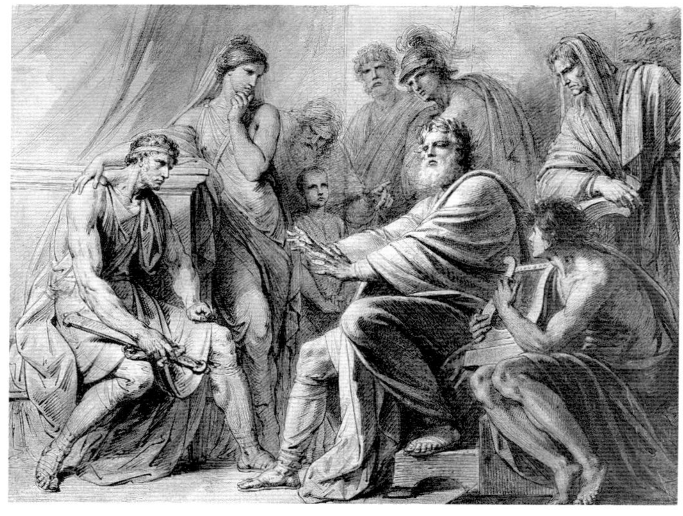

FIGURE 26
Friedrich Heinrich Füger
Germany, active Austria, 1751–1818

The Blind Homer Reciting His Verses
1798, pen, wash, white heightening, 49.5 x 68.9 cm (19 1/2 27 1/8 in.), Graphische Sammlung Albertina, Vienna (inv. no. 14.667)

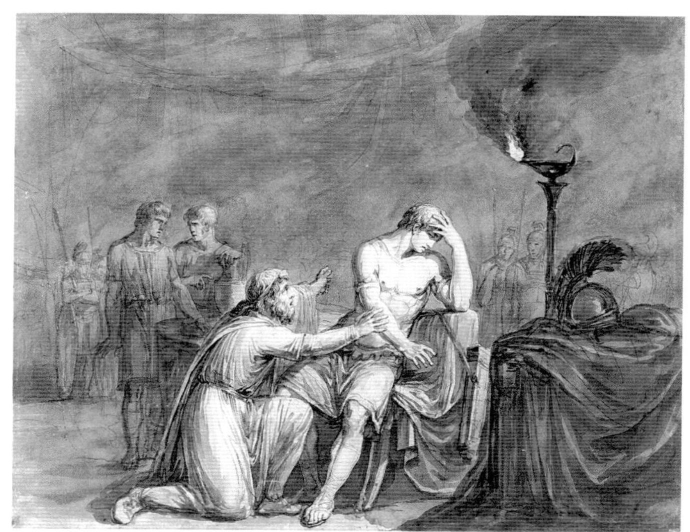

FIGURE 27
Philipp Friedrich Hetsch
Germany, 1758–1838

Priam and Achilles
Brush and brown ink over gray-black chalk, 48.8 x 65.1 cm (19 3/16 x 25 5/8 in.), Graphische Sammlung, Staatsgalerie, Stuttgart (inv. no. 5597)

Verse vortragend; FIGURE 26), 1798, in which ink wash and white heightening produce a dramatic chiaroscuro. The massive, sculptural figures, arranged in shallow space, are restrained and enclosed by simple contours. Interior modeling is created through a dense net of parallel strokes and occasional hatchings. Füger's new interest in plastic form was also reflected in his return to life drawing during the 1790s and his study of Michelangelo. Similar figures appear in his drawings for Klopstock's epic poem *Der Messias* (The Messiah) from 1797. *The Blind Homer*, with its tragic tone, may represent Füger's response to contemporary political developments as well as to the severe style and Homeric themes of Carstens and Wächter.[58] Füger rejected Carstens's generalized features, however, in favor of the individual physiognomies typical of a portraitist.

The Blind Homer, which is signed and dated, indicated the growing importance of the graphic medium to Füger. Initially, his drawings were only preparatory sketches or copies, but, increasingly, he produced finished works, frequently sold to engravers. Drawings provided his only opportunity to create neoclassical historical subjects in a country where commissions went to genre painters in the baroque style. Füger admitted in a letter to a friend that he survived financially only because of his portraiture.[59] The Akademie remained isolated in its advocacy of neoclassical standards and historical themes, a situation paralleled throughout Germany, though to a lesser degree. A contemporary writer deplored this situation in 1801, observing that "a favorable epoch for painters in Vienna may begin if aristocratic patrons collect according to standards of true art, rather than fashion, and purchase history paintings rather than hunting and animal pictures or landscapes."[60] Scholars have claimed that no true neoclassical period ever flourished in Austria but that the style coexisted with the rococo and, after 1800, with romanticism.[61] Füger's reliance on finished drawings, which were often engraved or completed as illustrations for books, was a solution increasingly popular with German artists after the turn of the century. His association with graphics was noted in a contemporary cultural survey, *Reise durch Deutschland . . . in den Jahren 1797, 1798, 1799* (Travels through Germany . . . in the years 1797–99; Leipzig, 1804), in which the author remarked that "Füger draws frequently and takes orders for his drawings as well as his paintings, which is unusual for a painter."[62]

Two other artists in Rome during the 1780s were the painter Philipp Friedrich Hetsch and the sculptor Johann Heinrich Dannecker, both of whom had studied at the Hohe Karlsschule in Stuttgart, founded by the duke of Würtemberg, Karl Eugen. This school, created in 1770, absorbed the previous Académie des Arts, established in 1761, and was intended to produce officers, physicians, and artist-craftsmen for the duke. Students were required to sign a lifetime pledge of service to him upon graduation, an arrangement rejected by Friedrich Schiller and the artist Joseph Anton Koch, both of whom fled the duchy. Karl Eugen modeled his educational and artistic policies on the program of the francophile Prussian king Frederick the Great, creating one of the most French-oriented centers of German neoclassicism. It is not accidental that the German artists cited as the closest followers of David—Hetsch and Schick—were from Würtemberg.[63]

Hetsch and Dannecker both entered the Hohe Karlsschule in 1771, where they studied under Guibal and the Belgian-born court sculptor Pierre-François Lejeune.[64] Hetsch departed for Paris in 1781, where he was exposed to the art of David, Jean-Baptiste Regnault, and Joseph-Marie Vien. He continued to work in a baroque style until his arrival in Rome in 1785.[65] His paintings from 1786, such as *The Death of Consul Papirius* (*Der Tod des Konsuls Papirius*; Germanisches Nationalmuseum, Nuremberg), are rigorously neoclassical, adopting the isolated sculpturesque figures, austere setting, and highly finished brush stroke of David and Drouais, both of whom were in Rome at the time. Hetsch's copies of antique statues, mostly done in pen or pencil, also contributed to the new manner.[66] His finished preparatory drawings, however, such as *Tullia Driving Away over the Corpse of Her Father* (*Tullia über ihres Vaters Leiche hinwegfahrend*; Staatsgalerie, Stuttgart), 1786, reflect a Poussin-inspired classicism similar to that of contemporary drawings by Füger and rely on fluid line and wash to emphasize movement.

Following Hetsch's return to Stuttgart in 1787 he became a professor at the Akademie, where he transmitted his Davidian manner to his students, who included the painter Schick. During the 1790s, when Hetsch completed such masterpieces as *Cornelia, Mother of the Gracchi* (Staatsgalerie, Stuttgart), 1793–94, his drawing style became more neoclassical. The undated *Priam and Achilles* (*Priamos vor Achill*; FIGURE 27) reflects the twin influences of David and Carstens, whose work he had admired at the latter's exhibition in Rome in 1795. The poses of the figures, the relief composition, and the solemn mood all echo aspects of Carstens's drawing of this subject, which was included in the Roman exhibition, as well as the style of their mutual friend, the Würtemberg artist Wächter, who also lived in Rome.[67] Hetsch alone among German artists painted and drew many subjects from Roman history, to which he added themes from German history and religious subjects in his later years. Drawing seems to have remained a subsidiary medium for him, employed mainly to copy or execute preparatory studies.

Dannecker was trained in a late baroque style of drawing both in Stuttgart in 1771–80 and in Paris with Pajou in 1783–85. Traces of this manner remain in early drawings finished in Rome, where he lived from 1785 to 1789. *Autumn/Bacchus* (*Herbst/Bacchus*; FIGURE 28), 1786, is a study for one of two allegorical figures representing the seasons that he completed for Duke Karl Eugen. The wash used for shading, especially in the eyes, and the delicate, slightly broken line have been modified by his study of the antique (the pose recalls the Apollo Belvedere) and life drawing at Trippel's academy. A similar style is used for drawings in his sketchbooks, where copies of female figures dominate, reflecting later preferences in his sculptures. Bacchus, despite his muscular torso, conveys an indolent voluptuousness befitting the god of wine and establishes Dannecker's aesthetic taste, shared with his friend Canova, for a Praxitelean softness. The drawing projects a melancholy mood, symbolic of autumn, which would characterize most of his later work.

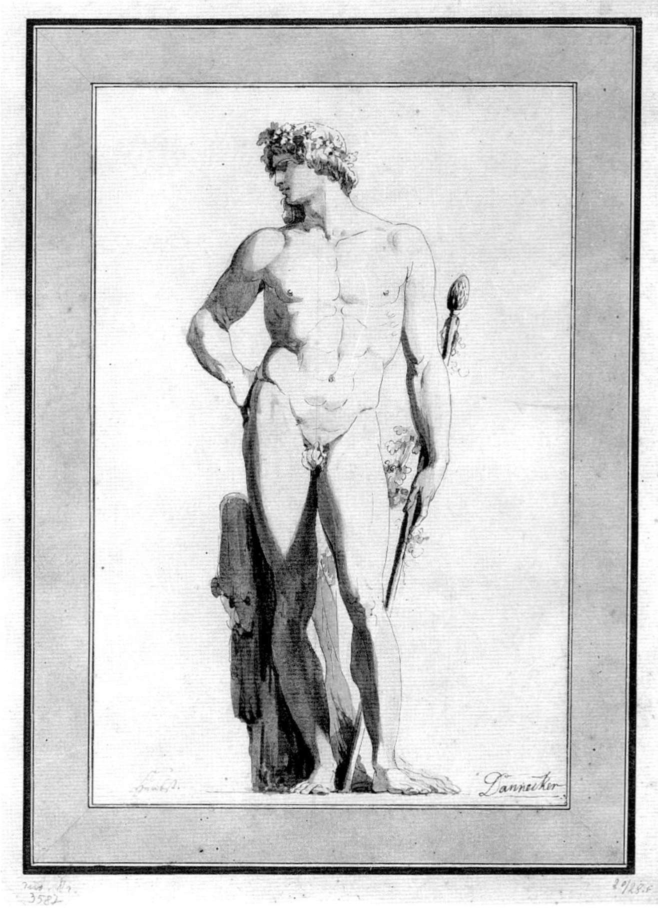

FIGURE 28
Johann Heinrich Dannecker
Germany, 1758–1841

Autumn/Bacchus
1786, pen and black ink, brush and brown ink over graphite, 23.8 x 15.5 cm (9 3/8 x 6 1/8 in.), Graphische Sammlung, Staatsgalerie, Stuttgart (inv. no. Heimatmuseum Ludwigsburg 3587)

Bacchus is one of the few sculptures in Dannecker's oeuvre for which sketches exist. To a remarkable degree, the two mediums remained unrelated; he preferred to develop his plastic ideas in clay *bozzetti*, a technique probably adopted from Canova. Nearly all of his drawings are "unfinished": copies of sculptures (never of paintings), life studies, and sketches for unrealized sculptures.[68] Despite their provisional nature, Dannecker valued his drawings, which he catalogued; at his death his estate contained two hundred drawings and five sketchbooks. After his return to Stuttgart all his sculptural commissions, mostly portraits, were controlled by the duke. His most famous sculpture, *Ariadne on a Panther* (Städtische Skulpturensammlungen im Liebieghaus, Frankfurt), for which no drawings exist, was his only independently conceived work and created a furor when the duke discovered his insubordination.[69] In this context, drawings were Dannecker's only means of free expression, and they comprise a "wish list" of sculptures never executed.

Among his most ambitious later projects were drawings of Homeric relief scenes completed during the late 1790s. *Aphrodite Rescuing Paris in Combat with Menelaus* (*Aphrodite rettet Paris im Kampf gegen Menelaos*; Graphische Sammlung, Staatsgalerie, Stuttgart) typifies the series in the violence of execution and the use of heavy lines of ink revising initial pencil sketches. Unlike Flaxman and Tischbein, whose works he knew, Dannecker rejected a pure outline style. Nearly all the drawings depict figures mourning or being rescued by gods and goddesses. Dannecker's interest in Homer's *Iliad* at this time may have been inspired by the visit of his friend Schiller in 1793 and their subsequent correspondence.[70] A new German translation of the *Iliad* was published by Heinrich Voss in 1793, which contributed significantly to the widespread interest in Homer among artists at the turn of the century. Goethe furthered this direction by choosing Homeric subjects for his Weimar art competitions held between 1799 and 1805. He expressed delight over Dannecker's projected series of Homeric drawings when he visited Stuttgart in 1797, although he was later critical of the sketch sent to him that depicted Andromache mourning Hector.

The most extensive Homeric project was completed by Tischbein. His six-volume *Homer nach Antiken gezeichnet* (Homer drawn after the antique) was published between 1801 and 1805, with later volumes (7–9) appearing in 1821–23. The books illustrated Homeric scenes reproduced from antique sculptures, reliefs, carved gems, and vase paintings in styles that varied from outline engravings to illusionistic painterly etchings. His goal was public moral education through heroic role models.[71]

The Berlin sculptor Johann Gottfried Schadow also lived in Rome from 1785 to 1787. His drawings from this period, unlike his sculptures, reveal a new precision and simplicity acquired through the study of antiquity, Raphael, and models at Trippel's academy. This experience sobered his earlier rococo style absorbed in Berlin at the Akademie and in the workshop of the sculptor Jean-Pierre-Antoine Tassaert. Schadow was a prolific draftsman who viewed the medium as a creative means of expression distinct from his sculptural activities. His drawings resemble those done by painters and are frequently finished works in which genre scenes from life are preferred to the classical themes characteristic of his sculptures.

Throughout the eighteenth century Berlin was renowned for its neoclassical architecture, while painting and sculpture remained in the hands of French rococo artists called to Berlin by Frederick the Great. Native talent, however, demonstrated a taste and aptitude for realism that continued into the nineteenth century. Schadow's sculptures, the most celebrated of which were done during the 1790s (for example, the tombs of Count van der Mark, formerly Dorotheenstädtisch Kirche, Berlin, and the princesses Louisa and Frederika, Nationalgalerie, Berlin), reflect a blending of neoclassicism with a realism suggestive of the work of Jean-Antoine Houdon. The same combination is seen in many of his drawings, such as *The Muse Thalia* (*Die Muse Thalia*; Deutsche Akademie der Künste, Berlin), one of three muses drawn in 1801 as studies for figures on a curtain in a new theater designed by Carl Gotthard Langhans. The floating muse more closely resembles a portrait of an actress dressed in Grecian clothing than a figure derived from antique sculpture.[72] Schadow's neoclassicism, informed by his daily observation of life, proved less popular in the nineteenth century, when the more austere style of Christian Daniel Rauch prevailed. Schadow's later career was concentrated on his administrative duties as director of the Berlin Akademie and on his drawings, which were frequently published as engravings.

Goethe lived anonymously in Rome in 1786–88, where he shed his earlier *Sturm und Drang* attitudes and experienced a classical "rebirth" guided by the spirit of Winckelmann.[73] His enthusiasm reflected a revival of interest in Winckelmann's theories by a younger generation that contributed to the flourishing of neoclassicism during the last decade of the century, especially in Weimar and Rome. Classical doctrine was propagated by Goethe and Schiller, who published the magazine *Propyläen* in 1798–1800 to advocate neoclassicism and sponsored the Weimar *Preisaufgabe* (open competition) from 1799 to 1805 to stimulate the depiction of subjects from classical literature.[74]

Several important theoretical texts appeared in the early 1790s, beginning with Kant's *Kritik der Urteilskraft* (*Critique of judgment*), 1790, which shaped the development of art during that decade. These writings merged neoclassical doctrine with attitudes derived from the *Sturm und Drang* movement to create a more conceptual classicism in which emphasis was placed on artistic genius and independence, on Greece as a moral paradigm, and on line as the transcription of idea. Most of this had been anticipated by Johann Georg Sulzer in his *Allgemeine Theorie der schönen Kunst* (*General theories on the fine arts*), 1771–74. More than any other publication, this multivolume aesthetic dictionary, which went through five editions, had popularized neoclassicism in Germany. Conceived in a true Enlightenment spirit, it had been compiled not primarily for scholars but to propagate good taste and educate the public.

Sulzer's presentation of neoclassicism was strongly flavored by the beliefs of his Swiss *Sturm und Drang* colleagues Bodmer, Breitinger, and Lavater, who wrote the literature entries. Fuseli was also a consultant and contributed an essay on the sublime. Sulzer, like Winckelmann, defined ideal beauty as the goal of art, although he did allow for the depiction of ugliness. Beauty was created through a study of nature, antiquity, and Renaissance art, especially the paintings of Raphael. The idealized human body epitomized beauty, form was superior to color, and drawing was "the foundation of art, without which taste and the highest perception of beauty can not be realized."[75] Sulzer broadened Winckelmann's Platonic notion of the ideal to incorporate genius, thereby anticipating theories of the 1790s. He defined the ideal as an *Urbild* (archetype) in the artist's imagination whose form is determined by genius: "The ideal is above all a work of genius."[76] Academic study and the application of rules (as of proportion) were useless in the creation and perception of beauty if unaccompanied by genius, which was necessary to absorb the spirit of antique art and "to feel the invisible within the visible."[77] (A decade later Carstens would dedicate his training to this pursuit.) Sulzer's opinions also had a strong ethical orientation, and he was one of the only writers to understand Winckelmann's theories as an attack on eighteenth-century politics and culture. Sulzer elevated the moral significance of the artist's task by ascribing divine power to the arts, whose purpose was to awaken a feeling for the true and good, and not the furtherance of "display and luxury."[78]

It was not Sulzer, however, but Kant who inspired the new wave of critical thinking during the 1790s. In *Kritik der Urteilskraft* Kant defined beauty in radically subjective terms, providing a foundation for future romantic theorists. Through his reading of David Hume and Jean-Jacques Rousseau, an important influence for *Sturm und Drang* writers, Kant became convinced that beauty did not exist in an object but in the perceiving mind. Because the mind, rather than the senses, was the source of knowledge and perception, the philosopher had to begin with an examination of inner consciousness in order to formulate universal principles. The many introspective figures depicted in German neoclassicism, beginning with Fuseli's, could be seen as emblematic of Kant's pursuit. Like Sulzer, Kant defined art as the outward manifestation of the initial aesthetic idea in the artist's imagination, which was formed through innate genius. Originality, rather than imitation, was characteristic of genius, which could not be acquired through study, although genius was dependent on academic skills for the realization of its visions. The separation of art into conceptual and technical areas would be reiterated in the defense of Carstens's drawings and would be used by Fernow and Carstens as proof of the superficiality of French painting.

Drawing was given renewed impetus through Kant, who considered it to be the essential part of painting. Colors might charm and gratify the senses, but they interfered with the perception of the delineation of form, which alone conveyed beauty and was worthy of contemplation. Kant's attitudes were repeated later in observations by Goethe, who wrote that drawings were "invaluable" because they transcribe "the artist's mental idea in all its purity," and by Schiller, who complained that color and light obscured true images that could be better represented through outline.[79]

Schiller's contribution lay in assigning new moral and political significance to the artist's actions. His aesthetic philosophy was articulated in two essays published in 1795 in his journal *Die Horen*: "Die naive und sentimentalische Dichtung" (Naive and sentimental poetry) and "Über die ästhetische Erziehung des Menschen" (The aesthetic education of man), which contained his response to Kant's *Kritik der Urteilskraft* and was based on a series of letters written to the duke of Schleswig-Holstein in 1793–94. Schiller believed that aesthetics were crucial to political change, and he wrote that "if man is ever to solve the problem of politics in practice, he will have to approach it through the problem of the aesthetic, because it is only through Beauty that man makes his way to freedom."[80] Schiller's goal was the restoration of society to a state of freedom and harmonious unity. This condition could only be achieved through the renewal of the individual, an internal process of healing arrived at through the resolution of the dualities (matter and spirit) of human nature. Self-renewal was to be accomplished through the contemplation of beauty, an act that transported the beholder into an intermediate state between sense and intellect. Art possessing such beauty could only be created from the inner being of an artist who had already experienced regeneration. Schiller believed that Greek art and society offered a model to the contemporary world because it had possessed a primal harmony now lost. Goethe also prescribed Greek art as a moral tonic for his ailing century. He wrote in 1788 that the contemplation of antique statues makes man "more human and authentic," whereby "it becomes impossible ever again to relapse into barbarism."[81] Schiller bequeathed to the artist an exalted status as social reformer and moral leader, which would be reflected in attitudes of independence and self-esteem by subsequent German artists, beginning with Carstens. His writings were also responsible for the popularity of Hellenistic themes at the end of the century.

Neoclassical theories incorporating the views of Kant and Schiller were presented to German artists in Rome by Fernow in a lecture series during the winter of 1795–96 at the Villa Malta.[82] Fernow's mission was to instill in his listeners a sense of the importance and nobility of art and to provide them with a theoretical foundation. His opinions were also contained in later articles and books in which he reiterated principles derived from Winckelmann with an emphasis on genius and artistic conception. He belittled technical excellence, academic training, and the imposition of any rules that would hamper the free expression of original genius.[83]

The oeuvre of Asmus Jacob Carstens, devoted principally to drawing, marks the culmination of four decades of German neoclassical art and theory, uniting Winckelmann's simplicity and grandeur with the emotional depth of the *Sturm und Drang* movement. His drawings reveal generalized forms precisely rendered to produce strong plastic and linear effects. Carstens's philosophical defense of his work as a draftsman, rather than a painter, also climaxes the sovereign position drawing occupied within classical doctrine.

Carstens was born in Schleswig-Holstein, then a province of Denmark. He remained throughout his life a proud and rebellious loner. His career and training were idiosyncratic, beginning with his first exposure to classical theory in the remote village of Eckernsförde, where he lived for five years as an apprentice cooper.[84] It was here that the foundations of his

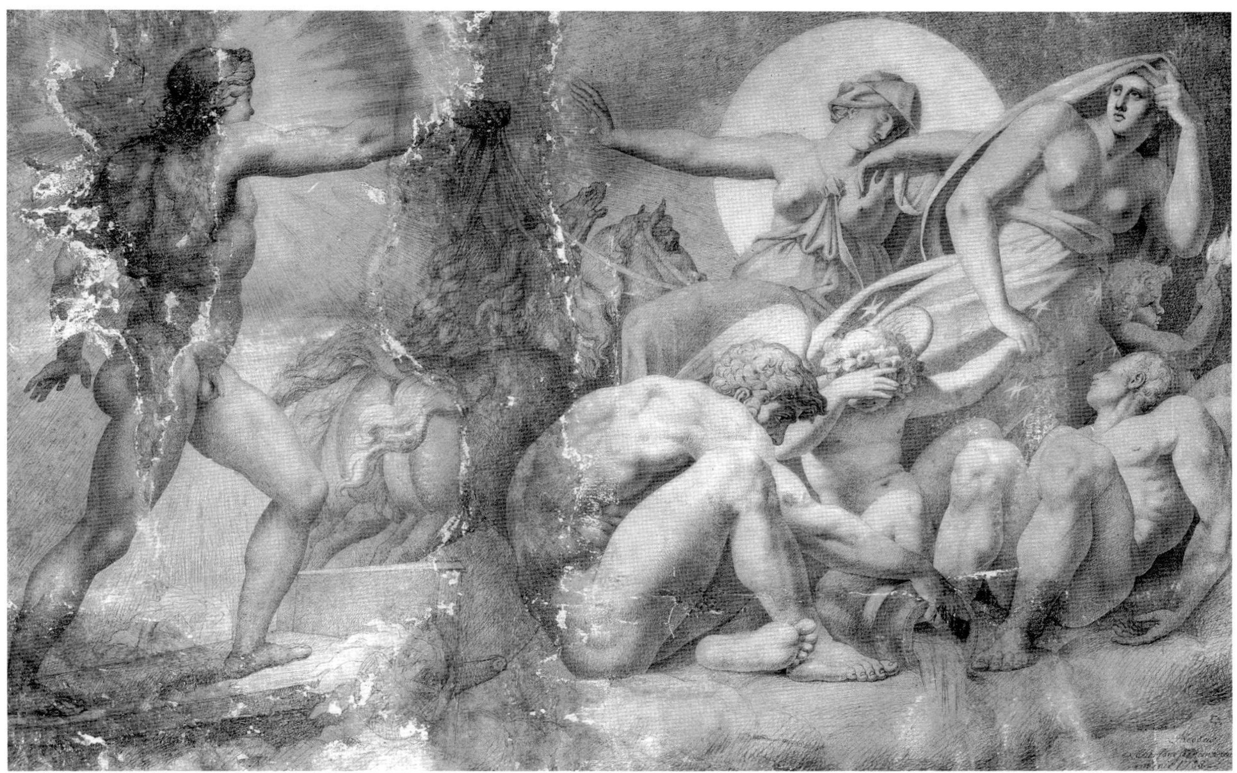

FIGURE 29
Asmus Jacob Carstens
Denmark, 1754–98

Morning
1788, black chalk, 38.7 x 63.2 cm (15 1/4 x 24 7/8 in.),
Kongelige Kobberstiksamling, Statens Museum for Kunst, Copenhagen (inv. no. 6788)

future beliefs were laid via the circuitous path of reading a German translation (1766) of Daniel Webb's *Inquiry into the Beauties of Painting*, 1760, which was partially based on ideas gleaned through the author's friendship with Mengs. Webb presented classical art as the epitome of ideal beauty, superior to modern forms in its depth of feeling, simplicity, and distilled expression. Like Mengs, Webb believed that the essence of beauty resided in curving lines. Webb articulated several themes that were later echoed in Carstens's writings: art was to be judged according to its inner spirit; the artistic concept was more important than the technical execution; and the human form was the central subject of art. Webb also maintained that nudity expressed man's freedom and nobility.

In 1776 Carstens moved to Copenhagen, where he lived until 1783, in order to pursue his artistic career. His relationship with the Kunstakademiet was stormy, and he attended classes only intermittently in order to qualify for participation in the Rome prize competition.[85] His overwhelming desire to reach Italy combined with his advanced age in comparison to the other students made him impatient with the incremental structure of academic advancement. He was also dissatisfied with the practice of teaching drawing by copying individual body parts, for which Johann Daniel Preissler's textbook on anatomy was used. Carstens termed this approach "piecemeal," anticipating already his future goal of creating unified art in the spirit of *Sturm und Drang* theory.[86] While he received encouragement from Wiedewelt, his interactions with Abildgaard were disappointing and he remained without training as a painter.[87]

The value of Carstens's artistic experience in Copenhagen lay in the program of study that he devised for himself. He attended anatomy classes, copied engravings after Raphael and Michelangelo, and, most importantly, studied the Kunstakademiet's plaster casts. The collection far surpassed his expectations, and he recorded his experience in terms suggesting a religious conversion: "I saw here for the first time the Vatican Apollo, the Laocoön, the Farnese Hercules, the Borghese Warrior, and others, and a holy feeling of adoration moved me almost to tears. . . . My prayers were answered."[88] The same merger of classical form and emotional depth would distinguish his mature drawings. Significantly, he made it a principle never to copy these statues but merely to absorb their spirit and draw from memory when he returned home. He wrote that copying would "cool my feeling" and that it would be more beneficial to "observe . . . and imprint their forms in my memory."[89] He would follow the same procedure in Rome and, like Fuseli, would rarely draw from life. This conceptual approach, which recalls the advice of Sulzer and Winckelmann, among others, enabled him to create generalized forms from ideal mental images.

Most of Carstens's earliest extant drawings date from his years in Lübeck, 1784–88, where he continued to represent themes from Nordic legends (as recounted by Ossian, Ewald, and Klopstock) and from Greek literature and history, as he had done in Copenhagen. He also completed many allegories, such as *Morning* (*Der Morgen*; FIGURE 29), in which meaning is symbolized through powerful muscular forms compressed in expressive poses. His Michelangelesque figures reflect a knowledge of

Fuseli and Abildgaard. They were also influenced by his study of Giulio Romano's frescoes at the Palazzo del Te during a brief trip in 1783 to Mantua and Milan, where he also saw Raphael's cartoon for *The School of Athens*. The figure of Apollo in *Morning* is based on the pose of the Borghese Gladiator but, typically for Carstens, remains anatomically flawed. Many of his future subjects and compositions can be traced to drawings from this period, and *Morning*, in which Night with her children, Sleep and Death, are depicted, contains the seeds of his famous later drawing of that theme (see FIGURE 31). The tragic mood and monumental quality of this work, possibly designed as a cartoon for a wall painting never executed, also anticipate future directions. His penchant for allegories, under the guidance of Winckelmann's *Versuch einer Allegorie besonders für die Kunst* (Meditations on allegory especially in art), 1766, reflected his desire to create images with profound philosophical content.

Carstens moved to Berlin in 1788 and two years later was appointed a professor at the Akademie der Künste, where he taught drawing in the plaster class using the detested Preissler book. As before, he rebelled against academic policy, demanding exemptions from customary practices.[90] Carstens's activities in Berlin were essential for the development of his mature style, in which his earlier mannered forms were regularized, contours emphasized, and compositions simplified. This discipline was achieved primarily through his work as an illustrator and mural painter.[91] In 1790 he completed fifty-nine sketches of antique statues of deities and heroes, including the Muses and the Fates, for a book by Karl Wilhelm Ramler entitled *Kürzgefasste Mythologie oder Lehre von den fabelhaften Göttern, Halbgöttern und Helden des Altertums* (A concise mythology, or fables of gods, demigods, and heroes of antiquity), and sixty-five drawings for Karl Philipp Moritz's *Götterlehre oder mythologische Dichtung der Alten* (Teachings of the gods, or ancient mythology). The Moritz engravings were based on copies of gems from the collection of Baron Stosch, acquired by Frederick the Great, and from the casts of gems owned by Philipp Daniel Lippert. This experience provided Carstens with a vocabulary of restrained figural poses, frequently presented frontally or in profile. The engravings, rendered in outline with minimal interior modeling, as in *Night with Her Children Sleep and Death* (*Die Nacht mit ihren Kindern Schlaf und Tod*; FIGURE 30), 1791, inspired many of his drawings completed in Rome.[92] Neoclassical directions in Carstens's work were also strengthened by his friendship with Schadow and the architects Hans Christian Genelli and Friedrich Weinbrenner, with

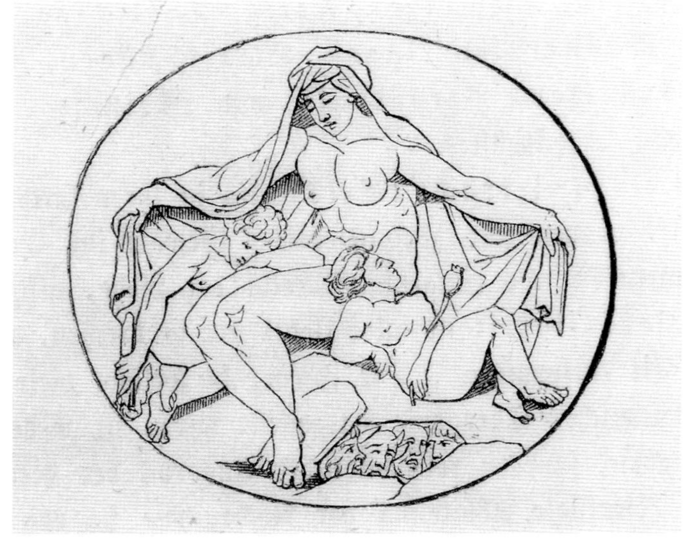

FIGURE 30
Asmus Jacob Carstens
Denmark, 1754–98

Night with Her Children Sleep and Death
1791, engraving, 5.3 x 6.1 cm (2 1/16 x 2 1/2 in.),
in Karl Philipp Moritz, *Götterlehre oder mythologische Dichtung der Alten*
(Berlin: F. A. Herbig, 1861),
General Research Division, New York Public Library,
Astor, Lenox, and Tilden Foundations

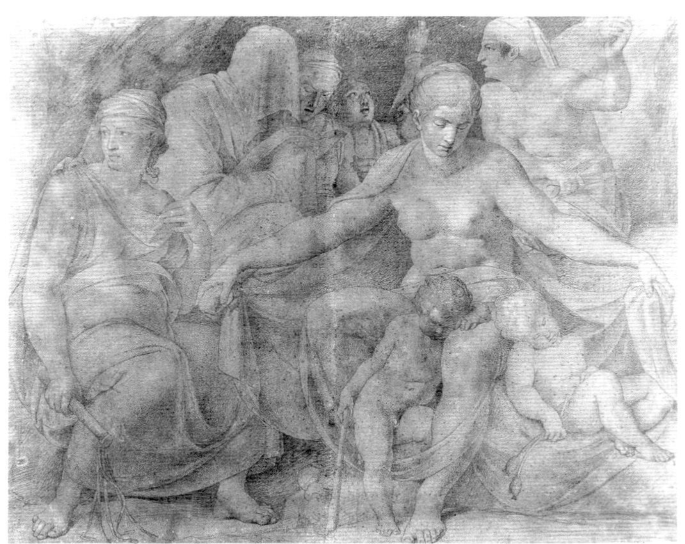

FIGURE 31
Asmus Jacob Carstens
Denmark, 1754–98

Night with Her Children Sleep and Death
1795, chalk, white heightening, 74.5 x 98.5 cm (29 5/16 x 38 3/4 in.),
Graphische Sammlung, Staatliche Kunstsammlungen, Weimar (inv. no. KK568)

whom he studied perspective. Carstens departed for Rome in 1792 with Weinbrenner on a travel grant secured by the Prussian minister of education, Karl Friedrich von Heinitz.

Carstens's final years in Rome (1792–98) were his most productive, and his reputation was established following a controversial exhibition of drawings in 1795. The centerpiece of the show was his ambitious *Night with Her Children Sleep and Death*, depicting allegorical figures of Night, Nemesis, hooded Destiny, and the Three Fates, adapted from the Sistine Chapel Sibyls, with softened forms and more generalized muscular structures.[93] The subject, which is an allegory of death, typifies Carstens's tragic worldview and defies easy categorization. Derived from classical sources, including Hesiod's *Theogeny* and Pausanias's *Description of Greece*, the theme transcends neoclassicism and evokes a dark, pagan, mythical world that anticipates the nocturnal gloom of romanticism.[94] The composition, in which space is displaced by the massive bulk of the figures, denies classical clarity and order. Nonetheless, the drawing conveys the nobility, restraint, and profundity that Winckelmann felt to be the essence of antique beauty. The slightly awkward appearance of the figures, due partly to anatomical inaccuracies, also suggests Carstens's admiration for Quattrocento art, whose primitivizing forms he felt evoked simplicity and honesty.[95]

The notoriety that surrounded Carstens following his exhibition was in large part due to Fernow's review in *Der neue teutsche Merkur* of May 1795. Fernow arrogantly proclaimed that Carstens's work announced "a new epoch in art," in which only his drawings embodied the simplicity and austere grandeur of antiquity. Anticipating criticism of Carstens's anatomical mistakes and the absence in the exhibition of oil paintings, Fernow used Kantian theory to define the essence of art as conceptual, while technical expertise was derided as mere mechanical skill. Carstens's work revealed the presence of genius that must be allowed to express itself unhampered by any petty rules.[96] The association between drawing and idea, established through four decades of critical theory, was also employed by Carstens in his own defense. Writing to Genelli, Carstens explained that his decision to exhibit drawings resulted from his desire to have his work judged on the basis of concept and plastic form rather than craftsmanship.[97]

Fernow framed his article as an attack against the neoclassical art of David and his followers, both French and German, whose work was contrasted to Carstens's and rejected as superficial and decorative, mirroring the current age of materialism. Fernow's opinions inspired considerable resentment among other Germans, whose views were later represented by Maler (Friedrich) Müller in his article published in *Die Horen* of 1797. Despite the popularity of David's style during the 1780s and 1790s among northern artists (with the notable exception of Trippel), a bias against earlier French art had been expressed by neoclassicists such as Abildgaard, Fuseli, and Winckelmann.[98] French art was disliked for a variety of reasons, and Goethe expressed the popular opinion when he criticized it as too theatrical, violent, and lacking in grace.[99] Attitudes toward French culture were complicated by constantly shifting political relationships, which seldom, however, deterred artists from studying in Paris.

The antiacademic bias contained within Fernow's article probably originated with Carstens and was more forcefully expressed in the latter's dealings with the Berlin Akademie. A series of letters between von Heinitz and Carstens in Rome resulted in the artist's refusal to fulfill any obligations attached to his travel stipend and his defiant proclamation that his divine talent belonged not "to the Berlin Akademie but to mankind." Carstens faulted the academies as well as the political powers they served for the degrading of art into decorative displays gratifying "the vanity of princes."[100] His posture of independence and moral superiority was heavily indebted to Schiller and Sulzer.

Carstens's drawings during the final two years of his life became more objective and traditionally classical. Themes from Greek literature and history predominated in works indebted to Raphael, such as *Homer Singing to the Greeks* (*Homer singt den Griechen*; Staatliche Kunstsammlungen, Weimar), 1796, whose composition, modeling, and facial expressions recall frescoes in the Vatican Stanze. Carstens's late works were frequently done in outline with slimmer figural proportions, a more relaxed mood, and simplified architectural settings, as in his drawing series of Jason and the Argonauts (CATALOGUE NO. 105).[101] New directions were also introduced in *The Golden Age* (*Das goldene Zeitalter*; Thorvaldsens Museum, Copenhagen), 1797. This drawing, which inspired paintings by Koch and Schick and was copied by Thorvaldsen, is unusual for Carstens in its inclusion of landscape and its optimistic sensuality. The circle of dancers, however, has sources in his Lübeck compositions. Carstens's outline drawings, in contrast to Flaxman's, always suggest plastic volume, but here the flowing contours anticipate the ability of Matisse to describe form through two-dimensional means. His portrayal of a natural, free life realizes a utopian vision common among late eighteenth-century writers as diverse as Heinse, Schiller, and Winckelmann.

Carstens's influence following his death was extensive both stylistically and theoretically. Those most indebted to his example included Wächter, Koch, Thorvaldsen, and Schick. The Swabian painter Wächter studied at the Hohe Karlsschule in 1773–75 under Guibal with fellow pupils Hetsch and Dannecker, followed by seven years of work in Paris (1785–92) with Regnault and Peyron. Wächter was one of the only Germans in France during the Revolution, an experience that caused him to flee the country in protest. No drawings or sketchbooks from this period remain, and his only extant painting reveals a style of late baroque classicism also characteristic of Hetsch.

Wächter's best work was completed in Rome (1792–98), and many later paintings were based on sketches he did there.[102] *Job and His Friends* (*Hiob und seine Freunde*; FIGURE 32), c. 1793–94, is a preparatory study for his most celebrated painting, begun in 1796 and completed in 1808, with further modifications added in 1824. This drawing, typifying his mature style, reflects an awareness of Carstens's work, although the two did not meet until 1795. Precisely detailed muscular forms are arranged like a bas-relief from which movement and setting are excluded.[103] Historical details are eliminated in favor of universal expression, and the mood is despairing and introspective.

The depth of feeling conveyed by the drawing reflects Wächter's belief that art should be judged according to inner spirit and poetic invention rather than technical proficiency, an attitude derived from Carstens and Fernow, whose lectures he attended.[104] Like Carstens he also championed the independence of the artist guided only by his vision and was a bitter opponent of academies. His conception of art as moral instruction fused Enlightenment precepts with personal religious convictions that resulted in his conversion to Catholicism and his preference for religious subject matter. Wächter particularly valued Quattrocento art, whose forms epitomized to him a naive artlessness that he equated with truthfulness and spiritual profundity. The massive simplified figures created by Giotto and Masaccio are echoed in Wächter's drawings. This appreciation of early Renaissance art as an embodiment of ethical values signals a move toward romanticism, and Wächter was a crucial influence on the Nazarene artists when he lived in Vienna from 1798 to 1808.

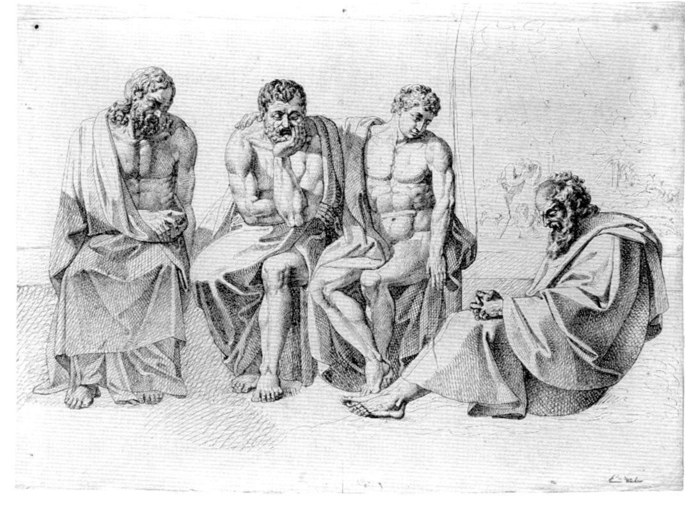

FIGURE 32
Eberhard Wächter
Germany, 1762–1852

Job and His Friends
c. 1793–94, pen and black ink over graphite,
60.3 x 85.6 cm (23 3/4 x 33 11/16 in.),
Graphische Sammlung, Staatsgalerie, Stuttgart (inv. no. C 1927/6 recto)

In contrast to Wächter, whose post-Roman work diminished in quality, Thorvaldsen and Schick emerged as leading neoclassicists after the turn of the century. When asked by Goethe for a report on the Roman art scene in 1804, Wilhelm von Humboldt, the Prussian ambassador, replied that Schick, Thorvaldsen, and landscapist Johann Christian Reinhart were the best among northern artists.[105] These men, together with Koch and the architect Karl Friedrich Schinkel, were part of a new circle of artists and intellectuals who frequently met at the home of von Humboldt and his wife, Caroline. Thorvaldsen and Koch, who shared lodgings in Rome from 1800 to 1803 and collaborated on pictures of themes from Dante, purchased and copied many of Carstens's drawings.[106] Both had known Carstens personally, and Thorvaldsen had been familiar with his work since 1781, when he was a student at the Copenhagen Kunstakademiet. Like Carstens, Thorvaldsen had been a student of Abildgaard's, and his early drawings reflect his teacher's style of extensive ink wash used to create shadows.

While Carstens's influence has been detected in Thorvaldsen's sculptures, particularly *Jason with the Golden Fleece* (see FIGURE 15), it is most evident in his reliefs and finished drawings, many of which were based directly on figures drawn by Carstens.

Thorvaldsen's drawings are rendered in a precise manner suggesting grisaille with forms softened and generalized, as in his reliefs. The occasional anatomical inaccuracies in his work may have resulted from his preference, like Carstens's, to work from an idea rather than nature. The plasticity of the figures further relates them to Carstens rather than to Flaxman, whose engravings Thorvaldsen also studied. These finished drawings, unusual for a sculptor, were often given as gifts to friends; they frequently depicted Raphaelesque Madonnas in a manner directly anticipating the Nazarenes.[107] The contemplative mood of the drawings is also characteristic of his sculptures and recalls the spirit of Winckelmann.

The majority of Thorvaldsen's drawings were quick sketches in which he worked out preliminary designs for sculptures before refining his ideas in clay *bozzetti*. Valued as process rather than finished product, the drawings were often sketched on scraps of paper and later thrown away. Because of their purpose they reflect the unguarded immediacy of creative inspiration and in their tangle of lines possess a dramatic intensity drained from Thorvaldsen's serene sculptures. Drawings such as Thorvaldsen's *Priam and Achilles* (Thorvaldsens Museum, Copenhagen) and *Achilles Dragging the Body of Hector around the Walls of Troy* (CATALOGUE NO. 109) reveal theatrical expressions and tensed poses eliminated in the reliefs. *Priam and Achilles*, whose composition was derived from drawings by Abildgaard, Carstens, and Flaxman, typifies Thorvaldsen's preoccupation with Homeric themes during this period. The slightly stiffened poses reflect his admiration for archaic Greek art. This enthusiasm for primitive artistic forms, which was not shared by his colleague Canova, linked Thorvaldsen with Carstens and Wächter.

The Swabian painter Gottlieb Schick contributed significantly to the development of German art through his fusion of the two main currents of neoclassicism (influenced by David and Carstens) and the creation of a new style that anticipated Nazarene romanticism in its emphasis on realism and religious subject matter. Schick studied at the Hohe Karlsschule from 1787 to 1794 with Hetsch and Dannecker. Like Dannecker, with whom he remained close friends, Schick later developed a style based on similar softened forms. Schick continued his training in Paris with David (1798–1802) and through museum study, where he first saw paintings by Raphael.[108] His most ambitious finished drawing, *Socrates in Prison* (*Sokrates, den Giftbecher entgegennehmend*; Staatsgalerie, Stuttgart), about 1800, is closely based on David's painting of the same subject, with harsh lighting, precise details, stiffened figures, and a relieflike composition.[109] Schick competed for the Prix de Rome in 1800 and 1801 and exhibited his painting *Eva* (Wallraf-Richartz-Museum, Cologne) in the Salon of 1800. This work reflects the sensual elegance of François Gérard, whose style influenced Schick's portraiture, and reveals Schick's dissatisfaction with the austere, archaic direction in much French neoclassicism. In a letter to Dannecker from July 1800 Schick discussed goals for which he would strive in Italy, explaining that he sought nature with a free reference to the antique (the Medici Venus as well as the work of Raphael) in order to avoid the "dry, cold, stiff, and emotionally insipid" style of contemporary schools.[110]

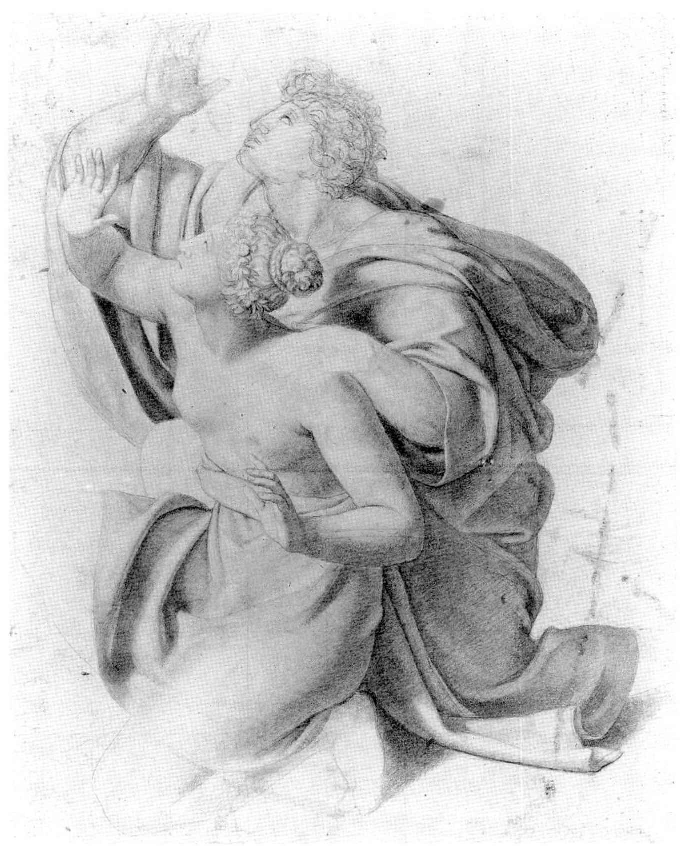

FIGURE 33
Gottlieb Schick
Germany, 1776–1812

Kneeling Pair with Faces Raised
1804, graphite and charcoal, 55.9 x 43.4 cm (22 x 17 1/16 in.),
Graphische Sammlung, Staatsgalerie, Stuttgart (inv. no. 2345)

Following Schick's arrival in Rome in 1802, he was introduced to the German artistic community by Hetsch and became part of the von Humboldts' circle. A close friendship developed with Koch, through whom he became familiar with Carstens's work. Schick quickly established his reputation in Rome with his paintings *David Playing before Saul* (*David spielt vor Saul*), 1802–3, and *The Sacrifice of Noah* (*Noahs Dankopfer*; both Staatsgalerie, Stuttgart), 1804, the latter exhibited in the Pantheon to great acclaim. The many sketches for these paintings, both outline composition studies and finished cartoons of individual figures, as in *Kneeling Pair with Faces Raised* (*Aufblickendes kniendes Paar*; FIGURE 33), 1804, a study for *The Sacrifice of Noah* (Staatsgalerie,

Stuttgart), differ from his earlier drawings in medium—pencil and chalk frequently replace pen—and in a reduction of detail, softening of light, simplification of contour, and more pronounced corporeality. These changes reflect the influence of Carstens as well as Michelangelo and Raphael. Unlike most neoclassicists he increasingly chose themes from the Old Testament, whose spiritual expression he believed to have greater populist appeal. These were praised by his friend the romantic critic August Wilhelm Schlegel for their "feeling of devotion."[111]

Like Carstens and Thorvaldsen, Schick disliked life drawing and preferred to compose from imagination, although he did complete a series of anatomical studies in 1804–5.[112] Schick's goals, however, were oriented toward greater naturalism, and he rejected working from studio models because he found the situation posed and artificial. He repeatedly advocated sketching in the streets and capturing the movement of life. In 1802 he wrote, "I believe that painters who only study nature in their studio are worthless. The seated model is only half of nature, from whom half of life has been drained; life is only found in movement, and painters must capture the moment of movement. I study form and character on walks, in the theater, and in public houses."[113]

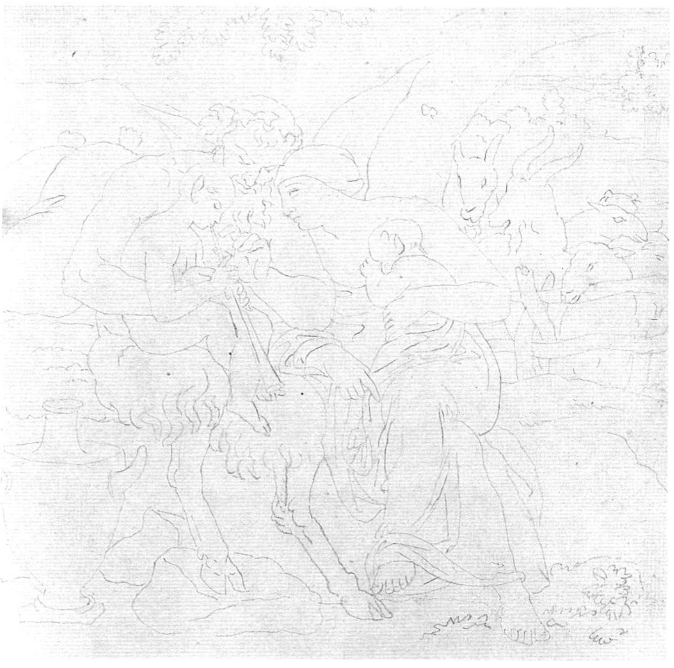

FIGURE 34
Gottlieb Schick
Germany, 1776–1812

Faun Family
c. 1809, graphite, 16.5 x 16.5 cm (6½ x 6½ in.),
Graphische Sammlung, Staatsgalerie, Stuttgart (inv. no. 2380)

The results can be seen in drawings like the charming *Faun Family* (*Faunenfamilie*; FIGURE 34), c. 1809, in which Carstens-like figures and spaces have been brought to life through a softened atmosphere and animated gestures. Antiquity is now re-envisioned through the domesticity of everyday life rather than tragic pathos. Schick ultimately subverted the neoclassicism of both Carstens and Winckelmann and provided a transitional basis for the development of Nazarene romanticism and Biedermeier realism.[114] *Faun Family*, believed to have been exhibited in Berlin in 1810, is one of many finished drawings by Schick purchased by Cotta for publication in his periodical *Taschenbuch für Damen*. The growing circulation of these magazines contributed greatly to the increasing number of finished drawings by painters in the early nineteenth century.

The neoclassical movement in painting, in contrast to architecture and sculpture, declined earlier in Germany than in France, with only Buonaventura Genelli continuing the style in the later nineteenth century.[115] Aspects of it survived, however, and were perpetuated by the academic curriculum of drawing from casts and life models. Many artists, including Christoffer Wilhelm Eckersberg and Johann Peter Krafft, began their careers as neoclassicists but matured as realists or romantics. Among the romantic painters, Runge, who studied with Abildgaard in Copenhagen, and the Nazarenes, most of whom trained under Füger in Vienna, retained a commitment to drawing the human form with neoclassical precision.

The Nazarene painters, despite their medieval, religious subject matter, owed a considerable debt to preceding neoclassicists. They valued drawing as much as painting and, like Winckelmann, emphasized contour and the depiction of the human body as a spiritual emblem. Many cherished beliefs and practices derived from Carstens, Schick, or Wächter: the conception of art as an expression of inner essence and feeling; the appreciation of early Renaissance painting (both northern and Italian) for its emotional depth and honesty; a preference for religious subject matter; an antiacademic attitude based on the rejection of drawing exercises considered to be sterile mechanical drills; and the habit of sketching people in the streets.

The Nazarenes, however, relied upon life drawing and studies from nature, while they valued technical skill and craftsmanship, derided by Carstens, which they found in the detailed precision of early Northern Renaissance art. As can be seen in their drawings of nudes, such as *Life Study of a Female Nude*,

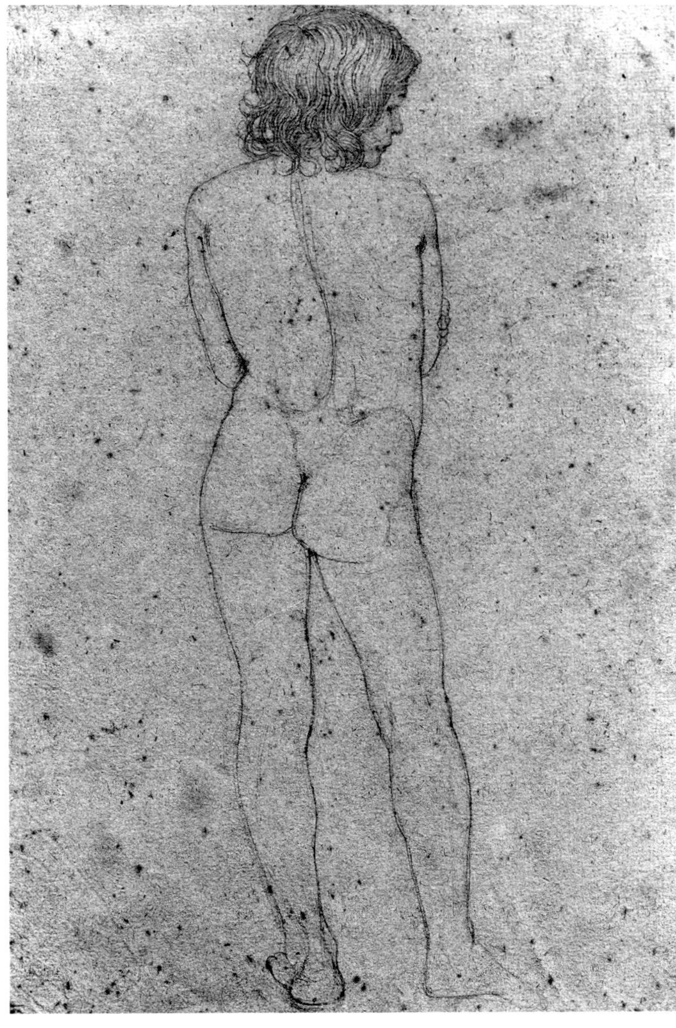

FIGURE 35
Franz Pforr
Germany, 1788–1812

Rear View of Nude Boy (Xaverio)
1810–11, graphite, 28.3 x 18.4 cm (11 1/8 x 7 1/4 in.),
Städelsches Kunstinstitut, Frankfurt am Main (inv. no. z.527)

by Julius Schnorr von Carolsfeld (CATALOGUE NO. 116), 1825–26, and *Rear View of Nude Boy (Xaverio)* (*Knaben-Rückenakt [Xaverio]*; FIGURE 35), by Franz Pforr, 1810–11, they rejected the generalized, softened plastic forms of Carstens, Schick, and Wächter for flatter, abstracted figures rendered with hard-edged clarity. This linear emphasis is related to the outline style popularized at the turn of the century and, in combination with the Nazarenes' characteristic accretion of detail, suggests parallels with Ingres's work. They preferred to draw with extremely sharp pointed pencils, thin brushes, or pens. Shading was created through hatching or parallel strokes contained within the dominant contour. Frequently this technique yielded results similar to engravings, as in Schnorr's *Life Study of a Female Nude*, and may have been influenced by their study of prints.

The Nazarenes drew nudes as life studies and as preparation for clothed figures in their paintings, according to academic tradition, but their drawings differed from chalk academies in a variety of ways. The art schools employed professional adult models with muscular physiques and placed them in dramatic, expressive poses suitable for incorporation in history paintings. The Nazarenes preferred to sketch local adolescent boys in natural, relaxed poses. Beginning in 1819 the Protestant faction of the group, known as the "Capitolines," also drew female models. The commitment of these artists to realism led them to emphasize individual personalities, in contrast to academic generalizations, evident in the portraitlike appearances and in the designation of names within the titles, as with Pforr's *Rear View of Nude Boy (Xaverio)*.

A similar detailed empiricism characterizes the graphic styles of Eckersberg and Krafft combined with a strong plasticity derived from their study with David. For the Nazarenes, however, nature remained the outer manifestation of a higher ideal and the human figure a reflection of spiritual truth. Schnorr wrote in 1823 that the artist "should form bodies and faces which witness to an inner spirit."[116] The desire of Nazarene painters "to see beauty as the stamp of the soul" is a reformulation of neoclassical goals attainable, according to Winckelmann, only when artists reject the use of hired academic models.[117] Despite differences in religious beliefs and artistic sources, the Nazarenes drew images of boys that most successfully realized Winckelmann's classical vision: the union of sensuous form with a delicacy of outline that embodied his Platonic definition of beauty as "impressions . . . made in the sand."[118]

❧

NOTES

1 Johann Wolfgang Goethe, cited in Otto Fischer, *Geschichte der deutschen Zeichnung und Graphik* (Munich: F. Bruckmann, 1951), vol. 4, 415.

2 Anna Maria Schwarzenberg, "Studien zu F. H. Füger" (Ph.D. diss., Universität Wien, 1974), 108–17. Others who frequently published drawings, or did them as commissioned illustrations, included Eberhard Wächter and Gottlieb Schick.

3 For a list of these schools with dates of their foundation see Nikolaus Pevsner, *Academies of Art Past and Present* (New York: DaCapo Press, 1973), 141, and Gisold Lammel, *Deutsche Malerei des Klassizismus* (Leipzig: E. A. Seemann, 1986), 127.

4 Lammel, *Deutsche Malerei* (NOTE 3), 21. For Goethe's response to the Mannheim casts see Goethe, *Italian Journey, 1786–1788*, trans. W. H. Auden and Elizabeth Mayer (San Francisco: North Point Press, 1982), 490.

5 Johann Heinrich Wilhelm Tischbein, cited in Franz Landsberger, *Wilhelm Tischbein* (Leipzig: Klinkhardt und Biermann, 1908), 19. His memoirs, *Aus meinen Leben* (Brunswick: C. A. Schwetschke und Sohn, 1861), provide an invaluable account of daily life in Rome during the 1780s.

6 Carl Ludwig Fernow, *Römische Studien* (Zurich: H. Gessner, 1806), vol. 2, viii.

7 This essay, written in Dresden, where Winckelmann worked as librarian and secretary to the Saxon minister Count von Bunau, resulted from his vast knowledge of classical literature and art studied through engravings. He was unable to view the antique collection in Dresden, which was in storage and remained so until 1785; see Carl Justi, *Winckelmann und seine Zeitgenossen* (Leipzig: F. C. W. Vogel, 1923), vol. 1, 296. Winckelmann first directly studied antique sculpture in 1755 in Rome, where he established a reputation as an antiquarian and historian through his influential appointment as secretary to Cardinal Albani in 1758 and the publication of books that included the *Geschichte der Kunst des Alterthums* (History of ancient art), 1764, and *Monumenti antichi inediti* (Unpublished ancient monuments), 1767.

8 Winckelmann, "Thoughts on the Imitation of Greek Art in Painting and Sculpture," trans. H. W. Janson and Elizabeth Holt, in *A Documentary History of Art* (Garden City, N.Y.: Doubleday Anchor Books, 1958), vol. 2, 341.

9 Winckelmann, *The History of Ancient Art*, trans. G. Henry Lodge (New York: Frederick Ungar, 1968), vol. 1, 30. For a brilliant analysis of Winckelmann's Platonic theories and their relation to drawing see Barbara Maria Stafford, "Beauty of the Invisible: Winckelmann and the Aesthetics of Imperceptibility," *Zeitschrift für Kunstgeschichte* 43 (1980): 65–78.

10 *Laokoon* was begun in response to a statement in Winckelmann's *Gedanken über die Nachahmung der griechischen Werke in der Malerei und Bildhauerkunst* that Lessing felt disparaged Virgil's presentation of Laocoön screaming. Lessing distinguished between poetry and the visual arts, maintaining that passions could be displayed in the former while prohibited in the latter, whose purpose was to create beauty. In fact, Winckelmann qualified his original statement when he wrote *Geschichte der Kunst des Alterthums*, stating that repose was also necessitated by the standards of beauty, but Lessing went ahead with his condemnation without acknowledging the fact; see Henry C. Hatfield, *Winckelmann and His German Critics, 1755-1781: A Prelude to the Classical Age* (New York: King's Crown Press, 1943), 52–53.

11 The influence of baroque theory has been discussed by many authors including Mario Praz, *On Neoclassicism* (Evanston: Northwestern University Press, 1969); David Irwin, *Winckelmann: Writings on Art* (New York: Phaidon, 1972); and Max Baeumer, "Klassizität und republikanische Freiheit in der ausserdeutschen Winckelmann-Rezeption des späten 18. Jahrhunderts," in *Johann Joachim Winckelmann, 1717–1768*, ed. Thomas W. Gaehtgens, vol. 7 of *Studien zum achtzehnten Jahrhundert* (Hamburg: Felix Meiner, 1986), 195–220.

12 Friedrich Gottlieb Klopstock, cited in Hatfield, *Winckelmann and His German Critics* (NOTE 10), 82.

13 For specific contrasts between Grecian and contemporary clothes see Winckelmann, "Thoughts" (NOTE 8), 339; for his descriptions of dancers and gymnasium athletes see 340–41.

14 Mengs assembled a collection of vases, which he gave to the Vatican Library, and two collections of plaster casts, one of which he presented to the king of Spain. The other was purchased after the artist's death for the royal collection in Dresden; Thomas Pelzel, *Anton Raphael Mengs and Neoclassicism* (New York: Garland Press, 1979), 72–73.

15 Similar thoughts were expressed by Sir William Hamilton in the introduction to his published collection of Greek vases in 1766. He wrote that young artists could only rise above mediocrity by "penetrating to the very source from whence these principles flow, that is the philosophical contemplation of the nature of things, by putting themselves in the place of the inventors" (*Collection of Etruscan, Greek and Roman Antiquities*, Naples, 1766–67; cited in Dora Wiebenson, "Subjects from Homer's *Iliad* in Neoclassical Art," *The Art Bulletin* 46, no. 1 [March 1964]: 34).

16 Pelzel, *Mengs* (NOTE 14), 242.

17 The best essay on this movement is by Isaiah Berlin, "The Counter-Enlightenment," 1973, reprinted in *Against the Current* (Harmondsworth, Middlesex: Penguin Books, 1982), 1–24.

18 In their anti-Gallic sentiment the members of the *Sturm und Drang* movement found common ground with Winckelmann, who was a notorious Francophobe.

19 Reprinted in Klopstock, *Sämtliche Werke* (Leipzig: Göschen'sche Verlagshandlung, 1855), vol. 10, 254–61.

20 Klopstock's interest in Teutonic history and literature was first stimulated in Copenhagen, where he lived from 1751 to 1771, through the writings of Elias Schlegel on Nordic sagas. His poetry, especially *Der Messias* (The Messiah) and his Hermann trilogy, was frequently illustrated by neoclassical artists such as Füger, Fuseli, and Carstens.

21 In Herder's advocacy of sculpture as a superior artistic medium he remained close to Winckelmann, differing only in his discussion of painting as an art form that allowed for the depiction of emotion and ugliness; see Herder, *Plastik* (Riga: Hartknoch, 1778), and B. Rupprecht, "Plastisches Ideal und Symbol im Bilderstreit der Goethezeit," *Kunstgeschichte und Kunsttheorie in 19. Jahrhundert*, ed. H. Bauer (Berlin: Walter de Gruyter, 1963), especially 203–11.

22 Herder's theories were influenced by Winckelmann's description of the evolution of Greek culture in *Geschichte der Kunst des Alterthums*.

23 This essay was written and submitted to the Kunstakademie in Kassel for a competition on the subject of Winckelmann and classical studies. It was later published in 1781 in the *Teutscher Merkur*.

24 Fuseli contributed illustrations to the French and English editions of Lavater's book, for which he wrote an introduction. Lavater greatly admired the work of Tischbein, whose Homeric engravings reflect the influence of *Physiognomische Fragmente*; for a full discussion see Charlotte Steinbrucker, *Lavaters "Physiognomische Fragmente" im Verhältnis zur bildenden Kunst* (Berlin: Wilhelm Borngräber, 1915).

25 Heinse, "Letters from the Düsseldorf Gallery," published in Lorenz Eitner, ed., *Neoclassicism and Romanticism, 1750–1850* (New York: Harper and Row, 1989), 82. This passage is contained in Heinse's description of Rubens's *The Flight of the Amazons*.

26 Heinse, *Diaries*, published in Eitner, *Neoclassicism and Romanticism* (NOTE 25), 79. Fuseli later echoed these sentiments when he observed that Winckelmann "reasoned himself into frigid reveries and Platonic dreams of beauty" (*The Life and Writings of Henry Fuseli*, ed. John Knowles [London: Colburn & Bentley, 1831], vol. 1, 14).

27 Heinse, "Letters from the Düsseldorf Gallery," in *German Essays on Art History*, ed. Gert Schiff, trans. Peter Wortsman, vol. 79 of *The German Library* (New York: Continuum, 1988), xvi.

28 Heinse, *Ardinghello*, 1787, translated in Eitner, *Neoclassicism and Romanticism* (NOTE 25), 85.

29 This drawing is generally believed to be a preparatory sketch for a sculpture never executed and may have been related to Sergel's work on another statue from this period, *The Rage of Achilles*. Nancy L. Pressly established its source in an antique relief of Achilles and Priam on view at the Villa Borghese; see Pressly, *The Fuseli Circle in Rome* (exh. cat., New Haven: Yale Center for British Art, 1979), 23.

30 Sergel claimed to have rejected his "abominable French manner" upon his arrival in Rome; cited in Per Bjurström, *Johan Tobias Sergel, 1740–1814* (exh. cat., Copenhagen: Thorvaldsens Museum, 1976), 94. For his early work and copies after antique sculpture and Renaissance paintings see Ragnar Josephson, *Sergels Fantasi* (Stockholm: Bokförlaget Natur och Kultur, 1956), and *Sergel* (exh. cat., Stockholm: Nationalmuseum, 1990).

31 Dyveke Helsted, "Sergel and Thorvaldsen," in *The Age of Neo-Classicism* (exh. cat., London: Royal Academy/Victoria and Albert Museum, 1972), lxxxiii.

32 For Fuseli's relation to the mannerists see Friedrich Antal, *Fuseli Studies* (London: Routledge & Kegan Paul, 1956), 28–65. This drawing may have been a pendant to *Seated Youth in a Storm*, also of 1774, in which another moody young man stares out the window at a bolt of lightning; see Gert Schiff, *Johann Heinrich Füssli, 1741–1825* (Zurich: Beuchthaus/Munich: Prestel, 1973), vol. 1, 128, no. 562. The autobiographical nature of this work may be suggested by the enormous feet (*Füssli* means "little feet") that clasp the visionary head. Similar personal symbols were contained in his drawing *Artist Overwhelmed by the Grandeur of Ancient Rome*, c. 1778.

33 This was in direct opposition to Winckelmann and Mengs. Winckelmann sent mixed messages, however, in his admiration for the Laocoön and the Belvedere Torso, both known to have been an inspiration to Michelangelo.

34 For a psychoanalytic interpretation of these drawings see Werner Hoffmann, "A Captive," in *Henry Fuseli, 1741–1825* (exh. cat., London: Tate Gallery, 1975), 29–37.

35 For Fuseli's drawings of themes from Dante see Schiff, *Füssli* (NOTE 32), nos. 418–26.

36 Fuseli's colleagues regarded him as the personification of *Sturm und Drang* principles. Lavater wrote to Herder that Fuseli was "everything in extremes—always an original; his look is lightning, his word a thunderstorm" (letter of March 25, 1775; cited in Gert Schiff, "Biographical Outline," in *Henry Fuseli, 1741–1825* [NOTE 34], 40).

37 On Wiedewelt see Karl Wilhelm Tesdorpf, *Johannes Wiedewelt* (Copenhagen: Levin & Munksgaard, 1933), and Charlotte Hintze, *Kopenhagen und die deutsche Malerei um 1800* (Würzburg: Konrad Trietsch, 1937), 28–30.

38 Abildgaard also copied figures by Raphael; under the terms of his travel grant from the Copenhagen Kunstakademiet he was required to send back forty-three copies of Raphael's paintings and antique sculptures for use as teaching aids.

39 Abildgaard began to depict many of these subjects in Rome, where he was reading Shakespeare in English, prior to its Danish translation in 1788, and Saxo Grammaticus's famous medieval *Historia Danica* (History of Denmark). After his return to Copenhagen he was involved with Danish historical themes through his commission to decorate the Rittersaal of the recently built Christiansborg Slot (palace) with paintings of scenes from the lives of Danish kings from pagan times to the contemporary period. His work was completed between 1778 and 1791 and destroyed in the palace fire of 1794; see *Von Abildgaard bis Marstrand* (exh. cat., Munich: Staatliche Graphische Sammlung, Neue Pinakothek, 1985), 10.

40 Abildgaard later acquired many publications about the French Revolution and other books that were banned in Denmark. In the early 1790s he supported movements for the abolition of slavery in the Danish West Indies, and he designed a relief for a monument commemorating this event in 1792; see Bente Skovgaard, *N. A. Abildgaard, Tegninger* (exh. cat., Copenhagen: Statens Museum for Kunst, 1978), no. 53, and Else Kai Sass, "The Temple of Fortune: A Painting by N. A. Abildgaard," in *Art the Ape of Nature: Studies in Honor of H. W. Janson* (New York: Abrams/Englewood Cliffs, N.J.: Prentice-Hall, 1981), 525.

41 For a lengthy analysis of Abildgaard's illustration for Ewald's poem, "The Temple of Fortune," and his painting of the same subject on a firescreen in 1785 see Sass, "Temple of Fortune" (NOTE 40), 513–30, and *Lykkens Tempel: Et malerei af Nicolai Abildgaard*, also by Sass (Copenhagen: Christian Ejlers, 1986). Sass and Patrick Kragelund ("The Church, the Revolution, and the 'Peintre Philosophe': A Study in the Art of Nicolai Abildgaard," *Hafnia* 9 [1983]: 25–65) were the first to perceive the political meaning of Abildgaard's art. This contrasts with earlier assessments of his art as apolitical; see, for example, T. Sloan, "Neoclassical and Romantic Painting in Denmark, 1754–1848" (Ph.D. diss., Northwestern University, 1972), 105.

42 These images first appeared in a vignette designed by Abildgaard for *Philosophische Versuche* (Philosophical investigations) by August Henning, a pupil of Moses Mendelssohn. They recur throughout many of his works but are most explicitly associated with anticlerical sentiment in *The History of Europe*, four allegorical paintings from the late 1780s for the Christiansborg Slot, and in a series of three drawings and paintings of allegorical female figures (Theology, Philosophy, and Justice) from the late 1790s; see Kragelund, "The Church, the Revolution" (NOTE 41), 28, 31, 54.

43 Abildgaard had suffered from censorship when several of his illustrations to Ewald's work were rejected for nudity; see *Von Abildgaard bis Marstrand* (NOTE 39), 30.

44 Ibid., 35.

45 For a discussion of Abildgaard as a teacher see K. Monrad, "Abildgaard and the Copenhagen Art Academy at the End of the 18th Century," in *Academies of Art between Renaissance and Romanticism* (*Leids Kunsthistorisch Jaarboek* 5–6, 1986–87; published 1989), 549–59.

46 Tischbein, *Aus meinen Leben* (NOTE 5); cited in Hermann Smidt, *Ein Jahrhundert römisches Leben* (Leipzig: Dyksche Buchhandlung, 1904), 10.

47 This pursuit was reflected in Tischbein's goal of acquiring a ready-made "alphabet of forms like Trippel" (Landsberger, *Tischbein* [NOTE 5], 19) to have at his disposal. Schadow nicknamed Trippel's proportional schema the "convenience man" and later published his own extensive study of anatomical canons, *Polyclet oder von den Maassen des Menschen nach dem Geschlecht und Alter* (Polycleitus or the proportions of the human body according to race and age), 1834. For a study of the late eighteenth century's preoccupation with ancient systems of proportions see Peter Gerlach, "Über das mittlere Mass oder der bürgerliche Kanon," in *Ideal und Wirklichkeit der bildenden Kunst im späten 18. Jahrhundert* (Berlin: Gebrüder Mann, 1984), 45–74. Goethe mentioned Trippel's study of proportions in his *Italian Journey* (NOTE 4) and remarked, "It gave me a unique opportunity for learning how far the human figure can be studied according to fixed canons of proportion and how much account should be taken of deviations caused by individual characteristics" (379–80). Carstens, with his abhorrence of any rules, scorned this type of study.

48 Schick frequently exclaimed over the beauty of the Italians and noted the similarity of their appearance to the figures in Renaissance art; see his letter to Dannecker from Rome dated October 21, 1802; cited in *Gottlieb Schick: Ein Maler des Klassizismus* (exh. cat., Stuttgart: Staatsgalerie, 1976), 27.

49 Goethe, *Das römische Carneval* (Weimar/Gotha: Carl Wilhelm Ettinger, 1789); "The Roman Carnival," *Italian Journey* (NOTE 4), 445–69.

50 Unlike Fuseli, Tischbein emphasized historical detail in his paintings of medieval themes. Johann Heinrich Merck published Tischbein's letter to him of February 23, 1782, in *Der teutsche Merkur*; see Landsberger, *Tischbein* (NOTE 5), 41, and Hermann Mildenberger, *Johann Heinrich Wilhelm Tischbein: Goethes Maler und Freund* (Neumünster: Karl Wachholtz, 1986), 21. Tischbein's uncle, Johann Heinrich Tischbein the Elder, had earlier painted Homeric themes together with subjects derived from Klopstock's Hermann trilogy during the 1760s; see *Aufklärung und Klassizismus in Hessen-Kassel unter Landgraf Friedrich II, 1760–1785* (exh. cat., Kassel: Staatliche Kunstsammlungen, 1979), 228–34.

51 Mildenberger, *Tischbein* (NOTE 50), 156.

52 Smidt, *Ein Jahrhundert römisches Leben* (NOTE 46), 12. For more on the influence of Davidian neoclassicism see Wolfgang Becker, *Paris und die deutsche Malerei 1750–1840* (Munich: Prestel, 1971), 46–47, and Lammel, *Deutsche Malerei* (NOTE 3), 140–43.

53 Volume 1 was published in 1791, followed by volumes 2 and 3 in 1795 and volume 4 in 1803. The collection itself was lost en route to England during a storm at sea; for further information see Landsberger, *Tischbein* (NOTE 5), 128–31; Wiebenson, "Subjects from Homer's *Iliad*" (NOTE 15), 33–35; and *John Flaxman: Mythologie und Industrie* (exh. cat., Hamburg: Kunsthalle, 1979), no. 255a.

54 See Goethe and Heinrich Meyer, *Winckelmann und seine Jahrhundert in Briefen und Aufsatzen* (Tübingen: J. G. Cotta, 1805; reprint Leipzig: E.A. Seemann, 1969), 174. Other artists who shared this interest during the 1780s and earlier included Meyer himself, Friedrich Bury, Aloys Hirt, Johann Heinrich Lipps, and the Englishman Thomas Patch. Their views would be continued by Carstens and Wächter and culminate in the art of the romantics.

55 The Vienna Akademie had recently been reorganized in 1772, merging three previously separate art schools; see J. T. C. Kuijpers, "Hofpreise der K. K. Akademie der bildenden Künste in Wien," in *Academies of Art between Renaissance and Romanticism* (NOTE 45), 378–96, and Walter Wagner, *Die Geschichte der Akademie der bildenden Künste in Wien* (Vienna: Brüder Rosenbaum, 1967).

Zauner's sculptures reveal a more mature neoclassicism than Füger's paintings, but the style of his drawings cannot be examined since none have been preserved; see Peter Gerlach, *Antikenstudien in Zeichnungen klassizistischer Bildhauer* (Munich: Wilhelm Fink, 1973), 12.

56 Füger drew figural groups from *Parnassus* and *The Expulsion of Heliodorus* and also completed one outline drawing that is no longer extant; see Alfred Stix, *Heinrich Füger* (Vienna/Leipzig: Manz, 1925), 34–40, and Schwarzenberg, "Studien zu F. H. Füger" (NOTE 2), 41–44.

57 Schwarzenberg, "Studien zu F. H. Füger" (NOTE 2), 45–46, 51, was the first to mention the importance to Füger of Hamilton and West. She has also cited the influence on Füger of the contemporary Italian artists Giuseppe Cades and Felice Giani. David was certainly familiar with Füger, whose work the former mentioned when he visited Tischbein's studio.

58 Alfred Stix, *Füger* (NOTE 56), 57, suggested that Füger's turn to tragic classical themes in the 1790s was in response to the repressive political situation in Austria following the death of Emperor Joseph II in 1790. The melancholy tone of his art—especially this painting, which depicts a blind man—may also have been caused by the necessity of giving up miniature painting in 1797 because of problems with his eyes.

59 In Füger's letter to Meyer, dated October 29, 1791, he confided "what I can't say at the Akademie . . . that history painting fills the mind but not the purse" (cited in Schwarzenberg, "Studien zu F. H. Füger" [NOTE 2], 112). The most important patron of neoclassical art in Vienna was not Emperor Joseph II, who preferred the softened style of Angelica Kauffman when forced to purchase a neoclassical painting, but Count Fries, who commissioned many of Zauner's sculptures and bought Canova's *Theseus and the Minotaur* (see FIGURE 10) and Füger's *Death of Germanicus*.

60 Unsigned article in *Zeitschrift für die elegante Welt*, June 4, 1801; cited in Schwarzenberg, "Studien zu F. H. Füger" (NOTE 2), 110–11.

61 Heinz Günther, "Die figürlichen Künste zur Zeit Josephs II," *Österreich zur Zeit Kaiser Joseph II* (exh. cat., Melk: Niederösterreichische Landesausstellung, 1980), 198.

62 C. G. Küttner, *Reise durch Deutschland* (Leipzig: Dybrisch, 1804), vol. 3, 224; cited in Stix, *Füger* (NOTE 56), 89.

63 Lammel, *Deutsche Malerei* (NOTE 3), 143.

64 The curriculum at the Hohe Karlsschule emphasized theory and proportion, using Guibal's textbook, *Traité sur les proportions du corps humain*; see R. Bernhard, "Nikolaus Guibal" (diss., Friedrich-Alexander-Universität, Erlangen, 1922), 14.

65 Hetsch's dates of study in Paris and Rome vary. Most sources agree that he was in Paris in 1781–82. Ulrike Gauss (*Die Zeichnungen und Aquarelle des 19. Jahrhunderts in der graphischen Sammlung des Staatsgalerie Stuttgart* [Stuttgart: Staatsgalerie, 1976], 88) places him in Rome in 1785–87, Becker, *Paris und die deutsche Malerei* (NOTE 52), 47, claims he arrived in 1784, and Herbert von Einem (*Deutsche Malerei des Klassizismus und der Romantik, 1760–1840* [Munich: C. H. Beck, 1978], 219) states that he was there in 1782–85. According to Werner Fleischhauer (*Phillip Friedrich Hetsch* [Stuttgart: Hugo Matthaes, 1929], 15), he arrived in Rome in 1785.

66 See Gauss, *Zeichnungen* (NOTE 65), for numerous illustrations of Hetsch's drawings as well as those of other Würtemberg artists.

67 Although *Priam and Achilles* is undated, Gauss, *Zeichnungen* (NOTE 65), 91, includes the drawing with other studies by Hetsch from the 1790s. It was one of several drawings depicting Priam. The influence of Carstens is also evident in Hetsch's *Job*, a painting that is related to Wächter's famous *Job and His Friends*, begun in the 1790s (see FIGURE 32). Both reveal a simplicity, corporeality, and melancholy reminiscent of Carstens; see Werner Fleischhauer, *Die Schwäbische Kunst im 19. und 20. Jahrhundert* (Stuttgart: Deutsche Verlags, 1952), 35–36.

68 Dannecker's few finished independent drawings were mostly done in Italy for proposed sculptures and are stylistically related to the *Bacchus*. Only two finished drawings after sculptures exist, and their attribution remains in question; see Ulrike Gauss, *Johann Heinrich Dannecker der Zeichner* (exh. cat., Stuttgart: Staatsgalerie, 1987), 11.

69 Adolf Spemann, *Johann Heinrich Dannecker* (Munich: F. Bruckmann, 1958), 14.

70 Ibid., 11. Other Homeric projects by Dannecker included several drawings for a statue of Hector never executed and drawings of twelve heads of Greek heroes.

71 Beate Grubert, "J. H. W. Tischbein: 'Homer nach Antiken gezeichnet' " (Ph.D. diss., Ruhr-Universität, Bochum, 1975). Wiebenson, "Subjects from Homer's *Iliad*" (NOTE 15), 36, notes the influence of Lavater on these illustrations; see also *John Flaxman* (NOTE 53), no. 256.

72 Schadow's interest in movement was manifested earlier in a series of drawings of dancers from the 1790s. The best study of Schadow as a draftsman is Annagret Janda, "Über den Zeichner Schadow," in *Johann Gottfried Schadow 1764–1850* (exh. cat., Berlin: Nationalgalerie, Staatliche Museen, 1964), 37–50.

73 Goethe, *Italian Journey* (NOTE 4), 136–37, entry for December 3, 1786: "I reckon my second life, a very rebirth, from the day when I entered Rome. . . . I immediately bought the new edition of Winckelmann's *History of the Art of Antiquity*. . . . I find it a great help"; entry for December 13, 1786: "This morning I came by chance on the letters which Winckelmann wrote from Italy, and you can imagine with what emotion I have started to read them. Thirty-one years ago, at the same time of year, he arrived here, an even greater fool than I was. But, with true German seriousness, he set himself to make a thorough and accurate study of antiquity and its arts. How bravely he worked his way through! And, in this city, what it means to me to remember him!"

74 Goethe's most significant articles on neoclassicism appeared in 1798 and included "Einleitung in die Propyläen" (Introduction to the Propyläen) and "Über Laokoon" (Observations on the Laocoön). He followed earlier classical doctrine, emphasizing man as the most appropriate subject for art, sculpture and drawing as superior mediums, and Greek art and culture as worthiest of emulation.

The most thorough study is Walter Scheidig, *Goethes Preisaufgaben für bildende Künstler 1799–1805* (Weimar: Hermann Böhlaus, 1958). The subjects were taken from the *Iliad* and *Odyssey*, and submissions included many drawings as well as paintings. The competition attracted few prominent artists, with the exception of the young Philipp Otto Runge, and results were generally considered to be poor in quality, testifying to the early impoverishment of the neoclassical movement in Germany.

75 Johann Georg Sulzer, *Allgemeine Theorie der schönen Kunste* (Leipzig: Weidmann, 1798), vol. 4, 827.

76 Ibid., vol. 2, 724.

77 Ibid., vol. 1, 198.

78 Sulzer, cited in Pevsner, *Academies of Art* (NOTE 3), 149. Sulzer expanded the application of "noble simplicity" beyond aesthetics to designate a Rousseau-based natural way of life opposed to the artificialities and over-elaborations of contemporary society; see Hatfield, *Winckelmann and His German Critics* (NOTE 10), 133.

79 Goethe, letter to J. P. Eckermann, July 5, 1827; cited in *Goethe on Art*, ed. John Gage (Berkeley: University of California Press, 1980), 74. Schiller's observations were made to Ludwig Tieck while touring the Dresden Museum and are published in *Biographische und literarische Skizzen aus dem leben und der Zeit Karl Försters*, ed. Luisa Förster (Dresden: H. W. Gottschalk, 1846), 155–56. For a discussion of Kant's praise of abstract line see Werner Busch, "Carstens und die Akademie," in *Berlin zwischen 1789 und 1848: Facetten einer Epoche* (exh. cat., Berlin: Akademie der Künste, 1981), 81–92.

80 Friedrich von Schiller, "The Aesthetic Education of Man," in *On the Aesthetic Education of Man*, trans. F. M. Wilkinson and L. A. Willoughby (Oxford: Oxford University Press, 1967), 9. See also James Sheehan, *German History 1770–1866*, The Oxford History of Modern Europe (Oxford: Clarendon Press, 1989), 329.

81 Goethe, *Italian Journey* (NOTE 4), 489, entry for April 1788.

82 Friedrich Noack lists the attendees and discusses their reading circle and library; see *Das Deutschtum in Rom* (Darmstadt: Scientia Verlag Aalen, 1974), 372.

83 The most comprehensive analysis of Fernow's work is Herbert von Einem, *Carl Ludwig Fernow: Eine Studie zum deutschen Klassizismus* (Berlin: Deutscher Verein für Kunstwissenschaft, 1935). Fernow was introduced to classical theory by Carstens in Lübeck, where he lived in 1786–88. He studied philosophy from the Kantian disciple Leonhard Reinhold at the University of Jena in 1791–93 and attended Schiller's lectures there in the winter of 1792–93. His later writings included a biography of Carstens (see NOTE 84), 1805, and *Römische Studien* (NOTE 6).

84 Carstens had rejected the offer of studying with the painter Johann Heinrich Tischbein because it entailed additional services as a valet that he found demeaning; see Fernow, *Carstens Leben und Werke*, ed. and enl. Hermann Riegel (Hannover: Carl Rümpler, 1867 [originally published in 1805]), 46–47.

85 For particulars regarding his interaction with the Kunstakademiet see Fernow, *Carstens* (NOTE 84), 55–63, and Alfred Kamphausen, *Asmus Jakob Carstens* (Neumünster in Holstein: Karl Wachholtz, 1941), 26–58.

86 See Heinse, *Ardinghello*, 1785; cited in Pevsner, *Academies of Art* (NOTE 3), 203; the artist-hero complains that academies teach with "disiecta membra": "eyes, muzzles, noses, ears and faces; and hands and feet, according to regulations."

87 Abildgaard admired Carstens's drawing *Baldur's Death*, based on a poem by Ewald, and agreed to accept him as a student, but he soon rejected Carstens as being too old and insufficiently talented to learn to paint. For his part, Carstens later criticized Abildgaard's drawing style for its elongated, mannered figures; Fernow, *Carstens* (NOTE 84), 60.

88 Ibid., 51.

89 Ibid., 52.

90 Lammel, *Deutsche Malerei* (NOTE 3), 137, and Pevsner, *Academies of Art* (NOTE 3), 195. Pevsner's book contains the only account in English of Carstens's intricate dealings with the Berlin Akademie.

91 Carstens was commissioned to paint relief friezes of classical figures in grisaille for the bedroom of Queen Friederike Luise in the royal palace. These included allegorical figures of the Three Fates, which reappeared in his later drawings in Rome. The preparatory studies were done in outline and repeated several poses also used in his engraved illustrations. The artist was also hired by the minister of education, Karl Friedrich von Heinitz, to paint murals in the salon of his Berlin residence, Dorville House.

92 Moritz's other theoretical writings, especially "Von der bildenden Nachahmung des Schönen" (On the pictorial imitation of beauty), 1788, which influenced Schiller, reinforced Carstens's attitudes through an emphasis on genius, inner spirit, and the creation of beauty as a moral imperative. According to Moritz, artistic genius was analogous to divine power; see Kamphausen, *Carstens* (NOTE 85), 106–7.

93 Other sources for this drawing include the Three Fates on Schadow's tomb for Count von der Mark, 1790, Carstens's own drawing of the Three Fates, and his sculpture *Atropos*, both completed earlier in Rome.

94 Fernow emphasized the quality of mystery in Carstens's work when he observed that "the pictorial arts speak a language that cannot be translated into words" ("Über einige neue Kunstwerke des Hrn. Prof. Carstens," *Der neue teutsche Merkur*, May 1795, 185).

95 Carstens had first seen this art in Florence in 1792, and his enthusiasm for Ghiberti, Ghirlandaio, and Masaccio was noted by Fernow, *Römische Studien* (NOTE 6), 98, and Goethe and Meyer, *Winckelmann und seine Jahrhundert* (NOTE 54), 181. Carstens was also a great admirer of Dürer.

96 The artistic spirit must be free to rise above rules if "the representation is to be free and beautiful, and not merely academically correct" (Fernow, *Carstens* [NOTE 84], 186). In his later book, *Römische Studien* (NOTE 6), vol. 2, 159, Fernow elaborated further, remarking that the creative idea was not a work of reason but of genius.

97 Carstens's letter is cited in Fernow, *Carstens* (NOTE 84), 129.

98 Carstens's opinions recall those of Abildgaard, who wrote in 1777 that French painting "gives offence to the thinking spectator, who does not view a painting as he would an embroidered cloth" (cited in *Danish Painting of the Golden Age* [exh. cat., London: National Gallery, 1984], 20).

99 Becker, *Paris und die deutsche Malerei* (NOTE 52), 48. During the 1780s, however, Goethe had been initially impressed with David and Drouais; see *Italian Journey* (NOTE 4), 379.

100 Pevsner, *Academies of Art* (NOTE 3), 195–97.

101 For a complete study see Markus Neuwirth, *J. A. Koch—A. J. Carstens: Die Argonauten* (Graz: Akademische Druck- und Verlagsanstalt, 1989).

102 Like many others, Wächter combined a study of antiquity and Renaissance art with drawing from models, although only one life drawing has been preserved; see Gauss, *Zeichnungen* (NOTE 65), 216, no. 1579.

103 The setting is also minimally depicted in the finished painting. A pendant to this work, *Belisarius*, was completed in Rome and features a similar composition in reverse. The drawing for *Job and His Friends* was etched in 1808. The dating of this work to 1793–94 was suggested by Paul Köster in "Eberhard Wächter (1762–1852)" (Ph.D. diss., Rheinischen-Friedrich-Wilhelm-Universität, Bonn, 1968), no. 58; see also Gauss, *Zeichnungen* (NOTE 65), 215.

104 Wächter, who was one of the few German artists to defend Carstens during his exhibition, later wrote that artistically he was always guided by the spirit of Carstens; see Köster, "Wächter" (NOTE 103), 58.

105 Cited in Karl Simon, *Gottlieb Schick: Ein Beitrag zur Geschichte der deutschen Malerei um 1800* (Leipzig: Klinkhardt und Biermann, 1914), 54.

106 Thorvaldsen purchased nine of Carstens's drawings as well as the Argonaut cycle. His copies included *Night with Her Children Sleep and Death*, *Homer Singing to the Greeks*, *The Golden Age*, and *Oedipus and His Daughter*, among others; see Fernow, *Carstens* (NOTE 84), 315–18, and Hubertus Froning, "Thorvaldsen und Carstens," in *Bertel Thorvaldsen* (exh. cat., Cologne: Wallraf-Richartz-Museum, 1977), 41.

107 The landscape of *Cupid and Bacchus*, once owned by Queen Caroline Amalie of Denmark, suggests sources in Quattrocento painting; see Dyveke Helsted, *Thorvaldsen: Drawings and Bozzetti* (exh. cat., London: Heim Gallery, 1973), 21.

108 Schick filled six sketchbooks in Paris and Rome with studies from life, copies of antique statues including the Parthenon frieze, and Renaissance paintings; see Gauss, *Zeichnungen* (NOTE 65), 173.

109 Schick also copied David's *Portrait of Madame Recamier* and Drouais's *Marius at Minturnae*; see *Gottlieb Schick: Ein Maler des Klassizismus* (exh. cat., Stuttgart: Staatsgalerie, 1976), 55, 69.

110 Schick, letter to Dannecker, July 10, 1800; cited in *Gottlieb Schick* (NOTE 109), 57. The comments were made in reference to his painting *Eva*.

111 Keith Andrews, *The Nazarenes: A Brotherhood of German Painters in Rome* (London: Oxford University Press, 1964), 95.

112 During the winter of 1804–5 Schick sketched dissected corpses in a hospital; for these and his few academies see *Gottlieb Schick* (NOTE 109), 105–6. Regarding *The Sacrifice of Noah*, Schick wrote, "I have rarely used models, and it is striking, how much better my work is when I paint from an idea" (cited ibid., 109).

113 Schick, letter to Dannecker, April 7, 1802; cited in *Gottlieb Schick* (NOTE 109), 25.

114 In his portraiture and genre drawings from daily life Schick directly anticipated Biedermeier art.

115 See Hans Ebert, *Buonaventura Genelli: Leben und Werke* (Weimar: Hermann Böhlaus, 1971).

116 Schnorr von Carolsfeld, letter to Johann Gottlob Quandt, January 30, 1823; cited in *Master Drawings from the National Gallery of Canada* (exh. cat., Washington: National Gallery of Art, 1988), 149. For a full discussion of nature and the ideal in Nazarene drawings see Peter Märker and Margret Stuffmann, "Zu den Zeichnungen der Nazarener," in *Die Nazarener* (exh. cat., Frankfurt: Städelsche Kunstinstitut, 1977), 181–82.

117 Schnorr von Carolsfeld (NOTE 116), 149. The means for achieving these goals differed from neoclassicism through an adherence to realism. In the same letter Schnorr von Carolsfeld wrote, "Only this one thing should not be desired from me—that I acknowledge an outer regularity, a superficial beauty, as true beauty. I want to see beauty as the stamp of the soul and will not take pleasing forms as beauty." Winckelmann's views are expressed in *Gedanken über die Nachahmung der griechischen Werke in der Malerei und Bildhauerkunst*; see Winckelmann, "Thoughts" (NOTE 8), 340.

118 Winckelmann, "Thoughts" (NOTE 8), 340.

OVERLEAF
Antonio Canova
Study for The Graces
Before 1815
(CATALOGUE NO. 89, detail)

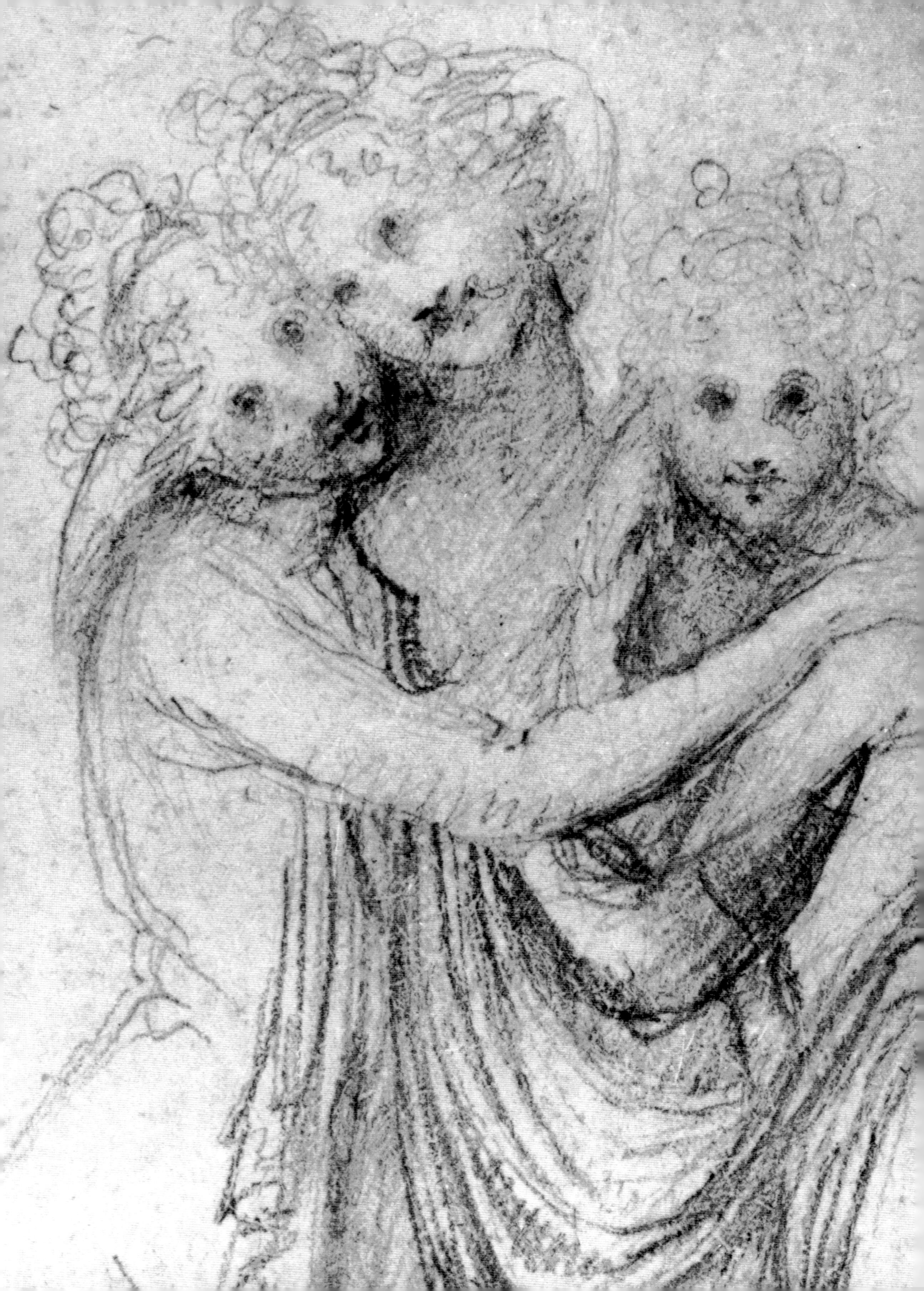

Academic Life Drawing in Rome, 1750–1790

Edgar Peters Bowron

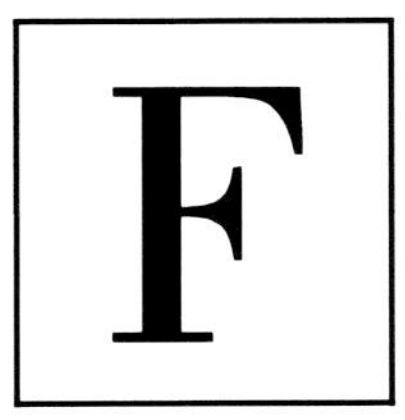

From the Renaissance until the end of the nineteenth century, life drawing was an essential part of nearly every artist's education in Rome.[1] Painters and sculptors progressed as students through a well-established series of instructional tasks that culminated in drawing from the live model. The importance of life drawing in art education is clear in this description of an ideal art academy by Johann Georg Sulzer, a popular late eighteenth-century German aesthetician:

> *The academy must be well supplied with objects necessary for learning the art of drawing. These consist chiefly of the following in sufficient variety: Books of drawings showing firstly separate parts of figures, form and proportion of heads, of noses, ears, lips, eyes, etc.; then larger parts of figures and complete figures. To copy these is the first task to be set to the beginner. They are to be followed by drawings of figures taken from the most outstanding works of art, correct drawings of classic sculpture, selected figures by the greatest masters, by Raphael, Michael Angelo, the Carracci, etc. In copying these the student receives a first insight into the higher spheres of art. Besides the stock of drawings a stock of plaster casts is necessary, representing the noblest works of Antiquity and some more recent works, in parts as well as in complete figures and groups. Students will have to draw from these assiduously, because this not only helps them to develop a just eye and an appreciation of beautiful forms, but also a knowledge of light and shade, of variations of attitudes and of foreshortenings. Furthermore, the academy must have models, men of beautiful form to pose on a raised platform or table in different attitudes according to the instruction of one of the leading teachers. . . . This will enable the teachers to explain almost everything that refers to the observation of light and shade on single figures. For the equipment of the room where life-drawing is to be held must be so that it can be used both by day-light and by artificial light.*[2]

For many seventeenth- and eighteenth-century artists life drawing was such an indispensable element of their training that they continued drawing from the nude well into maturity, both to maintain and sharpen their skills as draftsmen and to demonstrate their ability to draw from the live model. These drawings of "men of beautiful form"—highly finished red- or black-chalk studies of male nudes drawn in the studio for instructional purposes—were regarded in the late eighteenth century as independent works of art and admired as virtuoso performances of drawing.[3] The academy drawings of Domenico Corvi, for example, one of the chief exponents of the Roman classical tradition in the second half of the eighteenth century, were avidly sought by his contemporaries and, according to the historian Luigi Lanzi, were valued even more highly than his paintings.[4] Lanzi noted Corvi's incomparable command of anatomy, perspective, and design—strengths that the painter underscored in a self-portrait (FIGURE 36) in which he depicted himself holding a *porte-crayon* and maulstick and drawing the live model in the guise of Hercules on a sheet of paper tacked to an easel. A plaster cast of the Venus de' Medici, treatises on perspective and anatomy, and a proportional drawing of the human head allude to the intellectual and theoretical foundations of life drawing.

Corvi took an active interest in the training of young artists. He directed the life classes at the Accademia del Nudo and held a private drawing academy in his studio that was attended by Giuseppe Cades, Vincenzo Camuccini, Gaspare Landi, Teodoro Matteini, Luigi Sabatelli, and the poet, amateur artist, and patron of the arts Leopoldo Cicognara.[5] A black-chalk academy drawing from the 1760s by Corvi, now in Philadelphia, exemplifies his own competence before the live model (FIGURE 37).[6] Although similar poses, lighting, background, and devices for the model's support are found in the artist's other life drawings, this sheet is an especially fine example of his masterful command of human anatomy.

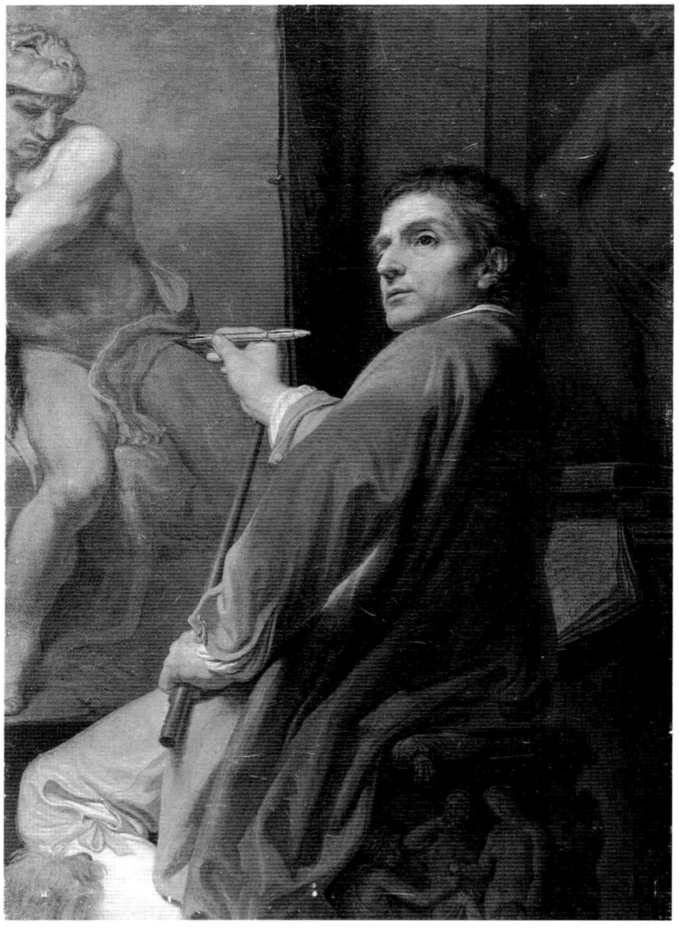

FIGURE 36
Domenico Corvi
Italy, 1721–1803

Self-Portrait
c. 1785, oil on canvas, 90 x 65 cm (35 7/16 x 25 5/8 in.),
private collection, formerly Richard Hellgren, Eskilstuna, Sweden

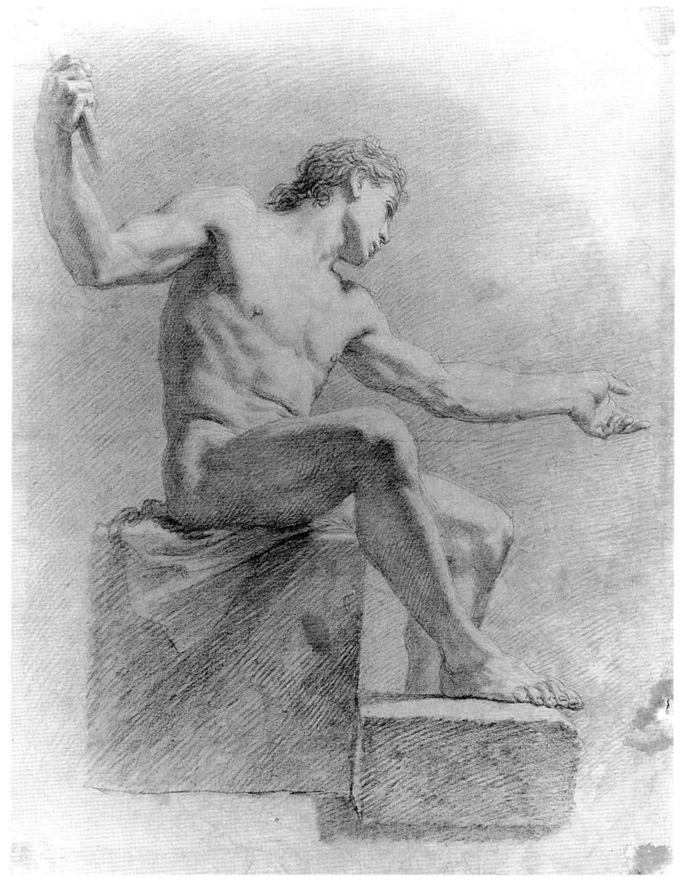

FIGURE 37
Domenico Corvi
Italy, 1721–1803

Academic Nude
c. 1760–70, black chalk, traces of white on tan paper,
55.3 x 42.6 cm (21 3/4 x 16 3/4 in.),
Philadelphia Museum of Art, bequest of Anthony Morris Clark
(inv. no. 1978-70-63)

An academy drawing of exquisite perfection by Giuseppe Bottani from his maturity represents the end of the arduous journey contemporary artists undertook in learning to represent the nude figure in pictorial space on paper (FIGURE 38).[7] When Bottani arrived in Rome in 1735 at the age of eighteen, he followed a traditional path that included the study of Raphael's Vatican Stanze, the Galleria Farnese, antique sculpture, and the live model. An unusually sensitive and conscientious draftsman, Bottani developed an exceptional command of the human figure in drawing terms. Proportional accuracy, foreshortening, detail-mass relationships, the use of light and shadow to establish the figure as a convincing volumetric and spatial form—Bottani demonstrates his mastery of these complex technical problems in this red-chalk drawing, in which the model strikes the attitude of a Praxitelean Apollo Lykeios, with a hand on his head to encourage attention to the muscular tension of the upraised arm and torso.

The techniques employed by each of these draftsmen to conceive and depict the human form in illusionistic three-dimensional space vary considerably. Bottani's representation of the characteristic swellings and contours of muscles is entirely different from that of Corvi or, for that matter, of Antonio Cavallucci, a painter from Sermoneta who spent most of his life in Rome. Giovanni Gherardo de' Rossi, one of the artist's contemporary biographers, described how Cavallucci arrived in Rome at the age of fourteen and under the direction of Stefano Pozzi progressed according to the method recommended by Sulzer—copying profiles, heads, hands, feet, and other details of the body from drawings and engravings; studying the entire figure *per se* through outline drawings; and representing three-dimensional objects, usually plaster casts of classical sculptures, before undertaking the live model.[8] A black-chalk academy drawing in Berlin (FIGURE 39) bears no resemblance to the tentative and uncertain efforts of the young artist but instead epitomizes the powerful grasp of the human form Cavallucci eventually attained—which de' Rossi praised for its exactitude, precision of contour, finish, and shading.

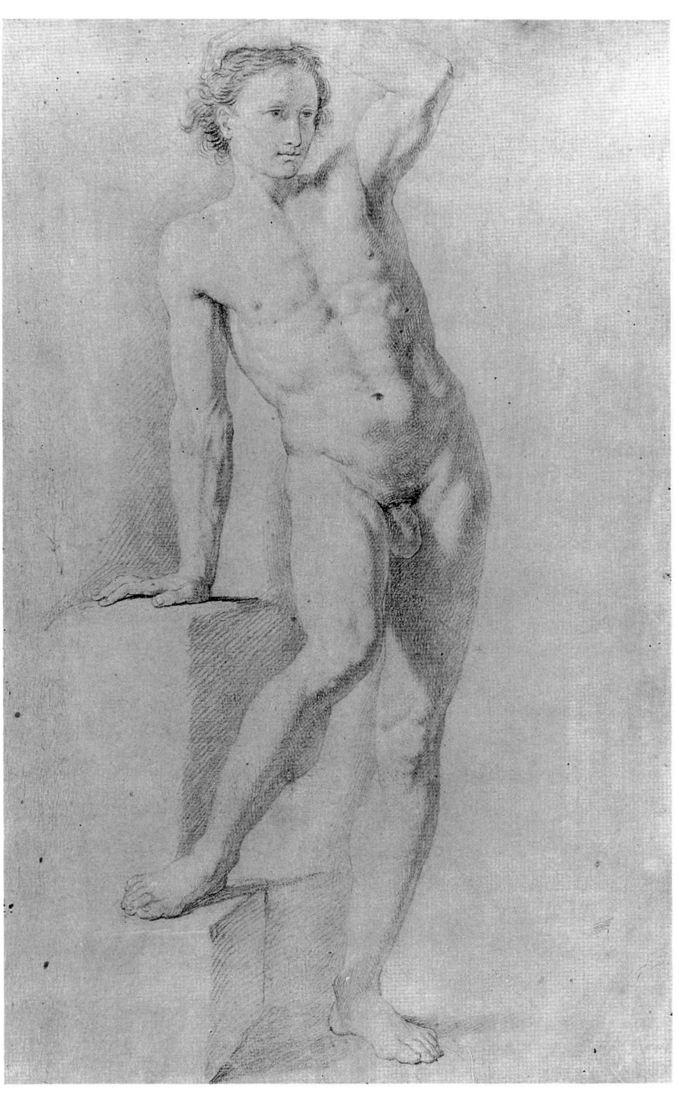

FIGURE 38
Giuseppe Bottani
Italy, 1717–84

Academic Nude
c. 1760–70, red and white chalks on red-orange prepared paper, 43.2 x 27 cm (17 x 10 5/8 in.), Philadelphia Museum of Art, bequest of Anthony Morris Clark (inv. no. 1978-70-197)

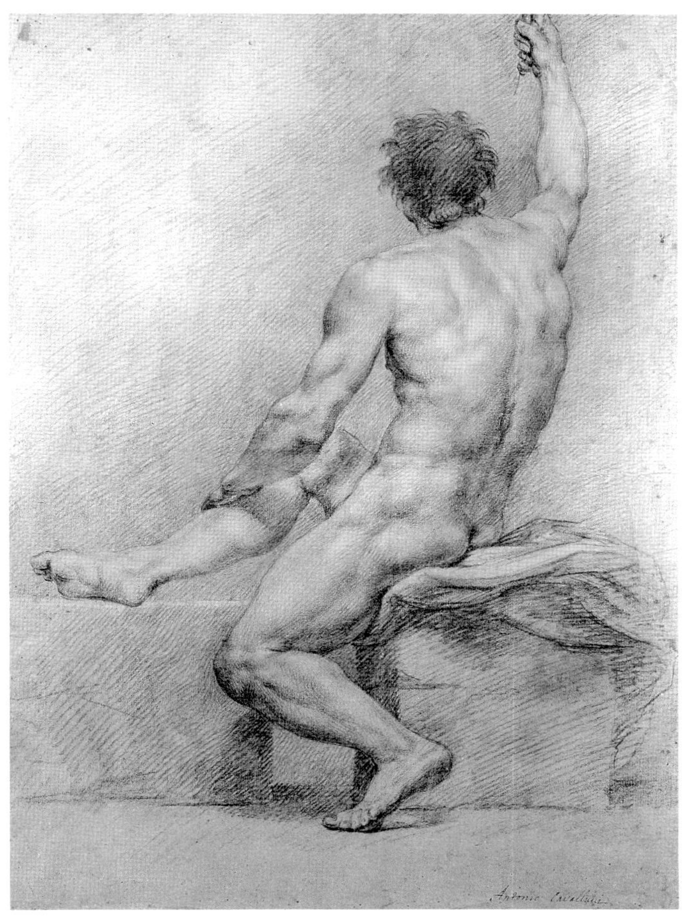

FIGURE 39
Antonio Cavallucci
Italy, 1752–95

Academic Nude
c. 1785, black chalk on blue paper, 55.2 x 40.6 cm (21 3/4 x 16 in.), Kupferstichkabinett, Staatliche Museen zu Berlin, Preussischer Kulturbesitz (inv. no. KdZ 22 254)

By the middle of the eighteenth century it had long been an established tradition for artists to travel to Rome to complete their education. The city remained unrivaled as a training ground for young artists, especially as a place where they could improve their ability to draw. Rome offered a wealth of artistic experiences unsurpassed elsewhere in Europe, and as the century progressed painters and sculptors considered a visit to Rome almost obligatory for their professional advancement. Although the number of art academies increased phenomenally from Paris to Saint Petersburg between 1740 and 1790,[9] Rome remained the "Academy of Europe," largely because of opportunities for instruction in life drawing. Artists could study from the model at the two "official" academies, the Académie de France à Rome and the Accademia di San Luca; they could enroll in one of the local evening drawing academies held by Rome's leading masters; and they could—and often did—organize their own independent life-drawing classes.

The Académie de France held evening classes in life drawing in its seat at the Palazzo Capranica and, after 1724, in the Palazzo Mancini on the Corso. Nicolas Vleughels, director of the Académie from 1725 to 1737, redecorated Palazzo Mancini with Gobelins tapestries and fine furniture and placed in every room paintings, students' copies of the Old Masters, plaster casts, antique vases, and portfolios of drawings. He introduced the practice of drawing from the draped model, as well as from life, and liberalized the curriculum.[10] Classes were open to the public as well as the *pensionnaires*, and numerous eighteenth-century sources indicate the popularity of the Académie for drawing instruction for young artists of many nationalities. The Scottish painter Allan Ramsay, for example, attended the life classes there on his first visit to Rome, in 1736–37, and also during his second visit, 1754–57. Immediately upon presentation of a letter of recommendation to Vleughels on the evening of November 15, 1737, Ramsay joined the life class, where students were engaged in drawing or modeling by lamplight from a handsome young Swiss model.[11]

The Accademia di San Luca, the official academy for Roman artists, was also open to students of all nationalities. They attended weekly classes and selected a master from among the academicians to whom their work would be submitted. The Accademia held competitions, which in the late eighteenth century alternated between the Concorsi Clementini and Concorsi Balestra, in which the younger artists were given a copying exercise, either from an antique or contemporary painting or sculpture, and the older artists were presented with the task of producing an elaborate, finished compositional drawing illustrating a theme from the Old or New Testament, classical history, or mythology.[12] The curriculum of the Accademia remains to be studied in detail, but it seems that instruction in perspective, anatomy, and drawing was provided intermittently and that a regular program of life classes was not established until the middle of the eighteenth century.[13]

The Accademia del Disegno—widely known as the Accademia del Nudo—was established by Pope Benedict XIV under the aegis of the Accademia di San Luca in 1754 in a large room below the Pinacoteca Capitolina in the Palazzo dei Conservatori. The pope, the eighteenth-century pontiff most energetic in support of the arts, had earlier founded the Pinacoteca Capitolina, in 1748, as "an exemplar and for the instruction of youth inclined to the study of the liberal arts." In 1747–48 architect Ferdinando Fuga expanded the Palazzo dei Conservatori for the display of the Sacchetti collection of paintings, and in 1752 he enlarged the building again to house the Pio collection. Beneath the gallery that under Pius VII became known as the Sala di San Petronilla a circular room was designed by Gian Paolo Panini for the "sala del nudo." The room exists today as the site of the Biblioteca della Avvocatura del Comune.[14]

The creation of an academy for young painters and sculptors to draw the live model appears to have been the inspiration of three men: the pope's secretary of state, Cardinal Silvio Valenti Gonzaga; Monsignore Riminaldi, *uditore* (magistrate) of the Camerlengo; and Francesco Mancini, *principe* (president) of the Accademia di San Luca. A papal brief of April 6, 1754 (*Gymnasium publicum seu Academia in Aedibus Capitolinus erigitur*), established the Accademia del Nudo with a stipend of 300 *scudi* a year for the employment of models, furniture, lighting and heating, and maintenance. The papal majordomo, Cardinal Girolamo Colonna, was named protector, and a constitution published in 1757 placed the institution under the authority of the Accademia di San Luca. Each year the president of the latter selected ten academicians—painters and sculptors—to direct the classes for a month each. The appointed professors were required to set the pose of the model, correct the students' drawings (and the sculptors' clay models), and attend the sessions three times a week. The students brought their sheets of drawing paper to the designated academician on Saturday; these were stamped, and at the end of the week the completed drawings were collected and corrected.

The Accademia del Nudo was open ten months a year, closing only in October and February, the month of Carnival. There were two terms, winter and summer, which determined whether classes began in the morning or in the afternoon. In the spring and summer the students drew the nude model; in the fall and winter a draped figure. At the end of each term, in March and September, competitions were held to which students submitted their drawings from the model during a given week. The winners were awarded silver medals designed by Placido Costanzi and engraved by Pietro Ortolani.[15]

The first ten directors of the Pontificia Accademia detta del Nudo, as it was also known, appointed by the *principe*, Ferdinando Fuga, are recorded in the minutes of the Accademia di San Luca on November 10, 1754. They included the painters Agostino Masucci, Anton Raphael Mengs, Gian Paolo Panini, Stefano Pozzi, Nicolò Ricciolini, and Giacomo Zoboli, and the sculptors Pietro Bracci, Carlo Monaldi, Filippo della Valle, and Francesco Vergara. Between 1754 and 1810 the *direttori* included the most important artistic figures in Rome: Domenico de' Angelis, Pompeo Batoni, Pietro Benvenuti, Giuseppe Bottani, Giuseppe Cades, Vincenzo Camuccini, Antonio Canova, Domenico Corvi, Placido Costanzi, Anton von Maron, Vincenzo Pacetti, and Stefano Parrocel. Many of these artists, who received no compensation for their duties beyond a medal from the Accademia di San Luca, were exceptionally generous with their time. Bracci and della Valle each supervised the model at least a month each year between 1755 and 1761; Corvi directed the life classes in 1757, 1760, 1775, 1777, 1778, 1792, 1801, and 1802, and Pozzi in 1754, 1759, 1761, and 1766.[16]

Between 1755 and 1800 the classes included, besides the Italians, twenty-four French, two Corsican, twenty German, twenty Spanish, sixteen Flemish, eight Swiss, eight Portuguese, about twenty English, four Polish, and two Russian students.[17] The activities of the British artists who frequented the Accademia del Nudo have been examined recently and their life drawings published.[18] Allan Ramsay studied there in the first winter term, during November 1754 to March 1755. Matthew William Peters, traveling in Italy with a stipend from the Society of Arts, wrote to an artist in London in 1762:

> *At the Pope's Academy, where I attend, the human figure is every day in the week, holidays excepted, free for any person to draw after without any expense—in the summer at half an hour after five in the morning and in winter after nightfall—two hours each time; near which are many large galleries erected for pictures and statues, where at any time people may study. . . . I am under the direction of Pompeo Battoni, from whom I shall hope to get some furtherance in drawing.*[19]

Other British artists who received prizes in the *concorsi* at the Accademia del Nudo included Nathaniel Dance, James Ennis, Joseph Nollekens, Thomas Jenkins, and Richard Wilson. For some, like the landscape painter Jonathan Skelton, the Accademia presented an opportunity to develop their skills in figure drawing. In October 1758 George James wrote from Rome to Skelton's patron, William Herring, about the artist's recent work:

> *I have seen the studies that he has just brought from Tivoli where he has been very busy all the hot weather & I waited to see them that I might with more certainty assure you that he is very much improved. . . . The thing he is most wanting in is figures but I can excuse him in that point because there are very few in an Italian country prospect—he proposes repairing this want by the help of the academy this winter, which I make no doubt he will do.*[20]

Few personal accounts survive to provide an impression of the students' experiences at the Accademia del Nudo. Johann Gottlieb Puhlmann, a Batoni pupil from Potsdam, lived in Rome from 1774 to 1787, and his letters to his parents comprise an important source of information about artistic life of the period.[21] He reports attending the Capitoline academy with about one hundred other students and describes the dates and times of his attendance, but otherwise provides little information about the mechanics of the life classes, except to note that during each five-month term the model was drawn in sixteen separate poses. The impression left by Puhlmann's account is the extraordinary importance of drawing for young artists in Rome—in his early years there he seems to have done little else. In addition to drawing at the Accademia del Nudo nearly every day, he drew at the Académie de France, Batoni's nightly academies, and the life classes of other local artists.

Antonio Canova attended a session on the evening of September 8, 1779, a few days after his arrival in Rome, and recorded the experience in his diary:

> *We then looked in at that [drawing academy] on the Campidoglio, which began this evening; there were about 150 young men but nothing new or clever; there were many sculptors there as well; it was so terribly hot that even though we stayed only a short time I was bathed in sweat, and indeed my two companions felt extremely ill.*[22]

Pius VI made alterations to the facilities of the Accademia del Nudo in 1780 in an attempt to alleviate the conditions criticized by Canova, but the room in which the classes were held remained unsuitable, and its location on the Capitoline was thought inconvenient and dangerously remote. Pius VII transferred the academy in 1804 to Santa Maria Maddalena delle

Convertite, an abandoned monastery on the Corso, and Canova was appointed permanent director. Eventually, with a wider curriculum, it became a practical school of art.[23]

In spite of the facilities offered by the Académie de France and the Accademia di San Luca, the most effective instruction in life drawing in eighteenth-century Rome took place in the informal evening classes conducted by individual painters and sculptors. Many young artists found the smaller private academies more congenial, places where they could meet and work more casually and with greater freedom. The members of these studio-academies met either in an artist's studio or in the palace of a patron, such as the drawing academies of Cardinal Ottoboni, Marchese Marcello Sacchetti, and Paolo Falconieri recorded in Rome at the beginning of the century.[24] These activities were held in the evening hours apart from the normal activities of the studio. For a small fee, the professor would supervise young artists in life drawing and even provide instruction in perspective, anatomy, geometry, and other subjects.

In the 1770s and 1780s artists seeking an *accademia privata del nudo* in Rome could choose from at least a dozen conducted by Pompeo Batoni, Joseph Bergler, Tommaso Conca, Domenico Corvi, Pietro Labruzzi, Anton Raphael Mengs, Stefano Tofanelli, Alexander Trippel, and a certain Abbate Conti, among others.[25] The best-known were those of Batoni and Mengs. Although the rivalry between the two most famous painters of the day has probably been exaggerated, their contemporaries were certainly conscious of a competition between the two. The German painter Christian Ludwig von Hagedorn noted in 1763, "Es sind Zwei Seiten—die Mengsische und die Battonische in Rom" (There are two factions in Rome—the Mengsian and the Batonian).[26] Fifteen years later the situation had not changed, as the English painter James Northcote, writing from Rome in 1778, confirmed:

> *Mengs and Pompeo Battoni, who are both in Rome, hold each other with the utmost possible degree of contempt, but Pompeo thinks that all that ever has been, is now, or ever shall be, is like the dirt of the street before him. But Mengs is by much more liberal and magnificent; he keeps two grand houses in Rome, in one of them he has a gallery with the finest collection of casts from the antique that I have ever seen, where anybody has full liberty to draw at all hours who are only just once introduced to him.*[27]

A distinction should be made between those who attended the evening drawing academies of these artists for a fee and the actual studio assistants of the master, which in Batoni's case were limited for the most part to his sons, Domenico, Felice, and Romualdo. Even a partial list of those who attended his drawing classes over the years indicates how popular these life classes were. Artists of all nationalities attended, from the obscure to those, like Giuseppe Cades, who achieved a significant reputation of their own: Domenico de' Angelis, John Astley, Angelo Banchero, Henry Benbridge, Vincenzo Cannizzaro, Antonio Canova, Adamo Chiusole, Antonio Concioli, Edward Francis Cunningham, Carlos Espinosa, Johann Dominik Fiorillo, Anne Forbes, Giovanni Gottardi, Franz Hillner, Gaspare Landi, Andrea Lazzarini, Teodoro Matteini, Niccola Monti, Bernardo Nocchi, Pietro Pedroni, Matthew William Peters, Frediano dal Pino, Giuseppe Pirovani, John Ramsay, Jean-Pierre Saint-Ours, Stephan Serdiukov, and Peter Sobolovski.[28]

Puhlmann's letters also provide a glimpse into Batoni's private academy. It was usually held one evening a week from November to March or April, although he apparently held no classes between 1768 and 1774 or in the winter of 1781–82. The classes were open to all for a small fee, and the primary purpose was to draw the live model in a variety of poses. Batoni's drawing academy was popular both because of the quality of the models and his gifts as a teacher. He occasionally presented other formal exercises for the students and encouraged them to draw after his own academy and preparatory drawings as well as from his paintings and casts after the antique. Following the formal session of instruction he frequently delivered an extemporaneous lecture on the principles of painting and other topics of interest to the young artists.

Batoni's academy drawings play a significant role in understanding his activities as a draftsman. He made these accomplished studies all his life: in his earliest years in Lucca at the drawing academies of Giovanni Domenico Lombardi and Domenico Brugieri; in Rome, shortly after his arrival in 1727, at Sebastiano Conca's evening life classes; in the drawing sessions held at the Accademia del Nudo, which he supervised in 1756, 1758, and 1759; and during his mature years, when he held private life-drawing classes in his own studio. He even drew in the life classes of his contemporaries in Rome, such as those held by the French painter Laurent Pécheux.

Batoni's surviving academy drawings, for reasons that are not clear, date mostly from the 1760s and 1770s.[29] He generally favored black and white chalks and blue prepared paper, but a few red-chalk academies survive to confirm that he occasionally employed other media. His drawings of the male nude are characterized by consummate technique and faultless anatomical description (FIGURE 40; CATALOGUE NO. 79). The realism is

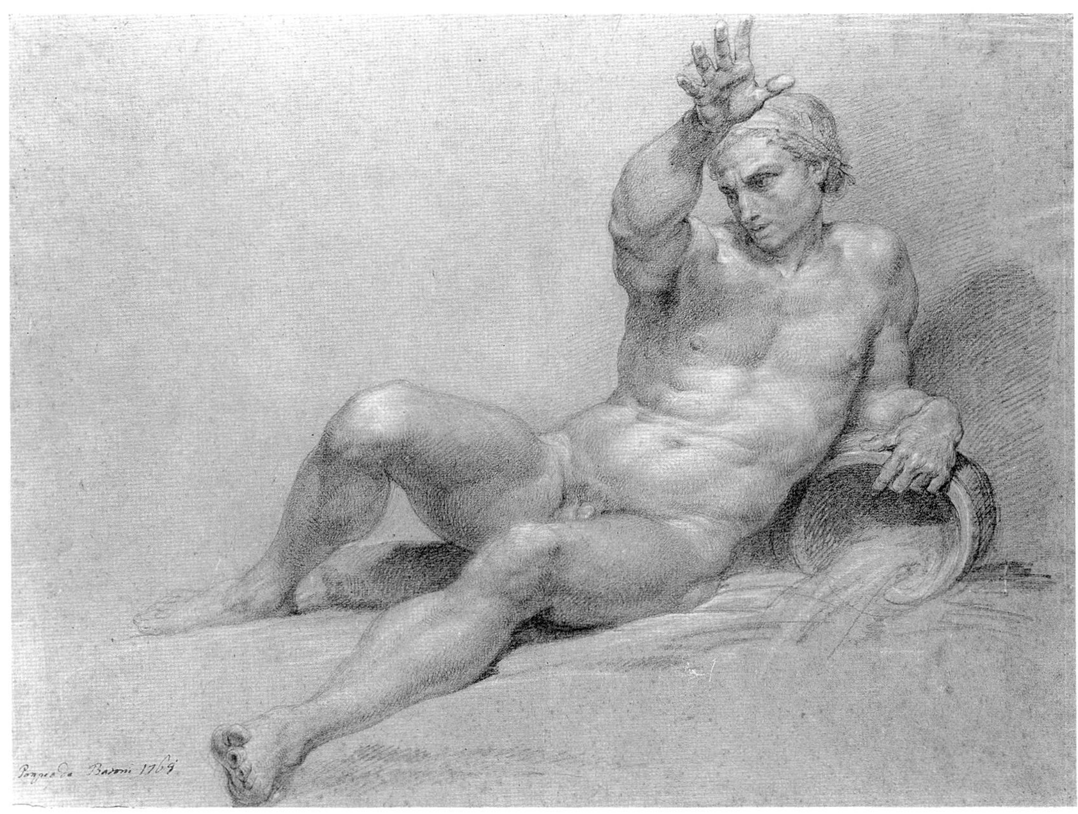

FIGURE 40
Pompeo Batoni
Italy, 1708–87

Academic Nude
1768, black and white chalks on grayish-green paper, 38.6 x 53.9 cm (15 3/16 x 21 1/4 in.), Kupferstichkabinett, Staatliche Museen zu Berlin, Preussischer Kulturbesitz (inv. no. KdZ 16 448)

deliberate and purposeful; rarely does one encounter the aggressive or exaggerated poses characteristic of Roman academy drawings of the first half of the century. The technical finesse and the mastery of the model's heavily muscled anatomy reflect Batoni's extraordinary ability to draw from life, and the pose, reminiscent of an antique river god, reflects his superb knowledge of ancient sculpture, knowledge that he had acquired in the late 1720s and early 1730s, when he supported himself in Rome as a professional copyist of antique statuary.

The subtly contoured cross-hatching Batoni employed to define the model's musculature was probably achieved by reworking, smoothing, and refining rapid, less precise sketches from life. The extreme detail and polish of these late academy drawings confirm that they are not the common product of a day's work in the studio but are demonstration pieces—virtuoso examples of the artist's skill as a draftsman. Batoni obviously regarded his academy drawings with great esteem, for they are remarkably well preserved. Most are signed and dated, and he frequently gave them to patrons and others as tokens of appreciation.[30]

Mengs resided in Rome periodically (1741–44, 1746–49, 1752–61, 1770–74, and 1777–79) and, like Batoni, was active in the official Roman art world. He supervised the life classes at the Accademia del Nudo in 1755, 1757, 1760, and 1771 and was selected *principe* of the Accademia di San Luca in 1771. In his last years in Rome, retired on a large pension as first painter to King Charles III of Spain, he lived in a grand manner and maintained a large and active academy in his spacious quarters in the Villa Barberini, near the Vatican. The landscape painter Thomas Jones described a visit to Mengs's studio on February 2, 1778: "All the Grand Apartments of the Palace being thrown open—in most of which were groups of Pupils making Studies after drawings pictures or Statues, according to their respective Classes."[31]

In a recent study of the Scottish pupils of Mengs, Basil Skinner noted that the artist was particular about whom he admitted to his academy. He refused to accept Pécheux as a pupil because he was French, and he held an antipathy toward British students in general because he considered them idle.[32] Moreover, his pedagogical approach to the teaching of young artists was extremely demanding, as Andrew Lumisden observed in 1756:

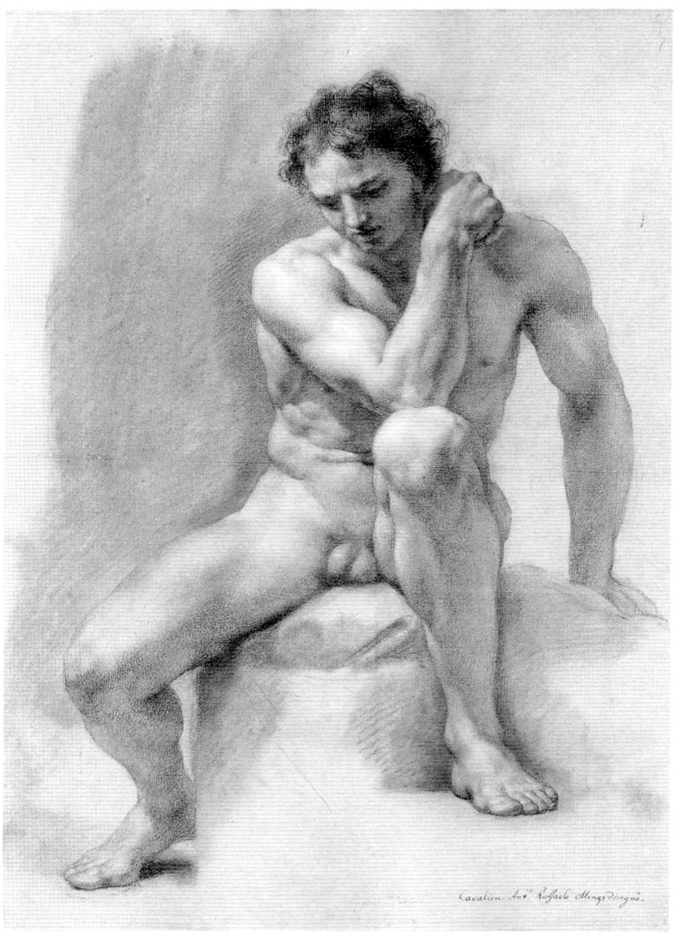

FIGURE 41
Anton Raphael Mengs
Germany, active Italy and Spain, 1728–79

Academic Nude
c. 1756, black chalk, heightened with white,
brown wash on gray-brown prepared paper, 54.7 x 39.7 cm (21 1/2 x 15 5/8 in.),
the Metropolitan Museum of Art, New York, Harry G. Sperling Fund
(inv. no. 1978.411.2)

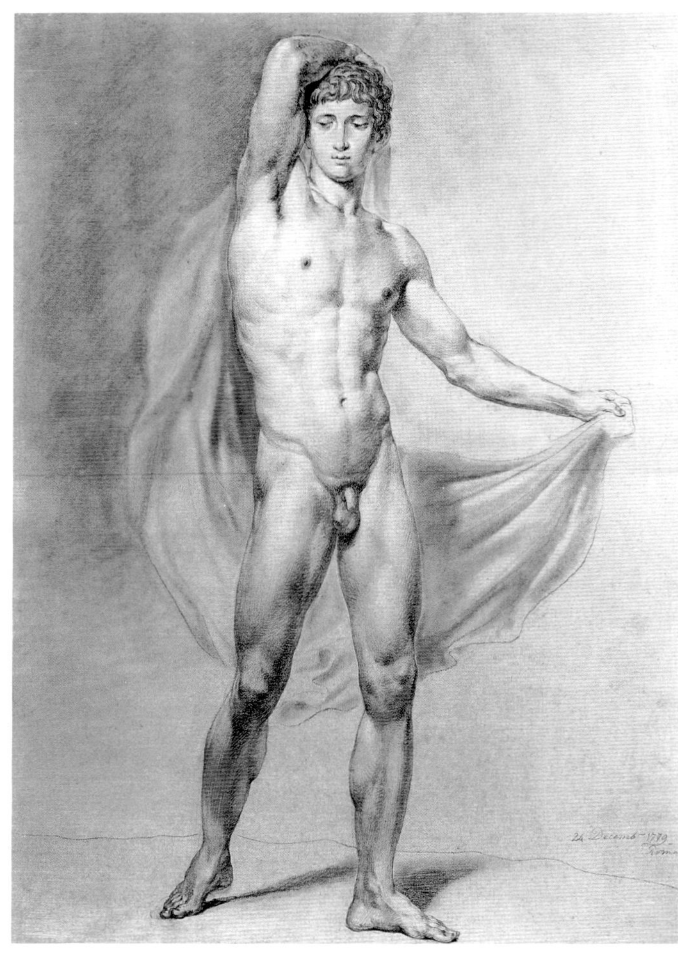

FIGURE 42
Jean Grandjean
The Netherlands, active Italy, 1752–81

Academic Nude
1779, graphite and black chalk,
heightened with white chalk on bluish-gray paper,
56.5 x 41 cm (22 1/4 x 16 1/8 in.),
Amsterdam, Rijksmuseum, Rijksprentenkabinet

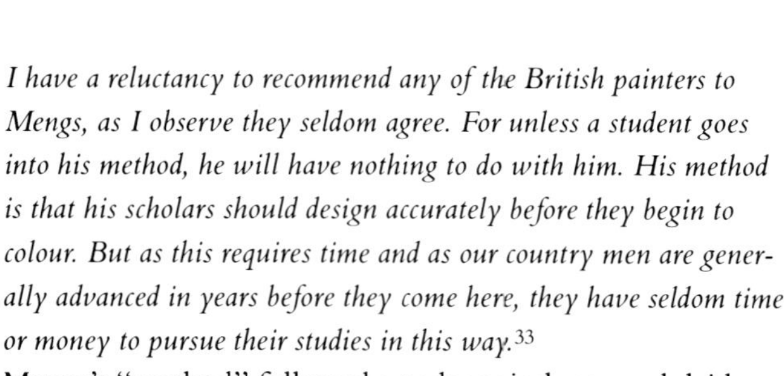

I have a reluctancy to recommend any of the British painters to Mengs, as I observe they seldom agree. For unless a student goes into his method, he will have nothing to do with him. His method is that his scholars should design accurately before they begin to colour. But as this requires time and as our country men are generally advanced in years before they come here, they have seldom time or money to pursue their studies in this way.[33]

Mengs's "method" followed a pedagogical approach laid down in the late Renaissance. He expected his students to follow the traditional artist's training and draw simple geometric figures without the aid of a rule or compass, copy the outlines of figures in prints and drawings, study perspective and anatomy, "without which it is not possible to reason upon the parts of a naked figure," and draw plaster casts of ancient reliefs and sculptures to learn shading and chiaroscuro in preparation for the live model. For Mengs and for many neoclassical theorists, only by concentrating on the human figure and "the exact imitation of all the forms and manners in which they present themselves to our sight" could the artist attain beauty and perfection in his work.[34]

His own academy drawings reveal an accomplished ability to represent the human figure on a two-dimensional surface and illustrate his belief that "the beauty of the outlines of the human figure depends on expressing rightly all the imperceptible lines and broken forms." Mengs's understanding of the body's underlying geometry and anatomical structure and his ability to represent the human figure on a two-dimensional surface is embodied in an early black-chalk academy drawing in the Metropolitan Museum of Art, New York (FIGURE 41).[35] The drawing summarizes all the qualities that characterized a successful drawing for Mengs: "exactness of eye," "correctness," "grace of contour," mastery of anatomy, perspective, and foreshortening. In his academic discourses he urged the artist to pay painstaking attention to shading, "minding to make his drawing with the utmost purity," and here he has used the stump, a piece of rolled-up paper or leather, to rub and blend the chalk into the clear areas of the paper, thus causing the lights and darks to melt into each other. It is evident that Mengs endeavored to create as brilliant an impression as possible through the cold precision of such drawings, investing them with the monumental and severe qualities that characterize his style of history painting. Little wonder that Pierre-Jean Mariette could write in the early 1770s, "I have seen some of his drawn academies; they are of ice."[36]

The German sculptor Alexander Trippel convened a much more modest academy than Mengs's in a house near the Trinità de' Monti that had formerly been the residence of Raymond Lafage, a seventeenth-century French draftsman and printmaker. Among the small group of draftsmen who attended regularly were Heinrich Füger, Franz Kobell, Jacob Wilhelm Mechau, Johann Heinrich Wilhelm Tischbein, Franz Zauner, and Jean Grandjean, a Dutch topographical draftsman who lived in Rome between 1779 and 1781 in the milieu of the Germans resident in the city. The importance for young artists like Grandjean of the life-drawing classes such as the so-called Trippelsche Akademie is confirmed by the immediate and decisive change that occurred in his drawing style. According to J. W. Niemeijer, who has resurrected Grandjean as an artistic personality, this was the result of both his study of the classical sculptures of Rome and the experience of drawing the live model.[37] Just as Grandjean in his landscapes abandoned a typical Dutch eighteenth-century manner for what Niemeijer calls an "international classicism," so did he acquire a grander, more monumental, and vigorous sculptural quality for the forms in his figure drawings. As was the case with all the artists discussed here, Grandjean made numerous drawings after antique statues, busts, and sarcophagi in addition to his assiduous study of the human figure. The influence of ancient art did not end with the copying of statues. Many of Grandjean's studies after the live model recollect classical prototypes in the pose of the model. As Niemeijer has observed, there can be no doubt that the models in Trippel's academy were deliberately placed in the poses of ancient sculptures.[38] The marmoreal polish Grandjean gave to the nude model posed like a classical statue in an academy drawing (FIGURE 42) executed during his Roman visit suggests the extent to which artists late in the eighteenth century had taken to heart Johann Joachim Winckelmann's dictum that there was "but one way for the moderns to become great, and perhaps unequalled: by imitating the ancients."[39]

Life drawing attained such popularity in Rome in the second half of the century that artists even organized drawing classes spontaneously and independently from either of the official academies or any of the established private academies. The painter James Russel reported in 1749 that he and sixteen English and Scottish painters and sculptors "formed an Academy among ourselves."[40] This academy presumably served as the basis for that promoted by Lords Charlemont and Bruce and Thomas Kennedy under the leadership of John Parker in May 1752 that included William Chambers, Gavin Hamilton, Thomas Jenkins, Thomas Patch, and Richard Wilson. Owing to dissension among the students, the academy was broken up on Lord Charlemont's orders in April 1758. The Swedish sculptor Johan Tobias Sergel noted that during his stay in Rome, after studying from the model at the Académie de France from 1768 to 1772, he too "had a special academy in association with other young artists." And in the late 1770s two British artists in Rome, Prince Hoare and Ozias Humphry, reported their participation in informal academies organized by groups of artists.[41]

The importance of life drawing in Rome in the second half of the century should be clear from this brief sketch. Yet, of the various categories of drawings that characterize the breadth and variety of drawing practice in eighteenth-century Rome,[42] academy drawings are among the least studied. Unlike the academy drawings produced at the Académie Royale de Peinture et de Sculpture in Paris, which have been the focus of an exemplary monograph by James H. Rubin,[43] a detailed study of life drawing and its role in academic training in the Roman Settecento has yet to be written. What is needed is an examination of the theoretical treatises and practical manuals on drawing published in eighteenth-century Italy, a closer look at the curricula and life-drawing classes at the Académie de France and the Accademia di San Luca,[44] and a survey of the extant academy drawings by the artists of the period, from Benedetto Luti to Canova. Especially useful would be a closer scrutiny of the minutia of the practice of academic life drawing—the draftsman's techniques, his use of materials and his sources for obtaining them, the social status and identities of the models, and the poses typically employed by a master during his life classes. Whether an investigation of the textual sources and the surviving drawings would produce as rich a picture of life drawing in Rome as did Rubin's work for eighteenth-century Paris is not clear, but the effort would certainly place these drawings in a more vivid context and illuminate their relationship to the art and artists of the period.

NOTES

1 The practice of drawing "dal nudo" or "dal naturale" in the studio is thought to have originated with the Carracci. Domenichino is also said to have held a drawing academy where Nicolas Poussin, among others, drew from the nude model, although no such drawings by either Annibale Carracci or Domenichino survive. Around 1630 the practice of making highly finished red-chalk studies of male nudes seems to have become established in Rome; Andrea Camassei, a pupil of Domenichino, held a drawing academy in a room in the Palazzo Barberini, and another pupil, Gian Angelo Canini, was highly regarded for his skill in life drawing. See Ann Sutherland Harris, "Drawings by Andrea Sacchi: Additions and Problems," *Master Drawings* 9, no. 4 (1971): 384, quoting Giovanni Battista Passeri, *Vite de' pittori, scultori ed architetti che hanno lavorato in Roma . . .* (Rome: Zempel, 1772), 386 n. 10: "Introdussero li Caracci lo studio di disegnare il nude, che chiamano Accademia" (the Carracci introduced the study of drawing the nude, which they call academy); see also Nikolaus Pevsner, *Academies of Art Past and Present* (Cambridge: Cambridge University Press, 1940), 75–79.

2 Johann Georg Sulzer, *Allgemeine Theorie der schönen Künste*, 2d ed., 5 vols. (Leipzig, 1792–99), vol. 1, 12–13, trans. Pevsner, *Academies* (NOTE 1), 172–73.

3 The authors of the *Encyclopédie méthodique des beaux-arts* claimed that a well-executed academy drawing "had as much right to become a precious collector's item as a work of any other category. Both one and the other should be beautiful and faithful images of nature, which ought to serve as models and concrete representations of the precepts of art, while attesting to the degree of perfection to which art has been brought" (*Encyclopédie méthodique ou par ordre des matières, dictionnaire des beaux-arts* [Paris, 1789–90], s.v. "*académie*," cited by James Henry Rubin, *Eighteenth-Century French Life-Drawing: Selections from the Collection of Mathias Polakovits* [exh. cat., Princeton: The Art Museum, Princeton University, 1977], 31).

4 Luigi Lanzi, *Storia pittorica della Italia dal risorgimento delle belle arti fin presso al fine del XVIII secolo*, ed. Martino Capucci, 3 vols. (Florence: Sansoni, 1968; originally published Bassano, 1795–96), vol. 1, 422.

5 For Corvi's private academy see Italo Faldi, "L'apice settecentesco di Domenico Corvi," *Pittori viterbesi di cinque secoli* (Rome: Ugo Bozzi, 1970), 84, and Luciana Ferrara, "Domenico Corvi nella Galleria Borghese," *Rivista dell'Istituto Nazionale d'Archeologia e Storia dell'Arte* 21–23 (1974–75): 211 n. 12.

6 *A Scholar Collects: Selections from the Anthony Morris Clark Bequest*, ed. Ulrich W. Hiesinger and Ann Percy (exh. cat., Philadelphia: Philadelphia Museum of Art, 1980–81), 71–72, no. 58.

7 Ibid., no. 47.

8 Giovanni Gherardo de' Rossi, *Vita di Antonio Cavallucci da Sermoneta pittore* (Venice, 1796), 12.

9 On the expansion of art academies in the eighteenth century see Pevsner, *Academies* (NOTE 1), 140–43.

10 Bernard Hercenberg, *Nicholas Vleughels: Peintre et directeur de l'Académie de France à Rome 1668–1737* (Paris: Léonce Laget, 1975), 24–31.

11 Alastair Smart, *The Life and Art of Allan Ramsay* (London: Routledge & Kegan Paul, 1952), 28–29. The Grand Tour literature is sprinkled with the observations of travelers such as Miss Mary Berry, who in 1784 found "the French Academy a noble institution: the rooms for the students are lined with beautiful Gobelins tapestry; they are full of models of all the finest statues of antiquity. Anybody, as well as the French artists, may draw from them" (*Extracts from the Journals and Correspondence of Miss Berry from the Year 1783 to 1852*, ed. Lady Theresa Lewis, 2d ed., 3 vols. [London: Longmans, Green, and Company, 1866], vol. 1, 109). The drawings produced by the French artists and the pensioners at the Académie were sent to Paris and remain in repositories such as the Cabinet des Dessins at the Musée du Louvre. Academy drawings produced by Italian artists and other foreigners in the life classes were not systematically collected and must be sought among the oeuvres of the individual draftsmen.

12 After 1754 the *concorsi accademici* were held in 1758, 1762, 1766, 1768, 1771, 1773, 1775, 1777, 1779, 1783, 1786, 1789, 1792, and 1795; see *Prize-Winning Drawings from the Roman Academy 1682–1754*, ed. Angela Cipriani (exh. cat., Rome: Accademia Nazionale di San Luca/State College, Penn.: Palmer Museum of Art/New York: National Academy of Design, 1989–90), and *I disegni di figura nell'Archivio Storico dell'Accademia di San Luca*, ed. Angela Cipriani and Enrico Valeriani (Rome: Casa Editrice Quasar, 1991).

13 Periodic attempts to provide instruction in life drawing at the Accademia di San Luca were made in the seventeenth century through the efforts of Pietro da Cortona and the architect Carlo Rainaldi, who as *principe*, or president, in 1673 attempted to initiate a program of life classes and anatomy lectures in the morning and architecture and perspective in the afternoon. See Pevsner, *Academies* (NOTE 1), 111, and Gaetana Scano, "Insegnamento e concorsi," in *L'Accademia Nazionale di San Luca* (Rome: De Luca Editore, 1974), 31.

14 Carlo Pietrangeli, "L''Accademia del Nudo' in Campidoglio," *Strenna dei romanisti* 20 (1959): 123–28, and "L'Accademia Capitolina del Nudo," *Capitolium* 37 (1962): 132–34.

15 Pietrangeli, "L'Accademia Capitolina" (NOTE 14), 134. On one side a bust of Benedict XIV was depicted; the reverse was inscribed *SCHOLA PICTORUM CAPITOLINA* and showed students drawing in the Accademia.

16 Luigi Pirotta, "I direttori dell'Accademia del Nudo in Campidoglio," *Strenna dei romanisti* 30 (1969): 326–34.

17 Pietrangeli, "L''Accademia del Nudo'" (NOTE 14), 125–26.

18 M. F. MacDonald, "British Artists at the Accademia del Nudo in Rome," in *Academies of Art between Renaissance and Romanticism* (*Leids Kunsthistorische Jaarboek* 5–6, 1986–87; published 1989), 77–94.

19 William T. Whitley, *Artists and Their Friends in England 1700–1799*, 2 vols. (London/Boston: Medici Society, 1928), vol. 1, 306.

20 Brinsley Ford, "The Letters of Jonathan Skelton," *The Walpole Society* 36 (1956–58; published 1960): 62–63.

21 Johann Gottlieb Puhlmann, *Ein Potsdamer Maler in Rom: Briefe des Batoni-Schülers Johann Gottlieb Puhlmann aus den Jahren 1774 bis 1787*, ed. Götz Eckardt (Berlin: Henschelverlag Kunst und Gesellschaft, 1979).

22 Antonio Canova, *I quaderni di viaggio (1779–1780)*, ed. Elena Bassi (Venice: Istituto per la Collaborazione Culturale, 1959), 30–31.

23 See Anna Maria Corbo, "L'insegnamento artistico a Roma nei primi anni della Restaurazione," *Rassegna degli Archivi di Stato* 30 (1970): 96–99, for Pius VII's *chirografo* (written agreement) of April 9, 1804, authorizing the change of location and the appointment of Canova as *presidente perpetuo*.

24 Melchior Missirini, *Memorie per servire alla storia della romana Accademia di S. Luca fino alla morte di Antonio Canova* (Rome, 1823), 159, cited in *A Scholar Collects* (NOTE 6), 6.

25 See note 5 and Stella Rudolph, "Felice Giani: Da Accademico 'de' Pensieri' a Madonnero," *Storia dell'arte* 30–31 (1977): 178 n. 8, and Heinrich Wilhelm Tischbein, *Aus meinem Leben*, ed. Lothar Brieger (Berlin: Propyläen Verlag), 1922, 134.

26 Hagedorn, letter of November 27, 1763, cited by Basil Skinner, "Scottish Pupils of Batoni and Mengs," unpublished paper read to the Scottish Society of Art Historians, June 1989 (typescript on file with the materials related to the forthcoming dictionary of British visitors to Italy in the eighteenth century based on Sir Brinsley Ford's Grand Tour archive, Paul Mellon Centre for Studies in British Art, London), 1.

27 Whitley, *Artists and Their Friends* (NOTE 19), vol. 2, 310.

28 Anthony M. Clark, *Pompeo Batoni: A Complete Catalogue of His Works with an Introductory Text*, edited and prepared for publication by Edgar Peters Bowron (Oxford: Phaidon, 1985), 37.

29 Clark/Bowron, *Pompeo Batoni* (NOTE 28), 378–79, 381–82, 383, 385–88; nos. D7, 17–18, 22–26, 81, 91, 93, 110, 124–25, 154–55, 176–77, 208–11, 213, 222–28, 231–34, 292–93, 295–96.

30 Clark/Bowron, *Pompeo Batoni* (NOTE 28), 61 n. 88.

31 "Memoirs of Thomas Jones," *The Walpole Society* 32 (1946–48; published 1951): 68. Friedrich Heinrich Füger, who entered Mengs's studio in March 1777, also reported on the artist's academy, which he described as "full of young men" (Alfred Stix, *H. F. Füger* [Vienna: Manz Verlag, 1925], 37).

32 Skinner, "Scottish Pupils" (NOTE 26), 1989, 2.

33 James Dennistoun, *Memories of Sir Robert Strange . . . and Andrew Lumisden* (London: Longman, Brown, Green, and Longmans, 1855), cited by Skinner, "Scottish Pupils" (NOTE 26), 2.

34 "Practical Lessons upon Painting," *The Works of Anton Raphael Mengs, First Painter to His Catholic Majesty Charles III. Translated from the Italian. Published by the Chev.r Don Joseph Nicholas D'Azara*, 2 vols. (London: G. G. and J. Robinson, 1796), vol. 2, 88–94.

35 Julius Böhler, *Ausstellung von Gemälden, Handzeichnungen, Plastiken in Holz, Terracotta und Bronze, Kunstgewerbe* (exh. cat., Munich: Julius Böhler, 1978), no. 32, citing Steffi Röttgen's date of about 1756 for the drawing.

36 *Abecedario de P.-J. Mariette et autres notes inédites de cet amateur sur les arts et les artistes*, ed. Ph. de Chennevières and Anatole de Montaiglon, 6 vols. (Paris: J. B. Dumoulin, 1851–56), vol. 3, 381.

37 J. W. Niemeijer, "Academies and Other Figure Studies from Grandjean's Roman Period," *Master Drawings* 12, no. 4 (1974): 351–58. The basis of the article, from which my account of Trippel's academy derives, is the discovery in the Rijksprentenkabinet, Amsterdam, of a portfolio containing forty-six large studies of figures and compositions by the artist entitled *Academie-beelden door J. Grandjean* (Academy drawings by J. Grandjean).

38 Niemeijer, "Academies" (NOTE 37), 356.

39 Johann Joachim Winckelmann, *Gedanken über die Nachahmung der griechischen Werke in der Malerei und Bildhauerkunst*, 1755; cited in David Irwin, *Winckelmann: Writings on Art* (New York: Phaidon, 1972), 61.

40 James Russel, *Letter from a Young Painter Abroad to His Friends in England*, 2d ed., 2 vols. (London, 1750), vol. 2, 361.

41 Per Bjurström, *Sergel Tecknar* (Stockholm, 1976), unpaginated; cited by Nancy L. Pressly, *The Fuseli Circle in Rome: Early Romantic Art of the 1770s* (exh. cat., New Haven: Yale Center for British Art, 1979), v.

42 For an excellent overview of the subject see Ulrich W. Hiesinger, "Drawings in Eighteenth-Century Rome," in *A Scholar Collects* (NOTE 6), 2–9.

43 See NOTE 3.

44 For an example of the use to be made of the correspondence of the directors of the Académie de France à Rome see Pierre Rosenberg, "Natoire directeur de l'Académie de France à Rome," in *Charles-Joseph Natoire* (exh. cat., Troyes: Musée des Beaux-Arts/Nîmes: Musée des Beaux-Arts/Rome: Villa Medici, 1977), 24–31.

OVERLEAF
Anne-Louis Girodet de Roussy-Trioson
The Ghosts of Evirallina and Oscar Gliding through the Evening Air
(CATALOGUE NO. 57, detail)

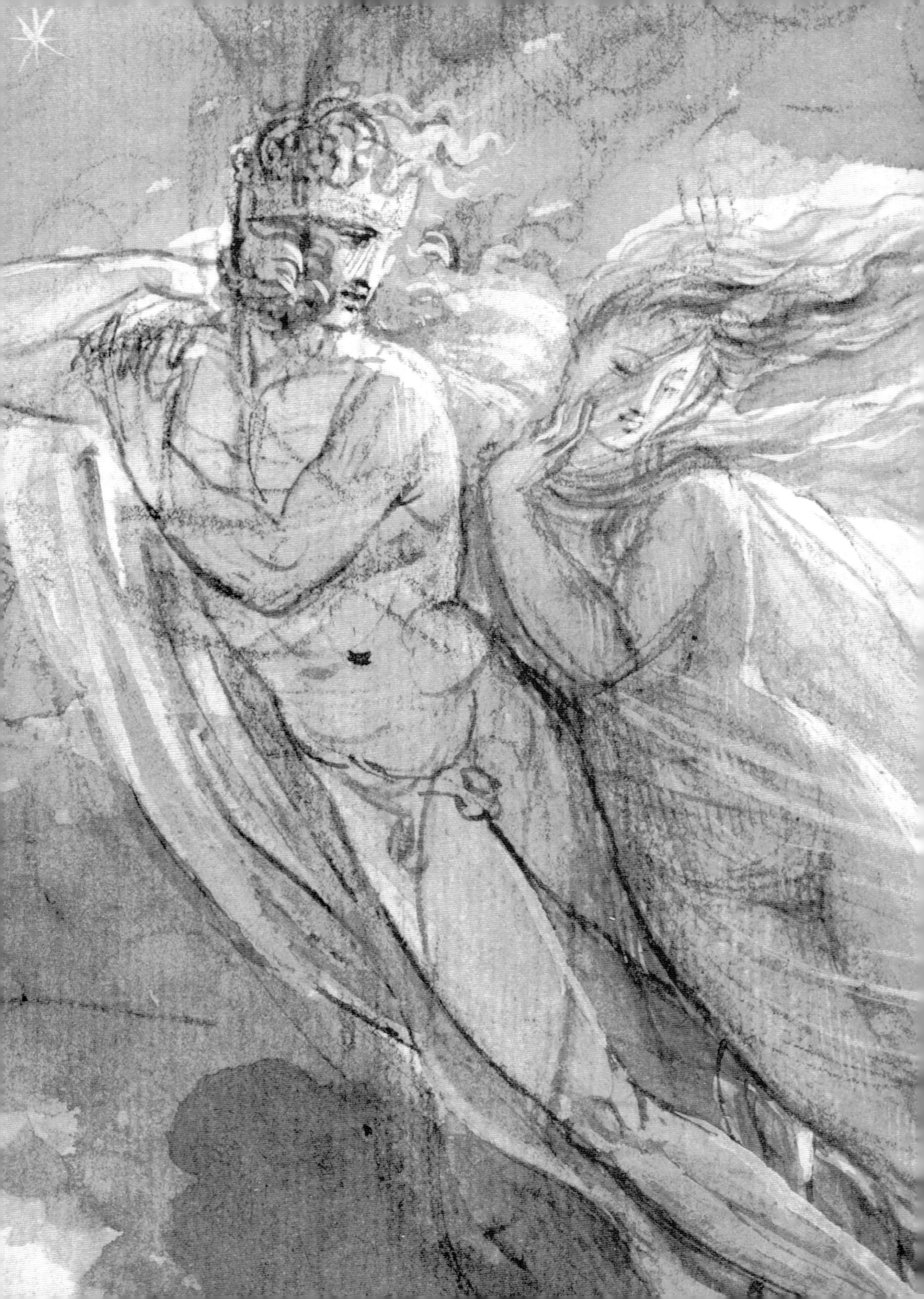

"It Is Not Right for Drawings to Be Nothing but Drawings"

Sylvain Bellenger

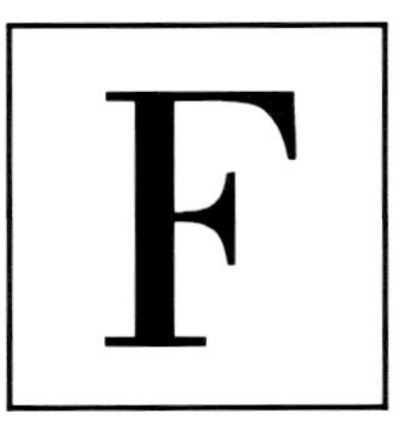riday, December 10, 1824: Artist, writer, and art critic Étienne-Jean Delécluze, celebrated memorialist of the school of Jacques-Louis David and editor of the liberal *Journal des débats*, directed by the Bertin family, wrote in his diary: "Girodet de Trioson died yesterday at 10:30 P.M. His agony lasted from 8:00 in the evening to the moment I have just indicated. . . . Tonight there was a gathering at the home of [Viollet] Le Duc. Sweeping discussion of romanticism. Beyle [Stendhal] was obscure and unable to be himself, reason with him though we would; he rambled continuously."[1]

"Romanticism," "reason," "Beyle"—we can scarcely imagine how the death of Anne-Louis Girodet de Roussy-Trioson echoes in those words. Born in Montargis in the age of Louis XV, in 1767, the most gifted of David's students—the one who with the death of Jean-Germain Drouais became the most esteemed of the master's disciples—left behind a legacy of pure neoclassicism, an "érotisme de frigidaire," as Mario Praz wrote of *The Sleeping Endymion* (*Endymion endormi, effets de lune*; FIGURE 43), 1791, shipped from Rome to the Salon of 1793.[2] In describing Girodet's funeral ceremony Delécluze helps us to better understand the situation of French painting in 1824, the year in which both Girodet and Théodore Géricault died, in which the exiled David finished his *Mars and Venus* (*Mars et Vénus*; Musées Royaux des Beaux-Arts, Brussels), in which Delacroix exhibited *The Massacre at Chios* (*Les massacres de Scio*; Musée du Louvre) at the Salon:

> *As the procession was forming, Girodet's students took up the body of their master and carried it through the doorway to the funeral carriage, after which the procession began. At the head of those who followed the body was Chateaubriand. Then came Gérard, pale and walking gravely with eyes downcast, carrying in his hand a laurel wreath. After him came Gros, also holding a laurel wreath. Tears rolling down his cheeks, he held his head high and walked quickly, like a man distracted. Isabey passed by alone at the end. Behind them marched a group composed of members of the Institute: Hersent, Vernet, Percier, Vaudoyer, Huyot, etc., then finally came the throng of artists, friends, and all who knew Girodet or who took interest in the glory of the arts. I do not believe it would be an exaggeration to say that there were more than four hundred people witnessing this procession and accompanying the body of Girodet, on whom the king had conferred the posthumous title of Officer of the Legion of Honor. . . . The Church of the Assumption is extremely small, and so many of the curious had already filed in that barely a third of those following the body were able to make their way into the interior. I was among those who remained outside. I took a coach that carried me to the cemetery of Père La Chaise. I visited this place, so sad in itself, where vanity, weakness, and human sensibility, according to how one views the matter, are embellished and rendered strange and interesting. . . . Meanwhile, from the height of the cemetery, which gave me a commanding view of the city of Paris, I perceived from afar in the main street a black line formed by the carriages and the people in mourning; lit torches surrounded the funeral coach, and a good many of those who wished to witness the interment took the lead as in silence I watched the procession advance with slow steps.*[3]

It would be a pleasure to continue quoting Delécluze's beautiful literature, which lays bare in the precision and self-effacement of his testimony the emotion of a community paying its last respects to a great artist. We wish, however, to resume our subject more directly, this time citing the words of Antoine-Jean Gros recorded by Delécluze in his diary a short while later.

After a long series of more or less sensible official speeches, wrote Delécluze,

> *Gros advanced to the edge of the grave and, tears in his eyes and laurel wreath in his hand, made it known that he wished to speak. We fell silent, and in a speech broken with sobs and frequent outbursts he spoke of the school of David as the greatest of all, and of the eternal regrets brought on by the death of such a one as Girodet, who had been the only painter whose talent and authority were able to offset the decline that was carrying the school to its death. Little by little, he became more animated. He spoke out vehemently against those who, taking advantage of a misleading facility, care*

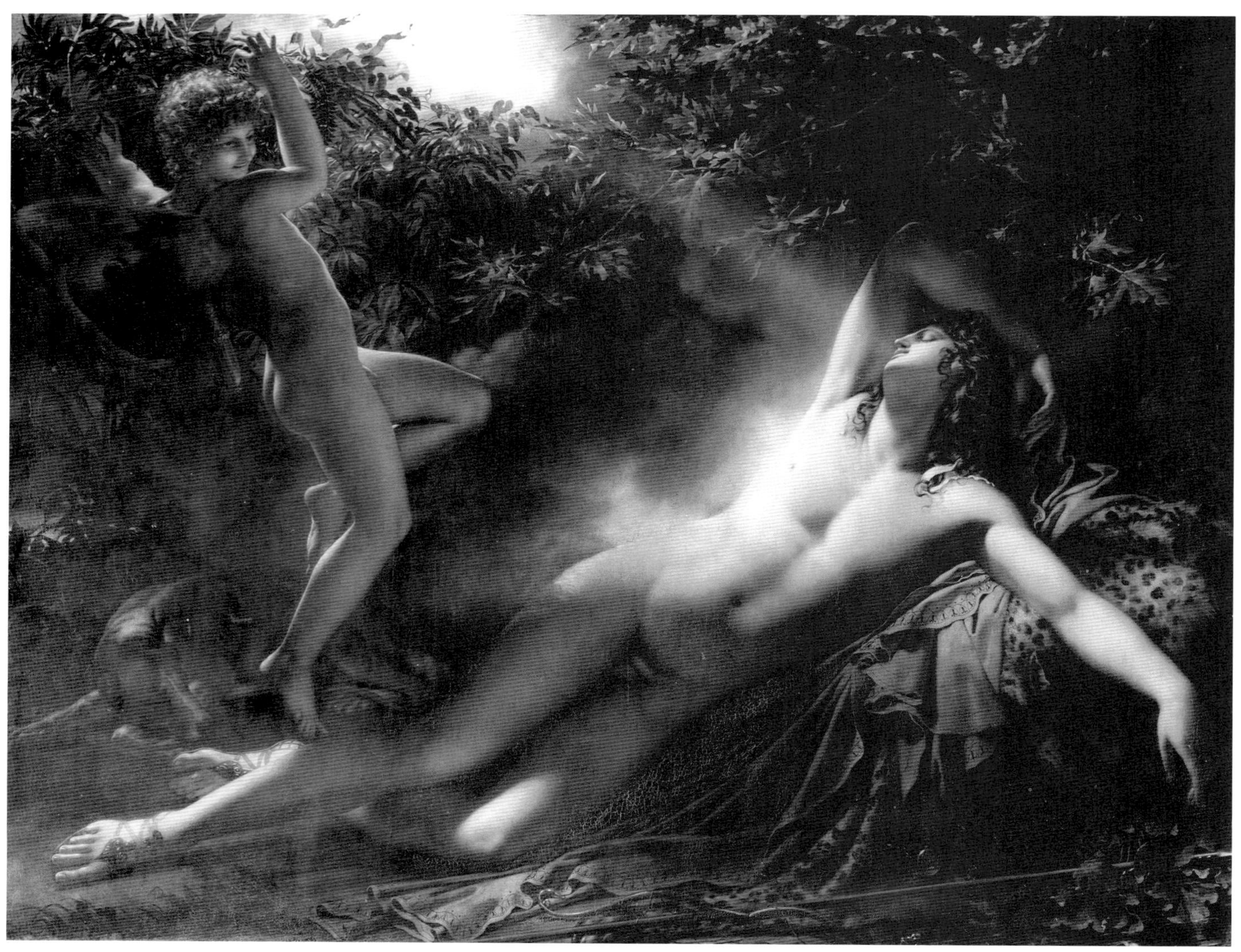

FIGURE 43
Anne-Louis Girodet de Roussy-Trioson
France, 1767–1824

The Sleeping Endymion
1791, oil on canvas, 197 x 260 cm (77 9/16 x 102 3/8 in.),
Musée du Louvre, Paris (inv. no. 4935)

nothing for study, on the contrary, they worship fleeting fame and fortune acquired without effort. Finally, upbraiding Vernet without actually naming him, he cried out, "Soon we will have convinced ourselves that a scrap of canvas we have smeared with color for a fortnight is a masterpiece worthy of sanctifying the memory of a prince."[4]

During these funeral ceremonies, which quickly came to symbolize those of the school of David itself, François Gérard admitted that he did not feel capable of putting the school back on its original course, since David was in exile and Gros had confessed to having been one of the first to set a bad example by not employing, either in his choice of subjects or in their execution, the severity recommended by David, who had demonstrated it unceasingly in his own work. Later, burdened with domestic sorrow and the grief of an artist mercilessly savaged by critics, Gros committed suicide. His last painting, *Hercules and Diomede* (*Hercule et Diomède*; Salon of 1835), in effect an allegory of the battle between classicism and romanticism, preserved in the Musée des Augustins, Toulouse, may be said to embody the theme of the present exhibition.

The "fall" of the French school, or, more properly, its mutation, is linked to the abandonment of a specific vision of antiquity and the hierarchy of genres upon which it depended. Gros had not misjudged himself; his *The Plague at Jaffa* (*Les Pestiférés de Jaffa*; Musée du Louvre), Salon of 1804, and to an even greater extent *The Battle of Aboukir* (*La Bataille d'Aboukir*; Musée de Versailles),[5] Salon of 1806, point toward the future. Contemporary politics, with its goal of colonial expansion, progressively "adulterated" the relevance of antiquity for artists whose subjects were grounded in the actualities of the present.

Even from a casual study of Girodet's art it is difficult to agree with Gérard or Gros that his death symbolized the demise of the school of David. Had he lived longer, probably nothing would have changed, even had David himself returned to Paris from exile in Brussels. Girodet's dissidence was manifest in his first efforts in Rome. The spectrum of French painting at this epoch is more complex than it might seem, and Davidian homogeneity, considering how little it was practiced, did not last long. Two of Girodet's most celebrated oils exemplify the shifting standards of the time. At the Salon of 1793 *The Sleeping Endymion* was received with great acclaim. Later in 1810 at the Institute's decennial *concours*, honoring the greatest artistic achievements of the Empire, the turbulence of Girodet's *Scene from a Deluge* (*Scène de déluge*; FIGURE 44), first presented at the Salon of 1806, was preferred to the Grecian purity of David's *The Sabine Women* (*Les Sabines*; FIGURE 13), 1799.

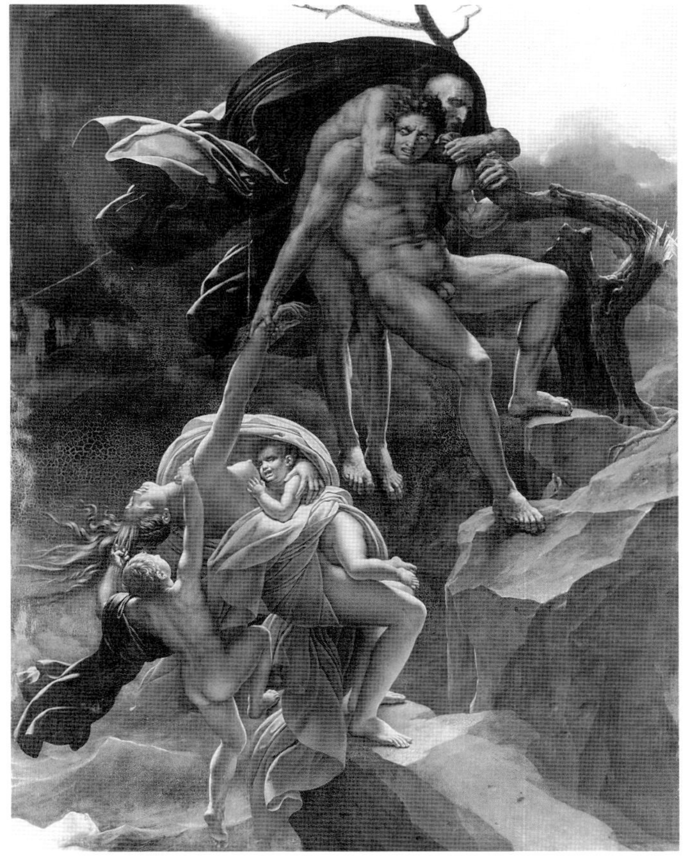

FIGURE 44
Anne-Louis Girodet de Roussy-Trioson
France, 1767–1824

Scene from a Deluge
1806, oil on canvas, 431 x 341 cm (169 11/16 x 134 1/4 in.), Musée du Louvre, Paris (inv. no. 4934)

When he won the grand prize of the Prix de Rome in 1789 with *Joseph Recognized by His Brothers* (*Joseph reconnu par ses frères*; FIGURE 45), Girodet had just completed four years in David's studio. Making his way to Rome in March 1790, he resided, like all pensioners of the king, at Palazzo Mancini on the via del Corso, seat of the Académie de France in Rome. From his arrival his behavior seemed to merit the remonstrances of the director of the institution, François-Guillaume Ménageot: "I am bored by the excess of the academic rules that apply to us," Girodet wrote to his tutor, Dr. Trioson,

> *and I confess to you that it displeases me in the extreme. It isn't that our director annoys us, since we see him, or at least I see him only on the stairway or in the street. He nevertheless wished to coerce me, from the first moments of my arrival, to go on drawing at the Académie. I begged him to spare me this requirement, and the more he insisted, the more I insisted, until he replied that perhaps this occupation was not at all to my liking, whereupon I demanded firmly that he leave it to me to direct my own studies, which he did.*[6]

Girodet's stay in Rome was short, for in January 1793 he was forced to flee to Naples with a number of other pensioners, the seat of the Académie having been attacked by the Roman population, whom Vatican authorities had roused against the French Jacobins after certain violent acts during the French Revolution, including the massacre of the Swiss Guards in August of 1792, the execution of the princesse de Lamballe, attendant to the queen, and the arrest and trial of the king, who was guillotined only a few days after the incidents in Rome. The letters sent by Girodet to Dr. Trioson are among the most valuable testimonies we have concerning these events, in which the ambassador of the French Republic, Joseph-Nicolas Hugou de Bassville, lost his life (Girodet's letters to his former fellow student Gérard are noticeably less respectful of institutional authorities, including David).[7]

Tired of copying "Etruscan jars,"[8] Girodet aligned himself with the most engaged French artists in Rome, sculptor Joseph Chinard and architect Ildephonse Rater. He was harassed frequently by the papal police, and he singled out with his pen the royal authorities or royalist exiles in Rome—"the aristocratic mob, that [Cardinal] Bernis, that Ménageot."[9] His painting manifests this same adversarial engagement, but the two paintings sent from Rome—*The Sleeping Endymion* and *Hippocrates Refusing the Gifts of Artaxerxes* (*Hippocrate refusant les présents d'Artaxercès*; FIGURE 46), executed at the same time in 1791 and early 1792—particularly testify to the duality of his work. The former was sent to the Salon after being shown in Rome. The Girodet who had written, "I seek to distance myself as far as I possibly

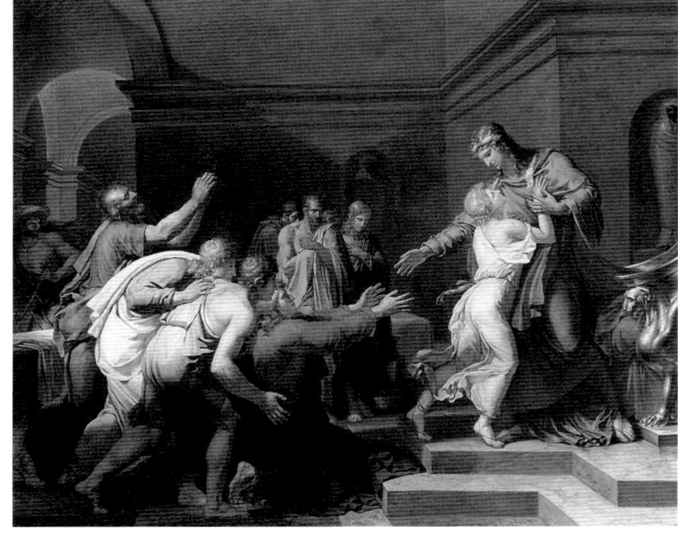

FIGURE 45
Anne-Louis Girodet de Roussy-Trioson
France, 1767–1824

Joseph Recognized by His Brothers
1789, oil on canvas, 120 x 155 cm (47 1/4 x 61 in.),
École Nationale Supérieure des Beaux-Arts, Paris

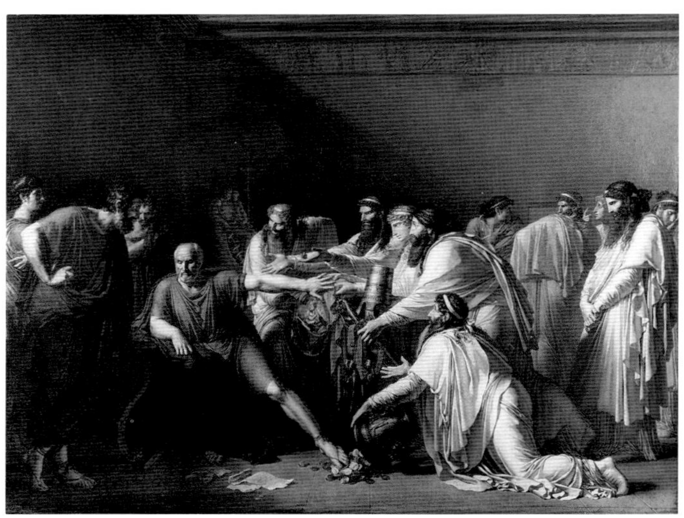

FIGURE 46
Anne-Louis Girodet de Roussy-Trioson
France, 1767–1824

Hippocrates Refusing the Gifts of Artaxerxes
1791–92, oil on canvas, 99.5 x 135 cm (39 3/16 x 53 1/8 in.),
Musée de l'Histoire de la Médecine, Paris

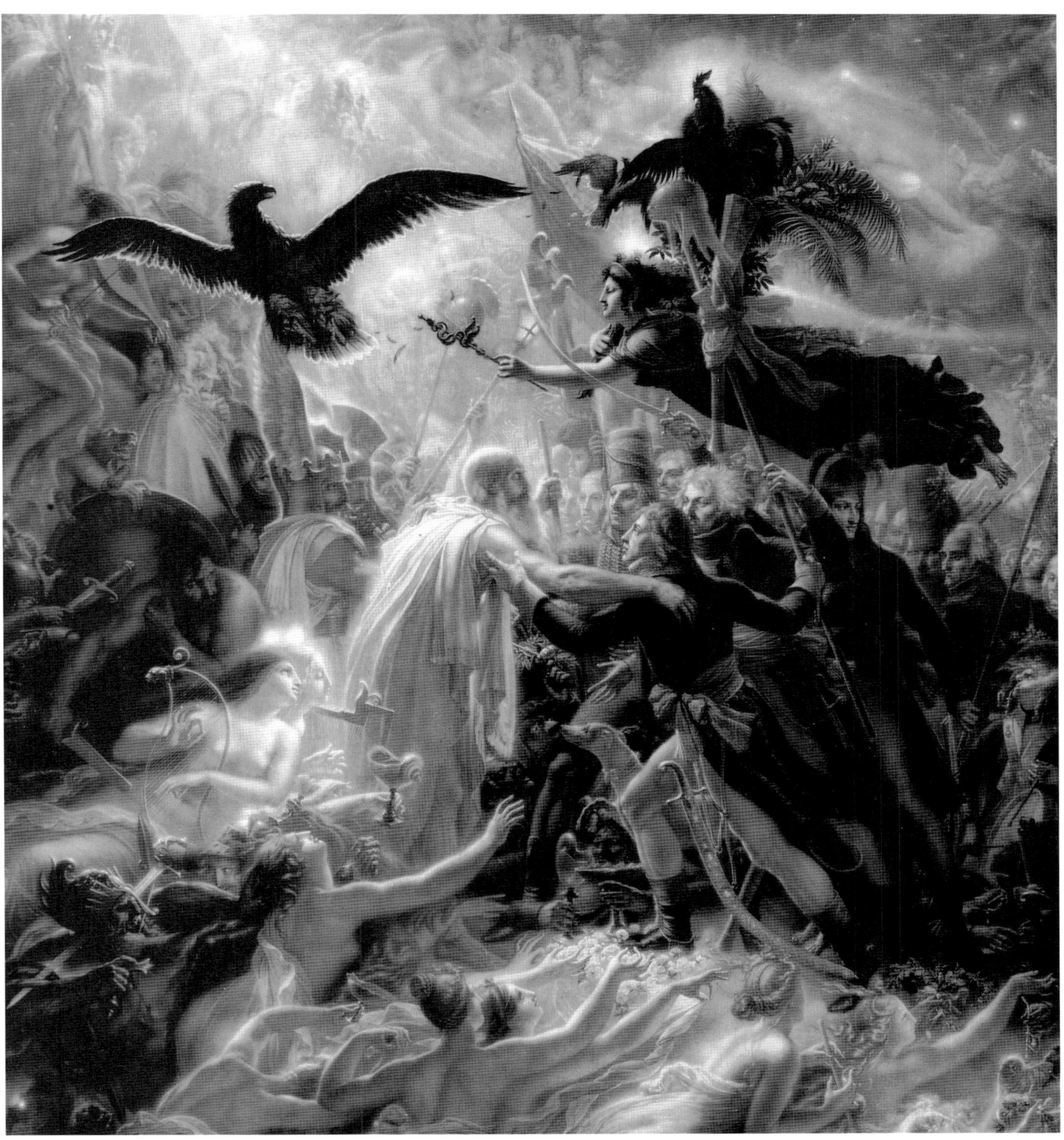

FIGURE 47

Anne-Louis Girodet de Roussy-Trioson

France, 1767–1824

Ossian Receiving the Shades of the French Heroes

1801, oil on canvas, 192 x 182 cm (75 9/16 x 71 11/16 in.),

Musée National du Château Malmaison, Rueil-Malmaison (inv. no. M.M.40.47.6955)

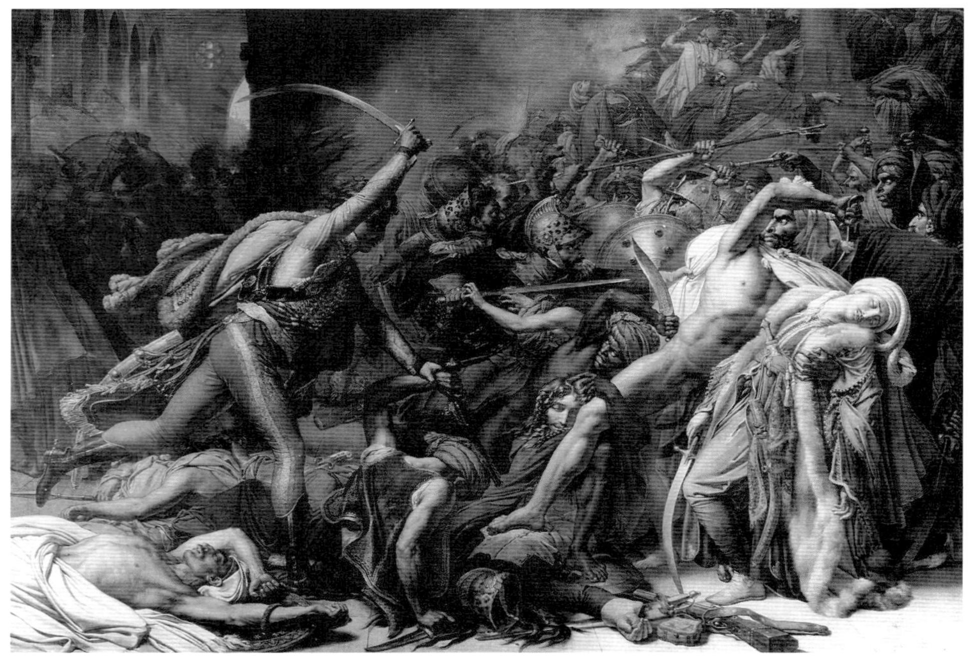

FIGURE 48
Anne-Louis Girodet de Roussy-Trioson
France, 1767–1824

The Revolt of Cairo
1810, oil on canvas, 356 x 500 cm (140 1/8 x 196 7/8 in.),
Musée National du Château de Versailles (inv. no. M.V. 1497)

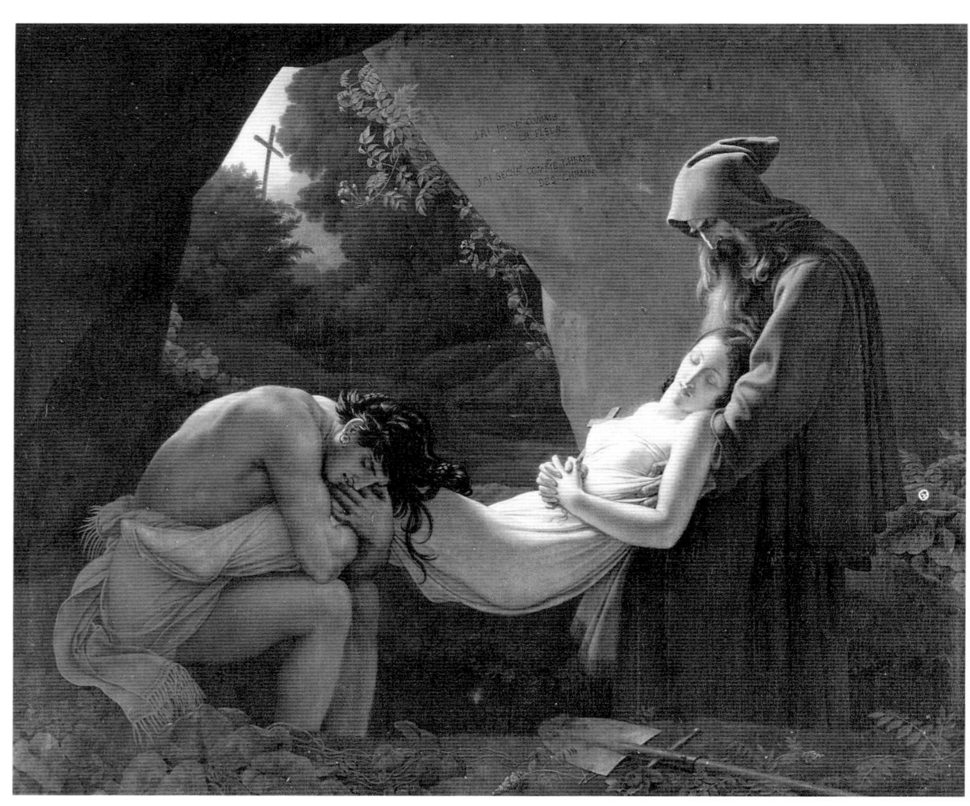

FIGURE 49
Anne-Louis Girodet de Roussy-Trioson
France, 1767–1824

The Funeral of Atala
1808, oil on canvas, 210 x 287 cm (82 11/16 x 113 in.),
Musée du Louvre, Paris (inv. no. 4958)

can from the genre of M. David, and I spare myself neither affliction, nor studies, nor models, nor paint" had rejoiced at the time of its presentation in Rome: "There was not even a single voice that said I resembled M. David in any way."[10] Much later, when the work's reception had secured its fame, he expressed himself in slightly different terms:

> *The earliest of my paintings is* The Sleeping Endymion. *It was painted in Rome in 1790, one year after I had carried off the grand prize in painting. The conceit came to me from a bas-relief at the Villa Borghese; I even all but copied the antique Endymion. It seemed to me improper to paint a goddess renowned for her chastity in the act of amorous contemplation. The idea of the ray [of moonlight] appeared to me more delicate, more poetic, besides which, it was then new.*[11]

Naturally, this argument was developed with certain ends in mind. In this letter Girodet's intention was to convince his correspondent of the importance of the imagination in the creation of his painting *Ossian Receiving the Shades of the French Heroes* (*Ossian recevant les ombres des héros français*, also called *Apothéose des héros français*; FIGURE 47), 1801.[12] It is easy to see that the disappearance of Diana, replaced by her luminous attribute—not the moon, but moonlight—creates the troubling, narcissistic eroticism of *Endymion*, linking it with the morbid and dreamlike sensibility of Henry Fuseli, Giuseppe Cades, and the illustrators of the legend of the Celtic bard Ossian.[13] One must add to this the adulteration of genres introduced by the painting, a traditional academic nude treated in the mythological mode, in a format required solely for the painting of history.

It is completely the opposite with *Hippocrates Refusing the Gifts of Artaxerxes*, painted for Dr. Trioson and left by him to the Faculté de Médecine at the University of Paris. An instance of the *exemplum virtutis*,[14] composed like a frieze, its costumes rendered with archaeological exactness, and painted with facial expressions embodying moral values, only the rarity of the subject and the presence of a painter at the left of the composition are details that refer to the recipient of the painting—a friend (later, a father) who was also a doctor.

Other examples allow us to extend this exploration of the contradiction in Girodet, but these do not admit of easy interpretation. The two set pieces destined to adorn the Galerie de Diane in the Tuileries palace, commissioned for the emperor by the director general of museums, Dominique Vivant Denon, format and subject probably prescribed, reveal the same duality. In *The Surrender of Vienna* (*La Reddition de Vienne*; Musée de Versailles), Salon of 1808, everything conceals the idea of military conquest: the portraits are formal, the poses serene, and there is respect for the imperial personage. In spite of its rigid conventionality, there is an element of lightheartedness. It is almost as if the saber held to the right side of the conquerors is brandished but without enough emotion to disturb the scene. On the left the Austrians, surrounded by deeply moved peasants, entreat and welcome the French army, while children climb trees to better view the scene. *The Revolt of Cairo* (*La Révolte du Caire*; FIGURE 48), Salon of 1810, expresses the repressed brutality of *The Surrender of Vienna*. In the background, in place of Vienna's Schloss Schönbrunn, are the walls of a mosque that might be El Hazar. The confusion of the scene and the disturbing violence of the composition clearly were intended to rival Gros's *The Battle of Aboukir*, shown at the Salon in 1806. These two paintings are among the most audacious colorist works to have come from the school of David.

Pictorial romanticism as expressed through color traverses Girodet's art in a vein at once radiant with sunlight, oriental, and brutal. But as we have seen with *Endymion*, the inner spirit, the search for an iconography of dreams, of disembodied *eros*, occupies an altogether different place in his work. The new literature of Ossian and of Chateaubriand would soon become the most poetic affirmation of Girodet's talent.

The Funeral of Atala (*Les Funérailles d'Atala*; FIGURE 49), Salon of 1808, an illustration from the famous novel by Chateaubriand, *Atala ou les amours de deux sauvages dans le désert* (Atala, or the loves of two savages in the wilderness), published in 1801, combines the world of the noble savage (whose grotto, dear to the planners of the Revolution, is the perfect architectural symbol), with the mute expression of suffering (the opposite of the theatrical expression of classical drama), organized as an antique

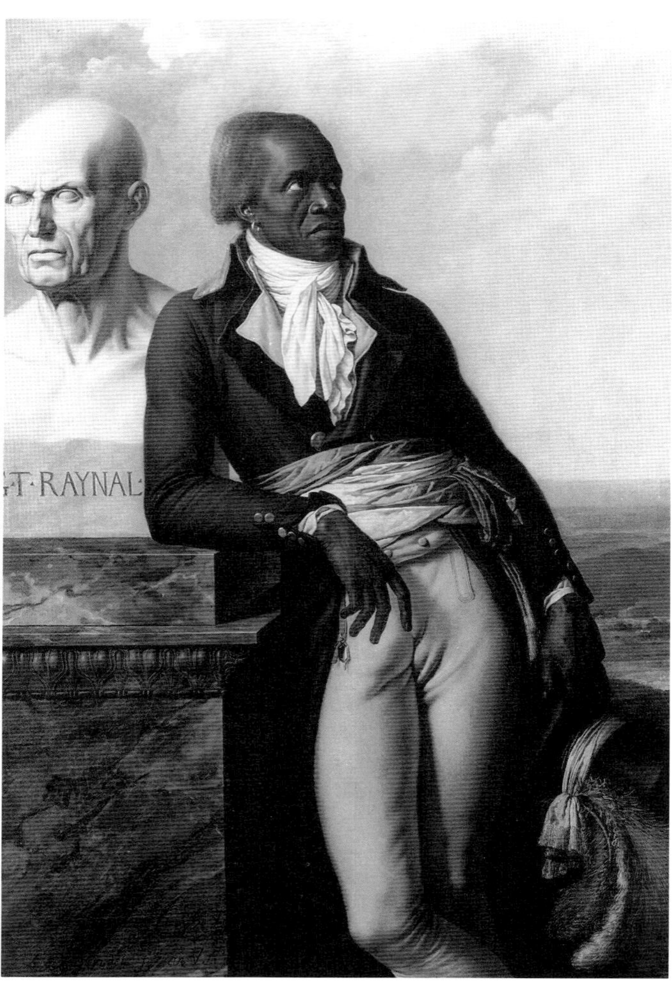

FIGURE 50
Anne-Louis Girodet de Roussy-Trioson
France, 1767–1824

Portrait of Jean-Baptiste Belley
1798, oil on canvas, 139 x 113 cm (54 3/4 x 44 1/2 in.),
Musée National du Château de Versailles (inv. no. 4616)

funerary bas-relief Christianized to serve the needs of contemporary literature. *Ossian*, 1801, was inspired by a more heroic literature. The poetry that James Macpherson had published in London in 1760 as the work of the bard Ossian (a folklore-inspired literary hoax that thrilled romantic Europe) was the Nordic transposition of Homeric antiquity and the myth of humankind's origin. However, the folkloric curiosity that was quite common in the Europe of the Enlightenment—with popular ballads published by Thomas Percy and *lieder* and stories collected by Johann Gottfried Herder, Clemens Brentano, and the brothers Jacob and Wilhelm Grimm—gradually devolved into archaeological duplicity and literary deceit.[15] Atala was Christian, Ossian a Celt, but the subject of both works was "primitive," and from them antiquity came to embrace an encyclopedic historicism that would find its echo in the Musée des Monuments Français, in which curator Alexandre Lenoir brought together the Gothic and Renaissance monuments threatened with destruction by the Revolution, as well as in the iconographic repertoire of that Winckelmann of Roman decadence, Séroux d'Agincourt.[16]

It was Napoleon and Germaine de Staël, who eulogized Ossian in her novel *Delphine*, 1802, who assured the success of Ossianic themes in France, and if of all the paintings commissioned by Napoleon on the subject Girodet's failed to win him over, it was because its ambiguous message, the modest presence of the first consul, and the coexistence of genres—contemporary history and mythology—were shocking.

We have seen Girodet as an expert in paradoxes; to this must be added his passion for portraits charged with symbolism to the point of making these, too, history paintings of moral import. So it is with the *Portrait of Jean-Baptiste Belley* (FIGURE 50), Salon of 1798, the black parliamentary delegate from Martinique leaning on a bust of Abbé Raynal, advocate of racial emancipation,[17] or with that of *Mademoiselle Lange as Danaë* (The Minneapolis Institute of Arts), Salon of 1799, a painting of a scandal that reveals the entire society of the Directory, flogged by Girodet in revenge for the unkind remarks that the actress was circulating about her portrait.

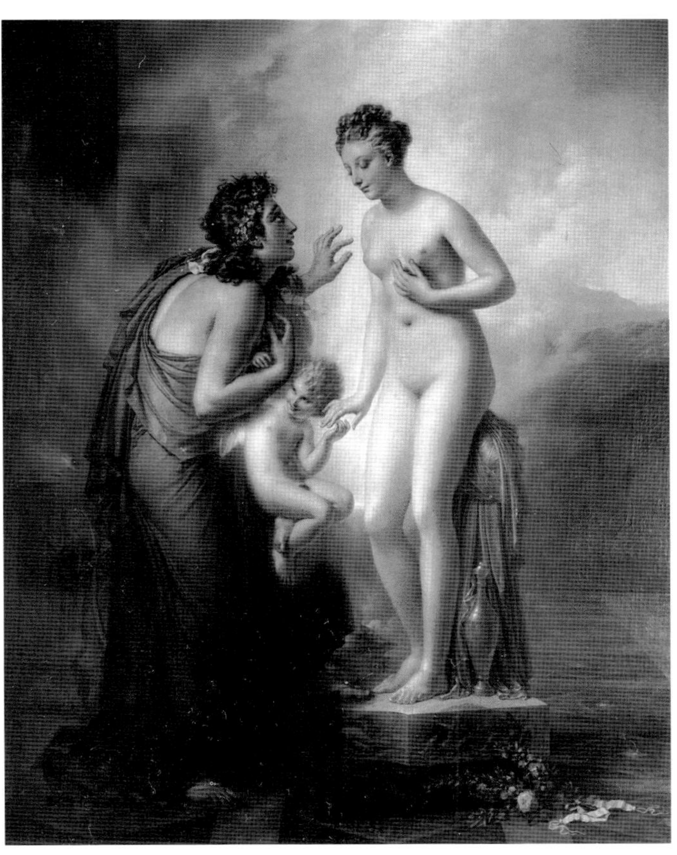

FIGURE 51
Anne-Louis Girodet de Roussy-Trioson
France, 1767–1824

Pygmalion and Galatea
1819, oil on canvas, 253 x 202 cm (99 5/8 x 79 1/2 in.), private collection, Château de Dampierre

At the Salon of 1819 the most well-received work in the exhibition, which included Géricault's *The Raft of the Medusa* (*Le Radeau de la Méduse*; Musée du Louvre), was without question Girodet's *Pygmalion and Galatea* (FIGURE 51). Was it this affirmation of the importance of classical art that nourished the regrets of Gérard and Gros after the passing of Girodet? His patron, the conte di Sommariva, had to wait a long time, since Girodet exhausted himself on the undertaking, which occupied him for seven years. With this painting the school of David seemed to have been completely revived, and with it the importance of drawing, which is inherent to this subject from antiquity. It is in his drawings that Girodet remained most faithful to classical principles. Indeed, the mastery of this technique was basic to the restoration of the ideals of David's school. All of Girodet's works were preceded by innumerable preparatory drawings, often quite finished. More than any other artist of his time, Girodet devoted himself to this art, leaving thousands of drawings in portfolios dispersed after his death. He lost, according to Delécluze, "a considerable amount of time making for the *Odes* of Anacreon and the poems of Virgil series of outline drawings that despite their importance do not recompense their author in fame for the time he spent in making them."[18] To this list we must add illustrations for works by Homer, Racine, Musaeus, and botanist Henri-Jacques Bernardin de Saint-Pierre. After his death Girodet's students—all of whom were great lithographers—chose among the hundreds of drawings that were to have illustrated an edition of the *Aeneid* and lithographed them in the state in which Girodet had left them. Thus, even in drawing, Girodet shuffled the cards and the categories: "It is an injustice for drawings to be nothing but drawings while they demand the same composition and nearly the same studies as a history painting."[19] The paradox reaches right to the heart of the principle: all of Girodet's greatness as an artist rests in these ambiguities.

NOTES

1 *Journal de Delécluze, 1824–1828* (Paris: Bernard Grasset, 1948), 48. The gathering was at the home of Emmanuel-Louis-Nicolas Viollet-Le-Duc, father of the architect Eugène Viollet-Le-Duc, Delécluze's brother-in-law and a major proponent of the Gothic revival. Henri Beyle, writing as Stendhal, was a defender of liberal romanticism.

2 Mario Praz, "Canova, or The Erotic Frigidaire," *Art News* 56, no. 7 (November 1957): 24–27.

3 *Journal de Delécluze* (NOTE 1), 48. The mourners mentioned by Delécluze included many important figures in the Parisian artistic milieu: author Vicomte François-Auguste-René de Chateaubriand, whose work inspired Girodet, painters Baron François Gérard, Baron Antoine-Jean Gros, Louis Hersent, Jean-Baptiste Isabey, and Horace Vernet, and architects Jean-Nicolas Huyot, Charles Percier, and Antoine-Laurent-Thomas Vaudoyer.

4 Ibid.

5 Girodet often commented on *The Battle of Aboukir*, praising it particularly in his *La Critique des critiques du salon de 1806: Étrennes aux connoisseurs* (Paris, 1807).

6 P. A. Coupin, *Oeuvres posthumes d'Anne-Louis Girodet-Trioson peintre d'histoire, suivies par sa correspondance . . .* (Paris: J. Renouard, 1829), vol. 2, 399. Benoît-François Trioson (1735–1815), general practitioner to the king and the duc d'Orléans at Montargis, enrolled at the school of medicine in Montpellier in 1754. Widowed in 1806, he adopted Girodet after the death in 1804 of his own son, Romainville.

7 *Lettres adressées au Baron François Gérard, peintre d'histoire, par les artistes et les personnages célèbres de son temps*, 2d ed. (Paris: A. Quentin, 1886), 2 vols.

8 Ibid., vol. 1, 33.

9 Ibid., vol. 1, 163. Cardinal François-Joachim de Pierre de Bernis was a protégé of Madame de Pompadour who later fell out of favor with her. He was sent to Rome to negotiate the election of a pope hostile to the Jesuits in 1769. He refused to swear allegiance to the Civil Constitution of the Clergy passed by the French Assemblée Nationale in 1791 and remained in Rome on a pension from the Spanish court until his death. François-Guillaume Ménageot (1744–1816), a painter, was director of the Académie de France in Rome from 1787 until 1792.

10 Coupin, *Oeuvres posthumes* (NOTE 6), vol. 1, 396.

11 Ibid., 340.

12 The full title of the painting is *Les ombres des héros morts pour la Patrie conduites par la Victoire viennent habiter l'Élysée aérien où les ombres d'Ossian et de ses valeureux guerriers s'empressent de leur donner dans ce séjour d'immortalité et de gloire la fête de la Paix et de l'Amitié* (The shades of the heroes who died for their country are led by Victory to dwell in the celestial Elysium where the shades of Ossian and his valorous warriors crowd around to express peace and friendship in this abode of immortality and glory).

13 For more on the illustrators of the legend of Ossian see the exhibition catalogues *Ossian* (exh. cat., Paris: Grand Palais/Hamburg: Kunsthalle), 1974, and *Girodet illustrateur de la légende d'Ossian* (exh. cat., Montargis: Musée Girodet/Boulogne-Brillancourt: Bibliothèque Marmottan, 1988).

14 For the development of the concept of the "exemplum virtutis" see Robert Rosenblum, *Transformations in Late Eighteenth-Century Art* (Princeton: Princeton University Press, 1967).

15 The English bishop Thomas Percy was eminent in literary circles for his revival of scholarly interest in the Celtic and Saxon languages. Herder, a German writer and philosopher, influenced the young Goethe and the formation of the *Sturm und Drang* movement. Brentano and the brothers Grimm were best known for tales derived from popular folklore.

16 Séroux d'Agincourt was the author of *Histoire de l'art par les monuments depuis sa décadence jusqu'à son renouvellement au XVIème siècle*, the first history of medieval art based on the evolution of style; it influenced Anton Raphael Mengs and Johann Joachim Winckelmann.

17 Guillaume-Thomas-François Abbé Raynal was the author of *Histoire philosophique et politique des établissements et du commerce des européens dans les deux Indes*, in which he preached the emancipation of black slaves. The book was burned by order of the *parlement* in 1781.

18 *Journal de Delécluze* (NOTE 1), 48.

19 Girodet, letter (c. 1806) to "P" (probably the future marquis de Pastoret), cited in Coupin, *Oeuvres posthumes* (NOTE 6), vol. 2, 338.

Color Plates

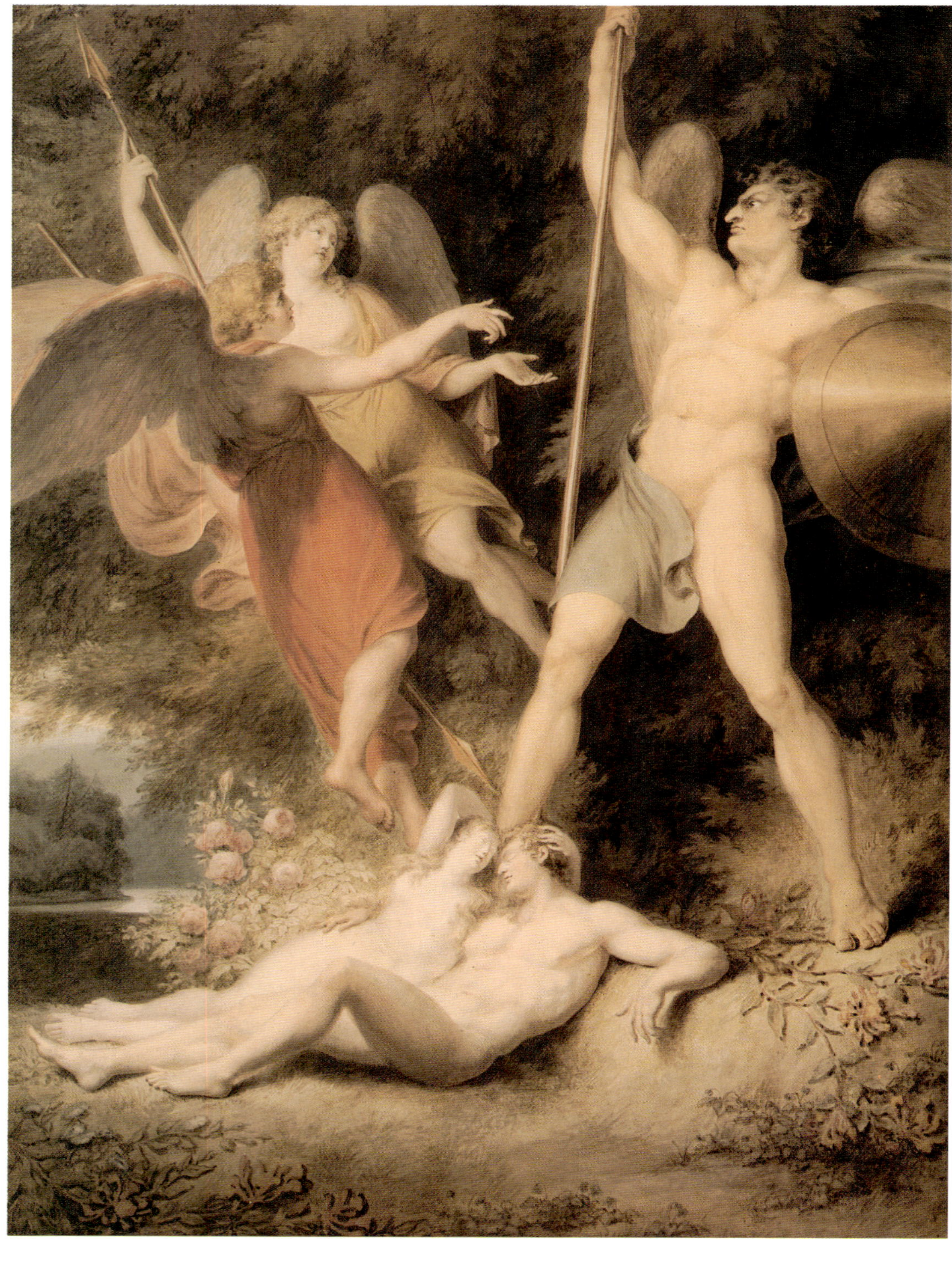

CATALOGUE NO. 13
Stephen Francis Dutilh Rigaud
Lucifer at the Bower of Adam and Eve
c. 1805

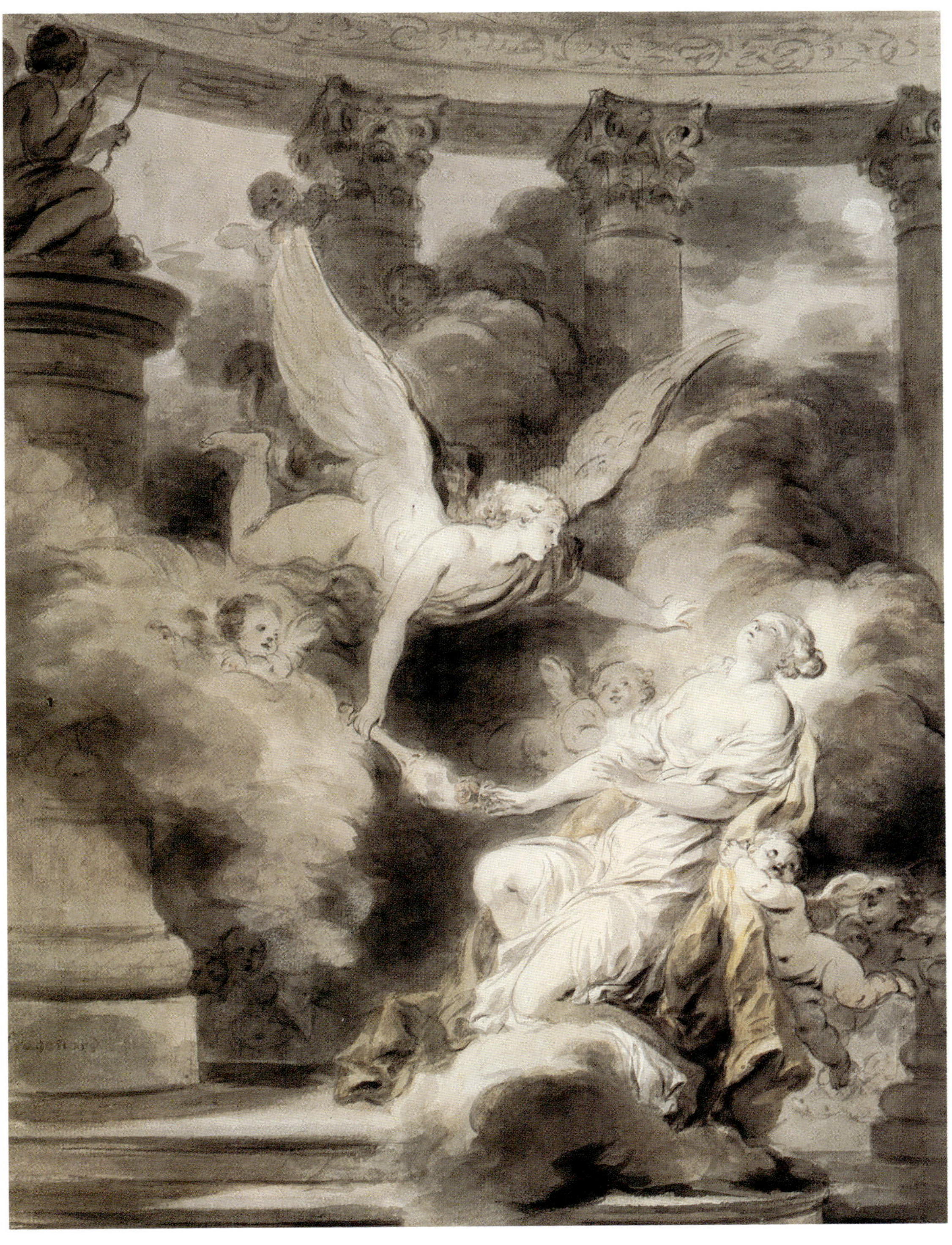

CATALOGUE NO. 21
Jean-Honoré Fragonard
The Sacrifice of the Rose
c. 1775–80

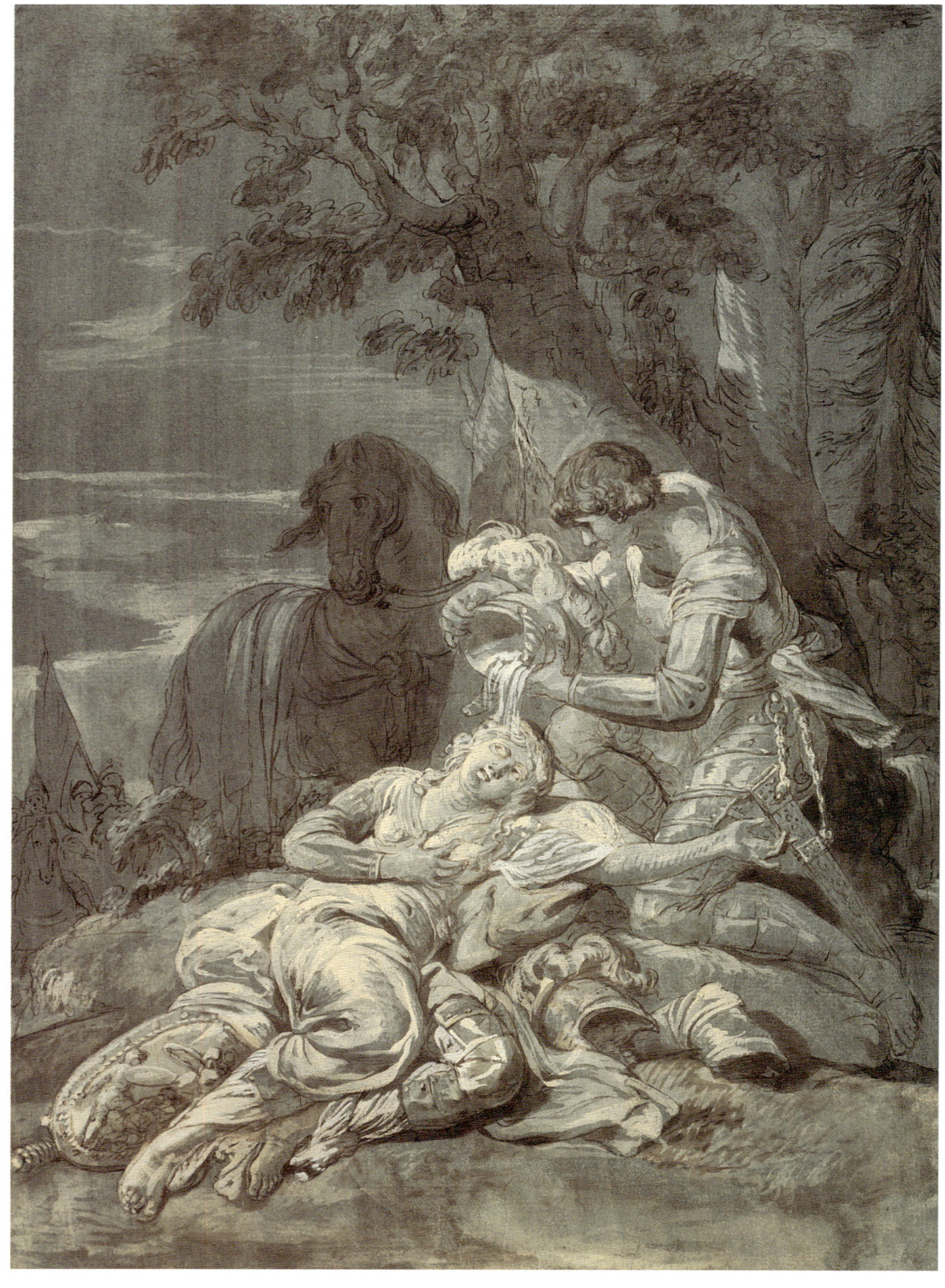

CATALOGUE NO. 25
Jean-Jacques Lagrenée the Younger
Tancred and Clorinda

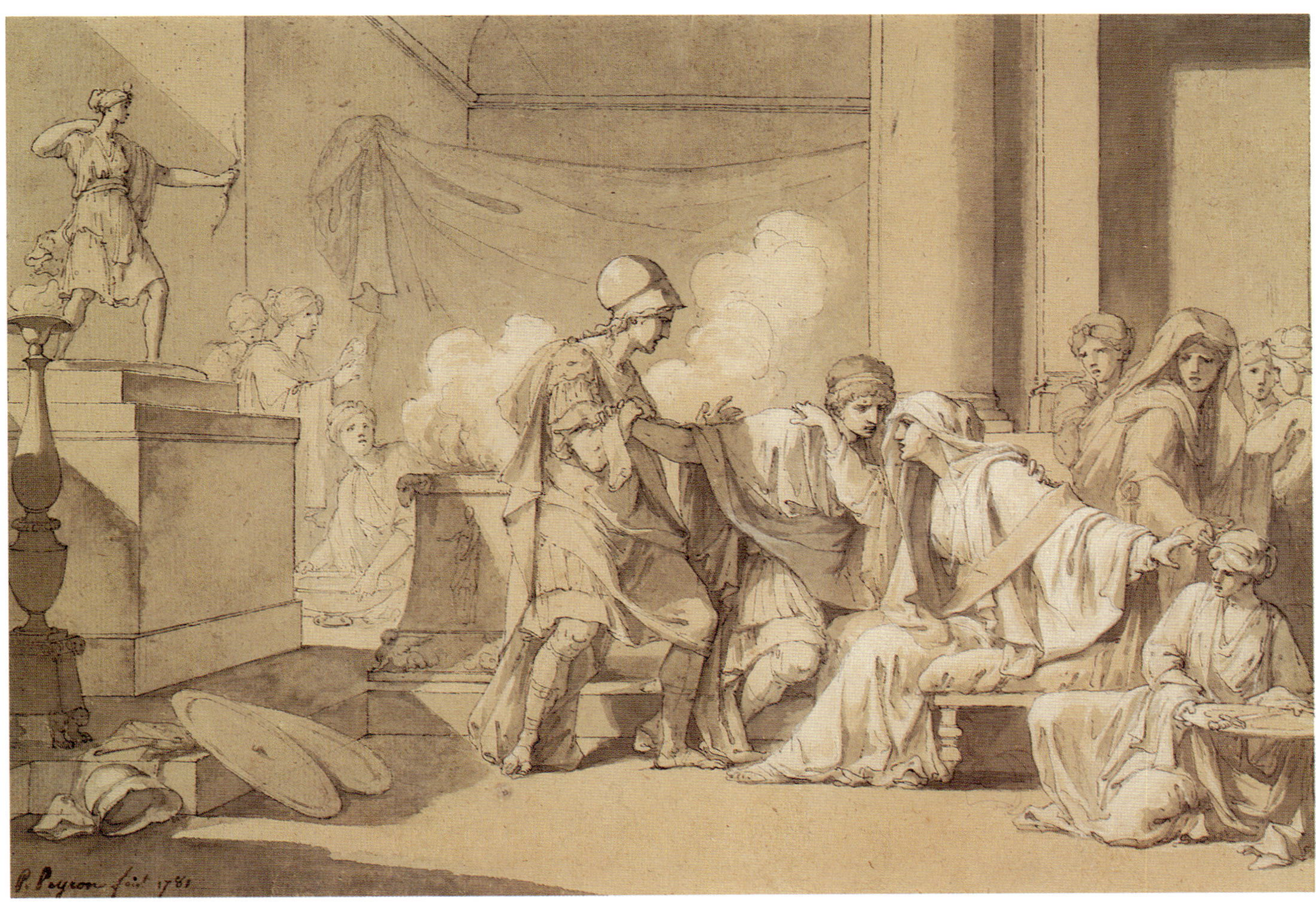

CATALOGUE NO. 31

Jean-François-Pierre Peyron

The Meeting of Orestes and Iphigenia

1781

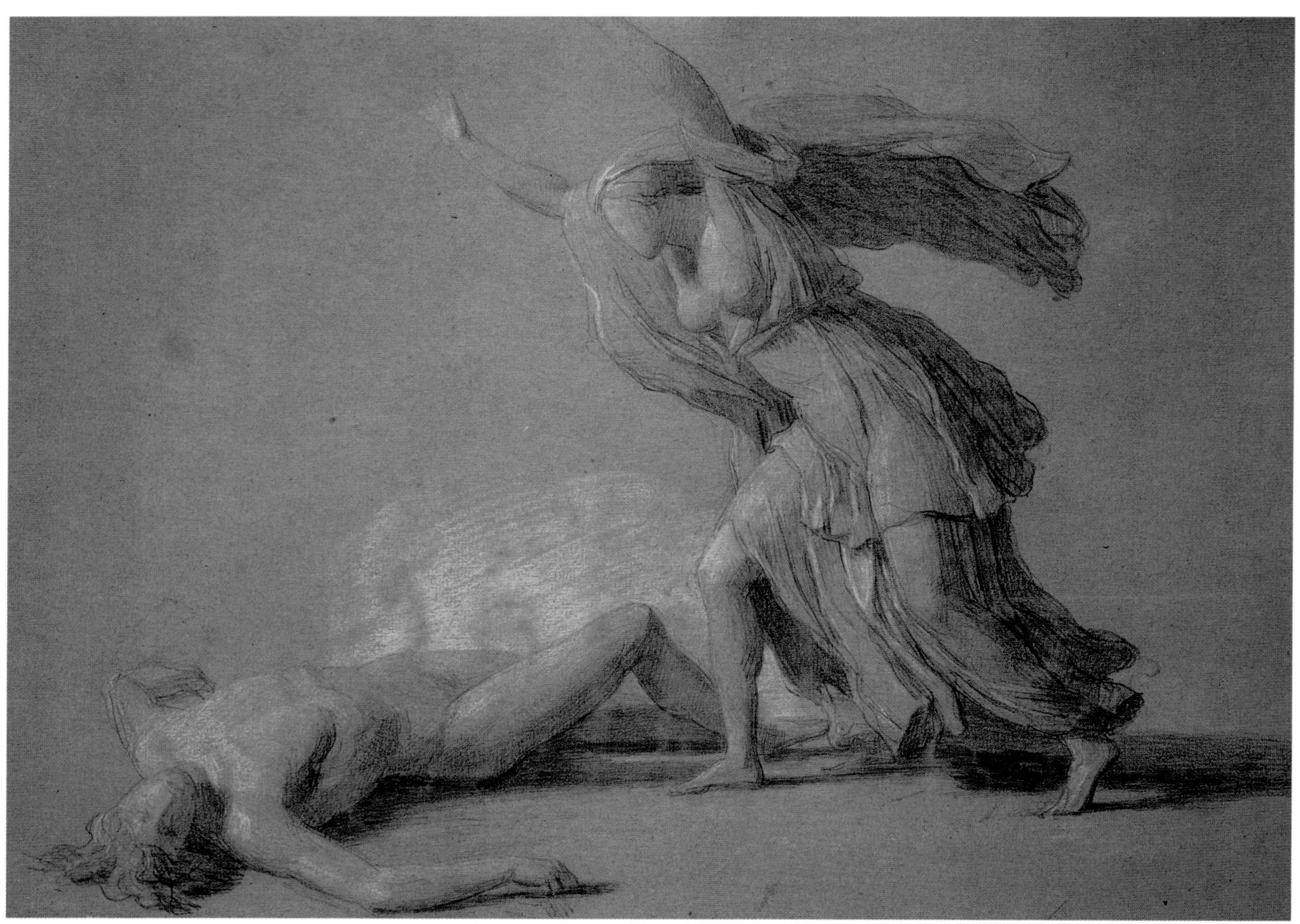

CATALOGUE NO. 33
Jean-Joseph Taillasson
Hero Discovering the Body of Leander on the Seashore
c. 1798

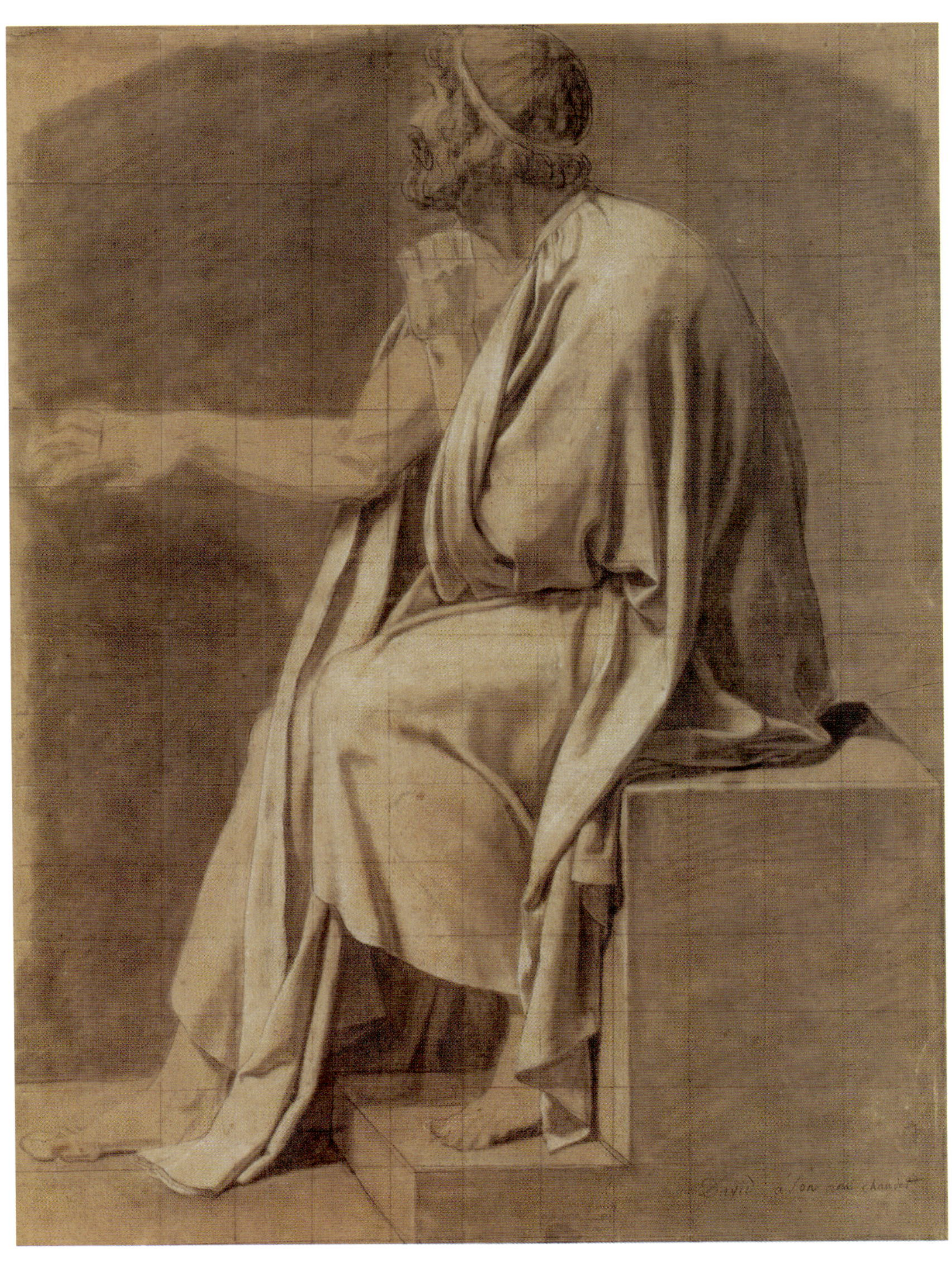

CATALOGUE NO. 40
Jacques-Louis David
Seated Draped Male Figure
c. 1787

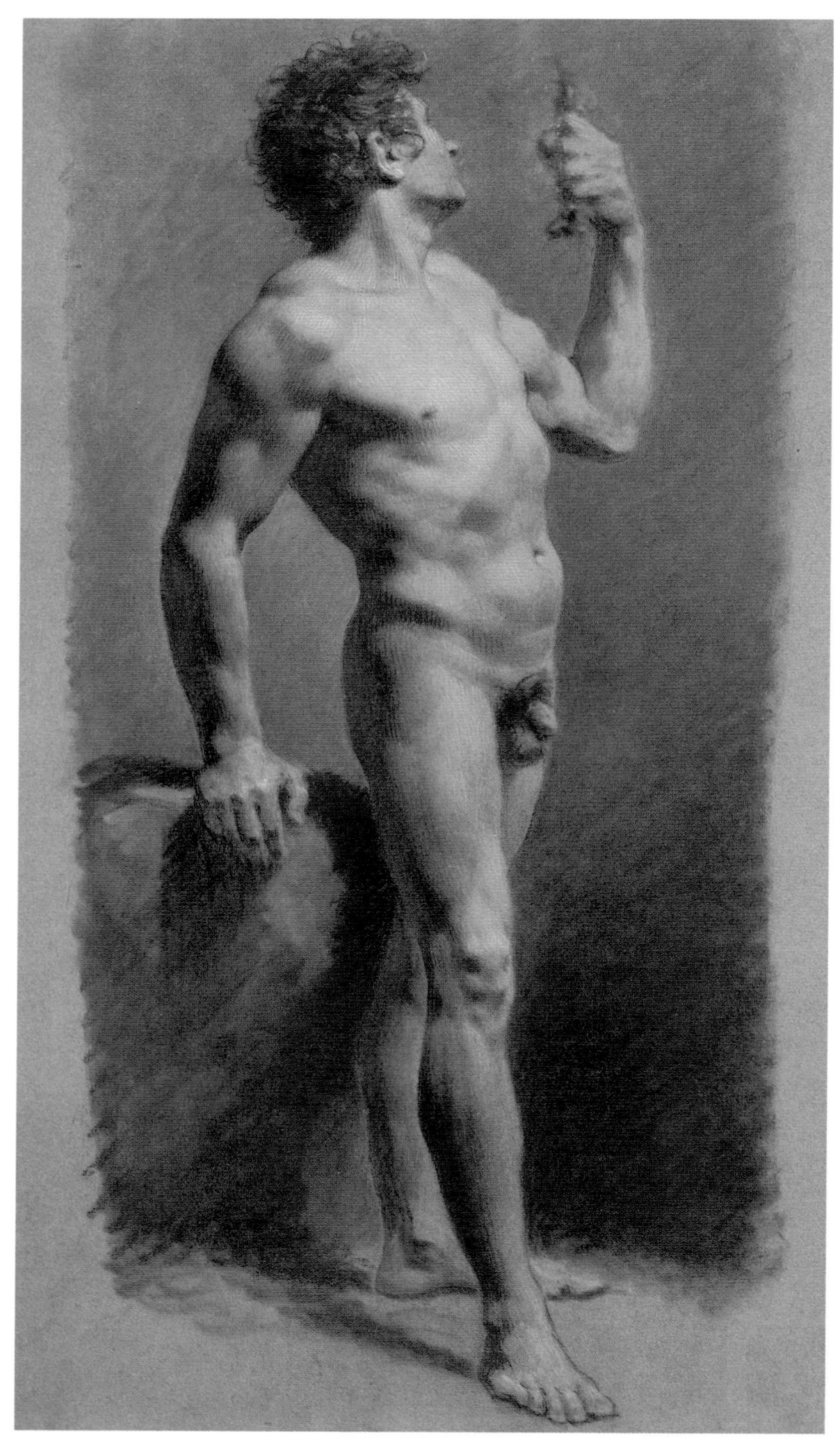

CATALOGUE NO. 49
Pierre-Paul Prud'hon
Study of a Male Nude

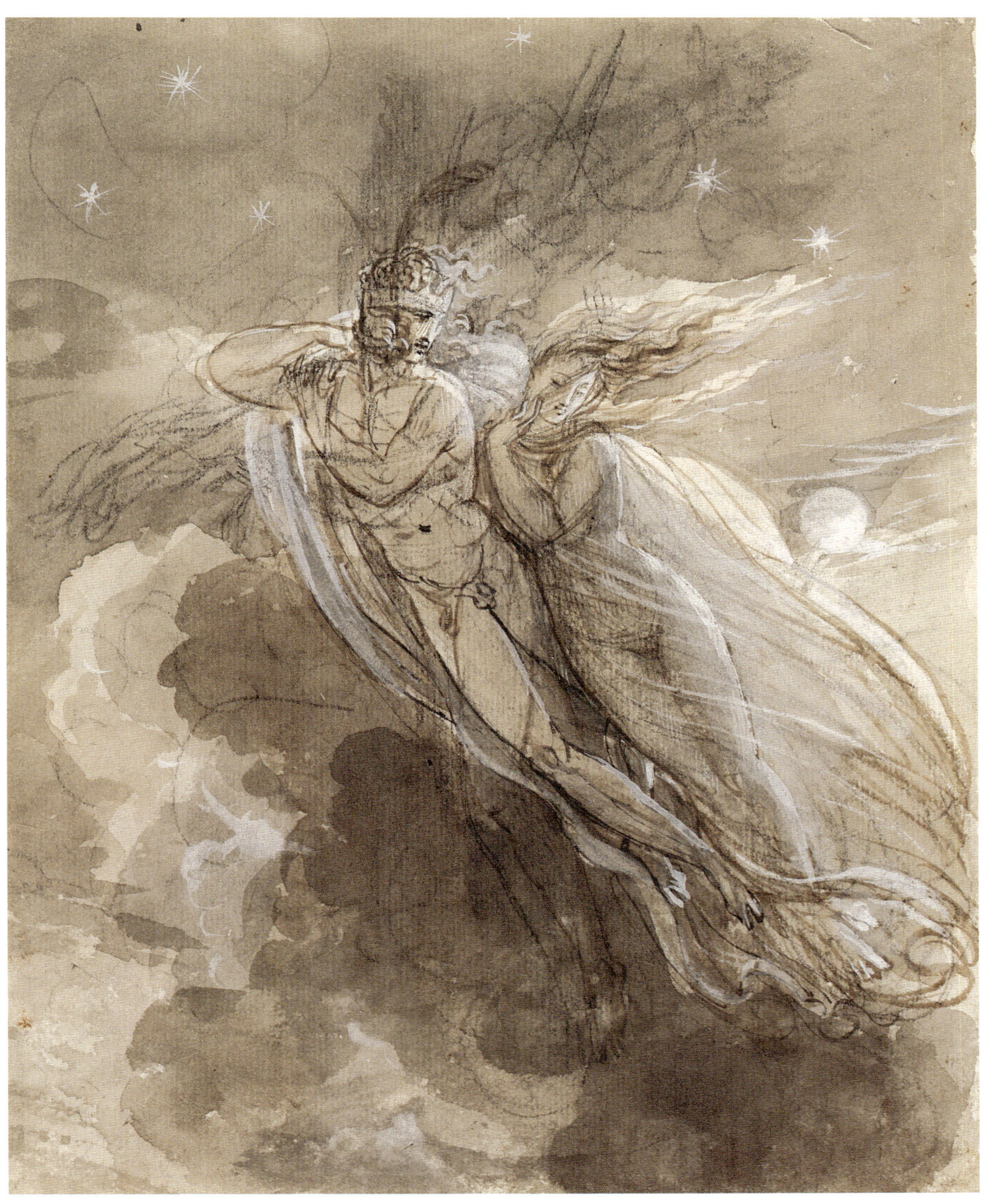

CATALOGUE NO. 57

Anne-Louis Girodet de Roussy-Trioson

The Ghosts of Evirallina and Oscar Gliding through the Evening Air

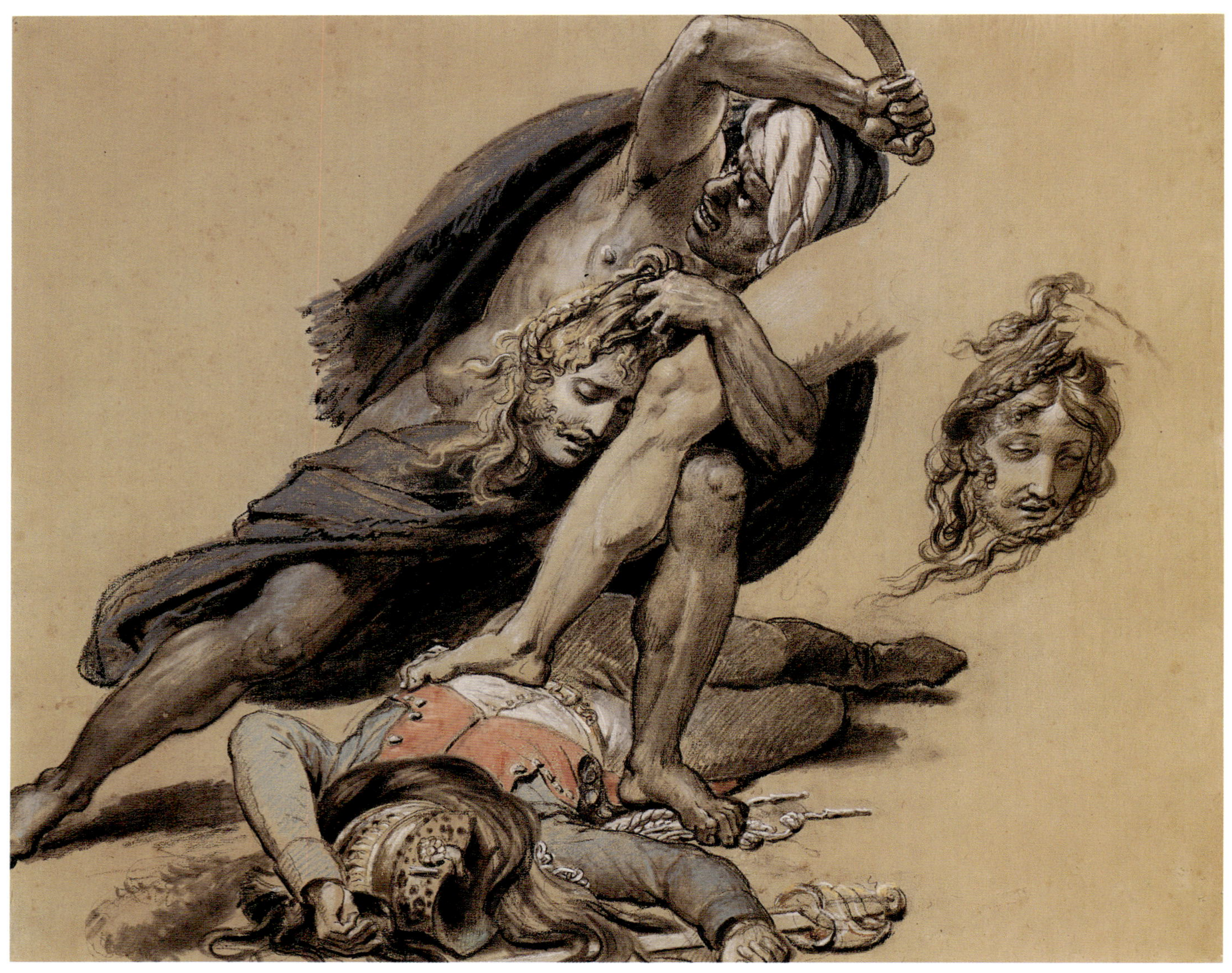

CATALOGUE NO. 59
Anne-Louis Girodet de Roussy-Trioson
Study for the Revolt of Cairo
c. 1809–10

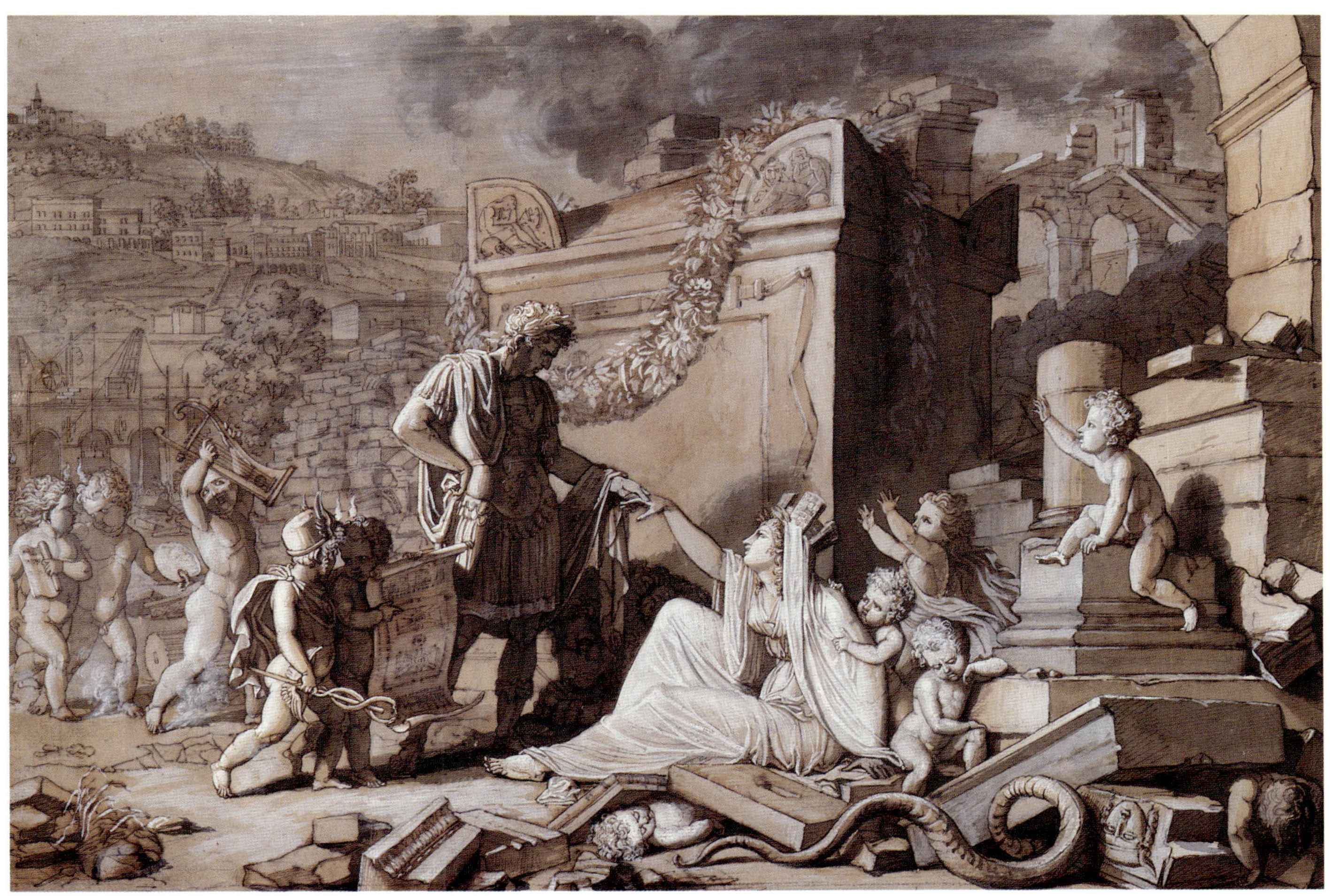

CATALOGUE NO. 67
Pierre-Henri Révoil
Bonaparte Relieving the City of Lyons
1804

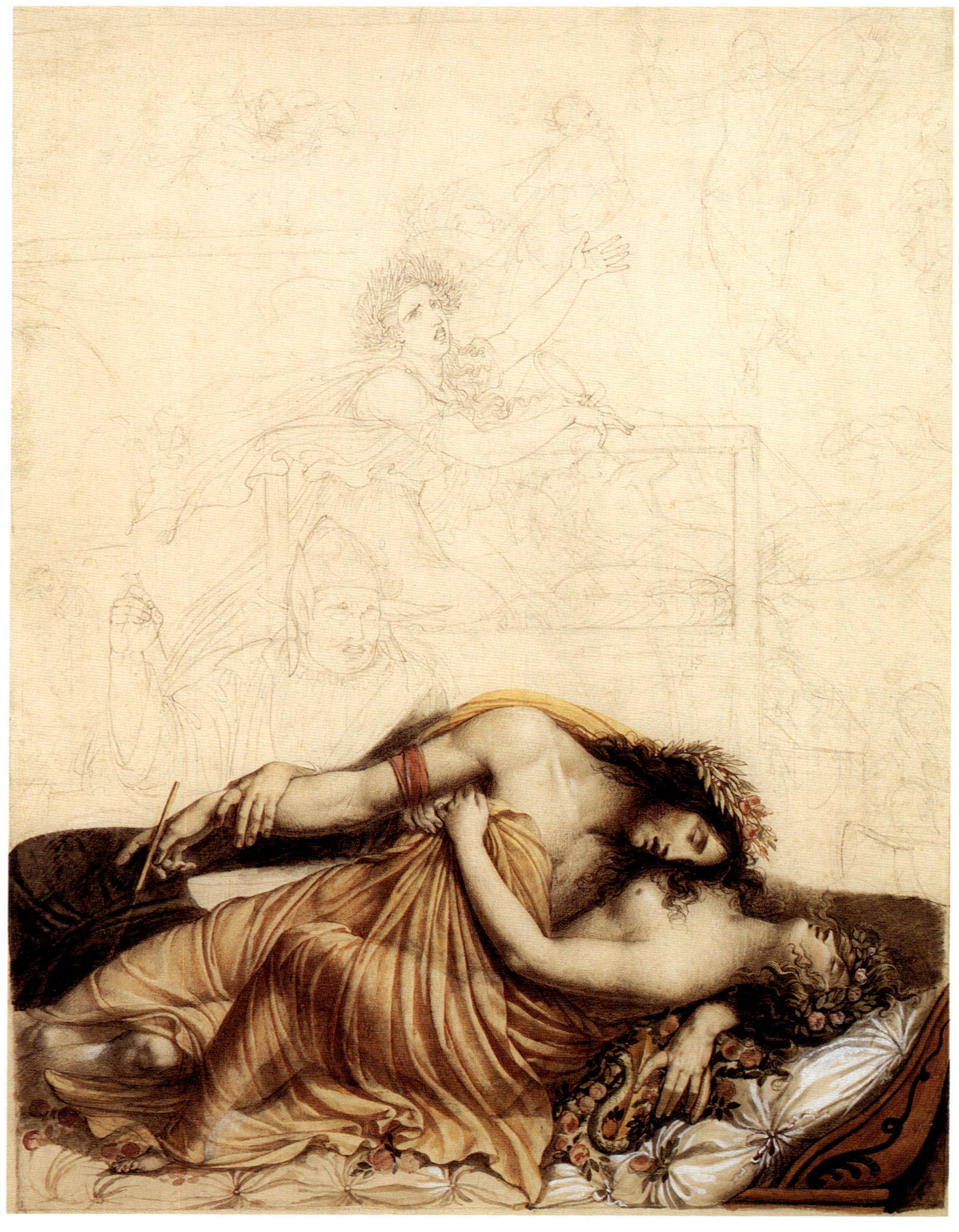

CATALOGUE NO. 69
Fulchran-Jean Harriet
The Death of Raphael
c. 1800–1805

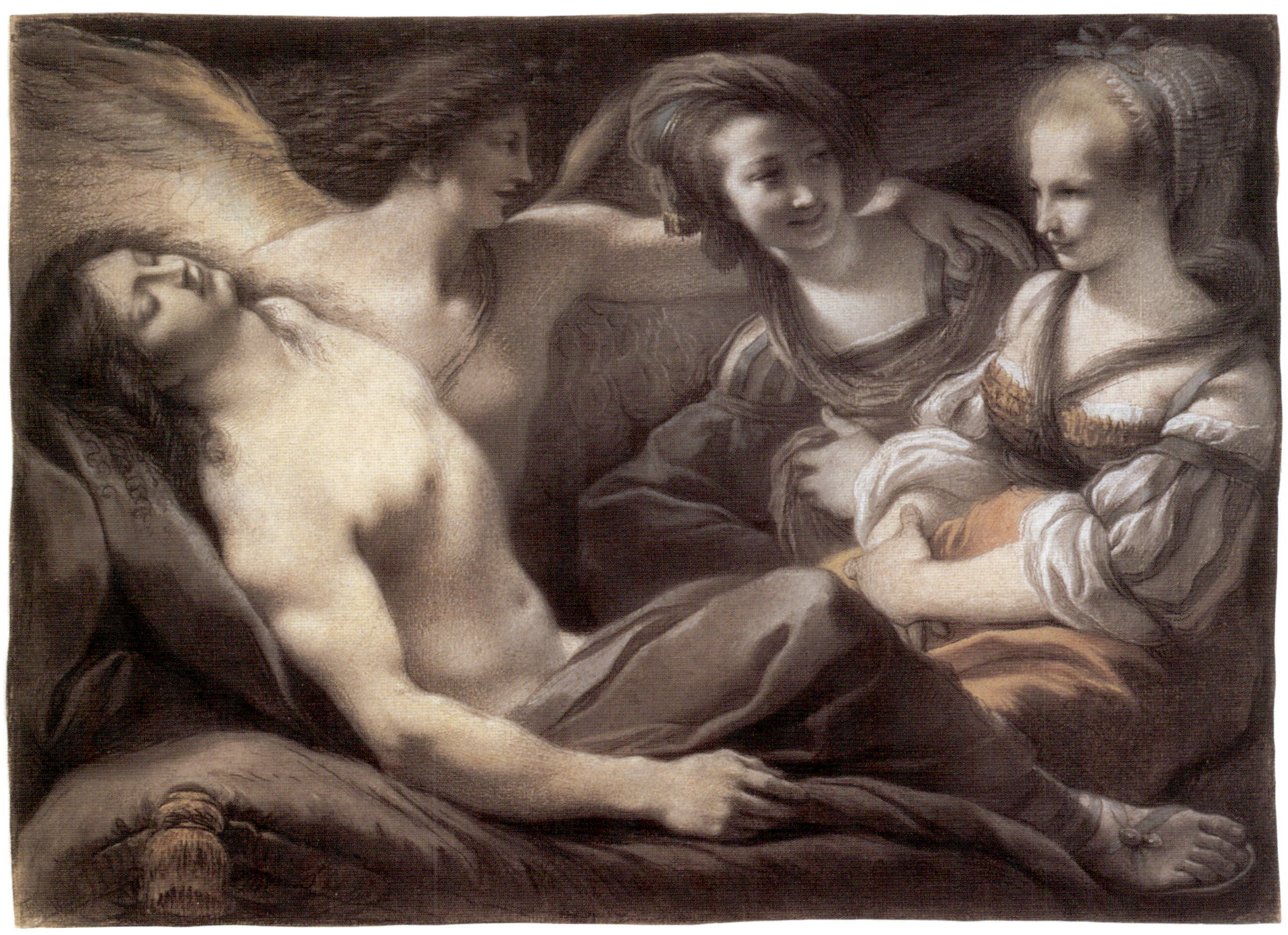

CATALOGUE NO. 81
Giuseppe Cades
Armida Abducting the Sleeping Rinaldo
c. 1785

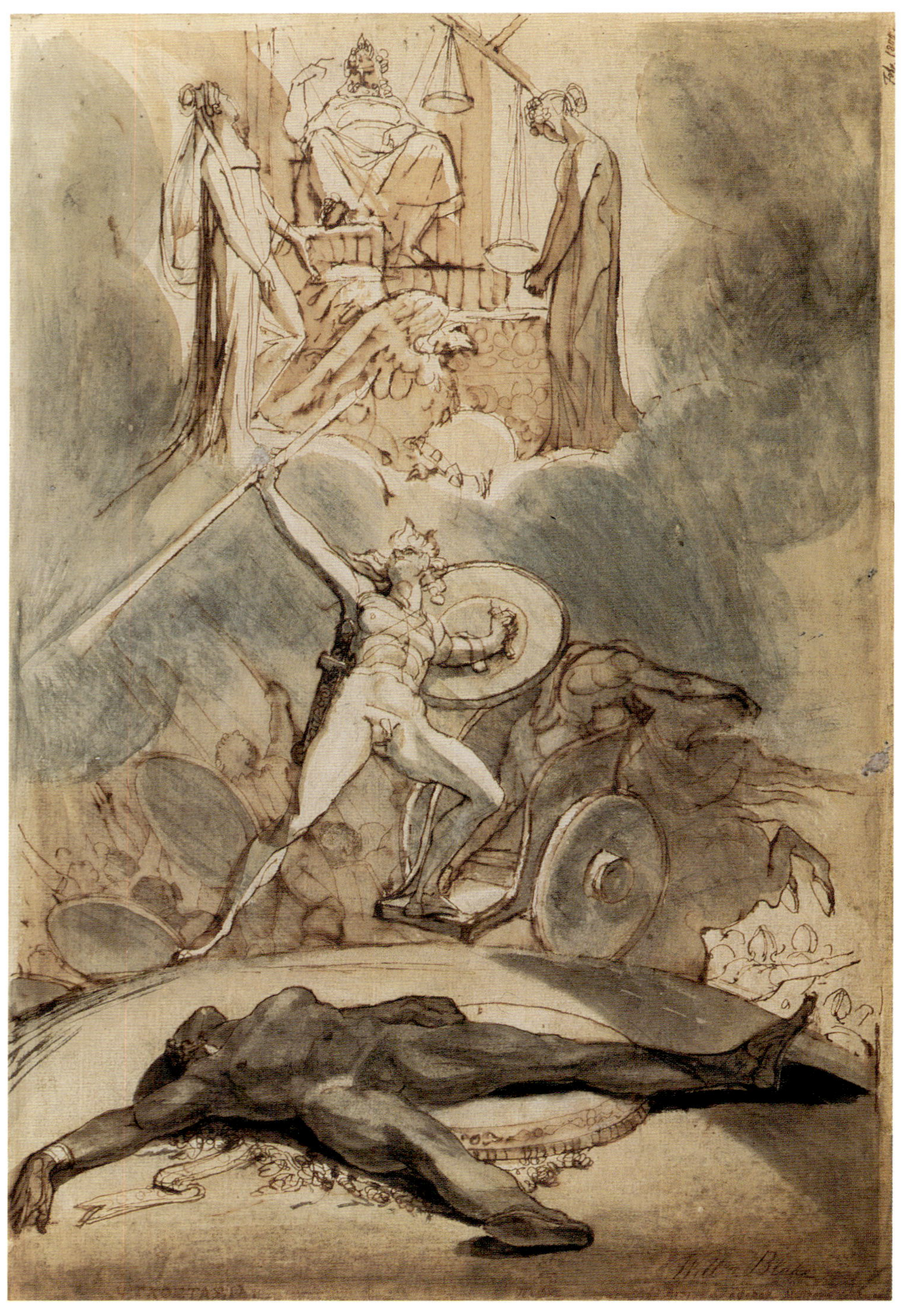

CATALOGUE NO. 98
Henry Fuseli
Psychostasy
c. 1800–1802

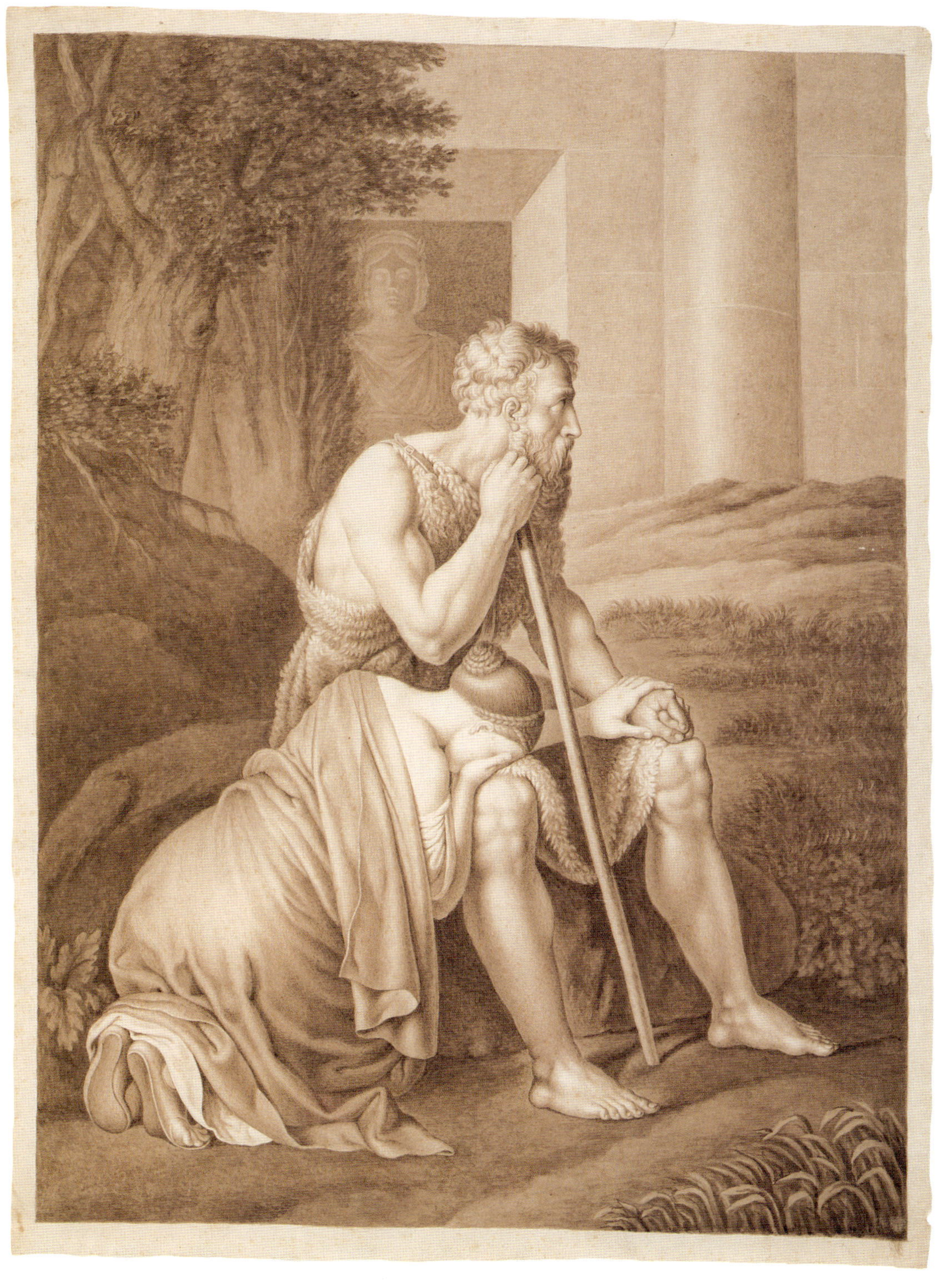

CATALOGUE NO. 113
Johann Peter Krafft
Oedipus and Antigone at Colonus
c. 1814

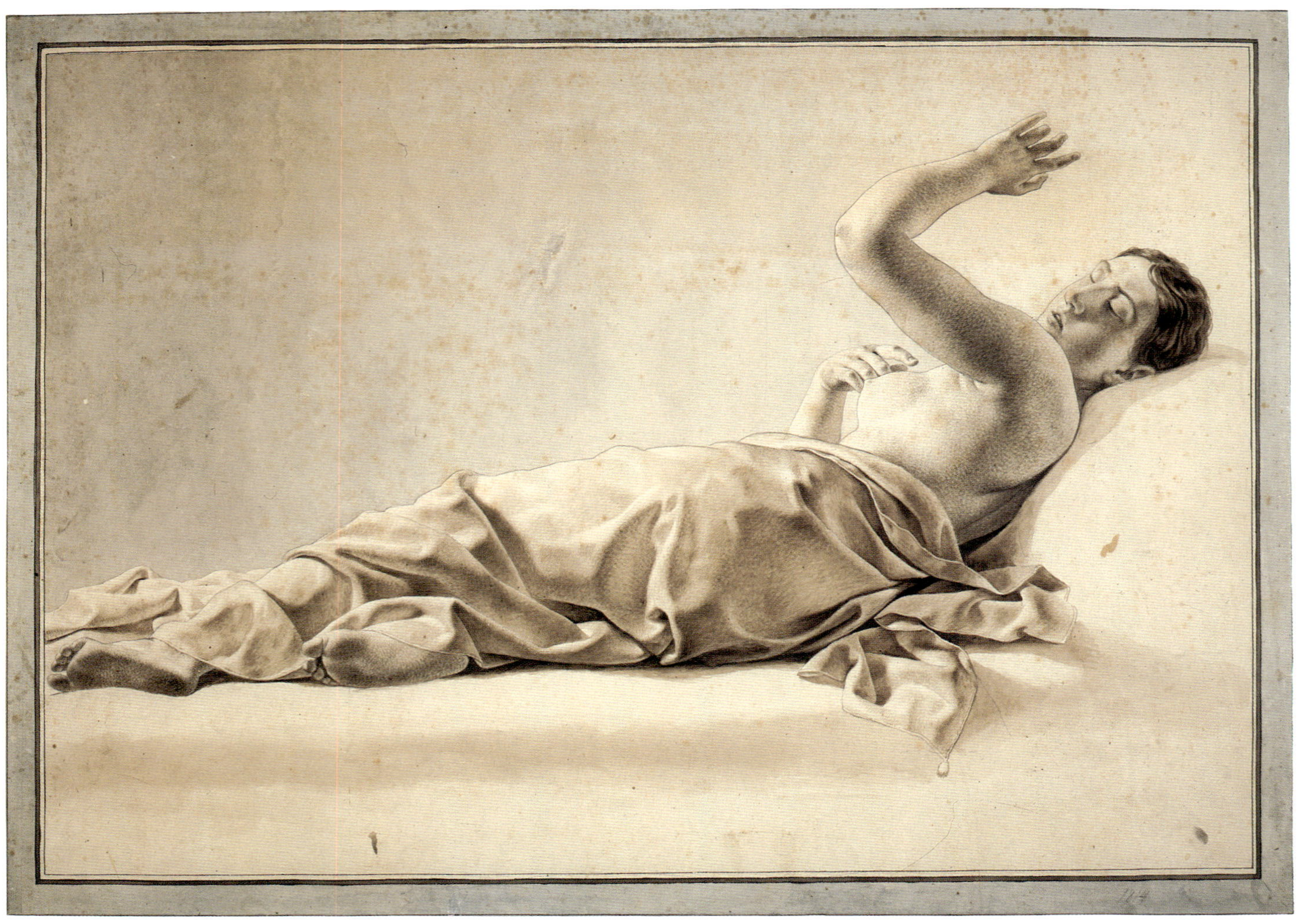

CATALOGUE NO. 115
Christoffer Wilhelm Eckersberg
The Dream of Halcyone
1813

Catalogue of the Exhibition

Key to Authors

BJ Bjarne Jørnæs

EPB Edgar Peters Bowron

LDM Lisa Dickinson Michaux

MM Marsha Morton

RJC Richard J. Campbell

SB Sylvain Bellenger

SM Stig Miss

VC Victor Carlson

Note to the Reader

Throughout the following entries the reader will find references (for example, "New York 1962") to publications that are fully cited in the Bibliography, which begins on page 331.

British Drawings

George Romney

❧

1734 Beckside (near Dalton-in-Furness)–Kendal 1802

AFTER AN APPRENTICESHIP with Christopher Steele from 1755 to 1757, George Romney worked in Kendal and Lancaster. In 1762 he left his wife and two children and moved to London, where he received awards from the Society of Arts for *The Death of General Wolfe* in 1763 and *The Death of King Edmund* in 1765. Romney set off for Rome with his fellow artist Ozias Humphry in 1773. He copied works by Raphael and Michelangelo in the Vatican and also studied the paintings of Giotto and Cimabue. Traveling throughout Italy to study classical antiquity, he became good friends with Henry Fuseli and Joseph Wright of Derby.

Romney returned to England via Florence, Bologna, Parma, and Venice in 1775. Enjoying success as a portrait painter, he became involved in London literary circles and produced several series of works based on the writings of Aeschylus, Virgil, Horace, and Boccaccio, among others. The wealthy engraver and print publisher John Boydell commissioned the painting *The Tempest* for his Shakespeare Gallery in 1786. In 1788 Romney became ill; although he never fully regained his strength, he completed a series of works based on Milton's writings in the 1790s. He soon suffered a series of strokes, however, and in 1799 he gave up painting and moved back to Kendal. LDM

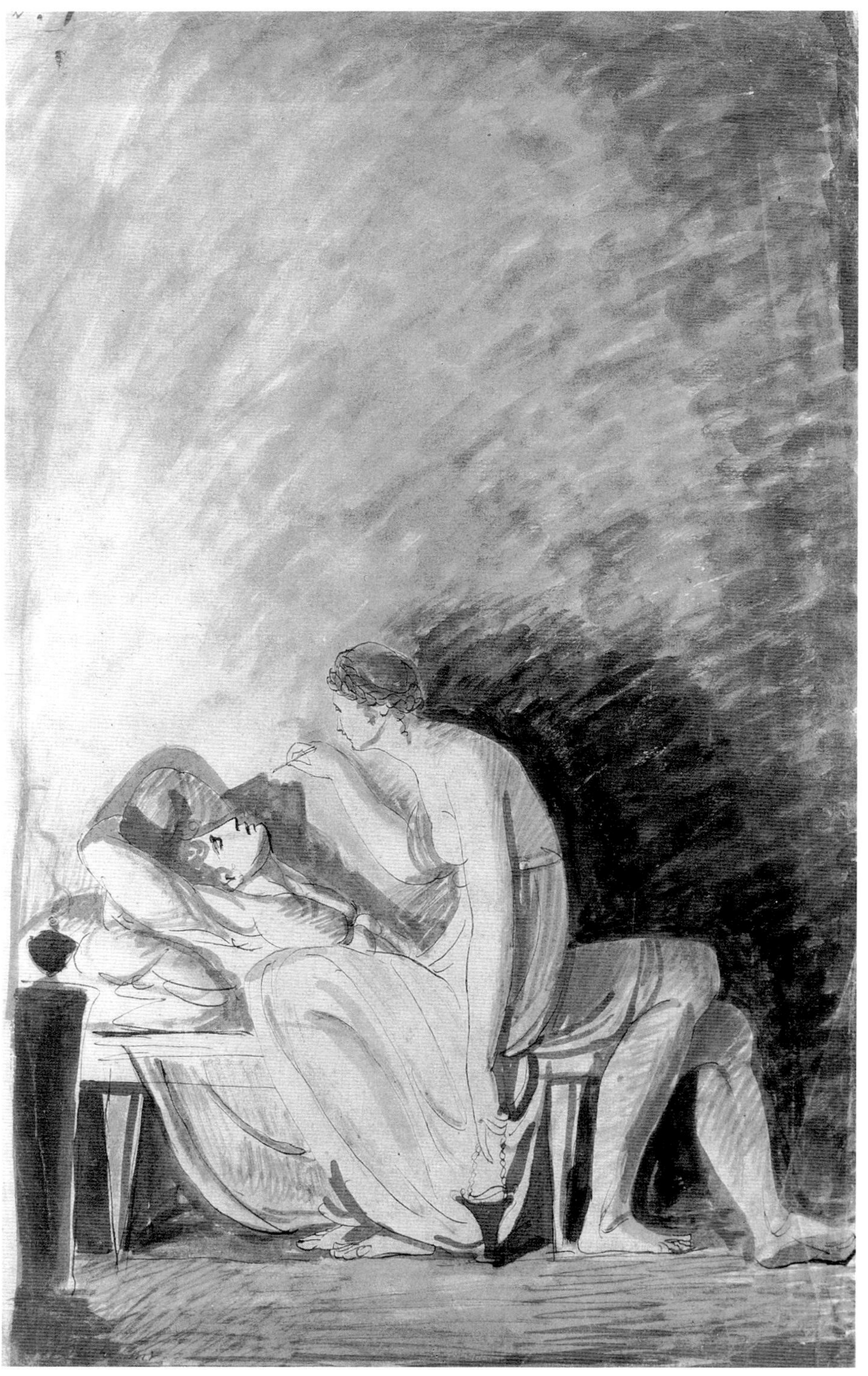

CATALOGUE NO. 1

George Romney
The Origin of Painting
c. 1775–80

I
Pen and brown ink, brush and brown and gray washes on off-white laid paper
52 x 32 cm (20 7/16 x 12 7/16 in.)
Inscribed at lower left in brown ink: *W Blake. inv.*; on the verso in brown ink: *N° 10*; in pencil: *G. Romney R.A./1789*
The Art Museum, Princeton University, gift of Frank Jewett Mather, Jr. (inv. no. x1947-28)

PROVENANCE
Frank Jewett Mather, Jr.

EXHIBITED
New Haven 1979, 126, no. 129.

The subject of Romney's drawing is taken from Pliny the Elder's *Historia naturalis* (Natural history; 35.151), which related that a maiden of Corinth, usually called Dibutade after her father, the potter Bitaudes, traced on a wall the shadow cast by her lover's face in order to preserve a memory of him before he left on a lengthy journey. Pliny's legend was amplified in the second century A.D. by the Greek writer Athenagoras, who specified that Dibutade drew her lover while he was asleep, as seen here (for a full discussion of this subject matter see Rosenblum 1957).

Pliny's tale was not often depicted until the later eighteenth century, when the story became popular among painters, first in Britain. John Hamilton Mortimer and Alexander Runciman both illustrated the subject in 1771. There would appear to be a connection between Romney's drawing and the writer William Hayley's verses (Hayley 1809, 346) in the first of his "Epistles" to Romney from 1778, which suggests an approximate date for this work:

Oh! Love, it was thy glory to impart
Its infant being to this magic art!
Inspir'd by thee, the soft Corinthian maid
Her graceful lover's sleeping form portray'd:
Her boding heart his near departure knew,
Yet long'd to keep his image in her view:
Pleased she beheld the steady shadow fall,
By the clear lamp upon the even wall:
The line she trac'd with fond precision true,
And, drawing, doated on the form she drew.

From Britain, Pliny's tale of the invention of drawing or painting spread to the continent, where Joseph-Benoît Suvée (see CATALOGUE NO. 30) and Anne-Louis Girodet de Roussy-Trioson, among others, took it as the theme for major paintings.

Romney's principal ambition was to paint religious or historical subjects—not the portraits for which he is best known today—but commissions were not forthcoming. The major evidence for the artist's thwarted goals can be found in his numerous drawings of subjects from classical mythology and literature or such favorite authors as Shakespeare and Milton.

The painter was one of the most prolific draftsmen of his time. Over five thousand sheets have survived to give a more complete view of the artist than do his paintings alone. The largest number of drawings come from sketchbooks, some of which have remained intact while many others were broken up and the pages sold separately. Seen out of context the sketchbook pages are usually quite modest, but when the books are still in their original condition, they give a vivid sense of the artist at work (Northampton 1962, introduction, unpaginated):

Thumbing through an unbroken series of sketches for a single subject, one often has the impression of the artist's seeing clearly in his mind's eye not only composition, but even animated scenes: if one figure in a group moves, all do—not with a cold sense of compositional arrangement imposed by the artist, but with a sense of dramatic necessity within the scene itself.

Romney also made more carefully finished drawings such as the present work, apparently unrelated to any painting or book illustration, as well as studies after the antiquities or Renaissance works of art he saw during his trip to Italy in 1773–75. In drawings such as these the artist's hand moved at a slower, more considered pace, and there is a more pictorial use of ink washes to suggest the play of light over forms. Other large subject drawings, though, are executed with great drama and gusto, the artist's heavily loaded brush moving in broad sweeping rhythms to lay down the essential features of the scene. Romney also left a number of large charcoal cartoons, principally of classical or Shakespearean subjects, which today are in the Liverpool Royal Institution as the gift of the artist's son John.

It is noteworthy that the artist seldom made drawings preliminary to his oils. Thus, one does not find among Romney's drawings the careful analysis of details that then are incorporated into a preparatory study for a picture, nor did he make drawings as finished independent works of art that could be framed and sold (compare Saint-Ours, CATALOGUE NO. 104). As John Romney wrote, "He only designed the general idea and effect, and executed the minor parts when he painted the picture" (Romney 1830, 130). VC

George Romney
Young Woman Holding a Lyre

2
Pen and brown ink, brush and brown wash over black chalk on wove paper
30.1 x 23.5 cm (11 7/8 x 9 1/4 in.)
Inscribed at the upper edge in brown ink: the remains of a final *t* from a cut-off inscription, legible when the sheet is turned to the right; at lower right: mark of the Laporte collection
National Gallery of Art, Washington, D.C., Julius S. Held Collection, Ailsa Mellon Bruce Fund (inv. no. 1984.3.55)

PROVENANCE
G. L. Laporte.
Julius Weitzner, New York.
Mr. and Mrs. Julius S. Held.

EXHIBITED
Binghamton 1970, no. 12.
Hartford/Hanover/Boston 1973, no. 41.
Williamstown 1979, no. 31.

This dashing sketch of a seated lady holding a lyre could be a study of a model posed either as Erato, muse of lyric poetry, or Sappho, sometimes known as the tenth muse, the ancient Greek poetess who lived on the island of Lesbos and was famed for her amorous lyrics. In Romney's time women were often painted with an attribute of one of the muses, and the artist could have made this drawing with such a painting in mind. The features of the artist's model recall in a general way Romney's portraits of Emma Hart, later the wife of Sir William Hamilton, the British envoy plenipotentiary to the court of Naples. Emma, formerly an actress, found a more circumspect outlet for her histrionic abilities in the creation of "Attitudes," as they were best known. Using little more than her shawl, Emma could dramatize a bewildering variety of subjects or psychological conditions. During a visit to Naples, Johann Wolfgang Goethe gave a memorable description of one of her performances: "In her [Sir William Hamilton] has found all the antiquities, all the profiles of Sicilian coins, even the Apollo Belvedere. This much is certain: as a performance it's like nothing you ever saw before in your life" (Kenwood 1972, 37–38). Romney's infatuation with Lady Hamilton had the effect of making her his ideal of feminine beauty, with the result that allegorical figures such as the present drawing inevitably reflect her likeness to some extent.

Whether figure studies such as this drawing were made in the course of working out an idea for a painting or were independent exercises, the artist concentrated on finding the most appropriate pose or the most telling gesture, rather than focusing on details of facial expression. Such "minor parts" would be perfected when the painter worked directly on his canvas, as the artist's son observed. In his drawings Romney sought "the general idea and effect," qualities that impressed John Flaxman. When he saw Romney's *Dream of Atossa*, a subject from Aeschylus, Flaxman exclaimed that it had "the fire and severity of a Greek bas-relief" (Hayley 1809, 309–10).

In London Romney felt the need to have at hand examples of classical sculpture and wrote to Flaxman, who was then in Rome, asking him to select and send off casts of as many choice and celebrated antiquities as funds would allow (Romney 1830, 230–31). Romney's study after antique models was not coldly analytical. The very lack of finish in his drawings suggests a parallel to a sculptor's *bozzetti* (rapidly executed waxes or terra-cottas), which Johann Joachim Winckelmann in his *Geschichte der Kunst des Alterthums* (History of ancient art), 1764, praised as actually superior to a carefully finished work: "For as the first gush of the grape-juice from the press forms the finest wine, so in the soft material, and on paper, the genius of the artist is seen in its utmost purity and truth; whilst, on the contrary, it is concealed beneath the industry and the polish required in a finished painting and a completed statue" (Winckelmann 1872, vol. 1, 144). In this view it is the artist's conception or idea that establishes the merit of his work, with mechanical skills relegated to a secondary level. Romney's drawings at their best, like those of the contemporary sculptors Antonio Canova, Johan Tobias Sergel, and Bertel Thorvaldsen, are distillations of the "fire" and "true spirit" of an artist's inventive powers. VC

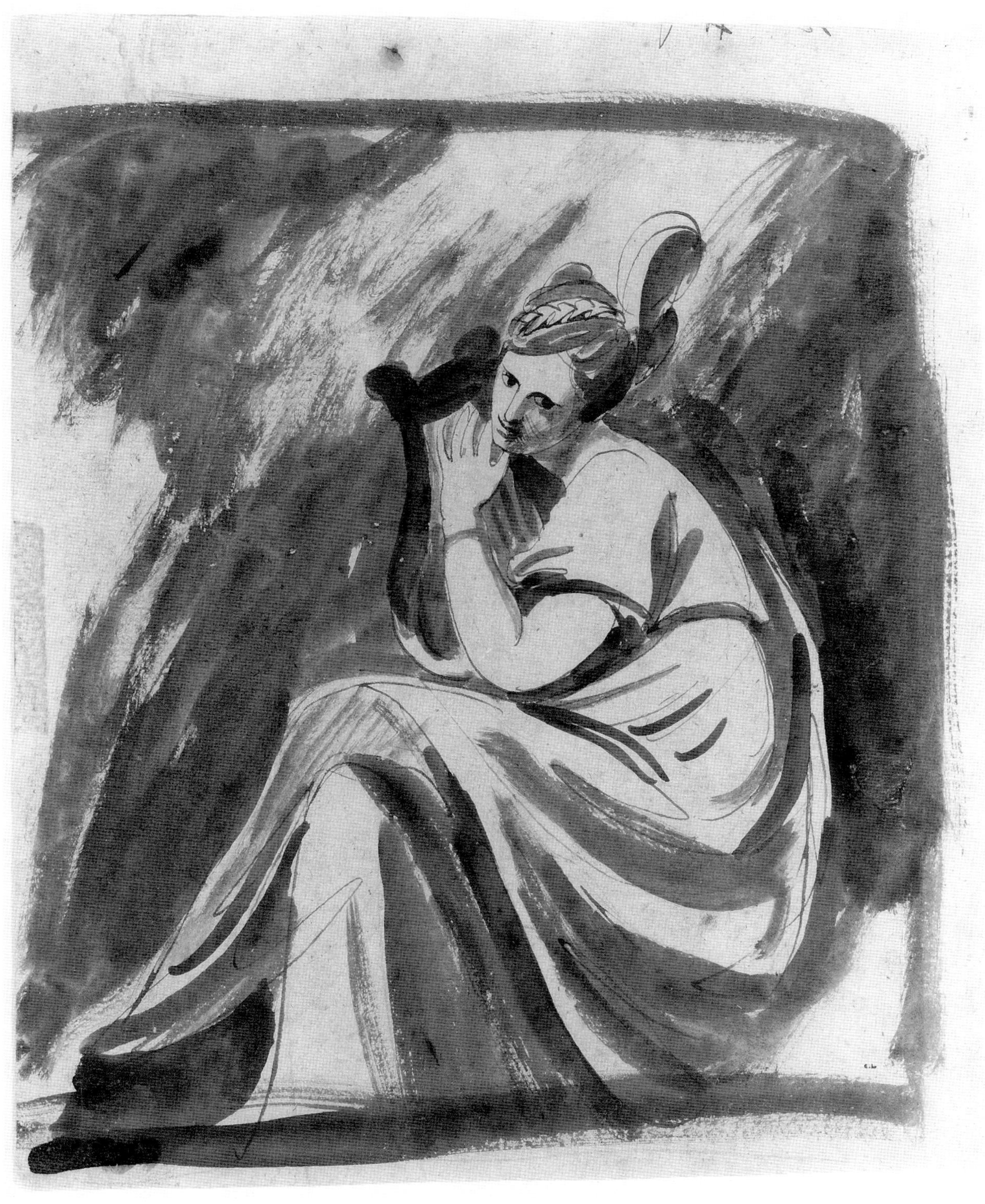

CATALOGUE NO. 2

Benjamin West

1738 Springfield, Pennsylvania–
London 1820

BENJAMIN WEST STUDIED with William Williams and later at the University of Pennsylvania with William Smith. He graduated in 1757 and painted portraits in Philadelphia and New York to earn money for a voyage to Rome. West arrived in Italy in 1760 as the first American artist to visit the country. He received introductions throughout Rome, where he stayed for three years and met Cardinal Albani, Pompeo Batoni, Anton Raphael Mengs, and Angelica Kauffmann and was befriended by Gavin Hamilton. West also traveled to Naples and viewed the discoveries at Pompeii and Herculaneum.

He opened a studio in London in 1763 and established himself as a portraitist and history painter. He became the most famous history painter in England by virtue of the success of *The Departure of Regulus*, shown at the first exhibition of the Royal Academy in 1769, and *The Death of General Wolfe*, exhibited in 1771. He was appointed historical painter to King George III in 1772 and executed many royal commissions. A founding member of the Royal Academy, he was its president from 1792 until 1815. LDM

Benjamin West
Antiochus and Stratonice
1777

3
Pen, brush, and brown wash, blue watercolor, heightened with white ink, over black chalk on tan paper
44.9 x 59.5 cm (17 11/16 x 23 7/16 in.)
Signed and dated at lower center in faint brown ink: *B. West 1777*
The Saint Louis Art Museum, museum purchase (inv. no. 4:1949)

PROVENANCE
Robert Frank, London.

EXHIBITED
Cleveland 1964, no. 78.

LITERATURE
Galt 1820, 226.
Leonard 1951, 48–50.

The story of Antiochus and Stratonice is a classical tale that enjoyed a resurgence of popularity in the arts from the seventeenth century to the opening decades of the nineteenth century. The prince Antiochus was mortally ill with an undiagnosed malady, and his father, King Seleucus, was in despair for his son's life. A physician, Erasistratus, was called in to find the cause of the mysterious illness. The doctor noticed that Antiochus's pulse quickened whenever his stepmother, Stratonice, entered the room, and realized that the prince was dying of repressed love. When Erasistratus told Seleucus the reason for his son's decline, the king agreed to renounce his claim on his second wife in favor of Antiochus, thus saving his son's life. There are several variants of the story, but the moral that parental love overcomes any obstacle is basic to all the versions (for a thorough discussion of the iconography see Stechow 1945).

West depicts Erasistratus, at center, taking Antiochus's pulse as Stratonice enters from left and King Seleucus sits grieving at right. This drawing has sometimes been thought to be a study for a painting that the artist signed in 1772 and exhibited at the Royal Academy in 1775. The canvas was reproduced by Valentine Green in a mezzotint dated 1776 (Leonard 1951, 50; Von Erffa/Staley 1986, 170, no. 15). There are only a few points of correspondence between the present work and the painting as it was engraved, and in fact they depict different episodes in the story. In the drawing Antiochus still has the strength to sit upright while Erasistratus makes the examination that leads to the discovery of the cause of the hero's illness. The event precedes the dilemma facing King Seleucus in which he must make a decision that inevitably will entail the sacrifice of either his wife or his son. West's painting is a deathbed scene, with Antiochus reclining at full length, his head turned to one side and cradled in his father's lap, as the latter ponders what decision to make. The moral dilemma acted out in West's painting is, in its basic conception, a familiar type of *exemplum virtutis* in praise of stoic behavior or heroic action, the sacrifice of personal pleasure or gain for a larger, moralizing principle.

West used the figure group of Stratonice and her attendants in both his drawing and painting; the variations in composition noted above are certainly to be explained in part by the difference in subject matter. West has more effectively organized the composition of his drawing to narrate the dilemma he chose to represent. The major figures—Stratonice, Antiochus and his physician, and Seleucus—each occupy clearly defined positions in the drawing, which are further reinforced by the details of the background architecture and the arrangement of draperies. West drew Stratonice and

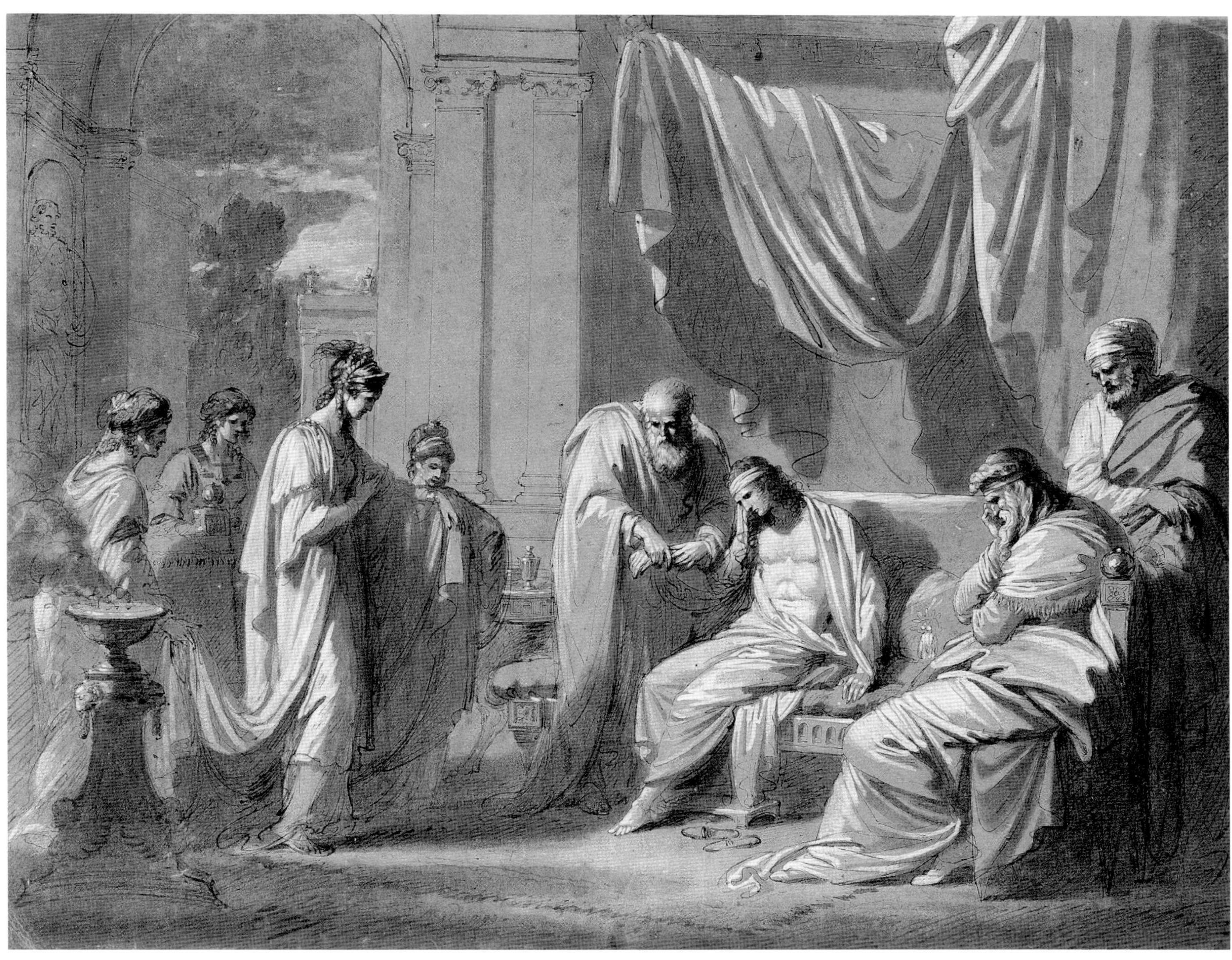

CATALOGUE NO. 3

Seleucus in profile, thereby framing the central group of the ailing Antiochus and Erasistratus. The artist's unambiguous presentation of the psychological states of the main figures marks an advance over the canvas in narrative clarity, which may suggest that the drawing postdates the artist's Royal Academy painting, even if there is no other evidence for this supposition.

Two plates from the English edition of Bernard de Montfaucon's *L'Antiquité expliquée et representée en figures* (Antiquity explained and represented in plates), 1721–24, offer striking parallels to the personages in this drawing. The figure of King Seleucus is virtually identical in pose to the mourning father in Montfaucon's engraving of a family lamenting the death of a young virgin (vol. 5, pl. 1), while the seated figure of Antiochus is strikingly like, although in reverse to, the figure of Diogenes in a bas-relief from an urn or sarcophagus (vol. 3, pl. 58). The shallow space of West's drawing reinforces the parallel to antique Roman bas-relief sculpture, as do the static poses of the figures who wait in quiet resignation to hear Erasistratus's diagnosis. Like many artists of his time, West admired such fragments of Rome's past as were then known. While he was in Italy from 1760 to 1763 he probably made his drawings after the reliefs of the Ara Pacis (Kraemer 1975, 4, no. 2, pl. 2, fig. 2), evidence of the profound impression these marbles made on him.

It has long been recognized that painters working in Britain, such as West and Gavin Hamilton, were in the forefront of those who looked to ancient Greece and Rome to give a new direction to their art. This was not simply a question of mastering archaeological niceties but of learning to think and see from an unfamiliar point of view. Jean Locquin (1921, 395) eloquently characterized the accomplishments of the first British neoclassical artists:

> *It is in the general conception of their work, in the arrangement of figures in the manner of bas-reliefs, in the serene and intelligible composition of groups and processions, in the stately rhythm of gestures and draperies, in the exact representation of architecture, furnishings, Greek and Roman costume, in the evocation of the forms of ancient sculpture, in the concise forcefulness of expressions, of which Poussin discovered the secret, that the English school presently asserts its superiority.*

VC

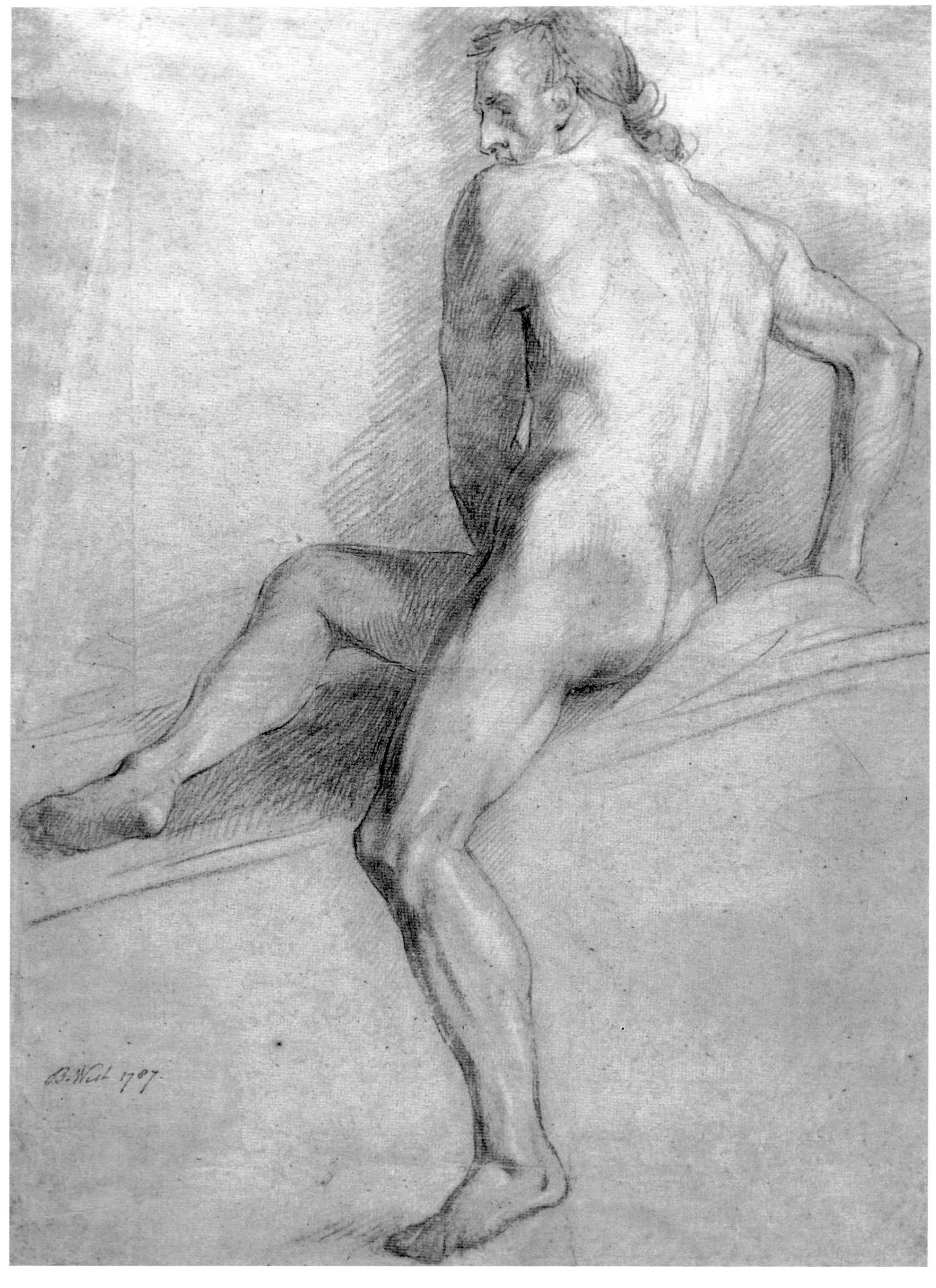

CATALOGUE NO. 4

Benjamin West
Male Nude: Academic Study
1787

4
Black chalk on off-white laid paper
60.4 x 44.5 cm (23 3/4 x 17 1/2 in.)
Signed and dated at lower left in brown ink:
B. West 1787
The Minneapolis Institute of Arts, the Richard Lewis Hillstrom Fund, 1989 (inv. no. 89.66)

PROVENANCE
Kennedy Galleries, New York.

West's study of a man seen from the back is a drawing after a live model, in which the artist has studied the muscular tensions created by the pose. The date on this drawing suggests that the work may have been executed during one of West's teaching sessions at the Royal Academy, where he was one of its most respected and influential professors. Other sheets similar to this in style and media are known (Kraemer 1975, nos. 113, 115, 117–18, pls. 70, 72–74), each of which appears to have been drawn as an end in itself.

When the British Royal Academy was established in 1768, there were facilities for members to draw after the living model, in addition to a collection of plaster casts of celebrated antique statues after which students worked as well. Both approaches were thought to be indispensable facets of the Academy's program.

The first president of the Royal Academy, Sir Joshua Reynolds, encouraged students to develop their command of the human figure through a careful and exact study of actual models,† although this was only an initial, but necessary, step toward the goal of attaining that "higher degree of excellence" to be found in the masterpieces of classical sculpture (Reynolds, *Discourse 3*, quoted in Eitner 1970, vol. 1, 43). In his third *Discourse* Reynolds explained that the true goal of a painter should be the creation of an ideal figure, composed of the most beautiful details to be found in nature, but imitating no specific individual. This position paralleled Winckelmann's proposition that ideal beauty is a mental construct attained by combining the finest parts to create a surpassingly perfect figure: "It is the mind, which the painter of genius desires to address; nor will he waste a moment on smaller objects, which only serve to catch the sense, to divide the attention, and to counteract his great design of speaking to the heart."

The position of the model in the present drawing recalls in a general way a figure from Annibale Carracci's ceiling of the gallery of the Palazzo Farnese, Rome, such as the crouching man to the right of the scene of Polyphemus and Galatea. It was not uncommon for artists, West among them, to have a live model assume a pose reminiscent of a celebrated work of art from the past, even when that figure was to have an entirely different identity in the artist's own work (Nottingham/Kenwood 1991, 58, no. 29). Carracci's celebrated fresco was familiar to artists, even those who never traveled to Italy, through several volumes of reproductive prints (Rome 1986, 111–200) and was generally admired by West's contemporaries (although there were dissenting voices, among them Henry Fuseli's, not surprising at a time when seventeenth-century Bolognese art was considered extravagant and barbarous [Irwin 1966, 116–17]). Carracci's figures, with their clear indebtedness to Michelangelo's *ignudi* on the Sistine Chapel ceiling, may have had a degree of reflected glory from the towering reputation of the earlier master. Winckelmann (cited in Eitner 1970, vol. 1, 11) declared Michelangelo to be the only modern artist whose work rivaled the grandeur of antique art, and Reynolds warmly praised him, devoting his final *Discourse* to the Royal Academy to an encomium of the artist. VC

†For an excellent study of figure drawing in England see Martin Postle, "The Artist's Model from Reynolds to Etty," in Nottingham/Kenwood 1991, 16–24.

John Hamilton Mortimer

1740 Eastbourne–London 1779

IN 1757 JOHN HAMILTON MORTIMER entered the London studio of Thomas Hudson, where he met his lifelong friend, Joseph Wright of Derby. Two years later he was a pupil of the portrait painter Robert Edge Pine and of Giovanni Battista Cipriani and Joseph Wilton at the duke of Richmond's sculpture gallery. He also studied at, and received prizes from, the Academy of St. Martin's Lane. Mortimer exhibited at the Society of Artists from 1762 until 1777 and won first prize in 1764 for best historical painting for his *Saint Paul Converting the Britons*.

In 1769–70 Mortimer collaborated with Thomas Jones, who painted the landscapes for his *Dido and Aeneas* and *Death of Orpheus*. He also worked with Francis Wheatley and James Durno on the ceilings of Brocket Hall, Hertfordshire. He completed his *Belisarius* in 1772 and his *Marius on the Ruins of Carthage* two years later; at this time he also began to illustrate the works of Shakespeare, Chaucer, and Cervantes.

Mortimer was elected a member of the Royal Academy in 1779, the same year that he died unexpectedly. He was only thirty-eight, but he had lived a flamboyant and wild life, often at the expense of his health. He had a reputation as a bohemian, and after his death his life was greatly romanticized. Despite his many adventures and the subject matter of many of his paintings, he never visited Rome. LDM

John Hamilton Mortimer
Lord North and Friends in Classical Dress: Allegory of Peace and Plenty

5
Pen and black ink, brush and brown and gray washes and watercolor on ivory paper
27.2 x 33.6 cm (10 11/16 x 13 1/4 in.)
Stanford University Museum of Art, the Committee for Art Acquisitions Fund (inv. no. 1984.159)

PROVENANCE
Christopher Powney.

LITERATURE
Sunderland 1988, no. 166, fig. 319.

Traditionally this drawing is thought to represent Frederick North, second earl of Guilford (1731–92), standing beside a statue holding a cornucopia and a sheaf of wheat, emblems of prosperity. Lord North himself wears classical dress and holds a fasces, a bound bundle of rods carried by ancient Romans to symbolize their position of authority and power. Six other unidentified figures complete the allegory, the composition of which is quite traditional and thus rather at odds with the eccentric, bohemian personality that the artist self-consciously cultivated. Perhaps the watercolor was a commission for an engraved frontispiece or book illustration, as John Sunderland suggests (1988, no. 166). Mortimer followed the conventions of his time in another respect, as well, by showing North and his attendant figures in classical attire. Sir Joshua Reynolds, then president of the Royal Academy, maintained that classical garments were more appropriate to "the inherent greatness" of the person being honored than were contemporary fashions (Irwin 1966, 148–49). And, as if to further surround North with the glory that only antiquity could confer, the artist added at the left the portico of an ancient Roman temple.

There is no evidence to provide a date for this watercolor, but during the artist's lifetime England's prosperity and North's political career flourished with the peace following the conclusion of the Seven Years' War in 1763. This was broken by the revolt of the American colonies in 1775. The British government's failure to negotiate successfully with the colonies led North, as a representative of the crown, to submit his resignation, which the king refused to accept. Mortimer's watercolor extolling North's wise and prosperous policies must have been drawn before this debacle. VC

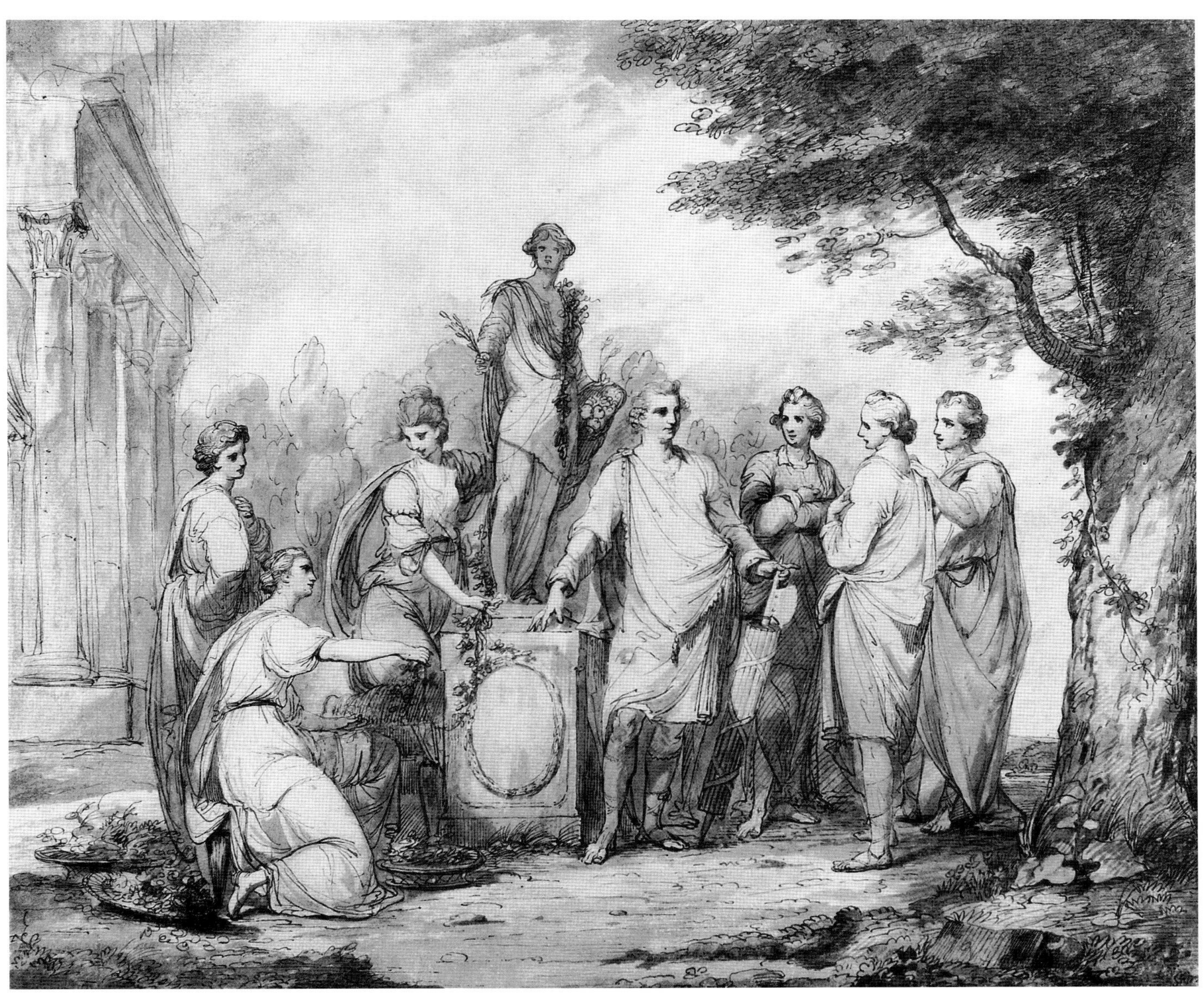

CATALOGUE NO. 5

Angelica Kauffmann

1741 Chur (Coire)–Rome 1807

KAUFFMANN WAS RECOGNIZED as a child prodigy. Her childhood was spent traveling through Switzerland, Austria, and northern Italy working with her father on small ecclesiastical murals. By the age of fifteen she was accepting her own commissions, and when she went to Rome in 1763, she was welcomed by the leading artists of the day. She exhibited her paintings *Bacchus and Ariadne* and *Penelope* in 1764, and Winckelmann proposed her election to the Accademia di San Luca in 1765. The next year Kauffmann left her father and began a successful career in London, where she was one of the founding members of the Royal Academy and sent pictures to their exhibitions from 1769 until 1797. She was very productive in England, painting *Last Interview of Hector and Andromache* and *Venus Showing Aeneas and Achates the Way to Carthage* as well as numerous portraits and four ovals for the new Royal Academy. In 1781, after the death of her first husband, Kauffmann married Antonio Zucchi, who accompanied her when she returned to Italy in 1782. She settled in Rome, where she had an international clientele, continuing to send pictures to London and contributing *Diomed and Cressida*, 1788–89, to publisher John Boydell's Shakespeare Gallery. After the death of Pompeo Batoni in 1787, Kauffmann was regarded as the most famous and successful painter in Rome. Her funeral in 1807 was planned in the tradition of that of Raphael by Antonio Canova. LDM

Angelica Kauffmann
Design for a Fan
c. 1775–81

6
Watercolor, with body color and gilding on off-white laid paper
17.2 x 53.3 cm (6 3/4 x 21 in.)
Yale Center for British Art, New Haven, Paul Mellon Collection (inv. no. B1975.3.1237)

PROVENANCE
Sale, Christie's, London, November 9, 1971, lot 96.

LITERATURE
Mayer 1972, fig. 45.
Mayor 1980, 50.

When Angelica Kauffmann went to England, her canvases of classical subjects or allegorical figures enjoyed a considerable vogue, which brought her a substantial income. Many of her patrons also employed the brothers Robert and James Adam to provide them with designs for stylish neoclassic interiors, in which the paintings of Kauffmann and Giovanni Battista Cipriani provided a tasteful and popular complement to the delicate tracery and pastel colors.

Notwithstanding her favorable reception in England's aristocratic and moneyed circles, some of her contemporaries voiced reservations about the outspokenly decorative and facile qualities of her art. In a bitter verse (cited in Irwin 1966, 52) Henry Fuseli wrote of Kauffmann and Francesco Bartolozzi, the engraver whose popular prints after her work were an essential aspect of her reputation:

Balzoned in Crystal, crowned with sculptured gold,
Imperious Fashion's central seat they hold:
Love without Fire; Smiles without Mirth; bright Tears
To Grief unknown; and without beauty, Airs;
Celestial harlots; Graces dressed by France;
Rosy Despair and Passions taught to dance
Irradiate the gay leaf—the charm-struck crowd
Devoutly gaze, then burst in raptures loud.

The center panel of Kauffmann's fan design is an allegory of the three arts of painting, architecture, and sculpture. The composition is a characteristic example of her art, a gracious evocation of a classical past that is closer in spirit to the work of seventeenth-century artists such as Guido Reni and Francesco Albani or of her own contemporaries Pompeo Batoni and Anton Raphael Mengs. Goethe's description of Kauffmann's personality is at the same time one of the most apposite commentaries on her art: "She is very sensitive towards all that is beautiful, true and tender, and also incredibly modest" (Irwin 1966, 51–52).

The central panel of this fan design was later used by Bartolozzi in his print *The Three Fine Arts* of 1783. The figures are exactly the same in each work, although Bartolozzi modified the background landscape, which Kauffmann had accommodated to the fan shape.

The panels on either side of the allegory are characteristic of the designs devised by the Adam brothers to ornament walls and ceilings. Details such as the pair of griffins facing one another on either side of an antique candelabrum occur throughout Adam interiors, which combine motifs from Greek and Roman

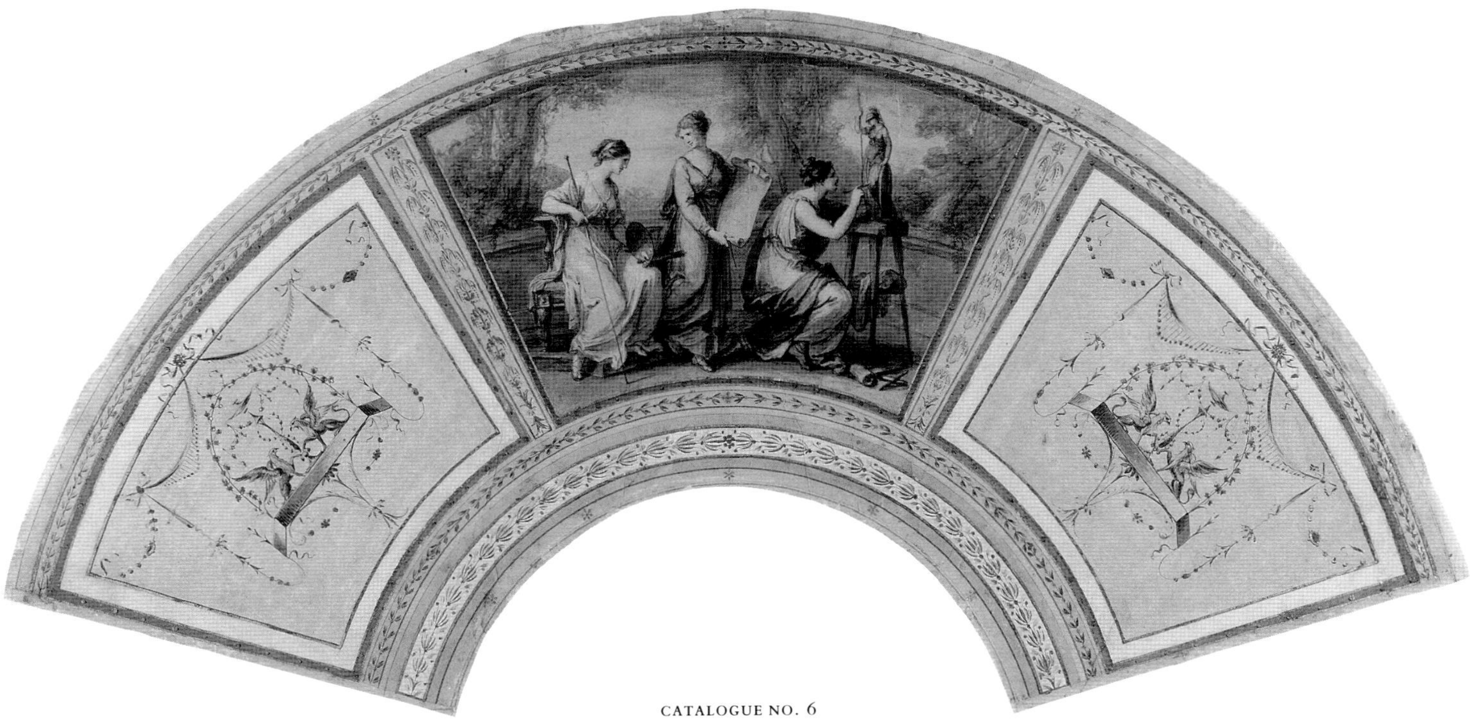

CATALOGUE NO. 6

art with references to the Italian Renaissance, especially Raphael's decorations of the Villa Farnesina in Rome. Kauffmann's fan design perfectly exemplifies on a small scale those qualities that made the Adam brothers' decorative schemes among the most important instances of neoclassic taste as evidenced in the applied arts.

Elegantly ornamented fans were quite popular at this time. Fanny Burney recalled in her diary going with Sir Joshua Reynolds to visit the workshop of the painter Antonio Poggi, one of whose specialties was painting fans, to see his work after designs by Kauffmann, Cipriani, and Benjamin West (Manners/Williamson 1924, 47). Burney specified that Poggi worked on leather, undoubtedly guided by watercolors such as the present example.

While still in London, prior to her final departure for Italy in 1781, Kauffmann exhibited some of her fan designs at the Royal Academy, although the specific examples are not identified. Consequently, it appears that these designs were at the height of their popularity during the late 1770s, which would be an acceptable date for this watercolor. VC

John Brown

1749 Edinburgh–Leith 1787

JOHN BROWN BEGAN his studies under Charles Pavilon at the School of Art in Edinburgh. He left for London in 1769 and later that year for Rome with his friend David Erskine; through Erskine's brother Charles the two artists were introduced into important artistic circles in Rome. During his twelve years in Italy Brown traveled throughout the country, including a trip to Sicily as draftsman to the antiquarian Charles Townley.

Brown returned to Edinburgh in 1781 and began one of his most important commissions: for five years he produced a series of life-sized pencil portraits of the leading members of the Society of Antiquaries in Scotland. He left for London in 1786 to work for Charles Townley again, this time drawing the marble sculpture in his collection. Soon after his introduction to the London scene, however, Brown fell ill; he was advised to return to Edinburgh and died in 1787 only four days after his boat landed in Leith. LDM

John Brown
The Geographers

7
Pen and ink, brush and gray-brown wash on off-white laid paper
18 x 25.2 cm (7 1/8 x 10 in.)
Inscribed on the right edge of the table in pencil: *John Brown Romae*; at the top right corner in pencil: *61*
Yale Center for British Art, New Haven, Paul Mellon Collection (inv. no. B1977.14.4152)

PROVENANCE
Sir Thomas Lawrence; sale, Christie's, London, June 17, 1830, lot 105 (bought by Knowles).
Lady North.
Leon Suzor.
Faerber and Maison, London, 1965.

EXHIBITED
Paris 1950, no. 94.
New York 1972, no. 59.
New Haven 1979, no. 61.

LITERATURE
Powell 1952, opp. 42.

John Brown's wash drawing shows four young men seated at a table with a globe at the far left. Two of the students are studying an atlas or folio open on the table, while the other pair is distracted by something outside the picture's composition. Behind the group absorbed by their book are two standing men who look over the students' shoulders. The scene, drawn in Rome, is lit by a candle or lamp that dramatically illuminates the figures at the table but casts into shadow the men who hover in the background.

Brown left for Italy in 1769 (not 1771 as is sometimes thought; see New Haven 1979, 54 n. 2), where he spent nearly twelve years, mainly in Rome and Florence. In Rome the artist made studies of character heads, a manifestation of his interest in human physiognomy that had its roots in the studies of Leonardo da Vinci and Albrecht Dürer or, closer to Brown, William Hogarth and Henry Fuseli.

The study of physiognomy theorized that facial expressions were a guide to human personality, a point of view expressed in Johann Kaspar Lavater's celebrated *Physiognomische Fragmente* (Physiognomical fragments), which was published in 1775–78. The present drawing reflects Brown's interest in physical types: the four students at the table are attractive youths, whereas the vaguely menacing character of the men in the background is conveyed by details such as a scowling expression or a hooked nose. The handsome profile of the seated student nearest the viewer is classical in its regularity and purity of outline, a conventional reference to indicate nobility of character or purpose. Thus, Brown probably intended that his drawing be more than a simple genre representation, although it is now impossible to suggest a specific subject or theme. VC

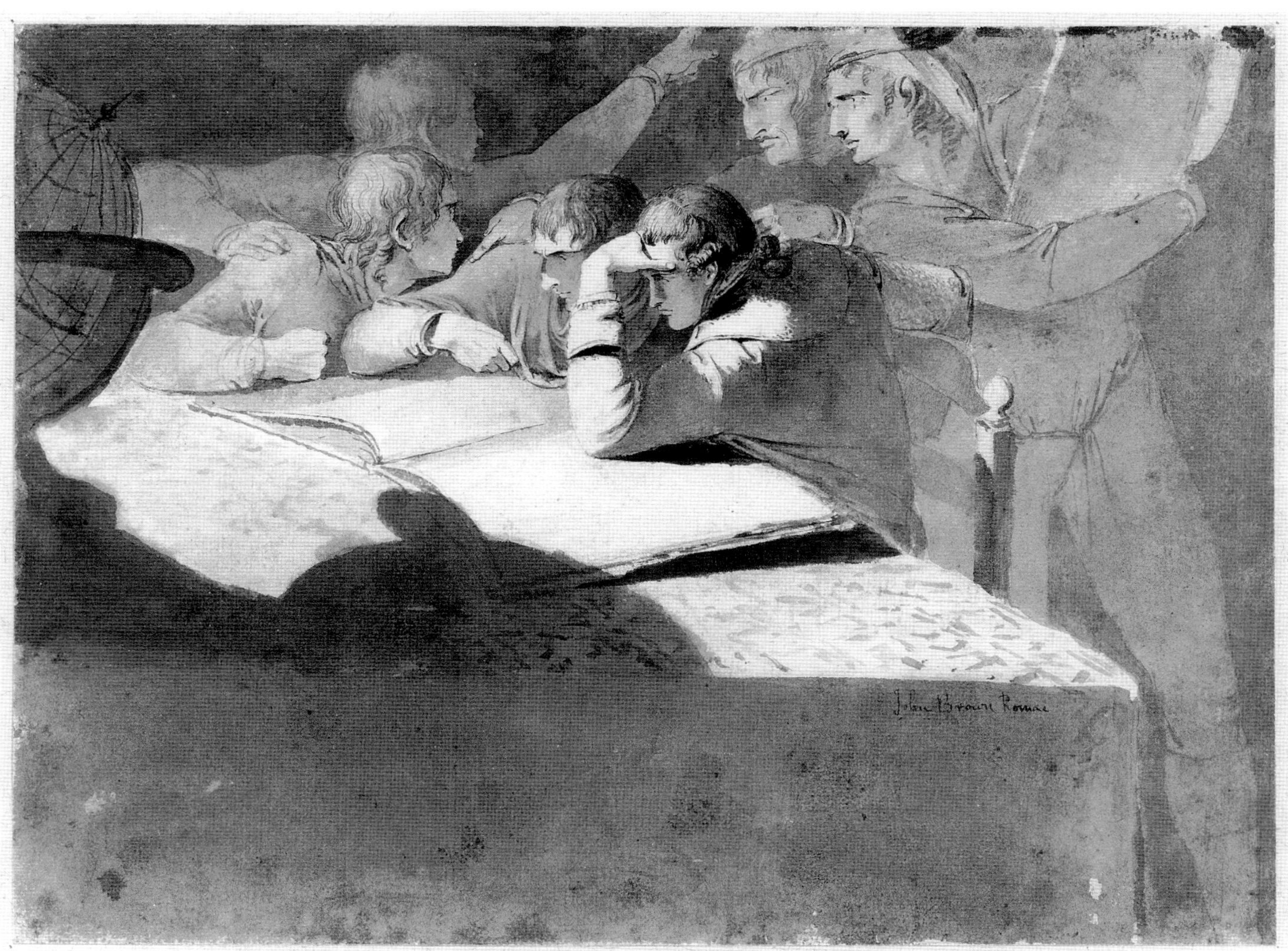

CATALOGUE NO. 7

John Flaxman

1755 York–London 1826

JOHN FLAXMAN'S FATHER was employed making and selling plaster casts and models in London, and the precocious young boy began his studies in his father's workshop, sketching and modeling his father's wares. By age twelve he had begun to exhibit models at the Free Society of Artists in London, and in 1770 he entered the Royal Academy school. Flaxman joined his father as a designer for Josiah Wedgwood in 1775; in 1787 he left for Rome as the company's superintendent in Italy.

Flaxman stayed in Rome for seven years studying ancient and Renaissance art. He was commissioned by well-known collectors of the time and completed the *Fury of Athamas* in 1790 for the bishop of Derry and *Cephalus and Aurora* for Thomas Hope. It was in Italy that Flaxman began his series of drawings illustrating the *Iliad* and the *Odyssey* and, later, the tragedies of Aeschylus and Dante's *Divina Commedia*. All four series were engraved by Tommaso Piroli; three were published in 1793, with the Aeschylus series appearing in 1795.

Flaxman returned to London in 1794 as an influential draftsman and sculptor and worked mainly on monumental sculptures. He became an associate of the Royal Academy in 1797 and a full member in 1800. In 1810 he became a sculpture professor at the Academy, a position he held until his death. LDM

John Flaxman
Leucothea Preserving Ulysses
1792

8
Pen and gray ink over graphite on white wove paper
21.1 x 27.2 cm (8 5/16 x 10 11/16 in.)
Inscribed below the lower margin of the design in ink: *Leucothea Ulysses 34/Swift as a Sea-mew springing from the floods/All radiant on the raft the goddess stood:/Odyssey. 5. line 429.*
Signed and dated to the right of the inscription in pen and ink: *J. Flaxman May 1792*
National Gallery of Canada, Ottawa
(inv. no. 1551)

PROVENANCE
Scott & Fowles, New York, 1919.

John Flaxman's drawings in unshaded outline, and the engravings made after them, represent the most distinctive type of draftsmanship to have developed in Europe at the end of the eighteenth century as a consequence of enthusiasm for the art of the classical past. Ironically, the artist wanted foremost to be remembered as a sculptor, but his illustrations engraved in outline brought him great renown and have remained the works for which he is most esteemed to this day.

Whether the themes are classical myths or Christian subjects derived from early Italian Renaissance art, the images in these outline drawings and engravings are united in formal terms by their great simplicity and economy. Unnecessary descriptive details were eliminated as useless distractions and meaningless demonstrations of virtuosity. It was argued that such a reductive approach brought the artist closer to unadorned truth, whether of the pagan or Christian worlds, a point made repeatedly by Johann Joachim Winckelmann in his *Geschichte der Kunst des Alterthums* (History of ancient art), 1764.

Flaxman first received a commission to design a set of illustrations to the *Iliad* and the *Odyssey* while he was studying in Rome (1787–94). His patron was Mrs. Georgina Hare-Naylor, the daughter of the bishop of Saint Asaph, who met the artist during her tour of Italy. At about the same time a Mr. Udney (probably Robert Fullerton Udney, a fellow of both the Royal Society and the Society of Antiquaries) also commissioned from Flaxman sets of illustrations to Homer's two epics. In the course of working on the two commissions, the artist made preparatory studies such as the present work for the plates.

The drawings for the first commission have remained intact and are today in the Royal Academy, London. Udney's drawings were dispersed at some point and are now identified at times with drawings scattered among various collections; their compositions may vary by comparison with those of the Royal Academy set. Furthermore, in the second group of drawings the figures are lightly modeled in ink wash, somewhat in the manner of bas-relief sculptures (Wark 1970, nos. 16–17; Irwin 1980, 58, pl. 89).

When Flaxman sold to Mrs. Hare-Naylor the drawings now in the Royal Academy, the transaction also included the copyright to all publications of them, a circumstance that the artist later bitterly regretted. The drawings were first engraved in outline by Tommaso Piroli (for the complicated history of the various editions of the Homer illustrations see London 1979b, 184–85).

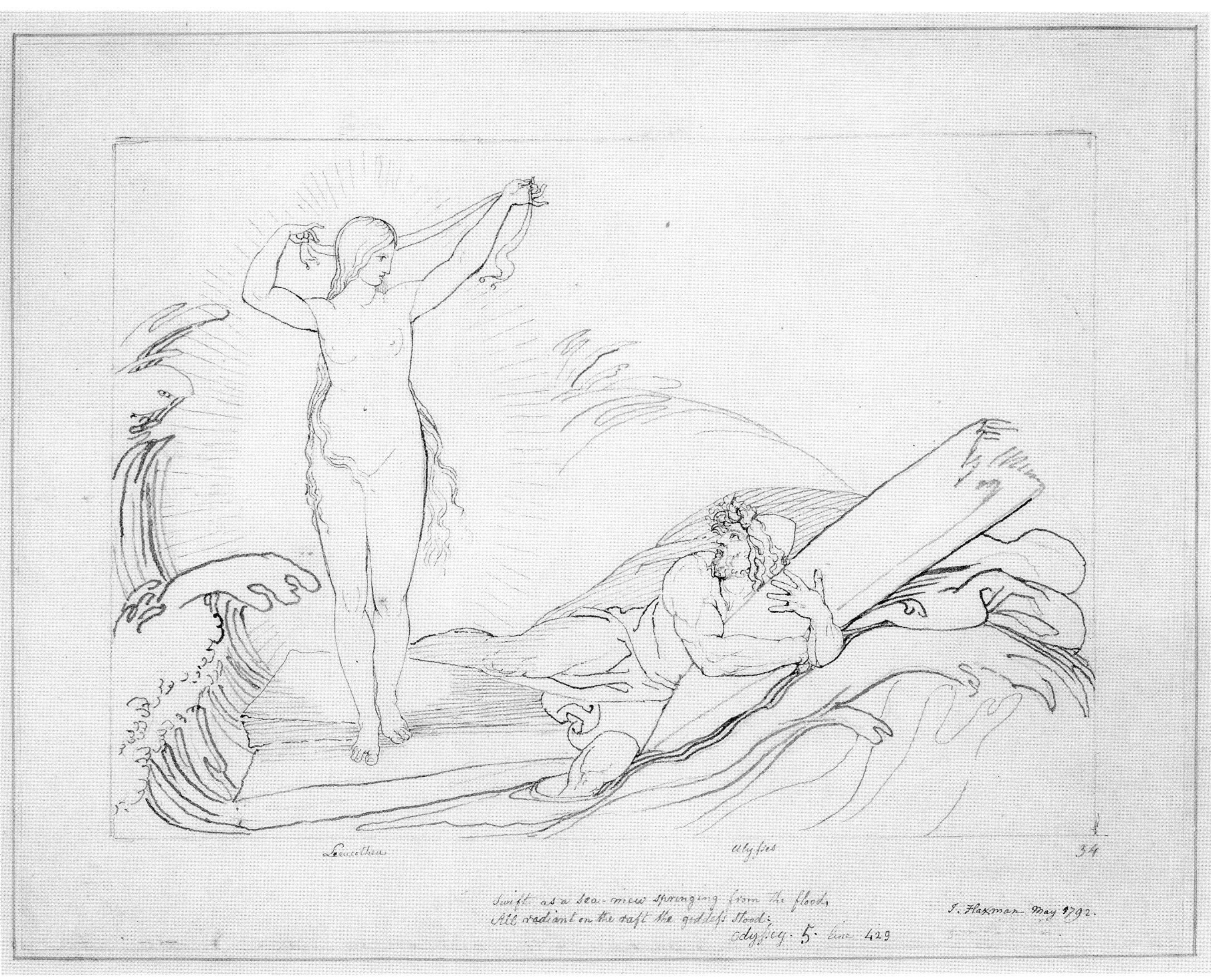

CATALOGUE NO. 8

This drawing illustrates the episode from book 5 of the *Odyssey* in which Leucothea (or Ino), a goddess who protects seafarers, comes to the aid of Ulysses, who is about to be drowned in a torrential storm. To save the hero she offers him a magic veil that will preserve him until he reaches shore. The present work is related to the outline engraving *Leucothea Preserving Ulysses* (pl. 7 of a 1795 edition of the *Odyssey* and pl. 9 of an 1805 edition) but differs from it in a number of respects. In the book illustration Leucothea stands at the center of the composition, with three personifications of the winds on the left and another on the right. Ulysses's posture is basically the same in both works, except that his left foot is visible in the illustration but trails in the water in this study. To judge by these changes, the Ottawa drawing must be a discarded idea for the engraved illustration. The drawing of this subject in the Royal Academy set is virtually identical to the Piroli engraving, except that all four winds are to the left of the goddess (see Essick/La Belle 1977, xxix, pl. 9 for the Piroli engraving). After Flaxman drew the study now in the Royal Academy, he must have made another version of the composition that Piroli followed carefully. The artist may also have made later replicas of the drawings, which he easily could have done by tracing the design from an impression of the engraving. (During Flaxman's lifetime other artists drew copies from his outlines, some of these being quite difficult to distinguish from the artist's own studies.) On the present drawing Flaxman inscribed the appropriate lines from Pope's translation of the *Iliad*, which had been reissued many times throughout the century, including the 1795 and 1805 editions for which he provided the designs.

Fortunately, the gamut of the artist's preparatory work for the Homer illustrations has been preserved. First, Flaxman made sheets of rapidly drawn sketches, usually in pencil. When he was satisfied with a composition, he then went over the figures with pen and ink and marked the small sketch along the margins for transfer to a larger sheet of paper (Wark 1970, nos. 7–15; Essick/La Belle 1977, vii–ix). Other drawings, approximating the dimensions of the engraved plates, may be provisional compositional ideas that were then either revised or discarded. At this stage Flaxman's pen line was tentative, and contours may have been worked over several times until a solution was found that then could be translated into outline drawings to serve as models for the engraver (London 1979b, nos. 97–98, 101). Flaxman thought of his outlines not as an end in themselves but rather as a repository of ideas useful to other artists, whether painters or sculptors. But in the end the elegance and expressive force of his linear designs overrode their potentially utilitarian function.

Unshaded outline drawings became popular throughout Europe and are virtually synonymous with neoclassical draftsmanship (for a full study of this phenomenon see Rosenblum 1976 and Symmons 1984). This style was particularly attractive to artists with an interest in the classical past, since the use of contour or outline could be traced back to the very origins of the representational arts. According to a legend recorded by Pliny the Elder in his *Historia naturalis* (Natural history), the art of painting was accidentally discovered by a Corinthian maiden when she traced in outline the shadow her lover cast on a wall (see CATALOGUE NO. 1; Rosenblum 1957, 279–90). Thus it could be argued that outline was the most ancient, and consequently the truest, mode of representation at an artist's disposal, a position further elaborated by Johann Joachim Winckelmann in his 1755 *Gedanken über die Nachahmung der griechischen Werke in der Malerei und Bildhauerkunst* (Thoughts on the imitation of Greek art in painting and sculpture), in which he stressed the importance of contour over color (Eitner 1970, vol. 1, 10–11). Flaxman's use of unshaded outline designs may well have been stimulated by earlier publications, such as the magnificent four-volume catalogue of antiquities in the collection of Sir William Hamilton published in Naples by Pierre-François Hugues d'Hancarville in 1766–67, which included numerous plates reproducing designs on Greek vases in which the images were created by contour alone against a blank ground. A year prior to the publication of Flaxman's first outline engravings in Rome in 1793, the French artist Bénigne Gagneraux, who spent most of his life working in that city, issued a set of eighteen *éstampes au trait* (etchings in outline), some of which were based on paintings by himself and his brother Claude (London 1979b, no. 223; Rome/Dijon 1983, nos. 70–87), and it is difficult to imagine that Flaxman was unaware of these prints. The Englishman's engravings, however, were the first conceived as original compositions to be executed and published in outline alone, and during his lifetime they enjoyed unrivalled popularity throughout Europe. When Philipp Otto Runge saw Flaxman's Homer illustrations, he particularly admired the nude Leucothea, writing to his brother Daniel on August 23, 1800, "Die ganze Idee is sehr überraschend und leicht" (The entire conception is startling and free; cited in London 1979b, 177). Consequently, it is not unlikely that Runge later recalled Flaxman's illustration when he drew his study *Der Morgen* (Morning), about 1807–8, for a painting in a cycle depicting the four times of day (Kunsthalle, Hamburg; London 1979b, 177, no. 251; see Symmons 1984, 214–15). VC

John Flaxman
Clytemnestra and Aegisthus
Before 1795

9
Pen and brown ink over a faint sketch in graphite on off-white laid paper
26.6 x 39.1 cm (10 1/2 x 15 5/16 in.)
Inscribed at lower center in pencil: *Clytemnestra Aegisthus*
The Pierpont Morgan Library, New York, gift of Miss Louise Crane in memory of Mrs. W. Murray Crane (inv. no. 1975.40.2)
(Los Angeles and Philadelphia only)

PROVENANCE
Louise Crane.

John Flaxman's illustrations to the tragedies of Aeschylus were drawn in Rome about the same time as his designs after Homer's *Iliad* and *Odyssey*. As in that publication, the plates were engraved by Tommaso Piroli, but the first edition of the volume appeared only in 1795, after Flaxman had returned to London. The engraver worked after a set of drawings owned by the dowager Countess Spencer, a cousin of Mrs. Georgina Hare-Naylor, who owned the *Iliad* drawings (see CATALOGUE NO. 8). A number of the Aeschylus drawings are now in the British Museum and the Royal Academy, London (London 1979b, nos. 105–10).

This drawing is related to plate 26 in the volume *Compositions from the Tragedies of Aeschylus Designed by John Flaxman*, titled "Behold this proud oppressor of my country; Choephora," which shows the entwined bodies of Clytemnestra and her lover, Aegisthus, who have been killed by Clytemnestra's son Orestes to avenge their murder of his father, Agamemnon. The engraved illustration includes at the left the figure of Orestes holding a sword and standing over the bodies; at the right is a robed figure that the artist labeled "chorus." A pen and ink drawing of the full composition as it was

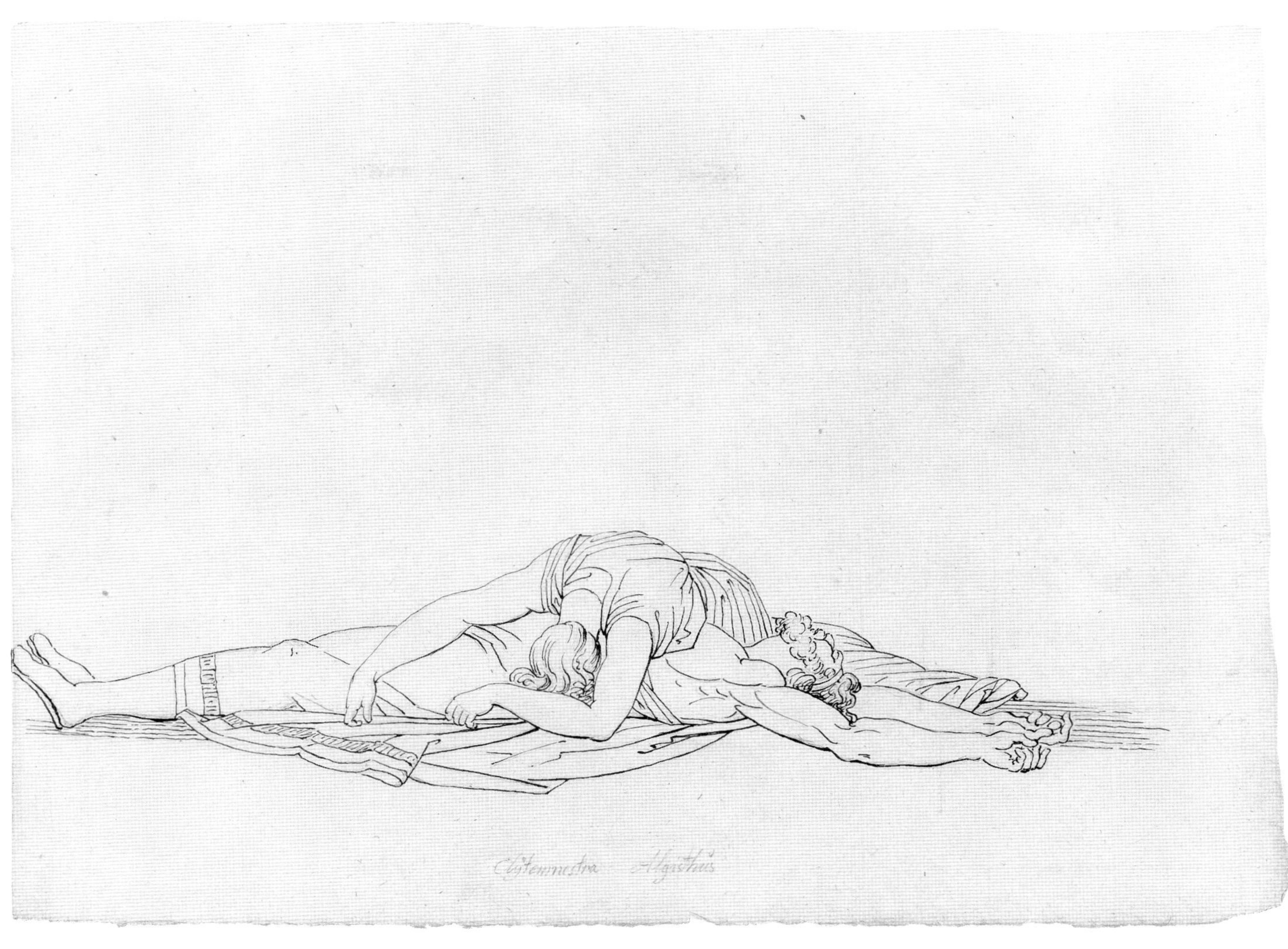

CATALOGUE NO. 9

engraved was on the New York art market (a photograph is preserved at the Henry E. Huntington Art Gallery and Library, San Marino, California).

The Morgan Library drawing is a study for the complicated figure group of Clytemnestra lying across the body of Aegisthus. Flaxman first made a preliminary sketch in graphite, which could easily be erased, before outlining the figures with pen and ink. Evidently the artist wanted to envisage the group separately from the rest of the composition, perhaps to judge his success in solving the difficult problem of representing with outline alone the foreshortened pose of Clytemnestra. He must have been satisfied, since the two figures are repeated in the engraving with only a few minor differences, most notably, their hands are less clearly articulated in the engraving. The ductile quality of the artist's pen lines is particularly effective. Minute variations in the thickness of pen lines establish the spatial relationship of the two figures with a conviction that is lost in the drier, more uniform lines of Piroli's engraving.

Other studies of details for Flaxman's outline composition drawings are known, but this sheet is notable for its power as a self-sufficient composition. The pyramidal figure group inevitably calls to mind a piece of pediment sculpture, and, in fact, the artist did intend that his outline designs be adapted for bas-reliefs to ornament "Sacred and Civil Architecture" (Flaxman in a letter of October 26, 1793, to William Hayley; cited in London 1979b, 86). This hope may have been prompted by his admiration for the panels of sculpture on Roman sarcophagi, because he observed that

the ancient sarcophagi . . . present a magnificent collection of compositions from the great poets of antiquity, Homer, Hesiod, Aeschylus, Euripides and Sophocles. . . . The study of these will give the young artist the true principles of composition, to produce the chief interest of his subject by grand lines of figures, without the intrusion of useless, impertinent, or trivial objects.

VC

John Flaxman
Adoration of the Magi
c. 1796

10
Pen, gray ink and wash over graphite on off-white laid paper
28.2 x 45.9 cm (11 1/8 x 18 1/16 in.)
Yale Center for British Art, New Haven, Paul Mellon Collection (inv. no. B1986.29.524)

PROVENANCE
Denman; sale, April 1876.
C. M. Palgrave.
Morton Morris and Company.

Flaxman's *Adoration of the Magi* is one of four drawings of this subject and composition, executed in imitation of a bas-relief sculpture, the dates and purposes of which are unclear. The earliest of the versions may well be two small brush and ink studies, one in the British Museum, London (Binyon 1900, vol. 2, no. 89b), and another, rapidly executed work in a private collection in California (Santa Barbara 1976, no. 77). The latter corresponds in all major details to the present sheet, which is considerably larger. Here the figures of the Virgin and Child are meticulously finished, although the Magi have been left incomplete, with hands barely indicated. This detail was fully resolved in a second *Adoration of the Magi* drawing in the British Museum, in which the robe of the magus in the foreground is more fully modeled; the drawing is also slightly larger than the present work (London 1979b, no. 145). It is impossible to establish a sequence for the execution of the four drawings because it was frequently the artist's habit to return to earlier ideas and rework them with few or no changes.

In the present drawing Flaxman clearly indicated at the bottom of the composition the shadow that would be cast against a wall by a bas-relief sculpture, and in fact the drawings are connected with such a project. A plaster relief of the composition is in the Sir John Soane Museum, London (Santa Barbara 1976, 82, fig. r); another plaster relief was at University College, London, but was destroyed during the Second World War. Such reliefs of molded plaster were often preparatory to Flaxman's larger works, but in this case there is no evidence that the artist ever executed versions in marble or bronze, nor is there any indication of when either plaster was cast. The large drawings of this composition at Yale and the British Museum are executed with greater detail and considerably more subtlety and refinement in the modeling of surfaces than the surviving plaster in the Soane Museum, thus raising the question whether the drawings might have been done after the sculpture, rather than preparatory to it. David Bindman has observed that the highly finished version in the British Museum is exceptional among Flaxman's drawings (London 1979b, no. 145). It remains uncertain whether Flaxman intended these drawings to serve some purpose (perhaps as a *modello* to show to a client) or whether they were simply virtuoso displays of his mimetic skill.

The figures in Flaxman's drawing are defined in large part by the disposition of their draperies, which fall in a series of rhythmic folds that complement the echoing poses of the kneeling magi. The monumental simplicity of the figures is heightened by the large expanse of blank space behind them, the shallow relief of Flaxman's design emphasizing the essential role of contour to define each figure. The simplified forms in Flaxman's *Adoration of the Magi* undoubtedly owe much to an awareness of Italian fourteenth- and fifteenth-century art that began to occur about this time. Several volumes illustrating works by Masaccio, Giotto, and Perugino appeared as early as the 1770s, such as Thomas Patch's publications after Masaccio's frescoes in the Cappella Brancacci in Santa Maria del Carmine, Florence, 1770, or his eleven plates after Ghiberti's "Gates of Paradise" for the Florentine baptistery, 1774 (Rosenblum 1976, 59–64). It is worth noting that the former volume was illustrated with outline engravings by Tommaso Piroli, who later would engrave Flaxman's *Iliad* and *Odyssey* outline drawings (see CATALOGUE NO. 8).

When a German admirer of Flaxman, the artist Ludwig Schorn, met the older master during a visit to London, Schorn expressed surprise that Flaxman, who was so famous for his designs after Homer and Aeschylus, was occupied with Christian subjects. Flaxman told him (London 1979b, 31):

> *Art in Christianity can rise higher than in paganism, since Christian ideas are more sublime than pagan ones, and the best that the art of Greece and Rome has produced is, to my mind, also contained in Christian ideas. . . . The sublimity of Greek art springs only from the memory of the idea of the single god and of the fall of man, which had remained from older times in the pagan world and which was only again made clear by Christ: truth, grace and the physical beauty of nature can be applied equally well to Christian subjects to be found in the Old and New testaments than in pagan mythology.*

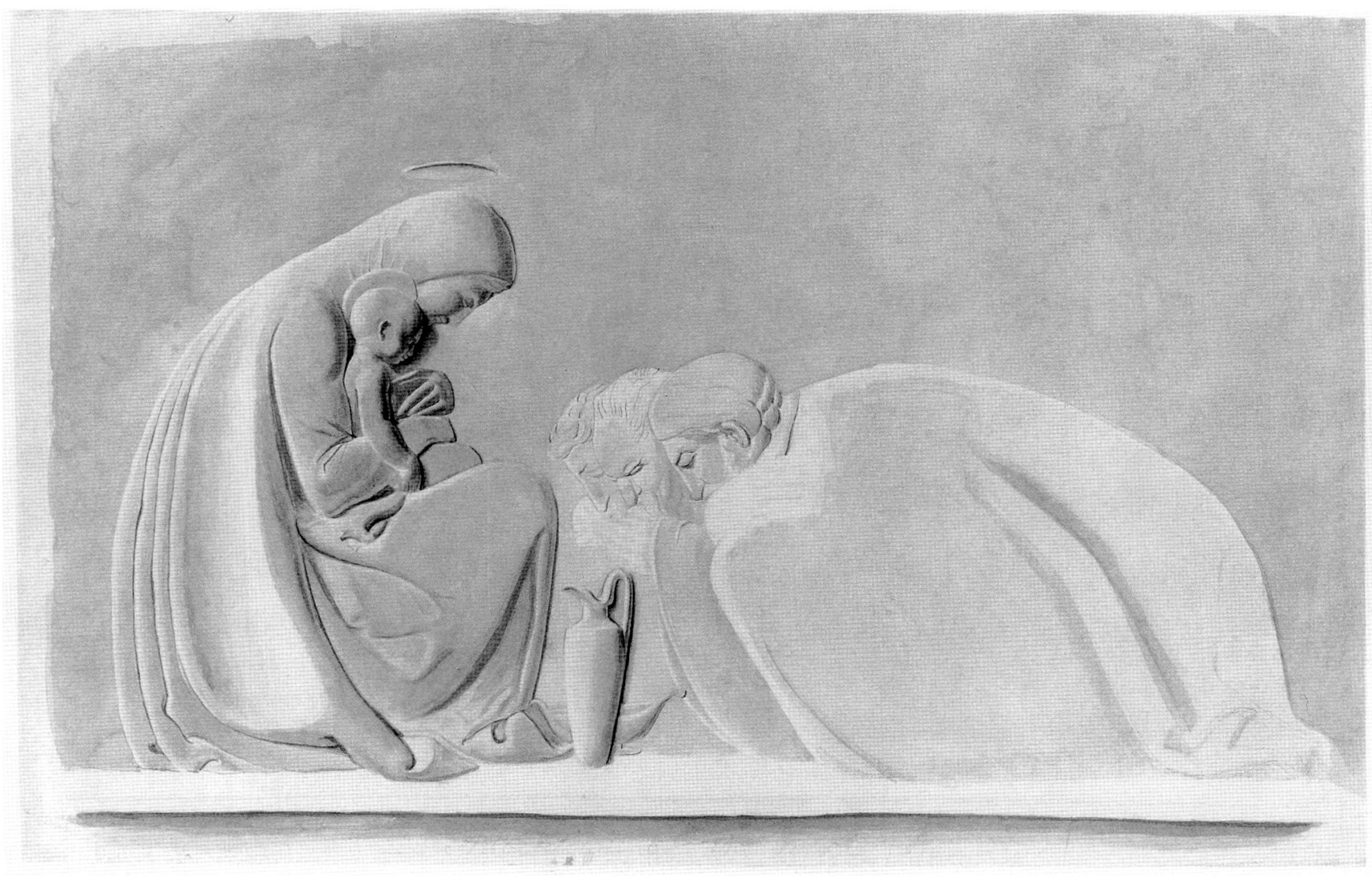

CATALOGUE NO. 10

Although Flaxman's *Adoration of the Magi* cannot be dated with any precision, the style of the composition has analogies to the pen and wash designs the artist prepared as illustrations to *The Eight Acts of Mercy*, 1831, which were issued only after the artist's death as a set of lithographs by F. C. Lewis. When compared to drawings such as *Comfort the Fatherless and the Widow*, the role of draperies in defining the figures is very similar, especially the way in which the folds of the figures' robes echo the contours of their forms. *Comfort the Fatherless* also places the figures against a blank ground with no indication of the setting, and the figures are modeled in shallow relief, as if the composition were a bas-relief (Wark 1970, 48, no. 30). *The Eight Acts of Mercy* was given by Flaxman to his wife on her birthday in 1796, and it is quite possible that the Yale drawing was executed at about the same time. VC

William Blake

1757 London 1827

THE PRECOCIOUS YOUNG Blake began his studies at age ten at Shipley's School under Henry Pars. In 1772 he was apprenticed to the engraver James Basire, where he eventually began work on the drawings for Richard Gough's *Sepulchral Monuments in Great Britain*, 1786–96. His apprenticeship ended, and in 1779 he enrolled in the Royal Academy school as an engraver and met John Flaxman, Henry Fuseli, John Hamilton Mortimer, and Thomas Stothard. Flaxman introduced him to the important patron Mrs. Matthew, who provided a venue for Blake to read his poetry and meet others interested in classical and medieval literature. Mrs. Matthew and Flaxman also financed Blake's first book of poetry, *Poetical Sketches by W. B.*, in 1783.

Blake sent two historical drawings to the Royal Academy in 1785 and followed this up the next year with four more. In 1789 Blake produced his first illuminated books, using a process he invented: *The Book of Thel* and *Songs of Innocence* were executed by drawing the design and the text on one surface, etching away the blank spaces, and hand-coloring the pages. Blake continued to engrave illustrations for his own books as well as those of other authors; in 1795 he executed twelve large color prints of subjects drawn from the Bible, Milton, Shakespeare, and his own writings. His engravings for *The Book of Job*, executed after a set of his own watercolors, were published in 1825. LDM

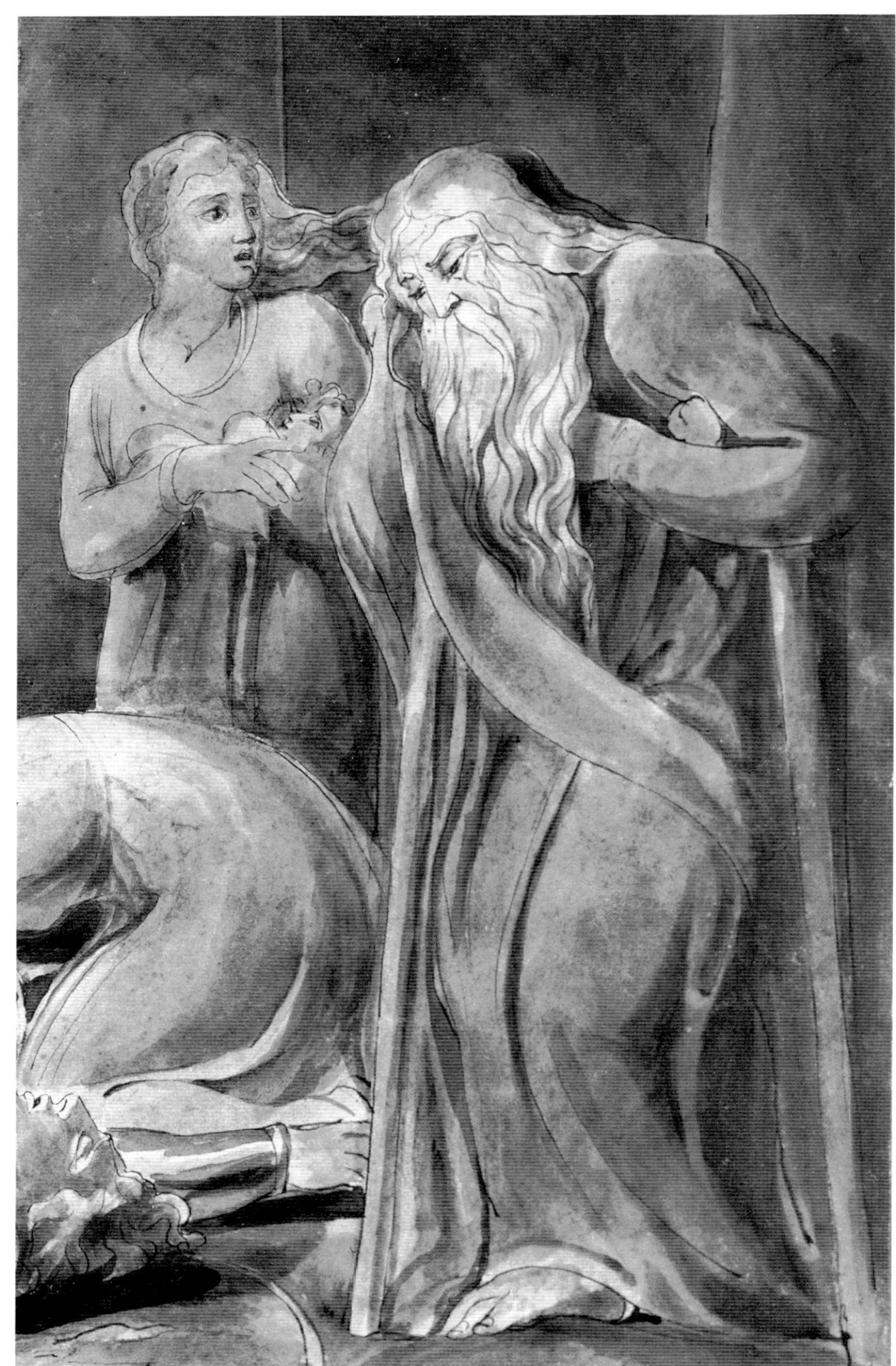

CATALOGUE NO. 11 (detail)

William Blake
A Breach in a City, the Morning after the Battle
c. 1795–1800

11
Pen and black ink, gray wash, and watercolor, with traces of stylus underdrawing on off-white wove paper
32.8 x 47.8 cm (13 x 18 13/16 in.)
Signed at lower right in ink: *W Blake inv. & d'b.r.*
Inscribed at lower right in ink: *A Breach in A City the Morning after the Battle*
Ackland Art Museum, University of North Carolina at Chapel Hill, Ackland Fund (inv. no. 62.16.1)

PROVENANCE
Alfred Aspland, by 1876; sale, Sotheby's, London, January 27, 1885, lot 62 (bought by Pincott).
Henry Young and Sons Ltd., Liverpool, July-August 1900, 8.
Quaritch, London, 1904, no. 313, and March 1904, no. 228.
W. Graham Robertson, 1904; sale, Christie's, London, July 22, 1949, lot 53 (bought by Agnew's).
H. C. Green; sale, Sotheby's, London, October 18, 1961, no. 14 (bought by Osmond).
Kerrison Preston.
Martin Breslauer, London, catalogue 96, 1962, no. 18.

EXHIBITED
London 1876, no. 157.
London 1906, no. 60.
Cambridge 1910.
London, Tate Gallery, on loan c. 1939–49.
London 1947, no. 75.
Bournemouth 1949, no. 15.
London 1950–51, no. 443.
London 1951–52, no. 521.
Charlotte 1963.
Lexington 1967, no. 37.
Raleigh 1967, no. 1.
Chapel Hill 1969, no. 69.
Chapel Hill 1975, no. 4, pl. 18.
Chapel Hill 1976.
New Haven 1979, no. 140.
Chapel Hill 1982.
Chapel Hill 1984, no. 2.
Chapel Hill 1990–91.

LITERATURE
Autotype, English Picture Publishing Company, 1876.
Rossetti 1880, 201, 208, no. 5.
Richter 1906.
The Bookman 30 (September 1906).
Gilchrist 1907, 54, 64, 415, no. 5.
Binyon 1922, 23, pl. 2.
Preston 1952, 175–77, no. 70, pl. 56.
Blunt 1959, 10–11, pl. 8b.
The Burlington Magazine 103, no. 703 (October 1961): i.
The Art Quarterly 25 (1962): 400, 407.
Detroit/Philadelphia 1968, 160.
Erdman 1969, 19, 75.
Schlumberger 1972, no. 62.
Mellor 1974, 107–8.
Bindman 1977, 31–32, 231 n. 19, pl. 59 (incorrectly identified as the version in the Fogg Art Museum).
Butlin 1978, 36–37.
Butlin 1981, no. 191, pl. 196.

William Blake's attitude toward the art of the classical past was ambivalent. At one point he wrote to the amateur artist and poet George Cumberland about "the immense flood of Grecian light and glory" that was sweeping across Europe. On other occasions he compared classical works of art unfavorably to those from the Middle Ages (Blunt 1943, 196). During Blake's years of apprenticeship to the engraver James Basire he most likely participated in the engraving of book illustrations for publications such as Jacob Bryant's *A New System, or, An Analysis of Ancient Mythology*, 1774–76 and 1775–76 (Easson/Essick 1979, vol. 2, 1–7). Later he contributed engravings to James Stuart and Nicholas Revett's *The Antiquities of Athens, Volume the Third*, 1794, as well as to George Cumberland's *Thoughts on Outline*, 1796, and his *Outlines from the Ancients*, 1829 (Easson/Essick 1979, 103–4, 109–12).

Blake was very much aware of Flaxman's outline drawings, in fact he made thirty-seven line engravings after Flaxman as illustrations to an 1817 edition of Hesiod's *Theogony* (London 1979b, 128, figs. 63a–b). The two artists knew one another, and it is not surprising to find Flaxman paying homage to Blake in a sheet of sketches drawn from memory after three Blake drawings. More importantly, as David Bindman noted (London 1979b, 78), "it is revealing that Blake should have been in Flaxman's mind at the time he was beginning work on the *Homer* and *Dante* outlines." In the

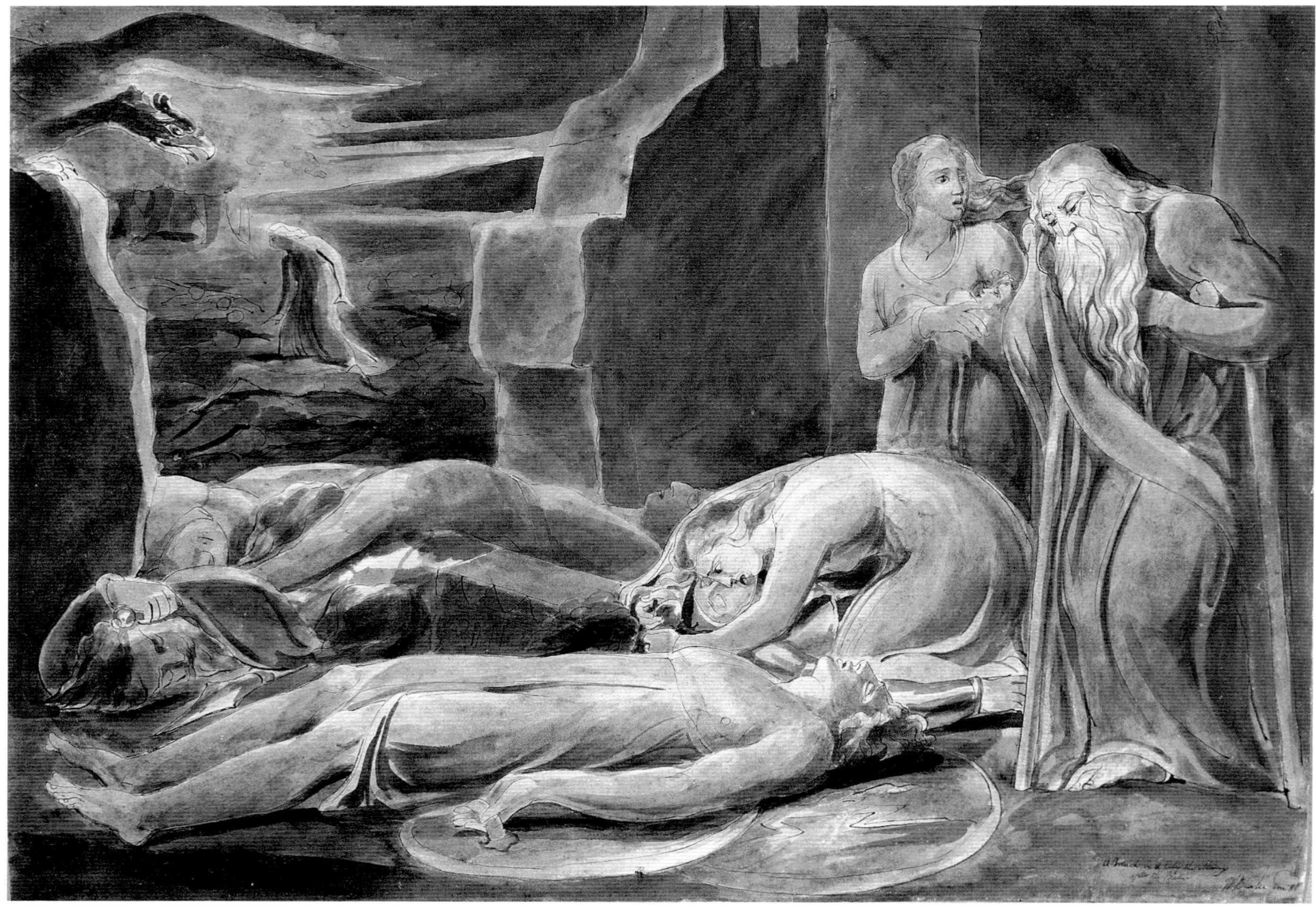

CATALOGUE NO. 11

main, Blake's interest in antique art was confined to small-scale works such as engraved gems or vase painting, excepting the engraving Blake executed after the Laocoön (Essick 1983, no. 19, figs. 51–53; a preparatory drawing for the print was recently acquired by the Yale Center for British Art). Blake knew about the classical past primarily through casts or reproductive engravings (since the artist never left Britain to study in Italy) and his own copy of *Reflections on the Painting and Sculpture of the Greeks*, Fuseli's translation of Winckelmann's *Gedanken über die Nachahmung der griechischen Werke in der Malerei und Bildhauerkunst*, published in London in 1765.

Ancient works of art were only one source of inspiration for Blake's development. He revered medieval art and the work of Michelangelo, whose influences in the creation of the artist's idiosyncratic style are obvious. Blake, like his compatriots Flaxman and Fuseli, found in classical art means of expression and motifs that could be taken up at will concurrently with references to the Middle Ages or the Renaissance.

In Blake's mature art classical works seldom appear in obvious quotations, although at times he assimilated references to his earlier studies after antiquities. A watercolor titled *A Breach in a City, the Morning after Battle* was exhibited by Blake at the Royal Academy in 1784; the present drawing has sometimes been identified with that work, although more recently a later date of about 1795–1800 has been proposed (Butlin 1981, no. 191). The gruesome scene shows the aftermath of battle, when the women come to search for their dead. At the right an old, bearded man woefully clasps his hands, while beside him a woman looks away, perhaps repelled by the slaughter. A second woman is bent nearly double as she despairingly embraces a dead man in battle armor. A gap in the city wall affords a view of the battlefield, where a distraught woman wanders among the fallen soldiers. A bird of prey in the upper left emphasizes the desolation of the scene. *A Breach in a City* has a complex iconography with references to the senseless consequences wrought by warmongering despots who would sacrifice their own subjects (Detroit/Philadelphia 1968, 159–60). Around 1780 Blake wrote several poems based on similar episodes from earlier British history, the reign of Edward III (1327–77) and his wars against the Scots and the French. A contemporary reader of Blake might have found implied in his writing an analogy to George III's recent oppression of the American colonies (Detroit/Philadelphia 1968, 159). Blake may have intended that such poems and watercolors be read as indictments of topical events, but the figures here are generalized beyond historical identification. The mourning woman in the foreground is shown in profile, the better to emphasize her classically regular features. The emphatic horizontality of the foreground figures inevitably carries with it the memory of classical bas-reliefs. Here Blake has carried linear stylization to an extreme degree, particularly in the figure of the kneeling woman, whose arched back recalls similar figures in earlier works by Romney and Fuseli. It has been suggested that in a general way Blake based his composition on a painting by Gavin Hamilton, *Andromache Mourning the Death of Hector*, which had been engraved by Domenico Cunego in 1764 (see FIGURE 4). In this watercolor, however, Blake has carefully avoided any historicizing references, with the result that the work is basically a commentary on the miseries of war, presented outside specific time and circumstance (Rosenblum 1976, 102–4).

There are at present three versions known of *A Breach in a City*. Blake's original submission to the Royal Academy in 1784 is now lost (Butlin 1981, no. 188). Probably about 1790–95 Blake drew the version now in the Museum of Art, Carnegie Institute, Pittsburgh (Butlin 1981, no. 189, pl. 195), followed by this watercolor. In 1805 he returned to the composition, which he considerably modified; this work is in the Fogg Art Museum, Harvard University, as part of the Grenville I. Winthrop Bequest (Butlin 1981, no. 195, pl. 193). VC

Richard Westall

1765 Hertford–London 1836

RICHARD WESTALL MOVED to London in 1779 and was apprenticed to a silver engraver until 1784. He exhibited at the Royal Academy from 1784 until his death and entered the Academy school in 1785. An accomplished watercolorist, he painted *Easu Seeking Jacob's Blessing* and *Mary Queen of Scots Going to Execution* in that medium. Westall painted five subjects for publisher John Boydell's Shakespeare Gallery and was a successful book illustrator, producing an edition of John Milton's works and a very popular version of the Bible. He was accepted as a full member of the Royal Academy in 1794, and late in his career he became the drawing master to Princess Victoria. LDM

Richard Westall
Fingal and Conban-Carglas
c. 1795–1805

12
Watercolor on off-white laid paper
50 x 58.1 cm (19 11/16 x 22 7/8 in.)
Princeton University Libraries, Department of Rare Books and Special Collections

PROVENANCE
Robert H. Taylor.

EXHIBITED
Princeton 1981, 85.

The subject of Westall's watercolor is based on an incident in *Fingal, An Ancient Epic Poem, In Six Books*, first published in 1762, which purported to be a translation of some of the earliest known Scottish poetry by Ossian, the son of Finn (or Fingal). James Macpherson claimed to have collected the verses while traveling in Scotland. After Macpherson's death a commission was formed, in 1805, to examine the authenticity of the poems, and it was found that Macpherson had fabricated them. Nonetheless, the imagery of the poetry created many German enthusiasts, among them Klopstock, Abel, Schiller, and Goethe, while in France Napoleon was a great admirer of the Ossianic legends, which became the basis for major paintings by Baron François Gérard (1801) and Anne-Louis Girodet de Roussy-Trioson (1801; see FIGURE 47). Something of Macpherson's intent behind the creation of this literary hoax may be deduced from his foreword to volume 2 of his *Works of Ossian*:

> *Without derogating from the fame of Greece and Rome, we may consider antiquity beyond the pale of their empire worthy of some attention. The nobler passions of the mind never shoot forth more free and unrestrained than in these times we call barbarous. That irregular manner of life, and those manly pursuits from which barbarity takes its name, are highly favorable to a strength of mind unknown in polished times.*

Not only did the author want to establish that the earliest writings of so-called primitive races such as the Celts merited comparison with Greek and Roman classics, but in addition he maintained that these early races possessed unique qualities that were actually superior to the "exalted manners" of Mediterranean cultures: "Their language is pure and original, and their manners are those of an ancient and unmixed race of men."

In spite of the dubious assumptions and chauvinistic character of Macpherson's arguments, the Ossianic legends were a rich source of pictorial subject matter (for a well-illustrated and documented study of this topic see Hamburg 1974). Somewhat ironically, however, the vast majority of artists using Ossianic themes still chose for the figures of their Gaelic heroes and gods the familiar typologies derived from classical Greek and Roman art.

Westall's watercolor illustrates this dilemma. He chose an incident from the poem "Cath-Loda," in which Fingal discovers hiding in a cave Conban-Carglas, daughter of Torcul-Torno, king of Crathlun, a district in Sweden, who had been killed in battle by Starno, the ruler of the neighboring territory. Macpherson goes on to relate that Starno had "confined [her] in a cave, near the palace of Gormal, where on account of her cruel treatment, she became distracted." Westall depicts Conban-Carglas relating her plight to Fingal.

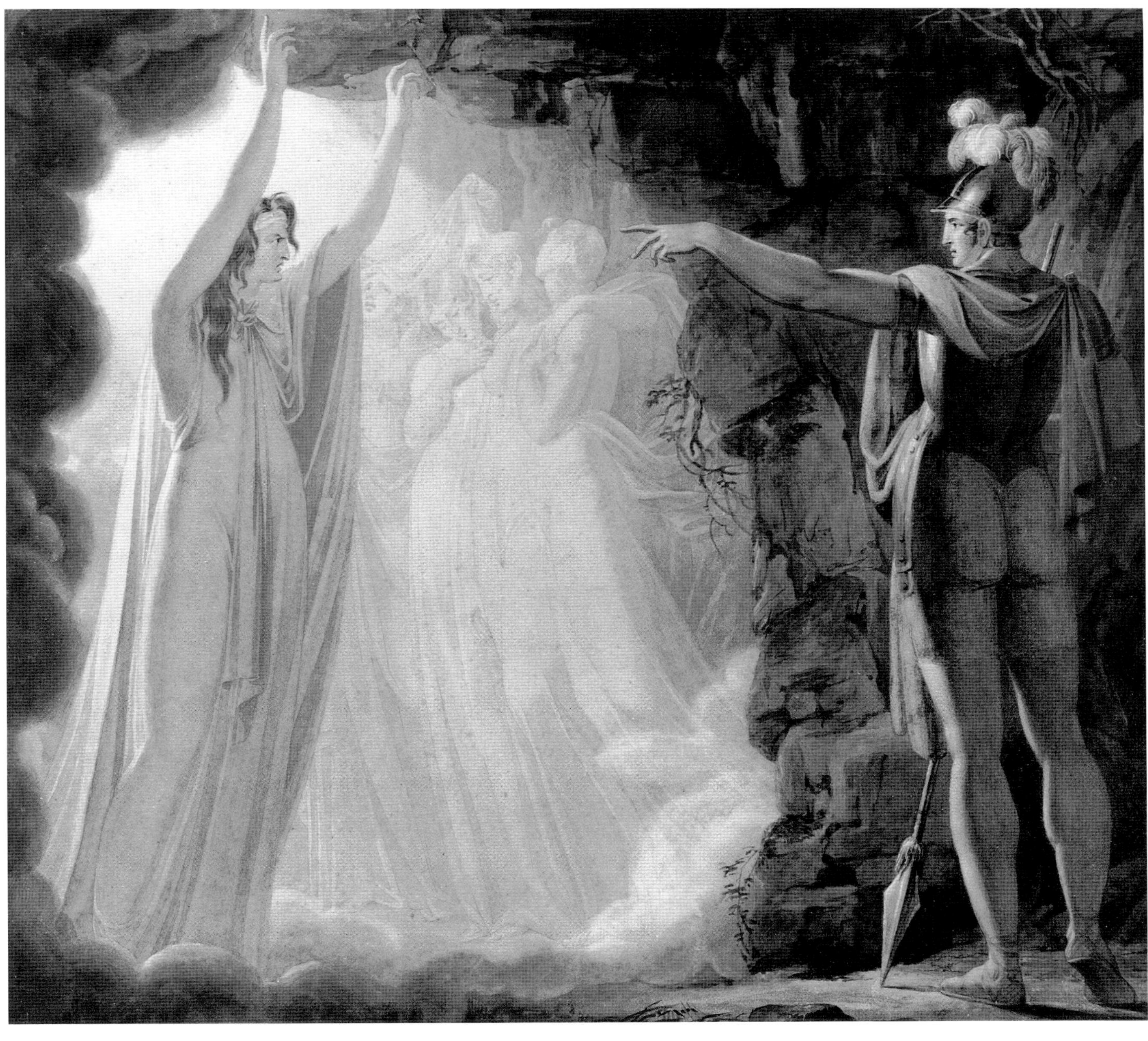

CATALOGUE NO. 12

Perhaps Westall knew Alexander Runciman's etching of this subject, based on the latter's Ossianic cycle at Penicuik House, near Edinburgh, which must have been completed by 1773 (New Haven 1979, 12, no. 8). Both artists represented Fingal as a Roman warrior, but the more sedate pose of Westall's figure is reminiscent of antiquities such as the statue of Pompey in Palazzo Spada, Rome, which at this period rivaled in fame celebrated sculptures such as the Apollo Belvedere, the Hercules of Glycon, and the Gladiator of Agasias (Haskell/Penny 1981, 296–98, no. 73, fig. 156). Westall went beyond simply using for his hero a pose that an educated viewer would readily associate with Roman art and dressed Fingal in specifically classical apparel, such as his plumed helmet. It is not known what sources Westall used for his knowledge of these details, since he did not go to Italy. But as a pupil at and, later, member of the Royal Academy in London he would have had access to its library of illustrated books on Greek and Roman art, its collection of casts of antique sculpture, and its lectures on various aspects of classical art.

Westall was better known for his watercolors than his canvases, and his finished works on paper, such as this example, together with his activity as a book illustrator, constitute the major part of his work. We do not know whether Westall executed the watercolor as part of a project to illustrate Ossian's poetry; the drawing may well be an independent work. VC

Stephen Francis Dutilh Rigaud

1777 London 1861

STEPHEN RIGAUD ENTERED the Royal Academy school in 1792 and first exhibited there in 1797. He won a gold medal for *Clytemnestra Exulting over Agamemnon* in 1801. Primarily known for his watercolors, he was one of the eight original members of the Society of Painters in Water-Colours in 1804; he exhibited with this group until he and others seceded in 1813. Little is known about his life after this point; he had a very long career and exhibited at the British Institution from 1806 to 1818 and again in 1850–52. LDM

Stephen Francis Dutilh Rigaud
Lucifer at the Bower of Adam and Eve
c. 1805

13
Watercolor over graphite on off-white wove paper
62.8 x 48 cm (21 3/4 x 16 3/4 in.)
The Minneapolis Institute of Arts, the David M. Daniels Fund, 1971 (inv. no. 71.53)

PROVENANCE
Alister Mathews, Bournemouth.

Book 4 of Milton's *Paradise Lost* contains a lengthy description of Adam and Eve in the garden of Eden (4.780–820), where Lucifer (or Satan) jealously observes their mutual happiness and their delight in such bountiful surroundings. He conceives a plot to destroy their bliss by whispering to Eve as she sleeps,

. . . distemperd, discontented thoughts,
Vaine hopes, vaine aimes, inordinate desires
Blown up with high conceits ingendring
pride.

But the angel Gabriel is aware that Lucifer is roaming through the garden and dispatches Ithuriel and Zephron, armed with spears, in search of the monster. They find him hovering over the sleeping couple, but he is startled and leaps back at the touch of Ithuriel's weapon. Rigaud's watercolor illustrates the moment when the two angels confront Lucifer, who recoils in anger. It is tempting to suggest that the present watercolor might be identical to *Satan in the Bower of Adam and Eve*, which the artist exhibited in 1805 at the inaugural exhibition of the Society of Painters in Water-Colours. Although Rigaud was one of the founding members of the Society, the catalogue description of his contributions is too brief to establish such an identification (Bryan 1904, vol. 4, 235; Hardie 1967, 113–14).

Works of art illustrating subjects from the works of Milton were very popular in Britain at the time, the most extensive and striking series being Henry Fuseli's Milton Gallery, more than forty canvases first exhibited in London in 1799 and again the next year. Among the subjects painted by Fuseli was *Satan Starts from the Touch of Ithuriel's Spear*. The painting is now lost but is known from a preparatory oil sketch and two engravings, one of which was included in F. J. Du Roverays's illustrated edition of *Paradise Lost*, which appeared in 1802 (Schiff 1973, nos. 895, 1212, 1301). Rigaud may have seen Fuseli's exhibition, and it is certainly likely that he would have read the 1802 volume with Fuseli's illustrations before essaying his own version. Rigaud's watercolor lacks the demonic fury of Fuseli's conception, although Lucifer's scowling profile is so like the Swiss artist's representation of the fiend as to suggest that he knew Fuseli's work. But the general posture of Rigaud's Lucifer, with his feet firmly planted on the ground, is more reminiscent of an etching of another Miltonic subject, James Barry's *Satan and His Legions Hurling Defiance toward the Vault of Heaven*, printed about 1792–94 (London 1983, 107, no. 50). The bold stance and dramatic gestures of both Rigaud's and Barry's demons were surely inspired by the often-engraved statues of the Dioscuri on the Quirinal Hill in Rome, even though both British artists exaggerate the figure's musculature, no doubt influenced by the example of Michelangelo.

In Britain artists were less ready to accept Winckelmann's stricture that representation of emotional extremes distorted the ideal harmony and balance of features found only when the face was in repose. Many Northern artists were unsympathetic to this position; they found in classical literature or the heritage of their own national writers a rich trove of dramatic subjects that contradicted the German historian's highly subjective characterization of antique art's most eminent characteristic, its "noble simplicity and quiet grandeur." VC

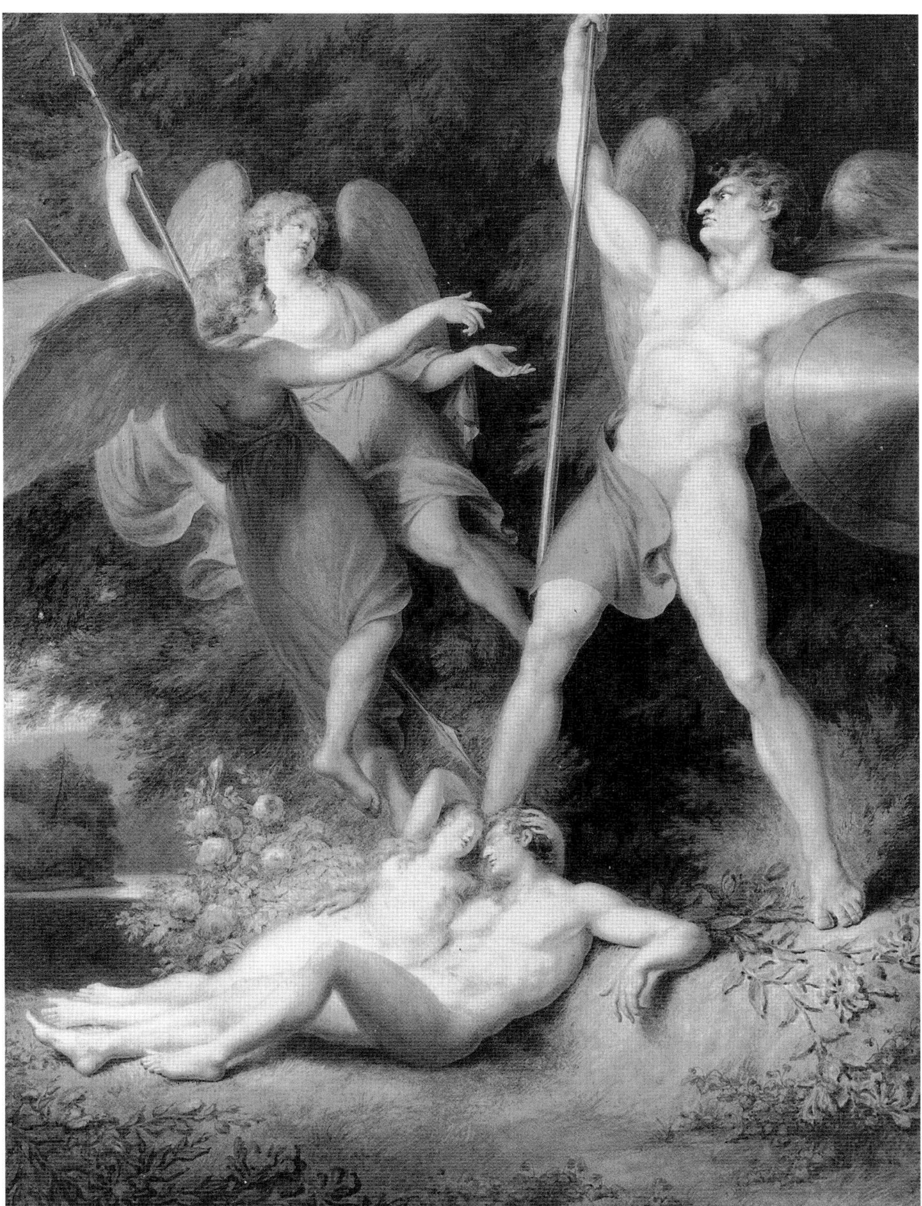

CATALOGUE NO. 13 (see color plate on page 98)

French Drawings

Joseph-Marie Vien

1716 Montpellier–Paris 1809

VIEN BEGAN HIS studies in 1740 at the Académie in Paris with Charles-Joseph Natoire and won the Prix de Rome on his first attempt, in 1743. He spent the next six years in Italy studying the Renaissance masters and classical antiquity and participated in the excavations at Herculaneum. After his return to Paris he was admitted to the Académie in 1754 with his *Daedalus and Icarus* (*Dédale et Icare*). *The Merchant of Cupids* (*La Marchande d'amours*), based on an ancient Roman wall painting and exhibited in the 1763 Salon, was a seminal work in the new style "à la grecque."

Vien's most important role was as a teacher. He was a full professor at the Académie in 1759 and became the director of the École Royale des Élèves Protégés in 1771. Serving as director of the Académie de France à Rome from 1775 until 1781, he restored strict discipline and a traditional curriculum. When he returned to Paris he was appointed *premier peintre du roi* and, in 1789, director of the Académie. Vien continued to paint throughout the Revolution. Although he lost his royal appointments in 1792, he was personally protected as the teacher and close associate of Jacques-Louis David. He flourished under Napoleon, who made him a senator in 1799 and a count in 1808. LDM

Joseph-Marie Vien
Maiden Offering Incense before a Statue of Juno
c. 1780–85

14
Oil paint over pen and brown ink, brush and brown wash on paper mounted on canvas
32 x 39 cm (12 5/8 x 15 3/8 in.)
The Metropolitan Museum of Art, New York, Van Day Truex Fund, 1983 (inv. no. 1983.429)
(Philadelphia and Minneapolis only)

PROVENANCE
Possibly Vien sale, Paris, May 17, 1809, and following days, part of lot 94 ("Esquisses sur papier, sujets grecs . . . une Vestale versant de l'encens sur le feu d'un autel").
Sale, Angers, April 30, 1980, lot 261 (attributed to Jean-Baptiste-Marie Pierre).

LITERATURE
New York: The Metropolitan Museum of Art. *Annual Report of the Trustees*, 1983–84, 24.
Bean 1986, 273, no. 308.
Gaehtgens/Lugand 1988, no. 39a.

This dashing oil sketch may have been among the works sold after Vien's death. His estate included several oil sketches on paper of "Greek subjects," one described as a vestal virgin burning incense at an altar; unfortunately, it cannot now be determined if this composition was once part of that group. The scene represented is very likely one of the festivals or rites that were held in honor of Juno, the wife of Jupiter. The goddess, who can be identified by the peacock at her side, is most customarily identified with the life of women, especially in ceremonies having to do with marriage and fertility. This is evidently the general theme of Vien's sketch, since only women and children are present to perform the ceremonies in homage to the goddess.

The figures in Vien's composition are dominated by the severely organized architecture of a vast temple, where the strong verticals of columns and pilasters reinforce the organization of the women into three groups. The austerity of the setting also enhances the solemnity of the event. Although this work cannot be precisely dated, it has been suggested by Thomas Gaehtgens and Jacques Lugand (1988, no. 39a) that it was executed about the first half of the 1780s. This seems reasonable from a comparison with Vien's paintings from that period, which often incorporate imposing architectural details, the placement of which echoes the positions of the major figures.

No artist of the time made a greater or more consistent success of "sujets grecs" or "sujets à l'antique" than Vien. The Salon of 1763 assured his reputation in this specialty, with Denis Diderot characterizing him in his commentary on that year's exhibition as "Apelle ressuscité au milieu d'une troupe d'Athéniennes" (Apelles reborn, surrounded by women of Athens) for paintings such as *Priestess Burning Incense in a Tripod* (*Une Prêtresse brûle de l'encens sur un trépied*; Musée des Beaux-Arts, Strasbourg) or *The Merchant of Cupids* (*La Marchande d'amours*; Fontainebleau), the latter based literally on a recently discovered Roman fresco at Stabiae, which had been reproduced the year before in an engraving in the third volume of *Le pitture antiche d'Ercolano* (Naples, 1755–92, this volume 1762; see Paris 1984–85, nos. 120–21). Quite probably Vien turned to this source at the advice of the comte de Caylus, at this time one of the most vociferous proponents of the superiority of ancient painting. The recovery of the Roman wall paintings was by no means greeted with unanimous enthusiasm, because the frescos were in poor condition, which made it difficult to judge the painters' command of such skills as mastery of perspective and chiaroscuro; nonetheless,

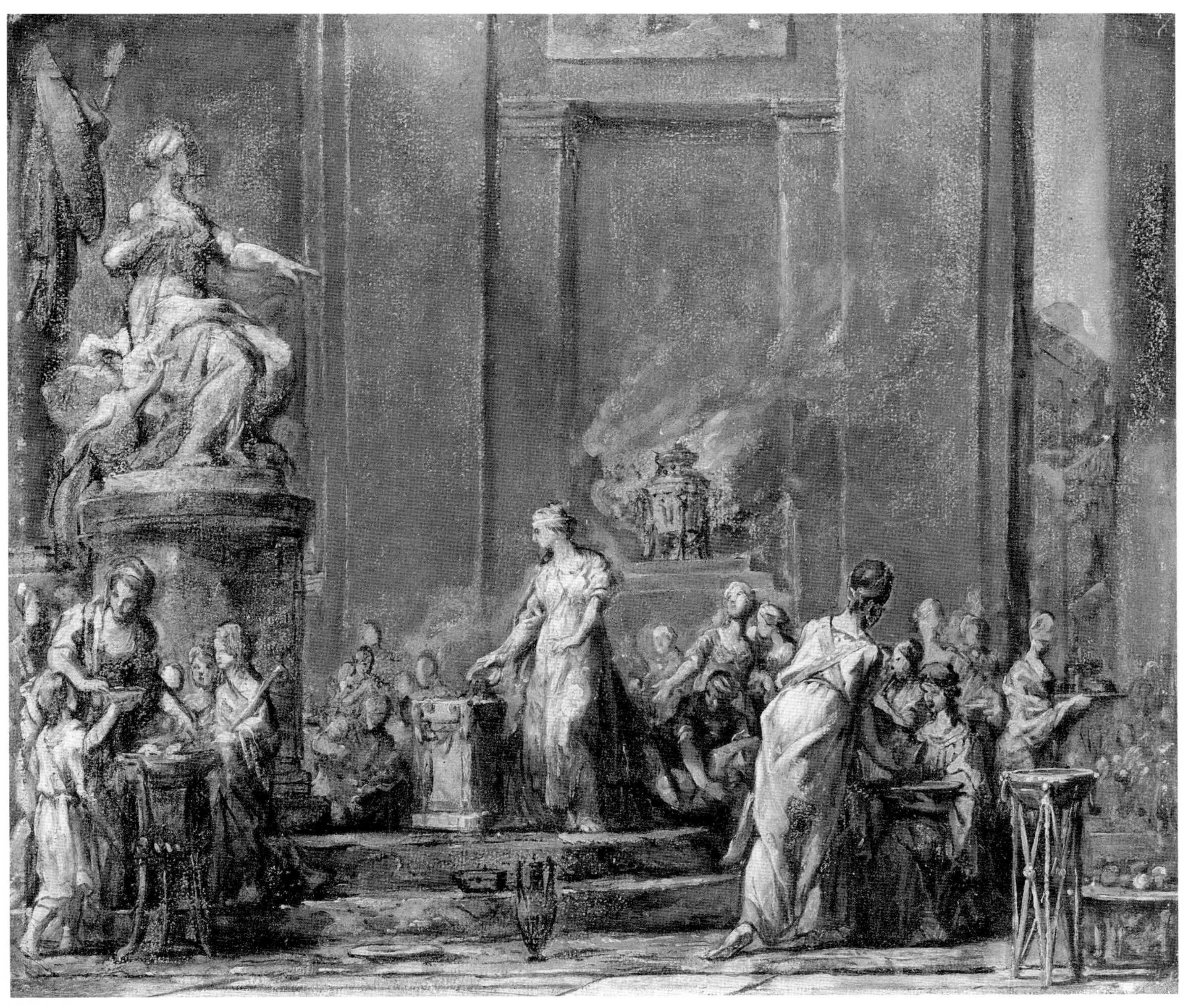

CATALOGUE NO. 14

in Caylus's opinion contemporary artists would benefit by studying them (Michel 1984, 105–17).

Toward the end of Vien's life it was recognized that the elder artist had set French painting on a new path that assured a return to its former glory and prestige. One of the best summaries of Vien's importance is contained in a list of important French artists compiled in 1800 and addressed to Napoleon. At the head of the list is Vien: "He is the father of the new school whose leader is David; Vien was the first to perceive that it was necessary to abandon the road traveled by the Bouchers, the Van Loos, etc., and to study only nature, antiquity, and the great masters of the various Italian schools" (Paris 1984–85, 410). VC

Joseph-Marie Vien
Love Adorned for His Triumph
1796

15
Pen and black ink, brush and brown wash on laid white paper
20.3 x 28.3 cm (8 x 11 1/8 in.)
Signed and dated below the niche at left in pen and black ink: *Vien 1796*
The Detroit Institute of Arts, Founders Society purchase, William H. Murphy Fund (inv. no. 34.135)

PROVENANCE
Edward Speelman, London, 1934.

EXHIBITED
Cleveland 1964, no. 31.

LITERATURE
Scheyer 1941, 191, fig. 1.
Rouen 1970, no. 48.
Paris/Detroit/New York 1974–75, 122.
Breazeale 1980, 458.
Gaehtgens/Lugand 1988, no. 163.

In 1792 Vien lost the position of *premier peintre* to Louis XVI—a post to which he had just been appointed on May 30, 1789—and, in consequence, an important source of income. The Revolution was a period of great hardship for many artists, who saw their sources of patronage literally cease to exist. Vien feared for his own safety, with good reason, because persons once associated with the crown were often viewed with suspicion and might be persecuted for that reason alone. The artist related that as a distraction from these worries he made three series of drawings: *Games of Nymphs and Cupids* (*Jeux des nymphes et des amours*), c. 1793–96 (Gaehtgens/Lugand 1988, nos. 144–81), *The Vicissitudes of War* (*Les Vicissitudes de la guerre*), 1795 (nos. 188–96), and *The Joys of Life, or The Union of Hymen and Love* (*Le Bonheur de la vie ou l'Union de l'Hymen et de l'Amour*), 1797–99 (nos. 197–253).

The present work was originally part of the first series, which contained twenty drawings, according to Vien's *Mémoires* (manuscript preserved in the Musée des Beaux-Arts, Béziers; published in Gaehtgens/Lugand 1988, 321–24). Only sixteen sheets are known today, in various public and private collections. Recently twenty-two smaller preparatory sketches for these compositions—several of which were not developed for the finished series—were given by the artist's descendants to the Musée des Beaux-Arts, Béziers; among them is a study for the Detroit drawing. The two sheets are identical in all major respects, although the rapidly executed study lacks the figures of the two standing nymphs offering wreaths to the hovering putto. The final, highly finished drawing is typical of Vien's late style in its finely detailed, virtuoso command of line, with discrete touches of ink wash used to define spatial relationships. The tight control so evident in Vien's pen drawings is a consistent aspect of his draftsmanship. Pen, brush, and ink were the artist's preferred media throughout his career. In general, Vien's manner of working was quite painstaking, whether on canvas or paper. Some contemporary critics praised his careful execution as a reflection of his scrupulous recreation of antiquity, although others found the artist's figures excessively reserved and lacking in vivacity.

The *Games of Nymphs and Cupids* drawings typify Vien's evocation of a serene antique world, an Arcadia of pleasure and amusing distractions. In this composition, also called *Love Decked with Flowers*

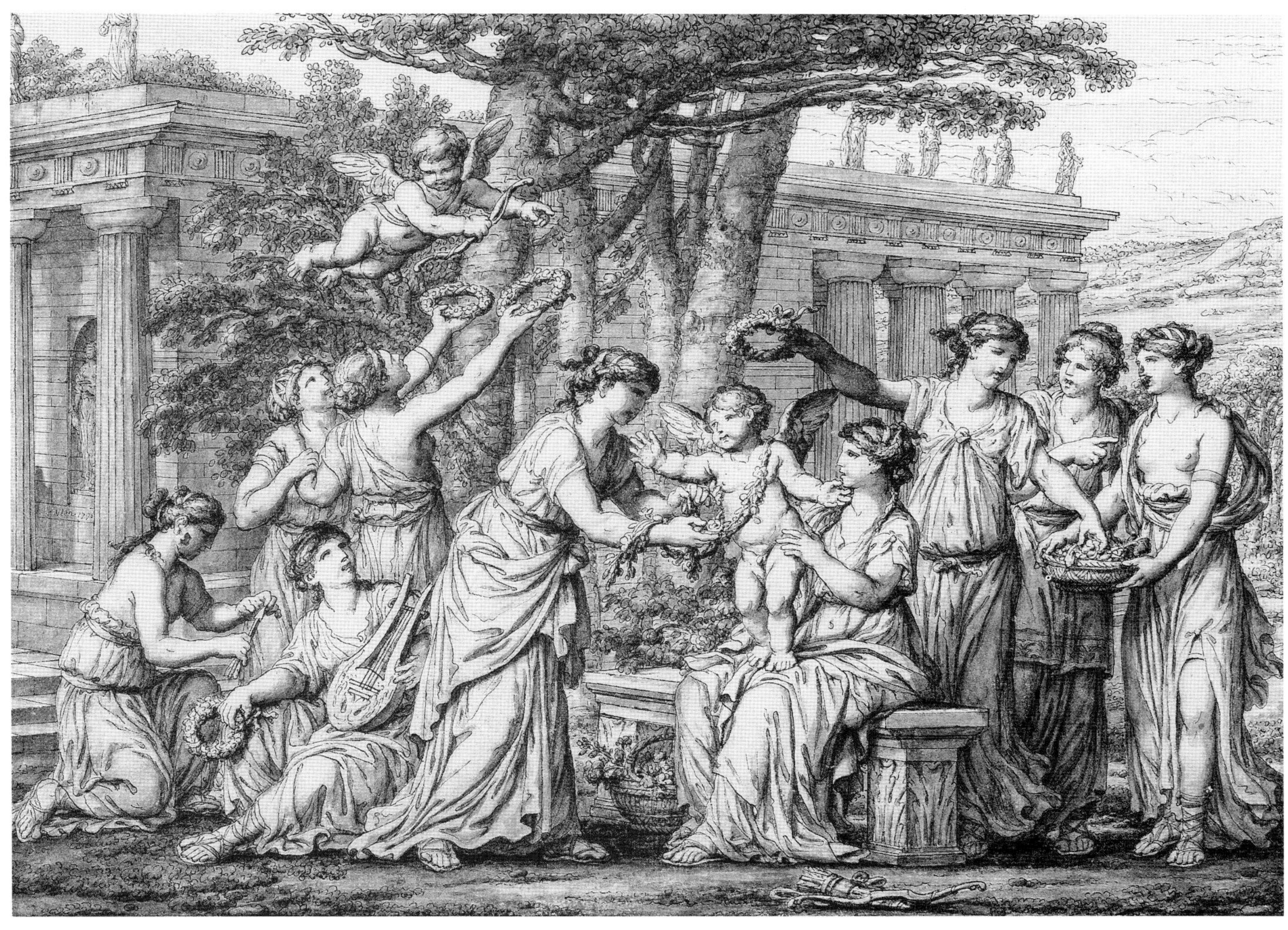

CATALOGUE NO. 15

by the Nymphs (*L'Amour paré de fleurs par les nymphes*), nine maidens adorn a putto with floral garlands and wreaths and offer wreaths to a second putto hovering above; at the left a crouching figure prepares an arrow for one of the cupids. Thus, the theme of the work is the preparation of Love to pursue his conquests. The graceful poses and lissome charm of Vien's figures in these drawings are the same qualities that had been praised in his first paintings *à la grecque* three decades earlier. To be sure, Vien at times painted heroic or morally uplifting episodes from ancient history, but these evocations of a classical world of idyllic pleasures are his most distinctive contribution to the revival of interest in antiquity. VC

Jean-Baptiste Greuze

1725 Tournus–Paris 1805

JEAN-BAPTISTE GREUZE began his studies in the studio of Charles Grandon in Lyons in the late 1740s. He was in Paris by about 1750, enrolled at the Académie, and became a member of that institution in 1755 on the strength of his moralizing *Reading the Bible* (*La Lecture du Bible*). Greuze accompanied the Abbé Gougenot on his travels throughout Italy in 1755 and remained in Rome until 1757 at the Palazzo Mancini, which housed the Académie de France.

Greuze returned to Paris and worked steadily for his patrons, including the marquis de Marigny, the comte de Vence, and Ange-Laurent Lalive de Jully. In 1769 he submitted *Septimius Severus Reproaching Caracalla* (see FIGURE 5) as his reception piece for the Académie. The work was a critical disaster, and the Académie accepted him as a genre painter, not at the higher status of history painter that he felt he deserved. He subsequently dissociated himself from the Académie and its exhibitions, preferring to hold private salons in his studio in the Louvre.

Greuze was, for a time, championed by Denis Diderot, and his works fetched high prices. He had great success with *The Father's Curse* (*La Malédiction paternelle*), 1777, and its pendant of 1778, *The Punished Son* (*Le Fils puni*). He remained in favor until the Revolution, when his works lost out in popularity to those of Jacques-Louis David. Greuze tried to return to the Salons after the Revolution, but his work was hopelessly out of fashion. He died virtually forgotten and destitute. LDM

Jean-Baptiste Greuze
The Return of the Young Hunter
c. 1775

16
Brush and black ink over black chalk, heightened with white gouache on cream paper
52 x 66.5 cm (20 3/4 x 26 1/4 in.)
The Minneapolis Institute of Arts, the John R. Van Derlip Fund (inv. no. 70.13)

PROVENANCE
Réjane (Madame Porel), Paris.
Comte Jacques de Bryas, Paris; sale, Paris, April 4–6, 1898, lot 72.
Lucien Goldschmidt, New York.

EXHIBITED
Toronto/Ottawa/San Francisco/New York 1972–73, no. 57.
Hartford/San Francisco/Dijon 1976–77, no. 79.

LITERATURE
Martin/Masson 1908, no. 365.
The Minneapolis Institute of Arts Bulletin 59 (1970): 81, 90.
The Art Quarterly 33 (1970): 324, 330, fig. 2.

Greuze's large, highly finished drawings such as this were avidly collected during his lifetime, selling for huge prices, according to the renowned collector Pierre-Jean Mariette. The present drawing was evidently made as an end in itself, because no painting of the subject is recorded. The artist made careful preparations for the composition: there is a smaller study in the British Museum, London (Hartford/San Francisco/Dijon 1976–77, 162, no. 79), in addition to a red-chalk drawing for the figure of the mother in the Musée des Beaux-Arts, Narbonne (Toronto/Ottawa/San Francisco/New York 1972–73, 164). Later, perhaps about 1800, Greuze may have recalled the figures of the young girl leaning on the shoulder of her brother when he submitted to the Salon of 1800 *The Departure for the Hunt* (*Le Départ pour la chasse*), now lost, in an unspecified medium. A superb ink-wash drawing of a hunter and his wife in a landscape (Musée du Louvre, Paris) is not dissimilar to the boy and girl in the Minneapolis work, although the relationship of the couple is reversed (Launay 1991, 145, no. 125, fig. 65). It is unknown whether the Paris drawing was a study for the work Greuze exhibited in the Salon, the exhibition piece itself, or a drawing made for some other reason.

The Minneapolis drawing should be dated to the mid-1770s, to judge from the Louis XVI-style furniture and the severity of the architectural background, although the oval painting of flying cupids on the wall is more characteristic of works done several decades earlier. The table with tapered legs at the far right of this drawing occurs again in a more outspokenly neoclassical drawing by Greuze, *The Love Letter* (formerly Émile E. Wolf, New York; Hartford/San Francisco/Dijon 1976–77, no. 78), in which the background is specifically based on ancient Roman architectural details. As a student in Italy Greuze drew after the antique (Hartford/San Francisco/Dijon 1976–77, 10, fig. 3; see also studies after heads from Trajan's Column, attributed to the artist [Paris 1989a, 34, no. 15]), but references to specific ancient works of art only rarely may be identified in his mature work (Hartford/San Francisco/Dijon 1976–77, 142–43, nos. 67–68). An exception is the figure of the father in this drawing, seated and turned to the right, his left arm nonchalantly resting on the back of his chair, whose pose is unmistakably based on the Roman marble figure of Menander, a statue that Greuze either might have seen in the Museo Pio-Clementino on the Capitoline Hill or known through an engraving in Diderot and d'Alembert's *Encyclopédie* (s.v. "Dessein," vol. 2, pl. 28). Whatever his source, Greuze reversed the antique Menander for his parental figure in con-

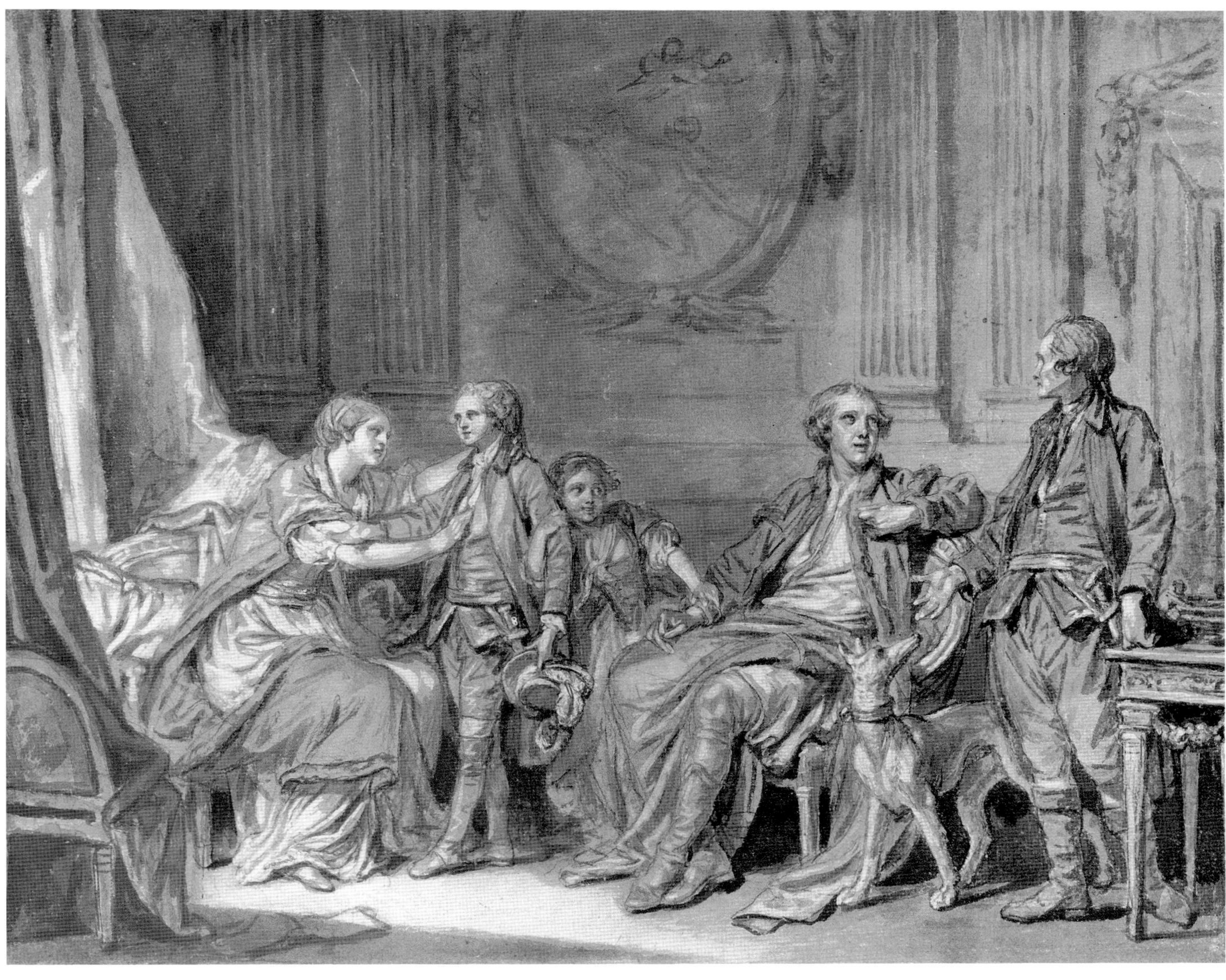

CATALOGUE NO. 16

temporary dress. In other respects, this modern domestic drama reflects Greuze's respect for classical principles of organization, whether based on the antique or his study of the work of Nicolas Poussin.

Greuze's admiration for Poussin is evident in the former's *Septimius Severus Reproaching Caracalla* (*L'Empereur Sévère reproche à Caracalla son fils . . .* ; FIGURE 5), the artist's 1769 submission to the Académie for election as a full member in the category of history painting. The Académie's decision to receive him only as a painter of genre subjects, together with the opprobrium of critics such as Denis Diderot (earlier a supporter of the artist), who castigated *Septimius Severus Reproaching Caracalla*, ended any ambitions Greuze had to rival Poussin's classicism. All the same, Greuze's study of the earlier master left traces on his composition of genre subjects, such as this domestic incident. The group is organized in a friezelike composition, occupying a shallow space defined by the interior architecture, which acts as a backdrop to the drama of the unsuccessful hunter returning empty-handed to his family. This type of composition can be found in other Greuze drawings from about the same epoch, such as his pen and wash *The Guilty and Repentant Daughter*, recently acquired by the Cleveland Museum of Art (*The Burlington Magazine* 133 [January 1991]: 65, fig. 11). VC

Jean-Baptiste Greuze
Anacreon in His Old Age Crowned by Love

17
Brush and gray wash, heightened with white ink on gray paper
31.4 x 41 cm (12 3/8 x 16 1/8 in.)
The Pierpont Morgan Library, New York, bequest of Therese Kuhn Straus in memory of her husband, Herbert N. Straus (inv. no. 1977.57)
(Philadelphia and Minneapolis only)

PROVENANCE
Possibly Gil de Meestre; sale, Paris, April 1, 1862. Jacques Seligmann and Company, New York. Mrs. Herbert N. Straus.

EXHIBITED
Hartford/San Francisco/Dijon 1976–77, no. 101.

LITERATURE
Martin/Masson 1908, no. 77

Jean-Baptiste Greuze
Study for Anacreon in His Old Age Crowned by Love

18
Pen and brown ink, brush and gray ink on white laid paper
23 x 36 cm (9 1/16 x 14 3/16 in.)
Private collection

The fifth-century B.C. Greek poet Anacreon was especially popular with French artists in the eighteenth and early nineteenth centuries. Diderot and d'Alembert's *Encyclopédie* defined the appeal of his verses (cited in Gaehtgens/Lugand 1988, 79):

> *Anacreon . . . is famous for the refinement of his thoughts and for the easy flow of his poetry, in which one finds above all simple and artless charm without apparent effort. His odes are noted for their tenderness, or better, for their delectable ingenuousness; they are short, pleasing, elegant, and exude only pleasure and amusement.*

The poet's celebration of life's pleasures, especially wine and love, found a sympathetic audience among those not yet prepared to adopt the rigorous moral philosophy embodied in the paintings of Jacques-Louis David or Jean-François-Pierre Peyron, for example. The most ambitious tribute to Anacreon's poetry was Anne-Louis Girodet de Roussy-Trioson's project to illustrate his works, a volume that remained incomplete at the artist's death but was finished by his students.

Greuze's highly finished drawing shows Anacreon interrupted in his writing by Love, who is about to crown him with laurel. The poet is at work in a setting that recalls the Louis XVI interiors of Greuze's drawings such as *The Return of the Young Hunter* (see CATALOGUE NO. 16). The copy of the Medici Venus on the table is no doubt the bronze-colored plaster reduction that the artist owned, as Edgar Munhall has observed (Hartford/San Francisco/Dijon 1976–77, 200). Greuze made no effort to research an archaeologically proper ambience but turned to stylish neoclassical references immediately at hand.

The unpublished preparatory drawing is in reverse to the final composition, with the addition of an enchanting study for the cupid's head rapidly sketched in the right margin. The boldly scumbled lines of Greuze's early study, with its dramatic additions of ink wash, are characteristic of his preparatory sheets, in which an idea is hastily set down, only to be immediately revised. This fresh, improvisational aspect of Greuze's draftsmanship is less familiar than the artist's more thoughtfully considered studies.

As C.-L.-F. Lecarpentier expressed in an obituary eulogy, Greuze's contemporaries thought there was a sympathetic bond between the artist's gallant behavior toward women and the gracious sentiments of Anacreon's poetry (Hartford/San Francisco/Dijon 1976–77, 200 n. 1). Greuze was not the only artist to be honored by a comparison with the Greek poet: his exact contemporary Vien received a similar accolade in a speech extolling his talents (Gaehtgens/Lugand 1988, 45). Greuze made only a few canvases or drawings that might be considered attempts at mastering a neoclassical style, but it is fortuitous that he and Vien should be linked through the vision of antiquity created by Anacreon. An important aspect of Vien's art celebrated the pleasurable domestic activities of antiquity, just as other works by him paid homage to the triumph of love. Greuze's own essays in a neoclassical vein are basically displays of familiar emotions: lachrymose sentimentality or glorifications of pleasure personified by Cupid, the god of love. The artist distanced these allegories from their immediate sources in rococo art through the device of references to a imaginary classical past, a tactic apparent in his canvases *The Votive Offered to Cupid* (Wallace Collection, London) and *Innocence Carried off by Cupid* (Musée du Louvre, Paris; Hartford/San Francisco/Dijon 1976–77, no. 100) and in Fragonard's drawing *The Invocation to Love* (see CATALOGUE NO. 22), each a paean to the pursuit of love. VC

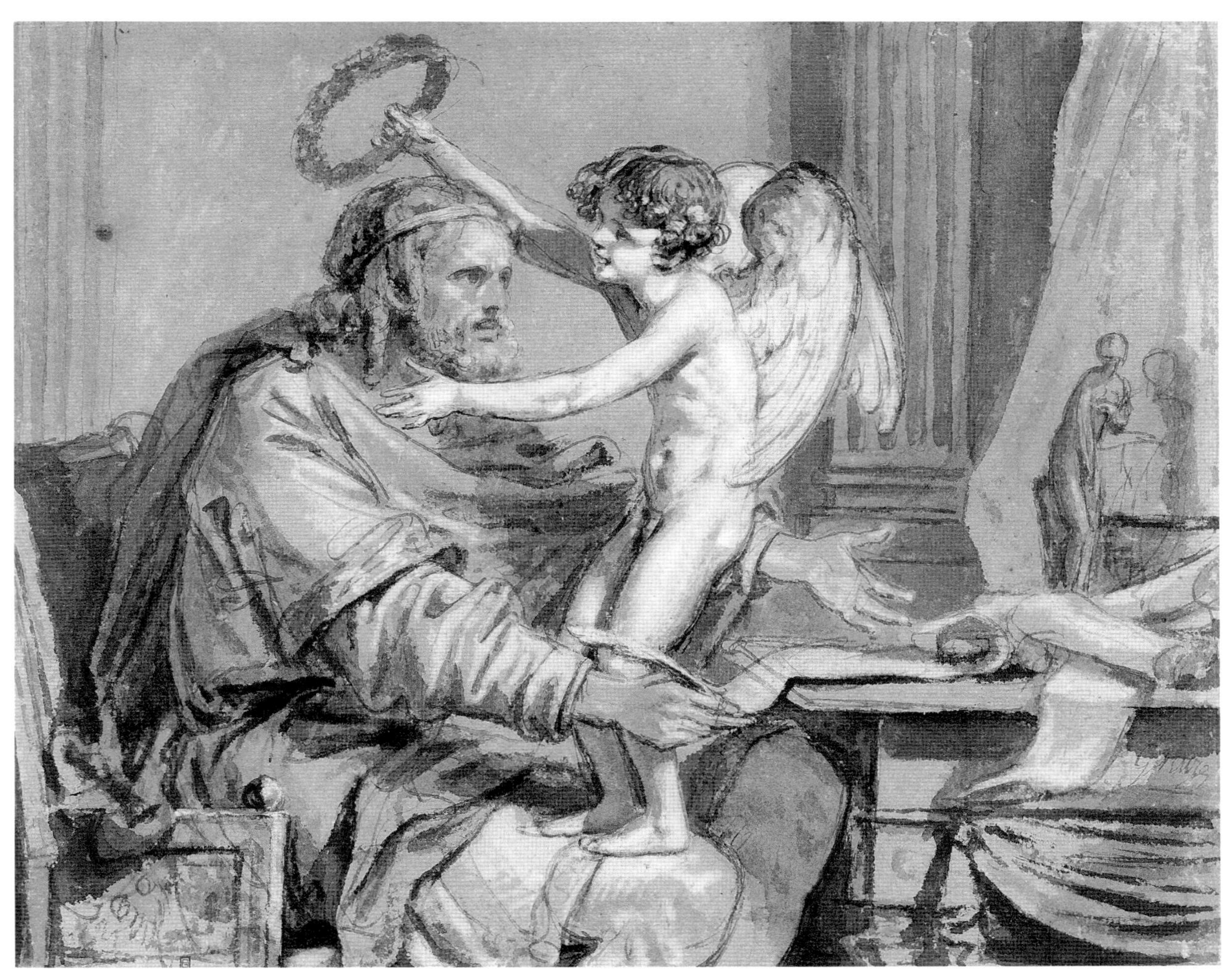

CATALOGUE NO. 17

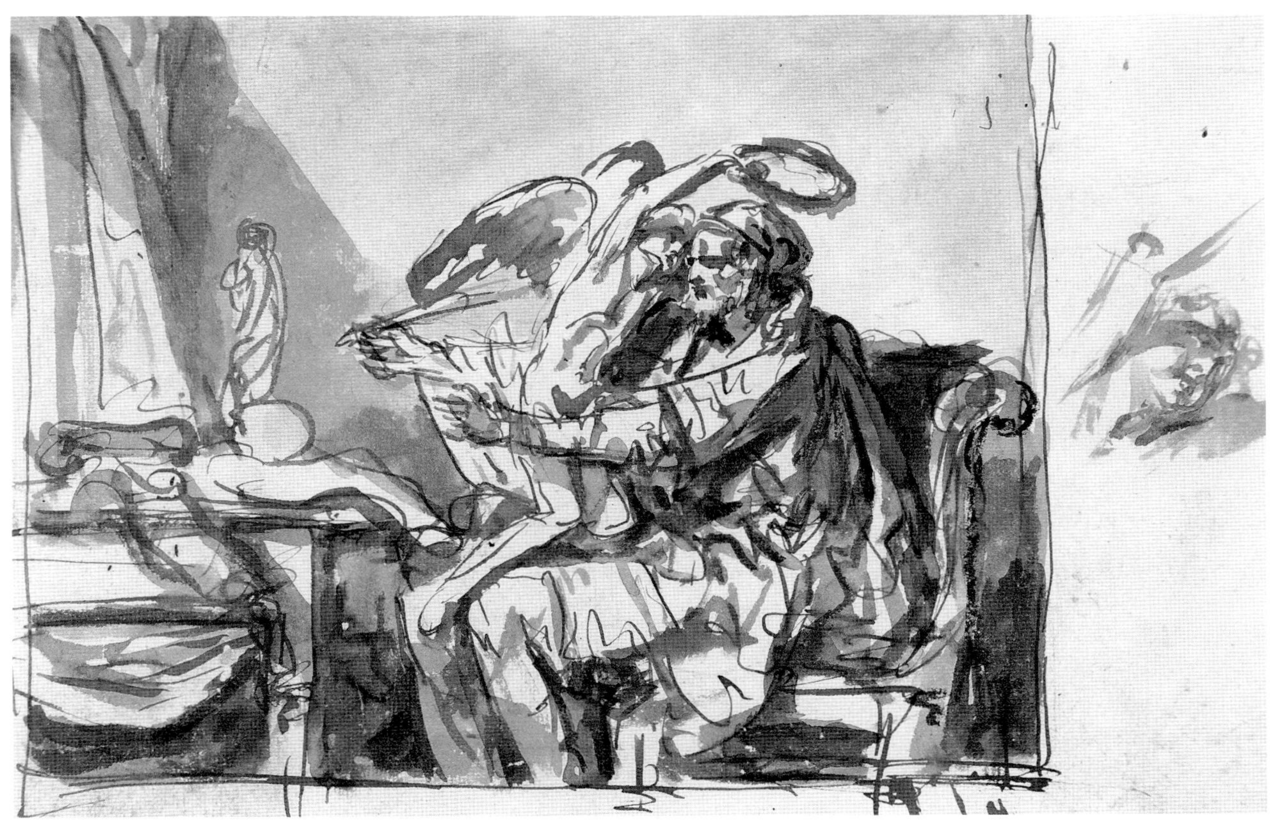

CATALOGUE NO. 18

Laurent Pécheux

1729 Lyons–Turin 1821

LAURENT PÉCHEUX ARRIVED in Rome in 1753 as an independent student but with a letter of introduction to Charles-Joseph Natoire, director of the Académie de France à Rome, whose life drawing classes were open to the public. Another letter put him in contact with Nicolas Guibal, who presented the young artist to Anton Raphael Mengs. Charles-Louis Clérisseau introduced Pécheux to Robert Adam when the latter needed someone to teach him figure drawing; in 1757 Adam commissioned *The Departure of Regulus* from the artist. Pompeo Batoni and Pécheux became close friends, the former even teaching classes at the private drawing academy Pécheux organized. The year after Pécheux's arrival in Rome the city's first publicly sponsored drawing academy opened, the Accademia del Nudo, where the artist later taught.

In 1762 Pécheux was elected to the Accademia di San Luca in Rome and the Accademia di Belle Arti in Parma; two years later he became a member of the Accademia Clementina in Bologna. He traveled throughout central and northern Italy for several years and returned to Rome for the years 1766–77, working in the Palazzo and Casino Borghese and the Palazzo Barberini. In 1777 he became *premier peintre* to the king of Sardinia and director of the Accademia in Turin. He remained there until his death, contributing paintings for the royal palaces, cartoons for the tapestry works, portraits, and ceiling decorations for the royal library. VC/LDM

Laurent Pécheux
The Assassination of Julius Caesar
1760

19
Pen and black ink, brush and gray wash, heightened with white on tan laid paper
27 x 36.8 cm (10 5/8 x 14 1/2 in.)
Signed and dated at lower left in pen and black ink: *Laur. Pecheux 1760. roma.*
Philadelphia Museum of Art, the Print Revolving Fund (inv. no. 1982-112-1)

PROVENANCE
Sale, Hôtel Drouot, Paris, December 19, 1973, lot 63.

The assassination of Julius Caesar is described in Plutarch's *Lives* and Suetonius's *Lives of the Caesars*, which relate that a group of Roman senators became alarmed by Caesar's increasing assumption of power and authority. When he attempted to have himself crowned king of Rome, the public roundly rejected the attempt, and a conspiracy was formed among several senators to put an end to his tyrannical ambitions by assassination. Pécheux's drawing focuses on the moment described by Plutarch, when the members of the conspiracy surge forward with their swords drawn (Plutarch 1821, vol. 6, 186):

> *All the conspirators now drew their swords and surrounded him in such a manner that wherever he turned, he saw nothing but steel gleaming in his face, and met nothing but wounds. Like some savage beast attacked by hunters, he found every hand lifted against him, for they all agreed to have a share in the sacrifice and a taste of his blood.*

The artist's drawing is a striking representation of Plutarch's description, a bold interplay of diagonals created by the upraised arms and swords of the attackers as they converge on the tyrant. Because Pécheux's drawing is such a vivid realization of Caesar's murder, it is tempting to suppose that it served as the model for a painting; however, the subject does not appear in the artist's manuscript catalogue of his principal works (published in Baudi di Vesme 1963–68, 796–99). Nor did artists prior to or contemporary with Pécheux depict it, with only rare exceptions that it is unlikely he knew.

Pécheux's tautly composed drawing is surprising in light of its date, 1760, which anticipates by some fifteen years works by Jean-François-Pierre Peyron and Jacques-Louis David based on subjects from classical history. In fact, the simplicity of the artist's draped figures and their eloquent gestures more likely reflect the continuing example and authority of such French artists as Nicolas Poussin or Charles Le Brun rather than a daring innovation. Engravings after Poussin's major works were widely distributed and could be found in all major artistic centers, where they played an essential role in maintaining his eminence. Moreover, paintings by Romans such as Francesco Trevisani and Marco Benefial, artists schooled in the conventions of seventeenth-century classicism, must also have been important for the formation of Pécheux's early style. Since Mengs studied with Benefial, and Pécheux knew Mengs, the Frenchman was surely aware of this Settecento Roman tradition during his early years in Rome. Also, like most artists studying in Rome, Pécheux

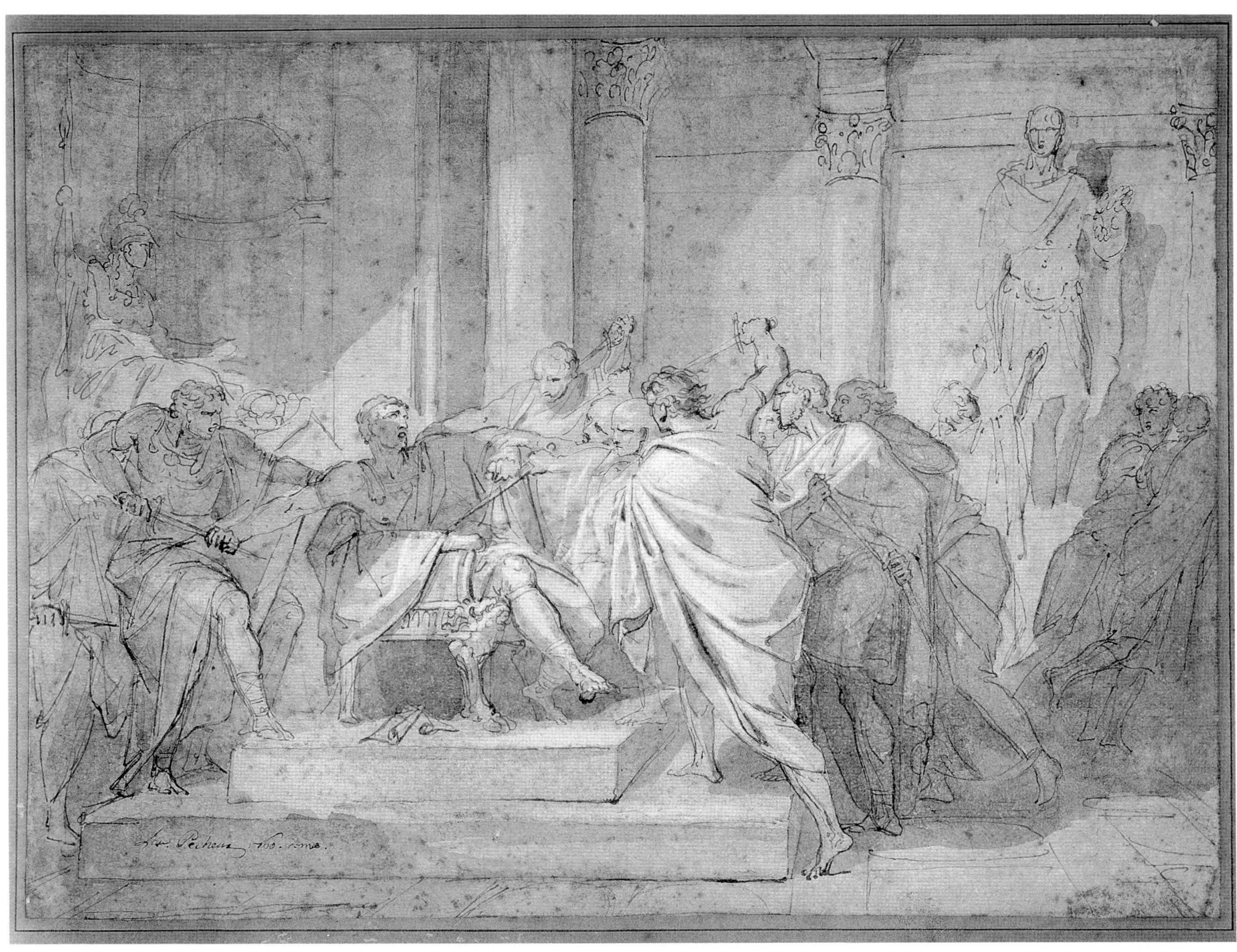

CATALOGUE NO. 19

drew after antique works of art and, in Mengs's studio, after casts of classical sculpture (Fleming 1962, 162–64; Philadelphia 1980–81, 73–74).

In addition to Pécheux's abilities as a painter, his active participation in the pedagogical life of Rome placed him in the midst of an international group of artists who visited or settled there, attracted by the rich legacy of Rome's past but as well by the stimulus of working with the city's resident artists, an experience that at this time no other European capitol could provide. VC

Augustin Pajou

1730 Paris 1809

TRAINED BY Jean-Baptiste Lemoyne from age fourteen, Pajou won the Prix de Rome in sculpture in 1748. After three years at the École Royale des Élèves Protégés he left for Rome, where he remained until 1756. Accomplished in both sculpture and drawing, Pajou first exhibited at the Salon of 1759, was elected to the Académie in 1760, became a professor in 1762, and taught for thirty years. Among his many works was decorative sculpture for the opera house at Versailles in 1768–70, in honor of the marriage of the dauphin and Marie-Antoinette, as well as for the Palais-Royale, Palais Bourbon, and Palais de Justice. He completed numerous portrait busts of Louis XVI, Madame du Barry, and the intellectual, military, and artistic figures of the time, including Comte Buffon, René Descartes, and Blaise Pascal. In 1777 he was appointed keeper of the king's antiquities. During the Revolution he served on the Committee on the Conservation of Works of Art and continued to exhibit at the Salons until 1802. LDM

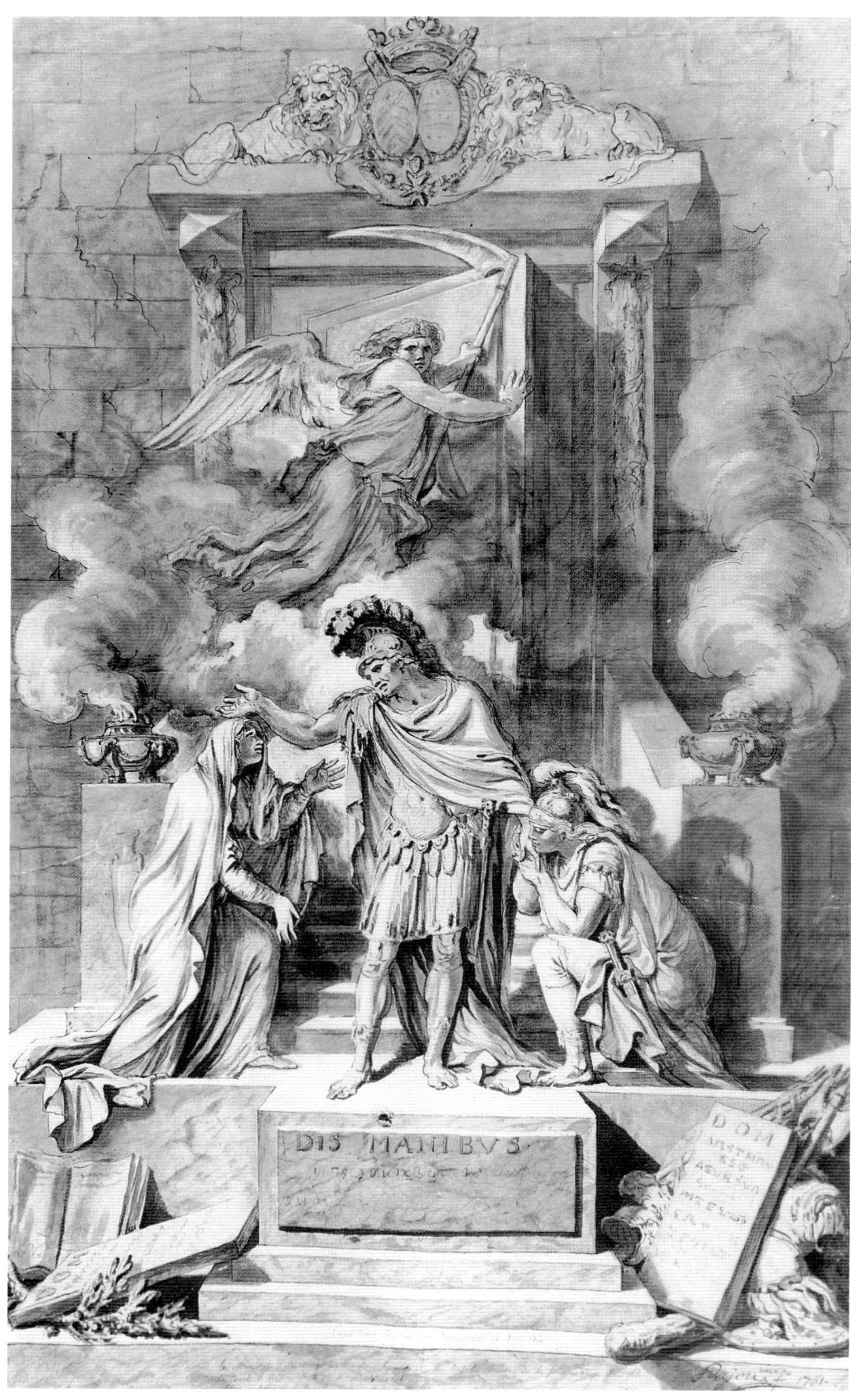

CATALOGUE NO. 20

Augustin Pajou
Project for the Tomb of the Maréchal Charles-Louis-Auguste Fouquet, Duc de Belle-Isle
1761

20
Pen and black ink, brush and brown and black inks, gray, brown, and red washes, with white gouache and black chalk on yellow-brown wove paper
90 x 56.9 cm (35 7/16 x 22 7/16 in.)
Signed and dated at lower right in pen and black ink: *Pajou inve f 1761.*
Inscribed on tablets in the foreground in pen and black ink: *DIS MANIBVS* (in the hands of the gods), *DOM* (*Deo optimo maximo*, to God, the best and greatest), and inscriptions in Greek (?); at the bottom in pen and brown ink: *Projet d'un Tombeau pour le Maréchal de Belle Isle/allegorie/Le Maréchal Entre dans la chambre sépulcrale ou Sont les tombes de sa femme et de Son fils/le Comte de Gisors tout deux morts avant lui/Leurs ombres Sont supposés sortire de leurs tombeaux pour le Recevoir, et L'ange de la mort ferme la porte/de la chambre Sepulcrale pour indiquer que le Marechal fut le Dernier de Sa famille.* (Project for a tomb for the marshal of Belle-Isle. Allegory. The marshal enters the sepulchral chamber containing the tombs of his wife and son, the comte de Gisors, who both predeceased him. Their spirits are supposed to have left their tombs in order to greet him, and the angel of death is shutting the door of the sepulchral chamber in order to indicate that the marshal was the last of his family [translation by Colin Eisler in New York 1981, no. 41].)
Cooper-Hewitt Museum, Smithsonian Institution, New York, gift of Sarah and Eleanor Hewitt (inv. no. 1931-73-234)
(Philadelphia and Minneapolis only)

PROVENANCE
Possibly Prunelé, comte André-Gaspard-Parfait de Bizemont, Paris, 1837.
Alfred Hubert; sale, Paris, May 24, 1876.
"E. H. R." (possibly Édouard Rodigues; sale, Paris, 1878).
Juan Jorg Peoli; sale, New York, May 8, 1894, lot 473.
Sarah Cooper Hewitt, New York.

EXHIBITED
Paris, Salon, 1765, no. 211.
Cleveland 1964, no. 38.
Washington 1967, no. 207.
London 1968, no. 526, fig. 332.
Ann Arbor 1969, no. 64.
New York 1981, no. 41.
Houston 1981, no. 41.

LITERATURE
Benisovich 1953, 295–98, fig. 10.
Benisovich 1959, 59–60, fig. 4.
New York 1962, no. 10.
Licht 1980, 97, fig. 96.
Eisler 1981, 67.
Cooper-Hewitt 1991–92.

In 1761 Pajou drew this extravagant idea for a funerary monument to the late *maréchal* Charles-Louis-Auguste Fouquet, duc de Belle-Isle, in the hope that his estate would erect the memorial. The sculptor's conception is quite startling, because he represented the deceased stepping through a massive door into the family mausoleum where his wife and only son welcome him. The family's military heritage is emblematized by the men's regalia as Roman warriors, reinforced by the club of Hercules, Roman cuirass, and other arms and trophies at lower right, while in the opposite corner an olive branch and an open book (of the law) symbolize the reign of peace and justice that followed conquest. Pajou's use of classical dress to indicate the family's nobility of character is sanctioned by tradition, but the dramatic illusionism of this design is the artist's innovation. The shadows cast by the figures indicate that if executed as a freestanding monument the work would have been complex and costly. In the end the design was never carried out.

Pajou must have been proud of the drawing, because he exhibited it at the Salon of 1765. The catalogue of the exhibition lists under number 211 three untitled drawings, one a design for a tomb, and the present work can be identified as that drawing, because a minute sketch by Gabriel de Saint-Aubin of a view of the installation shows it hanging on the wall (Dacier 1929–31, vol. 2, no. 1105; Diderot 1957–67, vol. 2, fig. 5). From time to time Pajou sent to the Salons drawings such as his large, highly finished *Lycurgus Presenting Their King to the Lacedaemonians* (*Lycurgue présente leur roi aux Lacédémoniens*; Musée des Beaux-Arts, Rouen; Paris 1974–75, 107, no. 108), seen at the 1763 exhibition, or in 1771 *An Event from the Life of Camillus* (*Épisode de la vie de Camille*; present location unknown; ex-collection Jean Masson; Stein 1912, 224–25).

The sculptor's drawings are numerous, varying in style and purpose from hasty sketches from life, unrelated to any sculptural project (undoubtedly many of these sheets are from sketchbooks that have been broken up), to complex, highly detailed designs for important sculptural projects, such as the Cooper-Hewitt drawing or his much later drawing for the tomb of the Russian prince Peter Borissovitch Cheremeteff and his wife, seen at the 1789 Salon (Staatliche Museen zu Berlin 1980, no. 20).

As a student at the Académie de France à Rome Pajou was criticized by its director, Charles-Joseph Natoire, for his failure to spend more time studying after the antique, a position endorsed by Natoire's superior in Paris, the marquis de Marigny (see letters from 1755 cited in Stein 1912, 5). Nonetheless, when Marigny was sent examples of Pajou's draftsmanship, he was impressed by the young artist's skills. These drawings cannot be identified, but they may have been similar to such accomplished works as his *Bas-Relief in the Antique Style* (*Bas-relief à l'antique*), signed and dated *Pajou, Roma 1756* (present location unknown, ex-collection L. Cardon, Brussels; Stein 1912, 7). The artist could not resist adding a group of putti pulling back some draperies to reveal the glory of this antique Roman battle scene, a flourish of anticlassical illusionism also evident in the Belle-Isle tomb design. VC

Jean-Honoré Fragonard

1732 Grasse–Paris 1806

FRAGONARD HAD A brief apprenticeship with Jean-Baptiste-Siméon Chardin and in about 1748 became a pupil of François Boucher, with whom he studied until 1752, when he won the Prix de Rome with *Jeroboam Sacrificing to the Idols.* After three years under the direction of Carle Van Loo at the École Royale des Élèves Protégés, he left for Italy in 1756. Fragonard studied with Charles-Joseph Natoire in Rome and spent a year sketching the landscapes of Tivoli and Naples with Hubert Robert and the Abbé de Saint-Non. He returned to Paris in 1761 with an established reputation and moved into a studio in the Louvre. His history painting *The High Priest Coresus Sacrificing Himself to Save Callirhoe* (*Corésus et Callirhoé*) was a great success at the 1765 Salon, prompting his membership in the Académie. By 1767, however, criticism of his subsequent work caused him to abandon the Salons for a private clientele.

The popularity of *The Swing*, 1767, made Fragonard in demand as a decorator for such clients as Louis XV and Madame du Barry. He returned to Italy in 1773–74 with his wife, Marie-Anne Gérard, and soon thereafter his sister-in-law, the artist Marguerite Gérard, moved into Fragonard's home, and the two collaborated on many works. Fragonard was active in the administration of the arts during the Revolution, and Jacques-Louis David appointed him curator of the new Conservatoire of the Musée du Louvre in 1793, a position he held until 1800. LDM

Jean-Honoré Fragonard
The Sacrifice of the Rose
c. 1775–80

21
Graphite, black chalk, brush and gray and brown washes, red and yellow watercolor on white laid paper
42.2 x 33.1 cm (16⅝ x 13 in.)
Inscribed at lower left in black chalk: *fragonard*
The Minneapolis Institute of Arts, gift of Mr. and Mrs. Clinton Morrison (inv. no. 83.109)

PROVENANCE
Daniel Saint; sale, Paris, May 4, 1846, lot 17.
Hippolyte Walferdin, 1860; sale, Paris, April 12–16, 1880, lot 189.
Bartholdy, 1889.
Baron de Neuflize and by descent Roberta, Countess of Bessborough.
Desmond Brown, Esq.
Sale, Christie's, London, July 5, 1983, lot 34.

EXHIBITED
Paris 1860, no. 7.
Minneapolis 1986, 96.
Paris 1987–88, 552, no. 286.

LITERATURE
Goncourt 1981, 281.
Portalis 1880, 308, 312.
Portalis 1889, 199, 312.
Réau 1956, 204.
Ananoff 1961–70, vol. 2, 151, no. 988; vol. 4, 156, no. 2427.
Ananoff 1984, 13–14.
"La Chronique des arts: Principales acquisitions des musées en 1983" *Gazette des Beaux-Arts*, ser. 6, 103 (March 1984): 29, fig. 182.
Tilly 1986, 18, no. 2.
Cuzin 1987, 215, fig. 266.
Roland Michel 1987, 197, fig. 234.
Campbell 1983–86, 18–47.

The Sacrifice of the Rose constitutes a key transitional work in the stylistic evolution of Jean-Honoré Fragonard. Significantly, this transformation can be attributed to the vogue for the so-called *goût grec* (Greek taste), the earliest manifestation of neoclassicism in France. At the outset of his "official" career Fragonard had achieved great success with his grand history painting based on an episode recounted by Pausanias, *The High Priest Coresus Sacrificing Himself to Save Callirhoe* (*Corésus et Callirhoé*; Musée du Louvre, Paris), his academic reception piece exhibited at the Salon of 1765. It has been conjectured that Fragonard intended to follow up on this painting with a similar "neo-classical-horrific" subject, *The Sacrifice to the Minotaur* (Paris 1987–88, 200). Negative critical response to his entries at the subsequent Salon of 1767, however, prompted him to embark on a "private" career and specialize in erotic subjects such as *The Swing* (Wallace Collection, London).

Between 1770 and 1773 Fragonard painted four large-scale canvases entitled *The Loves of Shepherds* (*Les Amours des bergers*; The Frick Collection, New York) for the drawing room of Madame du Barry's fashionable neoclassical pavilion at Louveciennes, which was designed for her by the architect Claude-Nicolas Ledoux. The panels sequentially depict an ebullient pastoral romance within a lavish floral garden. Although the paintings may be justly deemed Fragonard's masterpiece, they were completely out of character with the pavilion's classical architecture and decoration. Ultimately, Fragonard's panels were rejected and replaced by Joseph-Marie Vien's *Progress of Love in the Hearts of Young Girls*, a series in the antique taste, which featured sacrificial altars, an Ionic temple of Hymen, and figures clad in Greek garb. Hence, Fragonard for the first time came to recognize the economic implications of neoclassicism and was duly motivated to try his hand at the *goût grec*.

In his drawing *The Sacrifice of the Rose*, dating about 1775–80, Fragonard combined the vogue for the theme of ancient sacrifice and the traditional erotic symbolism of the rose. It is a study for a small panel painting now in a private collection (Paris 1987–88, 553; Campbell 1983–86,

20). Importantly, Fragonard transferred the setting of this amorous encounter from his hitherto typical boudoir to the interior of a temple of Eros. In the middle of the night a maiden wearing a *décolleté* chiton enters the temple to offer a rose before a statue of Cupid atop a lofty altar perch. In a dreamlike sequence Hymen, the adolescent god of marriage, wafts into the moonlit temple in a cloud of smoke and sears the rose with his burning torch as the young woman swoons. The bearer of the rose has thus been initiated into love's mysteries in this thinly veiled allegory of the loss of virginity. Fragonard's conception of the theme is entirely original, although he was undoubtedly inspired by the *Odes* of the ancient Greek lyric poet Anacreon and his late eighteenth-century French imitators such as Jacques Delille, Alexandre de Pézay, and Évariste Parny.

Despite its Anacreontic theme and "accessories" of antiquity Fragonard's *The Sacrifice of the Rose* is indebted to the baroque style of Pietro da Cortona and Gianlorenzo Bernini in its diagonal composition, billowing smoke, and surfeit of putti. When the Goncourt brothers described the composition as "an evocation of Saint Teresa in a metaphor of Parny" (Goncourt 1981, 281), they were comparing it to the sensuous marble sculpted by Bernini between 1645 and 1652 for the Cornaro family chapel in Santa Maria della Vittoria in Rome. Bernini's sculptural group represents the "transverberation" of Teresa of Avila. A smiling angel—similar to Fragonard's Hymen—makes ready to penetrate the saint's heart with an arrow as she swoons in ecstasy upon a cloud. As observed by the Goncourts, Fragonard had recast Bernini's masterpiece into the frivolous Anacreontic idiom of Parny, a poet of erotic verse.

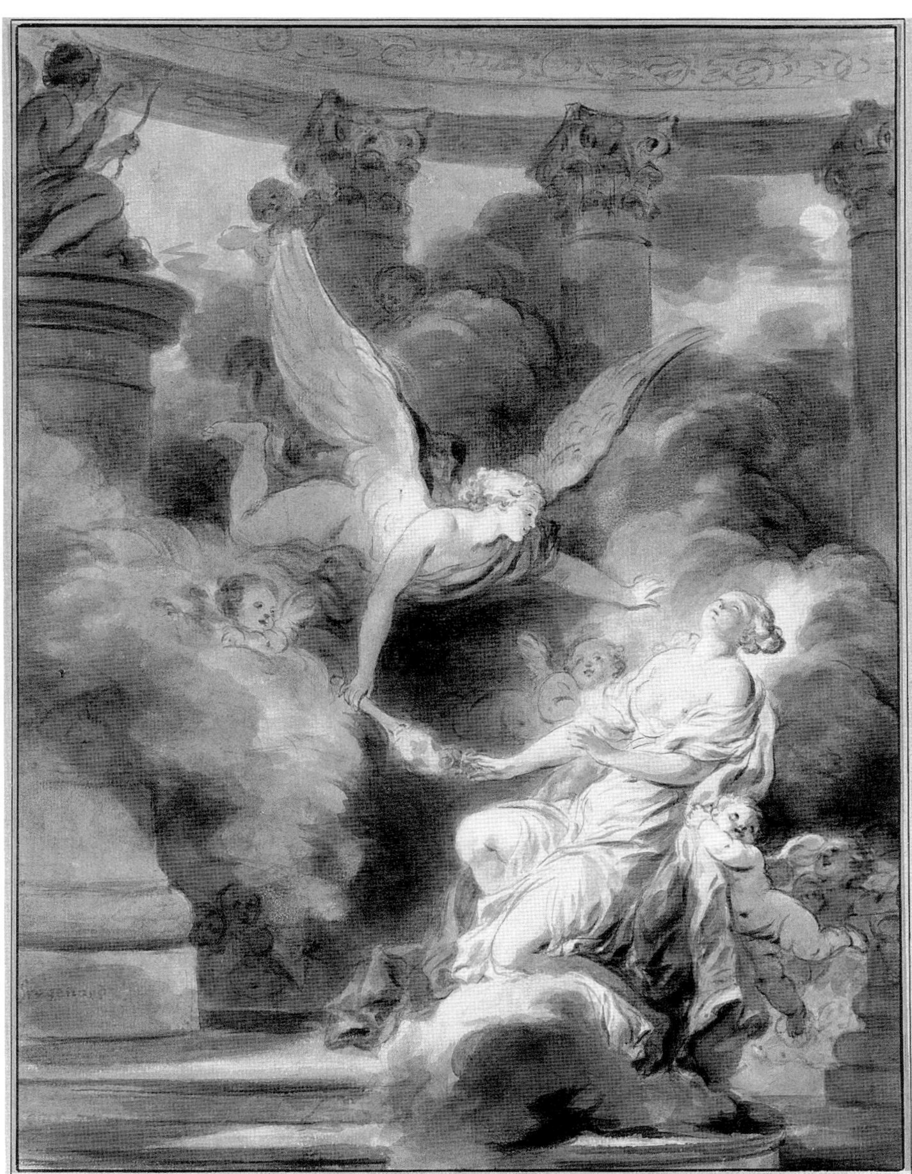

CATALOGUE NO. 21 (see color plate on page 99)

Fragonard's *The Sacrifice of the Rose* shares stylistic affinities with the neo-baroque tendencies of French religious paintings from the 1750s to the early 1770s, as typified by the work of masters Nicolas-Guy Brenet, Jean-Baptiste-Henri Deshays, Gabriel-François Doyen, and Louis-Jean-Jacques Durameau, who emulated Caravaggio, Lodovico Carracci, Pietro da Cortona, Domenichino, Guido Reni, and Peter Paul Rubens (Campbell 1983–86, 23–24).

Given its retrograde style, it is reasonable to assume that the Minneapolis drawing and its related panel painting constitute Fragonard's first conception of *The Sacrifice of the Rose.* The artist would reinterpret the subject in three subsequent paintings dating about 1785–88. In the later versions Fragonard abandons the temple setting and the statue of Cupid, and Hymen envelops the now upright maiden, who collapses against his wing as he torches the rose, which has been deposited on an altar—derived from an archaeologically correct *cinerarium* in the Capitoline Museum, Rome. Vermeule (1964, 129–30) traces the figural types in the later versions to the "New-Attic" school of Pasiteles. Importantly, they contrast strikingly in form to the awkwardly foreshortened, doll-like rococo beings in Fragonard's early treatment of the theme and herald the works of Pierre-Paul Prud'hon (see FIGURE 14). RJC

Jean-Honoré Fragonard
The Invocation to Love
c. 1780

22
Graphite, brush and brown wash, with touches of white gouache; black chalk squaring beneath the wash on white laid paper
33.5 x 41.6 cm (13 3/16 x 16 3/8 in.)
The Cleveland Museum of Art, Grace Rainey Rogers Fund (inv. no. 43.657)

PROVENANCE
Possibly François Renaud, mountmaker (Lugt 1956 [supplément], no. 1042).
François-Martial Marcille; sale, Paris, March 4–7, 1857, lot 416.
Sale, Paris, June 1–2, 1875, lot 333.
Pierre-Désiré-Éugène Franc Lamy (Lugt 1921, no. 949b) before 1922.
Wildenstein, New York.
Mrs. Grace Rainey Rogers; sale, Parke-Bernet, New York, November 18–20, 1943, lot 46.

EXHIBITED
Montreal 1950, no. 73.
Paris/Rotterdam/New York 1958–59, no. 51, pl. 67.
Los Angeles 1961, no. 46.
Toronto/Ottawa/San Francisco/New York 1972–73, no. 50, pl. 112.
Providence 1975, no. 56.
Washington 1978, no. 50.
Tokyo/Kyoto 1980, no. 156.
Paris 1987–88, no. 282.

LITERATURE
Portalis 1889, 64–65, 305.
Francis 1945, 88.
Vermeule 1964, 129, fig. 108.
Ananoff 1961–70, vol. 4, 154, no. 2422, fig. 612.
Williams 1979, 75, no. 5.

The Invocation to Love represents the apogee of Fragonard's "neoclassical" phase of the 1780s. The Cleveland drawing is a highly finished study after a painting now in a private collection, New York (Williams 1979, 128–29, no. 50; Paris 1987–88, 541–46, nos. 280–82). The drawing is similar in theme to *The Sacrifice of the Rose* (see CATALOGUE NO. 21), although the actual subject is enigmatic. In a park setting a distraught maiden lunges at a statue of an adolescent, blindfolded Amor, frenetically invoking the power of the divinity as she covers her face with her cloak and touches his leg. Has she come to dedicate herself to Eros, or does she implore his mediation to entice a lover? The artist alludes to love's domination over mankind by his depiction of a Cupid sprawled upon a terrestrial globe at the far left.

The fluid brushwork and brilliant gouache highlights convey the emotional intensity of the subject, which is unparalleled in Fragonard's oeuvre. The artist did not invent the theme: in a painting of 1775 Louis-Jean-François Lagrenée depicted an ingenue, clad in *palla* and *stola,* who kneels with her hands clasped in prayer before a statue of Cupid (Paris 1987–88, 542). Lagrenée's *Invocation to Love* is a routine exercise in the *goût grec,* however, and is far removed from Fragonard's conception. The sensual languor of *The Sacrifice of the Rose* series has been eclipsed by a new, passionate, proto-romantic sensibility, which heralds aesthetic currents of the nineteenth century.

Importantly, Fragonard's figures are disposed in a friezelike format. As indicated by Cornelius Vermeule (1964, 129–30), Fragonard quoted the figure of the wailing Creusa from a sarcophagus depicting the Vengeance of Medea for the supplicant pose of the maiden; he also cited Praxitelean Eros types and decorative bronze statuettes from Pompeii and Herculaneum as sources for the statue of Amor. It should be stressed, however, that Fragonard was neither a disciple of Johann Joachim Winckelmann nor an antiquarian by predilection (Thuillier 1967, 76–77, 136–37). His borrowings from antiquity were as eclectic and varied as his themes. It was the vision of antiquity that afforded him the formal means to transcend his erotic genre subjects and express a universal image of idealized love. RJC

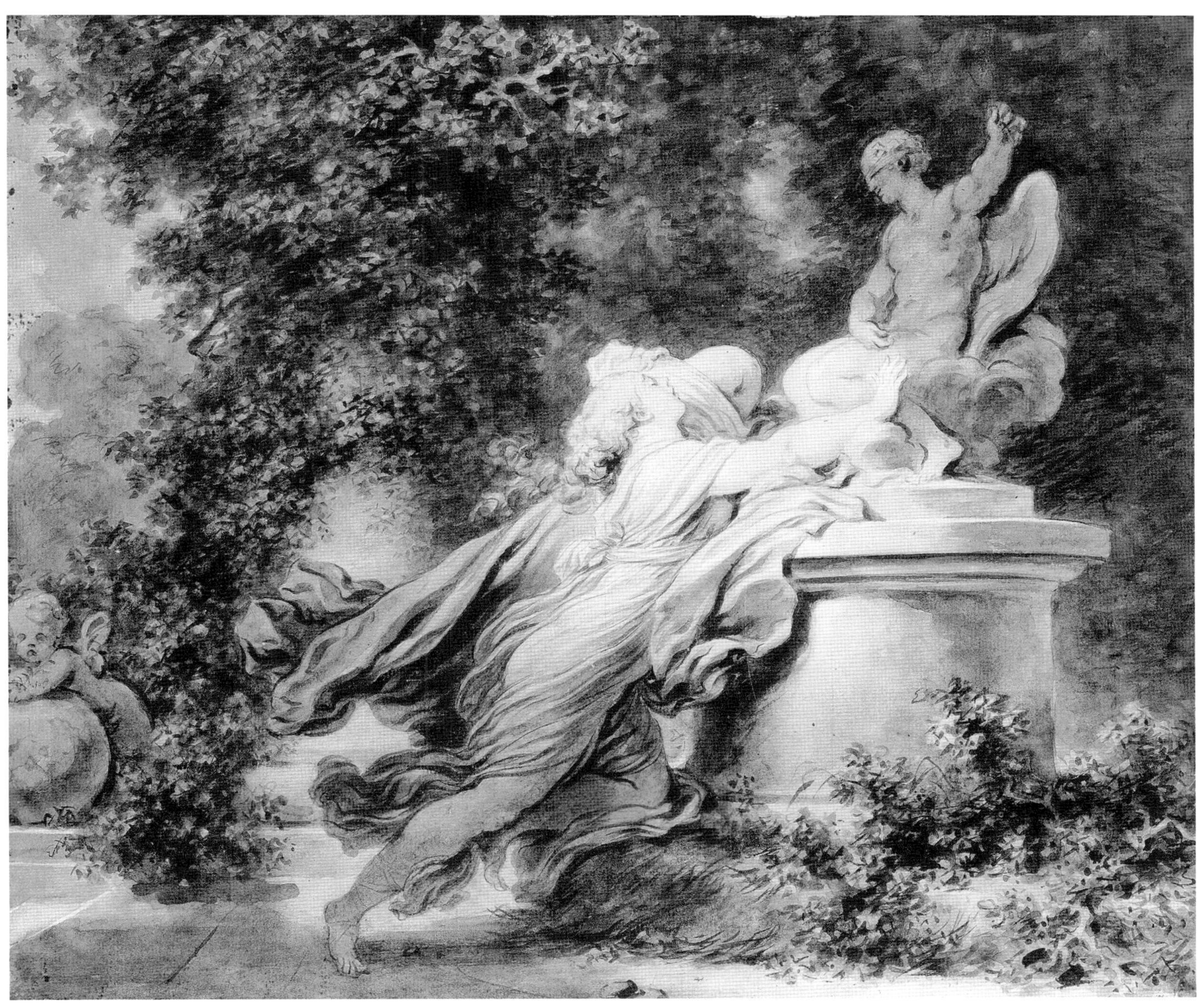

CATALOGUE NO. 22

Jacques Gamelin

1738 Carcassonne 1803

GAMELIN ACHIEVED HIS FAME working outside Paris in the southwestern region of France. Born in Carcassonne, he was the protégé of the baron de Puymaurin, one of the founders of the Académie of Toulouse and a major art connoisseur in the area. Gamelin studied in Toulouse under Jean-Pierre Rivalz and in Paris with Jean-Baptiste Deshays de Colleville. He competed unsuccessfully for the Prix de Rome, but the baron's generosity enabled Gamelin to study in Rome with Joseph-Marie Vien and Jacques-Louis David from 1765 until 1775. He won a prize for drawing at the Accademia di San Luca, the year after he arrived in Rome and was named a professor there in 1771. His success resulted in his appointment as the official painter to Pope Clement XIV.

Gamelin returned to Toulouse in 1775, and for three years he was the director of the Société des Beaux-Arts in Montpellier. He continued his painting of historical subjects and battle scenes and during the Revolution was the director of the Académie in Narbonne. In 1796 he moved back to Carcassonne, where he worked until his death as a drawing professor at the École Centrale de l'Aude. LDM

Jacques Gamelin
Odysseus Ordering Telemachus to Cleanse the Hall of the Dead
c. 1781

23
Brush and brown wash heightened with brush and white ink and black chalk, over black and red chalks on white paper
37 x 45.2 cm (14 9/16 x 17 13/16 in.)
The Detroit Institute of Arts, Founders Society Purchase, the William H. Murphy Fund (inv. no. 1934.123)
(Los Angeles only)

PROVENANCE
Marcell von Nemes, Munich.
Ch. Albert de Burlet, Berlin.

EXHIBITED
Detroit 1962, no. 22 (as by Antoine-François Callet).
Cleveland 1964, no. 39 (as by Callet).
Toronto/Ottawa/San Francisco/New York 1972–73, no. 52, pl. 124.

LITERATURE
Swarzenski 1921, pl. 27 (as by Clodion).
Scheyer 1941, 193–94, fig. 6 (as by Callet).

This drawing depicts Odysseus, who has just slain the suitors of his wife, Penelope, ordering his son, Telemachus, to carry away the bodies (*Odyssey* 22). The identification of the subject matter, which was previously thought to be *Achilles and Patroclus*, was proposed by Lindsay Errington (letter of May 1977, the Detroit Institute of Arts archives). Over the years the drawing has been attributed to various artists, including Clodion and Antoine-François Callet; however, Pierre Rosenberg's suggestion (Toronto/Ottawa/San Francisco/New York 1972–73, no. 52) that it is a work by Gamelin is now generally accepted. The problem of identifying this draftsman, whose abilities are so evident, is due to the obscurity that has surrounded the artist, most of whose career was spent far from Paris and the dominance of the Académie and its members. No doubt Gamelin's remove from this *centralisme parisien* also contributed to his development of a more idiosyncratic style.

With the recent rediscovery of Gamelin's entry for the 1764 Prix de Rome competition, *The Filial Piety of Cleobis and Biton* (*La Piété filiale de Cléobis et Biton*; Musée des Beaux-Arts, Carcassonne; Maynard 1991, 105, fig. 36), one can appreciate that at first the artist tried to work within the accepted conventions for history painting, his figures drawn with clarity of line and form and rendered with a clear, bright palette. Most of Gamelin's known drawings, however, date from his return to France, when he settled in the region of the Midi. His distinctive personal drawing style differs substantially from the polished mastery of academic conventions displayed in his canvas of 1764. Although Gamelin, like many artists of his time, used subjects from Homer, the artist often chose episodes of great complexity, which he treated in drawings with numerous figures gesticulating dramatically.

The attribution of this work to Gamelin is best supported by a comparison to two unpublished drawings, cited by Pierre Rosenberg (Toronto/Ottawa/San Francisco/New York 1972–73, 160–61), in the Musée des Augustins, Toulouse, each signed and dated 1781. Both are Homeric subjects—*The Return of Odysseus* and *Achilles and Hector*—drawn with the same media as the present work.

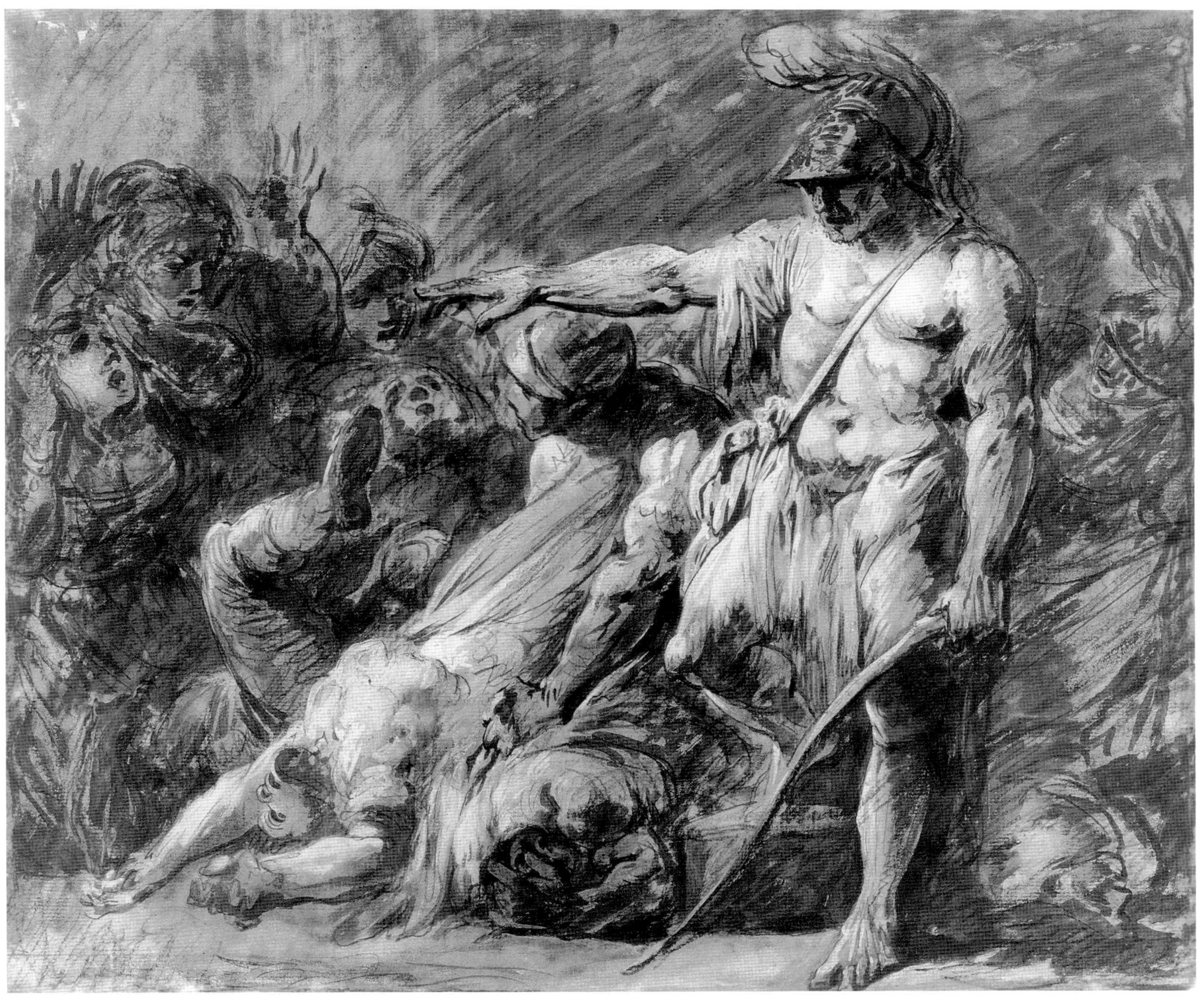

CATALOGUE NO. 23

The three drawings evidence a similar use of bold, slashing brushstrokes, dramatic lighting, and a preference for friezelike compositions. The bluntly characterized faces of the background figures are identical. The highly pitched emotional tenor of these scenes is enhanced by Gamelin's preference for chiaroscuro effects, which he sometimes achieved by covering a sheet of paper with a gray or blue ground, as did some of his Parisian contemporaries, such as Jean-Jacques Lagrenée (see CATALOGUE NO. 25). But Gamelin worked toward entirely different ends: his bold lighting effects, together with his bravura execution, give to these classical themes an emotional expressiveness that seems closer in spirit to the work of Henry Fuseli or James Barry than to any specifically French tradition.

Gamelin's drawings are seldom found in American collections, an important exception being his large, friezelike *Rape of the Sabines* in the Metropolitan Museum of Art, New York (New York 1986b, no. 116). Thus, the ascription of the Detroit drawing to this artist from the Midi provides a fine and powerful addition to his small oeuvre. VC

Jean-Jacques-François Le Barbier

1738 Rouen–Paris 1826

JEAN-JACQUES-FRANCOIS LE BARBIER began his studies in Rouen, where he won first prize for drawing at the local *académie* at age seventeen. He moved to Paris, where he was a pupil of Jean-Baptiste-Marie Pierre at the Académie. In 1776 he traveled to Switzerland, making sketches for Baron Zurlauben's *Tableaux topographiques, pittoresques, physiques, historiques, politiques, moraux, littéraires de la Suisse*, 1780–88, and went on to Italy in 1780.

Le Barbier became a member of the Académie in 1785, exhibiting *Jupiter Asleep on Mount Ida* as his presentation piece. Besides working as a history painter, he was a successful illustrator. He worked on his most financially and artistically successful publication, Salomon Gessner's *Oeuvres*, from 1779 until 1792 and also illustrated works by Cervantes, Confucius, Diderot, La Fontaine, Ovid, Racine, and Rousseau. LDM

Jean-Jacques-François Le Barbier
The Wedding Night

24
Pen and brown ink, watercolor on white laid paper
27.3 x 29.8 cm (10 3/4 x 11 3/4 in.)
The Phillips Family Collection

EXHIBITED
Ottawa 1976, no. 34.

Today Le Barbier is best known as a book illustrator, although his work and theoretical writings at the time of the French Revolution have been topics of recent research (Ray 1982; Wisner 1990). During the 1780s and 1790s the artist exhibited at the Paris Salons drawings and paintings based on classical subjects, such as his pen and wash composition of *The Combat between the Horatii and the Curiatii* (*Le Combat des Horaces et des Curiaces*), shown at the 1787 Salon, or *Coriolanus among the Volsci* (*Coriolan chez les Volsques*), executed in the same media, on view at the 1789 Salon (both are now in the Musée Tavet-Delacour, Pontoise; Paris 1974–75, nos. 89–90). The subject matter of his entries in the Salons of the revolutionary period is taken preponderantly from episodes of Roman history, an important exception being his book illustrations for the works of authors such as the second-century Greek Pausanius or the contemporary Salomon Gessner (Heim/Béraud/Heim 1989, 260–62).

Le Barbier's drawings have been lauded for their "purity, correctness and careful finish" (Portalis 1877, vol. 1, 332–33), desirable qualities in works destined to serve as models for engravers needing explicit guides to follow, even though these characteristics produce a certain chill uniformity. The present watercolor is a striking departure from the artist's works illustrating heroic deeds or stoic sacrifices from the classical past. At the left a man and his wife watch with a mixture of pride and anxiety as the young couple on the bed prepare to disrobe. Roses are scattered at the foot of the bed, which at the time would have been understood as a reference to the incipient consummation of a marriage. In fact, the watercolor is virtually an illustration to verses from Anacreon's *Epithalamium* (cited in Campbell 1983–86, 30):

The rose is the queen of flowers, and of virgins, the rose
is Myrilla—coy, yet with desire she glows,
Haste, groom, in thine amorous arms
thy sweet blushing bride enclose.

Le Barbier's drawing has antecedents in works created during the reign of Louis XV. This theme had been used by Pierre-Antoine Baudouin for a gouache that he exhibited at the Salon of 1767, where the work was roundly criticized by Denis Diderot for its lack of redeeming moral values. The critic insisted that morality was essential to good taste, and he advised artists to choose virtuous themes to assure that their work would embody worthwhile values. Whether or not Le Barbier read Diderot's essay, the artist certainly knew the celebrated engraving after Baudouin's gouache by Jean-Baptiste Simonet and Jean-Michel Moreau Le Jeune, one of the triumphs of rococo printmaking. It is doubtful that Diderot would have found Le Barbier's treatment of the subject more satisfactory, because his figures lack the qualities of tenderness and decorum that the critic found so praiseworthy in Greuze's painting of a similar event, *The Village Bride* (*L'Accordée de village*; Musée du Louvre, Paris), seen at the 1761 Salon (Diderot 1957–67, vol. 3, 197–98). The absence of redeeming moral value that Diderot deplored in Baudouin's gouache is here also, in spite of Le Barbier's use of classical references.

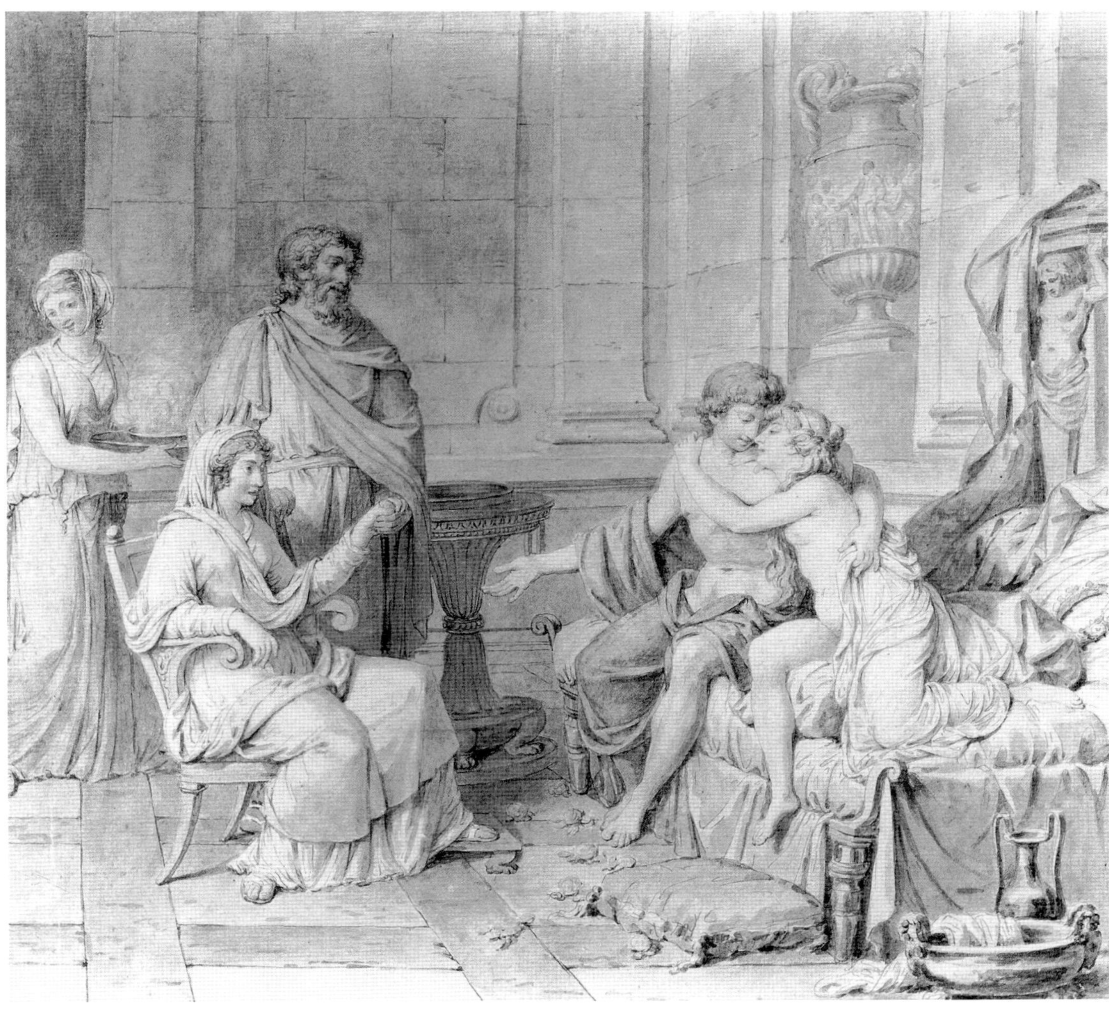

CATALOGUE NO. 24

In this watercolor the most specific reference to a celebrated work from classical antiquity is the stand behind the figure of the bride's father, which is copied directly from the *Aldobrandini Wedding*, a wall painting that for centuries was considered to be one of the finest works of art to have survived from classical times. The servant holding a brazier at the left in the drawing wears a costume very much like the corresponding figure in that painting. Le Barbier might have seen the original during his visit to Rome, but he also could have consulted Bernard de Montfaucon, who included an engraving of the work in his essay on ancient Roman wedding customs (Montfaucon 1976, vol. 2, 136–43, pl. 41).

It is difficult to propose a date for this watercolor on the basis of the artist's stylistic development, since the meticulous finish of Le Barbier's drawings creates a sense of consistency throughout his long and productive career. It may well have been executed during the 1770s or early 1780s, when neoclassical decorative arts like those seen here were at the height of fashion. In a general way the pose of the young couple embracing recalls the figures of Amor and Aphrodite on the relief of a Roman sarcophagus illustrating the *Death of Adonis* (Musée du Louvre, inv. no. 347), which was acquired from Prince Camillo Borghese in 1808. The comparison may be fortuitous, since this would indicate a rather late date for the watercolor. Even if the Louvre relief was probably not Le Barbier's prototype for these figures, he may have known similar antiquities, very likely through engravings.

Le Barbier's theoretical writings provide a clearer picture of his interest in antique works of art. His primary literary work is *Des Causes physiques et morales, qui ont influé sur les progrès de la peinture et de la sculpture chez les grecs* (On physical and moral reasons/factors that influenced the progress of painting and sculpture among the Greeks), 1801, in which the author acknowledged at the outset his debt to Johann Joachim Winckelmann, endorsing his theory that the quality of Greek art could be accounted for in large part by that country's temperate climate, which favored the development of physical perfection through outdoor exercise. Le Barbier avoided the thornier proposition made by Winckelmann that artistic excellence could only be attained through the study and imitation of ancient sculpture and instead suggested that artists should work after live models whose physiques conformed as closely as possible to the norms of ancient art. For all his sympathy with the reforms that could be brought about through a study of the classical past, Le Barbier ultimately remained very much a personality of his time, one whose works, often small in scale, have delicacy and charm and lack the rude vigor of a revolutionary statement. VC

Jean-Jacques Lagrenée the Younger

1739 Paris 1821

JEAN-JACQUES LAGRENÉE, called the Younger, was a student of his brother, Louis-Jean-François, called Lagrenée the Elder. In 1760, the year he won a second prize in the Prix de Rome, Jean-Jacques went to Saint Petersburg with his brother, who had been appointed *premier peintre* to the empress Catherine. The brothers worked in Russia until 1762 and then returned to Paris. In 1765 Jean-Jacques left for Rome, where he studied at the Académie de France (at his own expense until a stipend became available) and made engravings after classical remains. In 1769 he returned to Paris and exhibited at the Salons from 1771 until 1804. In 1775 he was accepted into the Académie for *Winter* (*Hiver*), a ceiling decoration for the Galerie d'Apollon in the Louvre; he became an assistant professor the next year and a full professor in 1781. LDM

Jean-Jacques Lagrenée the Younger
Tancred and Clorinda

25
Pen and brown ink, brush and brown wash, heightened with white ink on blue prepared paper
44 x 32.5 cm (17 5/16 x 12 13/16 in.)
Los Angeles County Museum of Art, Graphic Arts Council Fund and Donor Members (inv. no. M.89.75)

PROVENANCE
W. M. Brady and Company, New York.

EXHIBITED
New York 1988a, no. 7.

Torquato Tasso's poem *Gerusalemme liberata* (Jerusalem delivered), first published in 1581, is a vast, sprawling chivalric epic celebrating the First Crusade. Throughout the seventeenth and eighteenth centuries the poem was a rich source of imagery for European artists. The present drawing is based on one of the more obscure events described by Tasso, the baptism of Clorinda, a Saracen warrior, by the Christian knight Tancred, who was in love with her. Not recognizing her in her battle armor, Tancred mortally wounded her in combat. Dying, she begged for baptism into the Christian faith, and when Tancred removed her helmet and armor, he discovered that he had killed his beloved. He anointed her by gathering water from a nearby spring in his helmet (12.68):

> *and hastening in his anguish, he turned his efforts to giving life with water to her whom he had killed with the sword. While the sound of the holy words poured from him, she was transfigured with joy and smiled; and joyful and vibrant at the moment of death, she seemed to say: "Heaven is opening—I go in peace."*

Jean-Jacques Lagrenée's drawing follows the text quite literally, even to details such as Clorinda's outstretched arm: "And raising her bare, cold hand to the knight, in place of speech, she gives him a pledge of peace. So passes the beautiful lady, and seems asleep" (12.68).

Clorinda's conversion to the Christian faith was a theme only rarely favored by Lagrenée's contemporaries. The subject was used by the artist's elder brother, Louis, in a painting of 1761 that depicts Clorinda begging Tancred to baptize her (*Tancrède et Clorinde*, Tretiakov Museum, Moscow; Sandoz 1983, no. 102, pl. 21). This canvas was painted in Russia, where Louis worked from 1760 to 1762, accompanied by his younger brother, who thus certainly knew this painting. There are only slight analogies between the two works in background details, such as the horse and the approaching warriors, while the poses of the principal figures are completely different. Clorinda's baptism was also represented in one of the illustrations designed by Giovanni Battista Piazzetta for a magnificently printed edition of Tasso's epic published in Venice in 1745, which the Lagrenée brothers may conceivably have seen. Piazzetta, though, shows Tancred collecting the baptismal water, not the sacrament itself, hence the print lacks the compact figure group of both the painting by Louis and the drawing by Jean-Jacques.

Although in all probability Jean-Jacques had his brother's canvas in mind when he drew the present work, it would appear that the drawing was not executed in Russia but rather should date from the artist's full mastery of a pictorial language based on a study of Italian baroque art. The only surviving evidence of his stay in Russia is a group of etchings after compositions by his brother or artists

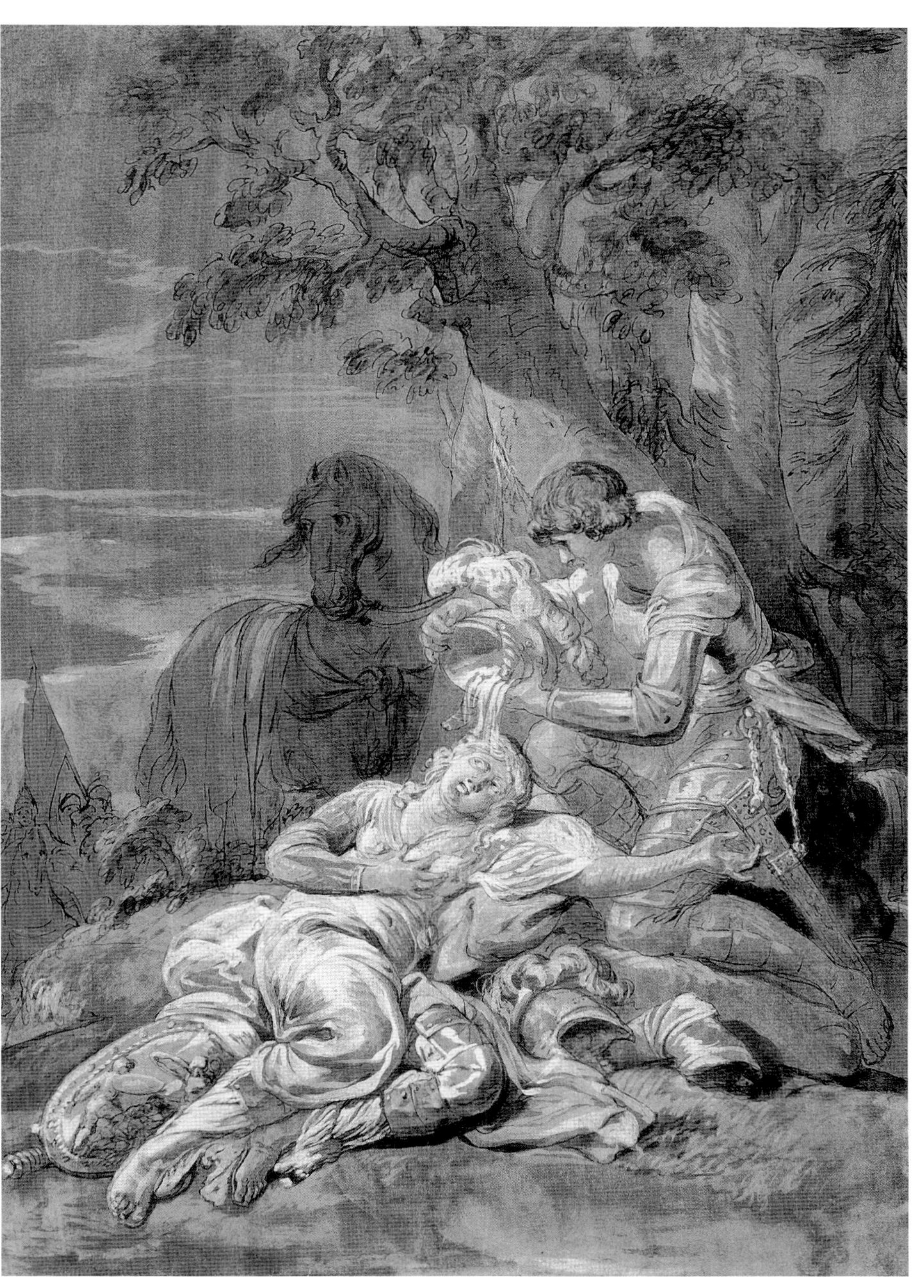

CATALOGUE NO. 25 (see color plate on page 100)

such as Nicolas Poussin, Rembrandt, and Guido Reni, as well as several original compositions (Sandoz 1988, 165–69).

In 1765 Lagrenée left Paris for Rome, where he worked and was housed at his own expense at the Académie de France until a stipend award became available for him, giving him official status. He remained in Italy for four years, returning to Paris in April 1769. Little is known of Lagrenée's work in Rome, aside from a few drawings and etchings after antique bas-reliefs and Roman or "Etruscan" sculpture and vases arranged in decorative compositions (Sandoz 1988, nos. 6–9, pls. 20, 22, 24). But as a student at the Académie de France, where pupils regularly made copies after masterpieces of the High Renaissance and baroque periods, he would have been exposed to these examples as a matter of course.

The accomplished anatomy of Tancred and Clorinda is similar to works from the artist's maturity, especially the Saracen's complicated pose, rather like an elongated Z, as she lies stretched out against a hillock. It would appear that the present drawing dates from the 1770s or early 1780s by comparison with documented paintings such as his tapestry cartoon *The Courage of Jubellius Taurea* (*Fermeté de Jubellius Taurea*), shown at the 1779 Salon (Musée Fabre, Montpellier; Sandoz 1988, no. 115, pl. 3), in which the facial type and fully rounded anatomy of the protesting woman at the right in the painting is comparable to the dying Clorinda. The cartoon and the drawing both clearly demonstrate the importance of Italian seventeenth-century artists such as Reni, whose work Lagrenée copied as a student, for history painters who looked to the past in an attempt to regain the "sober clarity of style" that some earlier critics claimed was sadly missing in the contemporary French school (for a discussion of this point see Crow 1985, 6–22).

One of the most delightful aspects of Lagrenée's art is his chiaroscuro drawings on blue paper, where the support is tinted with gouache or watercolor, as here, creating a ground against which the figures are defined with black ink and white highlights. This combination of media is used to evoke a scintillating play of light over surfaces, seen especially in Clorinda's robe and Tancred's armor. Artists before Lagrenée appreciated the seductive charm of these effects, notably Paolo Veronese. Closer to Lagrenée's epoch, pen and brush drawings on blue paper were frequently made by Jean-Baptiste Oudry and Charles-Joseph Natoire. Chiaroscuro drawings such as the present example continued to be popular with artists throughout the rest of the century and figured importantly in the work of such artists as Friedrich Heinrich Füger (see CATALOGUE NO. 102) and Tommaso Maria Conca (see CATALOGUE NO. 80). The fact that highly finished chiaroscuro drawings such as the examples just cited can be found throughout Europe at this time is one aspect of the growing preference for drawings as independent works of art. In France from the mid-eighteenth century onward glazed and framed drawings were often exhibited at the Paris Salons, and auctions frequently included framed drawings or watercolors. VC

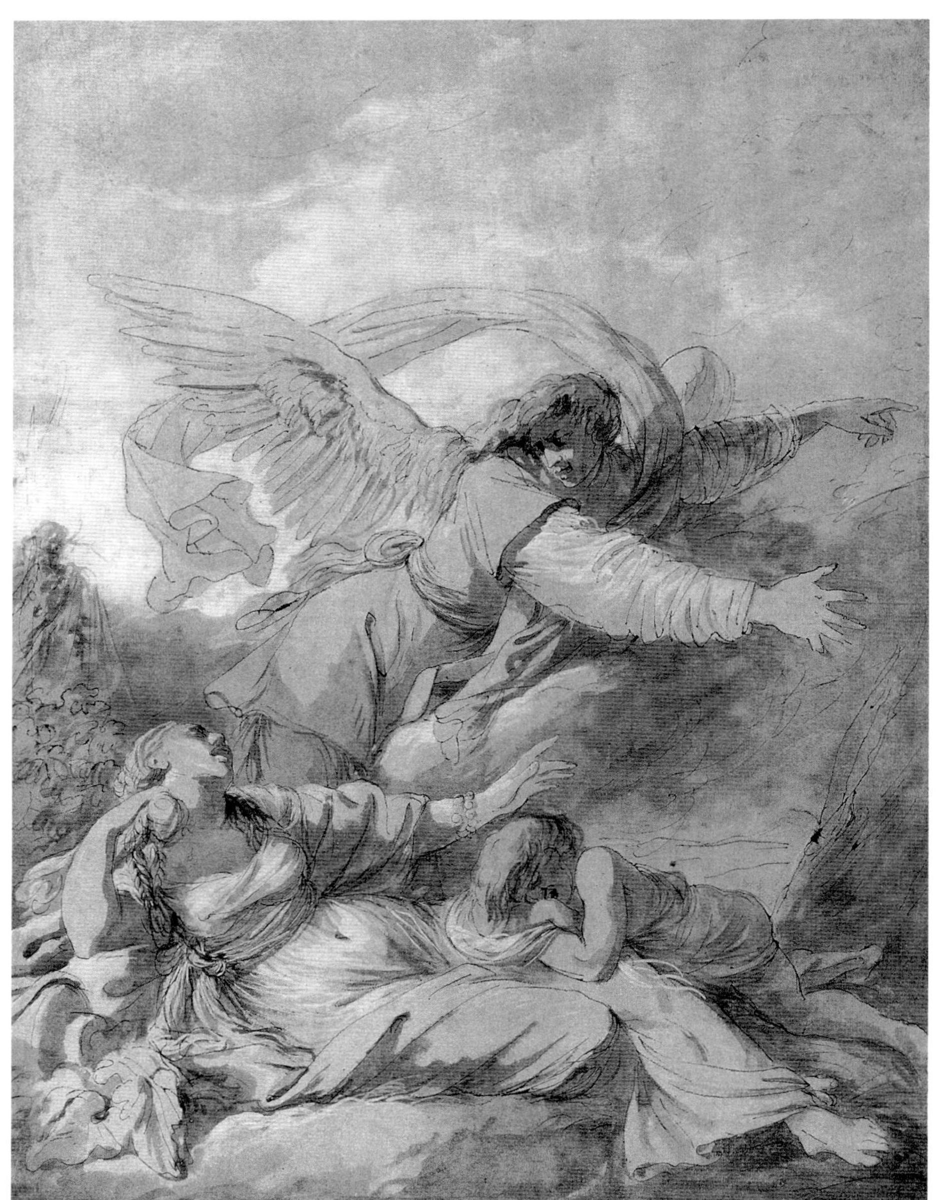

CATALOGUE NO. 26

Jean-Jacques Lagrenée the Younger
Hagar and Ishmael in the Desert
Probably before 1776

26
Pen and black ink, brush and brown wash, heightened with white ink on tan laid paper
53 x 42 cm (20 7/8 x 16 1/2 in.)
Lutheran Brotherhood, Minneapolis

PROVENANCE
Possibly Fournelle collection; sale, Paris, October 14, 1776, lot 178 ("L'Ange montrant une fontaine à Agar. Plume, lavé, et réhaussé de blanc au pinceau").
Sale, Hôtel Drouot, Paris, October 17, 1984, lot 120.

LITERATURE
Possibly Sandoz 1988, no. 59.

Lagrenée's drawing is based on an account from Genesis 21:9–21. In despair over her inability to conceive a child, Sarah proposed that her husband, Abraham, cohabit with her Egyptian maid Hagar, who bore the patriarch a son named Ishmael. Although Isaac was later born to the elderly couple in accordance with a promise made by God, Sarah was jealous of Hagar and feared that Ishmael would share the inheritance with her own son. She persuaded Abraham to send Hagar and her child away, and the outcasts were left to roam in the desert, eventually running out of water. When they were near death, an angel of the Lord appeared to point the way to a well. The drawing illustrates the moment when the angel indicates the source of water that will be their salvation.

Hagar's pose, reclining with her forearm supporting her head and one leg crossed over the other, which is bent at the knee, is an unmistakable reference, although in reverse, to the celebrated marble of a reclining Cleopatra that had been in Rome since the sixteenth century. During Lagrenée's years in the city the statue could be seen as part of the collection of antiquities on the Capitoline Hill that later became the Museo Pio-Clementino (today the sculpture is in the Vatican Museum; Haskell/Penny 1981, no. 24, fig. 96). Now thought to be a copy from the late Hadrianic or early Antonine period of a second-century B.C. masterpiece, perhaps from the workshop of Dionysios, the *Cleopatra* gave rise to a number of casts and copies, one of which was ordered by Louis XIV and is still in the gardens at Versailles. In addition, there were many bronze reductions, which helped spread knowledge of the work far beyond Italy. For artists, the marble was one of the most celebrated antiquities to have survived, and the figure's pose was echoed in many paintings, where it was frequently adapted to indicate the despair of an abandoned heroine. This is exactly the function of the pose in Lagrenée's drawing, with the modification that Hagar's left arm is outstretched as she follows the angel's gesture. Whether or not the artist found any anomaly in using a pose derived from classical antiquity for a biblical figure, the fame of the Cleopatra marble—with its connotations of dejection or despondency that any educated contemporary viewer would have recognized—must have overridden other considerations.

The drawing may be the work described in the auction catalogue of the Fournelle collection (sold Paris, October 14, 1776) as a pen, brush, and ink drawing of "L'Ange montrant une fontaine à Agar" (The angel showing a spring to Hagar; location unknown; Sandoz 1988, no. 59). The description is too abbreviated to permit a positive identification. (Another drawing in red chalk of this subject is also known, which was executed before 1787, in which year it was sold at auction [location unknown; Sandoz 1988, no. 216].) It seems likely that the Minneapolis drawing was made during the 1770s or the early 1780s, to judge from a comparison with a superb unpublished wash preparatory study (private collection, United States; ex-collection Galerie Cailleux, Paris) for an oil exhibited at the 1785 Salon, *Moses Saved from the River by Pharaoh's Daughter* (*Moïse sauvé des eaux par la fille de Pharaon*; Château de Chambéry). The style of the two ink drawings is identical, with pen used to define clearly the contours of each figure. Within these boundaries the artist manipulated his brush with great assurance to create patterns of drapery folds that suggest the ample volumes of each figure. Lagrenée's sense of form was firmly grounded in his study of seventeenth-century Bolognese masters (see CATALOGUE NO. 25).

As Marc Sandoz noted in his account of the artist's career (1988, 130), Lagrenée's paintings were characteristic of the standards favored by the Académie, which had a decisive role in awarding royal commissions. If the Académie was sympathetic to the essentially conservative style of Lagrenée's art, it should also be noted that this body was sufficiently broad-minded to recognize at the same time the work of more progressive artists. The Paris Salon of 1785 at which Lagrenée exhibited his *Moses Saved from the River by Pharaoh's Daughter* was also the venue for the public debut of Jacques-Louis David's *The Oath of the Horatii* (*Serment des Horaces*; FIGURE 9), itself a royal commission, and a work that critics, whether hostile or favorable, recognized as constituting a break with established conventions. VC

Jean-Antoine Houdon

1741 Versailles–Paris 1828

AFTER STUDY WITH Jean-Baptiste Lemoyne and Jean-Baptiste Pigalle, Houdon began his training at the Académie under Michel-Ange Slodtz and won the Prix de Rome in 1761. He spent the years 1764–68 in Rome, where he created the statue of Saint Bruno, 1766, for Santa Maria degli Angeli. Houdon was received into the Académie with his *Morpheus* (*Morphée*) in 1777 and successfully executed a number of works on mythological themes. There was a greater demand, however, for his half-length portrait busts, due in part to the success of his bust of Denis Diderot, 1771, and three works of 1778, a seated figure of Voltaire and busts of Jean-Jacques Rousseau and Benjamin Franklin.

Houdon spent the year 1785 in America working on a full-length statue of George Washington commissioned by the state of Virginia. Acknowledged as the leading portrait sculptor in Europe, he completed portrait busts of Napoleon and Josephine in 1806, and his last bust was of Czar Alexander in 1814. Houdon became a professor at the École des Beaux-Arts in 1805 and continued to teach there until 1823, when he retired at the age of eighty-two. LDM

Jean-Antoine Houdon
Sorrow Consoled by Justice Who Points to Fame (Project for the Tomb of Monsieur Guillard)
1774

27
Pen and black ink, brush and black wash, white heightening, over charcoal on tan paper
34.3 x 42.3 cm (13 1/2 x 16 5/8 in.)
Signed and dated at lower left in brown ink: *Houdon inve. 1774.*
Museum of Art, Rhode Island School of Design, Providence, gift of Mrs. Gustav Radeke (inv. no. 29.084)
(Los Angeles only)

PROVENANCE
Jacques Victor, comte de la Béraudière, Paris, 1883.
Marius Paulme, Paris, 1929 (Lugt 1921, no. 1910).
Martin Birnbaum.
Mrs. Gustav Radeke, Providence, 1929.

EXHIBITED
Versailles 1928, no. 78.
Paris 1928, no. 105.
Providence 1957, no. 83.
Cleveland 1964, no. 41.
Providence 1983, no. 50.

LITERATURE
Mireur 1911–12, vol. 3, 494.
Vitry 1928a, 100–101.
Vitry 1928b, 18, 20, 58–59.
Banks 1931, 66.
Arnason 1975, 30, fig. 73.

This is the only drawing by Houdon that scholars of his work have unanimously accepted as authentic; another sheet in the present exhibition, once thought to be by his hand can now be attributed to Antoine-Jean-Baptiste Thomas (see CATALOGUE NO. 78). A label formerly attached to the back of the frame, but now lost, explains the allegory inspired by the death of Monsieur Guillard, a member of the *grande chambre* of the *parlement* of Paris (cited in Providence 1983, 149, 151–52):

Cette allégorie fut composée au sujet de la mort de Monsieur Guillard, Conseillé de grande chambre au parlement de Paris, mort en 1772; le sujet est la Douleur au pied du tombeau, tenant d'une main l'urne elle est conseillé par la Justice qui lui montre la Renommée qui prend soin de sa gloire en attachant le médallion de celui qu'elle pleure entre les noms fameux des Talons, des Lamoignon, des Daguesseau, des Fleury et autre grand homme du parlement (This allegory was composed on the subject of the death of Monsieur Guillard, counselor of the great chamber of the parliament of Paris, who died in 1772; the subject is Sorrow at the foot of the tomb, holding an urn in her hand. She is counseled by Justice pointing to Fame, who assures the glory [of Guillard] by placing his [portrait] medallion among the famous names of the other great men of the parliament such as Talons, Lamoignon, Daguesseau, and Fleury).

Two years after Guillard's death in 1772, Houdon drew this project for a memorial, but the work was never carried further. It would have been a difficult and expensive project to execute the sarcophagus and three allegorical figures as freestanding sculpture. In fact, one may question whether Houdon's drawing might not have been intended as a design for a bas-relief or memorial plaque, a suggestion that has the merit of explaining the absence of shadows cast by the figures of Sorrow, Justice, and Fame. Furthermore, if Houdon had intended that the monument be freestanding, it would have been a work of considerable depth, as can be judged from the angle at which the tomb is placed. At any event, the rich pictorial values of this drawing show that the artist had a skillful command of the draftsman's materials; it is thus logical to

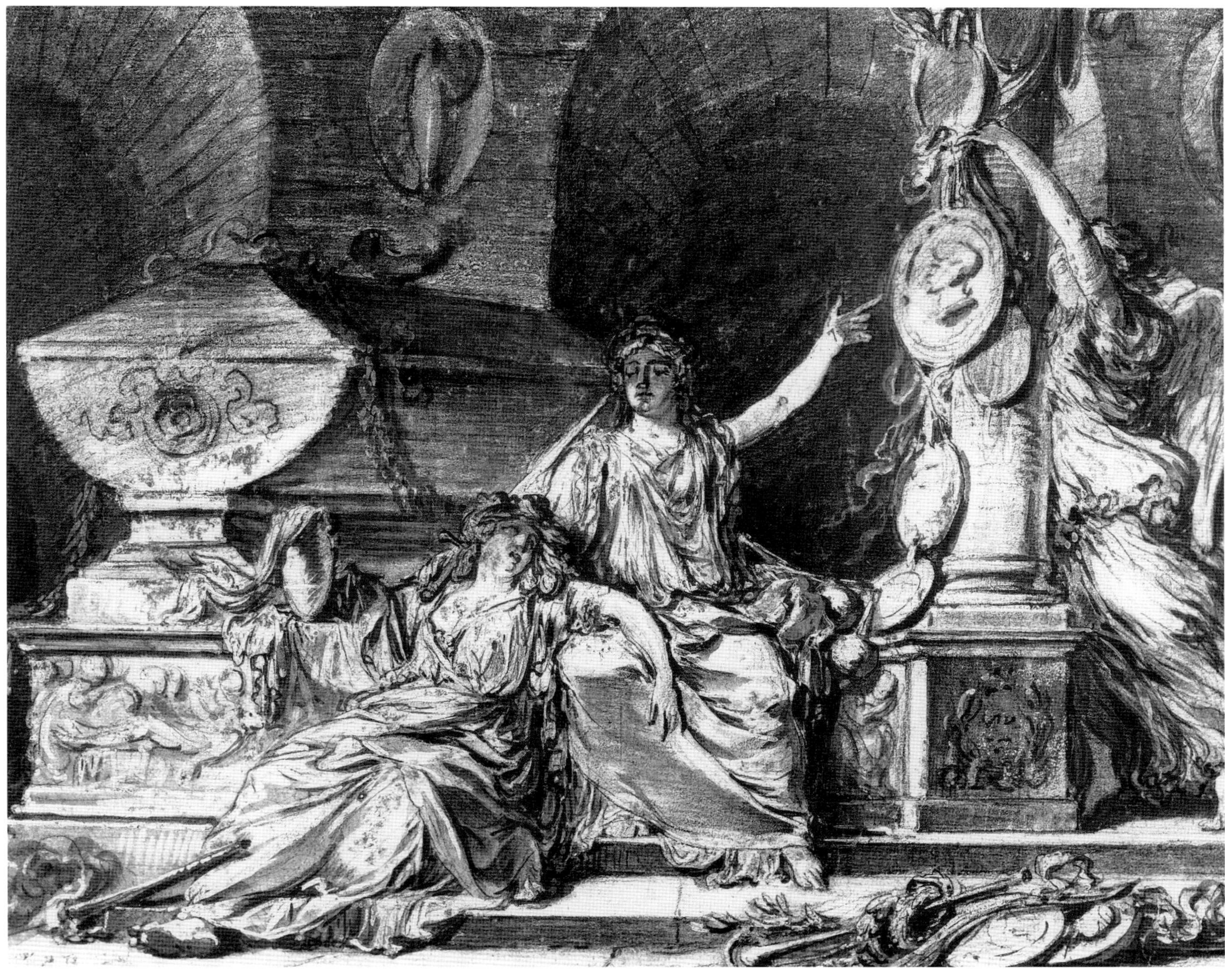

CATALOGUE NO. 27

assume that there must have been many other drawings by Houdon than this now isolated example.

The present drawing is concurrent with Houdon's most productive period as a tomb sculptor. By 1774 Houdon had completed two of his most successful monuments for the Russian Galitzin family, commissions given by Prince Dmitri Alekseyevitch Galitzin, the Russian ambassador to France from 1765 to 1773. Each tomb is a marble bas-relief, one in memory of Field Marshal Mikhail Mikhailovitch Galitzin, the other to Senator Alexis Dmitrievitch Galitzin (both are in the Donskoy Monastery, Moscow; Arnason 1975, 26–27, figs. 74–75). A third project, for the tomb of Prince Alexander Mikhailovitch Galitzin, survives only as a terra-cotta sketch in the Musée du Louvre, Paris (Arnason 1975, 29, fig. 96). Each of the three Galitzin tombs features allegorical figures in classical Roman dress, surrounded by appropriate attributes, very much like the figures in the present drawing. The use of classical figures to embody abstract ideas or virtues was commonplace in Western art from the Renaissance onward but at this time was endorsed not only by convention but as well by Johann Joachim Winckelmann's views about the supremacy of ancient art. When Houdon returned to Paris from Rome, he would have found French translations of Winckelmann's *Geschichte der Kunst des Alterthums* (History of the art of antiquity), 1764, translated in 1766, and *Versuch einer Allegorie besonders für die Kunst* (An essay on allegory, principally for artists), 1766, translated the same year.

Houdon came closest to realizing the German writer's ideal of "noble simplicity and sedate grandeur in Gesture and Expression" in his two marble reliefs for the Galitzin family. Winckelmann's characterization of works of ancient art posed a dilemma for an artist like Houdon, whose training with Jean-Baptiste Pigalle, followed by four years of study in Rome, exposed him to the baroque tradition of funerary sculpture, with its extravagant expression of emotions and use of illusionistic effects. In Houdon's works such as this design for a memorial to Guillard one senses a tension between the sculptor's gesticulating allegorical figures, their plethora of attributes a mixture of classical and Christian references, and the need to create an appropriately "antique" monument to eulogize the departed parliamentarian. VC

Jean-Michel Moreau, called Moreau Le Jeune

1741 Paris 1814

MOREAU—called Moreau Le Jeune to distinguish him from his older brother, Louis-Gabriel, also an artist—accompanied his teacher, Louis-Joseph Le Lorraine, to Saint Petersburg in 1758, when the latter was appointed director of the Russian Academy of Fine Arts. After Le Lorraine's death in 1760, Moreau returned to Paris and changed his course of study from painting to engraving, beginning studies with Jacques-Philippe Le Bas. He became so successful an illustrator that he soon had to abandon his engraving and confine himself to drawing; he was acclaimed for his work on La Borde's *Chansons*, Rousseau's *Oeuvres*, and Restif de la Bretonne's *Monument du costume* of 1789. He received royal appointments as a draftsman from both Louis XV, in 1770, and Louis XVI, in 1781. Traveling to Italy in 1785, he was influenced by his study of classical antiquity and the works of Jacques-Louis David. In 1789 he became a member of the Académie with *The Coronation of Louis XVI (Le Sacre de Louis XVI)*, an engraving after his own design.

Moreau was a supporter of the Revolution, despite the fact that he lost both his royal appointment and many personal possessions. From 1793 to 1798 he worked on the five volumes of his *Nouveau Testament*, and in 1795 he began working for the publisher Antoine-Augustin Renouard, illustrating the works of Ovid, Molière, Racine, Voltaire, and Rousseau. The last years of his life were unhappy; he could not draw because of illness and was thus penniless. He was finally reinstated as *dessinateur du cabinet du roi* by Louis XVIII in the year of his death. LDM

Jean-Michel Moreau Le Jeune
The Athenians Abandoning Their Camp after Their Defeat in Sicily
1808

28
Pen and brown ink, brush and bistre wash on white laid paper
16.2 x 9.8 cm (6 3/8 x 3 7/8 in.)
Signed and dated below the central image in brown ink: *J. M. Moreau Le Jr. 1808.*
Inscribed below the central image in brown ink: *les Atheniens abandonnet leur camp apres leur défaite/ en Sicile./Thucydide. liv. VII.*
Smith College Museum of Art, Northampton, Massachusetts, gift of Mr. and Mrs. Robert Lifton (Loretta J. Silver '52) and Dr. and Mrs. Ernst Greif (Carol Lynn Silver '55) (inv. no. 1971:15-6)

Jean-Michel Moreau Le Jeune
The Peloponnesians at Miletus Revolting against Admiral Astyochus
1808

29
Pen and brown ink, brush and bistre wash on white laid paper
16.2 x 9.8 cm (6 3/8 x 3 7/8 in.)
Signed and dated below the central image in brown ink: *J. M. Moreau Le Jr. 1808.*
Inscribed below the central image in brown ink: *les Péloponnésiens à Milet, ce révoltent contre/ Astyochus, géneral de la flotte./Thucydide Liv. VIII*
Smith College Museum of Art, Northampton, Massachusetts, gift of Mr. and Mrs. Robert Lifton (Loretta J. Silver '52) and Dr. and Mrs. Ernst Greif (Carol Lynn Silver '55) (inv. no. 1971:15-3)

PROVENANCE
Olry-Roederer collection.

These two drawings were intended to be engraved and published in an 1808 edition of *Histoire grecque de Thucydide* (Thucydides's History of Greece), translated from the Greek by Jean-Baptiste Gail, who had also published a Latin edition the previous year. At the Salon of 1817 five Moreau drawings, four of which were related to this publication, were exhibited posthumously. The Northampton sheets were listed as numbers 585: "Astyochus, poursuivi par des matelots révoltés, se réfugie près un Autel. (Il tient en main le bactérion, bâton de commandement.)" (Astyochus, pursued by mutinous sailors, seeks sanctuary at an altar. [He holds in his hand the bacterion, commander's baton.]); and 588: "Depart des Athéniens" (Departure of the Athenians). Also exhibited were numbers 586: "Le Prise de Mélos" (The capture of Melos); 587: "La Peste d'Athènes" (The plague of Athens); and 589: "Hercule étouffant le lion de Némée" (Hercules strangling the Nemean lion), the last unrelated to Thucydides's text (Janson 1977, 66). Guillaume Boichot and Jean-Jacques-François Le Barbier l'Aîné also exhibited drawings related to the Gail edition at the 1817 Salon (Janson 1977, 10; Salon nos. 82, 488–92).

The Smith College Museum of Art conserves four additional Moreau drawings for the 1808 edition of Thucydides (inv. nos. 1971:15-1, 15-2, 15-4, 15-5). Each of the six drawings is "framed" by a border of arabesques, trophies, and grotesques executed in pen and brown ink, brush and bistre wash, probably by Guillaume Boichot. Ten drawings by Le Barbier related to the Gail commission, now also in the Smith College Museum of Art (inv. nos. 1971:15-7 through 15-16), are adorned with borders by the same hand, and in the *livret* to the Salon of 1817 Le Barbier's entry number 489 indicates that Boichot executed the "arabesques."

Béraldi (1874, no. 236) documented that six designs by Moreau for Thucydides were engraved in 1808 by Jean Dambrun, Jean-Louis Delignon, and Louis-François Mariage. The present author has been able to verify only the Delignon engraving, *La Peste d'Athènes*, illustrating a scene from book 2 of the edition.

Moreau's illustration to book 7 of Thucydides's *Peloponnesian War* depicts the disastrous retreat of the Athenian army from Syracuse after suffering defeat at the hands of the Sicilian forces in this turning point of the war. As narrated by Thucydides (1934, 445):

> *The dead lay unburied, and each man as he recognized a friend among them shuddered with grief and horror; while the living whom they were leaving behind, wounded or sick, were . . . far more shocking than the dead, and more to be pitied than those who had perished. These fell to entreating and bewailing until their friends knew not what to do, begging them to take them and loudly calling to each individual comrade or relative whom they could see, hanging upon the necks of their tent-fellows in the act of departure, and following as far as they could, and when their bodily strength failed them, calling again and again upon heaven and shrieking aloud as they were left behind.*

Moreau is highly attentive to the archaeologically accurate details of the Athenian helmets, shields, swords, spears, and other accoutrements.

The other drawing depicts the revolt of the Peloponnesian sailors against the Spartan admiral Astyochus. After the debacle at Syracuse the Spartans, Sicilians, and Athens's vassal states banded together against the Athenians; the allies were subsidized by King Darius of Persia through his lieutenant Tissaphernes. The Peloponnesians became dissatisfied with the slow and irregular payment of their salaries and accused Astyochus of complicity with Tissaphernes. Thucydides (1934, 499) reported:

> *The army was engaged in these reflections, when the following disturbance took place about the person of Astyochus. Most of the Syracusan and Thurian sailors were freemen, and these the freest crews in armament were likewise the boldest in setting upon Astyochus and demanding their pay. The latter answered somewhat stiffly and threatened them, and when Dorieus spoke up for his own sailors, even went so far as to lift his baton against him; upon seeing which, the mass of the men, in sailor fashion, rushed in a fury to strike Astyochus. He however saw them in time and fled for refuge to an altar; and they were thus parted without his being struck.*

Although Moreau specialized early in his career in book illustration in the Louis XVI style, he came under the influence of Jacques-Louis David in the 1790s. His drawings for Thucydides are consummate examples of his new manner and veritable "history paintings" in octavo (Ray 1982, 87–89). From Charles Rollin's *Histoire ancienne* (Ancient history), 1738–48, illustrated by Hubert-François Gravelot, to the Didot editions of Jean Racine and the Latin classics, with engravings after François Gérard, Anne-Louis Girodet de Roussy-Trioson, and Jean-Guillaume Moitte, the importance of book illustration in the evolution and dissemination of neoclassicism throughout Europe cannot be overstated (Walch 1967, 226–27). RJC

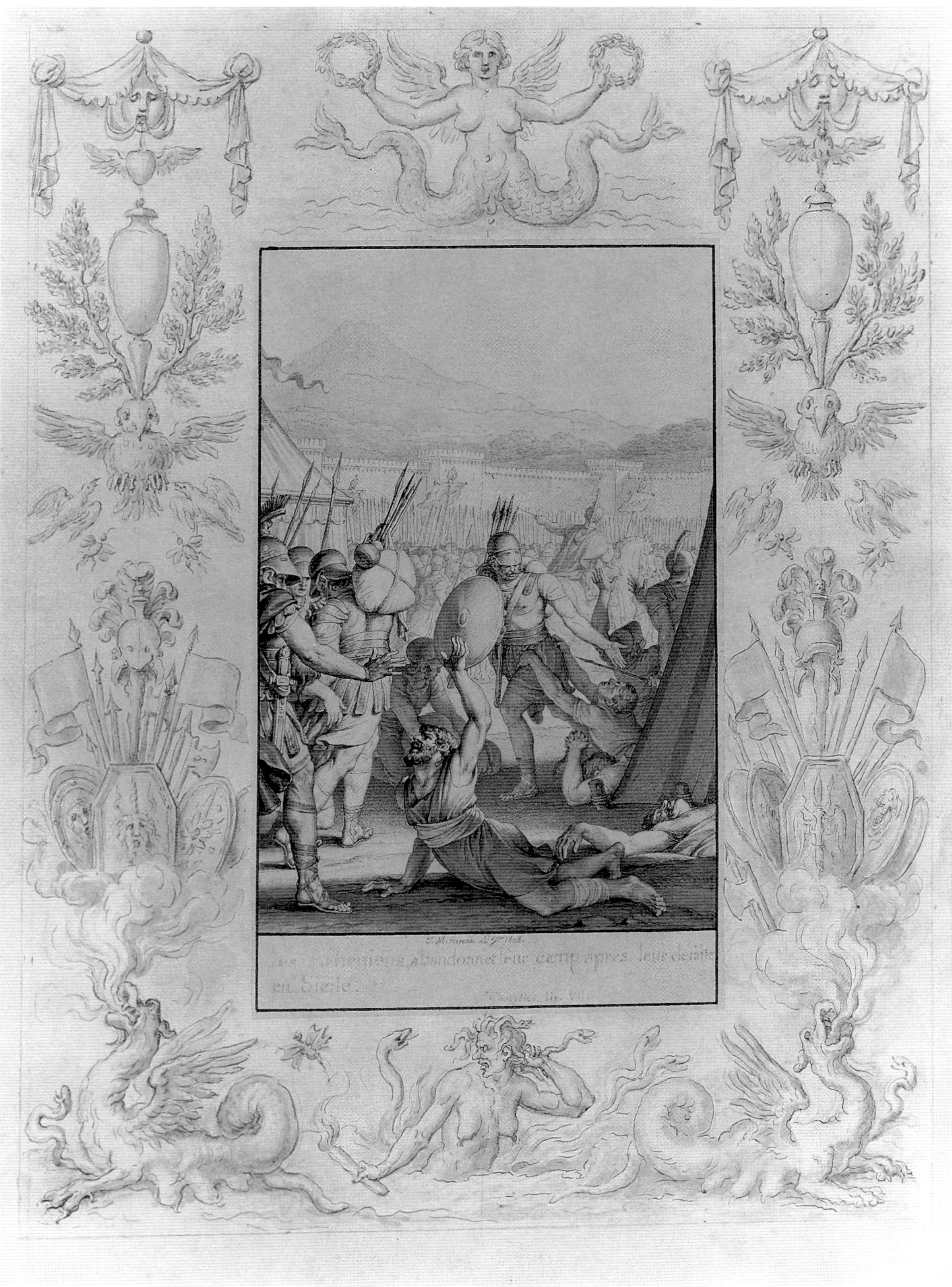

CATALOGUE NO. 28

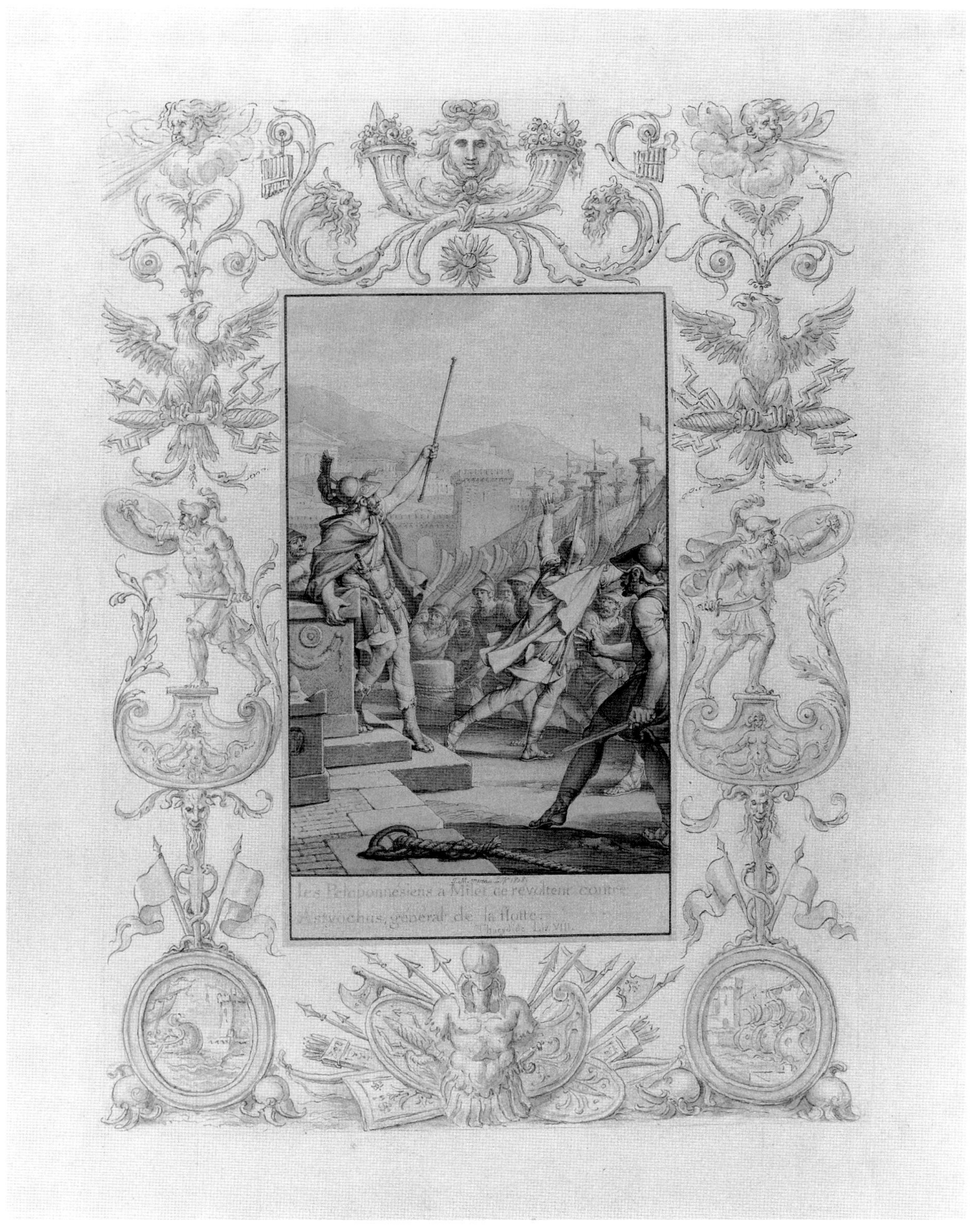

CATALOGUE NO. 29

Joseph-Benoît Suvée

1743 Bruges–Rome 1807

SUVÉE BEGAN HIS STUDIES at the Académie in Bruges. He relocated to Paris in 1763 and entered the atelier of Jean-Jacques Bachelier. After three attempts he won the Prix de Rome in 1771 with his *Combat of Minerva and Mars* (*Combat de Minerve contre Mars*) and arrived in Rome in 1772. Suvée returned to Paris in 1778 and exhibited at the Salons from 1779 until 1796. With his *Birth of the Virgin* (*La Naissance de la Vierge*) in 1779 he was awarded *agrément* status at the Académie and became a full member the next year. Enjoying royal patronage, Suvée executed official commissions for the king, as well as several tapestry cartoons for the Gobelins factory. He was elected director of the Académie de France à Rome in 1792, but his position was abolished after he been on the job for only five days by Jacques-Louis David during the Terror. Suvée was imprisoned in 1794 but was finally able to assume his position as director in Rome in 1801. He moved the Académie from the Palazzo Mancini to the Villa Medici and devoted his energy to his administrative tasks at the expense of his own painting. LDM

Joseph-Benoît Suvée
The Invention of Drawing
c. 1791

30
Black and white chalks on brown paper
54.6 x 35.5 cm (21 1/2 x 14 in.)
Inscribed on the original mount in graphite:
J. B. SUVEE. A SON AMI VAN SPAENDONCK MEMBRE DE L'INSTITUT NATIONAL
Collection of the J. Paul Getty Museum, Malibu, California (inv. no. 87.GB.145)
(Los Angeles only)

PROVENANCE
Gerard van Spaendonck; sale, Paris, July 15, 1822, lot 9.
Sale, Christie's, London, December 13–14, 1984, lot 150.

LITERATURE
Goldner/Hendrix 1992, 208–9, no. 87.

Pliny the Elder's story of the invention of drawing was a popular subject for artists during the last quarter of the eighteenth century, especially among British painters such as George Romney and David Allan (see CATALOGUE NO. 1 for a discussion of the iconography). The latter's canvas *The Origin of Painting*, dated 1773 (National Gallery of Scotland, Edinburgh; Irwin 1966, fig. 91), is strikingly close to Suvée's composition in that both artists show Dibutade's lover ardently embracing her as she traces his shadow cast against the wall of her father's pottery workshop, an uncommon interpretation of the legend, in which the young man is usually either asleep or oblivious to her actions. It is possible that Suvée saw the Scottish painter's work when both artists were in Rome, since Allan's painting won a medal at the Accademia di San Luca while Suvée was a student at the Académie de France.

In the Paris Salon of 1791 Suvée exhibited a painting, now in the Groeningen Museum, Bruges (Heim/Béraud/Heim 1989, 344), that corresponds in every detail to the composition of the present drawing. The artist exhibited at the same Salon a reduced replica of the canvas (present location unknown), which was shown again at the 1793 Salon, and there is a reference to a third painting of Dibutade once in the possession of Simon-Charles Boutin, treasurer of the Ministère de la Marine, who was guillotined in 1793 (Brussels 1985–86, 101).

The Getty Museum's drawing is a meticulously executed replica of Suvée's painting of 1791, one of several highly finished sheets made by the artist about this time, each of which is based on the composition of an earlier painting. At least six drawings of this type are known, all dated before 1801, when the artist left Paris to assume his post as director of the Académie de France in Rome. Suvée evidently gave these drawings to friends or artists whom he admired, since many are dedicated on their original mounts, such as the present example, which the artist gave to his compatriot Gerard van Spaendonck, a painter who specialized in still lifes of fruit and flowers. In addition to these replicas, Suvée executed several drawings of this theme, two sold after the artist's death in 1807, and another dedicated to his friend L. E. van Outryve (Goldner/Hendrix 1992, 208).

Suvée's drawing is a tour-de-force of chiaroscuro effects that effectively convey the tenebrous atmosphere of the potter's studio, lit only by an oil lamp. The dramatic lighting of the scene is an effective counterpart to the static pose of the embracing couple, whose ardor appears to have been arrested momentarily by the chill perfection of Suvée's draftsmanship. VC

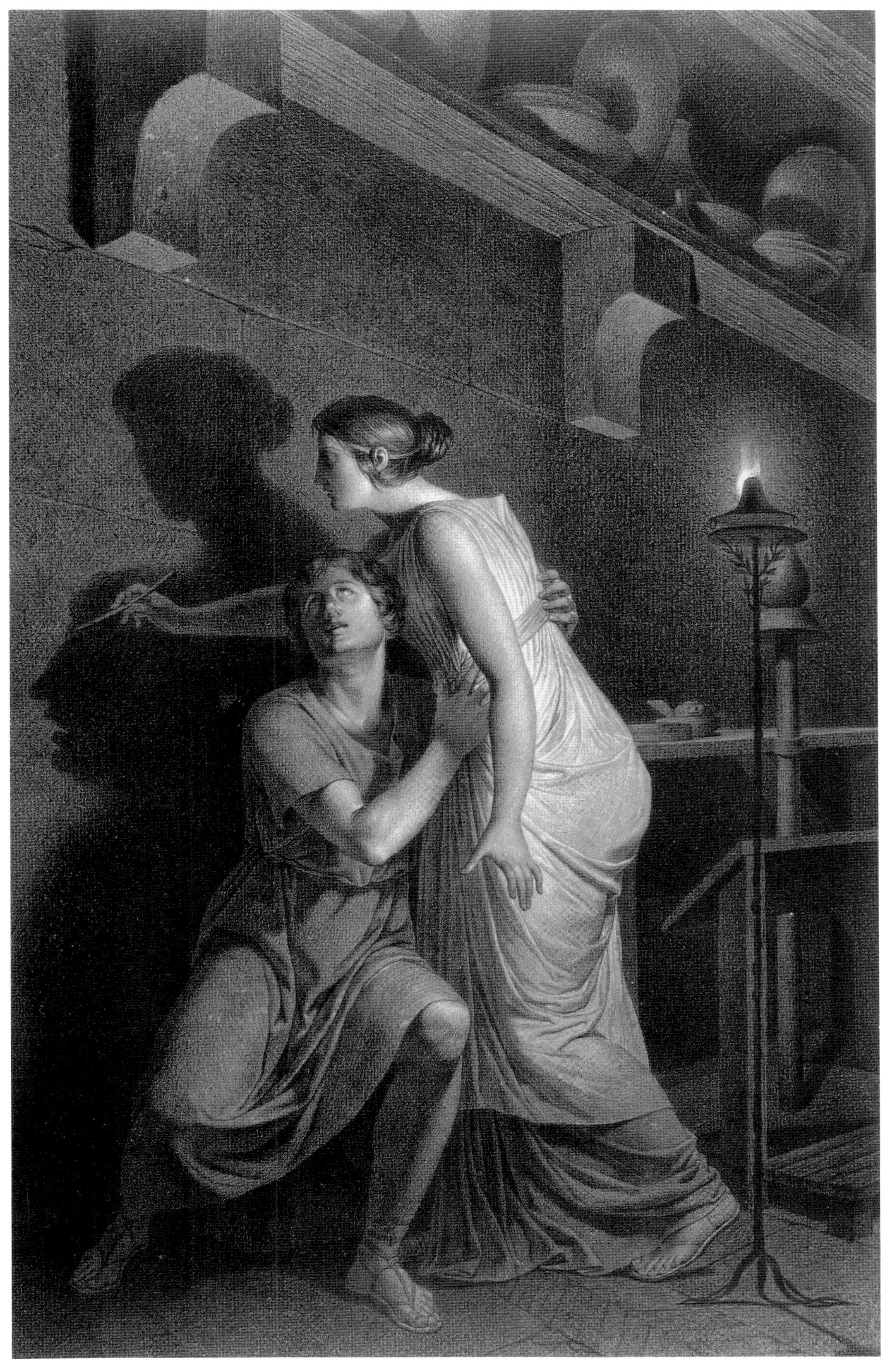

CATALOGUE NO. 30

Jean-François-Pierre Peyron

1744 Aix-en-Provence–Paris 1814

BORN INTO AN AFFLUENT FAMILY, Peyron began as a pupil in the local *académie* and, after 1767, studied in Paris in the studio of Louis-Jean-François, called Lagrenée the Elder. He won the Grand Prix de Rome in 1773, after three attempts, with his *Death of Seneca* (*Mort de Sénèque*); in doing so he was victorious over Jacques-Louis David, thus beginning their long-standing rivalry. Peyron studied at the École Royale des Élèves Protégés under Michel-François Dandré-Bardon until 1775, when he left for Rome. There he, not David, was considered the hope of the French school, and he was allowed to extend his stay in Rome to seven years. At the Palazzo Mancini under the direction of Joseph-Marie Vien he painted some of his most successful works, including *Hagar and the Angel* (*Agar et l'ange*), *Belisarius* (*Bélisaire recevant l'hospitalité d'un paysan qui avait servi sous lui*), and *Cornelia, Mother of the Gracchi* (*Cornélie, mère des Gracques*).

Thanks to the patronage of the comte d'Angiviller (see CATALOGUE NO. 32) and the equally influential Cardinal Bernis, the French ambassador to Rome, Peyron carried the day over David in Rome. Peyron returned to Paris in 1782 and exhibited his *Death of Alcestus* (*Mort d'Alceste*) at the Salon of 1785; however, it was overshadowed by David's *The Oath of the Horatii* (*Serment des Horaces*; see FIGURE 9), and his subsequent works suffered by comparison with those by David. Peyron continued to exhibit after the Revolution, but by then his work seemed old-fashioned, and he was soon surpassed by younger artists. At Peyron's funeral, however, David recognized his debt when he admitted, "Peyron opened my eyes." LDM

Jean-François-Pierre Peyron
The Meeting of Orestes and Iphigenia
1781

31
Pen and black ink, brush and gray wash, heightened with white ink, over faint traces of black chalk on pale tan laid paper
22 x 33.1 cm (8 11/16 x 13 in.)
Signed and dated at lower left in brown ink: *P. Peyron fecit 1781.*
Stamped on the back of the frame in red wax: *B J* within a rectangle)
Caron and Steven Broidy, Los Angeles

PROVENANCE
Sale, Paris, Nouveau Drouot, March 25, 1981, lot 19.

EXHIBITED
Possibly Paris, Salon, 1785.

LITERATURE
Gazette de l'Hôtel Drouot, March 20, 1981, 27.
Rosenberg/van de Sandt 1983, 107, no. 84, fig. 63.

Among the classical subjects that occupied Peyron during his time in Rome was this event from Euripides's tragedy *Iphigenia in Tauris*, in which the heroine recognizes her brother Orestes, from whom she has been separated since childhood. Iphigenia, the daughter of King Agamemnon of Mycenae, was sacrificed by her father in order to ensure favorable winds so that the Greek fleet could set sail for Troy. She was carried off by the goddess Artemis to be her priestess in the land of the Tauri, where all strangers were sacrificed. Orestes was ordered to sail to Tauris to capture the votive statue of Artemis in order to expiate his guilt for the murder of his mother, Clytemnestra. The dramatic recognition of the kinship of brother and sister is the episode chosen by Peyron, following which the pair devise a plan of escape for Orestes. Peyron may well have read Euripides's dramas, which were a rich source of thematic ideas for painters

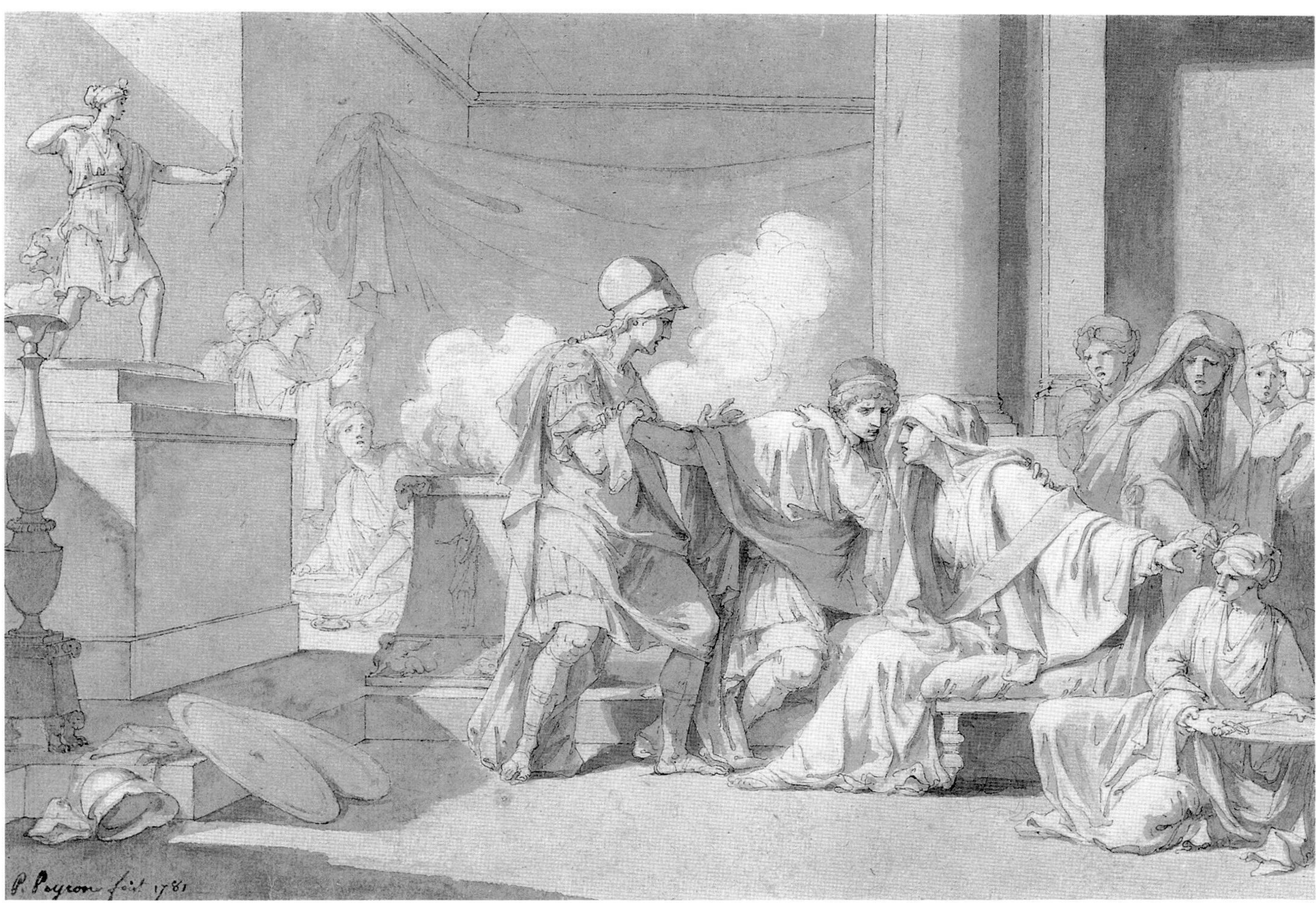

CATALOGUE NO. 31 (see color plate on page 101)

throughout the eighteenth century (see Bardon 1963, 236), but the story was also the basis for one of the most celebrated plays by Jean Racine, whose works were frequently performed at this time. Moreover, the drama was the basis for the libretto of Christoph Willibald Gluck's opera *Iphigénie en Tauride*, premiered in Paris in 1779. Since the story enjoyed a certain currency, Peyron may have been encouraged to show his drawing of the recognition scene at the 1785 Salon, where he made his Parisian debut. In all likelihood, Peyron drew another version of the present work, since customarily the drawings he submitted for exhibition at the Salons were larger in format (Rosenberg/van de Sandt 1983, 107).

Peyron's Roman drawings were the work of an artist fully in command of his style and means of expression, which subsequently served him without any dramatic changes. The assured modeling of his figures, their effective gestures, and the coherence of his compositions are evidence of the young artist's precocity. Most of Peyron's drawings are fully realized, complete compositions. Preliminary sketches for individual figures have rarely survived, although the artist's preparatory studies for the principal figure groups in his canvases are among his most appealing works on paper (see CATALOGUE NO. 32). Of course, like any student at the Académie, Peyron drew after the posed model; only recently has the first of these *académies* come to light, as, for example, a study inscribed *Rome 1780* (New York 1989a, no. 12). VC

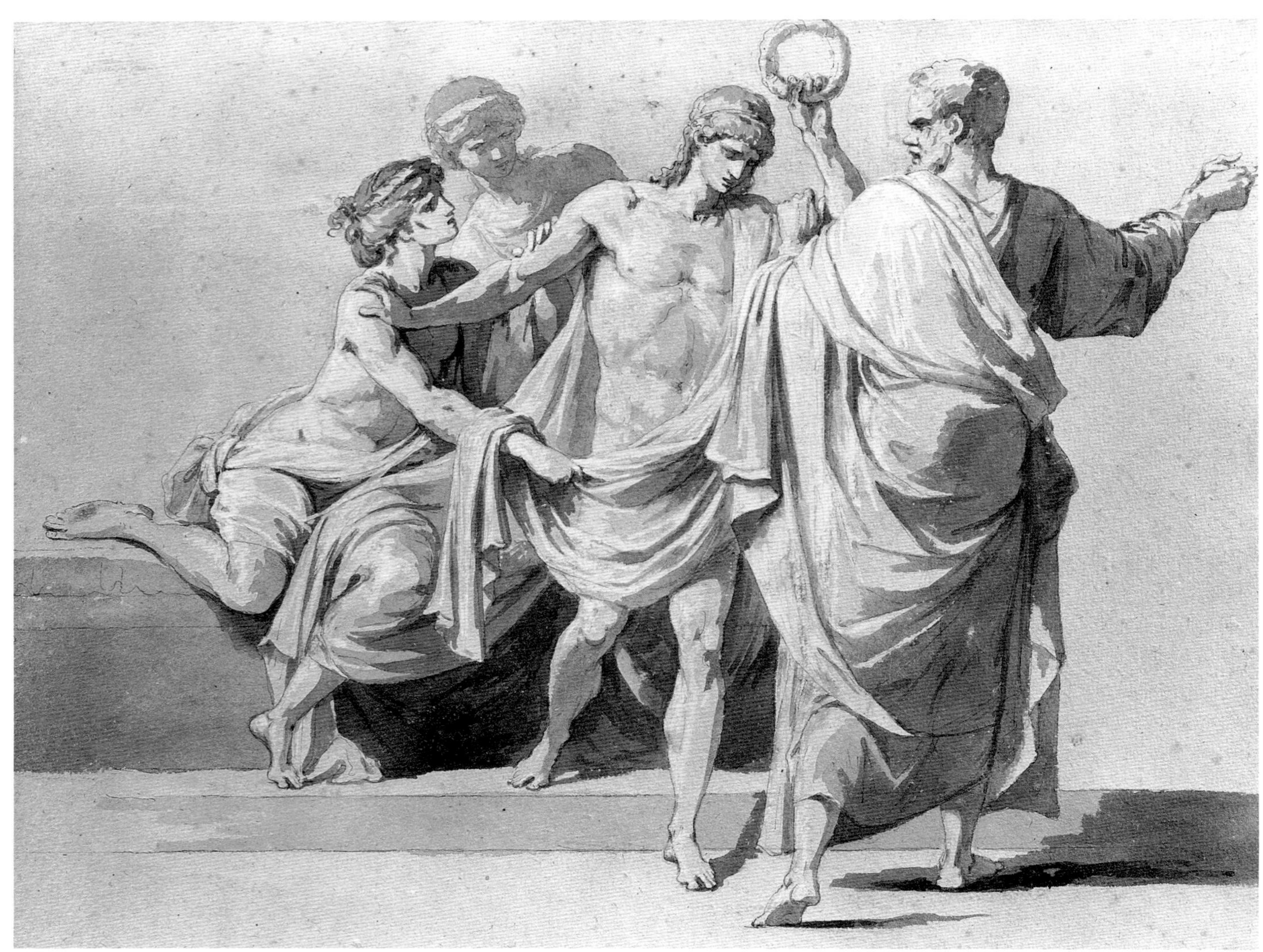

CATALOGUE NO. 32

Jean-François-Pierre Peyron
Socrates Leading Alcibiades from the Dangers of Sensual Life
Probably after 1785

32
Pen, brush, and brown ink, heightened with white ink, over faint indications of black chalk on gray-tan paper
23.3 x 31.1 cm (9 3/16 x 12 1/4 in.)
Ackland Art Museum, University of North Carolina at Chapel Hill, the William A. Whitaker Foundation Art Fund (inv. no. 69.18.1)

PROVENANCE
Sale, Paris, Hôtel Drouot, May 9, 1969, lot 40.
Henri Baderou, Paris.
Germain Seligman, New York.

EXHIBITED
Toronto/Ottawa/San Francisco/New York 1972–73, no. 109, pl. 132.

LITERATURE
The Art Quarterly 33, no. 2 (1970), 189, 193.
Rosenberg/van de Sandt 1983, no. 76, fig. 59.

As a student in Rome Peyron's exceptional abilities were recognized by Parisians such as the powerful superintendent of the king's buildings, the comte d'Angiviller, who wrote to Joseph-Marie Vien, then director of the Académie de France à Rome, that he would like from Peyron two "tableaux en pendant." In a letter of April 1780 d'Angiviller specified that one should have as its subject the death of Socrates in prison, which in the end was replaced by *The Funeral Rites of Miltiades* (*Les Funérailles de Militiade*; Musée du Louvre, Paris), while the other theme was to be chosen by Peyron but should include some female nudes. Two years later the second work, *Socrates Detaching Alcibiades from the Charms of Sensual Pleasure* (*Socrate détachant Alcibiade des charmes de la volupté*), was finished. Today the oil can no longer be identified, but its composition is known through two prints, one an etching by Peyron (Rosenberg/van de Sandt 1983, nos. 71, 80, figs. 57–58). He painted another version of the subject, in all probability after 1785, when d'Angiviller's commission was shown at the Paris Salon (Musée Guéret; Rosenberg/van de Sandt 1983, no. 72, fig. 60).

The present drawing is a carefully executed study for the four principal figures in the canvas, drawn when the artist had decided on the final position of each, since there are no signs of hesitation or change. There is a separate drawing for the figure of Socrates, part of a sheet of studies in black chalk for figures that appear in other paintings by Peyron. Even in this earlier sheet the artist had determined the pose he would use, with only very slight modifications (Rosenberg/van de Sandt 1983, no. 92, fig. 62). A highly finished drawing of the composition also exists (Musée Guéret), perhaps a replica after his painting drawn by the artist in preparation for an etching that was never executed (although he made an etching after the pendant *Funérailles de Militiade*, probably when it was seen at the 1785 Salon or shortly thereafter).

Studies of details such as this figure group are the exception among the small number of Peyron's known drawings. The exquisite interplay of contour and the delicate modeling of flesh and draperies, which both define form while helping to unite the figures as a coherent group, typify Peyron's draftsmanship at its best. Here the commanding stance of Socrates and the abashed expression of his favorite pupil—a youth of noble birth destined for a brilliant political career—communicate a clear moral lesson. The theme of Socrates leading Alcibiades away from the distractions of pleasure evidently was Peyron's innovation, as there is no classical or contemporary precedent for the subject. By the latter half of the eighteenth century the life of Socrates was a not uncommon source of subject matter for painters, who usually were attracted by the stoic death of the philosopher. His role as a teacher and moral counselor was less often represented. Although François-André Vincent's Salon entry of 1777, *Alcibiades Receiving Lessons from Socrates* (*Alcibiade recevant les leçons de Socrate*; Musée Fabre, Montpellier), predates Peyron's work, since the latter was in Rome at this time, it is difficult to imagine how he could have known Vincent's painting (Paris 1989a, 315, nos. 417–19). Subsequently, throughout the rest of the century the episode of Socrates admonishing Alcibiades attracted painters, although the philosopher's ethical imperative is diluted in Garnier's later drawing (see CATALOGUE NO. 50). VC

Jean-Joseph Taillasson

1745 Bordeaux–Paris 1809

TAILLASSON, whose provincial beginnings caused him to be overshadowed by many of his contemporaries, entered the atelier of Joseph-Marie Vien in 1764. He attempted to win the Prix de Rome three times, with only a third prize as a result. He did eventually go to Rome in 1773 and stayed for four years. He was made an academician in 1784 with *Ulysses and Neoptolemus Take Away the Arrows of Hercules from Philoctetes* (*Ulysse et Néoptolème enlèvent à Philoctète les flèches d'Hercule*) and exhibited regularly at the Paris Salons from 1783 until 1806. Many of his works showed the influence of Vien and were much admired for their sense of tragedy. He also translated and composed poetry and wrote commentaries on painting. LDM

Jean-Joseph Taillasson
Hero Discovering the Body of Leander on the Seashore
c. 1798

33
Black and white chalks on gray paper
36.2 x 50.5 cm (14 1/4 x 19 7/8 in.)
Los Angeles County Museum of Art, purchased with funds provided by Museum Associates Acquisition Fund and the Garrett Corporation (inv. no. M.85.191)

PROVENANCE
Henri Baderou, Paris.
Frederick J. Cummings, Detroit.
P. and D. Colnaghi, New York, 1985.

EXHIBITED
Chicago 1982, no. 28.

LITERATURE
Mouilleseaux 1974, 412.
Paris/Detroit/New York 1974–75, 626.
Bordeaux 1989, 319.

The story of Hero and Leander is a tale of ill-fated love. Hero, a priestess of Aphrodite at Sestos, met Leander at the celebration of the festival of Aphrodite and Adonis. They became deeply enamored, but her position as a priestess and the opposition of her family made their union impossible. Nonetheless, they met clandestinely. Every night Hero would put out a lamp at the top of the tower by the sea where she lived, and Leander, guided by the light, would swim across the Hellespont to her. One night a storm blew out the lamp, and Leander lost his way and drowned in the dangerous currents. When Hero found his body washed to shore the next morning, she committed suicide by throwing herself into the waves. The story is referred to by a number of ancient Roman writers, including Virgil (*Georgics* 3.258), Statius (*Thebias* 6.542–47), and Ovid (*Heroides* 18–19). Taillasson may also have read the version by the later Greek poet Musaeus (fourth-fifth century A.D.), which had often been translated into French. Before Taillasson the theme rarely occurred in French art, although a canvas by François-Savary Balthasard was exhibited at the 1791 Salon (Bardon 1963, 229). From the 1790s into the early nineteenth century, however, a number of French and English painters treated the subject, including William Etty, François-Xavier Fabre, Anne-Louis Girodet de Roussy-Trioson, and Joseph Turner (Mouilleseaux 1974, 412–13).

At the close of the eighteenth century many European artists were attracted to those aspects of classical literature that related dramas of morbid or hopeless emotional entanglements, such as Hero and Leander's mutual passion. Caught up in an overwhelming flood of despair, Hero chose to join her lover in death. This is a far remove from Johann Joachim Winckelmann's "noble simplicity and sedate grandeur in Gesture and Expression" (cited in Eitner 1970, vol. 1, 11). Ironically, classical literature could provide artists with numerous incidents illustrating violent emotions and irrational actions, "the very opposite of ideal beauty and perfect emotional equilibrium" (Rosenblum 1967b, 11). Taillasson apparently did not find it inappropriate to use classicizing formal means of representation for this type of iconography. The solidly defined figures of Hero and Leander, thrown into relief by dramatic lighting and isolated against a bleak seascape background, may well reflect the artist's admiration for Nicolas Poussin, whose art was an exemplar for many late eighteenth-century painters in their search for alternatives to the rococo style.

Taillasson's drawing is a preparatory study for the figures in his canvas *Hero and Leander* (*Héro et Léandre*; Musée d'Histoire et d'Art, Blaye), which was exhibited in the Salon of 1798 along with a smaller replica (Mouilleseaux 1974, 411,

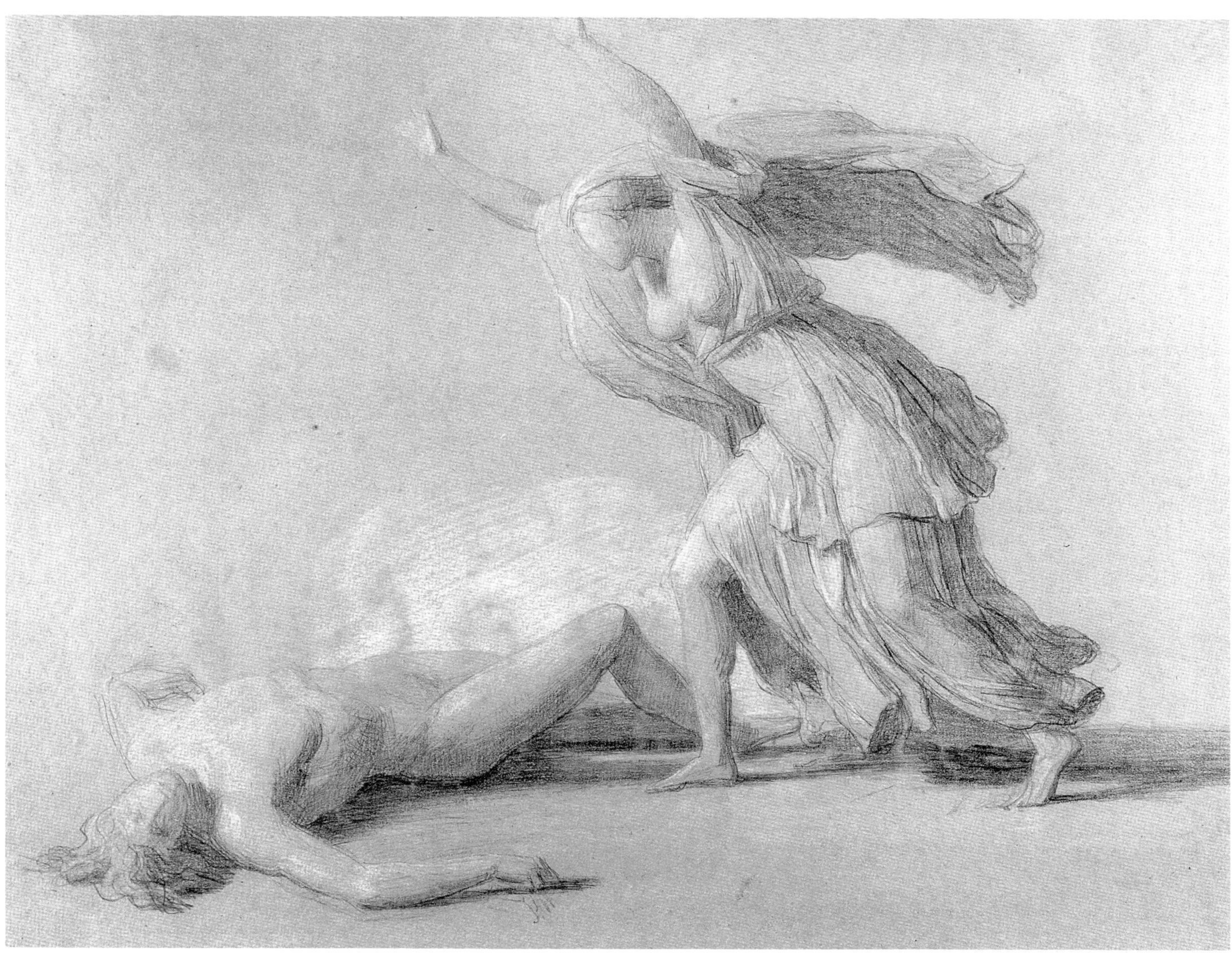

CATALOGUE NO. 33 (see color plate on page 102)

fig. 1). The guide to the Salon mentions that the larger painting was awarded a prize by the newly founded French Republic as part of a program to encourage artists (for the complicated history of this competition, see Paris 1989b, vol. 3, 830–51). Two years earlier Taillasson had painted an oil sketch of this subject, but differing from his Salon entries in composition and format; this work, in a private collection, remains unpublished (Mouilleseaux 1974, 412 n. 3).

In the present drawing Hero and Leander are posed as they appear in the 1798 canvas, even to such details as their shadows cast on the ground. This drawing is a forceful study of highly pitched emotion expressed through dramatic gestures illuminated by a source outside the composition. In the canvas the light also draws attention to Hero's anguished features as she discovers the dead body of her lover. The artist omitted facial details in his drawing, choosing instead to concentrate on how light would define the generalized forms of each figure. Because Hero's discovery takes place at dawn, Taillasson drew on colored paper, the function of which was to approximate the tenebrous background of the oil. By drawing on this ground with black and white chalks the artist could easily study the lighting effects he would transpose to his painting.

At present only a few drawings by or attributable to Taillasson are known. Among the largest and most important is his highly finished wash drawing *The Wounded Mezentius Receiving the Body of His Dead Son Lausus* (Musée des Beaux-Arts, Nancy), exhibited in the 1785 Salon and surely based on a painting by the artist done two years earlier (Bordeaux 1989, no. 97). The style of the Nancy drawing has provided the basis for the attribution to Taillasson of an elaborately realized sketch for a *Massacre of the Innocents* on the London art market (London 1975, no. 116). Our view of the artist's draftsmanship has recently been enlarged by the publication of a number of his works, mainly in French collections, several of which were heretofore unknown (Bordeaux 1989, nos. 102–3, 105, 111–12, 116, 121–22, 125–27). In the United States, in addition to the present work, a major Taillasson drawing was acquired by the Detroit Institute of Arts, *Bernice Reproaching Ptolemy* (*Les Reproches de Bérénice à Ptolémée*), a *modello* for the painting of the same title also in Detroit. Even this handful of works illustrates the strength of Taillasson as a draftsman, from the working study in Los Angeles, with its bold definition of figures, to the suave finish of his replica at Nancy after his 1783 Salon entry. VC

Jean-Guillaume Moitte

1746 Paris 1810

MOITTE BEGAN HIS TRAINING as a sculptor at age fifteen with Jean-Baptiste Pigalle, but because of Moitte's delicate health and the long walk to Pigalle's studio he changed to the nearby studio of Jean-Baptiste Lemoyne. In 1768 he won the Prix de Rome in sculpture for *The Triumphant David Carrying the Head of Goliath* (*David portant triomphant le tête de Goliath*) and subsequently spent three years at the École Royale des Élèves Protégés. He left for Rome in 1771 but studied at the Académie de France only for two years because of his poor health. Upon his return to Paris he worked for the king as an ornamental designer.

Moitte exhibited for the first time at the Salon in 1783, the same year he became an associate in the Académie. In 1787 he received his first important commission, for a statue of the seventeenth-century astronomer Dominique Cassini for the Paris Observatoire. During the Revolution he was awarded a commission for a statue of Jean-Jacques Rousseau to be raised on the Champs-Élysées, but the project was never executed. He executed a new pediment for the Panthéon in 1792 and became a member of the Institut de France three years later. Near the end of his life he was commissioned by Napoleon to execute the tomb of Général Desaix in the chapel of the Grand-Saint-Bernard hospice in the Alps. LDM

Jean-Guillaume Moitte
Theseus and Acheloüs
c. 1792–95

34
Pen and black ink, brush and greenish gray and black washes and white gouache on two joined sheets of white laid paper
26.8 x 64.5 cm (10 9/16 x 25 3/8 in.)
The Art Museum, Princeton University, museum purchase, Laura P. Hall Memorial Fund (inv. no. x1976-296)

Jean-Guillaume Moitte
Ceres and Cyane
c. 1792–95

35
Pen and black ink, brush and greenish gray and black washes and white opaque watercolor on two joined sheets of white laid paper
27 x 64.5 cm (10 5/8 x 25 3/8 in.)
The Art Museum, Princeton University, museum purchase, Laura P. Hall Memorial Fund (inv. no. x1976-297)

PROVENANCE
Spencer Drummond, London.

EXHIBITED
Princeton 1983, 30.

LITERATURE
Regnault 1808, 39, no. 276.
"Acquisitions of the Art Museum 1976." *Record of The Art Museum, Princeton University* 36, no. 1 (1977): 35.
Campbell 1981–82, 104, 108 n. 62.
Campbell 1982, 203–4, 311 nn. 25–27, 358, figs. 50–51.
Ross 1983, 30–31.

A protégé of Antoine-Chrysostôme Quatremère de Quincy and Jacques-Louis David, Jean-Guillaume Moitte achieved renown as a sculptor of monumental statuary and bas-reliefs from the *ancien régime* to the Empire. Earlier, however, he had established a solid reputation as a draftsman. His drawings, ranging from designs for ornamental arabesques for goldsmith's work to book illustrations and prints, were consistently exhibited at the Paris Salons from 1783 to 1791 to the acclaim of the critics.

The Princeton drawings are studies for a pair of *gravures aux outils* (tool-work engravings) printed in color on a dark background (*fond noir*) by Perdriaux and Ridé. The copper plates and ten proofs of each print were included in the 1808 atelier sale of the engraver Laurent Guyot (Paris, November 14, lot 276; impressions are conserved at the Bibliothèque Nationale, Paris).

The drawings illustrate themes from Ovid's *Metamorphoses*. One depicts the banquet hosted by the river god Acheloüs in his cavernous domicile for Theseus and his companions, who were returning to Athens after the hunt for the Calydonian boar (books 8 and 9). A discussion ensues about the power of the gods to effect metamorphoses, during which Acheloüs recounts his combat with Hercules for the hand of Deianira, at the climax of which he transformed himself into a fierce bull. Hercules nevertheless subdued Acheloüs and as a final humiliation broke off one of his horns, which was subsequently sanctified by naiads and enriched with fruits and flowers by the goddess of Plenty. Moitte represents the conclusion of Acheloüs's narrative, when a nymph of Diana approaches Acheloüs, Theseus, and his cohort Lelex with the cornucopia laden with autumn's harvest for their evening's dessert.

The identification of the subject of the second drawing has been problematic due to the title printed in the margin of the engraving: *Ceres demandant à Jupiter la permission de chercher sa fille Proserpine* (Ceres asking Jupiter's permission to seek his daughter Proserpina). It does not in fact represent Ceres and Jupiter, nor does it portray Ceres and Arethusa, as it is presently identified. Moitte actually depicts the Sicilian nymph Cyane displaying for Ceres the girdle of Proserpina.

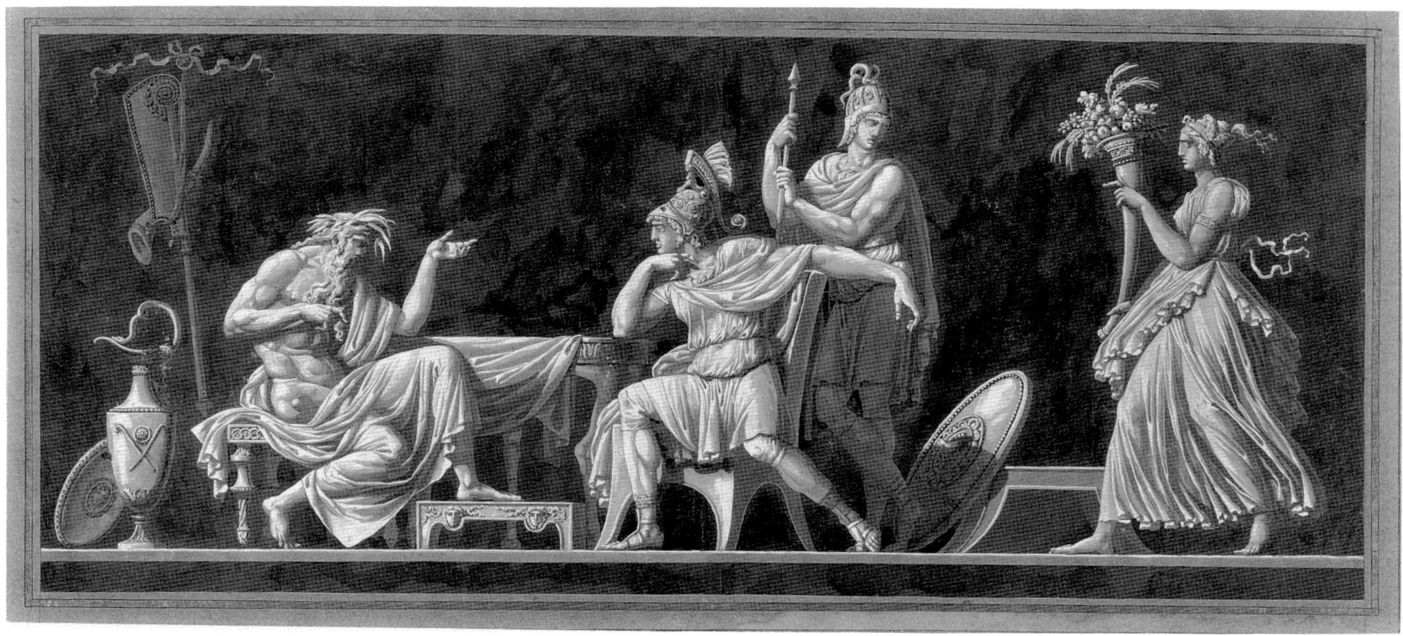

CATALOGUE NO. 34

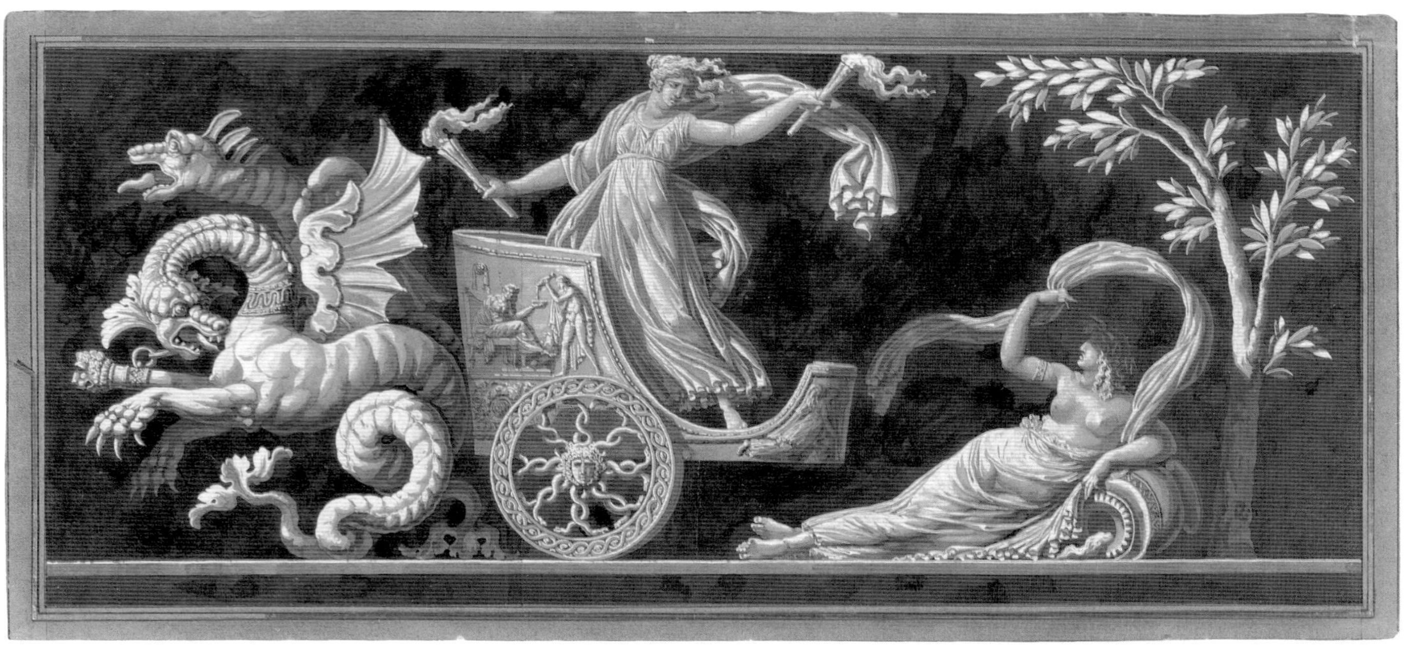

CATALOGUE NO. 35

Cyane had witnessed the abduction of Proserpina by Pluto and had attempted to intervene. The enraged Pluto hurled his scepter into the nymph's sacred pool of water and thus burrowed a crater through which to escape into his underworld domain. The grieving Cyane then dissolved into the pool that bears her name. When the distraught Ceres passed by in her dragon-drawn chariot in search of her daughter, the now voiceless Cyane provided a clue by floating a fragment of Proserpine's torn garment, which had fallen into her pool during Pluto's passage (book 5). The allusion to Jupiter in the title of the print may perhaps be explained by the image of Ganymede filling that god's cup in relief on the chariot.

Although the *gravures aux outils* by Perdriaux and Ridé are undated, the Princeton drawings were most likely executed about 1792–95, based on stylistic affinities with other *fond noir* prints on mythological and republican themes after Moitte (Guérinet n.d., pl. 118; Campbell 1982, 204–10, 311 n. 31, figs. 52, 54, 61; Minneapolis 1984, 302–3, no. 109; Gramaccini 1989, 67–69, figs. 14, 15, 17). It should be noted that Moitte designed for the publisher Joubert a *fond noir* engraving, *The Abduction of Proserpina*, which depicts simultaneously Proserpina gathering flowers with her companions, Cyane attempting to halt Pluto, and the pursuit of Ceres (Guérinet n.d., pl. 132, and Campbell 1982, 204, 311 n. 27).

Moitte drew upon two ancient sources for his *fond noir* compositions: Etruscan vase painting and Pompeiian mural painting. William Hamilton's *Collection of Etruscan, Greek and Roman Antiquities*, published in Naples in 1766–67, was illustrated with engravings of painted vases with figures highlighted against a black background, which provided models for artists and artisans throughout Europe, most notably Josiah Wedgwood and John Flaxman. Moitte designed an allegorical frontispiece for *La Galerie de Florence* with engravings after the collection of Leopoldo de' Medici, the grand duke of Tuscany, which included important examples of Aretine painted pottery; Moitte's design, engraved by Jean Marais, incorporated an Etruscan amphora and kylix (Campbell 1981–82, 104, 109 n. 68). Apart from the dark grounds of these vase paintings, Moitte was also influenced by the abstract, hermetic contours that defined the figures and the drapery.

Roman wall painting constituted a second source for the artist. He resided in Italy as a pensioner at the Académie de France in Rome from October 1771 until June 1773, but his chronically poor health was aggravated by the Italian climate, and he was forced to return to Paris. Consequently, his knowledge of Roman wall painting was most likely gleaned from the celebrated portfolio *Le pitture antiche d'Ercolano* (Naples, 1757–96) and Pietro Santi Bartoli's *Recueil de peintures antiques* (Paris, 1783). Moitte combined the black background and illusionistic ledges from the mural paintings in frieze drawings such as the present examples, which are in effect bas-reliefs on paper.

Moitte's designs are distinguished by a profusion of ornamental detail. Typical are the decorative elements of the chariot of Ceres. The elaborately wrought helmets, shields, ewer, and furniture in *Theseus and Acheloüs* resemble Moitte's contemporary corpus of designs for goldsmith's work and furniture executed for the entrepreneur Henri Auguste, which created a sensation among artists (Snodin/Baker 1980, 735–48, 830–34; Campbell 1982, 178–97). As observed by his early biographer, Joachim Le Breton (1812, 48):

> *Moitte produced perhaps more than a thousand designs in this genre, and he enjoys in this regard a special celebrity that later he would disdain to an inordinate degree; since he has restored to an industry of luxury, which the greatest masters did not shy away from doing honor, a degree of merit which has not existed in France for more than a century. Thus, Moitte had the foremost reputation as a draftsman for style, purity and composition.*

Lastly, the ornamental fantasy, attenuated figural proportions, and meticulous delineation of folds of drapery also reveal the impact of the sixteenth-century Roman mannerists on Moitte's compositions, a school that also profoundly influenced Henry Fuseli, who resided in Rome during Moitte's brief sojourn at the Académie de France (New Haven 1979, vii; Campbell 1982, 189–90, 302 n. 40).

In effect, Moitte's illusionistic frieze drawings constitute a synthesis of stylistic elements, unified by contour, that conveys a startling and highly original conception of antiquity (Paris 1989a, 87–89). As noted by his friend Quatremère de Quincy in the *Gazette nationale* of May 4, 1810, on the occasion of Moitte's funeral, "Moitte distinguished himself with a plethora of drawings, which simultaneously display his own taste and also exude the air of antiquity, of which he revealed himself a disciple." RJC

François-André Vincent

1746 Paris 1816

VINCENT BEGAN HIS CAREER as a student of his father, François-Élie Vincent, and later became a student of Joseph-Marie Vien at the Académie. He won the Prix de Rome in 1768 for *Germanicus Calming a Mutiny in His Camp* (*Germanicus apaisant la sédition dans son camp*), and after some time at the École Royale des Élèves Protégés he left for Rome in 1771. Vincent returned to Paris in 1775 and presented fifteen paintings at the Salon two years later. His entries were a success, and he was made an associate member of the Académie on the basis of his *Saint Jerome*. He followed this showing with the very popular *President Molé Seized by the Mob* (*Président Molé et les factieux*) at the Salon of 1779.

Vincent became a full member of the Académie in 1783, with his *Rape of Orythea by Boreas* (*Enlèvement d'Orythie*) as his reception piece. He continued to exhibit paintings at the Salon through the end of the century. From 1800 onward he devoted his energies to the large-scale *Battle of the Pyramids* (*La Bataille des Pyramides*), but his failing health prevented him from finishing the project. Late in life he continued to paint and draw portraits, a talent first seen in his drawings of his classmates in Rome. LDM

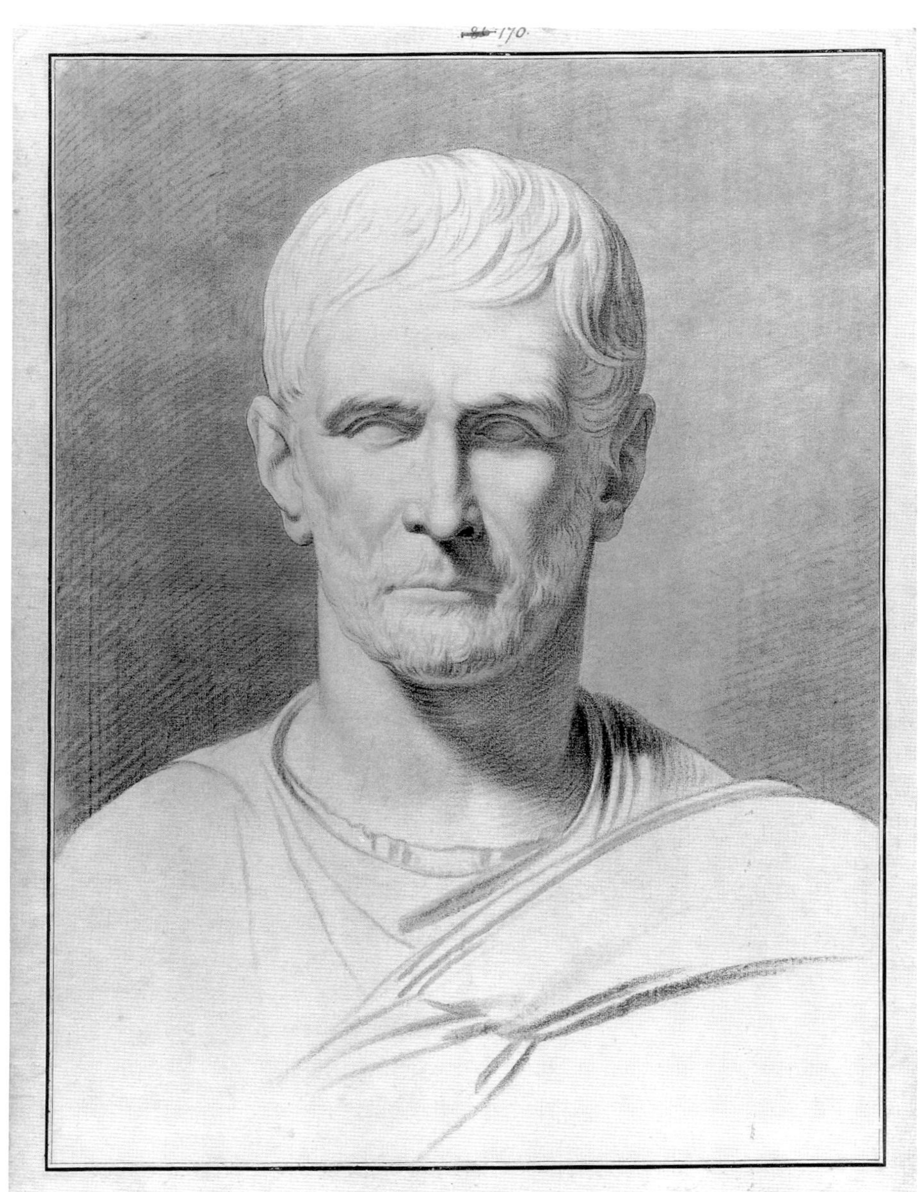

CATALOGUE NO. 36

François-André Vincent
Bust of Lucius Junius Brutus (The Capitoline Brutus)
c. 1774

36
Red chalk and red wash on white laid paper
52 x 39.3 cm (20 1/2 x 15 1/2 in.)
Hood Museum of Art, Dartmouth College, Hanover, New Hampshire, purchased through a gift from the Cremer Foundation in memory of J. Theodor Cremer and a gift from John W. Thompson, Class of 1908, and Dorothy M. Litzinger, by exchange (inv. no. D.988.16)

PROVENANCE
Theodore Allen Heinrich, Toronto (purchased in London, 1961); sale, Christie's, London, July 6, 1982, lot 230, pl. 26 (as Julius Caesar).
F. A. den Broeder, New York.

EXHIBITED
Toronto 1962, no. 56 (as Julius Caesar).
New York 1982a, no. 47, pl. XX (as Gaius Caesar).
New York 1988a, no. 8.

Vincent's drawing after the famous bust of Lucius Junius Brutus in the Capitoline Museum, Rome, was surely made while he was a student in that city. The finesse and control of the artist's modeling, here achieved basically through lines of varying densities enhanced with some brushwork, is comparable with a signed and dated chalk drawing of 1774 of a bust of Cicero now in Paris at the École Nationale Supérieure des Beaux-Arts (Cuzin n.d. [1988?], no. 14). Exercises such as these studies after the antique were a matter of routine for students at the Académie de France, although the high quality of Vincent's draftsmanship is impressive. The bust of Brutus was among the most celebrated antiquities in Rome, its fame attributable in part to its supposed representation of the man who overthrew his uncle, King Tarquin the Proud, to found the Roman Republic. But the sculpture was widely admired as a work of art because it vividly characterized a leader of "great character: melancholy, deep thought, firmness of soul, severity" (Abbé Coyer, cited in Haskell/Penny 1981, 164). Vincent's copy goes beyond the norms of competence to express a sense of individuality so emphatically conveyed by the portrait.

Only recently the research of Jean-Pierre Cuzin has revealed that many drawings formerly thought to be by artists as diverse as Jean-Honoré Fragonard and Jacques-Louis David are in fact by Vincent (see CATALOGUE NO. 38). As a student he was an immensely gifted and multifaceted personality. The reattribution to Vincent of several celebrated drawings traditionally regarded as masterpieces executed by Fragonard during his second visit to Rome, December 1773–June 1774, when the younger artist came to know him, is dramatic evidence of Vincent's precocious abilities (Rome 1990–91, 247–49, 251, nos. 173a, 175, 176, 178). The impact of Fragonard is nowhere to be found in a drawing such as this, however, which suggests that Vincent had an uncommon ability to switch from one manner of working to another, absorbing the characteristics of a style without the impulse to add a personal inflection. This situation is undoubtedly foremost a matter of the artist's character, but it also must reflect the lack of clear-cut options confronting a young artist in Rome at this moment. The authority of antique art, promulgated through Johann Joachim Winckelmann and Anton Raphael Mengs, was contradicted by the example of Fragonard, whose technical flair and immediate response to the everyday world clearly had a powerful attraction for Vincent. VC

François-André Vincent
The Clemency of Augustus
c. 1784–87

37
Pen and brown ink, brush and brown wash, over traces of red chalk, perspective lines in graphite (recto); red chalk, squared in red chalk (verso) on white laid paper
33.7 x 38.3 cm (13 1/4 x 15 1/16 in.)
Signed and dated at lower right in pen and black ink: *Vincent 1788*
The Metropolitan Museum of Art, New York, Harry G. Sperling Fund, 1985 (inv. no. 1985.245.2)
(Los Angeles and Minneapolis only)

PROVENANCE
Colnaghi, London, 1985.

EXHIBITED
London 1985, no. 46.

LITERATURE
Bean 1986, no. 319.
Montagu 1986, 91.
New York: The Metropolitan Museum of Art, *Annual Report 1986–1987*, 24.
Cuzin n.d. [1988?], no. 46.

This drawing and another study of one of the figures (see CATALOGUE NO. 38) illustrate the painstaking, methodical preparations made by Vincent for his major canvases. At the Salon of 1787 he exhibited a large oil, *The Clemency of Augustus to Cinna* (*Clémence d'Auguste envers Cinna*), which, according to the exhibition catalogue, was based on the final scene of Pierre Corneille's tragedy *Cinna* (v, 3), specifically, the moment when the emperor turns to his former enemy with an offer of reconciliation: "Soyons amis, Cinna, c'est moi que t'en convie" (Let us be friends, Cinna, I wish it so). The artist may well have seen the drama performed at the Comédie Française, where it was staged 186 times during the eighteenth century. This instance of royal magnanimity was chosen by the archbishop Clemens Wenzeslaus of Trier from a list of eight themes proposed to

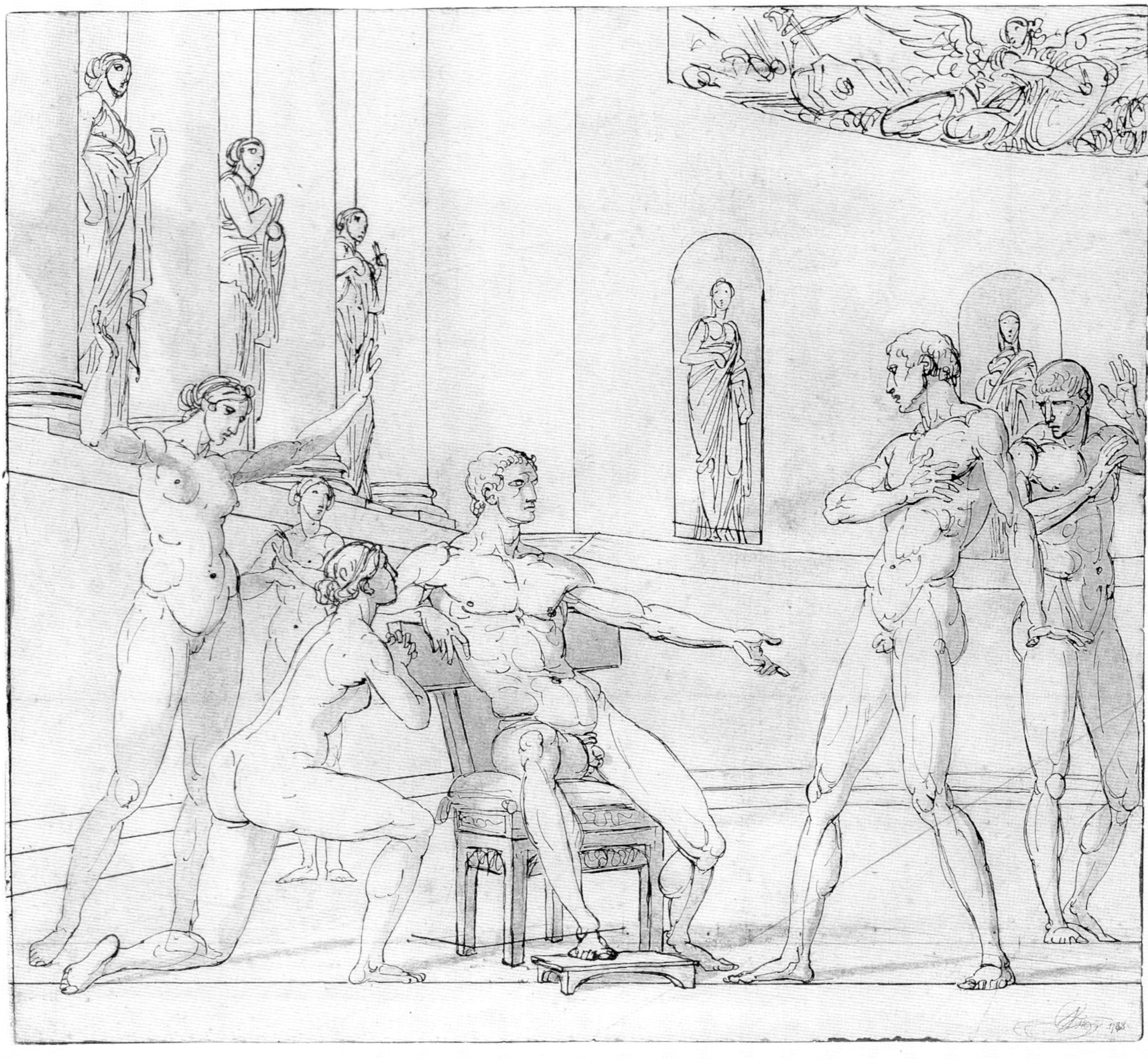

CATALOGUE NO. 37

him in 1784 for four large canvases to ornament the walls of the audience chamber in his residence in Koblenz (today the paintings are in the castle at Zidlochovice, Czechoslovakia; Lossky 1938, 47–53, fig. 2). Vincent's work was placed as a pendant to Jacques-Louis David's *Belisarius*. The archbishop had first thought of commissioning a painting from David but decided instead to purchase the already completed canvas (Seelig 1990, 52–58).

Vincent's drawing corresponds to the disposition of the figures in his painting, except that the figure of Maximus at the right is altered and the maid in the background to the right of the empress Livia, whose arms are raised in surprise, is omitted in the painting. The artist must have made a highly finished drawing, undoubtedly with the figures draped as they are in the canvas, or perhaps an oil sketch that was sent by the architect Antoine-François Peyre, the archbishop's agent, to his patron for his approval (Seelig 1990, 55). An earlier idea for the composition, with the three male protagonists shown in entirely different poses, was recently on the art market (Paris n.d., no. 20). Vincent's painting was shown in Paris in 1787 before being shipped to Koblenz, thus the date of 1788 on this sheet may well be a later, erroneous addition by the artist.

Other pen and ink composition studies of nude figures for several of Vincent's major history paintings have been identified (New York 1986b, no. 319). Separate studies for individual figures must have preceded these carefully realized designs. The rapidly executed chalk drawing for a figure of Rinaldo on the verso of this work, with its many signs of changes and indecision, illustrates an almost unknown aspect of the artist's draftsmanship. Cuzin has described Vincent as a "well-trained artist, with a broad curiosity and a concern for balance and good taste" (Paris/Detroit/New York 1974–75, 669), but lacking "the wonderful eccentricities, the flights of imagination that are found in the work of a genius" (Cuzin n.d. [1988?], 9). VC

François-André Vincent

Standing Man with His Right Hand on His Chest

c. 1784–87

38

Pen and brown ink, brush and brown wash, over red chalk, traces of squaring in graphite and red chalk on white laid paper

38 x 24.4 cm (14 15/16 x 9 5/8 in.)

Inscribed on the verso in pen and brown ink: *B/n° 12*; in pencil: *David.*

The Metropolitan Museum of Art, New York, bequest of Walter C. Baker, 1971 (inv. no. 1972.118.236)

(Los Angeles and Philadelphia only)

PROVENANCE

L.-J.-A. Coutan (Lugt 1921, no. 464).

Walter C. Baker.

EXHIBITED

Pittsburgh 1951, no. 155 (as by Jacques-Louis David).

Rotterdam/Paris/New York 1958–59, no. 109, pl. 87 (as by David).

LITERATURE

Mongan 1962, no. 104 (as by David).

Virch 1962, no. 88 (as by David).

Bean 1986, no. 320.

Cuzin n.d. [1988?], no. 47.

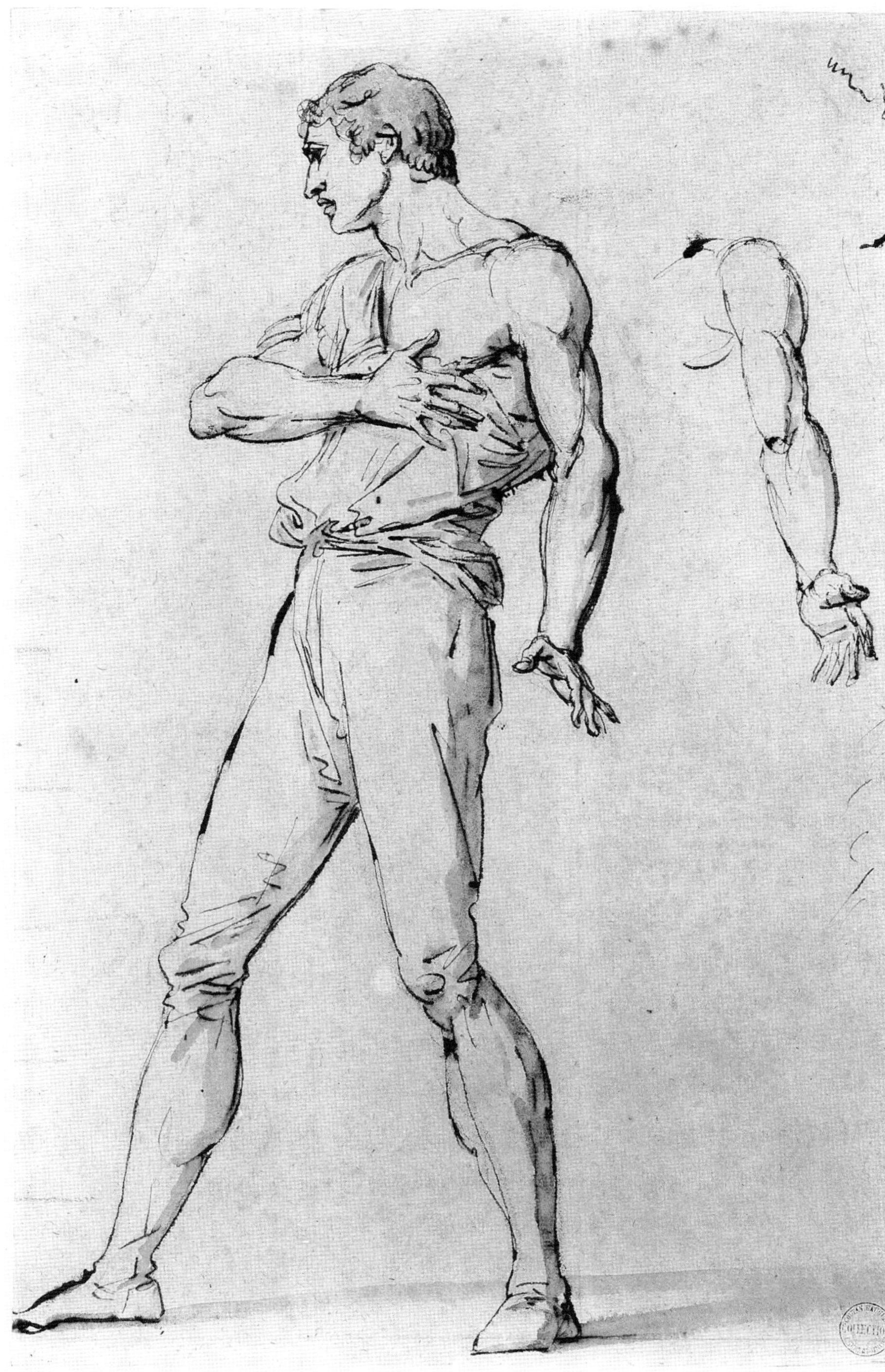

CATALOGUE NO. 38

For many years this handsome drawing of a model posed in an artist's studio was published and exhibited as a masterpiece by Jacques-Louis David, until Cuzin observed that the man, here wearing contemporary dress rather than a toga, is a study for Cinna in Vincent's 1787 oil *The Clemency of Augustus to Cinna* (*Clémence d'Auguste envers Cinna*). The same figure is shown nude in a study for the composition also in the Metropolitan Museum (see CATALOGUE NO. 37), and the pose is retained, with appropriate costume, in the canvas (now in the castle in Zidlochovice, Czechoslovakia). Cinna is shown reacting in astonishment that the powerful emperor Augustus would wish to settle amicably the differences between them.

At the time of the Cinna commission (see CATALOGUE NO. 37 for details of the commission) the history paintings of Vincent and François-Guillaume Ménageot were eclipsed only by David's work, in the judgment of the architect Antoine-François Peyre reporting to his patron Clemens Wenzeslaus, bishop of Trier (Seelig 1990, 53). Thus it is hardly surprising that Vincent's mature drawings such as this have been confused with works by his more celebrated contemporary. With hindsight, Vincent's somewhat nervous, mannered pen drawings have little in common with David's studies, although this sheet does have undeniable dash and spirit. But Vincent's drawings lack the grandeur of form, expressed with economy and conciseness, that characterize David's draftsmanship after Jean-François-Pierre Peyron had opened his eyes to the example of antique art. VC

Jacques-Louis David

1748 Paris–Brussels 1825

DAVID WON THE PRIX DE ROME on his fourth attempt in 1774 as a student of Joseph-Marie Vien. Since Vien had recently been appointed director of the Académie de France in Rome, David accompanied him to Italy in 1775. He remained until 1780, studying the art of the sixteenth and seventeenth centuries and the ruins of Pompeii and Herculaneum. After David's return to Paris his *Funeral of Patroclus* (*Les Funérailles de Patrocle*) and *Belisarius* (*Bélisaire, reconnu par un soldat qui avait servi sous lui au moment qu'une femme lui fait l'aumône*) created a sensation at the Salon of 1781. He was soon admitted into the Académie, and his studio was swamped with students. David returned to Rome in 1784–85 to work on the *The Oath of the Horatii* (*Serment des Horaces*; see FIGURE 9), commissioned by the king. Back in Paris, David worked on *The Death of Socrates* (*Socrate au moment de prendre la ciguë*), 1787, and *Paris and Helen*, 1788, as well as many portraits before the outbreak of the Revolution.

David stepped to the forefront of arts administration during the Revolution. He planned festivals and pageants, designed uniforms and coinage, and served on the committees for Public Instruction and Public Safety. Although he painted some of his greatest works at that time, such as *The Death of Marat* and *The Death of Le Peletier de Saint-Fargeau*, both 1793, his political activity prevented him from finishing the immense *The Oath of the Tennis Court* (*Serment du Jeu de Paume*). Due to his close association with Robespierre, David was briefly imprisoned after the former's fall. Soon after his release he was drawn to the heroic subject of Napoleon; he was appointed *premier peintre* of the Empire and was given commissions for several imperial portraits and *The Coronation* (*Le Sacre*), 1805–8, and *The Distribution of the Eagles* (*La Distribution des aigles*), exhibited 1810. The political climate after the fall of Napoleon forced David into exile in Brussels, where he lived from 1816 until his death. LDM

Jacques-Louis David
Paris and Helen
1786

39
Pen and black ink, brush and gray wash on white laid paper
18.3 x 22.9 cm (7 3/16 x 9 in.)
Signed and dated at lower right in black ink: *David 1786*
Collection of the J. Paul Getty Museum, Malibu, California (inv. no. 83.GA.192)
(Los Angeles only)

PROVENANCE
Jean-Guillaume Moitte; sale, Paris, June 7, 1810, lot 20.
A. Dumont; sale, Paris, February 13, 1854, lot 118.
L.-J.-A. Coutan; sale, Paris, April 18, 1860, lot 182.
Flury-Hérard; sale, Paris, May 13, 1861, lot 465.
H. Dreux; sale, Paris, February 4, 1870, lot 28.
Sale, Hôtel Drouot, Paris, March 22, 1983, lot 2.

EXHIBITED
Paris 1948, 54, no. 26e/f.
London 1948, 16, no. 7e/f.
Paris/Versailles 1989–90, 189–90, no. 83.

LITERATURE
David 1880, 656.
Korshak 1987, 108–9, fig. 18.
Goldner 1988, 154–55, no. 67.
Paris 1991, 416, 423, fig. 4.

The Getty Museum drawing is an advanced compositional study for David's painting *Paris and Helen* (*Pâris et Hélène*; Musée du Louvre, Paris), 1788, commissioned by the comte d'Artois, the future King Charles X and brother to Louis XVI, about 1786 and finally exhibited at the Salon of 1789 (Paris/Versailles 1989–90, 184–85, no. 79). In this composition David interprets a scene from book 3 of Homer's *Iliad*, a bittersweet conjugal encounter between Paris and Helen in Troy; it had been represented by Angelica Kauffmann and Gavin Hamilton in 1773 and 1783, respectively. To resolve the armed conflict between the Greeks and Trojans over the abduction of Helen, her seducer, Paris, reluctantly agrees to engage her aggrieved husband, Menelaus,

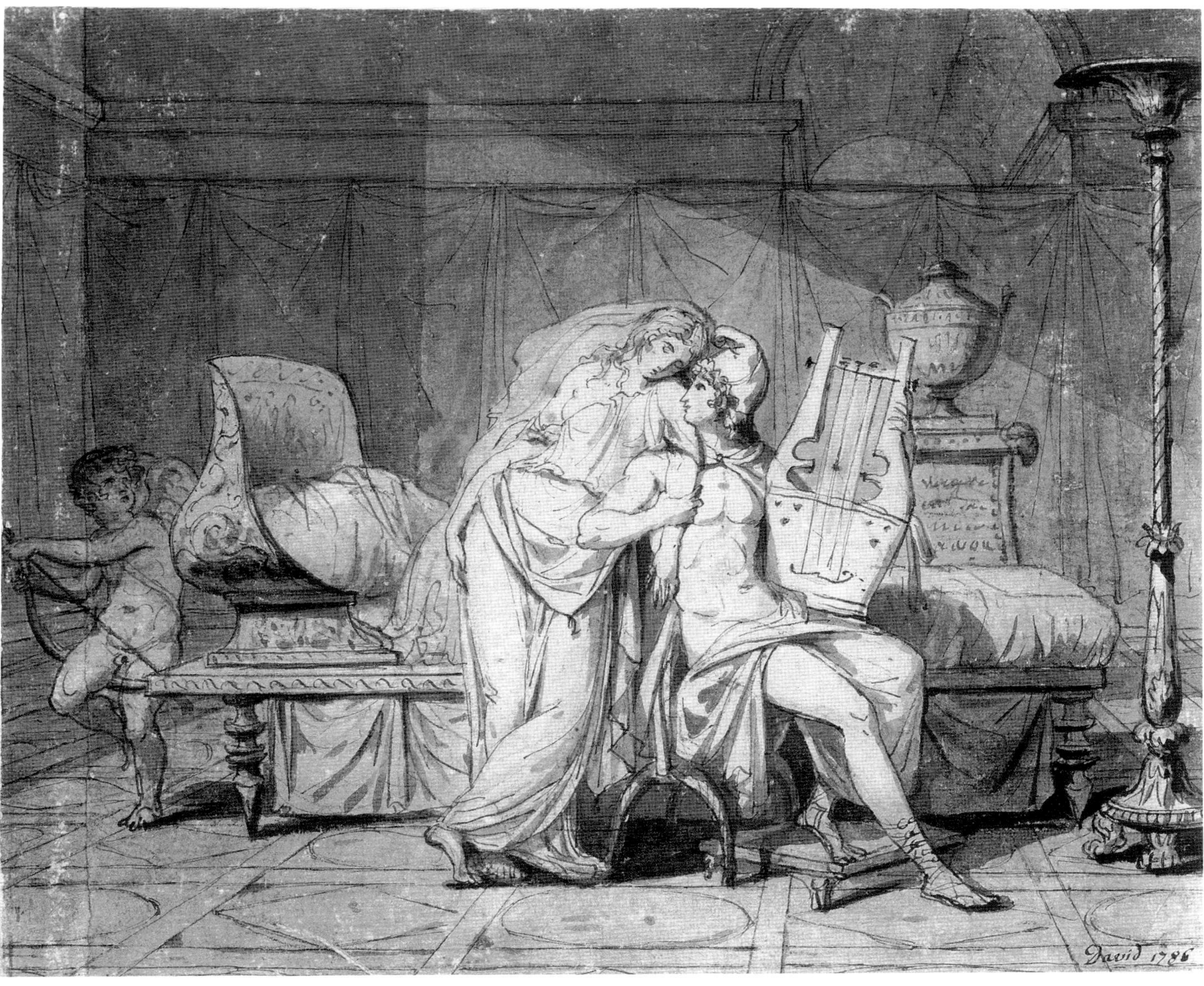

CATALOGUE NO. 39

in combat. In the course of the fray Paris is spared from Menelaus's spear and sword by the intervention of Venus, who spirits him away to Troy and settles him in his bed chamber. Venus then summons Helen and bids her to go to Paris; when Helen protests, Venus threatens her with a "miserable end." Withdrawing to the bedroom, Helen scolds Paris (Homer 1969, 71–75):

> *"So you are back from the battlefields—and I was hoping you had fallen there to the great soldier who was once my husband! You used to boast that you were a better man than the mighty Menelaus, a finer spearman, stronger in the arm. Then why not go at once and challenge him again? Or should I warn you to think twice before you offer single combat to the red-haired Menelaus? Do nothing rash—or you may end by falling to his spear!"*

In response, Paris declares:

> *"My dear, do not try to put me on my mettle by abusing me. Menelaus has just beaten me with Athene's help. But I too have gods to help me, and next time I shall win. Come, let us go to bed together and be happy in our love. Never has such desire overwhelmed me, not even in the beginning, when I carried you off from lovely Lacedaemon in my seagoing ships and we spent the night on the isle of Cranae in each other's arms—never till now have I been so much in love with you or felt such sweet desire." As he spoke, he made a move towards the bed, leading her to it. His wife followed him; and the two lay down together on the well-made wooden bed.*

David's painting of *Paris and Helen* was to undergo a complex evolution. In addition to the Getty drawing there exist two preliminary figurative sketches in black chalk, a compositional study in pen, ink, and wash, and a sketch in oil. In the first sketch David represents Helen seated and Paris standing by the bed (Nationalmuseum, Stockholm; inv. no. NM 43/1969; Paris/Versailles 1989–90, 188, 190, no. 80). In the second sketch Helen leans forlornly on a pedestal, resting her right hand on the left shoulder of Paris, who is seated looking back at her as he plays a cithara; Helen's cross-legged stance is here determined (Paris/Versailles 1989–90, no. 81).

In the first compositional study David established the definitive pose of the couple, which is based on an antique medallion representing Mars and Venus (Paris/Versailles 1989–90, no. 82; Paris 1991, 513). Helen now stands by Paris, who is seated to the right and clutches the cithara in his left hand; her left arm, hanging perpendicular, is grasped by Paris, who gazes upward at her face. The source for the figure of Helen is a bas-relief in the Galleria Borghese, and Paris is modeled after a figure on a vase formerly in the Hamilton collection (Paris 1991, 513). David also determined the final form of the nuptial bed, although he would later alter the griffin relief ornament. The chamber is relatively spare in conception. The rear wall is adorned with a spear, sheathed sword, and shield; simple tiles cover the floor. A large candelabrum is at the far right of the composition.

In the Getty sheet David creates a more sumptuous setting, with an entablature on the walls, a hanging drapery, and a barrel vault visible in the upper right of the composition. The floor tiles are decorated with lozenge and diamond motifs. In back of the bed to the right David depicts an urn atop a pedestal, and he substitutes a tall, slimmer-proportioned candelabrum in the right foreground. The figures remain essentially unchanged, although Helen wears a more prominent veil that cascades downward from her coiffure, and Paris's left foot is propped on a stool. In this version David expands the staffage with the presence of an impish Cupid, who steps through his bow as he observes the lovers.

Since the interior setting of the Getty drawing varies so significantly from that of the final painting, it may be surmised that David executed additional intermediate studies. In a subsequent oil sketch (Paris/Versailles 1989–90, 184, fig. 62), David added a *tribuna* of caryatids based on Jean Goujon's famous sculpted group at the Louvre, an elegant carved screen behind the bed, and a bath in the central foreground, all of which appear in the final painting. He also lavished attention on ornamental details that allude to the wedding of Paris and Helen: wreaths of myrtle, a *loutropharos* vase at the bath, a statue of Venus Pudica, from which is suspended Paris's bow and quiver of arrows, a motif of a veiled bride on the statue's base, and a relief of the Capitoline Cupid and Psyche on the right pilaster of the carved screen.

In the painting David provided details evocative of Helen's parentage—the Leda and Swan motif on the plinth of the bed—and events leading up to the dalliance between the couple—a relief depicting the Judgment of Paris on Paris's lyre. The artist adorned the walls with metopes of quivers, arrows, lamps, torches, and shields, and the bath is ringed with spouts spewing water. David replaced the candelabrum with a gilt tripod perfume-burner. Finally, the drapery previously covering Paris's loins has been removed; instead a piece of the drape over his shoulder is configured to form a *cache-sexe*.

In essence, David's *Paris and Helen* marks the culmination of the *goût grec* in its compulsive attention to archaeological detail, an accretion that may be followed in the studies for the painted composition. This aspect of the design and its heightened formal quality evoke the influence of Johann Joachim Winckelmann. As noted by Régis Michel (Rome 1981–82, 151), the composition anticipates David's equivocally erotic mythologies of the Brussels period (1816–25) and, in general, heralds the Ingrist, neo-Hellenic, and symbolist currents of the mid-to-late nineteenth century.

In recent years David's *Paris and Helen* has been interpreted as a manifestation of the artist's alleged protorevolutionary political views. Paris and Helen have been cast in the role of the comte d'Artois and Marie-Antoinette or Madame Polastron to castigate the immorality of the ruling aristocracy. In addition, the caryatids, phrygian cap, and even the spouting jets of water have been deemed allusions to slavery, liberty, and harbingers of revolution, respectively. As observed by Schnapper (Paris/Versailles 1989–90, 189) and Bailey (Paris 1991, 513, 517 n. 37), David's painting more likely constitutes an allegory of the triumph of love over war, especially given the preponderant nuptial symbolism. RJC

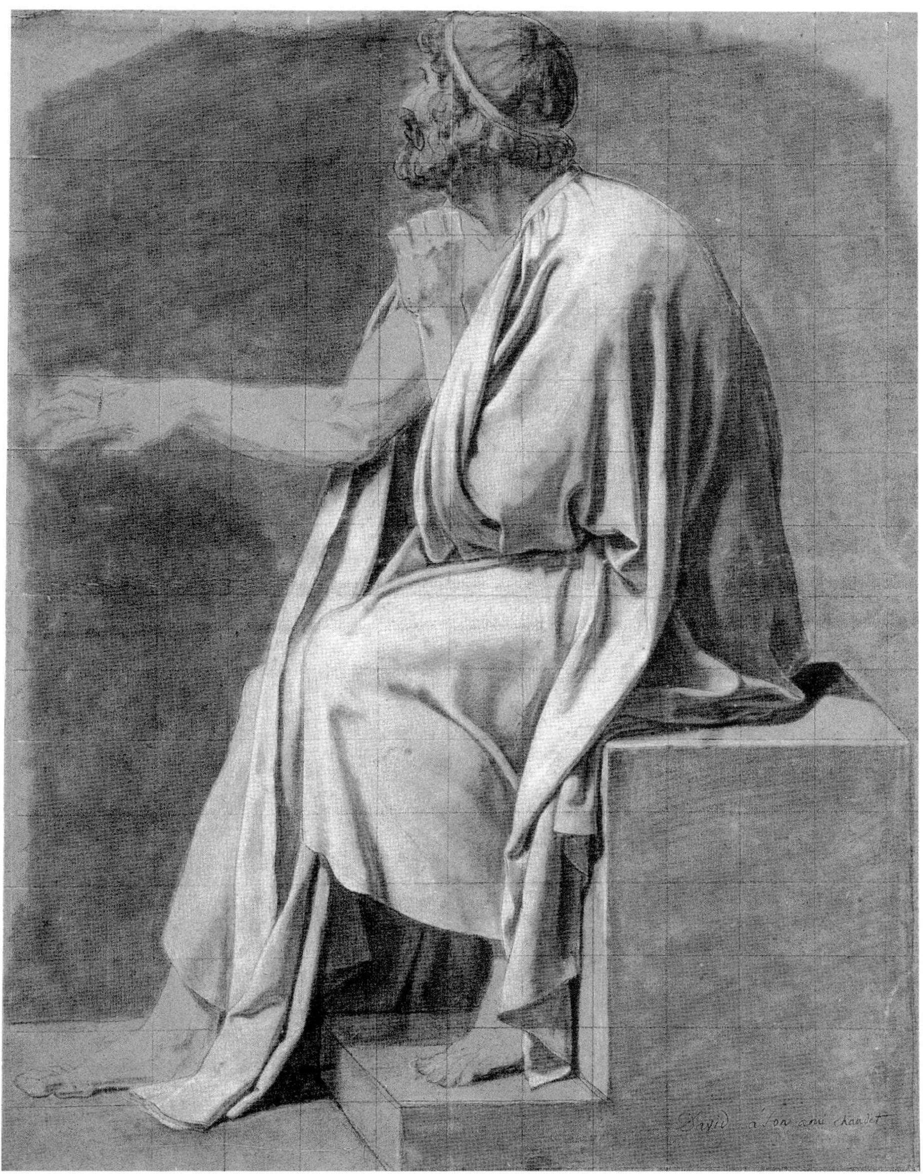

CATALOGUE NO. 40 (see color plate on page 103)

Jacques-Louis David
Seated Draped Male Figure
c. 1787

40
Black chalk, stumped, heightened with white on beige paper, squared in black chalk
53.5 x 41.4 cm (21 1/16 x 16 5/16 in.)
Inscribed at lower right in graphite: *David à son ami chaudet.*
The Metropolitan Museum of Art, New York, Rogers Fund, 1961 (inv. no. 61.161.1)
(Philadelphia and Minneapolis only)

PROVENANCE
Antoine-Denis Chaudet.
Wildenstein, 1961.

EXHIBITED
London 1968, 64, no. 182, fig. 330.
Paris 1973–74, no. 23.

LITERATURE
Bean 1962, 171, fig. 16.
New York: The Metropolitan Museum of Art. *Annual Report of the Trustees*, 1961–62, 67.
Bean 1964, no. 62.
Paris 1974–75, 36.
Paris/Detroit/New York 1974–75, 368.
Bean 1986, 87–89, no. 90.
Paris/Versailles 1989–90, 180.

David's drawing is a painstaking study for the draped himation worn by Crito in his painting *The Death of Socrates* (*La Mort de Socrate*; the Metropolitan Museum of Art, New York; London 1972, 41–42, no. 63, pl. 2; Schnapper 1980, 80–82), exhibited at the Salon of 1787. In the canvas Crito is seated upon a stone block at Socrates's bedside in prison and listens attentively to the last words of his mentor just before the latter drinks the cup of hemlock. With his right hand firmly poised on Socrates's knee Crito stoically expresses his devotion to his master. As related by Plato (*Crito*, 43–50), Crito, a wealthy Athenian disciple of Socrates, had planned the escape of the philosopher from prison, but Socrates refused to go. The depiction of Socrates was suggested to David by his consultant Jean-Félicissime Adry (Bonnardet 1938, 311–15).

In the painting David depicted a different, younger model for the figure of Crito; his beard is more closely trimmed and his head is not adorned with a fillet. In the New York sheet David lavishes his attention upon the elaboration of the folds of Crito's himation. As indicated by the squaring, the pattern of drapery was transferred precisely to the canvas.

Students at the Académie de France à Rome were required to produce meticulous studies of drapery in chalk as part of their regimen. David's drawing reveals his complete mastery of the genre. With a combination of black-chalk stumping and white-chalk heightening David creates infinitely subtle gradations of light and shade that define the folds of the drapery. There exist five additional large-scale studies of draped figures for *The Death of Socrates* in the collections of the Musée Bonnat, Bayonne; the Musée Magnin, Dijon; and the Musée des Beaux-Arts, Tours (Paris 1974–75, 36, 144–45; Paris/Versailles 1989–90, 180–81, no. 77). RJC

Jacques-Louis David
Sheets from a Sketchbook (Album 11)

41
FOLIO 83, TOP TO BOTTOM
The Embarkation of Orestes and Iphigenia from Tauris
c. 1780
Pen and black ink, brush and gray wash over black chalk
Inscribed at the bottom: *a venise a la librairie*

Asclepios and Hygieia
c. 1775–80
Black chalk
Inscribed on the plinth of the throne: *capitole*

Nuptial Ceremony
c. 1775–80
Pen and black ink, brush and gray wash
Inscribed at lower left: *sur un sarcophage au museum du pape*

FOLIO 200, TOP TO BOTTOM
Rider Toppling from a Rearing Charger
Pen and black ink, black chalk

Marius at Minturnae
c. 1785
Pen and black ink over black chalk

Figures Gathered at a Bedside
Black chalk

Private collection, courtesy Stephen Mazoh and Company, Inc.

PROVENANCE
Jacques-Louis David sale, Paris, April 17, 1826, lot 66.
Second Jacques-Louis David sale, Paris, March 11, 1835.
A. Chassagnole.
Sale, Sotheby's, Monaco, February 22, 1986, lot 106.

LITERATURE
"Inventaire après le décès de Mme. David," June 27, 1826 (Archives Nationales, Paris, Minutier central, fonds CVIII).
Thomé 1826, 12–13.
David 1880, 653.
Wildenstein 1973, 247, no. 2071.
Rome 1981–82, 65–70.
Paris/Versailles 1989–90, 65–71.
Sérullaz 1991, 12–13.

Album number 11 belongs to a corpus of twelve albums containing sketches executed by David during his two sojourns in Italy, 1775–80 and 1784–85. Only seven of the twelve inventoried in 1826 can now be documented: album 1 is in the Fogg Art Museum, Harvard University, Cambridge; 3 is in the Nationalmuseum, Stockholm; 7 and 9 are in the Musée du Louvre, Paris; and 6 and 10 have been dismantled (Sérullaz 1991, 11–13). The artist himself collated the albums from approximately 276 sketchbook sheets; the sketches, ranging in size from 7.7 x 6.9 to 29 x 43.5 centimeters, were arranged and pasted onto the album sheets. Each sheet is initialed by the artist's sons, Jules and Eugène David (Sérullaz 1991, 18–19).

Album 11 was acquired by Jules David's uncle, A. Chassagnolle, and remained in the possession of his descendants until 1986 (Sérullaz 1991, 13). It contains ninety-eight sketches, ranging from copies after ancient statuary, bas-reliefs, and vases and after the old masters, to original compositions, including Italian landscapes and townscapes (one of the latter is illustrated in the 1986 sale catalogue; see PROVENANCE).

The three sketches on folio 83 of the album are typical of David's copies after the antique. The study of a bas-relief of *Orestes and Iphigenia*, which was conserved at the Libreria Vecchia in Venice, is datable to David's visit to that city in late summer of 1780, as he traveled back to Paris (Reinach 1909–12, vol. 3, 432; Sérullaz 1991, 101, no. 94). The studies of the bas-reliefs depicting *Aesculapius and Hygieia* (Reinach 1909–12, vol. 3, 180) and a *Nuptial Ceremony* (Museo Vaticano 1908, 27, no. 522) were probably rendered during the artist's years as a pensioner at the Académie de France in Rome.

The drawings on folio 200 reveal a different aspect of David's activity as a draftsman. The artist had returned to Rome in 1784 to paint his *The Oath of the Horatii* (*Serment des Horaces*; see FIGURE 9). He was accompanied by his favorite pupil, Jean-Germain Drouais, who had just won the Prix de Rome. The precocious Drouais at once began work on his painting *Marius at Minturnae* (*Marius prisonnier à Minturnes*; Musée du Louvre), 1786, which would be the masterpiece of his short career (he died of smallpox in 1788). The progress of the painting, which is documented in a series of drawings by Drouais, was closely monitored by David (Rome 1981–82, 208–9, no. 58; Lille 1983, 90–92, nos. 66–68). The lower sheet on folio 200 of David's album includes a compositional study depicting Marius rebuffing the Cimbrian assassin sent by the Roman Senate that must relate to Drouais's painting (Sérullaz 1991, 18) and would have been rendered by David prior to his departure from Rome in September of 1785.

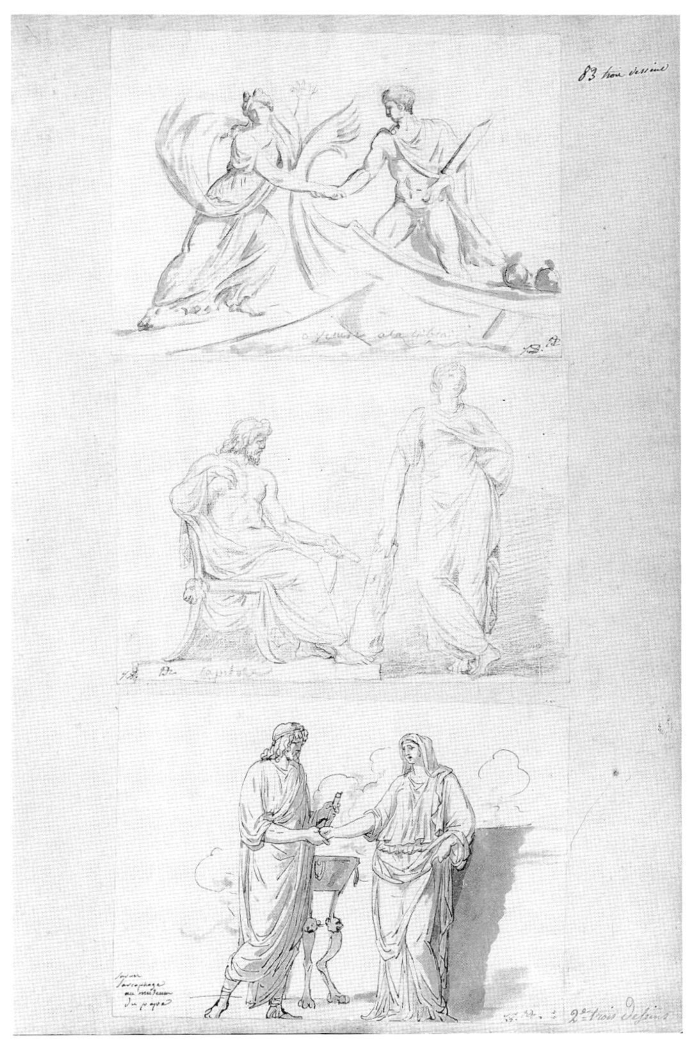

Folio 83

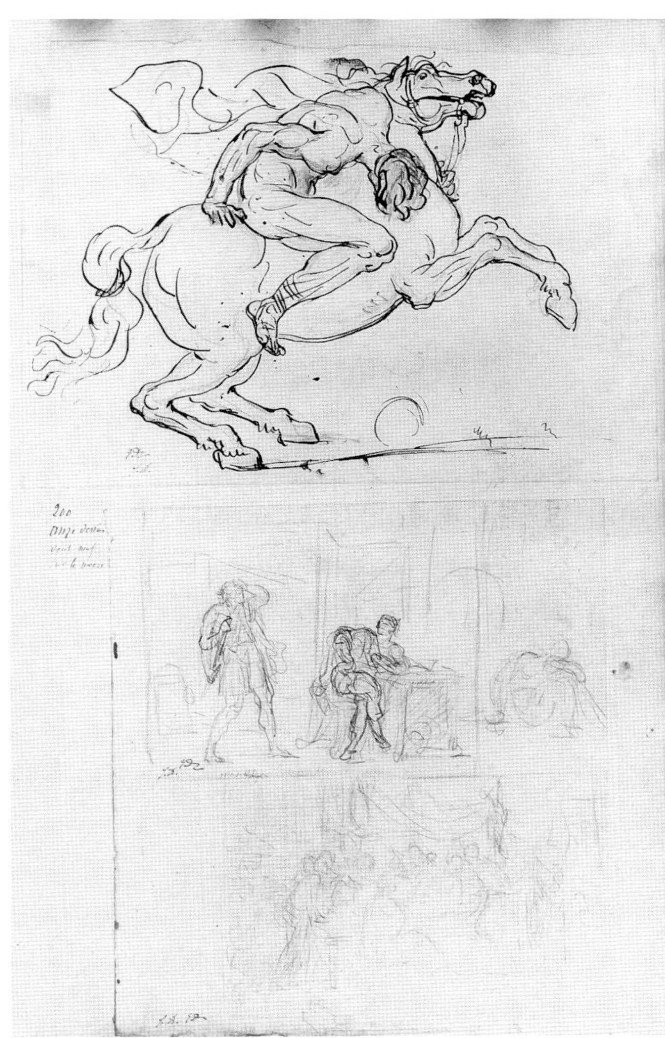

Folio 200

CATALOGUE NO. 41

Immediately below, on the same sheet, David faintly sketched in black chalk several figures gathered around a bed in a format suggesting the theme of Antiochus and Stratonice (see CATALOGUE NO. 3 for this theme; see also a black-chalk drawing, *Scène antique*, in Paris/Versailles 1989–90, 57, no. 12). On the top sheet of the album folio David depicted a nude rider toppling from a rearing steed. It may well be a *première pensée* for a representation of the death leap of Marcus Curtius. These Italian sketches reveal his complex assimilation of the arts of antiquity, which enabled him to create original works in the spirit of the ancients.

Recent research indicates that David systematically composed the albums as repositories to document his artistic evolution. Such methodical classification corresponds to Johann Joachim Winckelmann's art historical concepts as elaborated in his *Gedanken über die Nachahmung der griechischen Werke in der Malerei und Bildhauerkunst* of 1755 (Sérullaz 1991, 15, 20–23). RJC

Pierre-Paul Prud'hon

1758 Cluny–Paris 1823

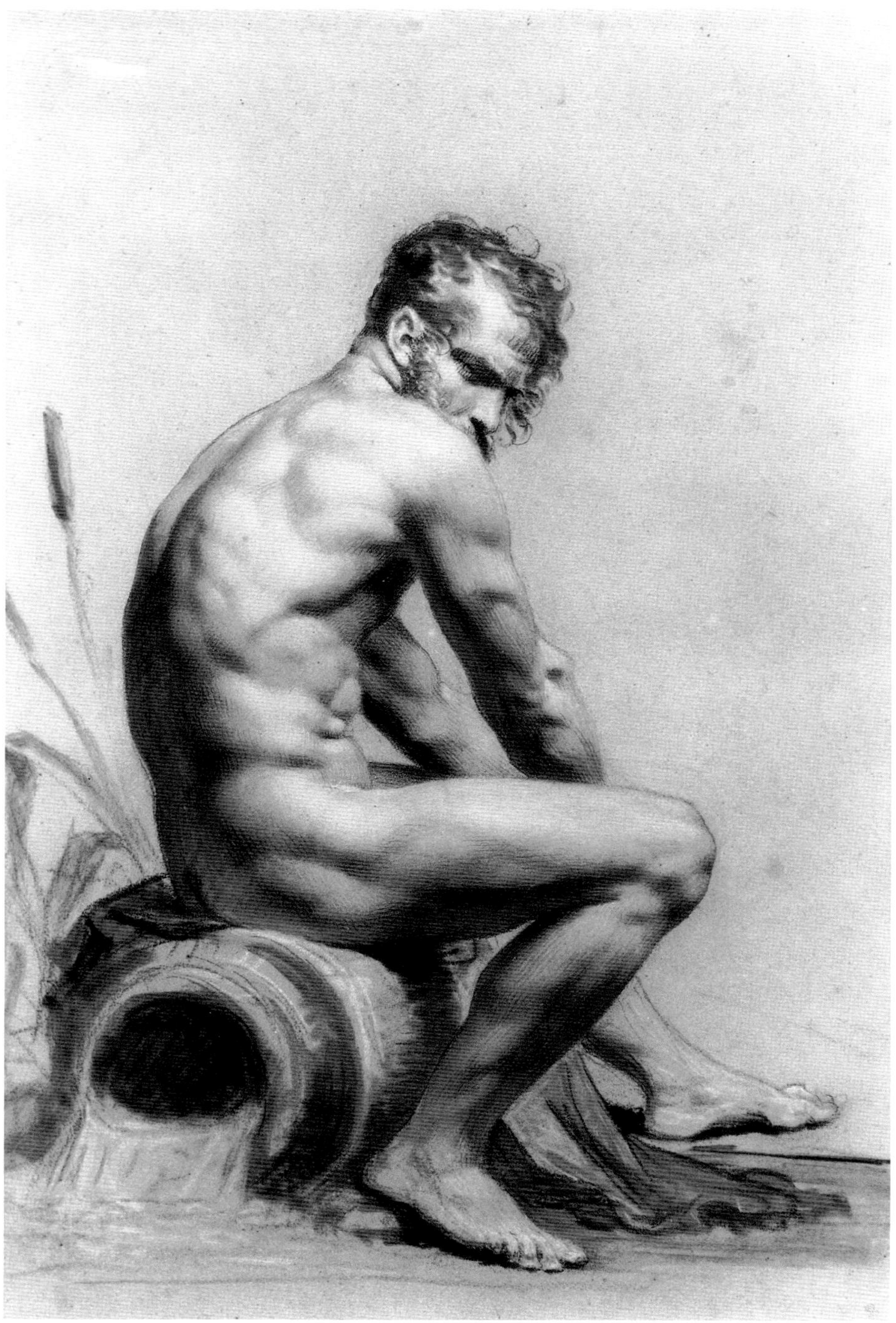

CATALOGUE NO. 42

RAISED BY THE MONKS of the abbey of Cluny, Prud'hon was allowed to draw and received an excellent education. His first teacher was François Devosge III at the Académie in Dijon, where he remained for six years until 1780, when he left for Paris. Three years later he returned to Dijon and then won the Prix de Rome offered by the estates of Burgundy in 1784. After his arrival in Rome in January of 1786 he began to study the works of Raphael and Michelangelo and was influenced by his contemporaries Antonio Canova, Angelica Kauffmann, and Anton Raphael Mengs.

Prud'hon returned to Paris in 1789 and began exhibiting at the Salon in 1791. He became involved in revolutionary activities, which probably motivated his abrupt move to the Franche-Comté in 1794. He returned to Paris two years later and worked for the publisher Pierre Didot illustrating Pierre-Joseph Bernard's *Oeuvres*, 1797, the French translation of Longus's *Daphnis and Chloe*, 1800, and Jean-Jacques Rousseau's *La Nouvelle Héloïse*, 1804. With the success of his *The Triumph of Bonaparte* (*Le Triomphe de Bonaparte*) at the Salon of 1801 he received many more commissions from Napoleon and his court. His first wife died in 1803, and he began a relationship with his former student, Constance Mayer. During this period he painted *Innocence Preferring Love to Riches* (*Innocence préfère l'amour à la richesse*) and *Psyche Carried Off by Zephyrs* (*Psyché enlevée par les zéphyrs*), both 1808, and was finally lauded by the critics. He was not well supported by the Restoration, however, and with the unexpected suicide of Mayer in 1821, Prud'hon went into a decline and died in 1823. LDM

Pierre-Paul Prud'hon
Study for an Allegory of the Rhine River
c. 1801

42
Black and white chalks with extensive stumping on blue paper faded to ocher
60.7 x 40.9 cm (23 7/8 x 16 1/8 in.)
Red stamp of the collector Charles Boulanger de Boisfrémont (Lugt 1921, no. 353) at the lower right
Private collection

PROVENANCE
The artist to Charles Boulanger de Boisfrémont, 1823.
Charles Boulanger de Boisfrémont *fils*; sale, Hôtel Drouot, Paris, April 9, 1870, lot 45 ("Dessins, croquis, études, tableaux et esquisses par Prud'hon").
Charles Bellanger.
Louis Michon.
Richard S. Davis, Minneapolis and New York.
Jacques Seligmann, New York.

EXHIBITED
Paris 1874, no. 457.
Paris 1922, no. 238.
New York 1959, no. 26.
Minneapolis 1960, no. 49.
Minneapolis/New York 1962, no. 91, pl. 3.
Minneapolis/Chicago/Kansas City/Cambridge 1968, no. 32.
New York 1981, no. 50.

LITERATURE
Goncourt 1876, 305.
Guiffrey 1924, 338, no. 902.
Preston 1960, 47, fig. 50.

Traditionally this drawing has been called *The Rhine* and associated with a project for a commemorative column to be located in the Place de la Concorde in Paris in honor of the French armies who fought in the Napoleonic wars. The competition for this monument, one of several to be placed in major cities throughout France, was directed by Napoleon's brother, Lucien Bonaparte, but in the end the work was never completed (Montaiglon 1858–60, 344–45). Prud'hon's drawing for the contest, signed and dated 1801, shows that he intended to feature at the base of the column allegorical figures of the rivers Nile, Po, Rhine, and Danube, representing territories conquered by Napoleon's armies (Musée Carnavalet, Paris; Guiffrey 1924, no. 899). In fact, the positions of the artist's reclining allegorical figures and this seated man are quite different, but the association is provocative. The presence here of an urn and river rushes suggests that the competition for the column was in the artist's mind, because he seldom added allegorical attributes to figure drawings made as ends in themselves. Another, much weaker version of this work, in black and white chalks and signed and dated (?) 1817, was on the Paris art market (sold Palais Galliera, June 20, 1969, lot no. 15).

As he thought about the monument, Prud'hon might have recalled the pair of second-century A.D. colossal river gods on the Capitoline Hill in Rome. He had drawn numerous studies of the city's antiquities, as evidenced by two of his sketchbooks (Weston 1984, 6–19). Also, at this period Prud'hon formed several friendships with sculptors, notably Antonio Canova, whose famous statues, based on his study of the antique and Johann Joachim Winckelmann's theories, were considered by some to surpass ancient Rome's most celebrated remains. In this drawing the muscular figure seated in profile and turned slightly away from the viewer recalls in a general way Michelangelo's *ignudi* on the Sistine Chapel ceiling or Annibale Carracci's heroic nudes in his ceiling fresco in the Palazzo Farnese. The powerfully defined volumes of Prud'hon's river god no doubt have their genesis in examples such as these.

From the first, Prud'hon chose to draw after the figure using black and white chalks on blue paper, now often faded to tan or ocher. Among his earliest known *académies* are a group of sheets in the Musée des Beaux-Arts, Dijon, from the bequest of Anatole Devosge. They undoubtedly date from the period of Prud'hon's study with François Devosge in the drawing classes he gave for the Académie des Sciences, Arts, et Belles-Lettres de Dijon. At this time the student's command of anatomy was still awkward and unclear (Dijon 1959, nos. 26–30, pl. 1). In these early drawings, one of which, *Ceres*, is dated 1781, Prud'hon had yet to attain the mastery of his drawing media so brilliantly evident in this figure. VC

Pierre-Paul Prud'hon
The Abduction of Psyche
c. 1808 or later

43
Black and white chalks on blue wove paper
29.8 x 23.8 cm (11 3/4 x 9 3/8 in.)
The Minneapolis Institute of Arts, the William Hood Dunwoody Fund (inv. no. 76.78)

PROVENANCE
Denesle; sale, Paris, March 30, 1860, 7.
Maximin Maurel; sale, Paris, April 10, 1865, lot 21.
Camille Marcille; sale, Paris, March 6, 1876, lot 95.
Derenancourt; sale, Paris, April 7, 1883, lot 103.
Possibly Ponce-Blanc; sale, Paris, February 11, 1887.

LITERATURE
Possibly Guiffrey 1924, no. 151.

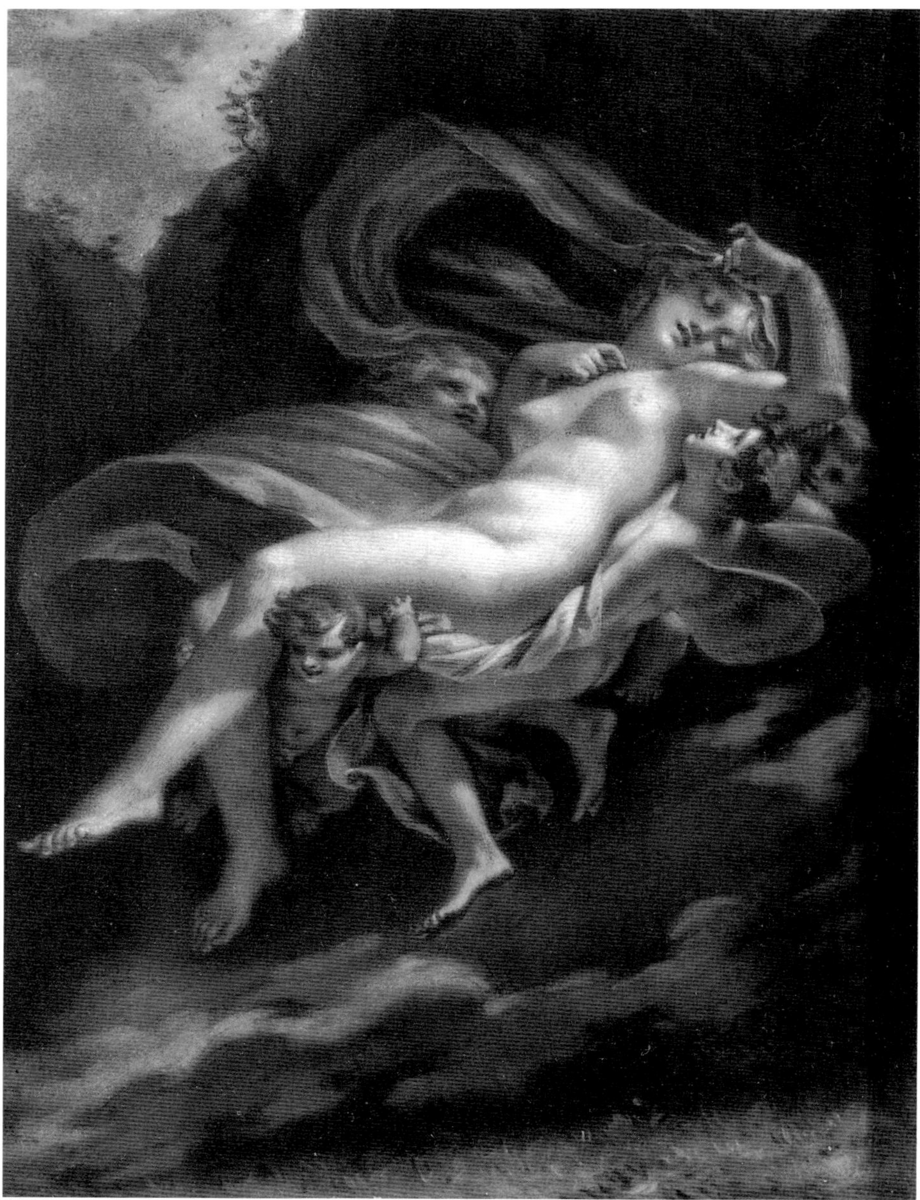

CATALOGUE NO. 43

Prud'hon's painting *The Abduction of Psyche* (*L'Enlèvement de Psyché*) was exhibited twice, at the Salons of 1808 (no. 485) and 1814 (no. 770), where the catalogue explained that the goddess, abandoned on a rock, was being transported by zephyrs to the realm of Love (Musée du Louvre, Paris; Guiffrey 1924, no. 146, pl. 5). The fable of Psyche has its origins in Lucius Apuleius's second-century A.D. romance *Metamorphoses, or The Golden Ass*, translated into French by Jean La Fontaine, among others, and was widely popular at this period. Psyche was celebrated for her beauty, which made her the envy of Venus, who sent Cupid to make her fall in love with a monstrously ugly creature. But Cupid himself succumbed to Psyche's charms and became her lover, only to leave her when she discovered his identity. The despairing Psyche sought him, undergoing a series of trials imposed on her by Venus until, at last, she was transported to Olympus where she married Cupid.

Prud'hon's canvas shows the sleeping Psyche borne aloft by zephyrs and carried to Cupid's palace. This incident from Psyche's legend was not often represented by artists in the eighteenth and nineteenth centuries, but Prud'hon probably knew Bénigne Gagneraux's *Psyche Borne Aloft by Zephyrs* (*Psyché transportée dans les airs par les zéphyrs*; Östergötlands Läns Museum, Löfstad), an oil completed in 1792, after Prud'hon had returned to Paris. He may never have seen the canvas, but he could have known the line etching after it included in Gagneraux's *Dix-Huit Éstampes au trait* (Eighteen line etchings), issued in Paris in the same year (Rome/Dijon 1983, nos. 50, 87). Gagneraux's Psyche is clothed, with only a breast exposed, in contrast to Prud'hon's nude figure, one hand resting provocatively on her breast. Only in a black-chalk and ink-wash drawing by Prud'hon, formerly on the London art market (Guiffrey 1924, no. 150), is the figure of the maiden partially covered by drapery.

It has long been recognized that Prud'hon's Psyche is a panegyric to the art of Correggio, whose *Venus, Cupid, and a Satyr* (or *Antiope*, as it was known in the eighteenth century) had been in Paris and on view in (what would become) the Musée du Louvre since 1785. Correggio's posthumous reputation was at its height; Anton Raphael Mengs thought that his command of chiaroscuro surpassed that of any other painter, and the Italian artist was idolized by writers such as Stendhal (Gould 1976, 158–59, 238–39, pls. 176–78).

There is a small oil sketch for the Salon painting (Musée de Chartres; Guiffrey 1924, no. 147), as well as numerous replicas of the canvas, which though of questionable authenticity are testimony that this was among the artist's most popular compositions during the nineteenth century. Guiffrey listed four drawings associated with the composition (1924, nos. 148–51), and a fifth has been subsequently identified today. A boldly drawn sheet in the Louvre appears to be a working study (53.5 x 40.5 cm; inv. no. R.F. 831; Guiffrey 1924, no. 148), while a slightly larger, highly finished drawing was on the Swiss art market (59 x 49 cm; Guiffrey 1924, no. 149). Another version of the composition, with Psyche supported by three zephyrs, not four as in the Louvre canvas, drawn in black crayon with extensive additions of ink wash and with a different landscape background, was on the London art market (51 x 42 cm; Guiffrey 1924, no. 150, there described as unfinished). Finally, there is a reduction of the composition (29 x 23 cm; Guiffrey 1924, no. 151) presently known in two versions, each of which corresponds in all details to the painting. Both drawings were executed in the artist's favorite medium of black and white chalks on blue paper but differ very slightly in size. One, in a private collection in Paris, measures 29.9 x 24.3 centimeters, while the Minneapolis drawing is 29.8 x 23.8 centimeters. Prud'hon occasionally made replicas of his drawings, and he may have had reason to do so in this instance. A year after the artist's death, in 1823, Hyacinthe Aubrey-Lecomte issued a lithograph reproducing the version of Psyche known from the Salon canvas (bought from the artist by the duca di Sommariva). The image of the lithograph is 29.4 x 23.7 centimeters (Inventaire 1930–85, vol. 1, 215). It is thus quite possible that Prud'hon drew a replica of his painting (then in the possession of Sommariva) to guide the printmaker. At any event, Guiffrey's statement that the larger, highly finished version (his no. 149) was the lithographer's model is not credible, given the very exact likeness between the present drawing and the print.

It was not unusual for an artist to form a business association with a printmaker and a dealer to distribute such images. Given the need of a printmaker to have a finished model from which to work, in addition to requests from private collectors who wanted a replica of a work acclaimed at one of the Salons, it is not surprising that Prud'hon made highly finished drawings after his most popular compositions. VC

Pierre-Paul Prud'hon
Venus
c. 1810–12

44
Black chalk with white chalk heightening on blue-gray paper
60.9 x 45.2 cm (24 x 17 7/8 in.)
The National Gallery of Art, Washington, D.C., Ailsa Mellon Bruce Fund 1972 (inv. no. 1972.48.2)

Pierre-Paul Prud'hon
Adonis
c. 1810–12

45
Black chalk with white chalk heightening on blue paper
60.8 x 45.7 cm (23 15/16 x 18 in.)
The National Gallery of Art, Washington, D.C., Ailsa Mellon Bruce Fund 1972 (inv. no. 1972.48.1)

PROVENANCE
Binder à l'Isle-Adam; sale, Paris, April 8, 1873, lots 60–61.
Jean Stern.
Dr. Fritz Nathan and Dr. Peter Nathan, Zurich.

EXHIBITED
Washington 1974, 99–100, no. 56.

LITERATURE
Goncourt 1876, 327.
Martine/Marotte 1923, nos. 61–62.
Guiffrey 1924, nos. 171–72.
Slayman 1970, pls. 56–57.

Only rarely can Prud'hon's figure drawings be dated, unless they are related to another documented work, as fortunately is the case here. Napoleon's second wife, Marie-Louise, daughter of the emperor Francis I of Austria, commissioned a painting of *Venus and Adonis* for a room in the Tuileries. The canvas was exhibited at the Salon of 1812 (no. 472), but the empress never took possession of it because the war with Russia made the purchase inexpedient. *Venus and Adonis* remained unsold at the artist's death (it is

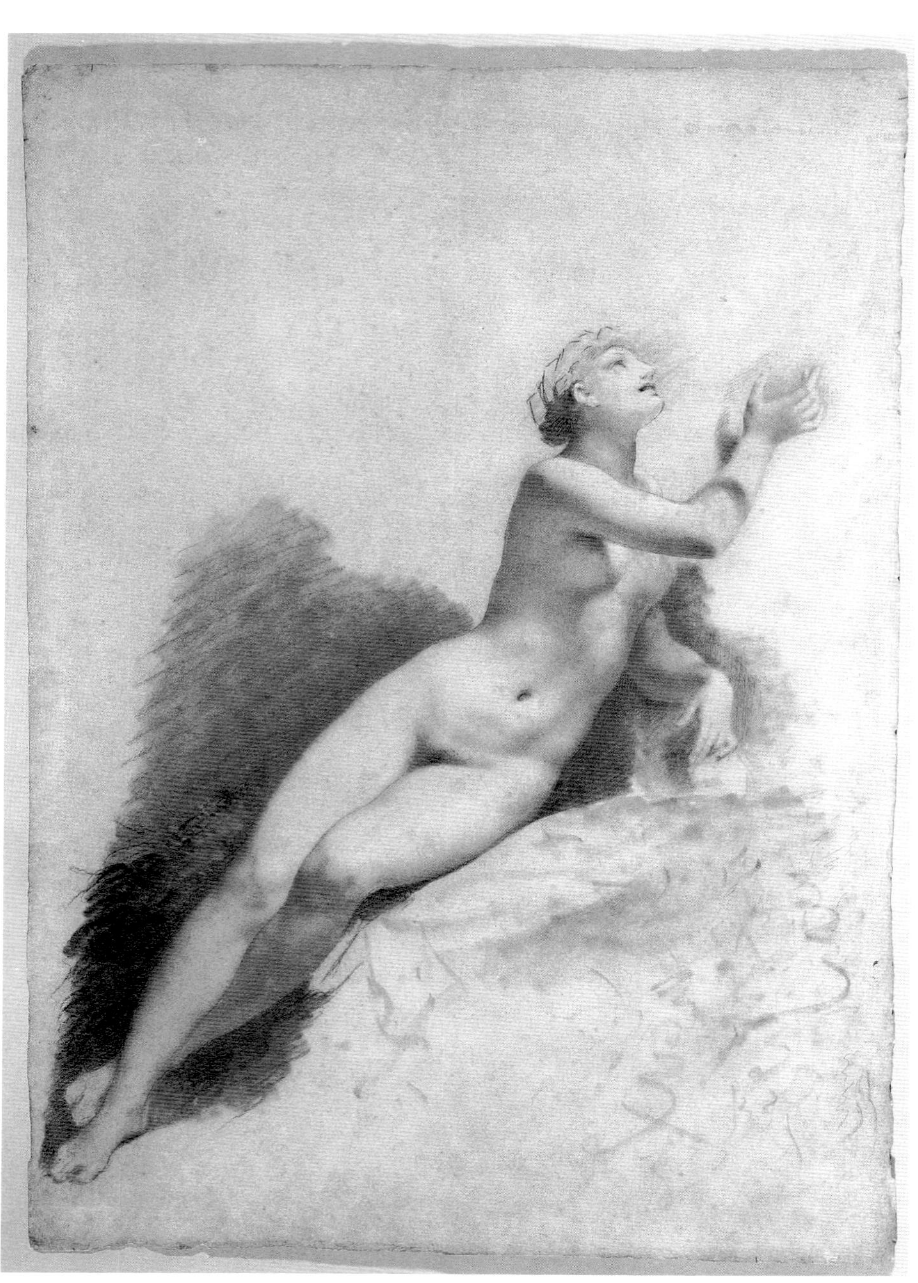

CATALOGUE NO. 44

now in the Wallace Collection, London; Wallace Collection 1968, no. P347). Marie-Louise, like her predecessor, Josephine, shared the emperor's taste for Prud'hon's work, which found expression not only in paintings but also designs for decorative objects, medals, and plans for the fêtes offered to Napoleon by the city of Paris in 1805, 1807, and 1810. Thus, when Prud'hon received the commission for this painting his reputation was at its height.

The myth of Adonis, a handsome Greek youth, exists in several versions, one of which relates that, having been brought up by nymphs, he was out hunting when Aphrodite (or Venus) met him and became entranced by his beauty. Possibly Prud'hon had this tale in mind, since he represented Adonis as a hunter roaming through a forest where he encounters Venus, who in both the canvas and this drawing gestures provocatively. This pair of studies shows the figures almost exactly as they appear in the final work, although the drawing of Adonis omits the detail of Venus's left arm resting on his thigh. Each figure was drawn from a model posed in the artist's studio, their ultimate poses already determined. For this major commission Prud'hon worked with his customary attention to details: aside from the present studies, there are five oil sketches of the full composition or of Venus only (Guiffrey 1924, nos. 163–65, 167–68), two drawings of alternative ideas for the composition (nos. 169–70), and four other preparatory drawings for Venus or various accessory figures (nos. 166, 173–75).

It has never been possible to satisfactorily characterize Prud'hon's art by any of the terms used to describe the various stylistic currents of this period, such as neoclassicism or protoromanticism, the validity of both of which is periodically called into question. Yet undeniably Prud'hon's exposure to antiquity was of vital importance to his maturity as an artist. It is somewhat surprising that the artist's library, sold after his death, contained such a costly publication as d'Hancarville's illustrated volumes (1766–67) of antiquities in the collection of Sir William Hamilton, whose famed Greek vases were reproduced in plates giving full emphasis to their flat, unmodulated figural decoration, defined only by contour against a blank ground (Prud'hon sale ["Notice de tableaux, dessins, gouaches et pastels éxécutés par feu Monsieur P.-P. Prud'hon"], Paris, May 13, 1823, lot 60). Also a part of the artist's library were six folios of prints by or after Alexandre-Évariste Fragonard (lot 58), whose suavely composed works, often of classical themes, may have appealed to Prud'hon because of the former's evocative use of chiaroscuro, which he handled with extraordinary technical finesse. Éugène Delacroix in his lengthy appreciation of Prud'hon published in the *Revue des deux-mondes* of November 1, 1846, defined the tenuous but palpable bond between classical art and the artist's work (Escholier 1926–29, 207):

> *Prud'hon . . . is above all a painter who is concerned with creating space by composing figure groups surrounded by atmosphere and light. He set out to master the greatest difficulty of his art, which is to create a sense of physical amplitude. The art of antiquity is characterized by the skillful mastery of forms that have a sense of animation, a grandeur of conception, and which are harmoniously composed. The true sense of antiquity does not consist in giving to each figure the isolated likeness of a statue.*

VC

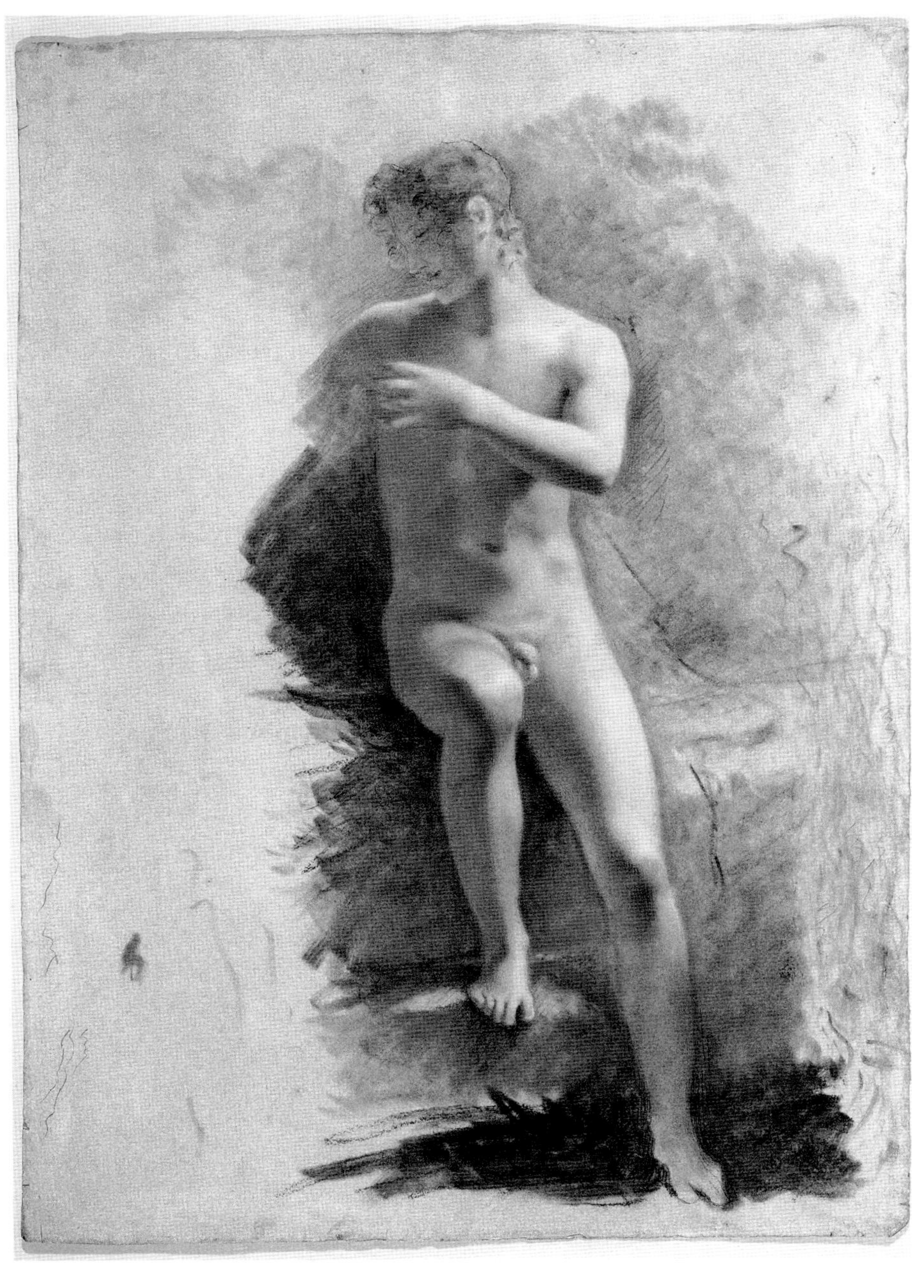

CATALOGUE NO. 45

Pierre-Paul Prud'hon
Young Nymph Teased by Cupids
c. 1811–12

46
Black and white chalks, squared in black chalk on blue paper faded to gray-green
53.5 x 41.5 cm (21 1/16 x 16 5/16 in.)
Fogg Art Museum, Harvard University Art Museums, bequest of Meta and Paul J. Sachs (inv. no. 1965.326 recto)
(Los Angeles and Minneapolis only)

PROVENANCE
Charles-Boulanger de Boisfrémont *fils*; sale, Hôtel Drouot, Paris, April 9, 1870, lot 30 (Lugt 1921, no. 353).
Denière.
Comte Jacques de Bryas; sale, Galerie Georges Petit, Paris, April 4–6, 1898, lot 141.
Stettiner.
Baron Maurice de Rothschild.
Wildenstein Galleries, New York.
Paul J. Sachs.

EXHIBITED
Paris 1874, no. 234.
New York 1922, no. III.
Cambridge 1929, no. 108.
Detroit 1951, no. 24.
Cambridge/New York 1965–67, no. 40.

LITERATURE
Goncourt 1876, 317.
Gueullette 1879, 530.
Guiffrey 1924, no. 83.
Mongan/Sachs 1940, vol. 1, no. 634; vol. 2, fig. 320.
Mongan forthcoming, no. 303.

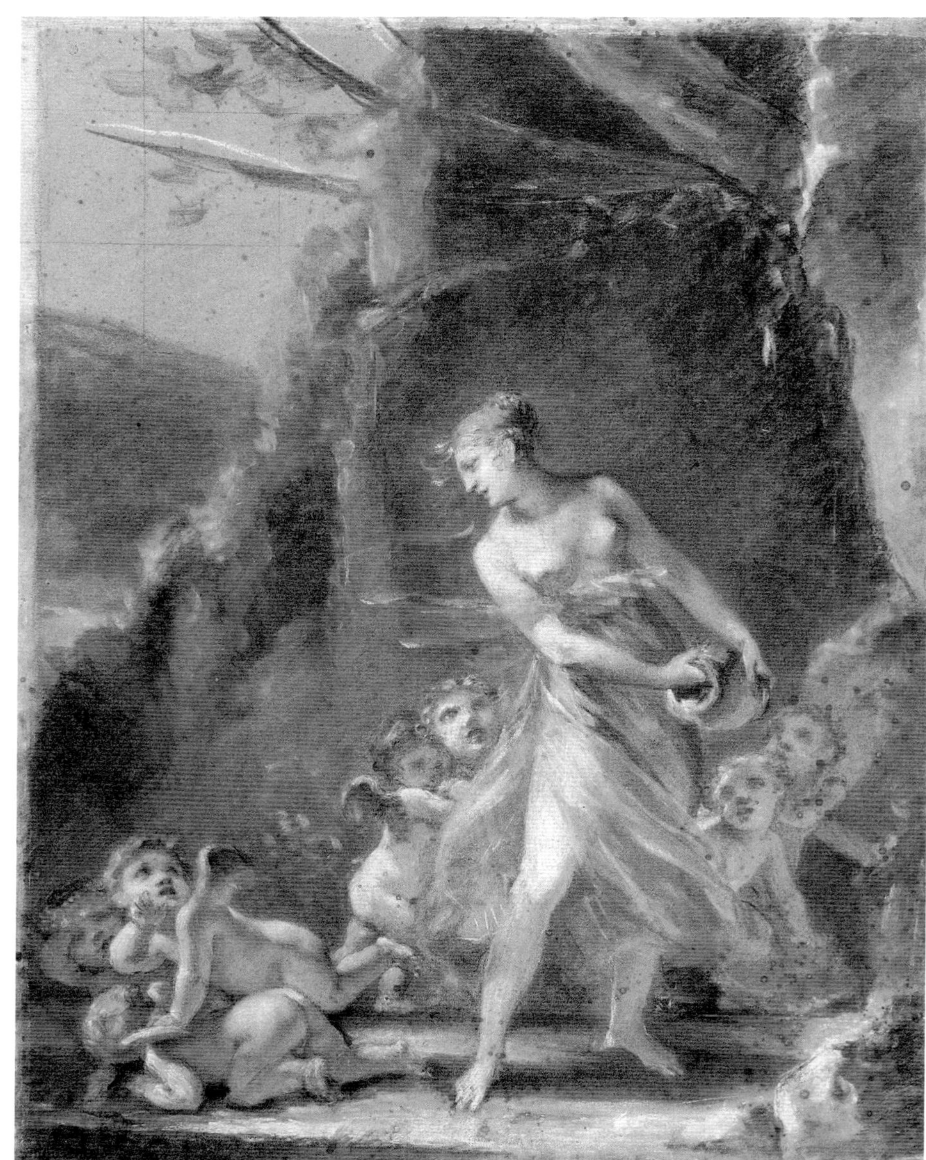
CATALOGUE NO. 46

This drawing, together with a smaller oil sketch now in the Musée du Louvre, Paris, and seven other drawings by Prud'hon (Guiffrey 1924, nos. 82–90) were made to assist the artist's pupil Constance Mayer in the preparation of her painting *Young Naiad Teased by Cupids* (*Une Jeune Naïade veut éloigner d'elle une troupe d'amours qui cherchent à la troubler dans sa retraite*; present location unknown), exhibited at the Salon of 1812 (no. 631). A smaller composition drawing, now in the Musée Cognacq-Jay, Paris

(Guiffrey 1924, no. 84), most likely preceded this larger work and perhaps the Louvre sketch, because there are variations in the figures of the *amorini*, which Prud'hon modified in favor of the composition seen here.

The present work clearly shows traces of a grid drawn in black chalk, visible in the upper left part of the sheet. The figures and landscape are drawn over the squaring, however, which suggests that the artist used this device as an aid to enlarge a smaller work. Had Prud'hon squared off the present study to assist Mayer in transferring the design to the larger dimensions of her Salon canvas, one would expect to find traces of black chalk over the figures (see observations by Eunice Williams in Mongan forthcoming).

A tonal drawing such as this would have aided the artist or his pupil in another respect. Prud'hon began his final canvases by first painting the figures in grisaille, to define the tonal relationships between each element. He then added thin glazes of color over this ground, slowly building up layers of paint, and finished his work by adding details and highlights (for a discussion of the artist's painting technique see Paris 1986, 93). Thus, independent of their beauty as drawings, these studies represent a preparatory stage at which the artist could easily test and modify value relationships before starting his grisaille underpainting.

Prud'hon's water nymph playfully rebuffing the cupids who have invaded her sanctuary is part of the gracious, pastoral view of life in antiquity celebrated in the poetry of Pierre-Joseph Bernard's *L'Art d'aimer* (The art of love) or Longus's *Daphnis and Chloe*. Both of these works, poems of youthful love in an arcadian setting, were published in editions with illustrations by Prud'hon that are among his finest achievements in that format. The commissions for the illustrations came from Pierre Didot, who in 1797 published Bernard's volume, followed in 1800 by a translation into French of Longus's novel as *Les Amours pastorales de Daphnis et de Chloé*. Also in 1800 the Parisian publisher Antoine Renouard asked the artist to provide a design for a frontispiece to an Italian edition of Longus's text (Cambridge 1980, 31–32, no. 17; Ray 1982, 128–30, nos. 75–76). Prud'hon's evocation of a serene antique world was formed as much by literary as by visual sources. The power of these images is the result of the artist's mastery of chiaroscuro drawing to create a luminous atmosphere that places these scenes outside the realm of the viewer's experience, in effect, a visual paraphrase of the poet's idealized, bucolic universe.

The verso of this sheet is an academic study of a male nude. VC

Pierre-Paul Prud'hon
Bust of a Female Figure
c. 1814

47
Charcoal and black and white chalks on blue paper
27.9 x 22.2 cm (11 x 8 3/4 in.)
Philadelphia Museum of Art, the Henry P. McIlhenny Collection in memory of Frances P. McIlhenny (inv. no. 1986-26-27)
(Philadelphia only)

PROVENANCE
His de la Salle.
Henriquel Dupont.
Eugène Laporte, Laroche Migennes, Yonne, 1937.
Henry P. McIlhenny, Philadelphia.

EXHIBITED
Paris 1874, no. 429.
Paris 1922, 42, no. 218.
London 1932, no. 866.
Paris 1937, vol. 2, 390, no. 153.
Philadelphia 1947, no. 109.
Philadelphia 1949.
Cambridge 1958.
San Francisco 1962, no. 31.
Allentown 1977, 12.
Pittsburgh 1979.
Atlanta 1984, no. 2.

LITERATURE
Clément 1872, 392.
Goncourt 1876, 297, no. 190 (as *Marguerite*).
Martine/Marotte 1923, no. 63.
Guiffrey 1924, 431, no. 1116.
Gradmann 1949, 29, 87, no. 53.
Shoolman/Slatkin 1950, 108, pl. 61.
Canaday 1959, 29, fig. 27.
Slayman 1970, 140, pl. 128.

One of Prud'hon's most hauntingly sensual images, this half-length study is traditionally thought to be of one of his favorite models, Marguerite. Originally, the artist may have planned to execute a full-length version of the figure, seated but with her head, arm, and torso exactly as shown here. This possibility is suggested by a recently published chalk drawing in the collection of Mr. and Mrs. John Jay Ide (San Francisco 1989–90, 35, 42). The Ide drawing cannot be identified with any of the female nude studies catalogued by Guiffrey, whose entries are

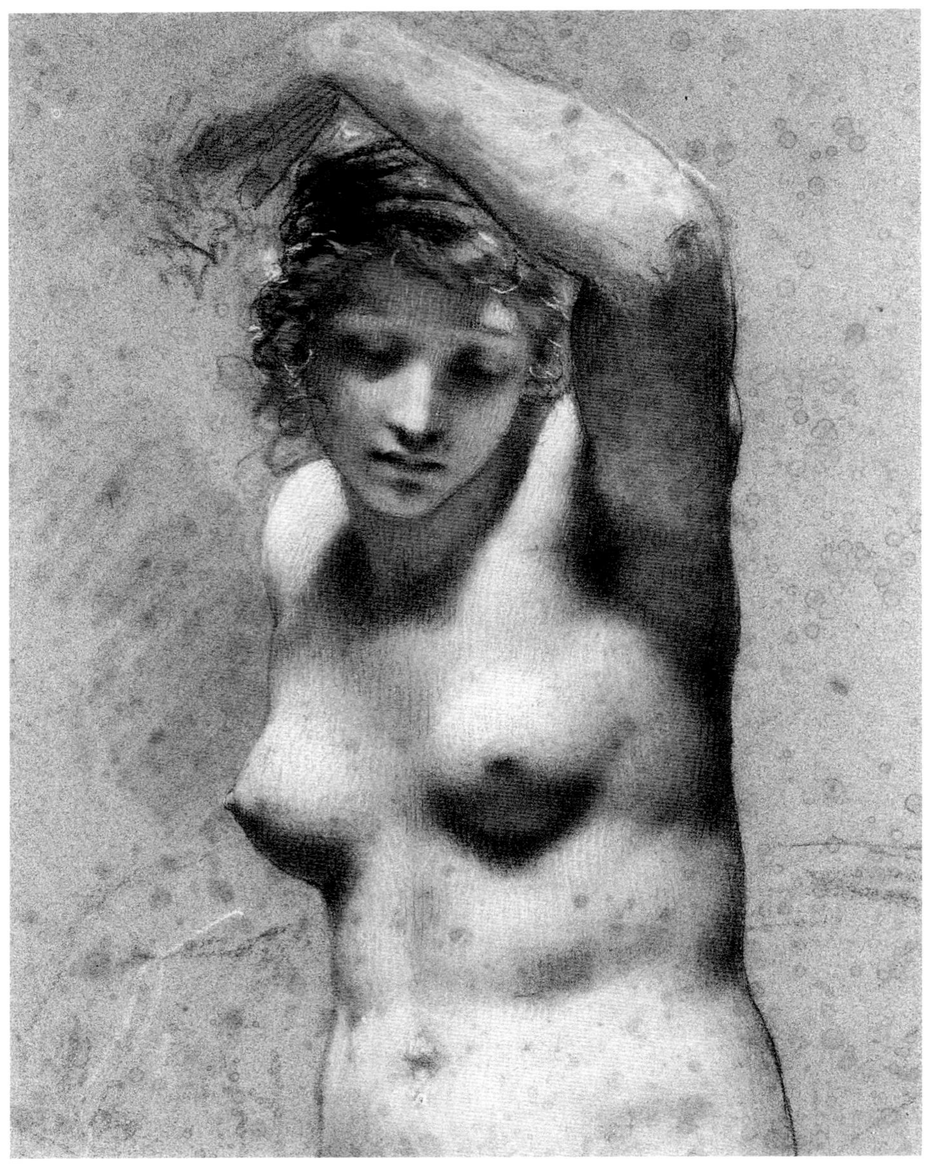

CATALOGUE NO. 47

sometimes imprecise and, in any event, must be incomplete. It is drawn in a manner typical of the artist's initial sketch for a figure or composition. Prud'hon's unfinished chalk drawings show that he first made a bold sketch of the contours, usually in black chalk, with slashing strokes of black and white chalks added to indicate in a general way the play of light over the volumes of the forms.

After having made an initial sketch of a figure or composition, Prud'hon then proceeded to blend together the black and white chalks to create the translucent *sfumato* modeling, with further details added in chalk, characteristic of drawings such as his *Young Nymph Teased by Cupids* (see CATALOGUE NO. 46). If he wanted a still more highly finished drawing, such as the present work, he combined additional layers of the two chalks to create more precisely detailed figures. The artist's modeling technique was to mix together the two chalks, working with short, parallel downward strokes that do not follow the contours of the figure, but nonetheless reveal its amplitude with a palpable sense for the physical, and at times sexual, character of the model. An unfinished drawing of a male nude at the Musée Bonnat, Bayonne, exhibits both stages of the artist's procedure, since the torso is carefully realized in his customary stipple manner, while the bold sketch of the legs remains unfinished (Paris 1979, no. 116). VC

Pierre-Paul Prud'hon
Cupid Testing the Flame of His Torch
Before 1814

48

Black chalk with white chalk heightening on blue paper
37 x 29 cm (14 9/16 x 11 7/16 in.)
The Baltimore Museum of Art, Nelson and Juanita Greif Gutman Collection, by exchange (inv. no. BMA 1981.18)

PROVENANCE

T. C. Bruun Neergaard; sale, Paris, April 29, 1814, lot 311.
Du Sommerard; sale, Paris, March 3–4, 1826.
Charles Turpin; sale, Paris, February 5, 1874, lot 166.
Alphonse et Édouard de Rothschild, after 1874.
Galerie Nathan, Zurich.

EXHIBITED

Paris 1874, no. 218.
Paris 1922, no. 96.

LITERATURE

Guiffrey 1924, no. 47.

Prud'hon's personification of Love as a cupid holding a burning torch (*L'Amour essayant l'effet de son flambeau*) has immediate antecedents in the imagery of works of art such as Jean-Honoré Fragonard's watercolor *The Sacrifice of the Rose* (see CATALOGUE NO. 21), c. 1775–80, in which the flambeau is a symbol for sexual conquest. Whether or not this was also Prud'hon's intention, his image is typical of the *galante* aspect of eighteenth-century art, glorifying the pursuit of pleasure and sensual gratification. The winsome, smiling putto makes it apparent why within his lifetime the artist was called the "French Correggio" (Nodet 1921, 408–16), but Prud'hon's letters from Rome frequently mention his admiration for Raphael and describe in glowing terms Leonardo da Vinci's *Last Supper*, which he knew through a tapestry woven after the fresco in Milan (Prud'hon 1857–58, 97–170). His veneration for these masters remained steadfast:

at his death the contents of his studio included a framed engraving by Raphael Morghen after the Leonardo, in addition to Morghen's reproductions of the Sistine Chapel ceiling and Raphael's *Madonna della Sedia* and *School of Athens*. Correggio was represented only by a print after a Magdalen; this and the other engravings were sold framed (sale, "Notice de tableaux, dessins, gouaches et pastels éxécutés par feu Monsieur P.-P. Prud'hon," Paris, May 13, 1823, lots 43, 44, 50, 45, 48, respectively).

In Rome Prud'hon certainly knew his fellow Dijonnais artist Bénigne Gagneraux, who also had been given a stipend by the estates of Burgundy to study in Italy. Before Prud'hon's arrival the latter had already painted *The Triumph of Love* (*Le Triomphe de l'amour*; Musée des Beaux-Arts, Dijon), 1779, after a canvas attributed to Ventura Salimbeni, a surprisingly vivid anticipation of the figure types and facial expressions Prud'hon developed in works such as the present drawing (Rome/Dijon 1983, 76, no. 7).

It is impossible to suggest a date for drawings such as this because both the figure types and handling of materials recur consistently throughout the artist's mature work. Two other versions of this drawing are known (Guiffrey 1924, nos. 48–49), as are three prints reproducing the composition by Jean Prud'hon *fils*, Julien Boilly, and C. Mendoze. In this instance a *terminus ad quem* is possible because the drawing was sold in 1814 by the Danish collector and admirer of Prud'hon, T. C. Bruun Neergaard, who had settled in Paris around 1800 (Lugt 1956 [supplément], no. 1939a; sale, Paris, August 29, 1814, lots nos. 308–18). He owned twenty-nine drawings by Prud'hon, many of them framed, as was the present work.

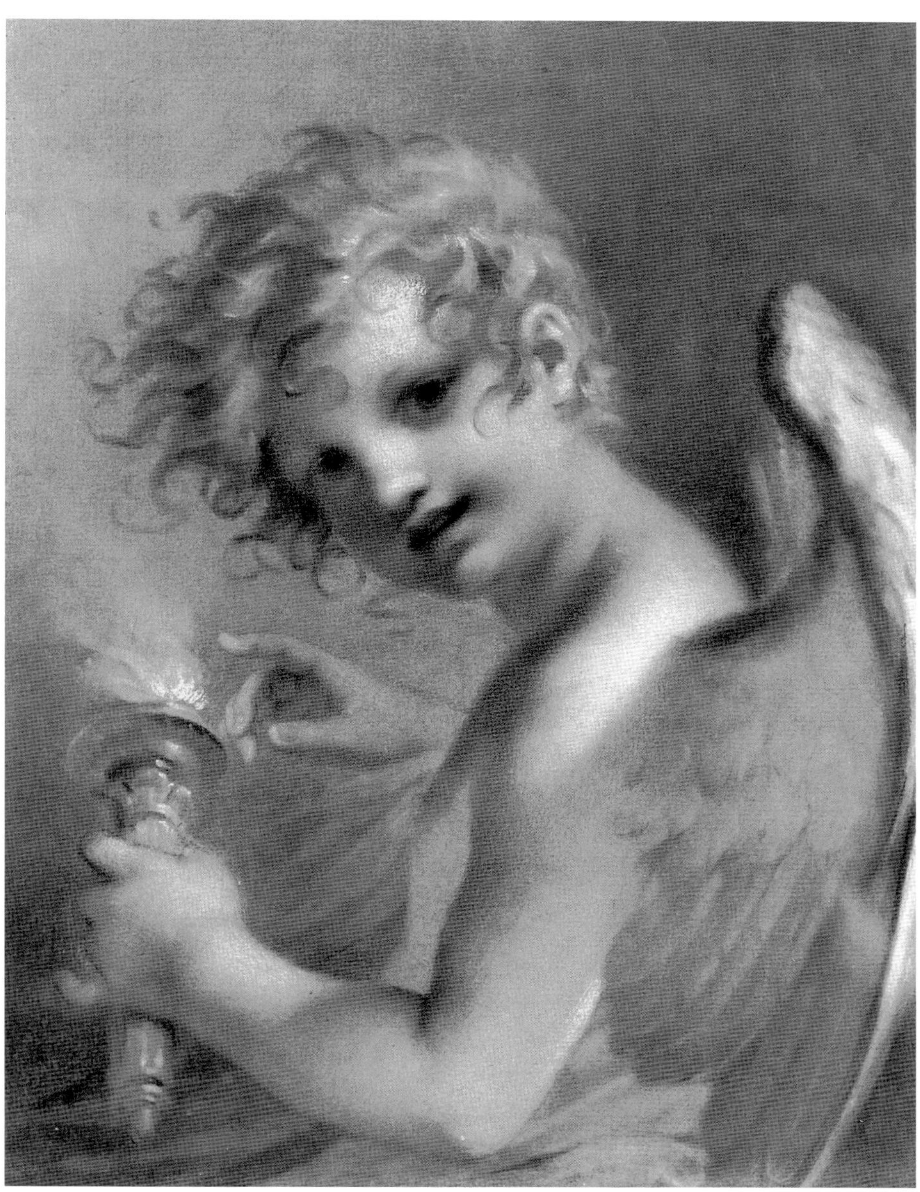

CATALOGUE NO. 48

With advances in the manufacture of plate glass during the eighteenth century it was possible to obtain the large sheets that were essential to protect the fragile surfaces of works on paper, which encouraged collectors to purchase and frame artists' drawings, watercolors, and pastels (Washington 1983, 20). Highly finished images such as this drawing would naturally appeal to a collector who wanted to enjoy an artist's drawings on his walls. Prud'hon had long been willing to respond to these requests: as an impecunious student in Dijon he wrote to his friend Fauconnier offering to provide drawings that the latter could frame (undated letter of c. 1784; cited in Clément 1872, 83), while in his Salon debut in 1791 he exhibited a framed, highly finished black crayon drawing, *The Genius of Liberty and Wisdom* (Fogg Art Museum, Harvard University, Cambridge; Heim/Béraud/Heim 1989, 314; Mongan forthcoming, no. 294). Through the end of the century the artist regularly included drawings among his Salon entries: designs for book illustrations in 1793, 1796, and 1798, drawings to be reproduced as prints in 1793 and 1798, and his four drawings for a frieze of the Seasons in 1799, part of the major commission to provide a series of decorative panels for the Hôtel de Lannoy (Guiffrey 1924, 294–300, nos. 800–53; Laveissière 1988, 2–23; Heim/Béraud/Heim 1989, 315–17).

One should not overlook the possibility that by exhibiting studies for other undertakings the artist was, in effect, announcing their availability or his readiness to accept like commissions. Perhaps with Napoleon's rise to power, the favorable reception Prud'hon's work found at court and among private collectors made this form of self-advertisement unnecessary. Significantly, at the Salon of 1801 his framed drawing *The Triumph of Bonaparte* (*Le Triomphe de Bonaparte*; Musée du Louvre, Paris; Guiffrey 1924, no. 1059) was an exception to the artist's now general habit of showing only his canvases. VC

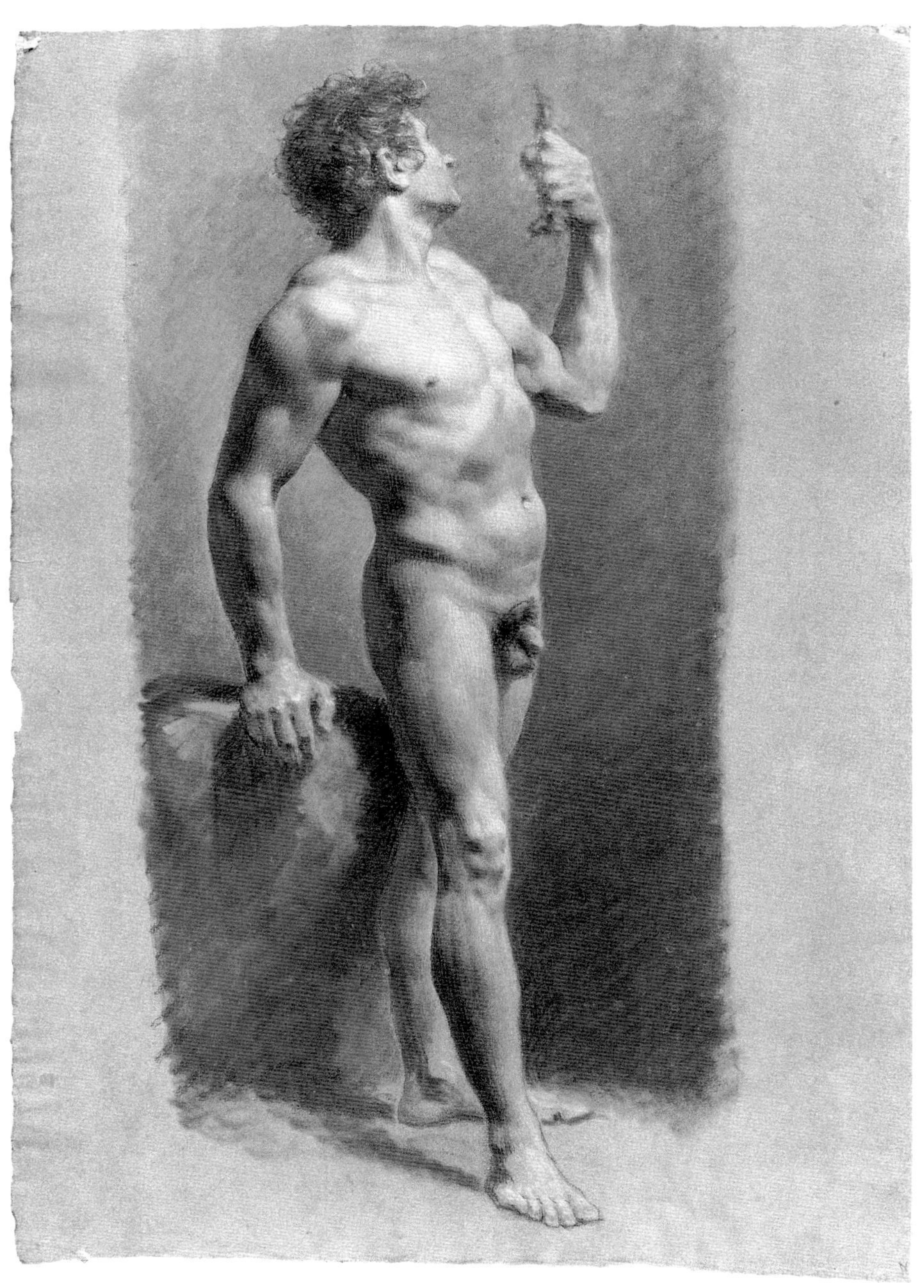

CATALOGUE NO. 49 (see color plate on page 104)

Pierre-Paul Prud'hon
Study of a Male Nude

49
Black and white chalks on blue paper
57.8 x 33.7 cm (22 3/4 x 13 1/4 in.)
Los Angeles County Museum of Art, the Graphic Arts Council Fund and Museum Acquisition Fund (inv. no. M.89.48)

PROVENANCE
François-Martial Marcille (1790–1856).
His son, Éudoxe Marcille (1814–1890).
Mme. Jahan.
Mme. Chévrier.
Meissonier collection.

EXHIBITED
Paris 1874, 132, no. 432.
Paris 1958, 57, no. 212.
Milwaukee 1977, 170–71.
Nishinomiya 1978, no. 46.
London 1981, 26.
New York 1982b, 26.

LITERATURE
Guiffrey 1924, 447, no. 1190.
Olson 1974, 74.
Weston 1981, 501.

Throughout his career Prud'hon consistently drew after a live model, even as an old man. Éugene Delacroix reported that late in life the artist spent much time working on figure studies such as the present example, either in his own studio or in that of his pupil Félix Trezel (Escholier 1926–29, 447). To appreciate Prud'hon's lifelong motivation to create these drawings requires an understanding of how the study of the human form was viewed in the eighteenth century. An ability to represent the figure was the most elementary task any art student was expected to master. Even artists of advanced experience and reputation drew after the model. In one sense, a mature artist's continual practice in figure drawing was simply a way to maintain an essential skill, which was basic to a painter's ability to function in the highly regarded category of history painting, the most elevated of all genres. Beyond this practical reason, at this period the art of draftsmanship was understood to be one part of the conquest of knowledge, which in turn shaped the personality of the artist.

The expression of a visual idea had to be based on a mastery of draftsmanship, defined in terms of knowledge and experience. This point of view may have impelled Prud'hon to continue studying the human figure as part of his painstaking search to perfect his art. These figure drawings were formed by the ideas of Prud'hon's time in another respect as well, the study of antique sculpture as a guide to the realization of the human form. In his discussion of two of the Musée du Louvre's finest Prud'hon drawings, Régis Michel noted classical prototypes for the figures, which were clearly executed after live models (Paris 1989a, 64–65). The individuality of Prud'hon's figures is immediately evident in spite of these references, an uncanny assimilation of palpable actuality and normative ideals derived from the antique. This is surely what Delacroix observed when he wrote that Prud'hon's study of ancient art went far beyond the dry replication of antiquities to the creation of an intensely personal vision that paralleled classical art in the grandeur of the artist's figures and the grace of his compositions.

These comments are relevant to the present study, which cannot be dated but may well be a work from the latter part of the artist's life. Prud'hon's masculine figure was drawn after a living model, who maintains his equilibrium by grasping with his left hand a cord hanging from the ceiling, while his other arm rests on a box to help stabilize this posture during a lengthy posing session. His right leg is slightly flexed, while the left limb assumes the weight of the stance. This was a standard position for a model to assume; in fact, it can be found in Charles-Nicolas Cochin's engraving *The Drawing School* (*L'École de dessein*), 1763, included in the article on drawing in Diderot and d'Alembert's *Encyclopédie*, where the model is shown from the back, with some drapery modestly added (Princeton 1977, 25, fig. 6). The pose taken by Prud'hon's and Cochin's models, with one leg forward, the arm outstretched on the opposite side of the body, and the head turned to one side, was often used for sculptures of freestanding figures. Celebrated above all was the Apollo Belvedere, on view in the Palazzi Vaticani by 1509, whose fame was propagated through innumerable copies and engravings (Haskell/Penny 1981, no. 8, fig. 77). Antiquities such as the Apollo established a norm for the pose assumed by the figure in this drawing by Prud'hon. By now, the reference to a precedent in classical art was thoroughly assimilated into standard academic practice. Artists such as Prud'hon understood as a matter of course the principles that underlay the composition of one of the world's most revered antique statues. VC

Étienne-Barthélémy Garnier

1759 Paris 1849

GARNIER WAS A STUDENT of Louis-Jacques Durameau, Gabriel-François Doyen, and Joseph-Marie Vien. He won the Prix de Rome in 1788 with *The Death of Tatius* (*La mort de Tatius*). The works he sent back for the Salons during his sojourn in Rome were very successful. He returned to Paris in March of 1793 and began in 1795 to exhibit regularly at the Salon. He worked with Pierre-Paul Prud'hon and Jean-François-Léonor Mérimée on the ceiling decoration of the Salle de Diane in the Louvre and painted *Burial of Dagobert I* (*Enterrement de Dagobert Ier*) for the new sacristy of the basilica of Saint-Denis, the traditional burial place of the kings of France.

During the Empire Garnier worked for Napoleon, completing such works as *Portrait of Napoleon I in His Study* (*Portrait de Napoléon Ier dans son cabinet de travail*) of 1808 and *Wedding Procession of Napoleon and Marie-Louise in the Tuileries Garden* (*Cortège nuptial de Napoléon et Marie-Louise dans le jardin des Tuileries*) of 1810. After the fall of the Empire he continued to exhibit history paintings, portraits, and religious commissions and became a member of the Institut de France in 1816. He was passed over in favor of Horace Vernet for the position of director of the Académie de France in Rome in 1829 and died in comparative obscurity twenty years later. LDM

Étienne-Barthélémy Garnier
Socrates and Alcibiades

50
Pen and black ink, brush and gray and brown washes, white highlights on tan laid paper, squared faintly in white chalk
30.5 x 44.7 cm (12 x 17 9/16 in.)
Inscribed on mount verso in pencil: *P. Guerin Donné par l'artiste à son ami Sylvestre, libraire rue du Bons Enfants, editeur du Brusset. De toute rareté et de tout premier ordre. Ne jamais donner les 2 pendants pour moins de 2,000 fr./en possession par heritage de M. Angoui [?] du Rey, petit fils de M. Sylvestre* (P. Guérin given by the artist to his friend Sylvestre, bookseller on the rue de Bons Enfants, Brusset's publisher. Quite rare and of the highest quality. Do not give up the pair of drawings for less than 2,000 francs. Acquired through the bequest of M Angoui [?] du Rey, grandson of M. Sylvestre)
The Art Museum, Princeton University, museum purchase, gift of Mrs. Rensselaer W. Lee, Mrs. David H. McAlpin, and Mrs. Hibben Ziesing (inv. no. x1978-6)

PROVENANCE
P. Guérin.
Shepherd Gallery, New York, 1978.

EXHIBITED
New York 1977, no. 48.

LITERATURE
Record of The Art Museum, Princeton University 38, no. 1 (1979): 22.
Ross 1983, 20–21.

At one point this drawing and its pendant, *Anacreon with His Mistress and the Young Bathyllos*, were thought to be works by Pierre-Narcisse Guérin because the inscription on the verso of the mount was thought to refer to that artist. The inscription, however, may refer to the fact that he once owned these drawings. At any event, Pierre Rosenberg (Ross 1983, 21) recognized that the drawings, both in Princeton, corresponded to a pair of small paintings once on the art market (sold Hôtel des Chevau-Légers, Versailles, September 20, 1970, lots 44, 45), there ascribed to Garnier, who exhibited oils of these subjects in the 1793 Salon. According to the Salon catalogue Garnier had painted *Socrates and Alcibiades* (*Alcibiade et Socrate*) in Rome when he was a *pensionnaire* at the Académie de France. Apparently he added the *Anacreon with His Mistress and the Young Bathyllos* (*Anacréon avec sa maîtresse et le jeune Bathylle*; present location unknown) to make a pendant composition. The two highly finished drawings may well be replicas of Garnier's canvases, rather than studies or *modelli* for the oils. In this drawing squaring in white chalk is visible in the background but is covered by the figures and draperies, which suggests that these elements were added later. Had the drawing been squared off to aid the artist in transferring the design to the larger dimensions of the canvas, one would expect to find traces of chalk on top of the drawing of the figures.

As a student in Rome Garnier made other complex pen, brush, and wash drawings with heightening in white that are related to paintings or oil sketches. Thus, the Princeton drawings conform to a characteristic aspect of Garnier's draftsmanship, although other artists also made elaborately detailed studies in these media. Such drawings, as well as oil sketches, were routinely sent to Paris to be reviewed as evidence of the students' progress (Paris 1974–75, 58, nos. 49–50).

The subject of Socrates leading his pupil Alcibiades away from vice or pleasure is not specifically mentioned in classical or contemporary sources but rather appears to be an innovation first realized by Pierre Peyron in an oil sketch and later in a 1785 Salon painting, both now lost. Peyron also painted another version of the theme, in which he substantially revised the composition (see CATALOGUE NO. 32 and Rosenberg/van de Sandt 1983, nos. 71–80, figs. 57–58, 60). In the 1791 Salon Jean-Baptiste Regnault exhibited a canvas of the subject recently

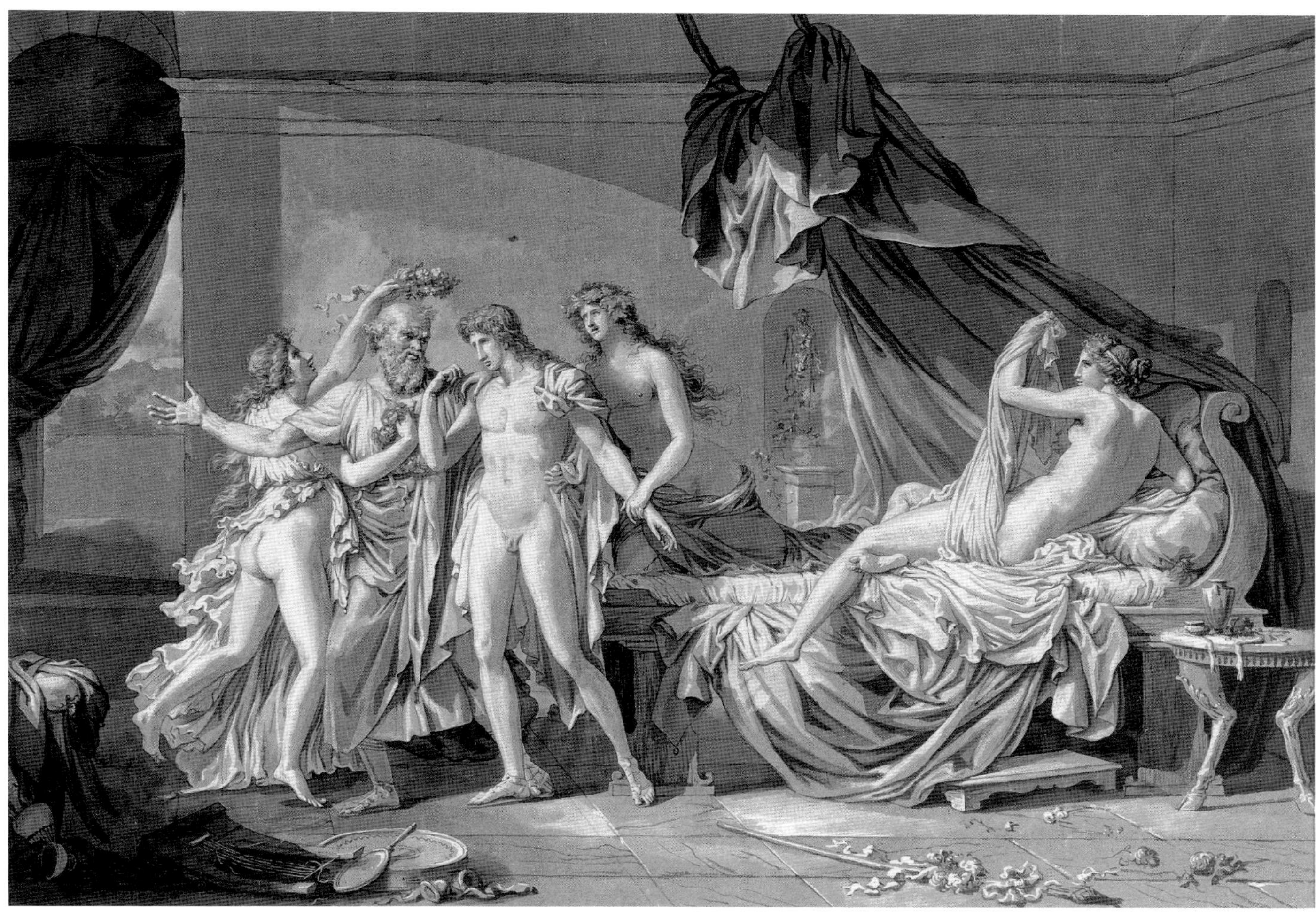

CATALOGUE NO. 50

acquired by the Musée du Louvre, Paris (Sells 1977, 354–57, nos. 5–6, fig. 1), followed two years later by Garnier's Salon entry. In the aftermath of the Revolution the legend continued to have a certain popularity, as attested by an oil by Jean-Charles-Nicaise Perrin seen at the 1801 Salon (Montargis 1989b, 60, no. 40) and drawings by Jacques Réattu, now lost (Simons 1985, 151, no. 15), and Louis-Simon Boizot (London 1975, no. 13). Regnault later painted another large-scale canvas of this moralizing subject, finished in 1810 and bought for the French royal collections in 1824 (Sells 1977, 354).

When Garnier set about developing the composition of his *Socrates and Alcibiades*, he certainly had in mind one of the most celebrated antiquities on view in Rome, the Capitoline Antinous in the Musei Capitolini, a statue admired for centuries as a paradigm of youthful male beauty; only the positions of Antinous's arms are changed slightly in Garnier's drawing (Haskell/Penny 1981, 143–44, no. 5, fig. 74). Adapting the perfection of the antique marble for his Alcibiades allowed the artist to display his considerable skills as a draftsman, abilities evident as well in the other figures in this composition. Garnier's canvases of *Socrates and Alcibiades* and *Anacreon with His Mistress and the Young Bathyllos* are typical of the small-scale works favored by private collectors, who admired these graciously composed scenes of historical or mythological subjects painted with a delicate, refined technique. In works of this kind, the artist's reference to the Capitoline Antinous is a flattering acknowledgment of both the painter's and his patron's erudition, even though the artist's evident pleasure in rendering the luxurious appointments of the setting negates the moral force of Socrates's importunity. VC

Guillaume Guillon, called Lethière

1760 Sainte-Anne, Guadeloupe–Paris 1832

LETHIÈRE WAS THE natural son of a French administrator in Guadeloupe, Pierre Guillon, and Marie-Françoise, a freed slave. In 1774 he left for France, where he enrolled in the drawing school of Jean-Baptiste Descamps in Rouen; by 1777 he was working in Paris in the studio of Gabriel-François Doyen. Lethière won second prize in the Prix de Rome competition in 1784 for his painting *The Canaanite Woman at Christ's Feet* (*La Cananéenne au pieds du Christ*). Even though he did not win a grand prize, he was awarded the status of a *pensionnaire* and left for the Académie de France à Rome in 1786, remaining there until 1791. In that year he returned to Paris, where he opened an atelier and received students; he proved to be a popular teacher.

Lethière exhibited regularly at the Salons from 1793 until 1831. In 1807 the minister of the interior named him director of the Académie de France in Rome (the artist's friendship with Napoleon's brother Lucien may have played a part in the award of this prestigious post). Lethière successfully directed the school until 1816, when he returned to Paris and was made a professor at the École des Beaux-Arts and again opened a private school. In 1822 he transferred his studio and school to the Institut de France, where he died ten years later. VC

Guillaume Guillon, called Lethière
Critias and Theramenes
1789

51
Pen and brown ink, brush and brown and gray washes heightened with white, over black chalk on off-white laid paper
65.2 x 101 cm (25 11/16 x 39 3/4 in.)
Signed and dated at lower right in pen and brown ink: *Lethière a Rome/1789*
Prat Collection, Paris

PROVENANCE
Art market, Paris.

EXHIBITED
Paris 1989b, 85–87, 158–59, no. 50.
New York/Fort Worth/Ottawa 1990–91, 169, no. 67.

Lethière, slightly younger than Jacques-Louis David, was one of a number of French painters active during the last three decades of the eighteenth century who based many of their works on themes from Greek or Roman history. Events from the classical past became increasingly popular at this period, in part as a conscious reaction against the rococo style. Criticism of contemporary art as decadent or frivolous had been voiced earlier by writers such as La Font de Saint-Yenne, who in 1747 and again in 1754 proposed that artists look to ancient writers for themes of virtuous action, generosity, courage, honor, and, most importantly, loyalty to one's nation or government. This theoretical position was adopted by many artists who followed this proposition for the reform of painting, although not necessarily guided by Saint-Yenne, whose voice was only one among several. As a consequence, artists read ancient history to find *exempla virtutis* that could be used to extol heroic personal conduct or exemplary forms of government.

When this drawing was exhibited for the first time in Paris in 1989, Régis Michel ingeniously and convincingly proposed that the subject of the work was a debate between the liberal Theramenes, one of the Thirty Tyrants appointed to govern Athens after its defeat in 404 B.C. at the end of the Peloponnesian War, and the more extreme oligarch Critias, who favored the imposition of military force to maintain civil order when necessary. Their debate is described in Xenophon's *Hellenica* (2.15-56). Lethière chose the dramatic climax of the verbal duel, when Critias orders his troops to seize Theramenes while their fellow governors sit powerless and immobile. As he is seized, Theramenes gestures toward the heavens, echoing the pose of the heroic statue of Athena in the background, clearly based on the marble Minerva Giustiniani, then still in that family's collection (Musei Vaticani, Rome; Haskell/Penny 1981, 269–71, no. 63, fig. 140). Since the drawing's execution was roughly coincident with the French Revolution, it is tempting to find a lesson in political morality in the artist's choice of this historical event. In fact, the very obscurity of the debate as a subject matter for painters led Michel to propose the identification only with prudently expressed reserve. It would not be out of character, however, for Lethière to find ideas for his subjects among some of the more recondite events of ancient history, as in his *The Condemned Metellus Saved by His Son* (see CATALOGUE NO. 52).

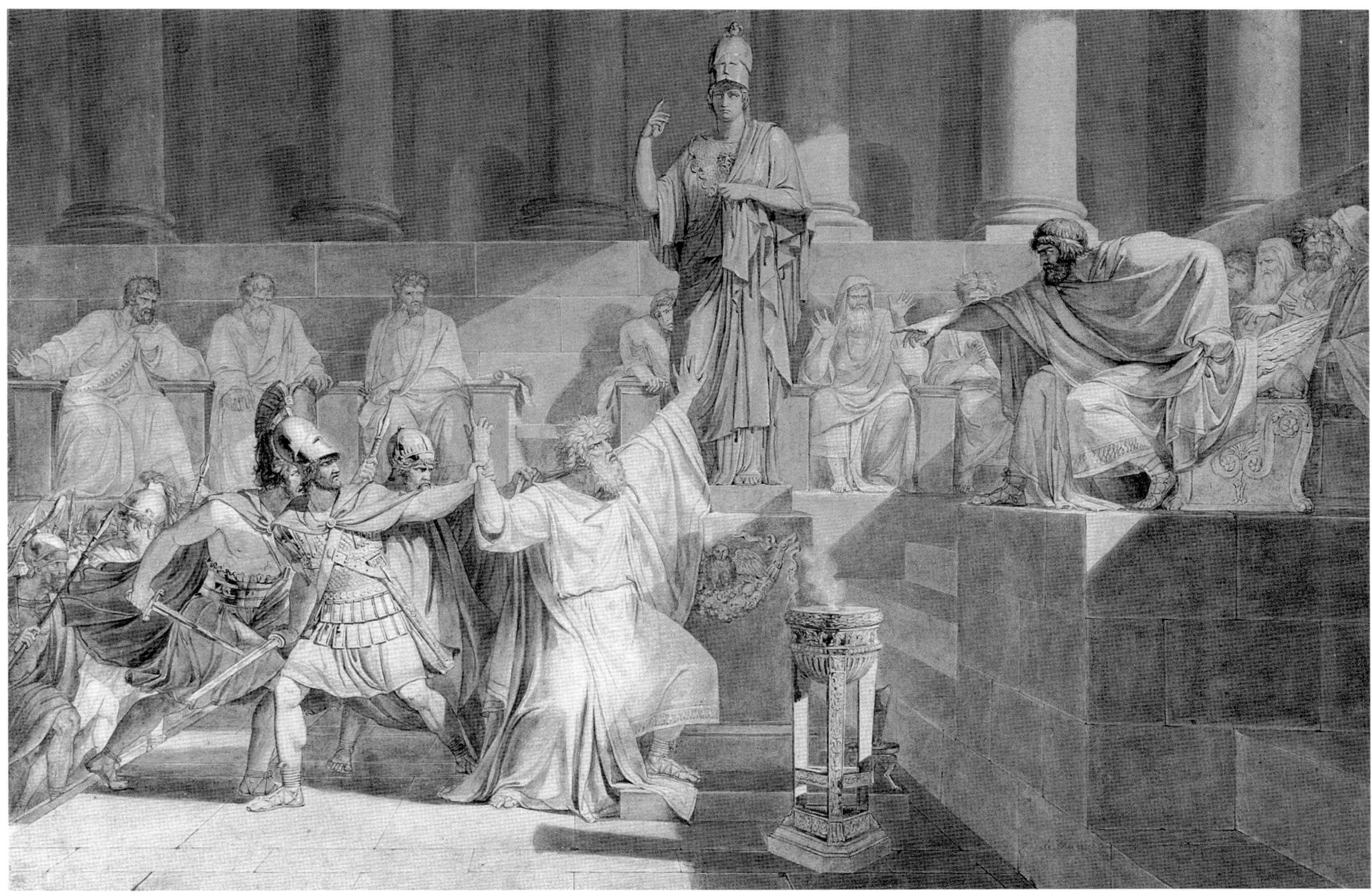

CATALOGUE NO. 51

It would be a challenge to any artist to represent the drama of a debate in visual terms. The expressive gesticulations of Lethière's two principal figures clearly define their roles as opponents, while the menacing soldier who grasps Theramenes with one hand and brandishes his unsheathed sword in the other forecasts the orator's imminent demise. But the artist's most imaginative visual paraphrase of this verbal drama is the background frieze of seated onlookers, who, Xenophon relates, sat rigid with fear. Their static postures are reemphasized by the regular, rhythmic repetition of the columns in the background architecture.

VC

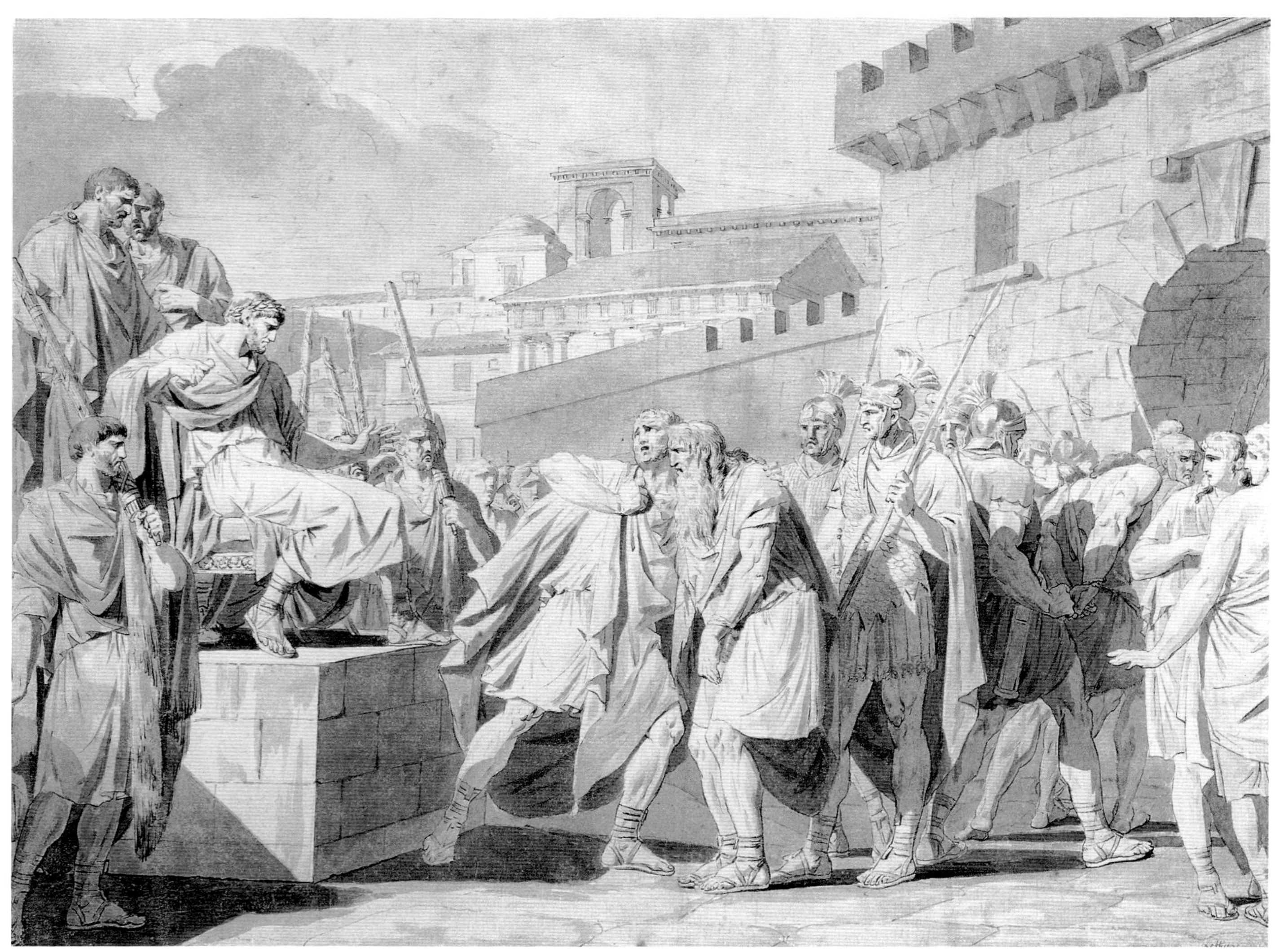

CATALOGUE NO. 52

Guillaume Guillon, called Lethière
The Condemned Metellus Saved by His Son
c. 1791

52
Pen and brown ink, brush and gray wash on off-white laid paper
45.7 x 62.5 cm (18 x 24 5/8 in.)
Signed at lower right in pen and brown ink: *Lethiere*
Los Angeles County Museum of Art, General Acquisition Funds (inv. no. AC1992.30.1)

PROVENANCE
Sale, Drouot-Richelieu, Paris, March 14, 1990, lot 89.
Sale, Sotheby's, New York, January 14, 1992, lot 149.

This drawing depicts an obscure event: the condemned Metellus is saved by his son, whom, ironically, the emperor Augustus had unwittingly appointed to be one of the judges in the case. This example of family loyalty is taken from the writings of the first-century B.C. historian Diodorus Siculus, a French translation of which was listed in the 1785 inventory of the library at the Académie de France in Rome (Bardon 1963, 225), where Lethière may have seen it.

Artists for the most part ignored this episode, except Nicolas-Guy Brenet, whose canvas *Metellus Condemned to Death by Augustus* (*Metellus condamné à mort par Auguste*; Musée des Beaux-Arts, Nîmes) was exhibited at the Salon of 1779 (Sandoz 1960, 44–45, fig. 2; Bardon 1963, 239). Lethière certainly knew Brenet's painting, since the figure of the seated Augustus is identical in the two works. A celebrated antique Roman marble of the poet and dramatist Menander was the prototype for Augustus, although both French artists reversed the pose of the statue; also Augustus's left arm is outstretched, whereas in the sculpture it lies across his lap. Lethière's drawing follows Brenet's oil exactly in these details, which surely cannot be a matter of chance, although in other respects the compositions are entirely different.

The composition of the present drawing follows the general plan of numerous antique Roman bas-reliefs, in which the principal figure is shown on a raised dais, below which a crowd of figures is paying homage or receiving a decision. It is possible to identify two specific prototypes used by Lethière. He may have seen the seated Menander on which Augustus is based in the Museo Pio-Clementino when he was a student at the Académie de France. It is also possible that he knew an engraving of the statue, such as the plate in Diderot and d'Alembert's *Encyclopédie* (vol. 1, pl. 28, fig. 1). The marble's fame was such that it was among the works taken from Italian collections by Napoleon under the terms of the Treaty of Tolentino; in Paris it was exhibited in the Musée Central des Arts when it opened in 1800.

The figure standing immediately below and to the left of the Augustus is derived from a late first-century A.D. relief of an *extispicium* (inspection of the entrails of a sacrificial offering), which in the eighteenth century was in the Borghese collection in Rome (Strong 1976, pl. 78); it is now the Musée du Louvre, Paris, having been included in the important purchase of antiquities made by Napoleon in 1807 from his brother-in-law Prince Camillo Borghese. It would appear that the artist worked after the original rather than the inept and somewhat inaccurate engraving published in Rome in 1767 by Johann Joachim Winckelmann in his *Monumenti antichi inediti* (reprinted 1967, vol. 2, 240, no. 183), since the lictor's draperies in the drawing and the sculpture are the same, whereas this detail is changed in the print. The Roman soldiers in the drawing, with their distinctive plumed helmets, recall similar figures on familiar Roman monuments such as Trajan's Column or the celebrated reliefs on the Arch of Constantine, although an exact source cannot be found. It has not been possible to identify an antique source for the figure of Metellus; in a general way he recalls one of the celebrated Farnese Captives (Haskell/Penny 1981, 169–72, figs. 87–88), although this figure may be a creation in the spirit of antiquity.

It is tempting to propose that Lethière's drawing was executed when both the statue of Menander and the Borghese relief were in Paris, but it was at just this time that the artist left France to assume the directorship of the Académie in Rome (1807–16). Of course, the artist could also have composed this drawing earlier on the basis of drawings and engravings after these monuments. Only a few drawings by Lethière are known today, among them the imposing *Critias and Theramenes* drawn in Rome in 1789 (see CATALOGUE NO. 51). The present drawing recalls David's pen and brush studies executed before 1800; both artists used brush to create crisp drapery folds and very bold, simple areas of shading, with pen work confined largely to the contours that define each figure and for details of expression and costume. It is likely that this drawing should be dated shortly after Lethière's return to Paris in 1791, when both Brenet's painting and David's works could have been seen by him. Although never actually a pupil of David, Lethière could not escape his example, which must have deeply impressed the younger artist when he saw the master's works again upon his return to France. VC

Philippe-Auguste Hennequin

1762 Lyons–Leuze 1833

HENNEQUIN WON THE Prix de Rome in 1788, while a pupil of Jacques-Louis David. As a fierce supporter of the Revolution, Hennequin remained only a brief period in Rome because of his republican sentiments. When he returned to his hometown of Lyons, he was imprisoned shortly after his arrival but escaped to Paris, where he was hidden by friends. After many brushes with death Hennequin abandoned politics in 1794 and devoted himself to his art. He painted throughout the Empire; during the Restoration he moved to Liège, where he painted *The Devotion of the Three Hundred Citizens of Franchimont*. He relocated to Tournai in 1815 and became the director of the Académie there. LDM

Philippe-Auguste Hennequin
The Disarming of Mars
1805

53
Pen and dark brown ink, brush and reddish brown wash on off-white laid paper
66 x 54 cm (26 x 21 1/4 in.)
Signed and dated at lower left in dark brown ink: *Phi. Aug. Hennequin an 14*
The Estate of Martin L. H. Reymert

PROVENANCE
Didier Aaron, Paris.
Martin L. H. Reymert, New York and Paris.

EXHIBITED
New York/Washington 1984, no. 4.
Hamburg 1989, 365, no. 501.

Hennequin was unusually adept at treating complex allegories commemorating political events and personalities, or, as this drawing illustrates, more abstract ideals intertwined with the consequences of the French Revolution. Here, Mars, the god of war, is sleeping exhausted in the lap of Peace. The "Tree of Liberty" shelters them, Mars's armor resting against its sturdy trunk. Putti, one with a trumpet, celebrate the beginning of an era of freedom, while in the right background the figure of Abundance signifies a prosperous future for the French nation. Allegories such as this were inextricably bound to Napoleon's rise to power. In fact, nearly contemporary with the present work is another drawing by Hennequin, dated 1806, specifically eulogizing "La Gloire napoléonienne" (Hamburg 1989, 365, no. 501).

Hennequin's Republican sympathies are manifest in his work, sometimes expressed through the guise of ancient history or as openly propagandistic allegory. His *Orestes Pursued by the Furies* (*Les Remords d'Oreste*; Musée du Louvre, Paris), exhibited in 1800, has been read as an allegory of revolution, personified by the Greek hero persecuted by antirevolutionary Furies (Paris 1989b, vol. 2, 639, no. 843). The artist's overt support of Napoleon is seen in an etching and mezzotint *Bonaparte Crowned in Egypt by Victory* (*Buonaparte couronné en Egypte par la Victoire*), c. 1798 (Los Angeles 1988, no. 173). The image of the etching and mezzotint is based on a drawing in the Bibliothèque Nationale, Paris (Paris 1989b, vol. 3, 719, no. 945), which is remarkably close in style to the present sheet, even to the repetition of details such as the figure of Victory holding a laurel wreath and the putto with a trumpet, which Hennequin lifted from his *Bonaparte Crowned in Egypt by Victory*. This coincidence reinforces the association of the present drawing with the glorification of Napoleon, one example among many of a propagandistic undercurrent that occurs in other works by Hennequin's contemporaries.

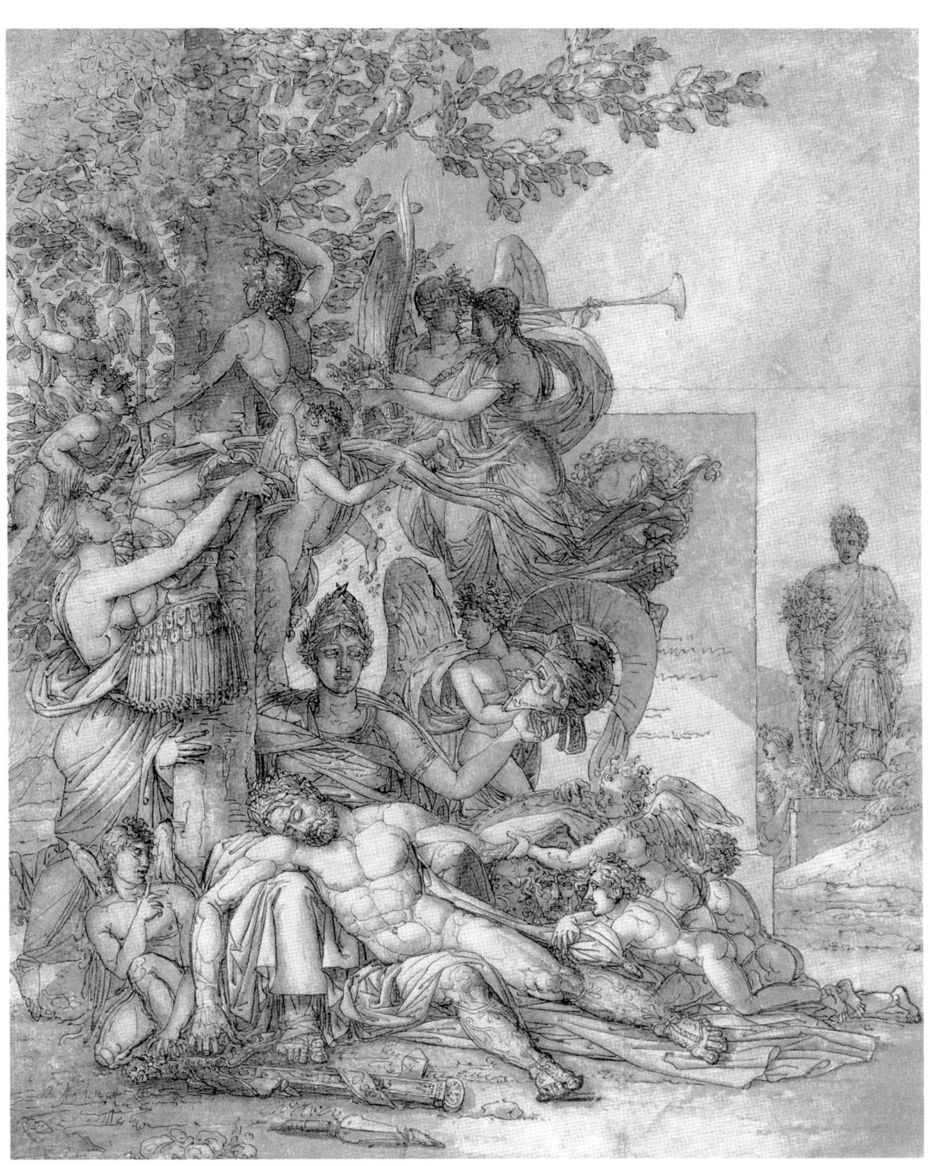

CATALOGUE NO. 53

Hennequin's drawings are quite distinctive, the artist's line thin and sinewy, especially in the contours of his figures. But he clearly took pleasure in the calligraphic flourishes that define accessory details such as Mars's armor and military equipment and the victory wreaths and cornucopias held by the Roman goddess of Abundance. At times the artist's command of anatomy is exaggerated to the point of grotesqueness, as, for example, in his preparatory drawing for *Orestes Pursued by the Furies* (The Snite Museum of Art, Notre Dame; Notre Dame 1987, 145) or the related study in the Musée Fabre, Montpellier (Paris 1974–75, 82, no. 81), to cite only two characteristic instances. The decorative linear flourishes of Hennequin's pen can be found, as well, in works by his contemporaries such as Charles Meynier (see CATALOGUE NO. 62; Paris 1974–75, 95, no. 94), Jacques Réattu, or Joseph-Marie Vien (see CATALOGUE NO. 15). Across the English Channel, John Flaxman's line engravings appear sparse and astringent by comparison, the Briton's outlines more sympathetic to the linear severity of Greek vase paintings, the character of which contradicts the elaborately executed pen drawings of Vien or Hennequin. VC

Anne-Louis Girodet de Roussy-Trioson

1767 Montargis–Paris 1824

GIRODET JOINED Jacques-Louis David's studio in 1784 and tried twice for the Prix de Rome before finally winning the prize in 1789 with *Joseph Recognized by His Brothers* (*Joseph reconnu par ses frères*; see FIGURE 45), a prize he shared with Charles Meynier. In 1790 he left for Rome, where he painted the highly successful *The Sleeping Endymion* (*Endymion endormi*; see FIGURE 43), 1791, shown both in Rome and at the Paris Salon of 1793. During the Revolution he spent time in Naples, Venice, and Genoa; he returned to Paris in 1795. Since 1791 he had worked for the publisher Didot, illustrating works by Anacreon, Virgil, and Jean Racine. His *Portrait of Mademoiselle Lange as Danaë* (*Portrait de Mlle Lange en Danaë*) caused a sensation at the 1799 Salon.

In 1801 Girodet was commissioned by Bonaparte to paint *Ossian Receiving the Shades of the French Heroes* (*Ossian recevant les ombres des héros français*, also called *Apothéose des héros français*; see FIGURE 47) for the Château de Malmaison. Between 1806 and 1810 Girodet painted *Scene from a Deluge*, *The Funeral of Atala*, *The Surrender of Vienna*, and *The Revolt of Cairo*. In the decennial competition of 1810 his *Deluge* triumphed over David's *Sabine Women*. By this time Girodet had painted most of his major works, and for the most part he spent the later years of his career making drawings, many of which are illustrations. Girodet, who was also a prolific writer and poet, became a member of the Académie in 1815. LDM

Anne-Louis Girodet de Roussy-Trioson
Study for Joseph Recognized by His Brothers
c. 1789

54
Charcoal with white highlights on tan laid paper
36 x 49 cm (14 3/16 x 19 5/16 in.)
Musée Girodet, Montargis (inv. no. 874.148)

PROVENANCE
Antoine César Becquerel.

EXHIBITED
Paris 1937, no. 608, not ill.
Montargis 1967, no. 54.
Montargis 1983, no. 7.

LITERATURE
Coupin 1829, iii.
Montargis 1864.
Montargis 1874.
Montargis 1885.
Montargis 1937.
Vaisse 1974, 82.
Paris 1983–84, 120, no. 110.

This drawing, one of the works that formed the basis of the Musée Girodet collection, was given to Montargis by the renowned physician Antoine César Becquerel, Girodet's cousin and executor. The work has great significance, for it was a preparatory study, along with two other works given by the same donor, for the painting that won for Girodet the grand prize in the Prix de Rome in 1789, *Joseph Recognized by His Brothers* (*Joseph reconnu par ses frères*; see FIGURE 45).

Few works by students demonstrate, as does this triple academic nude, such an excellent apprenticeship in drawing, in this case based on precepts of Jacques-Louis David; few students have shown such masterliness in the art of drawing. Three poses are shown, three attitudes of supplication, from the humblest to the most fervent, as if the artist broke a continuous movement into three stages. The art of expression, in which Girodet excelled as no other of his contemporaries, is wholly contained in this sculptural group, which is a study according to David's instructions—and more generally according to classical principles from Raphael to Lebrun—of anatomy and the effects of light on muscle mass before poses are finalized and figures clothed in the execution of the finished work.

Raphael and the antique were the watchwords of David returning from Rome; it was here that the classical method located perfection, grandeur, and propriety. In this dialogue Lebrun placed Raphael, "the god of painting," at the heart of artistic pedagogy. In Rome, David rediscovered these virtues: for him ideal beauty and grace did not exist apart from Raphael. As Jean-Pierre Cuzin has demonstrated, Girodet's model for grouping his figures was *The Adoration of the Magi* in the Vatican Logge decorated by Raphael (Paris 1983–84, 120, no. 110).

As a useful historical sidelight, noted by Philippe Bordes, we may recall that Girodet was excluded, on the basis of François-Xavier Fabre's denunciation, from the Prix de Rome in 1787 for having illegally introduced preparatory drawings corrected by David. P. A. Coupin (1829, vol. 1, iii) relates that after the *concours* Girodet "took to carrying a large cane [that] was hollow. . . . After the judgment in 1789 one of his competitors, Monsieur [François] Gérard, a comrade and friend, taking the cane from Girodet's hands, said to him laughing, 'Is this the Trojan horse?' Yes, he said, but it was necessary to hold on to it while the Greeks were still in there." The drawing from the museum in Montargis is perhaps one of those Greeks, rolled up in the cane taken by Girodet to the competition for the Prix de Rome. SB

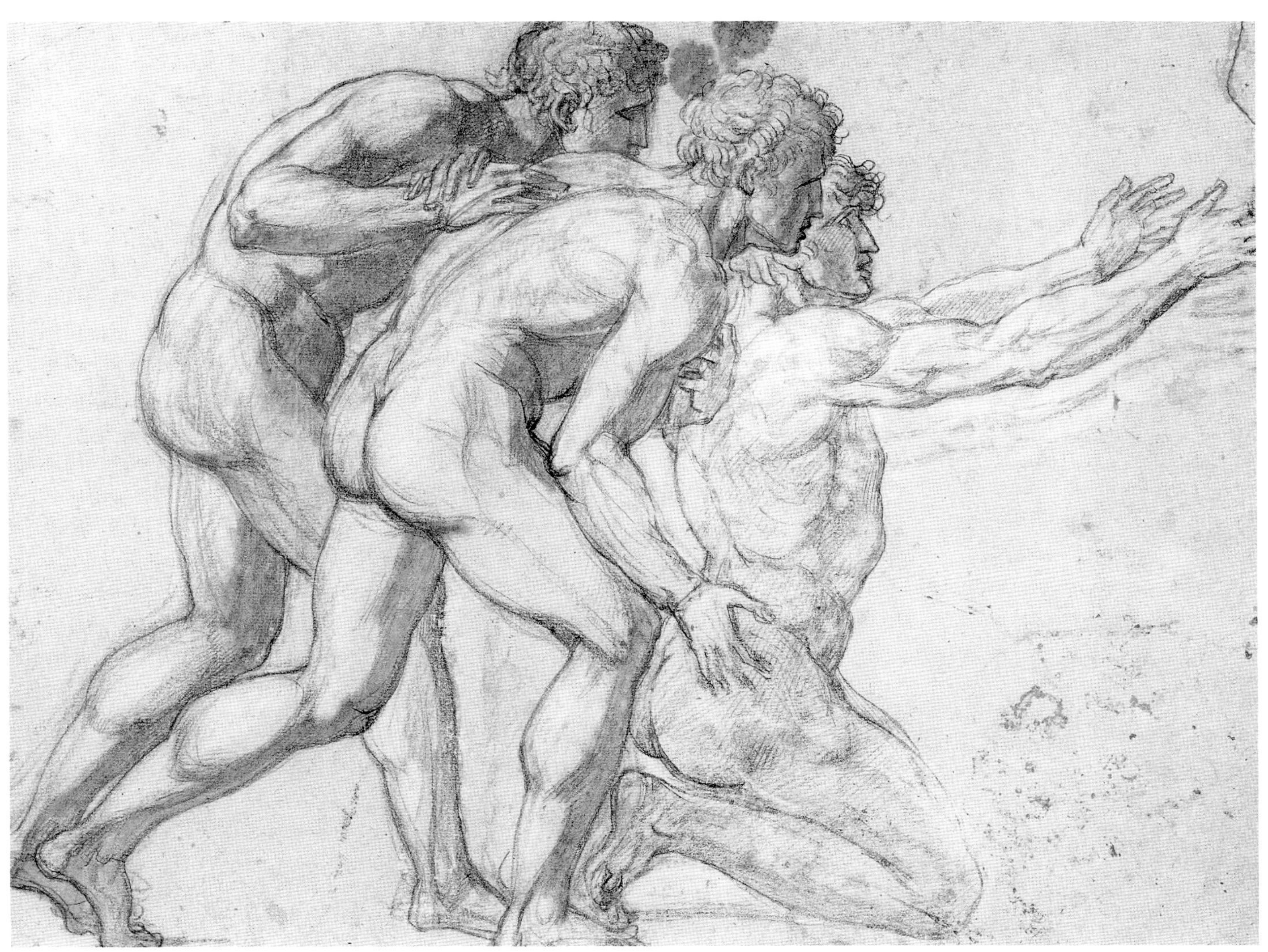

CATALOGUE NO. 54

Anne-Louis Girodet de Roussy-Trioson
The Meeting of Hermione and Orestes
c. 1800

55
Pen and brown ink, brush and gray and brown washes, with white and ochre highlighting on off-white wove paper
28.7 x 21.9 cm (11 5/16 x 8 5/8 in.)
The Cleveland Museum of Art, Leonard C. Hanna, Jr., Fund (inv. no. CMA.89.101)

PROVENANCE
Pierre Didot L'Ainé (1761–1853).
His brother, Firmin Didot (1764–1836).
Marquis de Chateaugiron (purchased c. 1814).
Probably Honoré Theodore Paul Joseph d'Albert, duc de Luynes (1802–67), Château de Dampierre (Seine et Oise) and by descent to his heirs.
Comtesse Marie de Luynes, Château de Dampierre, until 1988.
The Cleveland Museum of Art.

EXHIBITED
Paris, Salon of 1800, no. 170.

LITERATURE
Osborne 1985.

In the painting section at the Salon of 1800 Girodet showed five drawings for the illustration of an edition of Jean Racine's play *Andromache* prepared for the publisher Pierre Didot; among then was the Cleveland sheet, titled *Entrevue d'Oreste et d'Hermione* (no. 170). According to Didot, this project was to be his most ambitious to date. It was dedicated to Napoleon, at that time first consul of the French Republic. "In your two names, children of victory, France with pride will contemplate her glory," Didot wrote in the publisher's announcement, linking the names of Racine and Bonaparte in his patriotic endeavor (Osborne 1985, 113).

At the Salon of 1804 Girodet exhibited five other drawings, this time destined for an edition of *Phaedra*, the second of Racine's works he would illustrate. Didot's first choice of illustrator for *Andromache* had been Pierre-Paul Prud'hon, his favorite artist. We owe the selection of Girodet to the intervention of Jacques-Louis David; the influence of the master of the new school of painting upon Firmin Didot, Pierre's younger brother and business partner, had already become manifest with the publication of the works of Virgil in 1798 (Osborne 1985, 84).

Recently, several masterpieces of drawing by Girodet have appeared on the art market, and, due to the perspicacity of the late Frederick J. Cummings, the best have gone to American collections. Among these is *The Meeting of Hermione and Orestes*. Hermione, daughter of Helen of Troy, suffered because of the love Pyrrhus bore for the Greek captive Andromache. Left forlorn, Hermione used the love of Orestes for her to carry out a vendetta, creating herself a guardian of the ancient order that had promised her to Pyrrhus. In Girodet's composition Hermione, her caryatidlike pose echoed by the columns of the temple, is a masterpiece of ambiguity. Her body and expression restrained, alluring, full of duplicity, they combine both self-denial and a devious will to please. Behind her is the only furnishing in the austere dwelling, a small gueridon with its support in the form of a siren, conveying the allegorical attributes of seduction and danger of death. Orestes, naive and spontaneous, marvels at his good fortune. A mute, supplicating presence in the scene is the servant Cleone, who assists in the tragedy unawares.

The logic of Racine's narrative and the implacability of destiny are reflected in the austere Doric architecture—antiquity in its purest and most primitive form—and in the floor mosaic, the geometric echo of the narrative's rational severity. The architectural frieze shows the lower halves of the bodies of a man and a woman on the backs of seahorses, separated by a putto riding a dolphin, as if to suggest that even at this point we are still in the midst of a game.

Girodet wrote, "If one takes pride in imbuing them with style and character, drawings require the same composition and the same studies as a painting, differing only in the method of execution" (Coupin 1829, vol. 2, 343). The many preparatory drawings for his illustrations of Racine (a sale of his work after his death, in 1825, accounted for thirty) reveal the same process as that for the painting of history. The study of facial and gestural expressions, of anatomical truth via the nude, is demonstrated here and in another drawing from the series, *Hermione Rejecting Orestes*, from the Art Institute of Chicago (inv. no. 1986.428).
SB

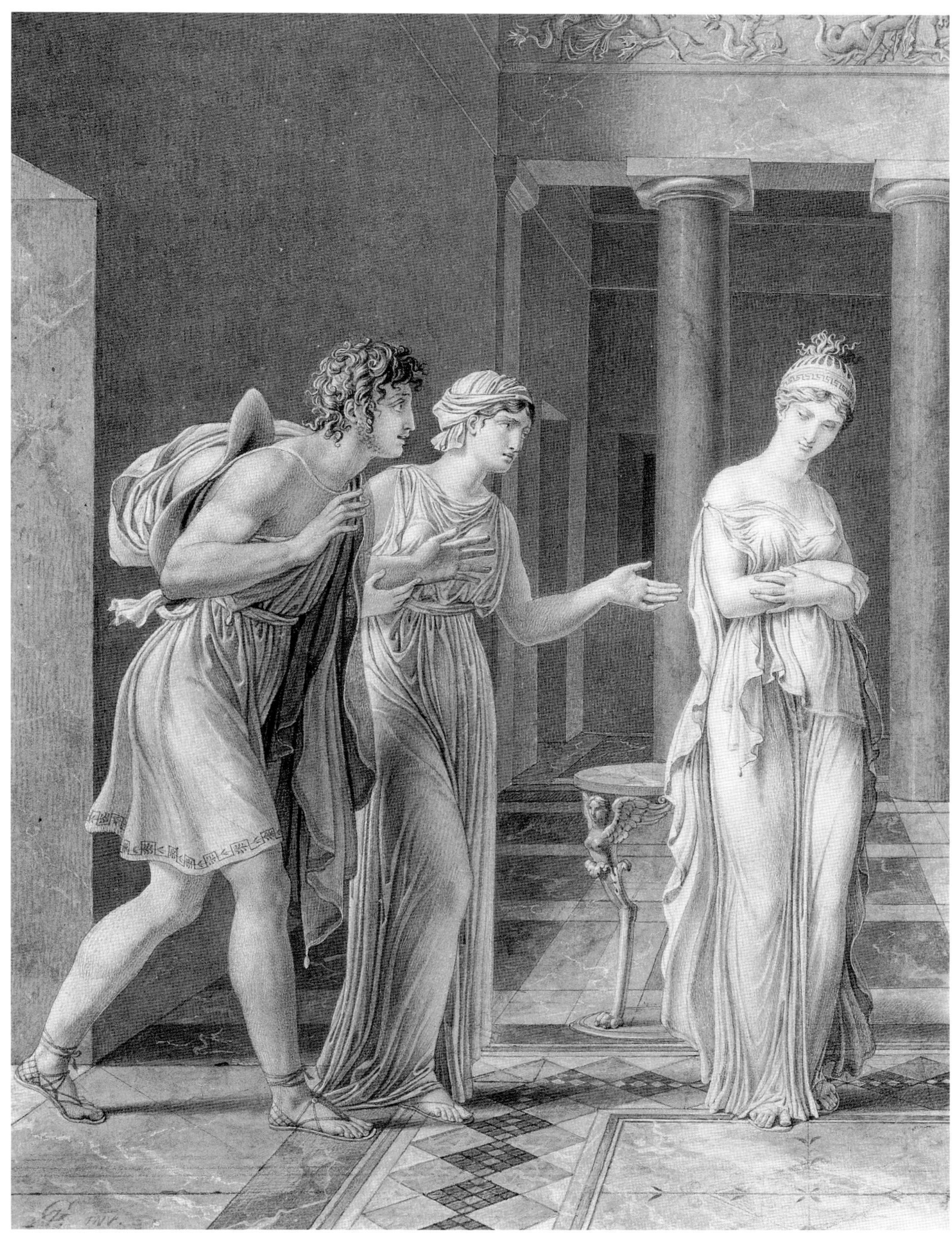

CATALOGUE NO. 55

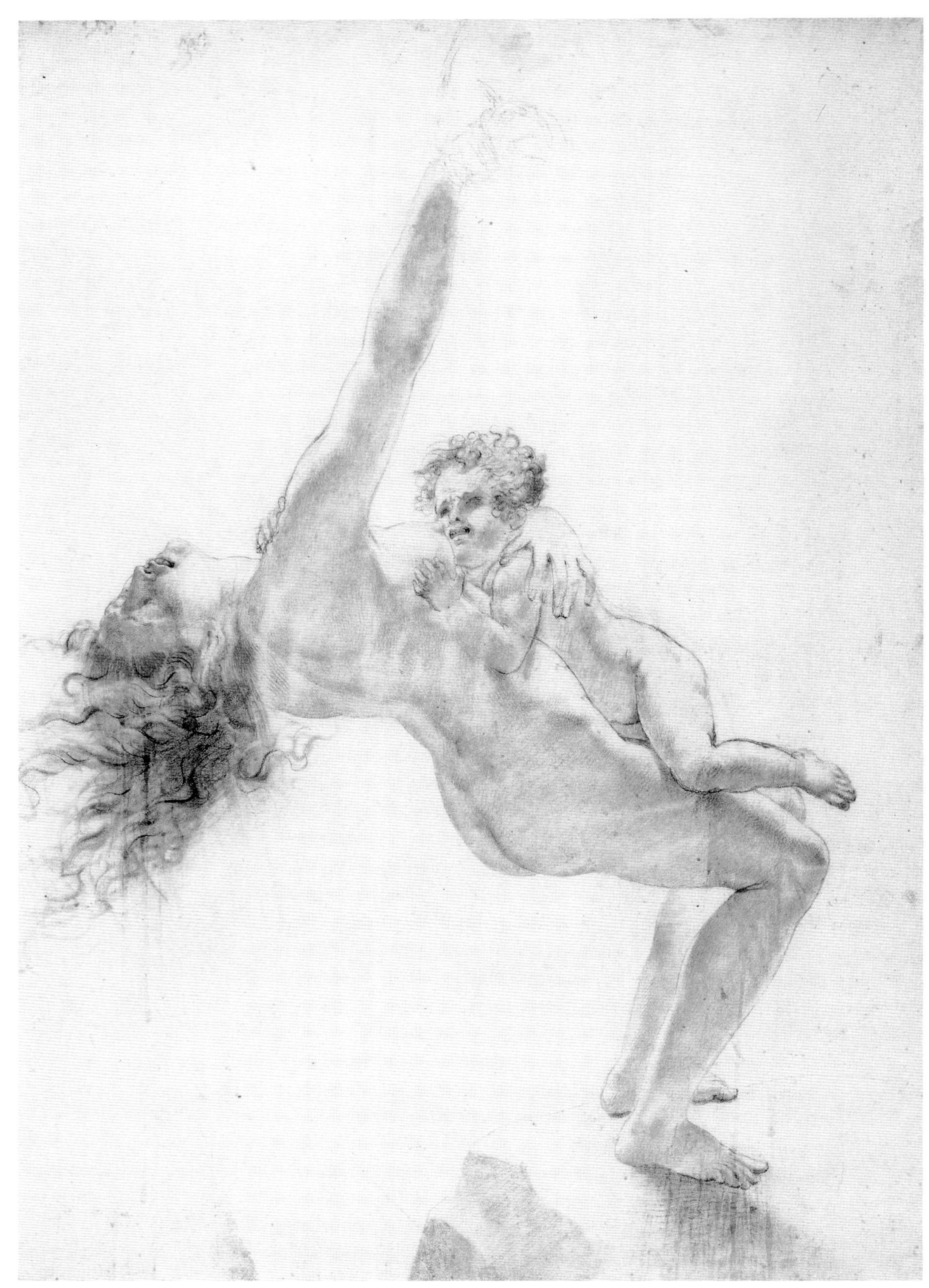

CATALOGUE NO. 56

Anne-Louis Girodet de Roussy-Trioson
Study for Scene from a Deluge
c. 1806

56
Charcoal, graphite, and stump on off-white laid paper
60 x 44.5 cm (23 5/8 x 17 1/2 in.)
Musée Girodet, Montargis

PROVENANCE
Acquired by the museum in 1982.

EXHIBITED
Montargis 1983, no. 51.
Paris 1989a, no. 56, ill. 96.

LITERATURE
Girodet 1807.
Rubin 1972, 211–37.
Montargis 1983, no. 51.

Scene from a Deluge (*Scène de déluge*; see FIGURE 44), exhibited by Girodet at the Salon of 1806, occupies a special place in the iconography of floods, shipwrecks, and catastrophes (see Rubin 1972, 211–37). The alarming nature of the composition was readily perceived by both public and critics:

Truly Girodet has too hard a soul!
To show in public such a painting!
It's the desire, without regard for their plight,
to make salon-going ladies give birth out of fright! (Girodet 1807, 19)

Or, elsewhere, "strictly speaking, we may very well consider the painting by M. Girodet the result of a nervous condition" ("F. P.," *Journal de Paris*, no. 268, September 25, 1810).

Girodet responded curiously, not by defending the violence of the scene, but by withdrawing himself from any moral interpretation of the title. "Would you prefer a family surprised in the night, surprised by an inundation and on the point of being engulfed by the waters?" he wrote a few months after the exhibition, probably to the future marquis de Pastoret (Coupin 1829, vol. 2, 391). What did he mean by this apparent banalization of a scene that had been the sensation of the Salon and carried off the prize for best historical painting at the decennial *concours* in the year 1810?

The drawing from the Musée Girodet is a study, before the addition of the draperies, for the figures of the mother and young child, a crucial element in the final composition. The academic pose of the model suspended in the studio is made apparent by the absence of draperies. Also evident is the maternal reality of the body, the prominent abdomen, the exaggerated dimensions of the breast and protective hand. The opposing motion of the hair, the arm extended but slack, the closed eyes, these alone embody a large part of the drama: the imminence of a fall, suspense rendered more expressive by the contortion of the figures. In the painting the woman, surrounded by her children, is held by the wrist by the father, carrying on his back an aged relative. The branch that holds them is about to break; in a few moments the family will be swallowed in the waves swirling below the rocks. It is a theatrical, baroque scene. Girodet wished it to be without moral import, "a family surprised by the flood." There is no serpent to signify the biblical deluge, and therefore no redemption; the suspense is not compatible with a moral lesson. All that counts here is the horror of the individual in the face of chaos, the dreadful, nature—and, thus, the sublime.

The modernity of 1810 was expressed through its myths: Michelangelo against Raphael, Cinna against Berenice ("F. P.," *Journal de Paris*, no. 266, September 23, 1810), paradigms of the quarrel that raged violently in an otherwise silenced crowd between the partisans of the perfection of composition and purity of taste of David's *The Sabine Women* (*Les Sabines*; see FIGURE 13), for which the artist had undertaken archaeological research—naked warriors, horses without harnesses, the exemplary civic behavior of the defenders—and the partisans of Girodet, painter of the sublime. After the originality of the arrangement, contemporaries admired in the *Deluge* the splendor of its draftsmanship (Marie Boutard, *Feuilleton du journal de l'Empire*, October 6, 1806). P. A. Coupin (1829, vol. 1, xli) stated that "without exception, for all of the individual figures that compose *Scene from a Deluge*, Girodet made skeletal studies for each of the articulations, as well as myologic drawings, in order to take into account with precision the movements of the deep, hidden layers of muscles that play, unbeknownst to us, such a great role in the appearance of the form."

It is through his exaggeration, therefore, that Girodet parted with classical logic. Amplifying Raphael, he approached Michelangelo, of whom he wished to make a cult. The homage evident in *Scene from a Deluge* makes of Girodet an atypical artist of the French school, one who pushed the boundaries of the Davidian circle out to those of German and English Romantic art. SB

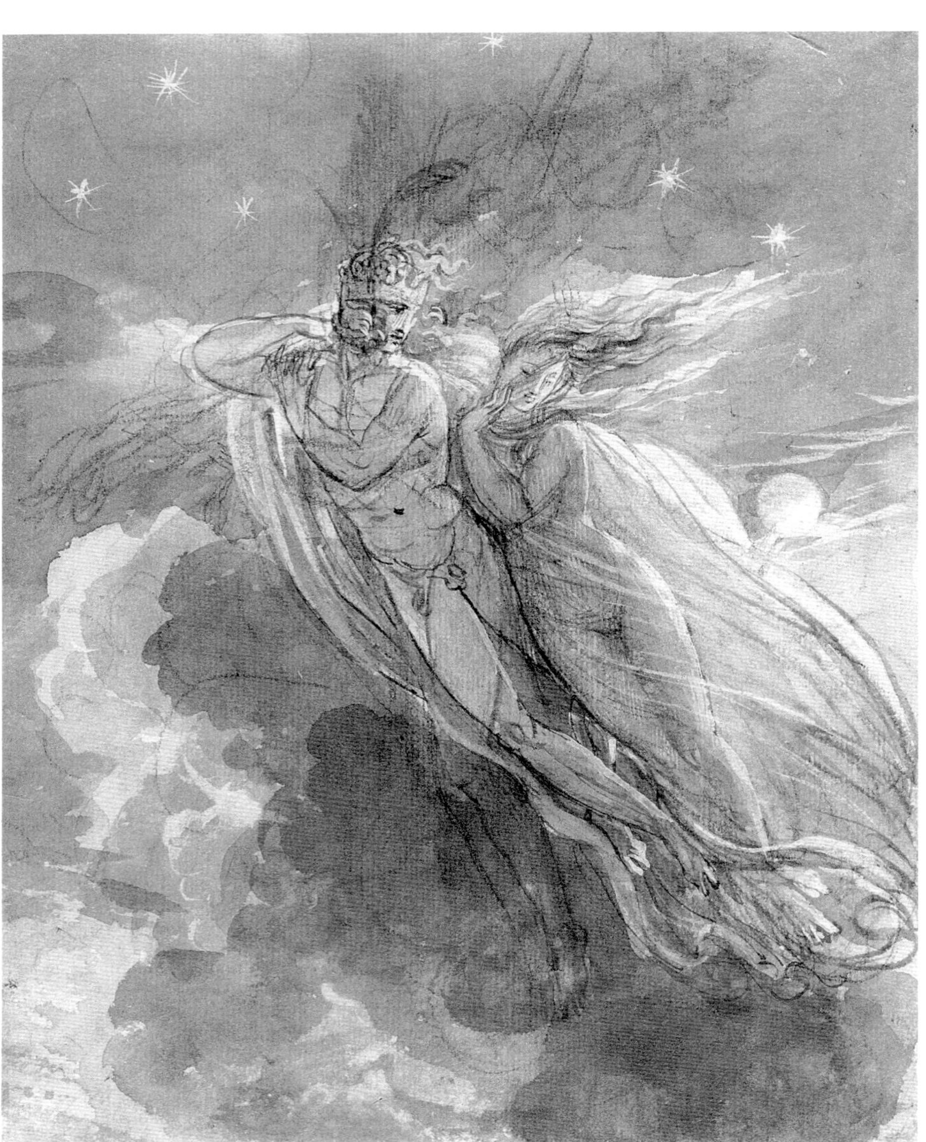

CATALOGUE NO. 57 (see color plate on page 105)

Anne-Louis Girodet de Roussy-Trioson
The Ghosts of Evirallina and Oscar Gliding through the Evening Air

57
Brown and gray wash, heightened with white gouache, over black crayon on off-white laid paper
21.1 x 17.7 cm (8 5/16 x 7 in.)
Musée Girodet, Montargis (inv. no. 71-15)

PROVENANCE
Mme. Becquerel, a descendant of the artist's heirs, purchased by the museum in 1971.

EXHIBITED
Hamburg 1974, no. 104.
Paris 1974b, no. 90.
Paris 1974–75, no. 67.
Copenhagen 1975, no. 50.
Montargis 1983, no 46.
Montargis 1989a, no. 9, ill. 35.

LITERATURE
Porée 1907, 285.
Auzas/Ternois 1973, 265, ill. 265, fig. 4.
Toussaint 1974, 4.
Vaisse 1974, 82.
Joannides/Sells 1974, mentioned 361.
Bernier 1975, 65–66, ill. 97.
Rubin 1979, 720, not ill.

Anne-Louis Girodet de Roussy-Trioson
Fingal before the Corpse of Fillan

58
Brown and gray wash, heightened with white gouache, over black crayon, on off-white laid paper
22.4 x 18.3 cm (8 13/16 x 7 3/16 in.)
Musée Girodet, Montargis (inv. no. 71-14)

PROVENANCE
Mme. Becquerel, a descendant of the artist's heirs, purchased by the museum in 1971.

EXHIBITED
Paris 1974b, no. 87.
Hamburg 1974, no. 101.
Montargis 1983, no. 47.
Montargis 1989a, no. 6, ill. 29.

LITERATURE
Porée 1907, 285.
Joannides/Sells 1974, mentioned 361.
Toussaint 1974, 4.
Vaisse 1974, 82.
Bernier 1975, 65–66, ill. 69.
Rubin 1979, 720, ill. fig. 52.

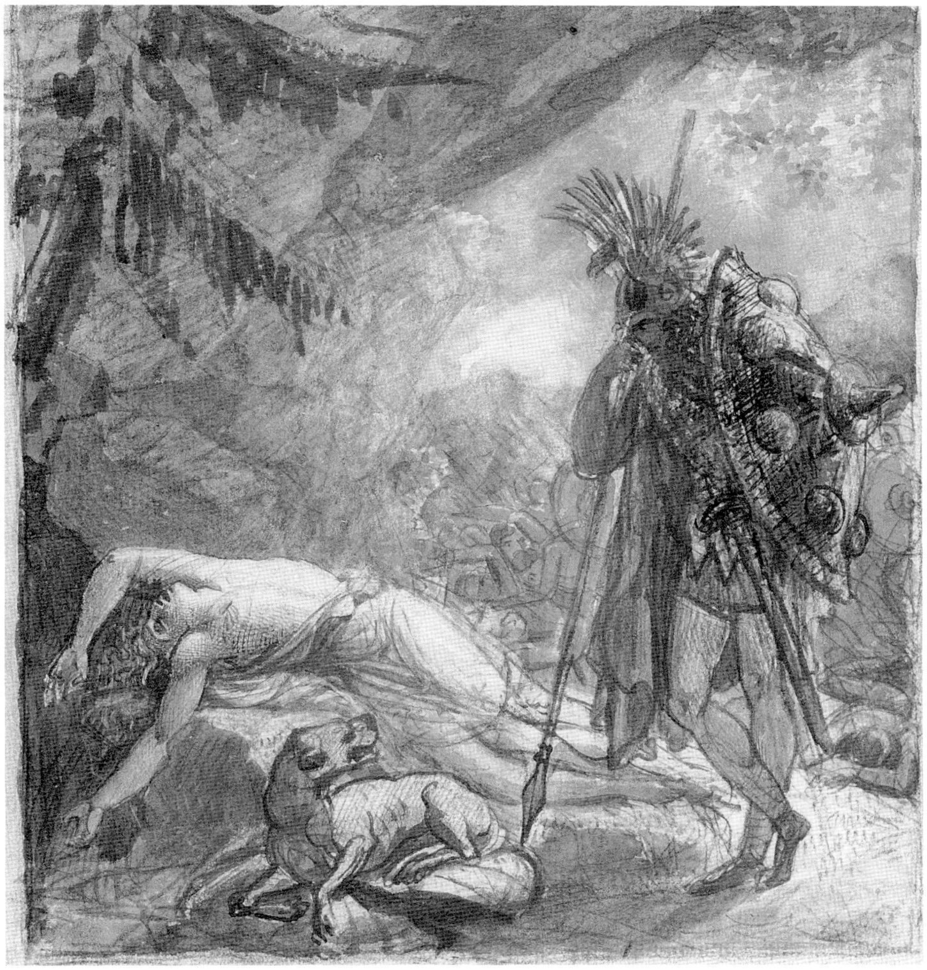

CATALOGUE NO. 58

Of all the ancient myths that haunted the end of the eighteenth century in Europe, the most eloquent and unusual was without doubt the one that prompted the literary hoax of the poems published by James Macpherson in London in 1760. Born among Scottish peasants in 1736, Macpherson owed the beginnings of his fame and fortune to a circle of Scottish literary adepts who instructed him in the Gaelic legends of the Highlands. Familiar with the accounts circulated in the countryside, he composed poems and attributed them to the ancient Celtic heroes who had survived in popular stories; he then pretended to have discovered and translated the Gaelic manuscripts. Immediately translated into French by Anne-Robert-Jacques de Turgot, Physiocrat and famous finance minister under Louis XV, and later, more notably, by Pierre Le Tourneur in 1777, *The Poems of Ossian* had a considerable impact throughout Europe for nearly half a century. From Germany to Denmark Ossian was perceived as a new Homer with a legitimate Nordic identity of the kind Goethe had developed in the *Sturm und Drang* movement. In France the legend of the Gaelic bard owed its fortunes to Napoleon, who said, "I've had none but Ossian, the others were taken!" (Montargis 1989a, 11). Hymns, operas, and paintings were inspired by Ossian. When in 1801 architects and designers Charles Percier and Pierre-François-Léonard Fontaine chose him as the subject for the decoration of the empress Josephine's salon at Malmaison, they approached François Gérard and Girodet. In Rome in the Palazzo del Quirinale, which served as Napoleon's residence, *The Dream of Ossian* (*Songe d'Ossian*) was commissioned from Jean-Dominique-August Ingres for the emperor's bedroom ceiling.

The poem *Ossian* recounts the deaths of young heroes. Here, Fingal, king of Morven, meditates over the corpse of his grandson, Fillan. Evirallina and her husband, Oscar, the son of Ossian, are invoked by the song of the blind poet. The latter has the power to return the couple to the shadows of death through the power of his verse and his chants.

A recent exhibition at the Musée Girodet in Montargis dedicated to the theme of Girodet's illustrations of Ossian brought to light the permanent interest that the painter had in this legend, in both literature and the visual arts. Between the painting at Malmaison (see FIGURE 47)—its strange sophistication repelled the public—and the *Collections de têtes d'étude* . . . (Collection of studies of heads; Paris, 1822) that Aubry-Lecomte lithographed twenty years later under the master's direction is an entire series of drawings, seventeen according to the inventory of Girodet's work, published at the time of the dispersal of his estate in Paris in 1825. *The Ghosts of Evirallina and Oscar Gliding through the Evening Air* (from the poem "Duthona") and *Fingal before the Corpse of Fillan* (from "Temora") are the finest of the eight drawings on the subject of Ossian in the Montargis collection. The revelation of two works painted on paper and the discovery of several other drawings and lithographs since the Ossian exhibition confirm the hypothesis that here was an illustration project that Girodet did not bring to completion, as with a number of other efforts. With regard to this infatuation with Ossian we may point out one fault: Girodet's inability to hold himself to one style. What could be more romantic than this series of drawings, their complex, original technique showing a preference for coloristic effects rather than linear purity, a conflict between line and color that blurs the distinctive hallmarks of neoclassicism and romanticism?

In his poem "The Painter" Girodet glorified geographical curiosity. The subjects furnished by Italy were not enough, he said. Greece and the Orient ought also to nourish his genius, but so must Egypt, Israel, and the New World, "which neither time nor man have yet tarnished" (cited in Coupin 1829, vol. 1, 135). Among the regions that Girodet knew only from literature were the summits of Cromla, Arven, and the rivers of Lubar, and the gloomy clouds and the harp of Ossian were but a historical and geographical extension of the repertoire of Zeuxis, the ancient painter savant, symbol of the selective initiation into the beauties of nature reconciled in art. Seen in this light Girodet's Ossianic drawings are to romanticism what Ossian is to primitive wildness. Both are molded from classic models, and if the theme of the grotto as the abode of primitive man—recurrent in Girodet's work—seems to break with the vocabulary of the antique, like the pine tree that recurs in the paintings of Caspar David Friedrich, it is only in making a travesty of it. The body of Fillan, like that of Endymion, finds its origin in the bas-relief of a sarcophagus (according to a letter of Girodet probably to the marquis de Pastoret; Coupin 1829, vol. 2, 338–92). Fingal's grief—contained, stoic, in a word, Winckelmannesque—and the frieze construction of this mourning scene are direct descendants of Roman antiquity.

For their part, Evirallina and Oscar—a transposition of Orpheus and Eurydice or Mercury and Psyche into the ambit of Ossian—arise from a Flaxmanesque treatment of line and aerial composition. Fingal's classical pose is easily recognized behind the "Nordicized" helmet and shield. We must remember that for Ossian's universe Girodet had no archaeological model; it was necessary to rely on his imagination. SB

Anne-Louis Girodet de Roussy-Trioson
Study for the Revolt of Cairo
c. 1809–10

59
Charcoal and pastel on tan laid paper
54.4 x 66.3 cm (21 7/16 x 26 1/8 in.)
Musée de l'Avallonnais, Avallon

LITERATURE
Paris 1974–75, 149.

In 1809 Dominique Vivant-Denon, director-general of Napoleon's museums, commissioned from the best-known artists of the Empire a series of works to redecorate the vast Galerie de Diane in the Tuileries palace (Zieseniss 1966, 199–235; Lacambre 1975, 39–48); it burned in 1870. The commission specified the formats and themes of the compositions (Tinti 1936, vol. 1, 107), which were to glorify the highest military achievements of Napoleon in his Italian and Egyptian campaigns, to promote his legend in his own lifetime. Few works of this epoch emphasized the violence of the conquests of the Republic as did *The Revolt of Cairo* (*La Révolte du Caire*; see FIGURE 48), 1810, with the result that it is difficult to see in this painting any of the civilizing virtues that the conquerors associated with their victories.

At the Salon of 1806 Pierre-Narcisse Guérin had shown *Bonaparte Pardoning the Rebels of Cairo* (*Bonaparte pardonnant aux Révoltés du Caire*; Musée de Beaux-Arts, Caen), a treatise much better suited to the propagandistic purposes at hand. More than a political response to Guérin or Vivant-Denon, *The Revolt of Cairo* was an artistic challenge, vying with *The Battle of Aboukir* (*La Bataille d'Aboukir*; Musée de Versailles) exhibited by Antoine-Jean Gros in the same Salon (1808). Among the innovations that shook Davidian convictions, this work in particular introduced the most radical modernity:

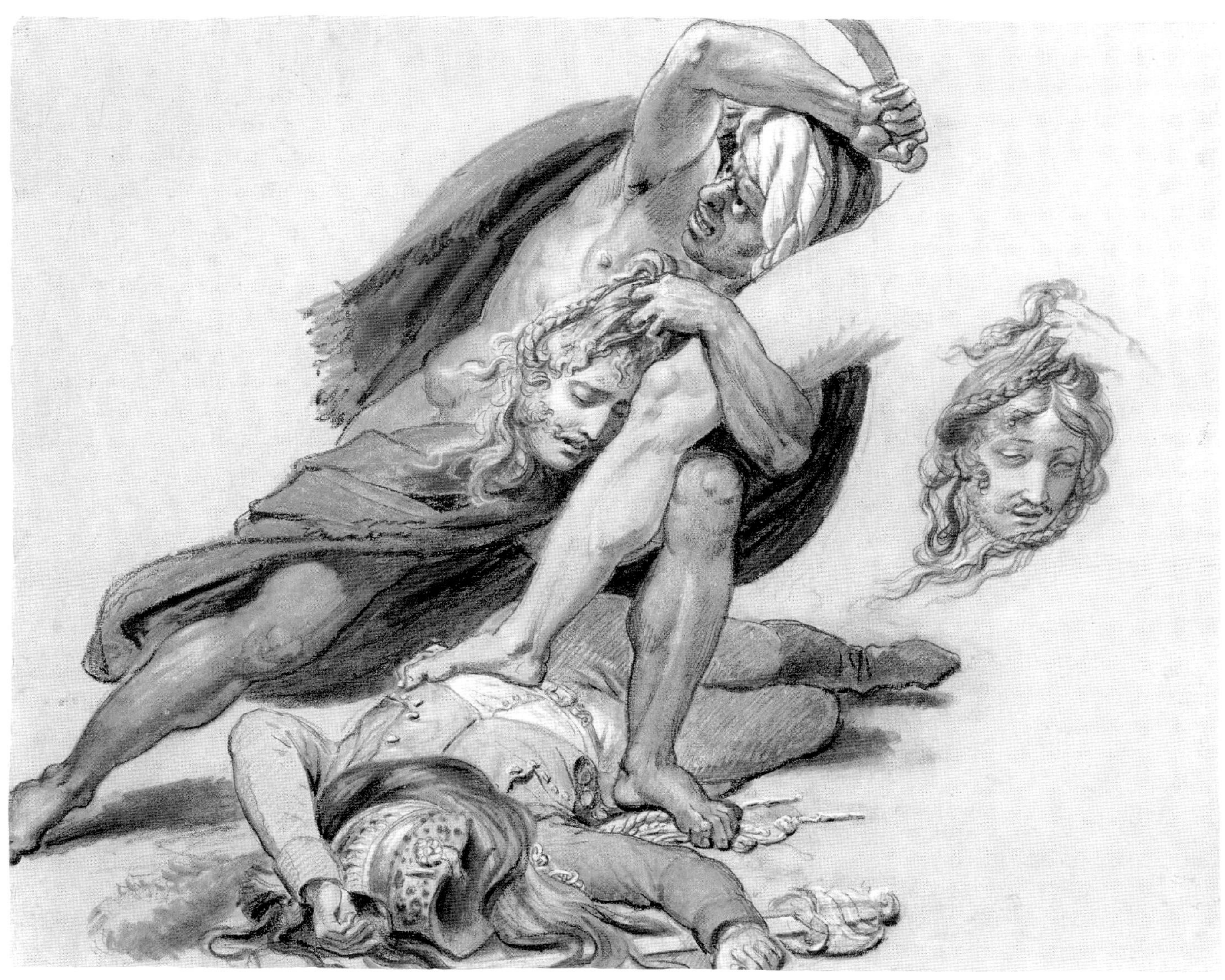

CATALOGUE NO. 59 (see color plate on page 106)

colorism. Girodet well understood it, and in the many preparatory drawings that have been accounted for—more than eighteen—he used pastel for the first time. The result was a series of spectacular sheets, of which the example in Avallon is the jewel.

The rebellion of the Mamelukes that broke out in Cairo was an obscure but bloody episode in the Egyptian campaign. In 1798 the French took possession of the city, which was delivered into their hands at the Battle of the Pyramids. Several months later, at midday on October 21, a revolt exploded and took the lives of three hundred French soldiers. The insurrection lasted two days, and Bonaparte, who was conferring with his general staff on the island of Boudah, came with all possible speed and viciously punished the rebels. Four thousand insurgents died in a bloody affair generally omitted from history textbooks.

It cannot be imagined what pleasure the emperor could have taken in a painting in which neither he nor any of his generals appeared on the canvas (Rubin 1980, 95–105). The French dragoon remains an unknown soldier—although his artistic source is clear: the *Mercury* of Giambologna by way of the dragoon in Jacques-Louis David's *Distribution of the Eagles* (*La Distribution des aigles*; Musée de Versailles; Paris/Versailles 1989–90, no. 187, pl. 187). But *The Revolt of Cairo* has no real accusatory value—it is not the *Guernica* of the nineteenth century. The violence depicted in the work, as well as its relief composition, connects it to the artistic production of the Revolution. Its concentrated energy is that of David, its violence heroic. Above and beyond its coloristic effects and the tumult of the scene, it is essentially a neoclassical composition. In a closed, architectural space it offers a second reading, from left to right, the dragoon set against the slave—naked, heroic, "antique." The movement is reminiscent of Antonio Canova's *Hercules and Lichas* (Galleria d'Arte Moderna, Rome; Honour 1960, 230), 1793–1815, preparatory studies for which date from Girodet's sojourn in Rome. Finally, the decapitated head brandished by the black slave finds its origin as much in Perseus's display of the head of the Medusa as in the military history of the conquest of Egypt. The horror of the act is also reflected in the Avallon study.

If the classical references of the work are clear, and we can see its relation to Canova or the head of the Medusa, those of the Orient are more difficult to track down. It is probable that Girodet found models in *Description de l'Égypte* (Description of Egypt), which had been recently (1809) published by Vivant-Denon, who had been with Napoleon on the campaign. Girodet's private collection, dispersed after his death, contained a number of Oriental cashmeres, helmets, and turbans (sale, Pérignon, Paris, 1825, lots 902–14). Lastly, the portrait he made of the architect and poet Louis-Charles Balzac, recently acquired by the Dallas Museum of Fine Art (see Colin B. Bailey in New York 1989b, 236–39), points to the identity of at least one eyewitness who guided Girodet in his compositions. The Avallon drawing indeed stands out in the group of drawings shown in this exhibition, by virtue of its spirit and subject, but we must be sure to recognize beneath the Oriental disguise a history painting and, expressed through modern history, the heroism of antiquity. SB

Anne-Louis Girodet de Roussy-Trioson
Venus Leaving Aeneas
After 1811

60
Graphite on off-white laid paper
35 x 42.3 cm (13 3/4 x 16 5/8 in.)
Musée Girodet, Montargis

PROVENANCE
Pannetier.
De la Bordes (sold Paris, Hôtel des Commissaires-Priseurs, April 15, 1867, lot no. 11).
Firmin-Didot family (sold Paris, Hôtel Drouot, November 17, 1971, lot no. 7).

EXHIBITED
Montargis 1983, no. 56.

Girodet, himself the author of thousands of verses, was haunted by literature and—under the influence of neoclassical poet Jacques Montanier, called Delille—by poetry. No work captivated him more than Virgil's *Aeneid*, which Delille had translated. Although there are reasons to distrust Girodet's biographer Coupin, it is believed that, as he has said, the artist's vast effort to illustrate the ancient text was begun before 1811 (Coupin 1829, vol. 2, 309–10). The work remained unfinished at the time of Girodet's death, and of the 200 planned illustrations—for whom is not known—only 150 were finished and 78 published. The provenance of few graphic ensembles has been as thoroughly documented; we owe this to the Firmin-Didot family of publishers (Osborne 1985), who nevertheless broke up the set in a sale held at the Hôtel Drouot in Paris 1971 (Paris 1974–75, 73). For the past twenty years drawings from this sale have appeared on the market, to the benefit of public and private collections.

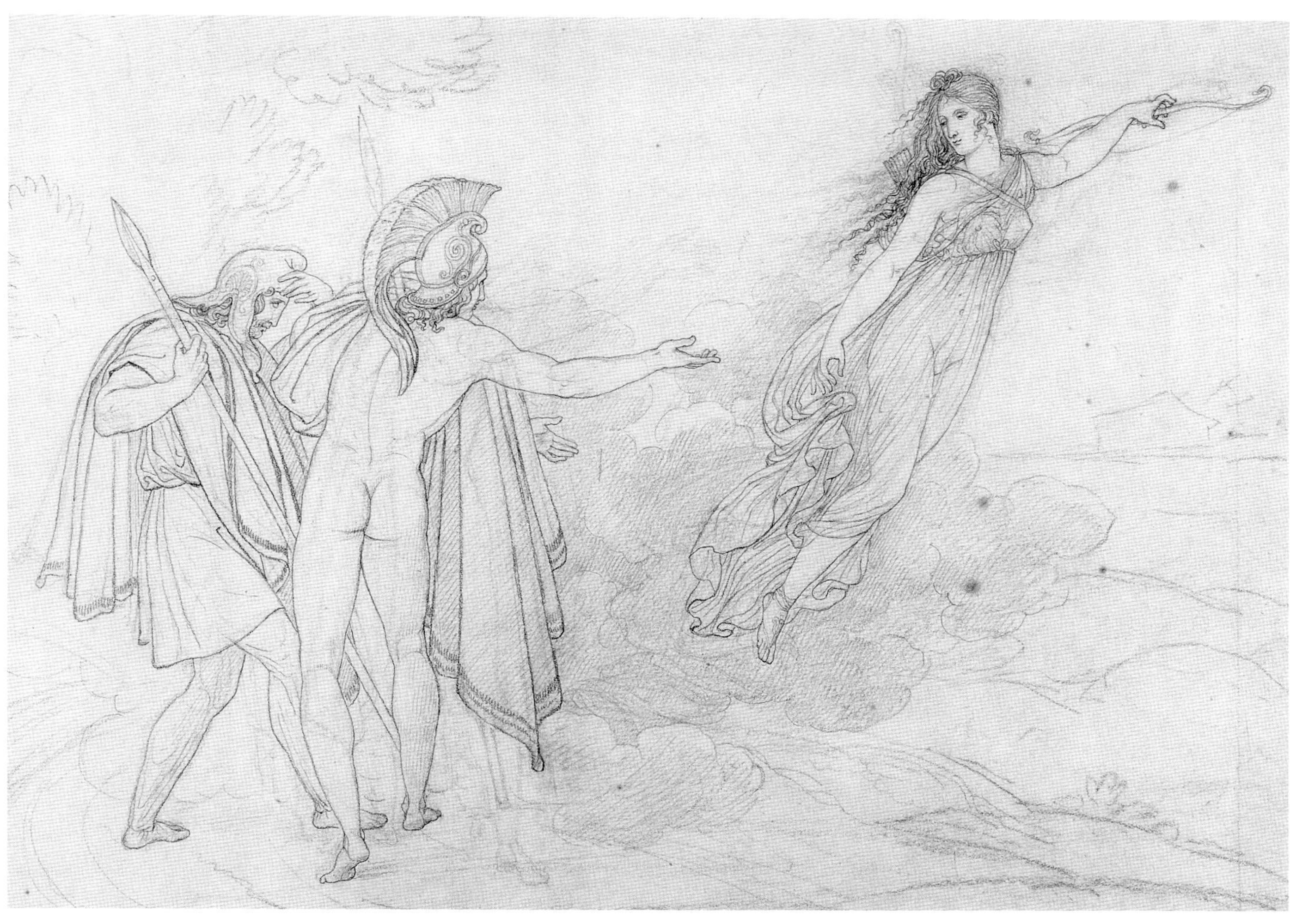

CATALOGUE NO. 60

Girodet was passionate about lithography, which had been invented in 1796 in Germany by Aloys Senefelder. Publishers who during the eighteenth century had specialized in illustration took up lithography for the same reason as did artists: its extraordinary and limitless power of reproduction (Cousin 1872, 19). Contrary to engraving, which requires an elaborate consideration and calculation of the effects to be achieved, lithography preserves the texture of the pencil and the immediacy of the design.

The romantics seized upon it. The facility with which they could achieve rich blacks and suggestive shadows served the colorists' sensibility, in addition to which lithography assured large print editions and a guaranteed income. It was not only these qualities, however, that interested Girodet. The lithograph illustrations for the *Aeneid* were published in a posthumous edition by his students Dejuine, Aubry-Lecomte, Châtillon, Monanteuil, and Pannetier as an homage. It is not known whether this was an instance of respect for the artist's wishes or the choice of a medium that would most faithfully reproduce his work. Paradoxically, however, Girodet's line drawings were reproduced in this inherently tonal medium.

The contour engraving and the plasticity of line were at the center of an aesthetic debate at the end of the eighteenth century. It was contour that evoked antiquity, not only through the popularization of painted vases discovered in Herculaneum—for example, the collections of Sir William Hamilton, published in 1766–67 and 1791–1803—and researched so diligently by antiquomaniacs then and now, but also through sculpture, the proportions and poses of which henceforth came to govern the formal repertoire of the studio. The pose is the form expressed by contour and therefore by line. The paintings of antiquity having disappeared (other than mural painting), it was through the statuary seized in Italy that the practice began to spread of working "d'après la bosse" (from the round), a practice inseparable from the return to the art of antiquity. Two names in particular are associated with the linearity debate: Bénigne Gagneraux, who set a precedent with the publication in Rome in 1792 of a selection of eighteen outline engravings, and John Flaxman, whose edition of the *Odyssey* engraved by Tommaso Piroli came out in Rome in February 1793. Although we know that Girodet had left the city in January, two letters from him to Flaxman confirm the meeting of these two artists in Rome and underscore the influence of Flaxman upon Girodet (Banks 1979, 100–101).

If this English artist's importance for the imitators of Ingres is well known, a study remains to be made of spiritual affinities with "les Barbus," the fanatical primitives from Jacques-Louis David's studio whose ambiguous works glorified line for its purity, its simplicity, its truth—in a word, for its primitiveness (Levitine 1978). It is this linearity that created in their work the glorification of the young male, to which must be added Girodet's *The Sleeping Endymion* (*Endymion endormi*; see FIGURE 43), 1791, and his outline drawings for the *Aeneid*.

The *Aeneid* is the greatest poem of Latin antiquity. The first six books of the epic, based loosely on Homer's *Iliad*, trace Aeneas's voyage to Latium (or Italy). Here, Girodet illustrates the episode from Book I when Venus, Aeneas's mother, departs from him and his friend Achates. SB

Anne-Louis Girodet de Roussy-Trioson
Head of a Mustachioed Man, Three-Quarter View
1817

61
Charcoal, graphite, and stump with white highlights on tan laid paper
19.4 x 18.4 cm (7⅝ x 7¼ in.)
Inscribed at lower left in ink: *Girodet fecit 1817*
The Minneapolis Institute of Arts, gift of funds from an anonymous donor, the Print and Drawing Council, and the Fiduciary Fund, 1986 (inv. no. 86.39)

EXHIBITED
New York 1986b.

LITERATURE
Levitine 1954, 32–44.

"The painter of history is the king of the portrait" (Girodet, cited in Coupin 1829, vol. 1, 396). Such remarks seem at odds with the hierarchy of genres otherwise recognized so clearly by Girodet (cited in Coupin 1829, vol. 1, 391):

Descend from history and sketch portraits,
Shine brightest in this secondary art.

If we speak first of portraiture while assessing this study of a head, it is because it surpasses the limitations of a traditional academic study of a model. The popular "gaulois" style of mustache was rarely retained in the studios of 1817. This current fashion, hardly reconcilable with ideals of neoclassical beauty, would be depicted only much later with the advent of realism. The head is most reminiscent of a "Grognard," one of Napoleon's "Old Guard" demobilized from the ruin of the Empire. The fierce expression seems to come more from the universe of Théodore Géricault than from the grace of Girodet.

Girodet was deeply interested in the portrait. For proof we have only to consult the list of works drawn up by his biographer P. A. Coupin or by Alexis Nicolas Pérignon the younger, a student of Girodet, in 1825 after the artist's death. This aspect of his art was generally neglected by historians until Georges Levitine (1954) first underscored the importance of Swiss scientist Johann Kaspar Lavater's writings for Girodet's own psychological investigations. It was through Girodet's adoptive father, Dr. Benoît Trioson, that the artist kept up with medicine, the avant-garde of nineteenth-century sciences.

Girodet possessed in his library Lavater's *Physiognomische Fragmente* (Physiognomical fragments), 1775–78, "leading to the understanding and the appreciation of man." This theory, which augmented and raised to the level of a science Charles Lebrun's treatise on the expression of the passions, exerted two contradictory effects upon the genre of the portrait. The unifying principle that made of the face a mirror of a psycho-spiritual reality was at odds with the ideal of beauty that reunited, in the themes of grace and perfection, heterogenous morphologies. Also, as a decoding handbook of humanity, physiognomy gave to the human face a moral reading reserved for history painting. A veritable incarnation of the fierce soul, this mustachioed head bears no relation to any other of Girodet's known works, yet the extraordinary cyclopean effect of the three-quarter view, which places the eye a third of the way along the height and width of the composition, recalls certain heads from *The Seven against Thebes* (*Le Serment des chefs de Thèbes*). An unfinished work known only from a drawing (École Nationale Supérieure des Beaux-Arts, Paris) and a lithograph (Musée Girodet, Montargis), it brings together a prodigious assembly of grimaces. SB

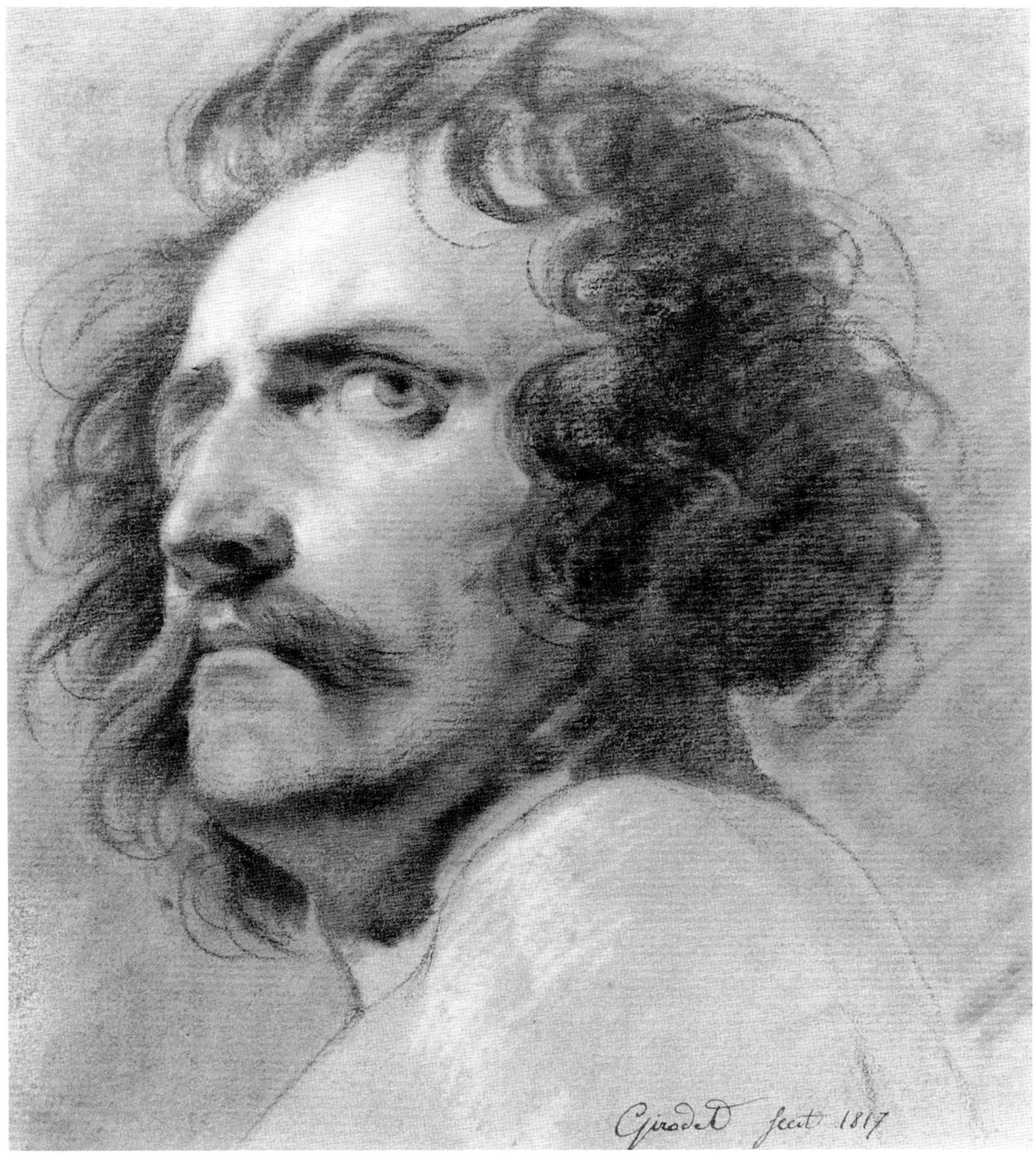

CATALOGUE NO. 61

Charles Meynier

1768 Paris 1832

MEYNIER STUDIED UNDER François-André Vincent and shared the Prix de Rome in 1789 with Anne-Louis Girodet de Roussy-Trioson, whose entry was *Joseph Recognized by His Brothers* (*Joseph reconnu par ses frères*; see FIGURE 45). He remained in Rome only briefly because of the political upheaval of the French Revolution and returned to Paris in time to exhibit at the 1795 Salon. He was a regular exhibitor until 1827, displaying several works executed on imperial commission during the Empire, including *Marshal Ney and the Soldiers of the 76th Regiment* (*Les soldats du* 76e *régiment de ligne retrouvant leurs drapeaux dans l'arsenal d'Inspruck*), 1808; *Entry into Berlin* (*Entrée dans Berlin*), 1810; and *The Emperor on the Island of Lobau* (*L'Empereur dans l'île de Lobau*), 1812. One of the major designers of decoration in the neoclassical style, Meynier supplied drawings for reliefs and figures for the Arc de Triomphe du Carrousel, which were carried out by a team of sculptors including Clodion and Le Sueur. Meynier's oeuvre included portraits and religious works, but he was most in demand for his skills as a decorator, especially during the Restoration. He was responsible for *The Birth of Louis XIV* (*Naissance de Louis XIV*), 1819, for the ceiling of the Grand Salon of the Tuileries, several ceiling paintings in the Louvre, and the grisaille decoration of the main room of the Paris Bourse, 1826. LDM

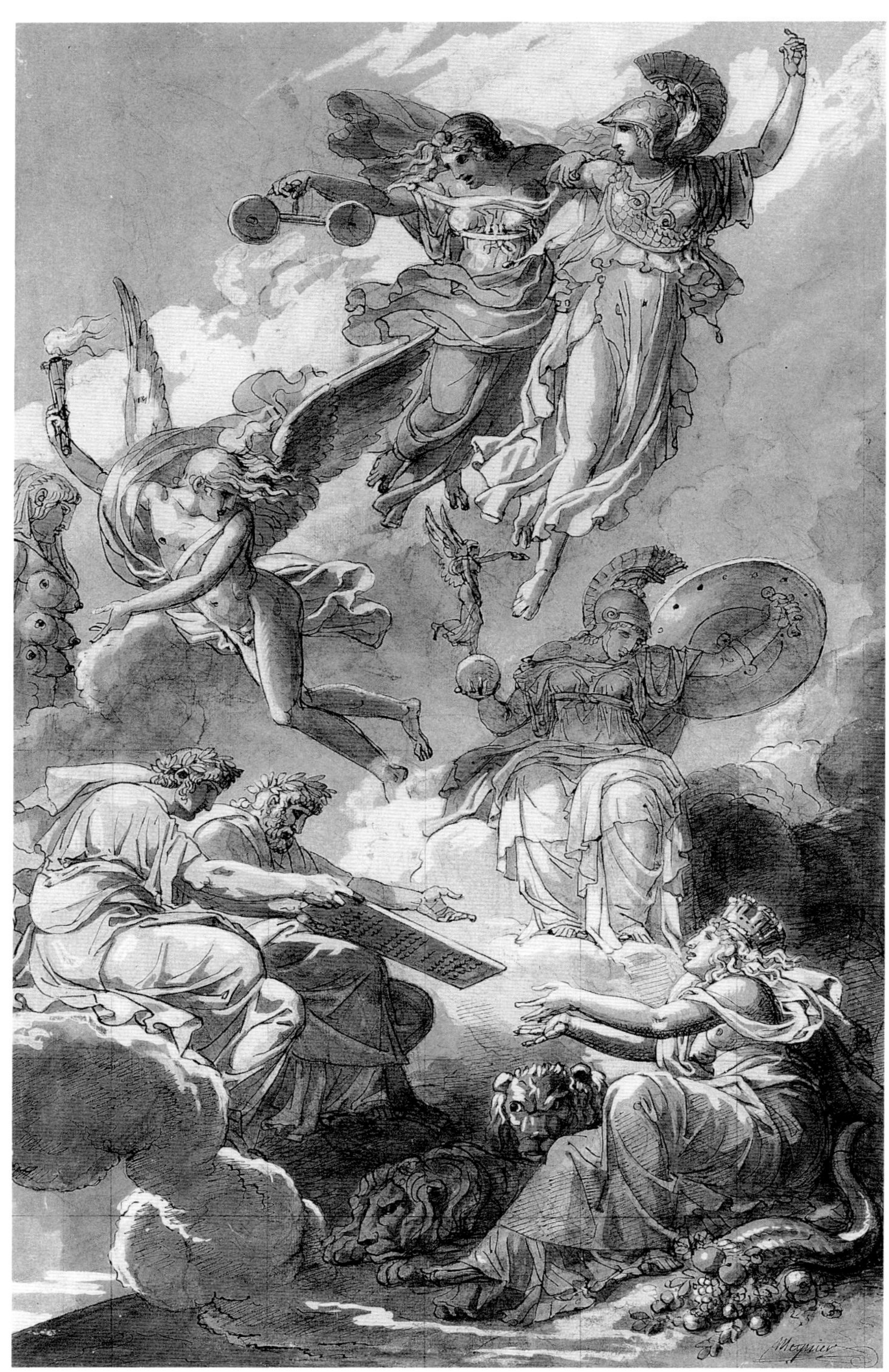

CATALOGUE NO. 62

Charles Meynier
Earth Receiving from the Emperors Hadrian and Justinian the Digest of Roman Law
Before 1808

62
Pen and brown ink, brush and brown wash heightened with white ink, over black chalk on brown paper, squared in black chalk
62.5 x 40.5 cm (24 5/8 x 15 15/16 in.)
Signed at lower right in pen: *Meynier*
The Metropolitan Museum of Art, New York, purchase, Mr. and Mrs. David T. Schiff Gift, 1977 (inv. no. 1977.372)
(Los Angeles and Minneapolis only)

PROVENANCE
Colnaghi.

Meynier's impressive drawing is a preparatory study for his ceiling painting *La Terre reçoit des empereurs Adrien et Justinien le code des lois romaines* installed in 1808 in the Salle des Empereurs in the Louvre. In the lower right of the composition, the personification of Earth, wearing a crenelated crown, is flanked by a cornucopia and two lions to symbolize prosperity and power. With outstretched hands she is about to receive a tablet engraved with Roman law from the emperors Hadrian and Justinian. Above her the figure of Rome is seated on a bank of clouds, holding in one hand a shield and in another a statuette of Victory. Justice and Wisdom soar upward to spread the reign of enlightenment across the land.

This is a working study for the painting described by the comte de Clarac (Clarac 1826–53, text vol. 1, 517–18, 664; plate vol. 1, pls. 70, 74), since faint traces of black chalk were added over the finished sheet to square it for enlargement. A highly finished drawing such as this could have served as a *modello* to be shown to those in charge of the renovation of the Salle des Empereurs before Meynier was given permission to execute the final work. Another drawing for an 1820 ceiling painting in the Salle Dûchatel, *The Triumph of French Painting* (Coutances; Paris 1974–75, 97, no. 96), is analogous to this example. Both compositions are characterized by dynamically posed figures whose vigorous gesticulations and soaring postures would easily be visible from a distance. Each drawing was executed with the same chiaroscuro technique, the white ink highlights broadly applied both to define the form and gestures of the principal figures and to indicate the dramatic lighting of the scenes that would be essential to the legibility of the allegories when the canvases were installed in the ceiling of the galleries.

Today highly finished chiaroscuro drawings, typified by these ceiling designs, are the most familiar aspect of Meynier's draftsmanship, but originally his oeuvre was more varied. The Danish collector T. C. Bruun Neergaard, who knew Prud'hon and had an important group of his drawings (see CATALOGUE NO. 48), also knew and avidly sought Meynier's sheets. The Dane describes his acquisition of studies after antiquities such as an Apollo (perhaps the Apollo Belvedere) and the Laocoön, drawn when the artist was in Rome. But more interesting and relevant to the artist's thoughtful preparation of complex works such as the allegory represented by this drawing is Bruun Neergaard's observation that Meynier made separate studies for each figure in his paintings, resolving not just facial expressions and poses but also details such as the disposition of draperies and "petits accessoires" (Bruun Neergaard 1801, 162–63). It is a reflection of our scant knowledge of Meynier's work, and of our incomplete understanding of neoclassical drawings generally, that such studies can no longer be traced. The collector concluded his comments by praising the perfection of Meynier's drawings, which were important to the formation of his interest in the fine arts. The result was Bruun Neergaard's collection of drawings by contemporary artists, one of the most important to be formed in Paris at this period. VC

Louis Lafitte

1770 Paris 1828

LAFITTE WAS A PUPIL OF Jean-Baptiste Regnault and Gilles Desmarteau. He was the last student sent to the Académie de France in Rome under the régime of Louis XVI, having won the Prix de Rome with *Regulus Returning to Carthage* (*Regulus retournant à Carthage*), 1791. He arrived in Rome but soon left for Naples and Florence with a group of French artists to wait out the Revolution and the Terror. He returned to Paris in 1796 and produced many highly finished drawings, which he sent to the Salons between 1791 and 1817. He worked on the decoration of the dining room at Malmaison and from 1802 to 1815 designed a series of medallions commemorating Napoleon and the events of the Empire. During the Restoration he was appointed as *déssinateur du cabinet du Roi* by Charles X.
LDM

Louis Lafitte
Orestes Pursued by the Furies
1790

63
Black and white chalks with touches of white opaque watercolor on tan laid paper
22.6 x 39.4 cm (8 7/8 x 15 1/2 in.)
Signed and dated at lower left in brown ink: *Lafitte 1790*
Ackland Art Museum, University of North Carolina at Chapel Hill, Ackland Fund (inv. no. 65.20.1)

PROVENANCE
G. S. Seligmann (verso: intertwined GS stamp). Jacques Seligmann and Company, New York, 1965.

EXHIBITED
New York 1965, no. 27.

Although Lafitte's drawings are not well known and have never been the subject of a major study, such works on paper as have been identified show the artist as a talented and versatile draftsman. Two preparatory studies for figures in the artist's *Regulus Returning to Carthage* (École Nationale Supérieure des Beaux-Arts, Paris), which won him the Prix de Rome in 1791, have been on the art market. One drawing depicts two nude models posed as the supplicants begging Regulus not to fulfill his promise to return to Carthage (New York 1991, no. 2); on the reverse of the sheet are three rapidly sketched ideas for the full composition, a type of drawing only rarely found in the work of the artists represented in this exhibition but which originally must have been fairly commonplace. The kneeling men, now clothed, occur in another study for this canvas (London 1975, no. 79). A more finished preparatory drawing for the composition is in the Musée des Beaux-Arts, Rouen (Paris 1989b, vol. 1, 301, no. 398). An exhibition at the Heim Gallery also presented a superb portrait drawing of Marie-Joseph Chenier, a dramatist and revolutionary patriot (London 1975, no. 80), as well as an unidentified scene from classical history (no. 81).

Lafitte received commissions from the newly founded republican government for projects such as designs for a calendar, and under Napoleon he painted decorative panels for Malmaison. These few citations are by no means complete, but they do indicate that the artist worked in a variety of manners, sometimes dictated by the function of the drawing, while the suave, rather decorative character of his later work (the calendar illustrations, for example) surely reflects the popularity of the Empire style under Napoleon's reign.

It is not known whether any specific project lay behind Lafitte's execution of this highly finished work. It is unlikely that a publisher would have risked the expense of issuing an engraving after a work by a young artist who had yet to make his reputation. In the Salon of 1791, the year he won the Prix de Rome, the artist exhibited six drawings: a landscape, a religious subject, and four history subjects, which suggests that he may have hoped to find collectors who would appreciate finished drawings such as this theatrical interpretation of a scene from Euripides's drama (Heim/Béraud/Heim 1989, 249).

The present work was drawn in Paris a few years in advance of the enthusiastic revival of Jean Racine's tragedies, greatly admired for their references to antiquity and acted with an effusion of emotions that stirred audiences and critics alike. Certainly Lafitte could have read in translation Aeschylus's trilogy of the tragedies of Agamemnon, Clytemnestra, and Orestes, or Euripides's drama *Orestes*, but he might have been familiar with Racine's

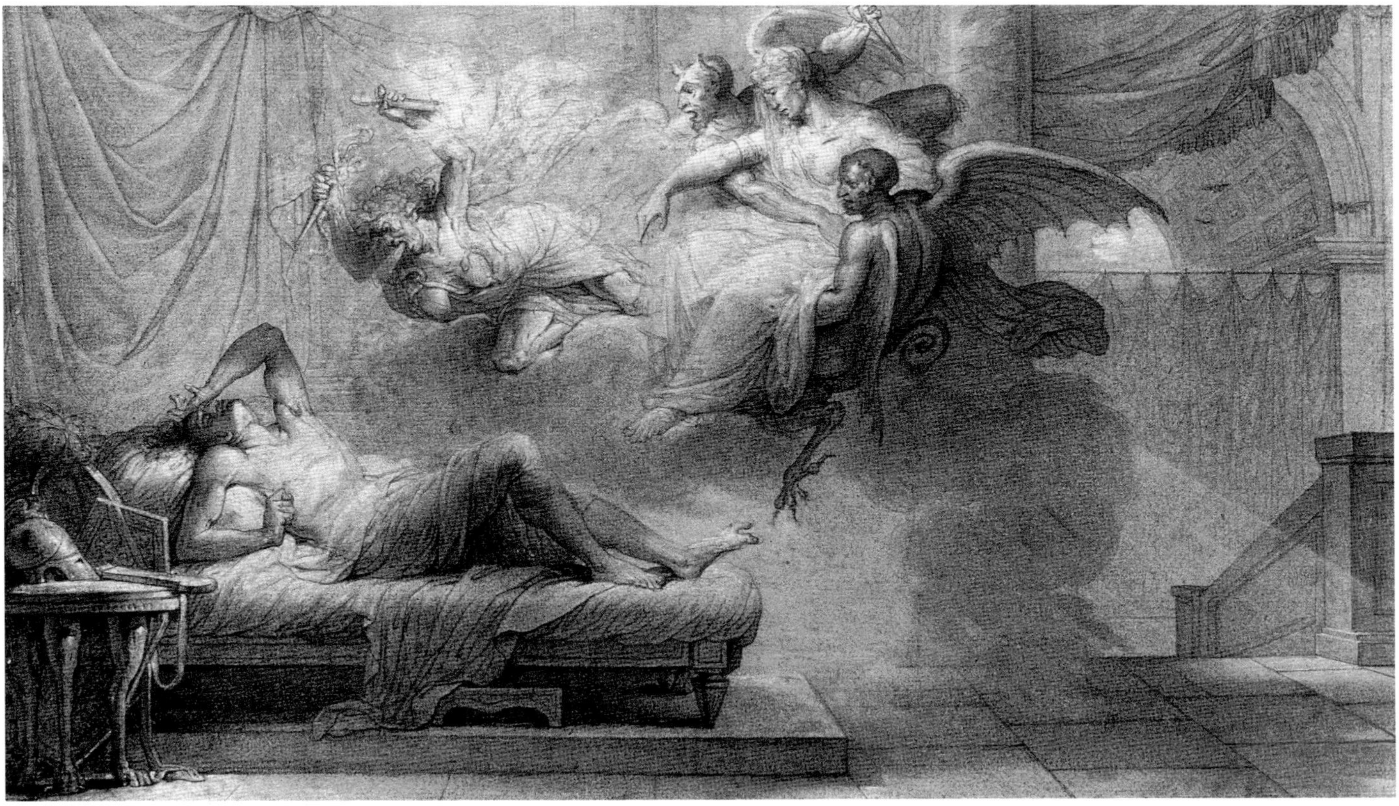

CATALOGUE NO. 63

Fureurs d'Oreste (Rage of Orestes), based on the Greek text, or, nearer his own time, Voltaire's tragedy *Oreste*, 1750. Lafitte's drawing illustrates the scene in which, Orestes having killed his mother Clytemnestra in revenge for her complicity in the murder of his father, Agamemnon, a band of avenging Furies arrives to haunt him. The nightmarish brood hovers over Orestes's writhing body, their boldly expressive gestures enhanced by the nocturnal ambience, lit only by torchlight and the faint disc of the moon in the right background.

Lafitte's drawing is several years in advance of Flaxman's outline illustrations to the *Tragedies of Aeschylus*, first drawn in Rome about 1792–93 but not published until 1795, after his return to London. His version of Orestes pursued by the Furies shows the protagonist as a classical figure inspired by the artist's study of antiquities (pl. 27), as does his later (1809) drawing of the same subject (London 1979b, 130, no. 159). Flaxman's works lack the pathos of Lafitte's tormented hero. This drawing is a textbook illustration for Rosenblum's "*Neoclassic Horrific*. . . a vehicle for expressing the most overtly Romantic impulses, this late eighteenth century current offers the most vigorous denial of Winckelmann's characterization of the antique" (Rosenblum 1967b, 11). Thus, theatrical rhetoric undermined the authority of classical canons of beauty and propriety. VC

Pierre-Maximilien Delafontaine

1774 Paris 1860

DELAFONTAINE WAS BORN into a celebrated family of bronze casters; his father established himself in Paris and by 1787 was elected a syndic of the guild of casters, gilders, and engravers. Pierre-Maximilien, however, had aspirations to become a painter and for a while studied with Jacques-Louis David. He was extremely loyal to his master, even escorting him to the prison door when he was arrested in 1794, and his letters and other writings have been very helpful in the documentation of David's life. Delafontaine exhibited at the Salon for the first time in 1798, showing *The Deluge* (*Le Déluge*) and *Portrait of Andrieu*, among other works. He exhibited for only four years, subsequently entering the family business, from which he retired in 1840, passing it to his son. LDM

Pierre-Maximilien Delafontaine
The Return from the Race
c. 1808 or later

64
Black chalk, heightened with white gouache on off-white paper
57 x 87 cm (22 7/16 x 34 1/4 in.)
Signed at lower right: *Delafontaine*
The Fine Arts Museums of San Francisco, Achenbach Foundation for Graphic Arts purchase (inv. no. 1985.2.6)

PROVENANCE
David and Constance Yates, New York.

LITERATURE
Paris 1991–92, 8, fig. 14.

Delafontaine's impressive, meticulously executed drawing no doubt is based on an etching and stipple engraving *The Return from the Race* (*Le Retour de la course*) by Jean Godefroy, which reproduces a drawing by Carle Vernet. Recently Vernet's drawing *Le Retour de la course* and its pendant *La Mort d'Hyppolite* have reappeared on the art market (each work is executed in black chalk, heightened with white, and signed at bottom center: *Carle Vernet*; 23 3/4 x 37 in. [sight]). [It is a pleasure to thank Alan Salz of Didier Aaron, Inc., for his help and Paul Jeromack, who brought the drawings to my attention.] In 1808 Godefroy showed at the Salon his print after Vernet, which is the source for Delafontaine's drawing (Bibliothèque Nationale, Paris; Inventaire 1930–85, vol. 9, 216, no. 16). The dimensions of the Delafontaine drawing and the Godefroy print are slightly different (the Godefroy is 55.5 x 85.7 cm), although the compositions of the drawing and the print correspond even in minute details. It remains a puzzle why Delafontaine should have spent the considerable time required to execute such a large and elaborately finished drawing when anyone at the Salon who admired Vernet's work could easily have bought Godefroy's reproductive etching and stipple engraving.

In Delafontaine's first Salon his canvas *The Deluge* (*Le Déluge*; Musée Baron-Martin, Gray) was warmly praised. The painting, which shows a couple about to be overcome by a natural cataclysm, anticipates Girodet's oil of the same theme (see FIGURE 44). One of the few important drawings thus identified as by Delafontaine is his study for this oil (Sérullaz 1976, 380, fig. 1).

After exhibiting at the Salons during a five-year period, he ceased to show his works, no doubt discouraged by a lack of sales and commissions, as were many other artists who experienced hardship during this time of political instability. Delafontaine returned to his family's business, which he took over with great success, often collaborating with the cabinetmaker Jacob Desmalter in the production of some of the finest examples of furniture design and craftsmanship to be executed in the Empire style.

It is not difficult to imagine that Delafontaine would have admired Vernet's composition of an ancient Roman couple returning in triumph from a race, as indicated by the wreath of victory tucked in the man's belt and symbolized by the winged Victory holding a wreath decorating the chariot. The stylized elegance of the pair in their luxurious vehicle must have appealed to the designer and manufacturer of decorative bronzes. But such classical references are unusual in Vernet's work, although his views of contemporary equestrian subjects were widely popular. Vernet's drawing is a fanciful re-creation of an incident from domestic life in the classical past using figure types that recall those of Pierre-Paul Prud'hon or Alexandre-Évariste Fragonard, set in a

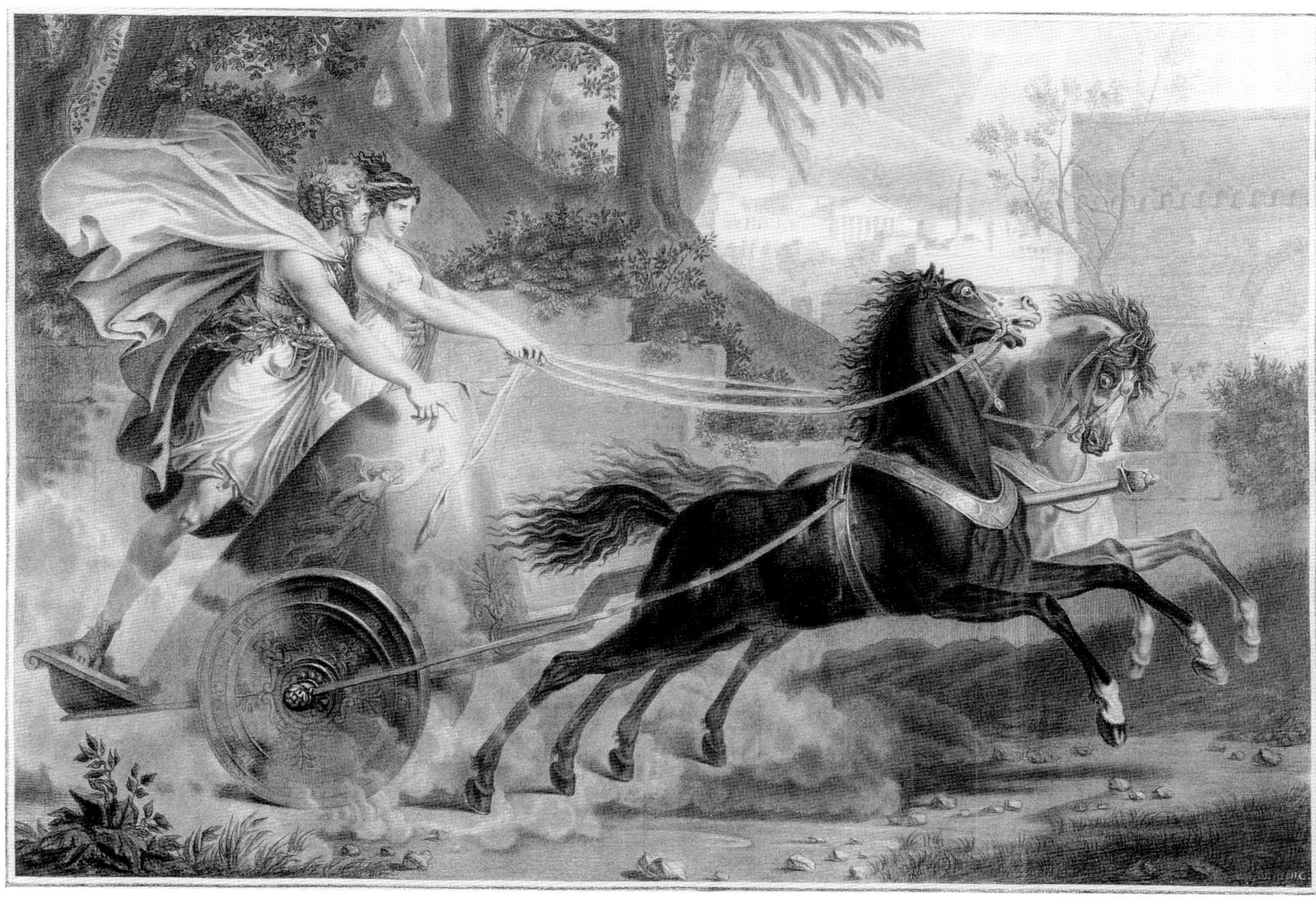

CATALOGUE NO. 64

landscape inspired by Nicolas Poussin. Here antiquity is seen through the eyes of Vernet's and Delafontaine's contemporaries, who collectively contributed to create the Empire style.

Delafontaine was not the only artist to have made use of Godefroy's print after Vernet. More surprisingly, the young Géricault knew this work and made a vigorously painted copy based on the etching. The young artist was more intrigued by the problem of rendering the dynamic, prancing poses of the horses than by the antiquarian references so meticulously detailed by Godefroy and Delafontaine (Paris 1991–92, 9, no. 8, fig. 13). VC

Pierre-Narcisse Guérin

1774 Paris–Rome 1833

GUÉRIN STUDIED WITH BOTH Nicolas-Guy Brenet and Jean-Baptiste Regnault. He won the Prix de Rome in 1797 with *The Death of Cato of Utica* (*Le Mort de Caton d'Utique*), but because of the suspension of the Académie de France à Rome during Napoleon's Italian campaign Guérin did not leave Paris until 1803. While still in Paris he had great success at the Salons with *The Return of Marcus Sextus* (*Le Retour de Marcus Sextus*), 1799, and works inspired by the theater, such as *Phaedra and Hippolytus* (*Phèdre et Hippolyte*), 1802. He finally spent two years at the Académie in Rome, visiting Naples twice. After his return to Paris in 1805 he continued to execute epic history paintings. A successful teacher, Guérin was named director of the Académie in Rome in 1816 but did not take up the appointment until 1822. In Rome he worked on the huge *The Last Night of Troy* (*La Dernière Nuit de Troie*), which he abandoned, exhausted, after his return to Paris. He left for Rome again in 1828 in the company of Horace Vernet, the new director of the Académie de France, and lived there until his death. LDM

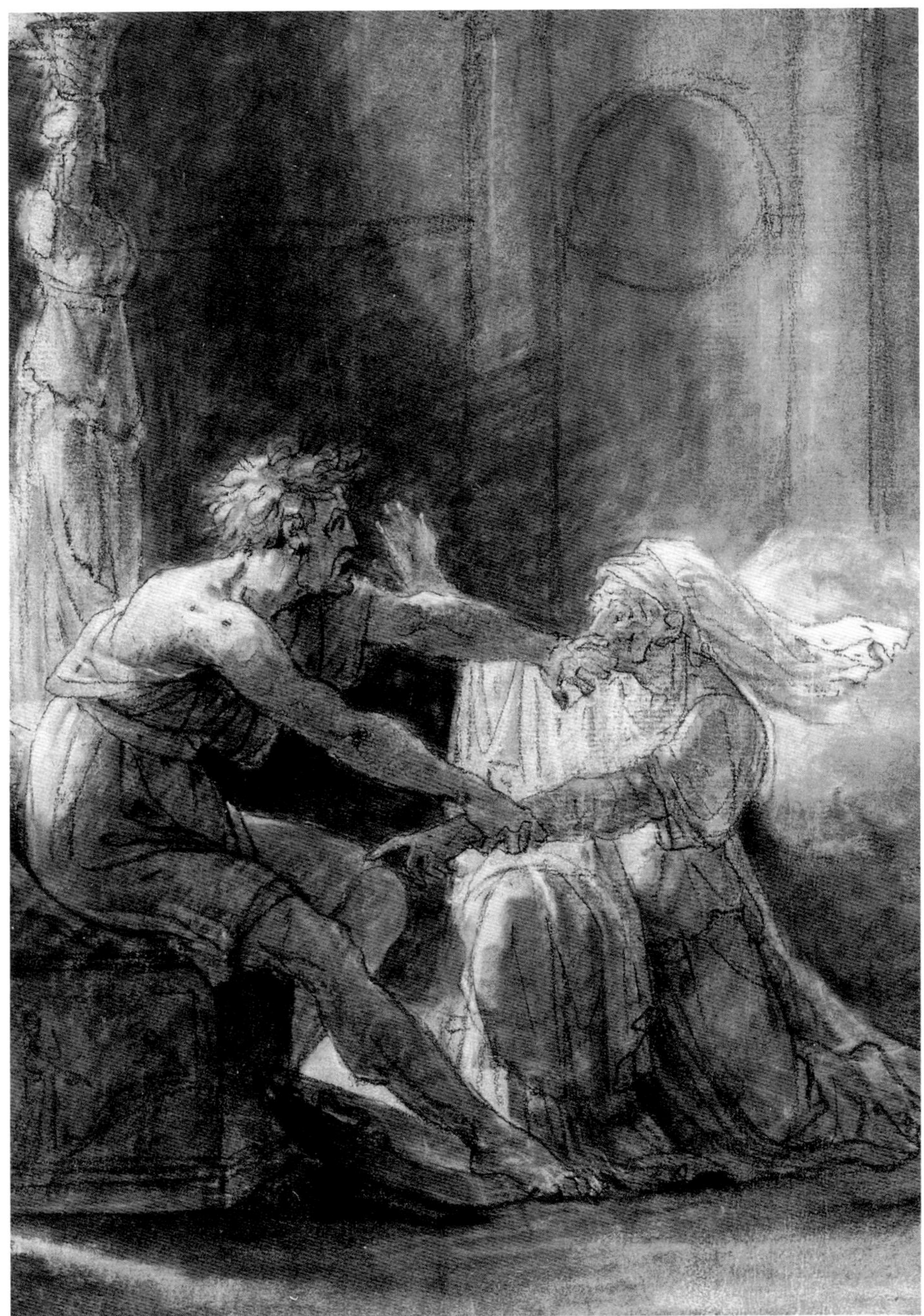

CATALOGUE NO. 65 (detail)

Pierre-Narcisse Guérin
Odysseus Recognized by His Nurse
1797

65
Charcoal, stumped and heightened with white on light brown laid paper
46 x 57.8 cm (18 1/8 x 22 3/4 in.)
Inscribed on the verso in black chalk: *Vincent*
The Pierpont Morgan Library, New York (inv. no. 1961.36)
(Los Angeles and Philadelphia only)

Traditionally, this drawing has been attributed to François-André Vincent because that artist's signature is on the verso; however, this does not necessarily indicate that Vincent was the author of the work. It is not surprising that Vincent's name was attached to this sheet, since until recently his work as a painter and draftsman was very little known, and works by him were attributed to names as varied as Jean-Honoré Fragonard and Jacques-Louis David.

The subject matter of the Morgan Library drawing is an important clue to uncovering the identity of the draftsman. In Homer's *Odyssey*, when the weary Odysseus returned from the Trojan war and his twenty years of wandering, he found that his wife, Penelope, who remained faithful in the belief that her husband would one day reappear, was besieged by suitors attracted by her beauty and the prospect of her wealth and power. Disguised in the rags of a beggar, Odysseus went to his palace to assess for himself the loyalty of his wife, who out of pity offered him a bath and a bed. When Odysseus's old nurse, Eurykleia, bent down to wash his feet and saw the scar on his leg from a childhood accident, she recognized the hero. Odysseus cautioned her to say nothing until he could get rid of Penelope's suitors and reveal himself to his wife.

This episode from the *Odyssey* was rarely depicted by artists (Pigler [1956, vol. 2, 316–21] does not include it in his list of Odyssean themes), but it was from time to time assigned to students competing for the Prix de Rome, which after the 1789 Revolution was administered by the Académie des Beaux-Arts; the subject was chosen by the Académie in 1797, 1816, 1843, and 1849 (Grunchec 1986, vol. 1, 34). The first post-Revolutionary competition, in 1797, is of interest for establishing the authorship of this drawing. During the initial stage of the competition the students had to paint an oil sketch (see Grunchec 1986, vol. 1, 27–31, for a detailed account of the Prix de Rome tests). The records of the Académie show that nineteen students met with the professor in charge of that day's test, who was François-André Vincent. The latter signed the works submitted to him as proof that they satisfied the requirements. Thus, Vincent's signature is on the reverse of this drawing because he was in charge of that day's competition and has nothing to do with the authorship of the work. After two further trial periods three students were awarded the Premiers Grands Prix: Louis-André-Gabriel Bouchet, Pierre Bouillon, and Guérin for their paintings of *The Death of Cato of Utica*.

Fortunately, Guérin's preparatory drawing in black and white chalks for his winning canvas exists and presents strong stylistic analogies with the present sheet (Musée du Louvre, Paris; inv. no. RF 12.844; Bottineau 1989, 305–6, fig. 12, and Paris 1989a, 115–17, 156, fig. 68). The drawings were executed with the same materials employed in an identical manner, using a continuous outline in black chalk to define each of the principal figures. Modeling is carefully contained within these boundaries, the draftsman working with a stump (*estompe*) to create a range of transparent grays to suggest the play of light over each figure, with highlights added in white chalk. Details such as Odysseus's right hand grasping the wrist of his nurse and Cato's left hand tearing at his wound are identical, the fingers simply blunt forms with no attempt at foreshortening. The head of Homer's hero in profile is quite similar to that of the onlooker at the left of Cato, who recoils in horror at the sight of the grisly suicide. The similar style of the draftsmanship in each work suggests that they have a common author.

Only recently have Guérin's early drawings been studied by Josette Bottineau (1989), who shares this writer's view that the Morgan Library's drawing may be attributed to that artist (letters to the author, December 3, 1991, and February 23, 1992). The possibility that this study is by one of the other participants must be considered (for cautionary advice on using the Prix de Rome archival data as the basis for attributions see Grunchec 1986, vol. 1, 32–36). Unfortunately, few drawings by these artists are known, while the similarities to Guérin's *Death of Cato* in Paris (Musée du Louvre) are compelling in the absence of other evidence.

The drama of Odysseus's recognition is enhanced by the artist's use of a single source of light from a massive fireplace at the left, which casts into shadow Odysseus's face while highlighting his nurse, a clever reemphasis of the role of each character. However, this architectural feature is an anomaly, since Greek houses were not heated by this means. In fact, the armless caryatids are similar to the figures supporting Jean Goujon's rostrum, which even was in the Musée du Louvre and could have been seen by the artist (Vitry/Brière 1969, pl. 110).† Such a reference would be a solecism in any attempt to create an appropriate "antique" or "Greek" setting for the event, although the artist might have been aware of Jacques-Louis David's oil *Paris and Helen* (*Les Amours de Pâris et Hélène*; Musée du Louvre, Paris; see CATALOGUE NO. 39), dated 1788 and engraved by Gérard Vidal in 1790, in which Goujon's four caryatids dominate the background of the setting, which is otherwise replete with classical references (Paris/Versailles 1989–90, 185, no. 79).

The only specifically classical figure in Guérin's drawing is the goddess Athena standing to the left of Penelope, who befriended the hero and assisted him throughout his travels. Although it has not been possible to identify a specific model for the goddess, the artist must have been aware of such a famous antiquity as the Minerva Giustiniani, which had been engraved and published in several anthologies of antique sculpture to be found in Roman collections (Haskell/Penny 1981, 269–71, no. 63, fig. 140). A description of the Prix de Rome competition specifies that before beginning their work the students were first shown appropriate examples of ancient art, most likely engravings or casts of sculpture.

The appeal of the Odyssean legend within the context of the Prix de Rome had less to do with the fame of Homer's epic or its moral lessons than with the fact that an episode such as this necessitated that the students demonstrate their command of expression. From this point of view each of the three figures has a clearly defined role in the drama that, to be visually effective, had to be expressed through certain facial expressions and gestures. The codification and mastery of an appropriate visual language to express emotions had been one of the concerns of the Académie since its founding in the seventeenth century, and the post-Revolutionary Prix de Rome contests reflect the continuation of this interest.
VC

†I am grateful to Mary Levkoff, assistant curator, Department of European Painting and Sculpture, Los Angeles County Museum of Art, for this observation and reference.

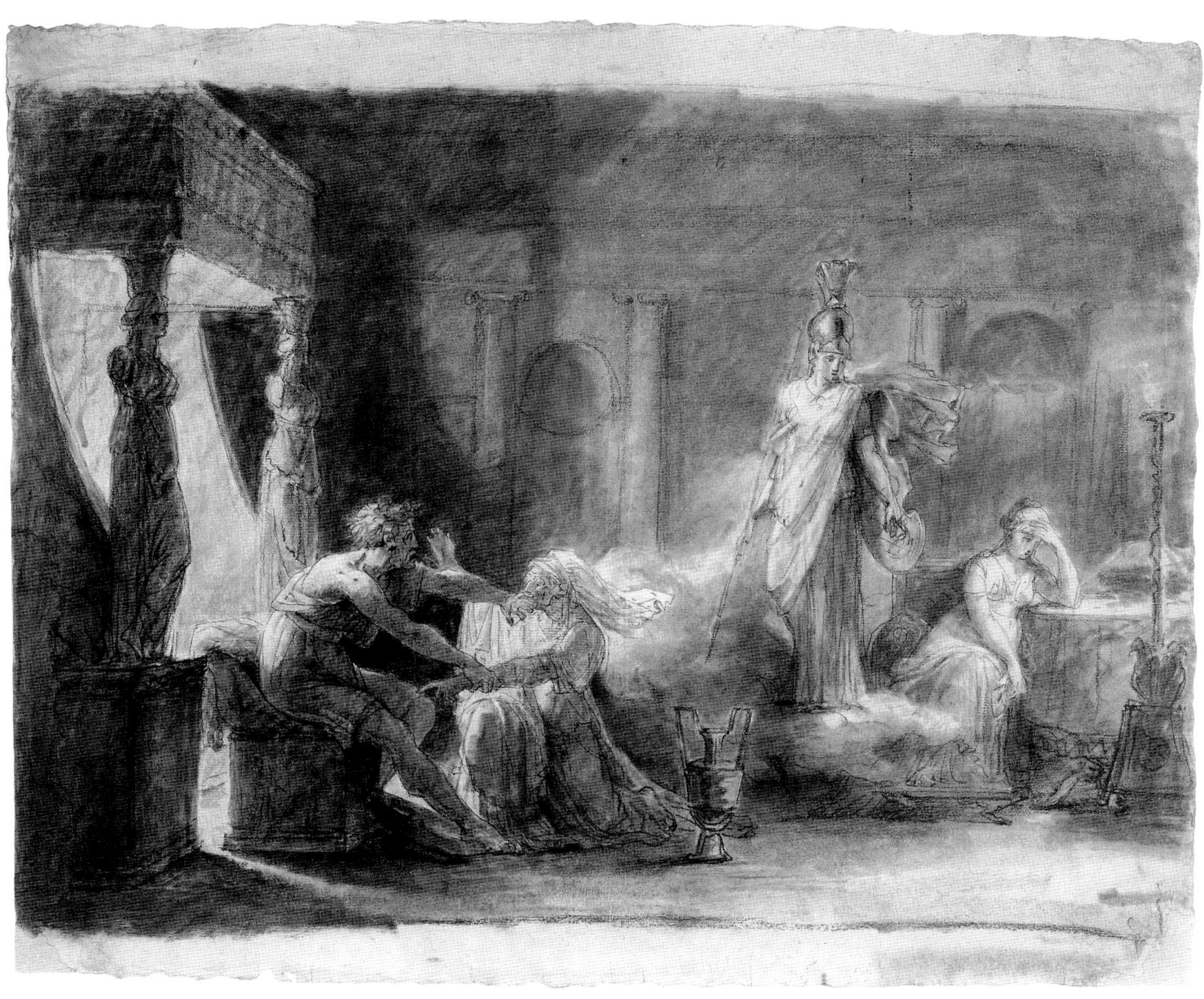

CATALOGUE NO. 65

Pierre-Henri Révoil

1776 Lyons–Paris 1842

RÉVOIL COMPLETED HIS preliminary training at the drawing school in Lyons in 1791–95 with Alexis Grognard before he went to Paris and entered the studio of Jacques-Louis David in 1796. He developed an interest in medieval and Renaissance subject matter, and he and his friend Fleury-François Richard developed the so-called *style troubadour*. He began exhibiting in the Salon as early as 1804 and continued through 1842, the year of his death. In 1807 he returned to Lyons, where he was a professor of painting until 1818, when he moved to Aix-en-Provence. Révoil's first success at the Salons came in 1810 with *The Ring of the Emperor Charles v* (*L'Anneau de l'empereur Charles Quint*), followed in 1812 by *A Fourteenth-Century Tourney* (*Un Tournoi au XIVeme siècle*) in 1812. He returned to his teaching in Lyons in 1823 and was an influential force in the artistic life of that city until 1830, the year of his retirement. Révoil was also a prominent collector of medieval and Renaissance art, and in 1828 his collection was bought by Charles x for the Louvre. LDM

Pierre-Henri Révoil
Allegory of the Reconstruction of the City of Lyons
1800

66
Black chalk and stumping, heightened with gouache on cream wove paper
64 x 84 cm (25 3/16 x 33 1/16 in.)
Watermark: *2794/J. Whatman*
Inscribed at the top: *O·FORTVNATI·QVORVM·IAM·MOENIA·SVRGVNT! VIRG·ENEI·LIB·I* (O happy they whose city already rises! Virgil *Aeneid book 1*); at the bottom: *GENIO·BONAPARTIS/ET·R·VERNINACO·PRÆFECTO·ANDRODO·OPTIMO/P·P·RÉVOIL·PICTOR·LVGDVNEVS~HANC·TABVLAM·GRATO·ANIMO/OFFERT·DICAT·CONSECRAT·* (To the genius of Bonaparte and to R. Verninac, prefect and noble Androcles, P. P. Révoil, painter of Lyons, offers, dedicates, consecrates this painting in the spirit of gratitude); on the shield at lower right: *QVA·VICIT·ARTES·PROTEGIT·ILLE·MANV·* (Whoever conquers protects the arts with the same hand)
Inscribed on the verso: *Faciebam anno aetatia meae XXIV P.R.* (I did [this] in my twenty-fourth year P[ierre] R[évoil])
Private collection

PROVENANCE
Raimond de Verninac, prefect of Lyons.
Private collection.
Sale Sotheby's, Monaco, December 8, 1984, lot 125.
Frederick J. Cummings, New York.

EXHIBITED
New York 1985a, no. 13.
New York 1989b, 270–71, no. 43.

LITERATURE
Chaudonneret 1977, 16–17.
Chaudonneret 1980, 142, no. 62, fig. 233.
Tillyard 1987, 350, fig. 102.
Lyons 1989–90, 49–51, fig. 8.

On June 28, 1800, Révoil offered this magnificent presentation drawing to the prefect of Lyons, Raimond de Verninac, to commemorate Napoleon's visit to the city on that day. The First Consul stopped at Lyons on his return from the Battle of Marengo to lay the cornerstone for the rebuilding of the Place Bellecour, which had been razed during the savage bombardment and demolition of the town by a Republican army under General Kellermann in August of 1793. Révoil's gesture was prompted by his desire to receive a commission for a painting of the subject, which celebrated the rebirth and prosperity of Lyons under the rule of Napoleon (Chaudonneret 1980, 148).

Révoil conceived of his painting as a *trompe l'oeil* bas-relief with a ledge and projecting base. Prominently in the foreground of the composition is the artist's portrayal of Verninac as Androcles pulling a thorn from the paw of a lion, in a punning and remarkably poignant allusion to the "healing" of Lyons.

In a story recounted by Appion (*History of Egypt*, book 5) and Aulus Gellius (*The Attic Nights* 5.14.16–26), Androcles, a Dacian slave of a tyrannical Roman proconsul of Africa, fled to the desert and took refuge in a cave. A lion, crippled by a thorn in its paw, limped into the cave, where Androcles tended to its wound. For three years the slave resided in the cave with the lion until he was captured and brought to Rome. Condemned to be devoured by wild beasts in the Circus Maximus, Androcles was reunited with his lion, who gently licked his hands and feet. Ultimately, the two were released by the emperor Caligula and subsequently traversed Rome together, where everyone who met them exclaimed, "This is the lion that was a man's friend, this is the man who was physician to a lion" (Aulus Gellius 1970, vol. 1, 423–27).

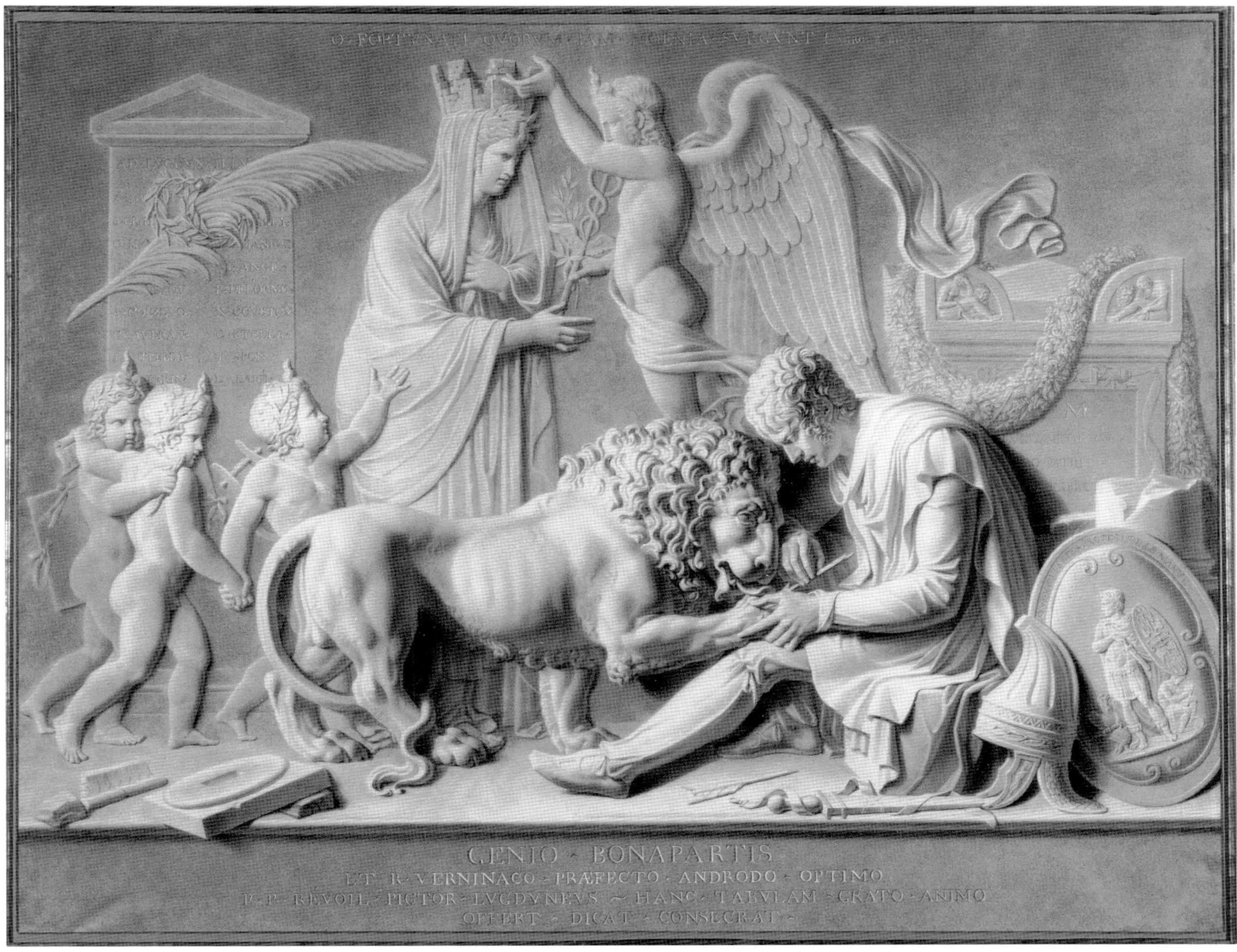

CATALOGUE NO. 66

In a tract composed by Révoil to explain the iconography of his drawing, the artist designed an *en-tête* representing Androcles and the lion with a dedication to Napoleon quoting Aulus Gellius: *À l'Androclès moderne, Hic est homo medicus leonis* (To the modern Androcles, this is the man who was physician to a lion; Lyons 1989–90, 49–51). Two years later *tableaux vivants* of Androcles and the lion were staged at *fêtes* in honor of Napoleon during a subsequent visit to Lyons.

Although the theme was rarely depicted in French art, Jean-Baptiste Stouf exhibited a plaster entitled *Androclus, esclave fugitif d'un proconsul d'Afrique, pansant la blessure d'un lion, après avoir tiré une épine de la patte* (Androcles, fugitive slave of a proconsul of Africa, curing the wound of a lion, after having taken a spine from its paw) at the Salon of 1789, and Charles Meynier sent an *Androclès* to the Salon of 1795. Subsequently, a painting, *Androclès arrachant l'épine de la patte d'un lion*, by Loras, and a sculpture, *Androclès ou le Lion reconnaissant*, by Sébastien Caldelary, were shown at the Salons of 1806 and 1817, respectively (Janson 1977, Salon of 1789, no. 253; of 1795, no. 367; of 1806, no. 138; of 1817, no. 801).

In a subtle variation of the Androcles theme Révoil here depicts Verninac as a Dacian warrior who extracts an arrow—not a thorn—from the lion's paw; its broken, feathered shaft lies at the prefect's feet. The implication of the military assault on Lyons is thus made clear. Verninac himself is garbed in a cloak, leggings, slippers, and with a curved helmet based on ancient prototypes of "barbarians" or "captives," alternatively identified as Dacians, Parthians, or Armenians. While Révoil never traveled to Italy as a pensioner of the Académie de France, he would have known copies of the celebrated Farnese Captives (Museo Nazionale, Naples) executed for Versailles (Reinach 1897–1910, vol. 1, 520, no. 2163; Haskell/Penny 1981, 169–72, no. 17, figs. 87–88). Curiously, Androcles's shield conforms to a common Roman type borne by legionaries in the reliefs on Trajan's Column; it is adorned with the figure of a Roman warrior who resembles Napoleon and appears to observe Androcles and the lion. Révoil's lion is modeled on the famous Medici Lions in the Loggia dei Lanzi, Florence, dating from the second century A.D. (Haskell/Penny 1981, 247–50, no. 53, figs. 126–27), casts of which were made in bronze for Louis XIV.

In the second plane of his composition Révoil portrays Napoleon as a nude winged genius with fiery brow, who descends to present the caduceus of commerce and the olive branch of peace and public tranquility to an allegory of the city of Lyons in the traditional guise of an ancient municipal deity, wearing a crenelated mural crown (Reinach 1897–1910, vol. 1, 11, no. 301). With his right hand the genius restores the mutilated crown. To the left of Lyons are three young genii, who represent music, literature, and the visual arts, distinguishable by their attributes: the lyre, the scroll, and the burin and portfolio. Behind the three genii is a stele displaying the names of Lyons's most illustrious artists, architects, musicians, and men of letters, among which can be read: *A. COIZEVOX, G. AVDRAN, J. STELLA, [GER]MANICUS, M. ANGE, P. DEL'ORME, N. COVSTOV, C. STELLA, J. SPON, L. LABÉ* (a laurel wreath and palm frond superimposed on the top of the stele partially obscure the roster of names). In the right background of the composition is a sarcophagus dedicated to the victims of the siege; it is adorned with a pair of reliefs of seated mourners and lions. The inscription is obscured by a large garland and the figure of Verninac.

Révoil's presentation drawing failed to secure for him the desired commission for a painting. It may be surmised that the prominence allotted to Verninac in the composition led to its rejection by Napoleon; moreover, heroic nudity was anathema to the First Consul. Nevertheless, Révoil extensively reworked his composition in a series of drawings, culminating in a painting of a similar subject, which he exhibited at the Salon of 1804 (see CATALOGUE NO. 67). In essence, the neoclassical orientation of *The Allegory of the Reconstruction of Lyons* was a thematic aberration for Révoil, who was an aficionado of medieval art and a major innovator of the *style troubadour*.

RJC

Pierre-Henri Révoil
Bonaparte Relieving the City of Lyons
1804

67
Pen and brown ink, brush and brown wash, heightened with white gouache, over black chalk on cream laid paper
35.5 x 55 cm (14 x 21 5/8 in.)
Private collection, Memphis, Tennessee

LITERATURE
Chaudonneret 1977, 15–16, fig. 4.
Chaudonneret 1980, 149, no. 63, fig. 224.

Révoil's drawing is a preliminary compositional study for a painting entitled *The Passage of His Majesty the Emperor to Lyons* (*Le passage de S. M. l'Empereur à Lyon*), exhibited at the Paris Salon of 1804 and subsequently purchased for the Hôtel de Ville in Lyons (Janson 1977, Salon of 1804, no. 75). The painting was destroyed on January 9, 1816, during the Bourbon Restoration by order of the prefect of the Rhône (Lyons 1989–90, 49). Révoil completed two additional highly finished compositional drawings prior to his execution of the painting.

The present study constitutes a radical progression from Révoil's earlier conception of the theme, in the format of a bas-relief, to a purely painterly vision. The composition is seen from a diagonal perspective. The artist clearly identifies the setting as the Place Bellecour in Lyons by depicting the Coteau de Fourvière in the left background. This scenic, light-suffused landscape passage contrasts starkly with the demolished architectural ruins overcast with clouds in the right foreground. The sarcophagus depicted in the earlier *Allegory of the Reconstruction of the City of Lyons* (see CATALOGUE NO. 66) is now set at an angle and divides the composition. In the center Napoleon, in the guise of a Roman emperor with a laurel crown, ancient *lacerna* (mantle), *lorica* (cuirass), and sandals, extends his left

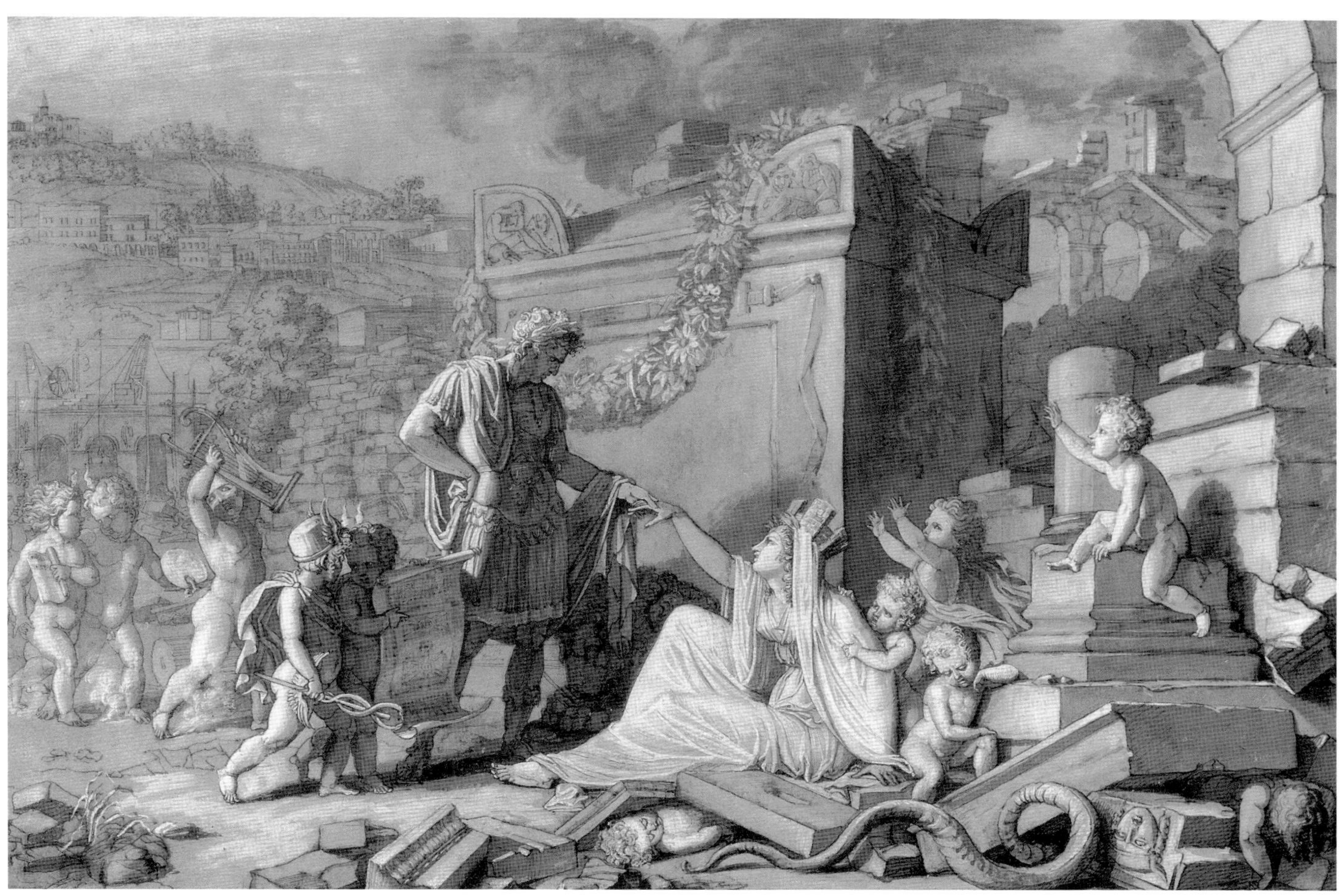

CATALOGUE NO. 67 (see color plate on page 107)

hand to raise up the seated allegorical figure of Lyons. The lion, an arrow piercing its paw, lies passively at the feet of Napoleon. Lyons is attended by despondent putti, two of whom hail with upraised arms the approach of Napoleon. Two more genii lie dead, crushed by fallen blocks, through which slithers an enormous serpent. In contrast, Napoleon is accompanied by a retinue of energetic genii representing literature, painting, music, commerce, and architecture; the last bears a plan for the reconstruction of the Place Bellecour. As Napoleon advances from the left, sunlight illuminates Lyons and her putti.

In a subsequent drawing, now in the collection of the Musée des Beaux-Arts, Lyons (Pittsburgh 1992, 152–53, no. 79), Révoil again radically changed his composition. The landscape of the Coteau de Fourvière is shifted to the right and the demolished architecture to the left foreground. In the central middleground Révoil placed the sarcophagus at a less oblique angle; it is totally redesigned as a rectangular slab surmounted by a roundel adorned with a lion in relief and its facade bears the inscription, *VIVORVM LVDG./ MANIBVS/PATRIA MORENS* (From the surviving people of Lyons to the shades of those who died for their country). Napoleon, clad in a contemporary military uniform, approaches from the right to raise the allegorical figure of Lyons. He is draped in a Roman mantle, however, and still wears a laurel crown, and his pose conforms to that in the Memphis sheet, but his entourage of genii has been expanded to include an allegory of prosperity and a bearer of the victorious standards from the Battle of Marengo. Also, the genius of music raises a scroll inscribed with Virgil's quotation, *O FORTVNATI QVORVM IAM MOENIA SVRGVNT* (O fortunate they whose walls already rise). A putto at left hailing Napoleon from atop a ruined stereobate (at the right in the Memphis drawing) has been transformed in the Lyons drawing into an allegory of the École de Dessin founded by Napoleon and symbolized by the presence of a cast of a torso. A corresponding genius of painting on the right of the composition holds flowers in an allusion to the ornamental patterns for the designers at the silk factories of Lyons.

Révoil rendered a final preparatory study for the 1804 painting, in which he modified slightly the light and shade of the composition (Chaudonneret 1980, 149–50, no. 64; Lyons 1989–90, 119, no. 76). Otherwise, with his Lyons drawing he had arrived at his final formula for the commission (Chaudonneret [1980, 129–30, no. 2] indicates that in the painting Révoil depicted the broken keys to the city in a bronze basin in which can be seen the physiognomy of Henri IV, an early restorer of Lyons). The Salon critics were indifferent, however, and merely criticized Révoil for the mixture of modern and ancient costume worn by Napoleon (Chaudonneret 1980, 130). Subsequently, the artist turned to medieval themes and worked in the historicizing, romantic *style troubadour*. RJC

Pierre-Henri Révoil
Woman Painting Designs on the Body of a Warrior
After 1809

68
Pen and brown ink, brush and wash, watercolor on off-white laid paper
19.7 x 26 cm (7 3/4 x 10 1/4 in.)
Signed at lower left in brown ink: = *P. Révoil*
Private collection, New York

PROVENANCE
Shepherd Gallery, New York.

EXHIBITED
New York 1986a, no. 6.

In Révoil's romanticized vision of Romano-Gallic antiquity, a druid woman paints symbols on the brow, chest, and arms of a triumphant warrior. The pair are depicted within a sanctuary of prehistoric trilithic monuments, set in a grove of oak trees, which were sacred to druidic sects (Bertrand 1897, 3–15, 42–50; Spence 1949, 77–78). Typically, Révoil is highly attentive to archaeological detail, such as, for example, the golden sickle tucked into the bronze belt of the woman, which was used to harvest mistletoe for rituals (Spence 1949, 79–80).

The painted ornaments on the left biceps of the warrior appear to be solar symbols (Bertrand 1897, 241, fig. 35). He grasps in his left hand a shattered eagle standard, which alludes to a recent victory over a Roman legion. Révoil represents a mastiff, a breed introduced by the Romans to Gaul as a guard dog, at the feet of the woman (Appianus 1911, 115). The dog's paws rest protectively on a battle-ax in the form of a fleur-de-lis, a reference to Gaul. Curiously, the Gaul wears the pantaloons and slippers characteristic of ancient sculptures of Dacians and other eastern barbarian tribes (see CATALOGUE NO. 66).

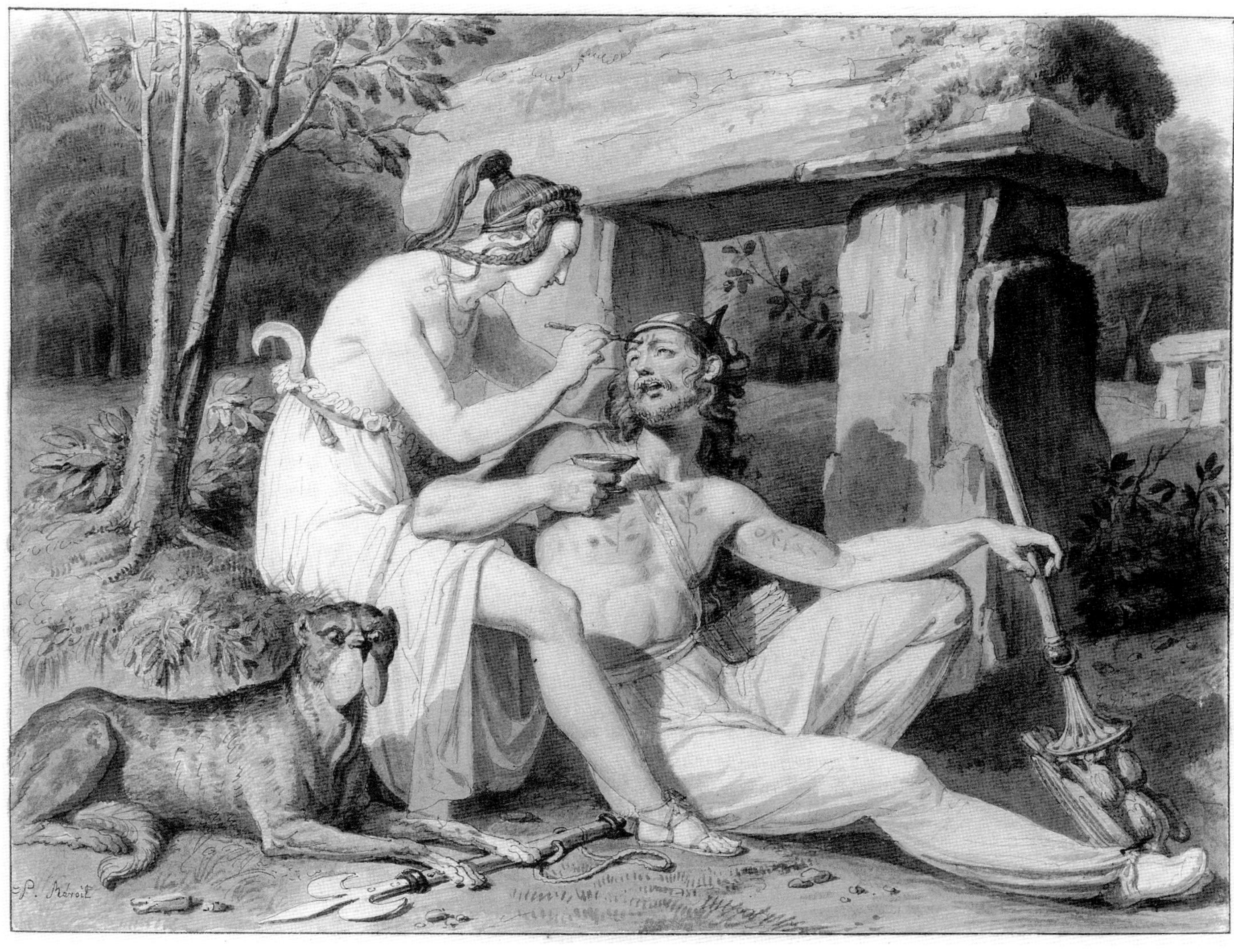

CATALOGUE NO. 68

In essence, Révoil's watercolor manifests a *style troubadour* sensibility in the tender exchange between the druidess and the warrior, who leans upon her knee and gazes fondly at her. The composition could be a Gallic variation of Dibutade and her lover in depictions of the theme of *The Origin of Painting* (see CATALOGUE NOS. 1, 30).

The revival of interest in ancient Gaul had nationalistic overtones and can be traced to Bernard de Montfaucon and especially the comte de Caylus (Boime 1987, 149). The romantic vogue for druidism was inspired by the novel *Les Martyrs, ou Le Triomphe de la réligion chrétienne* (The martyrs, or the triumph of the Christian religion) published in Paris in 1809 by the vicomte de Chateaubriand. Early in his novel Chateaubriand chronicles the tragic passion of the Roman Eudore for the druid priestess Velléda; the setting evokes oak groves, megalithic monuments, and druidic sacrificial rites in Brittany during the reign of emperor Diocletian (see especially books 9 and 10). At the Salon of 1814 Charles-Nicolas-Raphael Lafond exhibited a painting entitled *Velléda, prêtresse druide*, based on the Chateaubriand novel (Janson 1977, Salon of 1814, no. 555), and Révoil himself executed before 1836 the painting *A Young Gallic Woman at the Tomb of Her Husband* (*Une Jeune Gauloise au tombeau de son époux*), which is now lost (New York 1986a, no. 6). RJC

Fulchran-Jean Harriet

1778 Paris–Rome 1805

HARRIET STUDIED WITH Jacques-Louis David and exhibited portraits and history paintings at the Salons from 1796 until 1802. He won the Prix de Rome in 1798 for his *Battle of the Horatii and Curiatii* (*Combat des Horaces et des Curiaces*) and lived at the Villa Medici in Rome from 1802 until his unexpected death in 1805, when he was only twenty-seven, apparently caused by overwork and the change of climate (he had never been in good health). One of his last projects was a large *Horatius Cocles Defending the Sublician Bridge* (*Horatius Coclès défendant le pont Sublicius*), which was shown at a posthumous exhibition at the Académie de France à Rome in 1805. LDM

Fulchran-Jean Harriet
The Death of Raphael
c. 1800–1805

69
Watercolor, gouache with white heightening, over black chalk on pale tan paper
45.4 x 37.7 cm (17 7/8 x 14 13/16 in.)
Private collection, New York

PROVENANCE
Traditionally, from a descendant of Girodet.
Hazlitt Gallery, London, 1982.

EXHIBITED
Paris 1983–84, no. 113, fig. 362.

LITERATURE
London 1982, no. 8, fig. 9.
Verdi 1982, 521, fig. 37.

According to Giorgio Vasari, the tragedy of Raphael's death came about because his doctor mistakenly bled him when the artist complained of fatigue surely brought about by overwork. His frequent visits to the house of his mistress—"a light attachment to which he was enchained," as one translator delicately phrased it—also was thought to have contributed to the painter's weakness (Vasari 1897, vol. 3, 221). Harriet shows Raphael expiring atop his mistress, their figures intertwined and his head resting on her breast. Roses are strewn on their bed, a symbol of amorous conquest, with a snake to reinforce the legend that Raphael's sexual excesses were as much responsible for the painter's end as his workload. Lightly sketched behind the couple is the painter's doctor, with ass's ears, and an allegorical figure (perhaps the muse of painting, although if she is holding a mirror, she could be the personification of Prudence or Lust) who points to Raphael's *Transfiguration* (Musei Vaticani, Rome), a painting which, according to Vasari, was placed at the head of the corpse when the artist's body was displayed prior to burial (Johann Joachim Winckelmann thought that this example of Raphael's work in oils, in contrast to his frescoes, was supreme of its kind [Winckelmann 1972, 101]).

The death of one of the Renaissance's most celebrated artists was one aspect of the late eighteenth-century artist's exploration of history and exotic foreign lands for new subject matter. But to convey to Harriet's audience an image of the venerated artist, the former resorted to the classically harmonious features of a profile view recalling renowned antiquities such as the Antinous bas-relief in the Villa Albani in Rome, expropriated by the French in 1798 and placed on view in Paris by 1802–3 (Haskell/Penny 1981, 144–46, no. 6, fig. 75). Classical sculpture was still the referent to define the nobility of Raphael's art, an admixture of allusions that "permitted a growing chronological and geographic mobility in painting" (Rosenblum 1967b, 34).

Harriet's *The Death of Raphael* (*Mort de Raphaël*), shown at the Salon of 1800, was a *dessin allégorique*, a pendant to his *The Death of Virgil* (*Virgile mourant*; present location unknown). It is most unlikely that the artist would have submitted an unfinished drawing such as this, which may very well be an incomplete replica of the Salon work (Paris 1983–84, no. 113). The work was followed by other representations of the same subject: Nicolas-André Monsiau's Salon entry four years later and Pierre-Nolasque Bergeret's *Raphael Honored after His Death* (*Honneurs rendus à Raphael après sa mort*; Château de Malmaison, Reuilly), a canvas sent to the 1806 Salon (Rosenblum 1967b, 36).

The modeling of the figures in his drawing recalls the finesse of Pierre-Paul Prud'hon's stipple technique, particularly as used in his designs for book illustrations. Harriet's ideal of classical beauty is similar to Prud'hon's facial types, as well as to those of Gérard and Girodet.

Very little is known about Harriet, except for a list of his works and the facts that his health was delicate and that his work in Rome was admired by members of the German resident community, including Schlegel, who praised him to Goethe (Paris/Detroit/New York 1974–75, 483–84, and Grunchec 1986, vol. 1, no. 39; vol. 2, 16). Ironically, he died young, probably of overwork, like the subject of this drawing. VC

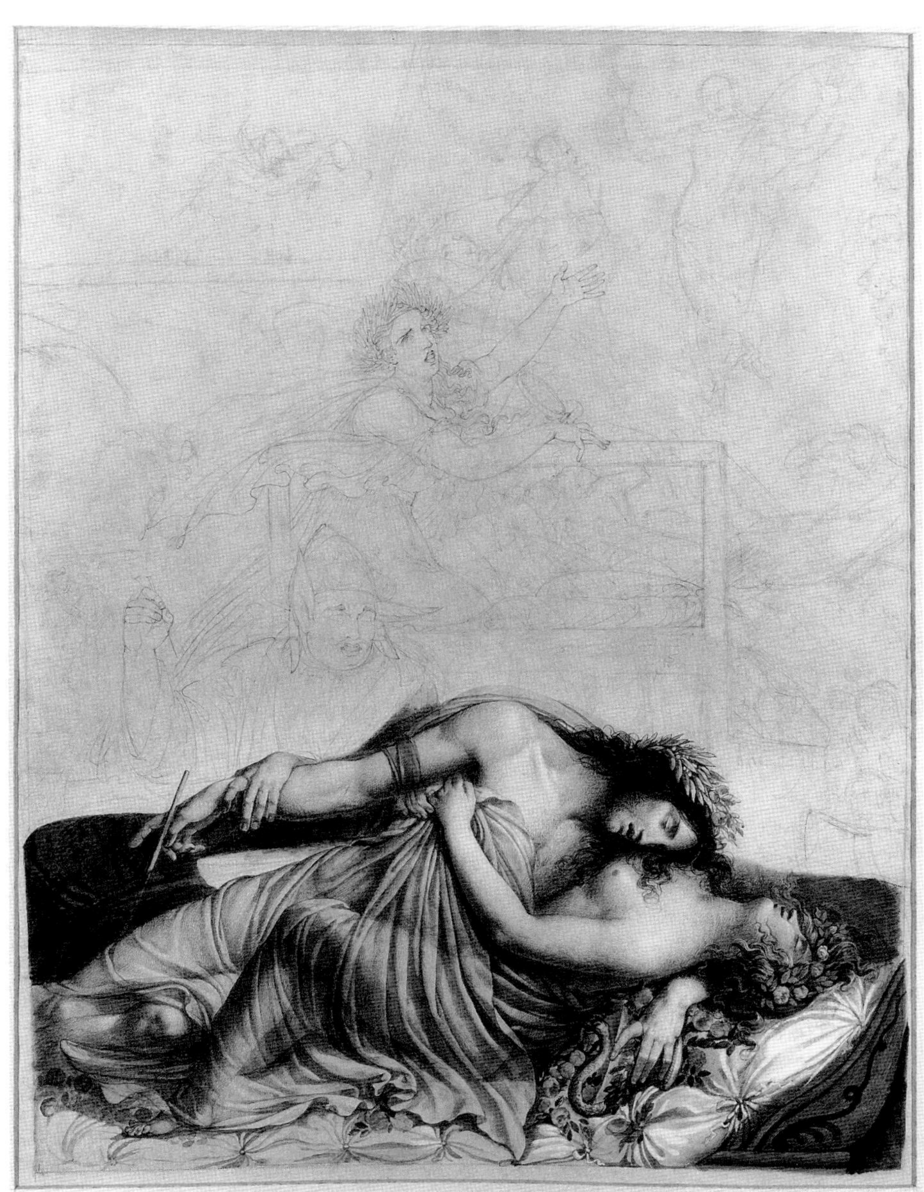

CATALOGUE NO. 69 (see color plate on page 108)

Jérôme-Martin Langlois

1779 Paris 1838

LANGLOIS WAS A PUPIL, assistant, and imitator of Jacques-Louis David. He won the Grand Prix de Rome in 1809 for *Priam at the Feet of Achilles* (*Priam aux pieds d'Achille*) and remained in Rome until 1815. He assisted his master on areas of *Leonidas at Thermopylae* (*Léonide à Thermopyle*) and painted the horse in *Napoleon Crossing the Alps* (*Le Passage du Grand-Saint-Bernard*). Langlois was awarded the Legion of Honor in 1822, the same year he exhibited his *Diana and Endymion*. He remained faithful to David, and in 1824 he traveled to Brussels to paint the portrait of his exiled master, which he exhibited in the Salon of 1827. He was made a member of the Institut de France in 1838, the year of his death. LDM

Jérôme-Martin Langlois
Alexander Ceding Campaspe to Apelles
1819

70
Black and white chalks, brush and gray wash, heightened with white gouache on off-white laid paper
39 x 51.4 cm (15 3/8 x 20 1/4 in.)
Collection of the J. Paul Getty Museum, Malibu, California (inv. no. 86.GG.475)
(Los Angeles only)

PROVENANCE
Zangrilli, Brady and Company, Ltd., New York.

EXHIBITED
New York 1986b, no. 23.

LITERATURE
Goldner/Hendrix 1992, 154–55, no. 62.

Apelles was usually described as the greatest painter of antiquity, whose excellence was recognized by Alexander the Great. The latter honored the artist by making him painter to his court (c. 332–329 B.C.) and was said to have held Apelles's art in such esteem that when he noticed that the painter and his own mistress, Campaspe, had fallen in love during their sittings, he ceded his claim to her in favor of the artist. This episode is found in such widely read and translated sources as Pliny's *Historia naturalis* and Raffaello Borghini's *Il riposo*, 1584, either of which might have been available to Langlois. The theme occurs with some frequency in western European art from the work of Primaticcio and the school of Fontainebleau to contemporaries of Langlois such as Girodet (Pigler 1956, vol. 2, 351–53). In one sense, the story is a tribute to the generosity of rulers, but the tale also carries with it the implication that the painter is a personage of some standing in Alexander's court, whose genius is recognized and esteemed by the sovereign.

Langlois's painting *Generosity of Alexander: Alexander Ceding Campaspe, His Mistress, to Apelles* (*Générosité d'Alexandre: Alexandre cède Campaspe, sa maîtresse, à Apelle*), was exhibited in Paris at the 1819 Salon (it is now in the Musée des Augustins, Toulouse; Roschach 1920, 87, no. 137). A line engraving after the canvas was included in the review of the exhibition by C. P. Landon (Landon 1820, vol. 2, 17, pl. 4). Although their compositions are identical, the relationship between the painting and the Getty Museum drawing is unclear. Artists sometimes made highly finished drawings like the present example during the preparatory stages of work, prior to putting the composition onto canvas. At this stage it might also be useful to have such a drawing to show to a prospective patron. But artists also drew replicas of their paintings to have a record of their work before it left the studio. Because the early history of Langlois's oil is unknown, it cannot be determined which circumstance applies to this drawing. The extreme scarcity of Langlois's drawings makes it impossible to generalize about their role in his development of a compositional idea. A preliminary pen and ink study for the 1819 oil (Musée Magnin, Dijon; Dijon 1938, no. 581) shows several compositional elements that vary from the final painting: Campaspe faces right and thus looks at a point outside the composition—a fault corrected in the painting—and Apelles is kneeling. In addition to these modifications the style of the Dijon work points to an earlier, less developed stage in Langlois's thinking. The pen lines are fluid and searching in their attempt to situate and characterize the figures, which lack entirely the suave finish seen in the Getty Museum drawing.

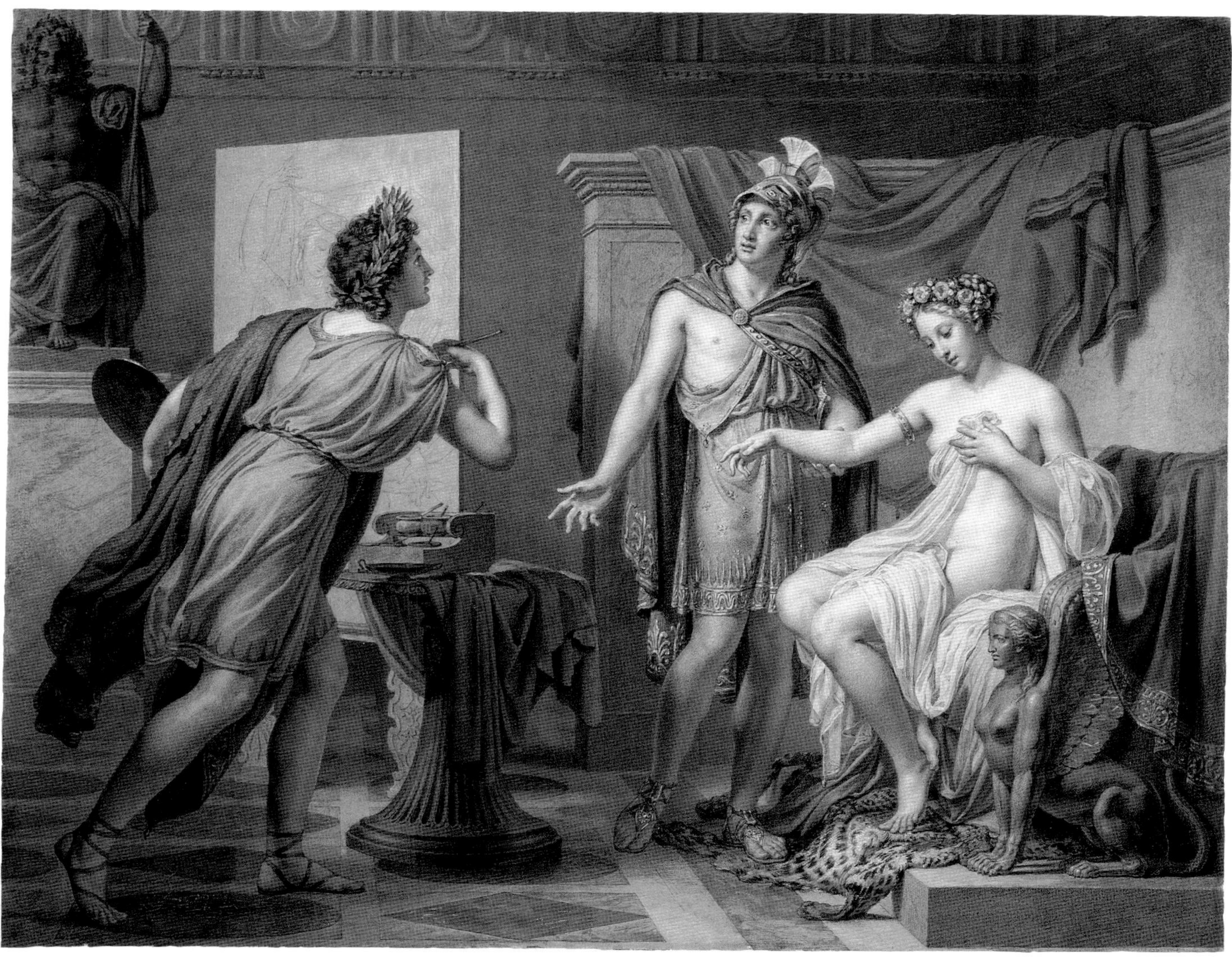

CATALOGUE NO. 70

When *Alexander Ceding Campaspe to Apelles* was first exhibited, the Salon critic Landon voiced some reservations concerning the male figures, but he found the heroine to exhibit Langlois's abilities at their finest: "The head of Campaspe is charming, full of grace and simplicity; in all respects her figure is an excellent academic study. One rarely finds these works as knowledgeably composed and painted with such delicacy and accuracy." An anonymous account of the 1819 Salon sent to Jacques-Louis David, who was in exile in Brussels, by one of his other former students called the canvas one of the best paintings in that year's exhibition (Lettres 1819, 218). It is not surprising, however, that Langlois's work was favorably noticed, since he had studied in David's atelier earlier in his career, and this collection of letters written by former pupils quite naturally praised the master's work and aesthetic doctrines. As a member of David's studio Langlois had assisted his mentor during the initial stages of transferring onto canvas the physically vast and complex composition *Leonidas at Thermopylae* (*Léonidas aux Thermopyles*; Musée du Louvre, Paris), which occupied David from about 1800 to 1812 (Paris/Versailles 1989–90, 486–97, no. 215). David made major changes in the composition during these twelve years, and presumably Langlois was of assistance during the early stages, since by 1805 the younger artist was described as a "demi élève" of the master, suggesting a certain degree of independence (Delécleuze 1855, 229; Grunchec 1986, vol. 2, 33). The interest of the 1819 Salon commentaries extends far beyond information about the works exhibited, because at this Salon Géricault exhibited his *Raft of the Medusa* (*Radeau de la Méduse*; Musée du Louvre, Paris), which attracted more favorable attention from the officials of the Académie des Beaux-Arts than Langlois's submission (Paris 1991–92, 153, 284–87, pl. 242). In retrospect, Géricault's Salon entry challenged the authority of works of art based on a study of classical prototypes; the vast canvas appalled a conservative critic such as Landon, who praised Langlois's entry for its academic correctness and "good taste." VC

Augustin-Alphonse Gaudar de Laverdine

1780 Bourges–Rome 1804

GAUDAR DE LAVERDINE was a pupil of François-André Vincent in Paris and won the Prix de Rome in 1799 with *Manlius Torquatus Condemning His Son to Death* (*Manlius Torquatus condemnant son fils à mort*). He shared the prize with Alexandre-Romain Honnet and left for Rome in 1803, where he studied with Joseph-Benoît Suvée at the Académie de France. He died at the age of only twenty-four in Siena and was buried in Rome. LDM

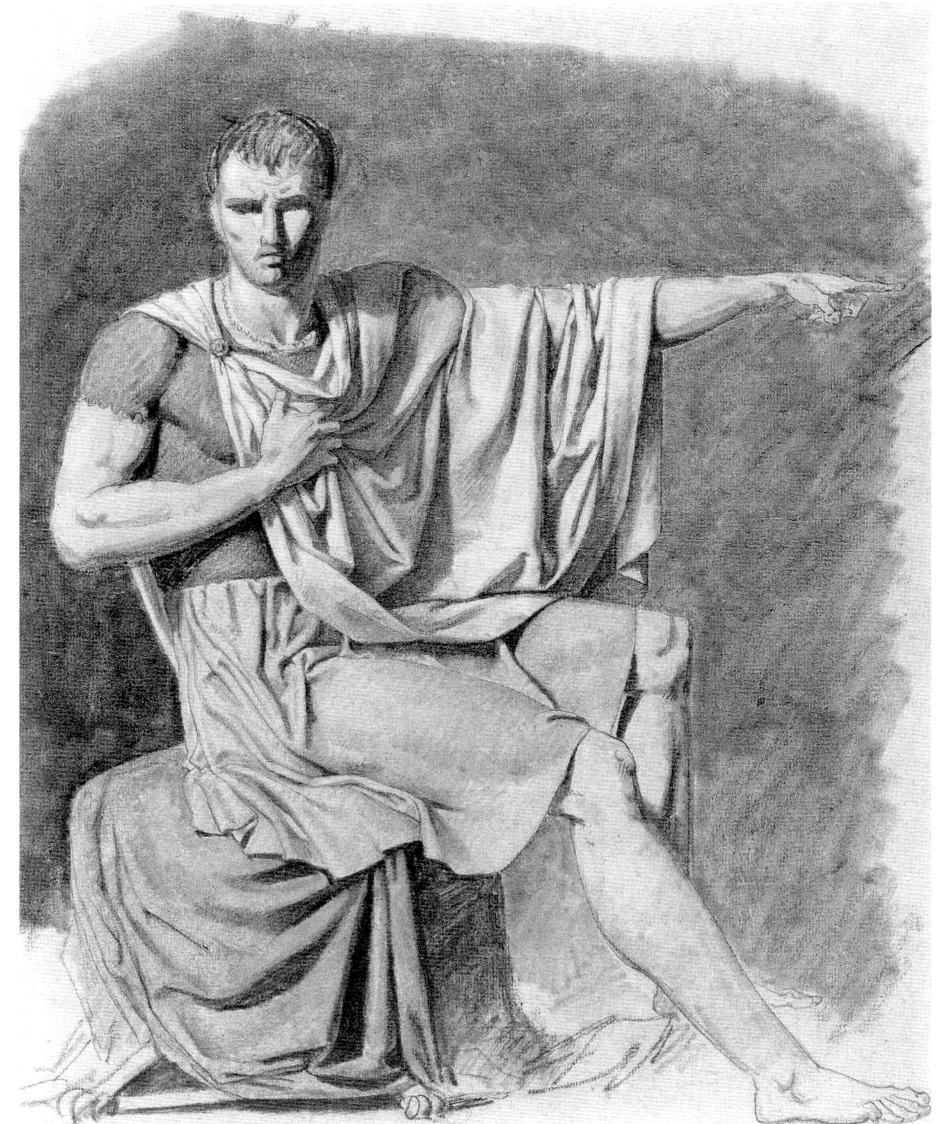

CATALOGUE NO. 71

Augustin-Alphonse
Gaudar de Laverdine
Manlius Torquatus Condemning His Son to Death
c. 1799

71
Black and white chalks on tan laid paper
47.1 x 37.4 cm (18 9/16 x 14 3/4 in.)
Inscribed on the verso in red and blue chalks: *Etude faite pour le tableau qui a [indecipherable] le [indecipherable] par Gaudar de Laverdine*
Fogg Art Museum, Harvard University Art Museums, Paul Geier and Agnes Mongan Funds and through the generosity of Maida and George Abrams (inv. no. 1989.22)
(Los Angeles and Philadelphia only)

EXHIBITED
New York 1989a, no. 14.

Gaudar de Laverdine is virtually unknown as an artist except for his painting *Manlius Torquatus Condemning his Son to Death* (*Manlius Torquatus condemnant son fils à mort*), which won him the Prix de Rome in 1799 (Paris, École des Beaux-Arts; Grunchec 1986, vol. 1, 71; vol. 2, 17–18). Three drawings by the artist have been published, each a study for the principal figure of the Latin consul Manlius Torquatus; two sheets are in the Musée des Beaux-Arts, Tours (Grunchec 1986, vol. 2, 17–18), while the present drawing appeared on the art market only in 1989. In each drawing the pose of the model is identical, but the smaller of the works in Tours (probably the first to be executed) depicts the figure wearing a different costume with a fringe of straps (usually leather) at the waist, a detail that can be found in Bernard de Montfaucon's description of military dress (Montfaucon 1976, vol. 4, 12–17), although Gaudar de Laverdine's drawing is not based on any of the illustrations to this article. The larger drawing in Tours is virtually identical to the present one, differing from it only in medium (black and red chalks) and shading in the background, which covers the full sheet of paper. In these two drawings the model wears what appears to be a studio costume, which the artist modified in his painting to conform more closely to descriptions such as Montfaucon's of military uniforms with bands of fillets hanging below a girdle covering the torso.

It is exceptional that an artist would make two drawings so nearly alike, but the Prix de Rome was the most prestigious award a young painter could receive, and, consequently, the student may have taken the greatest care in his preliminary work. Further, as a pupil of François-André Vincent, Gaudar de Laverdine might have followed his teacher's habit of meticulous preparation. The rhythmic pattern of the heavy, dignified folds of drapery that clothe the otherwise rigid figure of Manlius Torquatus in the drawings and the canvas reflect Vincent's example, as in his 1787 painting *The Clemency of Augustus to Cinna* (*Clémence d'Auguste envers Cinna*; now in the castle at Zidlochovice, Czechoslovakia; see CATALOGUE NO. 37), in which the costumes of five classically draped figures are skillfully arranged to create a dynamic counterpoint to their frozen poses.

The subject of Gaudar de Laverdine's painting is taken from Livy's *History of Rome* (*Ab urbe condita*), book 8, which recounts that during the Latin War of 361 B.C. the Roman consuls forbade single combat with the enemy. When their leader Manlius Torquatus, who insisted on strict military discipline, found that his own son had undertaken such a battle without authorization, he condemned him to death for disobedience, even though he had emerged victorious. This condemnation was seldom depicted by eighteenth-century artists, an exception being Jean-Simon Berthélemy in 1785 (Musée des Beaux-Arts, Tours; Bardon 1963, 232). But such an example of stoical sacrifice, placing duty to the state above familial bonds, was an ideology current during Gaudar de Laverdine's epoch, exemplified most notably by Jacques-Louis David's *The Lictors Returning to Brutus the Bodies of His Sons* (Musée du Louvre, Paris), finished in 1789. After the French Revolution duty to the state as embodied in Livy's Roman commander was still a topical issue, because during the period of the Directory (1795–99), the authority of the five-man executive head of the legislative assembly was challenged by pro-monarchical forces in an attempt to disrupt the already tenuous stability of the Republican government. VC

Jean-Auguste-Dominique Ingres

1780 Montauban–Paris 1867

INGRES BEGAN HIS STUDIES at the Académie Royale in Toulouse in 1791. He moved to Paris and entered Jacques-Louis David's studio in 1797 and the École des Beaux-Arts in 1799. In 1801 he won the Prix de Rome with *The Ambassadors of Agamemnon* (*Les Ambassadeurs d'Agamemnon*), but his trip to Rome was delayed for five years. In the interim he lived in the ex-Capuchin monastery in Paris, submitting works to the Salon and working on his commissions. He finally left for Rome in 1806, and after his four years as a student expired, he remained in Italy working on portraits and history paintings. After the fall of the Empire many of Ingres's patrons left Italy, but he remained, spending time in Naples and relocating to Florence in 1820. He received a commission for *The Vow of Louis XIII* (*Le Voeu de Louis XIII*) for the cathedral in Montauban; it was his first critical Salon success when he returned to Paris in 1824. Shortly afterward he received the Legion of Honor and was made a member of the Académie des Beaux-Arts. He opened his own studio in 1826 and began teaching at the École des Beaux-Arts in 1829, but his bitterness at the Salon's reception of the *Martyrdom of Saint Symphorien* (*Martyre de Saint Symphorien*) in 1834 resulted in his request to be sent to Rome, where he served as director of the Académie de France from 1835 until 1841. He continued to paint until his death for private clients and the governments of Louis-Philippe and Napoleon III. LDM

Jean-Auguste-Dominique Ingres
Belisarius
c. 1797

72
Charcoal with stumping under black chalk and graphite on heavy cream wove paper
62.7 x 49.3 cm (24 11/16 x 19 3/8 in.)
Inscribed at lower right in pen and brown ink over graphite: *offert à Léon Bonnal/30 janvier/1887 Ve Ingres* [inscribed by Mme. Ingres]; at upper right in black chalk: *J D Ingres/1793*; at lower right in blue crayon: *1793*
Private collection, courtesy Phyllis Hattis Fine Arts

PROVENANCE
Gift of the artist to his wife, Delphine Ingres, née Ramel (Veuve Ingres).
Gift of Mme. Ingres to Léon Bonnal, January 1887.
Pierre Bonnal (grandson of Léon).
American collection, 1970.

EXHIBITED
Cambridge 1973, 67, no. 8.

This is one of Ingres's most spectacular early drawings, a study of the heads of the blind Roman general Belisarius, falsely accused of conspiracy, and his young guide as they return to their homeland in Thrace. Ingres copied this detail from François Gérard's painting *Belisarius* (present location unknown), which had been exhibited to great acclaim at the Salon of 1795. The young artist could have seen Gérard's canvas when he arrived in Paris in the fall of 1797 to study in Jacques-Louis David's school; its popularity was so great that it was returned to the Salons to be exhibited again at various times between 1796 and 1801. Drawings after three-dimensional objects, known as *dessins en bosse*, were used by David to judge the skills of his new students. Since in Toulouse Ingres had already made a number of these drawings, working after plaster casts or engravings, he may have felt that the heads of Belisarius and his wounded guide posed a greater challenge to his skills than the more routine copy after an antique sculpture (for a study of these early drawings, many of which were later inscribed with erroneous dates, see Cambridge 1973). As a pupil newly arrived in David's school, Ingres might well have preferred to prove his abilities by working after a celebrated canvas, since its artist also was a pupil of David. Nor could it have escaped Ingres's attention that the master himself had in 1781 painted another incident from the hero's life, Belisarius asking for charity (*Bélisaire, reconnu par un soldat qui avait servi sous lui au moment qu'une femme lui fiat l'aumône*; Musée des Beaux-Arts, Lille).

At this period, the immediate source for an artist's knowledge of the Roman general's heroism and stoic courage was most likely the novel by Jean-François Marmontel, *Bélisaire, Roman moral et politique* (Paris, 1767). However, for his Salon painting Gérard invented an incident in which the general's guide was bitten by a snake, imposing an additional burden, quite literally, on the old man. By focusing only on the heads of the two figures Ingres created a drawing in the tradition of *têtes d'expression*, in which the young artist could demonstrate his ability to render the expressive pathos of the situation and characterize differences of age and physical type.

The Belisarius drawing is one of a group of eleven recently discovered sheets, the provenance of which suggests that they are youthful works ranging in date from a study of about 1789–91,

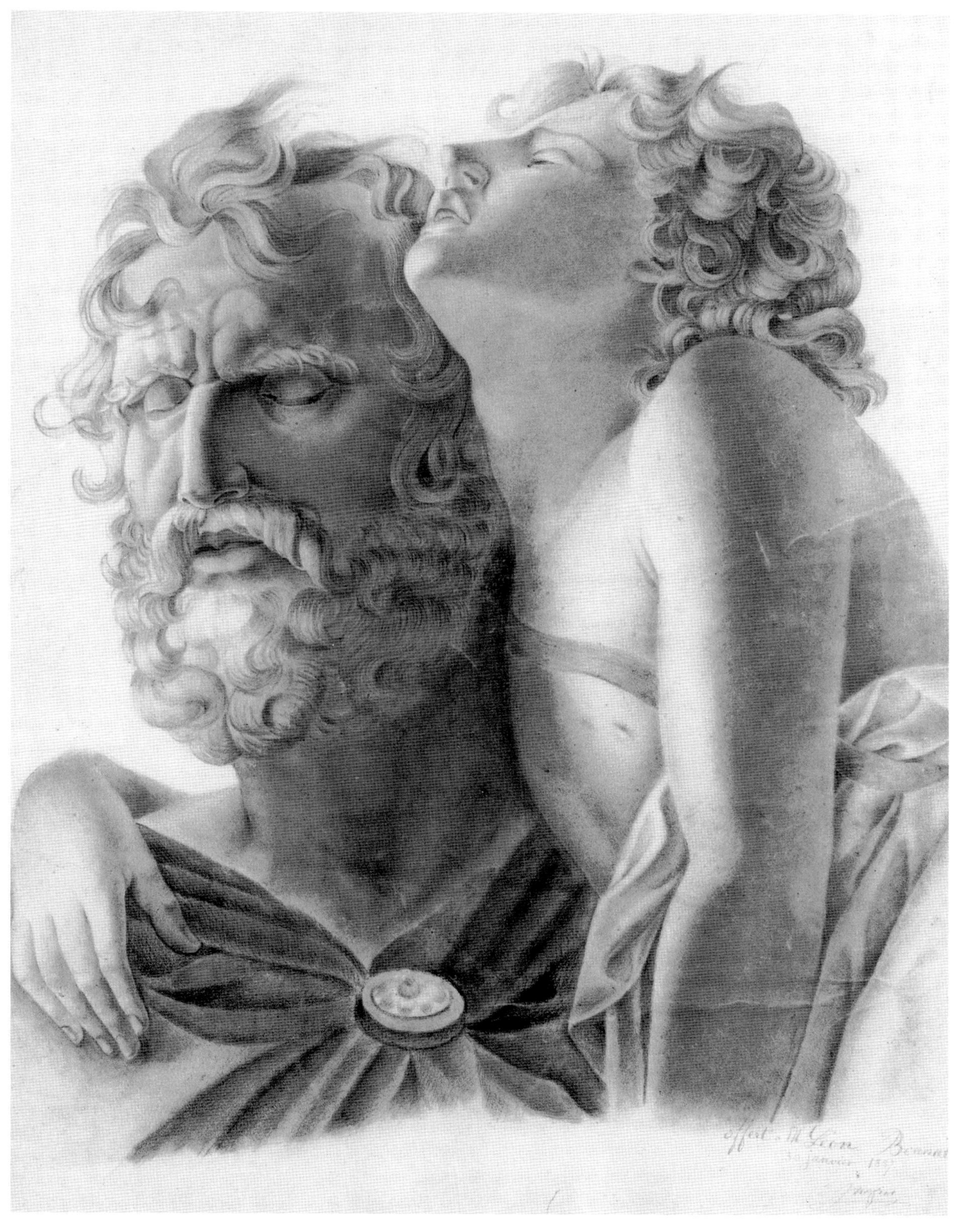

CATALOGUE NO. 72

when the student was under the tutelage of his father in Montauban, to a head after a portrait bust of a woman by Antonio Canova, probably executed between 1797 and 1806. Excepting the present work and the copy after Canova, these drawings clearly demonstrate how basic was the study of antique art to Ingres's training from the very outset. Working in Montauban and Toulouse, he must have known these monuments only through plaster casts or engravings. The skill and labor so evident in these drawings show that even at this remove from original antiquities Ingres could find in the classical past lessons that would be essential to his mature work. VC

Jean-Auguste-Dominique Ingres
Romulus Victorious over Acron
c. 1812

73
Graphite, brush and gray wash on tracing paper
26 x 51.2 cm (10 1/4 x 20 1/8 in.)
Inscribed at lower right in pen and ink:
Ingres à M. Haro
Private collection

PROVENANCE
The artist to Étienne-François Haro, Paris; sale, Hôtel Drouot, Paris, April 2–3, 1897, lot 175.
Henri Haro, Paris; sale, Hôtel Drouot, Paris, February 3, 1912, lot 147.
Henry Lapauze, Paris; sale, Hôtel Drouot, Paris, June 21, 1929, lot 46.

EXHIBITED
Paris 1911, no. 190.
Paris 1913, no. 337.
London 1934, no. 49.
New York 1947–48, no. 34.
New York 1976, no. 27.
Ithaca 1978.
London 1981, 9.
New York 1982b, 11, 113.
Louisville/Fort Worth 1983–84, 42, 157, no. 6, fig. 1.

LITERATURE
Delaborde 1870, 275, no. 190.
Cambridge 1967, no. 12.
Rome 1968, 46–48.

As a young artist working in Rome, Ingres received an important commission to execute two large history paintings to be placed in the Palazzo del Quirinale in preparation for Napoleon's occupation of the Italian capitol. The first canvas Ingres had to complete was intimately allied to the history of Rome itself. The subject of *Romulus Victorious over Acron* (*Romulus vainqueur d'Acron*; École des Beaux-Arts, Paris) is taken from Plutarch's *Life of Romulus*, the founder of Rome. Among the many concerns of Romulus was the shortage of wives for his soldiers to father a future generation of Roman warriors. At a festival honoring Neptune, the Roman soldiers kidnapped and took as their wives the unmarried Sabine women assembled there. In retaliation, King Acron declared war on the Romans, but the Sabines were vanquished and Acron was killed. In this drawing Romulus prepares a triumphal procession, removing the armor as a trophy from his fallen adversary. The parallel between Romulus the victorious conqueror and Napoleon, who planned to install himself in place of the pope in the Quirinale made this an obvious, albeit arrogant, theme for the decoration.

For the ceiling of his bedroom the emperor chose the *Dream of Ossian*, a nocturnal fantasy of warriors and muses chanting of heroic deeds while the warrior-poet sleeps, a subject taken by Ingres from the Gaelic poems of Ossian, the "Homer of the North," a favorite book of Napoleon (which was later found to be an eighteenth-century fabrication; see CATALOGUE NO. 12). With the collapse of the empire Napoleon never reached Rome, and the palace decorations were dismantled when the Quirinale was occupied by Pope Pius VII in 1815.

A contract for the *Romulus* was signed on February 26, 1812. In spite of the fact that Ingres had little time in which to finish his *Romulus* (the painting was delivered in November of the same year), he prepared the work with customary attention to even minute details. A number of preparatory studies survive for details of the figures (see CATALOGUE NO. 74), in addition to five elaborately finished drawings of the full composition, of which the present work is generally agreed to be the first (Louisville/Fort Worth 1983–84, 42–45, 157, no. 6, figs. 2, 4, 5, 7). The traditional chronology for Ingres's preparatory work antedates his actual receipt of the commission, because two of these drawings are dated 1808 and 1810 (both Musée du Louvre, Paris; Paris 1989a, nos. 84–85).

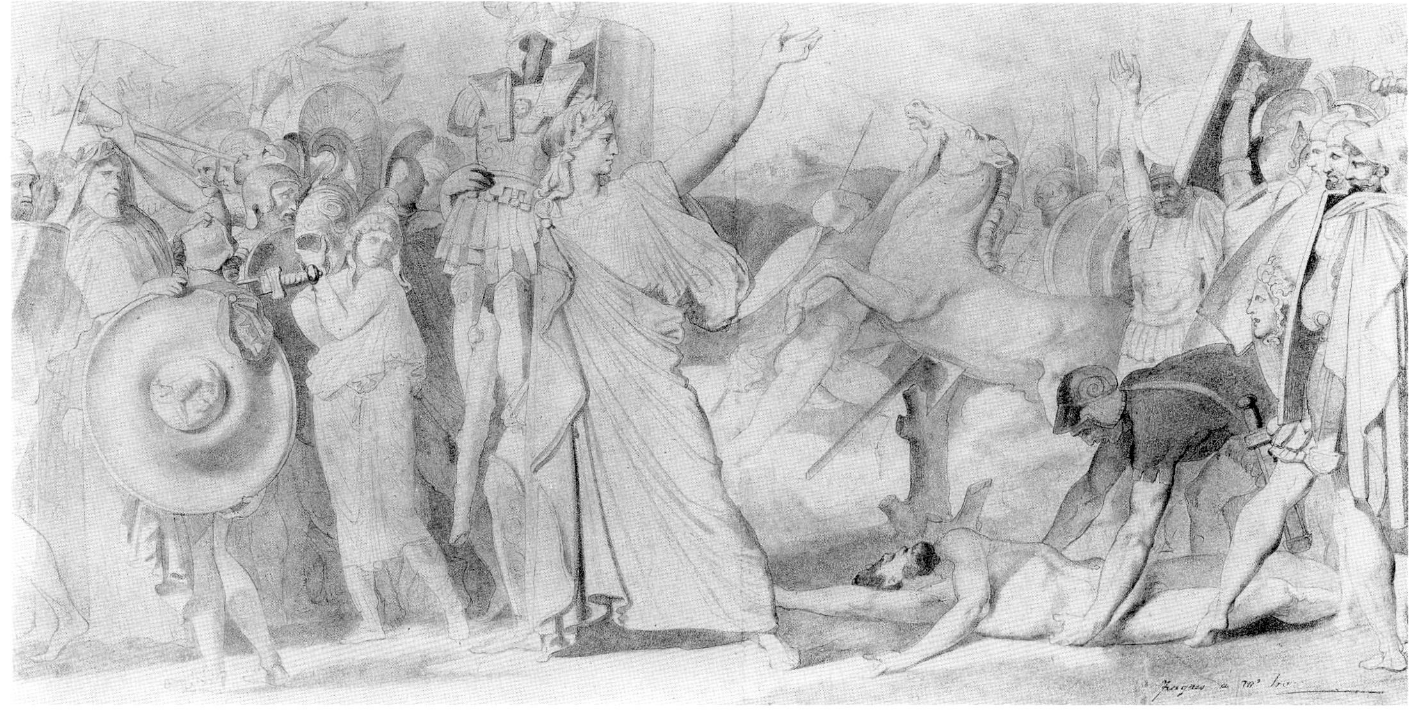

CATALOGUE NO. 73

The suggestion made by Régis Michel (Paris 1989a, 142) that these were erroneous inscriptions added later, as sometimes happened (see CATALOGUE NO. 72), is more satisfactory than the assumption that Ingres had ready to hand the Romulus and Acron composition that propitiously could serve Napoleon's propagandistic needs. The artist again took up the composition in preparation for an etching on steel that was published by Achille Réveil in 1851. He modified his earlier composition in a number of respects, the most dramatic being that the rearing horse at the right in the present sheet and the painting was moved to the left.

Ingres's hero, his left arm outstretched in a victorious salute, may have been inspired by one of the Dioscuri, the monumental antique Roman marbles of horse tamers that stand outside the palace where the *Romulus* was to hang. A drawing (or tracing?) at the Musée Ingres, Montauban, although undated, indicates that Ingres was familiar with the sculpture, which as one of the most visible antiquities in the city he could hardly have avoided (see Montauban/Reuilly 1991, 9, no. 41); the marble group may also have suggested that Ingres include the figure of a prancing horse.

The shallow space of the composition, with the main figures aligned across the foreground, inevitably recalls the Roman relief sarcophagi that abounded in the city. As if in homage to David, Ingres borrowed the position of Acron, lying on the ground with his left arm across his chest, from a fallen soldier in David's *The Sabine Women* (*Les Sabines*; see FIGURE 13), a canvas finished in 1799, while Ingres was a student in his school. Although the Dioscuri may have impelled Ingres to add a similar figure group to his composition, he seems to have turned to one of the line engravings after Flaxman for his drawing of the animal. Ingres's horse is nearly identical to a figure in plate 22 of the Englishman's illustrations to Homer's *Iliad*, save for a minor change in the position of the forelegs.

After having painted *The Sabine Women* David told Eugène Delécluz, one of his first historians, that he had wanted to paint a work in a pure Greek style, with figures of archaic simplicity that would be less "anatomique" than those in his previous canvases (Paris/Versailles 1989–90, 328). This shift of emphasis in the older artist's goals was also shared by Ingres, as witness his knowledge of John Flaxman's line engravings, his tracings after Greek vase paintings, and acquisition of panel paintings by Italian Quattrocento painters. Admiration for a more remote epoch of antiquity was a credo for a number of artists at this time, some of whom were David's students. They called themselves *primitifs*, as if to signal a break with the accepted canons of antiquity and the classicism of Raphael and Poussin. "In the earliest and simplest Greek vase paintings and reliefs, in Quattrocento masters like Perugino, they found images of refreshing flatness and linear purity, of lucid geometric stylizations that offered the visual equivalent to their literary taste for the stark drama, the vigorous grandeur, the legendary remoteness of Homer, Aeschylus, and Ossian" (Rosenblum 1967a, 17). This vivid evocation of the *primitifs*' goals helps account for the singular character of *Romulus Victorious over Acron* within Ingres's work. Painted in tempera on canvas, the figures are modeled in shallow relief, an effect enhanced by the rather dry, flat surfaces characteristic of tempera. For these reasons the work remains an isolated experiment in his oeuvre, an exception to the artist's oil paintings, with their vivid palette and subtle glazes. VC

Jean-Auguste-Dominique Ingres
Studies of a Male Nude (Acron)
c. 1812

74
Graphite on white wove paper
19.7 x 37.5 cm (7 3/4 x 14 3/4 in.)
Signed at lower left in black chalk: *Ing*
The Metropolitan Museum of Art, New York, Rogers Fund, 1919 (inv. no. 19, 125.2)
(Los Angeles and Minneapolis only)

PROVENANCE
Édouard Gatteaux (died 1881).
Édouard Dubufe.
François Flameng; sale, Galerie Georges Petit, Paris, May 26–27, 1919, lot 126.

EXHIBITED
Paris 1867, no. 177.
Paris 1911, no. 191.
Cambridge 1967, no. 12.
Paris 1968, 86, no. 56.
London 1972, no. 659.
Paris 1973–74, no. 50.

LITERATURE
Gatteaux 1875, pl. 45.
Burroughs 1919, 246–47.
New York 1942–43, vol. 2, no. 38.
Millier 1955, 20.
Bean 1964, no. 64.
Waldemar George 1967, pl. 64.
Ternois 1970, 81, 83, fig. 27.
Hamburg 1977–78, 109–10, fig. 15.
Ternois 1980, 46.
Mráz 1983, 42, no. 16.

This sheet of four studies for the cadaver of Acron for the composition *Romulus Victorious over Acron* (see CATALOGUE NO. 73) was surely drawn after a model posed at Ingres's studio. Only the position of the legs in the topmost sketch and the turned head of the figure below were retained by the artist as he continued to refine the pose. A sheet of six drawings for the dead man's legs, with a sketch of his left hand, is less closely related to the final image than the present work, and no doubt preceded it (Musée Ingres, Montauban; Montauban/Reuilly 1991, 8, no. 35). A drawing in Bayonne of Acron's torso in the position finally adopted shows that even at this advanced stage of his thinking Ingres experimented with alternate positions for the figure's arms (Musée Bonnat, Bayonne; Paris 1979, 66, no. 89). In the end the artist placed the dead Acron's left arm across his chest, a pose that so closely parallels that of a fallen warrior to the right in Jacques-Louis David's *The Sabine Women* (*Les Sabines*; see FIGURE 13) that the similarity cannot be a matter of chance. David's masterpiece was first publicly exhibited when Ingres was a student at his school; there can be no doubt that Ingres admired the work, since at one time he owned one of David's most elaborately finished preparatory drawings for *The Sabine Women*, which he later gave to the Louvre (Paris/Versailles 1989–90, 347, no. 152). In Rome, in the absence of David's canvas, Ingres may have had an engraving after the oil to which he could refer. Six additional studies for *Romulus Victorious over Acron* are in Bayonne, and five others in Montauban (Montauban/Reuilly 1991, nos. 36–40).

The several studies for the figure of Acron demonstrate that Ingres essayed alternatives for each detail of the figure before making his final decision. If in the end his solution recalled a work from antiquity or by a contemporary such as David, the reference may have been chosen because after trial and indecision it provided the best solution. Ingres's admiration for the classical past was not motivated by a need to display his erudition through easily recognizable references, but his faith in the classical tradition did impel him to rival the excellence of these works of art he so much admired. VC

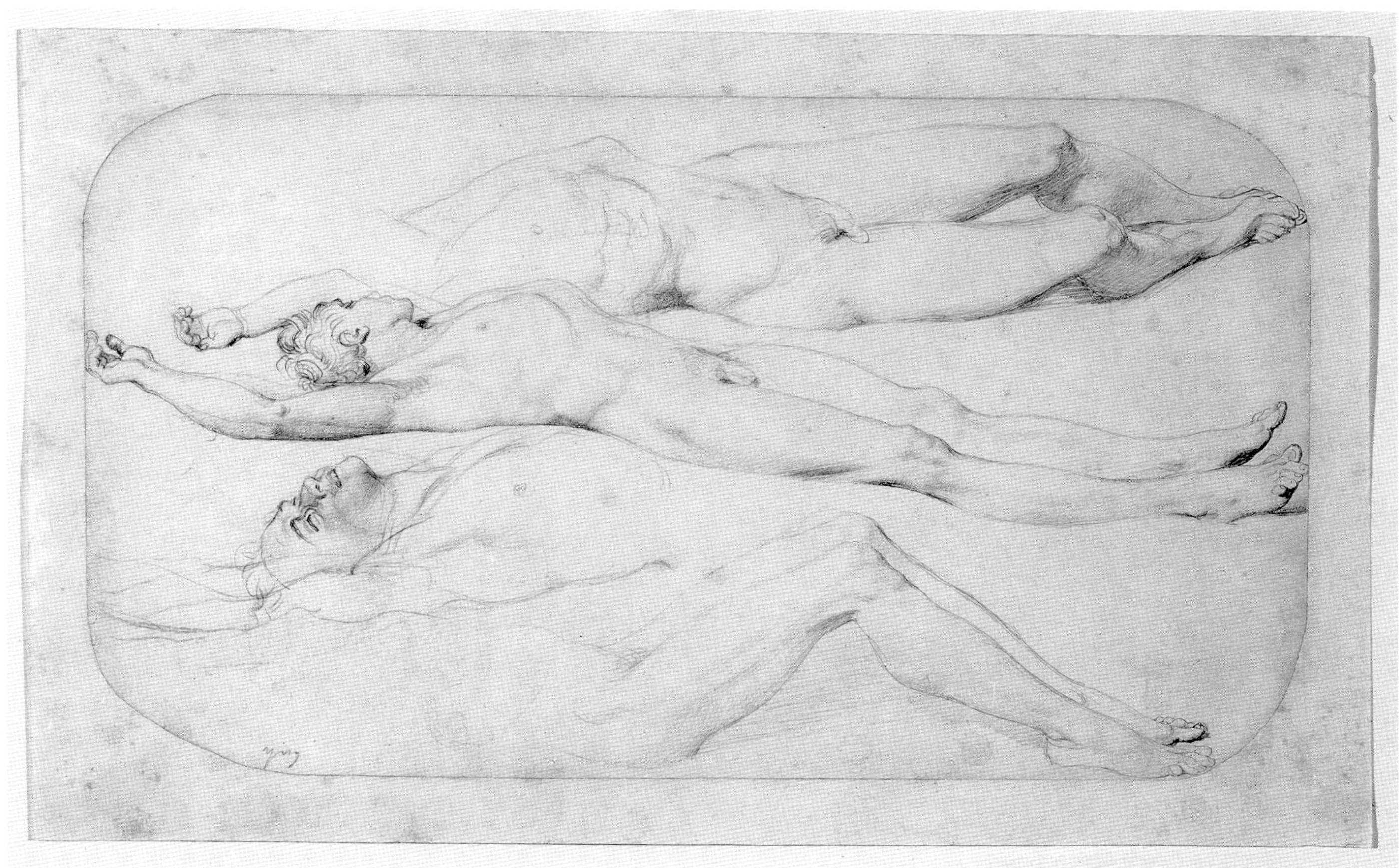

CATALOGUE NO. 74

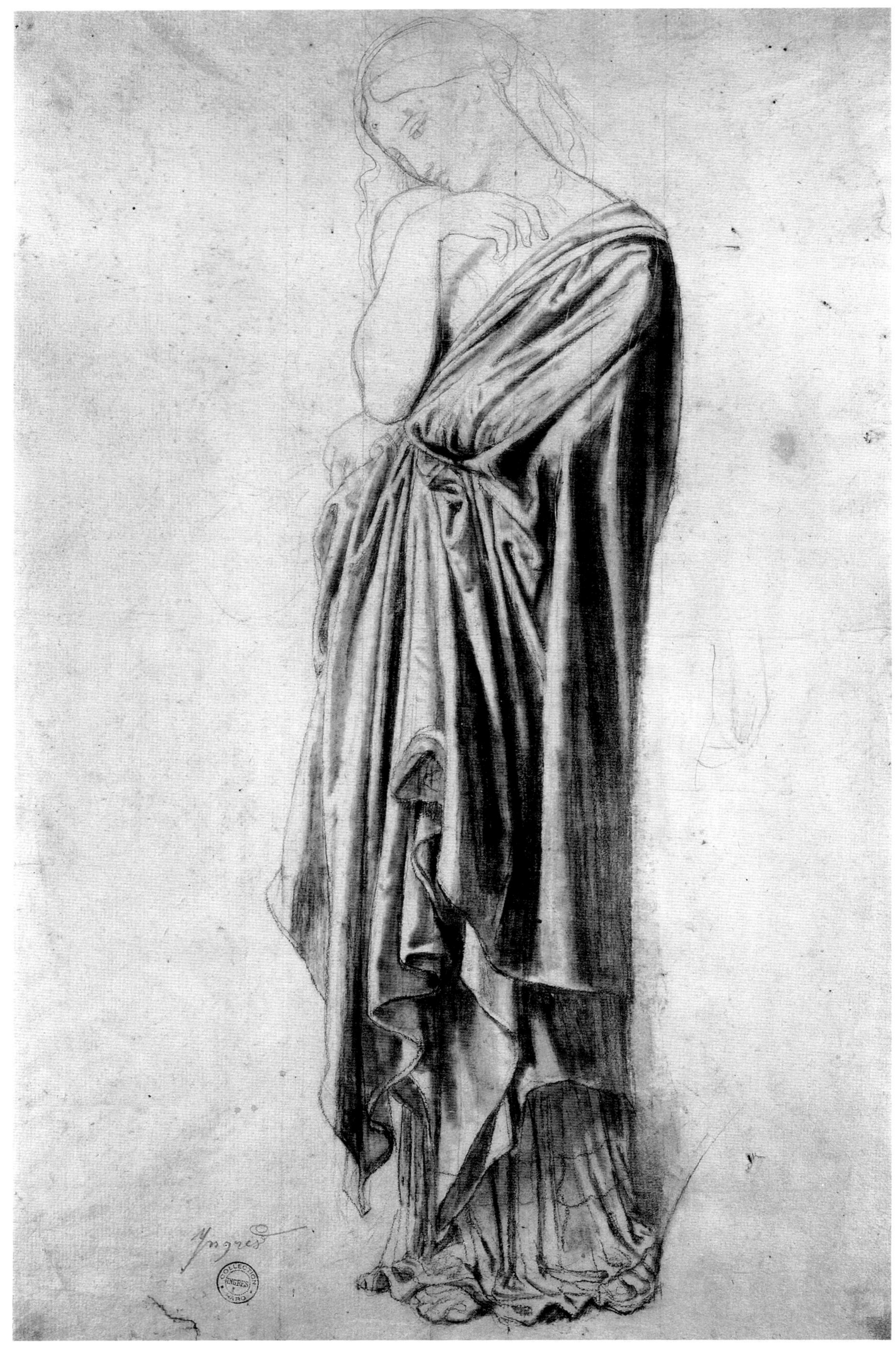

CATALOGUE NO. 75

Jean-Auguste-Dominique Ingres
Study of Classical Drapery
c. 1835–40

75
Soft graphite and black chalk over stylus contours on heavy cream-colored laid paper, partially squared for transfer
49.2 x 32.1 cm (19 3/8 x 12 5/8 in.)
Signed at lower left in black chalk: *Ingres*
The Metropolitan Museum of Art, New York, Gustavus A. Pfeiffer Fund, 1963 (inv. no. 63.66)
(Philadelphia and Minneapolis only)

PROVENANCE
Étienne-François Haro.
Jan Heyligers, Rotterdam.

EXHIBITED
Paris 1867, no. 192.
Cambridge 1967, no. 79.
New York 1985–86, 75, 76, 138, no. 58, fig. 50.

LITERATURE
Choix de dessins 1926, no. 33 (wrongly said to belong to the Musée Ingres at Montauban).
Alazard 1950, pl. 71.
Bean 1964, no. 66.
Mathey n.d., no. 42.

In 1834 Ingres received from Ferdinand-Philippe, duc d'Orléans and son of King Louis-Philippe, a commission for a painting on the subject of Antiochus and Stratonice. In the same year the artist left for Rome, where he had been appointed director of the Académie de France at the Villa Medici, a position he held until 1841. The finished painting, now at Chantilly (Musée Condé), was sent to Paris in 1840, where it was exhibited to great acclaim. Thus Ingres's preparatory work must have been carried out in Italy from about 1834 to 1840. His labor over the commission was intense; more than three hundred drawings for every aspect of the work have survived, most of them in the Musée Ingres, Montauban.

Four drawings of a nude model posed as Stratonice have been published: two are magnificent sheets of studies, one at the Museum Boymans-van Beuningen, Rotterdam (Baltimore/Los Angeles/Fort Worth 1986–87, no. 58), and the other recently on the art market (ex-collection John Gaines; Louisville/Fort Worth 1983–84, 168, no. 17). Closely related to these is another drawing of Stratonice's head and upper torso in the Musée des Beaux-Arts, Tours (Rome 1968, no. 112), and a sketch of only her torso in the Musée Ingres (London 1979a, 60). The present highly finished drapery study is almost identical, even in its dimensions, to the corresponding detail in the Chantilly painting, suggesting that here the artist is close to realizing his final solution for Stratonice's robes.

The plight of the lovesick Antiochus was a popular subject for artists (see Benjamin West's drawing of 1777, CATALOGUE NO. 3, or Jacques-Louis David's 1774 oil [Paris/Versailles 1989–90, no. 10]). Probably while Ingres was a pupil in David's school, he drew a highly finished pen and wash version of the subject (Musée des Beaux-Arts, Boulogne-sur-Mer; Louisville/Fort Worth 1983–84, 60, fig. 2). In a drawing executed around 1807 (Musée du Louvre, Paris; Louisville/Fort Worth 1983–84, 61, fig. 3), Ingres placed Stratonice in isolation from the other figures, leaning against a pillar, her gaze averted from the sickbed, a solution that anticipates her position in the much later Chantilly painting.

Stratonice's pensive expression, her head downcast, with her right arm supporting her chin, is paralleled in ancient Roman wall paintings such as the figure of Penelope in a mural of Ulysses and Penelope in Pompeii, a pose that the artist adopted for his portrait of Madame d'Haussonville (see New York 1985–86, 69–72, for a discussion of this and other antique sources). Later, in conversation with Théophile Silvestre, Ingres acknowledged that he had studied the frescoes from Herculaneum and Pompeii but immediately added that his love for antiquity was always tempered by his study of nature and the masterpieces of artists such as Raphael (New York 1985–86, 69). VC

Henri-Joseph de Forestier

1787 Santo Domingo–Paris 1872

FORESTIER WAS A PUPIL of both François-André Vincent and Jacques-Louis David. He won the Prix de Rome in 1813 for *The Death of Jacob* (*La Mort de Jacob*). He studied in Rome, and upon his return to Paris he exhibited at the Salon for the first time in 1819. He was decorated with the Legion of Honor in 1832. Forestier became involved in politics after the Revolution of 1848: he was made a colonel of the sixth legion of the Garde Nationale and was subsequently arrested after a revolutionary demonstration in June of 1849, although he was acquitted by the Haute Cour of Versailles. The only Salon to which he contributed after that was the one of 1855. LDM

Henri-Joseph de Forestier
The Wrath of Saul against David
c. 1817

76
Pen and brown ink, heightened with white gouache over graphite on dark tan paper
16 x 24.4 cm (6 5/16 x 9 5/8 in.)
The Baltimore Museum of Art, Dr. and Mrs. William W. Magruder Fund (inv. no. BMA 1984.21)

PROVENANCE
Sale, Paris, Hôtel Drouot, December 6, 1982, lot 118.

Forestier's *The Wrath of Saul against David* (*La Colère de Saül contre David*) is another example of the chiaroscuro drawings that were popular in this period. Traditionally an artist working in this manner would use the tinted paper as a middle tone, adding shadows and highlights with black and white chalks or inks. The present drawing departs from this procedure, since Forestier employed the dark tan paper to suggest a dimly lit interior space. His figures were then built up from layers of white ink washes of varying density, with opaque highlights defining the major contours of the figures, their facial expressions, and costumes. As a result, Forestier's modeling with white inks is cameolike in its delicacy and sense of shallow relief, especially by contrast to the fully realized volumes of Pierre-Paul Prud'hon's figures, for example, whose approach respected the honored conventions of chiaroscuro drawing.

The dramatic lighting typical of chiaroscuro drawings is ideal for representations of incidents such as Saul's wrath against his armor-bearer and eventual son-in-law, David, as told in 1 Samuel 18–19. King Saul became increasingly enraged by David's superior prowess in battles against the Philistines; on two occasions Saul tried to kill David with a javelin while the young warrior was playing his harp. Here, the figure to the right of David holds his harp while the young warrior prepares to defend himself. The artist evidently did not feel constrained by the usual conventions for representations of biblical personages, since David is dressed as a Roman warrior, while the vaguely "antique" furnishings of the scene reinforce the sense that these figures could easily be used to represent an event from classical Greek or Roman mythology or history.

Such works by Forestier as have been identified show a preference for compositions with figures arranged across the foreground in a shallow, friezelike space. They are sometimes posed in profile, as here, which emphasizes the analogy to classical bas-reliefs, even when Forestier is depicting biblical subject matter. The dramatic gestures of Saul and David recall in a general way the figures in John Flaxman's outline engravings or in the Greek vase paintings that inspired them. In fact, Saul's pose is close to that of a figure on a krater reproduced in an outline engraving in Wilhelm Tischbein's illustrations of Greek vases in the collection of Sir William Hamilton, published in Naples between 1791 and 1795 (Reinach 1922–24, vol. 2, 333, fig. 3). At the very least the comparison points to the kind of source Forestier must have used to inform himself about the classical past.

In all likelihood this drawing was executed in Rome, as was another slightly larger version of the composition, signed and dated 1817 (present location unknown; London 1975, no. 30). The two drawings are almost identical, the major difference being the addition of Saul's daughter Michal to the left of her father in the dated example. In the same year in Rome Forestier also drew another work using this technique, *Antique Scene:*

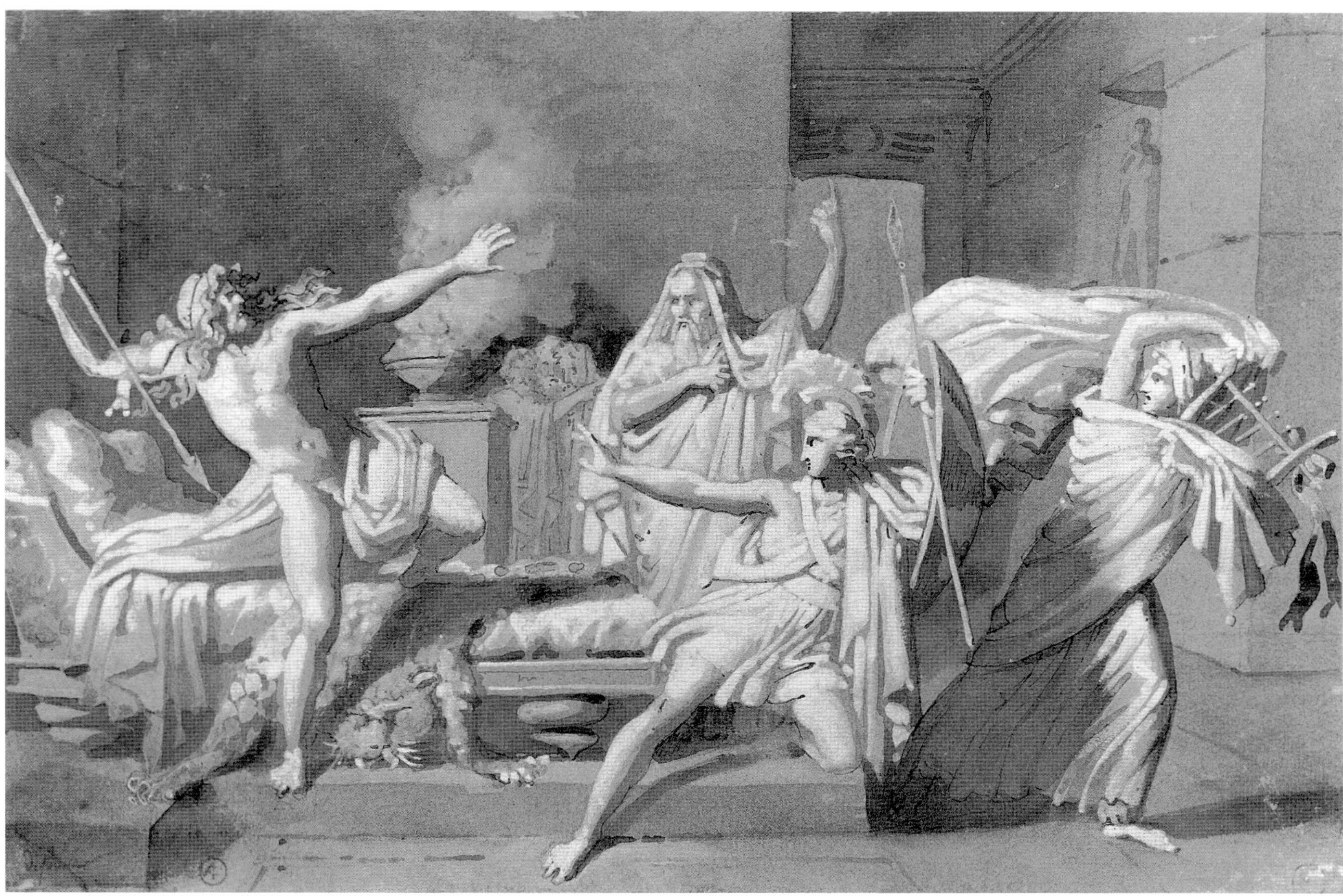

CATALOGUE NO. 76

Allegory of Pleasure (*Scène antique: Allégorie de la volupté* [?]; Musée Bonnat, Bayonne; Paris 1979, no. 66), which bears comparison to the present sheet, as does the artist's *Allegory of the Arts* (*Allégorie des arts*; Musée du Louvre, Paris; Inventaire 1907–75, vol. 5, 99, no. 4040), dated a year earlier. Aside from these four drawings, little else is known by the artist, the major exception being the canvas that won him the Prix de Rome in 1813, *The Death of Jacob* (*La Mort de Jacob*; École des Beaux-Arts, Paris; Grunchec 1986, vol. 2, 50–51).

Other French students with Forestier at the Villa Medici also made chiaroscuro drawings, among them Jean-Victor Schnetz, who was a friend of Théodore Géricault. There is a certain amount of confusion surrounding the authorship of certain of these Roman drawings, which have been optimistically ascribed to the more celebrated Géricault (Grunchec 1979, 37–58). The latter artist had known both Forestier and Schnetz in Paris and saw them again in Rome in 1816–17. Géricault's own chiaroscuro drawings are quite distinctive in their greater reliance on contour to define each figure, with white highlights used to indicate light modeling the figure, not the body of the figure itself, as was Forestier's habit. Chiaroscuro drawings such as those by Forestier mentioned in the preceding paragraph catered to the preference for highly finished works drawn in a variety of media that artists made independently of other projects. It is not clear whether students at the Villa Medici hoped to find clients for drawings that could be framed and hung on the wall, although it is known that older, more established painters such as Prud'hon did have patrons who bought their framed drawings (see CATALOGUE NO. 48). In any case, the finished chiaroscuro drawings of Forestier, Géricault, and Schnetz were part of the widespread appreciation of drawing as a self-sufficient art form, a striking feature of European neoclassical draftsmanship. VC

Jean-Louis-André-Théodore Géricault

1791 Rouen–Paris 1824

AGAINST HIS FATHER'S WISHES Géricault entered the studio of Carle Vernet in 1808. After two years he changed to the studio of the neoclassicist Pierre-Narcisse Guérin but left in 1810 to begin independent studies copying the paintings of Rubens, Rembrandt, Titian, and Velasquez in the Musée Napoléon. He exhibited at the Salon for the first time in 1812 with his *Charging Chasseur* (*L'Officier de chasseurs à cheval de la guarde impériale chargeant*) and won a gold medal, but when he exhibited the pendant to this painting, *The Wounded Cuirassier* (*Cuirassier blessé, quittant le feu*), at the Salon in 1814, it was not well received. Géricault failed also in his attempt to win the Prix de Rome in 1816 but left that same year for Italy at his own expense, partly to escape a scandalous affair with his aunt. In Florence and Rome he continued drawings of satyrs and nymphs he had begun in Paris and painted the *Riderless Horse Race* (*Course de chevaux libres à Rome*) in 1817 after a visit to the Roman carnival.

Géricault returned to Paris in 1817 and experimented with lithography and sculpture. After a five-year absence from Salon exhibitions he presented in 1819 the huge *Raft of the Medusa* (*Radeau de la Méduse*), which caused an aesthetic and political scandal. Géricault was mentally and physically exhausted from his work on the painting and his disappointment over its reception; in 1820 he left Paris for London, where he remained for two years, working on genre paintings and portraits. He returned to Paris at the end of 1821, but his self-destructive behavior endangered his health and financial security. He spent his last years painting portraits of the insane for Dr. Étienne Georget, a brilliant young psychiatrist who may have treated him for depression. He died at the age of thirty-two.
LDM

Jean-Louis-André-Théodore Géricault
Studies of Hercules Casting Off the Cloak of Nessus
c. 1817

77
Pen and brown ink on white paper
18.1 x 26 cm (7 1/8 x 10 1/4 in.)
Robert Tuggle

PROVENANCE
Christopher Powney, London, 1968.

EXHIBITED
Princeton 1981, 91.

At the outset of his artistic career Géricault was attracted to the military painting of Antoine-Jean Gros and his contemporaries, a "modern" genre then being fostered by the lavish patronage of Napoleon. Due to his informal and largely self-directed training he lacked the traditional academic instruction of mainstream history painters.

A corpus of studies in the so-called Zoubaloff sketchbook in the Musée du Louvre, Paris, documents Géricault's revived interest about 1814–15 in the academic drawing exercises and classical themes he had first encountered under the tutelage of Pierre-Narcisse Guérin. The pen, ink, and wash drawings are copies of engravings after ancient sculpture, figures from works by Michelangelo, Nicolas Poussin, and Raphael, and John Flaxman's outline illustrations to the *Iliad* and the *Odyssey* (see CATALOGUE NO. 8). Stylistically, they are heavy-handed and exaggerated in execution and reflect the routine exercises of a student copyist (Eitner 1983, 78–86).

Géricault intended this new regimen of drawing to prepare him for competition for the Prix de Rome in 1816. He was successful in the first stage of the contest—a compositional sketch, *Aeneas Stopped by Venus as He Attempts to Kill*

Helen Who Has Sought Refuge at a Statue of Vesta—but he was eliminated after the second round of the competition—a painted study from life. Despite this reversal Géricault executed a series of five drawings depicting *The Dying Paris Rejected by Oenone*, the subject decreed for the final and decisive stage of the contest (Paris 1991–92, 60–65, figs. 110–16). (The Prix de Rome was awarded to Antoine-Jean-Baptiste Thomas for his treatment of the theme [see CATALOGUE NO. 78].) In addition to these compositional studies Géricault rendered an extraordinarily vigorous group of drawings representing *Horatius Cocles Defending the Sublician Bridge*, *Mars and Hercules*, and *The Procession of Silenus*, which date from this period (Paris 1991–92, figs. 137–39, 142–43).

In late September or early October of 1816 Géricault departed for a projected two-year sojourn in Italy at his own expense. In Rome the artist occupied himself by producing drawings "for albums" (Clément 1879, 84). The present sheet dates from Géricault's Roman period, 1816–17, and illustrates an episode from book 9 of Ovid's *Metamorphoses*. Unwittingly, Hercules donned a cloak smeared with the blood of the centaur Nessus, who was infected with the venom of the Lernaean hydra. The poisoned garment inflamed Hercules's blood and seared his skin. His attempts to remove it were in vain and resulted in the laceration of his flesh. Overcome with pain and resigned to his cruel fate, Hercules constructed his own funeral pyre; when his human form had been consumed by the fire, he was deified by Jupiter and carried up to Mount Olympus.

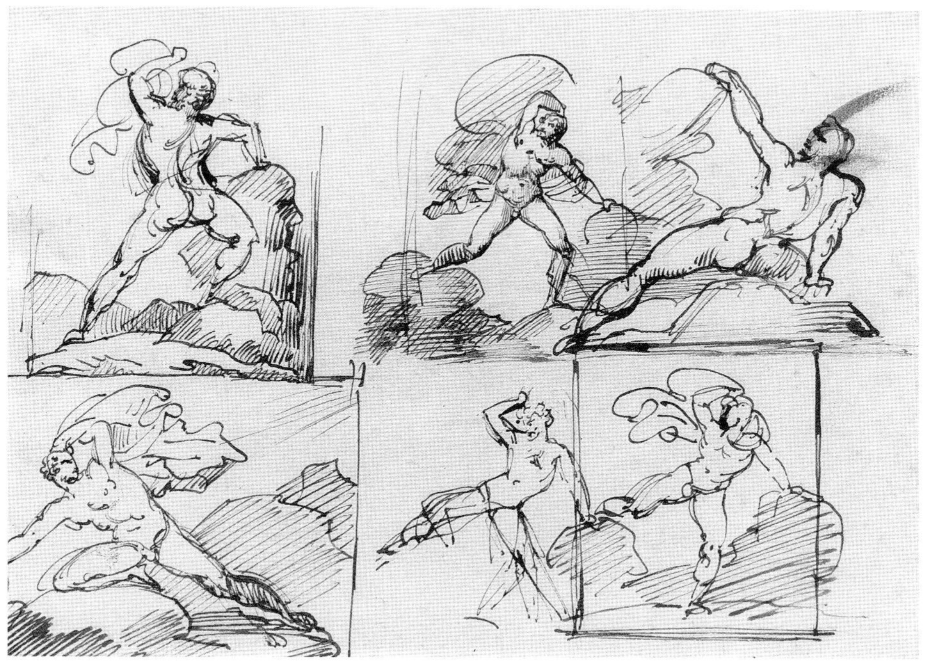

CATALOGUE NO. 77

Géricault depicts Hercules's futile attempts to cast off the tainted mantle in a staccato sequence of six individually "framed" sketches on the same sheet. His assured, even exuberant shorthand in pen and ink succinctly establishes space, defines form, and conveys the frenzy of Hercules. Another figure of Hercules casting off the cloak within a "frame" also appears in the lower left corner of a sketchbook sheet now in a London private collection (Los Angeles 1971, 80, no. 41). The pen and ink technique and dimensions (17.8 x 26.2 cm) of the London sketch are identical to the Tuggle sheet. Significantly, the London sheet includes preliminary sketches for the *Riderless Horse Race*, which suggests a date of 1817. There also exists in the collection of the Cabinet des Dessins at the Louvre a sheet of five variant sketches of a centaur carrying off a woman, ostensibly Nessus and Hercules's wife, Deianira, the episode that began the chain of events culminating in Hercules's death (Eitner 1983, 104–5, fig. 90; New York/San Diego/Houston 1985–86, no. 39, fig. 39b).

Géricault's representation of Hercules attempting to cast off the cloak is unusual; traditionally, artists chose to depict Hercules taking revenge on his servant Lichas, who had unwittingly presented him with the cloak. Géricault's conception of the emotive suffering of Hercules parallels that of Laocoön and Philoctetes, other ancients noted for vociferously bewailing their misfortunes. It constitutes the eclipse of the "noble" and "sedate" neoclassical ideals of Johann Joachim Winckelmann and Gotthold Ephraim Lessing. The Tuggle sketch and the related sketches pave the way for Géricault's dark vision of antiquity that is fully manifest in a series of highly finished "paintings" in chalk, wash, and gouache, which the artist inscribed *Rome, 1817* (see FIGURE 19; Eitner 1983, 106–7, 336, no. 37; Paris 1989a, 138–42; Paris 1991–92, 72–75, figs. 131, 141, 144.). RJC

Antoine-Jean-Baptiste Thomas

❧

1791 Paris 1834

THOMAS BEGAN HIS STUDIES as a pupil of François-André Vincent and entered the École des Beaux-Arts in 1814. He won the Prix de Rome in 1816 with *Oenone Refusing to Help the Wounded Paris* (*Oenoné refusant de secourir Pâris blessé au siège de Troie*). He studied in Rome for two years and returned to Paris in 1818. He exhibited at the Salons between 1819 and 1831, but he is best known today for his series of lithographs, *One Year in Rome and Its Environs* (*Un An à Rome et dans ses environs*). LDM

Antoine-Jean-Baptiste Thomas
The Dying Paris Rejected by Oenone
c. 1816

78
Verso: Half-length Study of a Male Nude
Black and white chalks on blue laid paper
22.2 x 31.8 cm (8 3/4 x 12 1/2 in.)
Inscribed at lower right in black chalk: *houdon.*
Fogg Art Museum, Harvard University Art Museums, bequest of Meta and Paul J. Sachs (inv. no. 1965.334)
(Philadelphia and Minneapolis only)

PROVENANCE
Georges Bourgarel; sale, Hôtel Drouot, Paris, November 13–15, 1922, lot 107.
Richard Owen.
Paul J. Sachs.

LITERATURE
Parker 1930, 39.
Mongan/Sachs 1940, no. 626, fig. 315.
Boucher 1952, no. 116.
Eitner 1963, 25, fig. 2.
Grunchec 1983, 161, pl. 2.
Grunchec 1986, vol. 2, 59, pl. 2.
Paris 1991–92, 349.
Mongan forthcoming, no. 319.

For many years this was thought to be one of the few drawings known by the sculptor Jean-Antoine Houdon (see CATALOGUE NO. 27). In 1952, however, James Fowle proposed the present attribution and title for the work (letter in museum files, April 12, 1952). Subsequently Eitner published the drawing as a preparatory study for Thomas's painting *Oenone Refusing to Help the Wounded Paris* (*Oenoné refusant de secourir Pâris blessé au siège de Troie*; École des Beaux-Arts, Paris), which won the Prix de Rome competition in 1816. Among the unsuccessful aspirants was Théodore Géricault, who nonetheless made several drawings based on the story of Paris and Oenone (Eitner 1963, 24–25, fig. 2; Grunchec 1986, vol. 1, 106–7; vol. 2, 58–60, pl. 2; Paris 1991–92, 62–64, nos. 71–74). The warrior Paris is dying from injuries received during the siege of Troy. He appeals to the nymph Oenone to give him the remedy for his wounds that only she possesses. Since she had once loved Paris, who spurned her in favor of Helen of Troy, she now refuses to aid the hero, although eventually she relents, but not in time to save his life.

The drawing is a rapidly executed compositional sketch that sets out all the major details of the final canvas, excepting the figure of Oenone, who is shown here facing the viewer, while in the canvas she is seen from the back. Thomas based the pose of his dying Paris on the figure of the hero in Charles Lebrun's painting *The Death of Meleager*, which had been placed on view in Paris and engraved a few years earlier (Musée du Louvre, Paris; Jouin 1889, 514; Rosenberg/Reynaud/Compin 1974, 209; Paris 1991–92, 349, no. 70). The inspiration to represent Oenone from the back may have been suggested by the figure of a servant bringing aid to Meleager in Lebrun's oil. Moreover, the balletic grace with which Oenone turns away from Paris recalls dancing figures such as are often found on reliefs of bacchic revels, one of the most celebrated examples being the Borghese Vase, recently acquired for Paris by Napoleon and placed on view by 1811 (Musée du Louvre; Haskell/Penny 1981, 315, no. 81, fig. 166). Whether or not the renown of the vase was a factor in Thomas's decision to revise the figure when he set to work on the canvas, in its final form Oenone's gesture of repudiation is far more elegant than her abrupt denial of aid seen in this drawing.

The Fogg Museum drawing is one of the few works by Thomas to have been identified. Another facet of his draftsmanship while he was a student at the Villa Medici is shown by the artist's

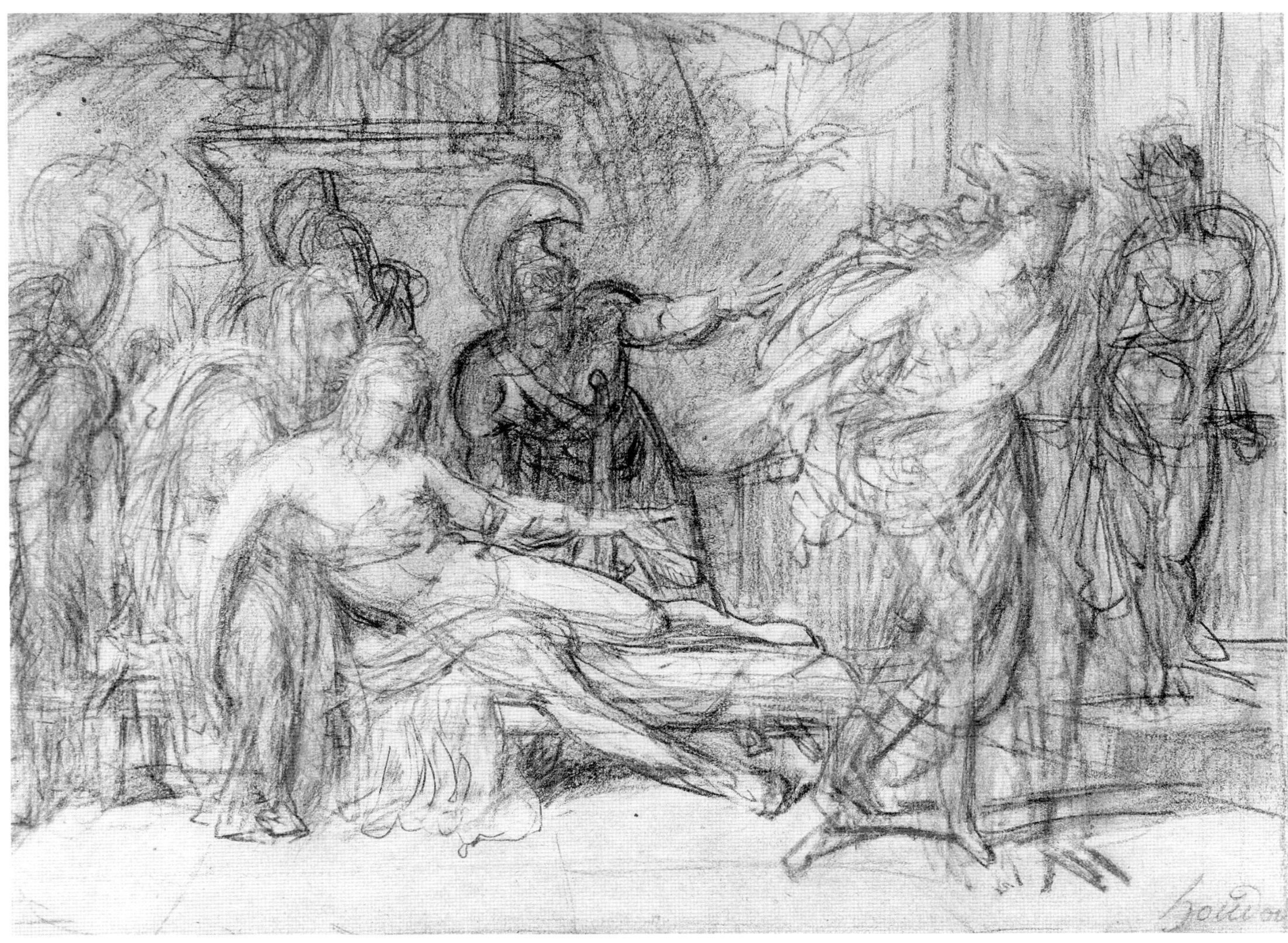

CATALOGUE NO. 78

The Oath of Brutus (present location unknown), executed with pen, brown wash, and body color, signed and dated 1818, which is very much like the chiaroscuro drawings of Forestier (see CATALOGUE NO. 76) in its dramatic contrasts of light and shadow (London 1975, nos. 118–19). Thomas and Forestier were students in Rome at the same time, when Géricault also made his trip to Italy at his own expense. All three artists were making chiaroscuro drawings at the same time and in the same place.

Rapidly executed compositional studies such as Thomas's sheet are fairly uncommon in comparison with the more widely known highly finished neoclassical drawings. Originally these spontaneously executed notations must have been commonplace, however, since this type of drawing has usually been an artist's initial step in planning a complex project. The Académie des Beaux-Arts, the body that awarded the Prix de Rome, customarily judged the works submitted to it on the basis of the correctness and expressiveness of the aspirant's command of anatomy, the harmony of the composition, and the skill with which the work was painted. That too-rigid insistence on these qualities could have stultifying consequences was recognized by Johann Joachim Winckelmann, who warned that "[the genius of the artist] is concealed beneath the industry and the polish required in a finished painting and a completed statue" (Winckelmann 1872, vol. 1, 144), a pitfall not entirely avoided by Thomas in his painting. The German writer praised sketches, whether modeled in clay or drawn on paper, exactly because they were the purest expression of an artist's thought, at this preliminary stage free from the encumbering discipline of technical execution. VC

Italian Drawings

Pompeo Girolamo Batoni

1708 Lucca–Rome 1787

BATONI BEGAN HIS CAREER as a goldsmith working with his father. In 1728 he moved to Rome, where he studied with Sebastiano Conca, Agostino Masucci, and Francesco Imperiali and copied the paintings of Raphael and works of classical antiquity. He was a friend of Johann Joachim Winckelmann and Cardinal Albani, and by 1740 his reputation was established as one of the most important painters in Rome. He was first acclaimed for his history paintings such as *Triumph of Venice*, 1737, and his large-format religious work such as the *Fall of Simon Magus* for Saint Peter's Basilica, 1746–55. In the 1750s, however, he became renowned for his portraits of wealthy foreigners visiting Rome on the Grand Tour. He had no shortage of clients and often depicted the tourists among the antiquities they had come to admire. He was responsible for the decorative schemes in the Villa Borghese, Palazzo Colonna, and Casino of Benedict XIV. He continued to paint until 1780, when his health began to fail. He partially recovered from a stroke in 1786 but died shortly after a second stroke the next year. LDM

Pompeo Girolamo Batoni
Male Nude Leaning on a Pedestal
1765

79
Black chalk on blue prepared laid paper
52.5 x 38.7 cm (20 11/16 x 15 1/4 in.)
Signed and dated at lower right in brown ink: *Pompeo Batoni 1765*
Philadelphia Museum of Art, Anthony Morris Clark Bequest (inv. no 1978-70-171)

PROVENANCE
Possibly David Allan, Edinburgh; sale, Edinburgh, February 6, 1797, lot 77.
Sale, Sotheby's, London, February 22, 1961, lot 10.
Marcello and Carlo Sestieri, Rome, 1961.
Anthony M. Clark.

EXHIBITED
Philadelphia 1980–81, 53, no. 42a.

LITERATURE
Clark/Bowron 1985, 376, no. D177.

Batoni's pedagogical activities included the directorship of the life-drawing class at the Accademia del Nudo at Rome in 1756, 1758, 1759, and 1762 (Clark/Bowron 1985, 20–21). The artist also conducted a private life-drawing class in his own studio one evening per week from November through April. Batoni's academy rivaled that of Anton Raphael Mengs in popularity for both Italian and foreign art students. Giuseppe Cades, Gaspare Landi, Johann Gottlieb Puhlmann, and Jean-Pierre Saint-Ours figured among his more illustrious pupils (Clark/Bowron 1985, 36–37).

The high degree of finish and virtuosity of execution suggest that the Philadelphia *Male Nude Leaning on a Pedestal* was intended to be copied by students. In Batoni's academy the pupils were assigned to copy the master's own academies and preparatory studies in addition to drawing the live nude model.

As observed by Bowron (Clark/Bowron 1985, 37), Batoni reworked his rapid, less precise sketches from life with subtly contoured cross-hatching to achieve the refined modeling of the musculature evident in these masterful late academies. There is a pendant to the present sheet, a *Male Nude Leaning on a Ladder*, also in the collection of the Philadelphia Museum of Art (inv. no. 1978-70-170; Philadelphia 1980–81, 53, no. 42b; Clark/Bowron 1985, 386, no. D176). RJC

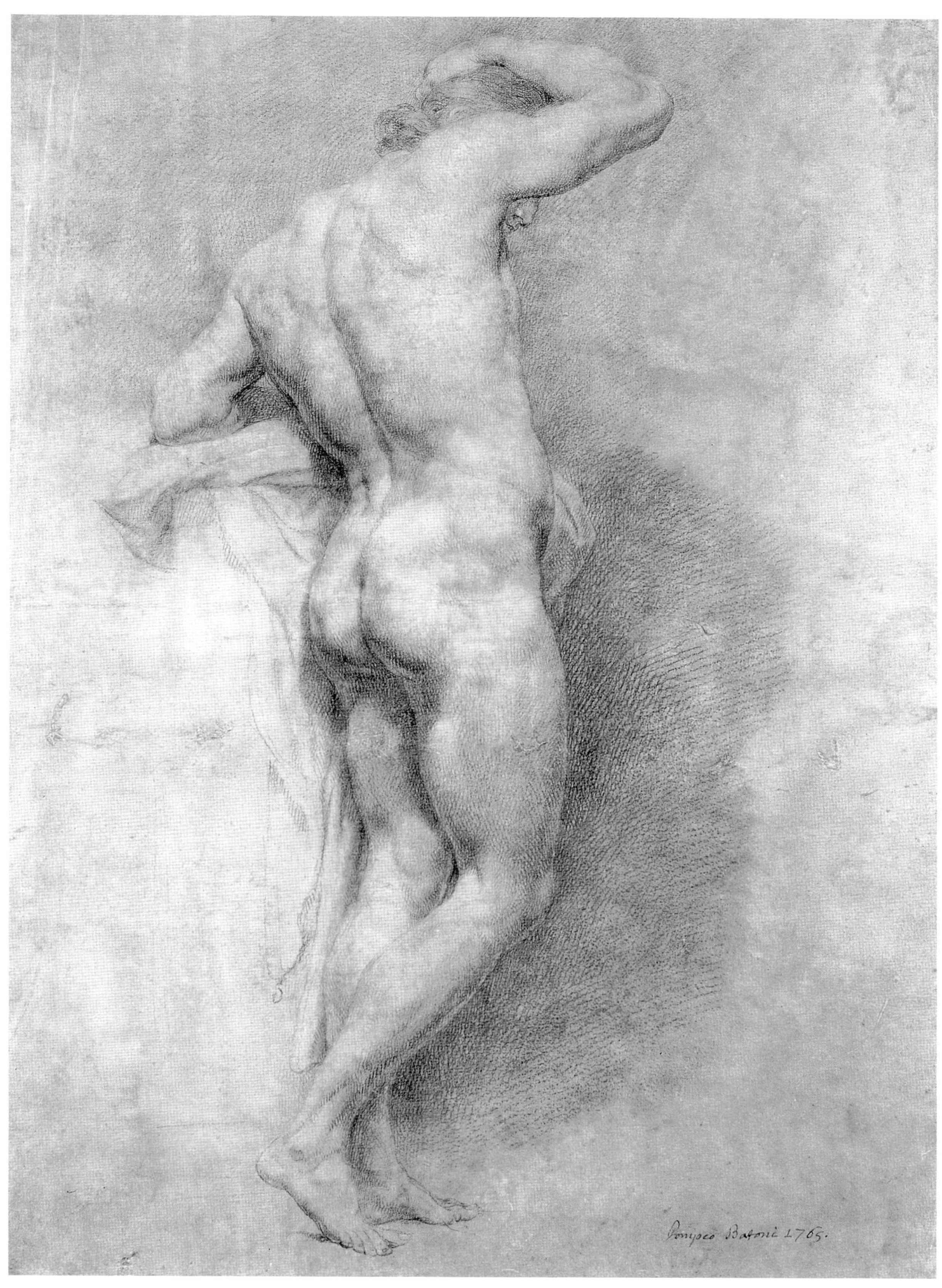

CATALOGUE NO. 79

Tommaso Maria Conca

1735 Gaeta–Rome 1822

CONCA WAS THE nephew and pupil of Sebastiano Conca. He arrived in Rome in 1760 and soon came under the influence of Anton Raphael Mengs. He became a member of the Accademia di San Luca and, like his uncle, an important decorative painter. Conca contributed mythological scenes and grisaille decoration to the Casino of the Villa Borghese and was acclaimed for his work in the Sala delle Muse of the Museo Pio-Clementino, 1782–87, and the dome of the cathedral of Città di Castello, 1789. Later in life he contributed to the decoration of the Palazzo del Quirinale. LDM

Tommaso Maria Conca
The Finding of Moses
c. 1810–20

80
Brush and brown wash, gouache on blue wove paper
35.4 x 49.7 cm (13 15/16 x 19 9/16 in.)
Inscribed at lower left in pencil:
Raff, Mengs 1728–1779
Philadelphia Museum of Art, Bequest of Anthony Morris Clark (inv. no. 1978-70-250)

PROVENANCE
Possibly Piancastelli.
Mary Brandegee (Lugt 1956 [supplément], no. 1860c).
Lucien Goldschmidt, New York, 1959.

EXHIBITED
Minneapolis 1967, no. 32.
Philadelphia 1980–81, 89–90, no. 78.

LITERATURE
Wood 1978, 4.

In this elegant wash drawing Conca depicts a theme from the Book of Exodus (2:1–10). Upon Pharaoh's command each Hebrew male child born in Egypt was to be cast into the Nile River. A son born to a Levite was sheltered for three months and then concealed in a basket and hidden in the reeds along the river bank, watched over from a distance by his sister. The child was retrieved from the river by Pharaoh's daughter, who adopted him as her son, whom she called Moses. The baby's sister came forward to ask if a Hebrew nurse should be sought for him; when the princess consented, Moses's own mother was hired to nurse him. Conca represents the moment when the infant is presented to the Egyptian princess as her handmaidens look on with delight. At the right of the composition the artist depicts Moses's young sister inquiring about a nurse. The figures are arranged in a frieze in the front of the picture plane; their expressions and gestures properly conform to academic precepts.

The Philadelphia drawing cannot be related to a painted commission. It is interesting to note that a drawing by Conca of *Moses and Joshua* (Deuteronomy 31), which appeared on the New York art market in 1978 (*The Burlington Magazine* 120, [May 1978]: lvi), was related to the artist's decorations for the Palazzo Doria in Rome. Conca collaborated with Stefano Pozzi, Domenico Corvi, and Luigi Agricola in this project in the late 1760s (Clark 1981, 132). The *Moses and Joshua*, which reflects the dual influence of Annibale Carracci and the artist's uncle and master, Sebastiano Conca, provides a fascinating comparison with the resolutely neoclassical *Finding of Moses*. A date of about 1810–20 has been suggested by Thomas William Sokolowski for the Philadelphia sheet (Philadelphia 1980–81, 89, no. 78).

The Egyptian statue that appears at the far left of Conca's composition is based on a plate from Giovanni Battista Piranesi's *Diverse maniere* (1767; pl. 45, decoration for the "Caffé degli Inglesi"). It also has affinities with the similar "Egyptian Revival" concoctions of Anton Raphael Mengs (Pelzel 1979, 101–3) and Felice Giani (see CATALOGUE NO. 91). The friezelike composition is also evocative of works by Giani, such as his pen, ink, and wash drawing *The Child Moses Trampling Pharaoh's Crown* (Faenza 1979, no. 11, fig. 11) and Bartolomeo Pinelli (see CATALOGUE NOS. 93–94). The bravura wash and gouache passages in Conca's drawing are technically comparable with sheets by French artists Jean-Jacques Lagrenée (see CATALOGUE NO. 25), Jean-Guillaume Moitte (see CATALOGUE NOS. 34–35), Henri-Joseph de Forestier (see CATALOGUE NO. 76), and Théodore Géricault (see FIGURE 19). RJC

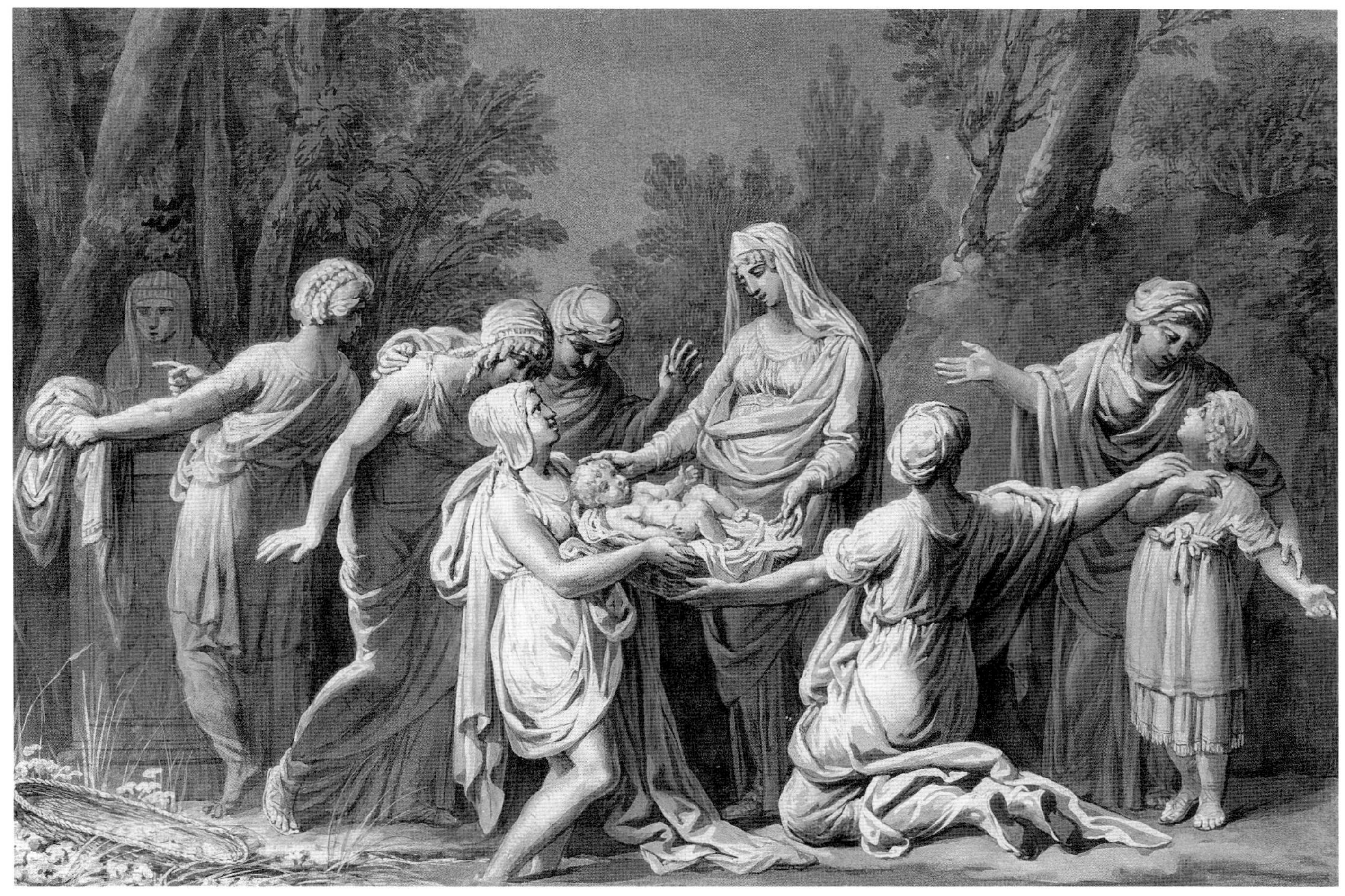

CATALOGUE NO. 80

Giuseppe Cades

1750 Rome 1799

EVEN AS A YOUNG PRODIGY Cades was self-reliant and controversial. His first teacher, Domenico Corvi, expelled him from his studio in 1766 for being too independent, the same year that he won first prize at the Accademia di San Luca for his *Tobias Recovering His Sight*. Two years later Cades sent an altarpiece to San Benedetto in Turin and by the age of twenty had received his first public commission in Rome.

In the 1770s Cades achieved a reputation as one of the best history painters in Rome, and by the end of the decade his studio was an important stop for foreign visitors. Cades was denied admission to the Accademia di San Luca until 1786, but this did not hinder his commissions from wealthy foreigners and the most important Roman families. He contributed to the decoration of the Palazzo Chigi in Ariccia, the palazzina of the Villa Borghese and the appartamento neoclassico in the Palazzo Altiere. Cades also completed religious works, including his *Birth of the Virgin*, 1784, for the choir of Santa Maria della Vigne in Genoa.

It has been said that Cades sold more drawings than any other Roman artist of his day, and these included both copies of and drawings done in the manner of the Renaissance masters. These drawings helped to augment his income, especially in his last years when the political events of the Roman Republic reduced the amount of foreign visitors and consequently his commissions. LDM

Giuseppe Cades
Armida Abducting the Sleeping Rinaldo
c. 1785

81
Black, white, yellow, orange, blue, and gray chalks on cream laid paper
31.3 x 44 cm (12 5/16 x 17 5/16 in.)
Philadelphia Museum of Art, the Henry P. McIlhenny Fund in memory of Frances P. McIlhenny, funds contributed by George Cheston, and funds from the sale of deaccessioned works (inv. no. 1990-49-1)
(Philadelphia only)

PROVENANCE
Private collection, England.
W. M. Brady and Company, Inc., New York.

EXHIBITED
New York 1990, no. 10.

LITERATURE
New York 1990.

Cades's drawing represents an episode from canto 19 of Torquato Tasso's epic poem, *Gerusalemme liberata* (Jerusalem delivered; 19.68), 1575. During the Crusades the beautiful sorceress Armida, ally of the Saracens, had seduced and enslaved warriors who were subsequently liberated by the heroic knight Rinaldo. The vengeful Armida stalked Rinaldo, planning to kill him. The knight was lured to an enchanted islet in the Orontes River and lulled to sleep by a water sprite. As Armida approached the sleeping Rinaldo, the seductress became seduced by the beauty of her victim. The sorceress then transferred the hero to her chariot and brought him to her magic island in the Atlantic (Tasso 1852, 434):

With bluebells, lilies, woodbines and wild roses,
That flower'd in thousands through those pleasant plains,
She next with admirable skill composes
Garlands, festoons, and odoriferous chains,
Which round his neck, and arms, and feet she strains
Tight yet tenderly; and o'er his eyes
While sleep her shadowy government maintains,
Bears upon tiptoe the imprison'd prize
To her enchanted car, and, mounting cuts the skies.

Cades has obviously embellished Tasso's text. Armida sits and observes the seminude, somnolent Rinaldo, who reclines on tasseled cushions, presumably in her "enchanted car." She is attended by a turbaned female figure, possibly the water sprite cited in the previous stanzas, who coyly gazes at her mistress. In the background Cades depicts an adolescent amor who has kindled Armida's passion for Rinaldo. This scene is not described in Tasso's poem, unlike the subject of a painting executed in 1784 by Angelica Kauffmann, who presented a literal interpretation of Armida preparing to bind Rinaldo with garlands (Buzzoni 1985, 373). In terms of iconography, the most plausible source for Cades's composition is a painting executed about 1620 by Alessandro Tiarini, *Rinaldo Abducted by Armida* (*Rinaldo rapito di Armida*; Galleria Borghese, Rome), in which Rinaldo reclines in the cushioned carriage of the chariot as Armida grasps reins in her left hand and gestures with her right to a female attendant who bears Rinaldo's helmet (Buzzoni 1985, 278; Guercino, Nicolas Poussin, and Simon Vouet also depicted the theme; see Lee 1967, 48–56, figs. 8, 11, 14).

Like his drawing *Bacchus and Ariadne* (see CATALOGUE NO. 82), Cades's *Armida Abducting the Sleeping Rinaldo* cannot be related to a specific commission. There exists a red-chalk drawing, *Rinaldo and Armida*, in the collection of the Crocker Art Museum, Sacramento, which Anthony Clark (Sacramento 1971, 25, 135, no. 94) speculated was somehow

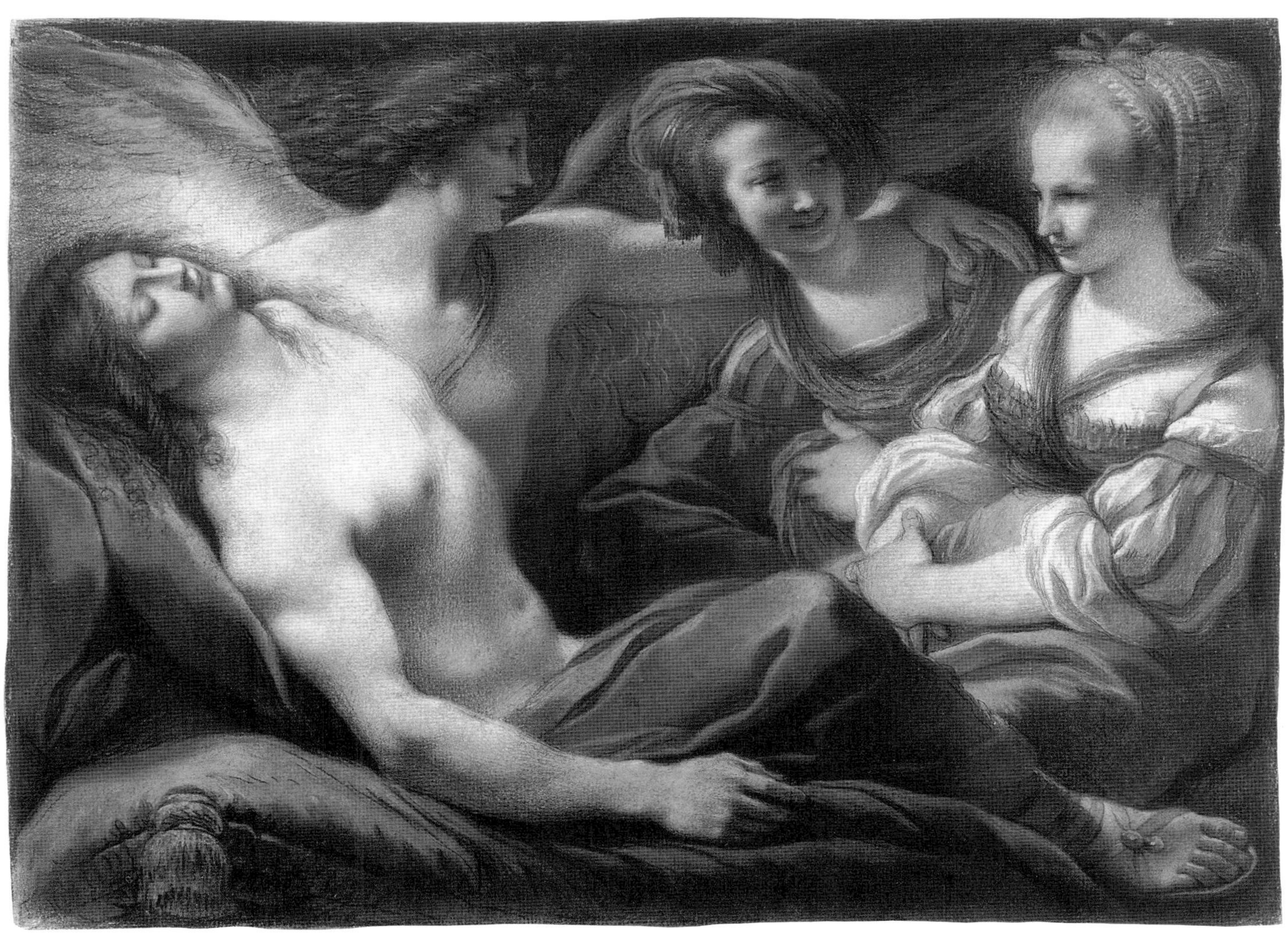

CATALOGUE NO. 81 (see color plate on page 109)

connected with Cades's painted decorations for the Palazzo Chigi in Ariccia, 1787–90, which included an *Orlando furioso* cycle (Caracciolo Arizzoli 1977, 246–65). Maria Teresa Caracciolo Arizzoli (New York 1990, no. 10) dates the Philadelphia drawing to about 1785. The high degree of finish manifest in the Philadelphia drawing, however, suggests that Cades intended it as a complete work of art, rather than a study.

While ancient precedents existed for Cades's composition—for example, a relief of *Diane* [Selene] *and Endymion*, now in the Louvre (Reinach 1897–1910, vol. 1, 63, no. 70)—the artist was clearly more influenced by seventeenth-century prototypes like Simon Vouet, Pietro da Cortona, and Guercino (Lee 1967, 50–51, figs. 8, 10, 14). The winged Amor may have been a concession to the current neoclassical taste. It is interesting to note that themes from Tasso's sixteenth-century epic poem remained popular with European artists despite the popularity of subjects from ancient history (see CATALOGUE NO. 25). RJC

Giuseppe Cades
Bacchus and Ariadne
c. 1785–90

82
Pen and black ink, brush and brown wash over black chalk on cream laid paper
34.5 x 44 cm (13 9/16 x 17 5/16 in.)
Inscribed at upper right in pencil: *89*
Philadelphia Museum of Art, Anthony Morris Clark Bequest, 1978-70-213

PROVENANCE
Walker's Gallery, London 1962.
Keith Andrews, Edinburgh.
Anthony M. Clark, New York.

EXHIBITED
Cleveland 1964, no. 99.
Minneapolis 1967, no. 18.
Bregenz/Vienna 1968–69, no. 132.
Minneapolis 1971, no. 13.
Philadelphia 1980–81, 82–83, no. 69.

Cades's *Bacchus and Ariadne* cannot be related to a commission for a painting. The artist, however, enjoyed renown as a prolific and brilliant draftsman, whose original compositions and drawings "in the style of" the old masters were eagerly sought by collectors and Grand Tourists. Anthony Clark speculated that "he sold more drawings than any other living Roman" (Clark 1981, 150–54). A vast quantity of his drawings were thus conceived as complete works of art (Philadelphia 1980–81, 5).

Here Cades depicts the discovery of Ariadne by Bacchus on the isle of Naxos. Ariadne, daughter of King Minos of Crete, had been abandoned by her beloved, Theseus, even though she had aided him against her father in his escape from the labyrinth after he had slain the Minotaur. In the narrative recounted with variations by Homer (*Odyssey* 11.275–334), Apollodorus (*Bibliothēkē*, "Epitome" 1.7), and Ovid (*Metamorphoses* 8.140–75; *Ars amatoria* 1.525–80; *Heroides* 10), Bacchus was immediately smitten by Ariadne and spirited her away to the isle of Lemnos and produced several children with her.

A Roman bas-relief depicting the encounter of Bacchus and Ariadne, subsequently brought to the Louvre (Reinach 1897–1910, vol. 1, 26, no. 148), was Cades's source of inspiration for the figure of the god with a putto hovering beneath his upraised right arm. As Caracciolo Arizzoli observed, however, the physiognomy and torso of Bacchus are derived from Annibale Carracci's painting of Bacchus and Ariadne in the Palazzo Farnese (Philadelphia 1980–81, 82–83).

Cades's conception of a seated versus a reclining Ariadne conforms to eighteenth-century versions of the theme, such as those by Pompeo Batoni and Angelica Kauffmann (Clark/Bowron 1985, no. 333, pl. 321; Clark 1981, fig. 62). He may also have been influenced by ancient prototypes of seated muses, such as Mnemosyne or Clio, for the pose of Bacchus's consort (Reinach 1897–1910, vol. 1, 256–57). RJC

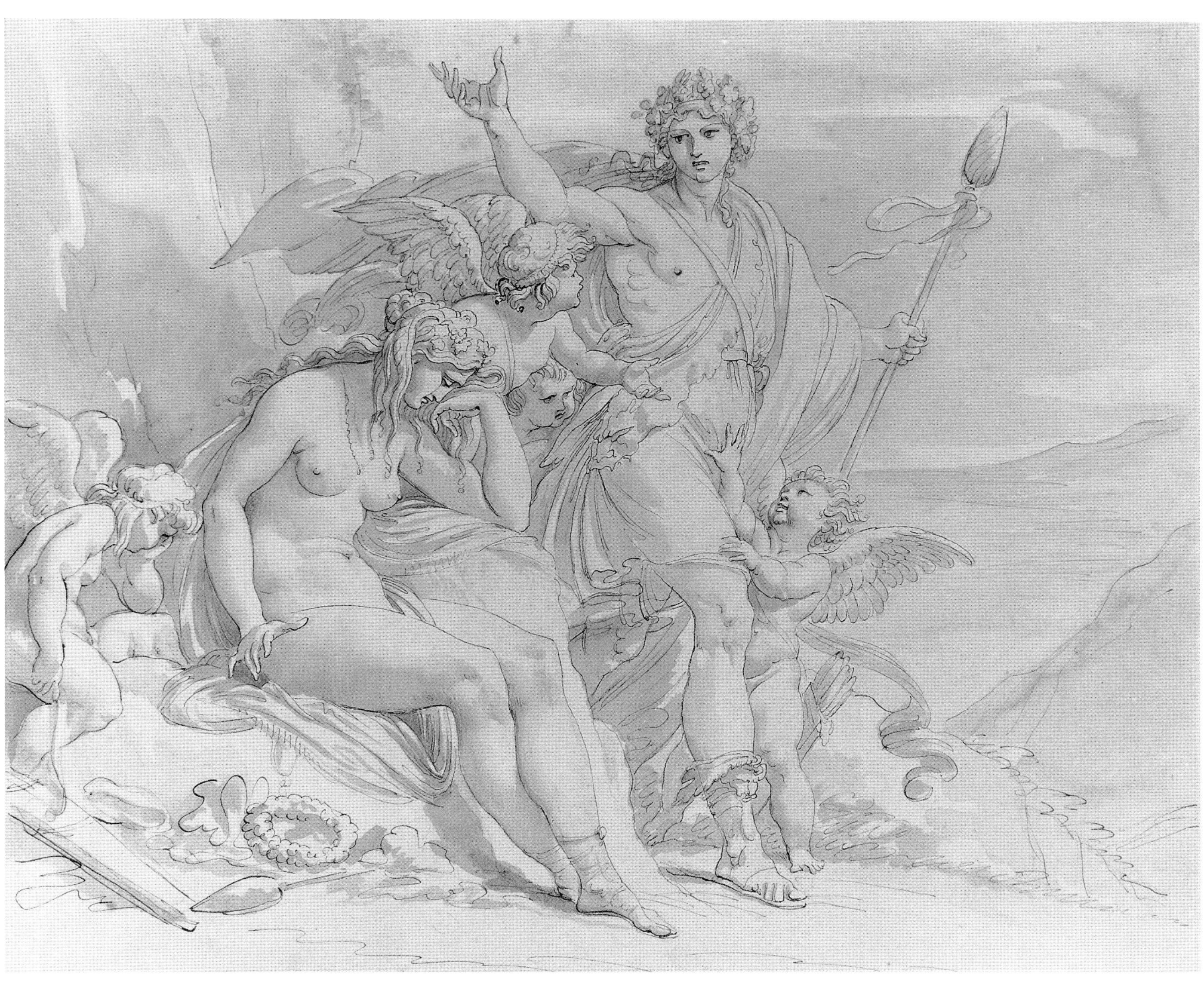

CATALOGUE NO. 82

Antonio Canova

1757 Possagno–Venice 1822

CANOVA BEGAN HIS CAREER in 1768 as an apprentice in the Possagno studio of Giuseppe Bernardi, called Il Torretti. Torretti soon moved Canova to his Venice studio, where the young artist was exposed to the collections of the city as well as to new patrons. Canova opened his own studio in 1775 and established his reputation in 1779 with the exhibition of his *Daedalus and Icarus*. The sale of this work enabled him to travel to Rome, where he settled permanently by 1780. There Canova met Gavin Hamilton and his circle of antiquarians and traveled to Herculaneum and Pompeii. His first great public commission was for the tomb of Pope Clement XIV; when it was unveiled in 1787 it brought him an international clientele.

Canova's success continued through the 1790s. He was elected to the Accademia di San Luca in 1800 and soon began to work for Napoleon, traveling to Paris to model the emperor in 1803. On his return he completed the tomb of Maria Christina in Vienna, which he had begun in 1798. He continued to produce works for the Bonaparte court and remained in favor after 1814. He acted as an agent for Pope Pius VII at the Congress of Paris in 1815, the same year he began work on his famous *Three Graces*, completed in 1817. Canova spent most of his time in Possagno after 1820 working on the "Tempio," a new church for the city. At the time of his death he was considered by virtue of an impressive 176 finished works the greatest contemporary sculptor in Europe. LDM

Antonio Canova
Female Nude Seated on the Ground, Clutching Her Knee

83
Black chalk on off-white laid paper
32.1 x 41.9 cm (12 5/8 x 16 1/2 in.)
Museo Civico di Bassano del Grappa (inv. no. A.22.22)
(Minneapolis only)

PROVENANCE
The artist.

EXHIBITED
Paris 1983, 34, no. 3.

LITERATURE
Bassi 1959, no. A.22.22.

A posed studio model is the subject of Canova's drawing of a female nude. The artist depicted the same model seated on a platform in a pen and ink study (inv. no. E.a.36.949; Bassi 1959, 110) and seen from behind on the left side of another sheet (see CATALOGUE NO. 88) from the same album, both in Bassano. The present study is not related to a specific sculpture or painting by Canova.

The Museo Civico at Bassano del Grappa is a major repository of approximately 1,800 drawings by Canova conserved in eighteen albums. Included in this corpus are male and female academies, copies after Graeco-Roman antiquities, studies of draped figures, sketches for Canova's executed statuary, tombs, and monuments, and formal and informal portraits. The drawings were bequeathed to the museum by the artist's half-brother, G. B. Sartori-Canova (Bassi 1959, 15–20). RJC

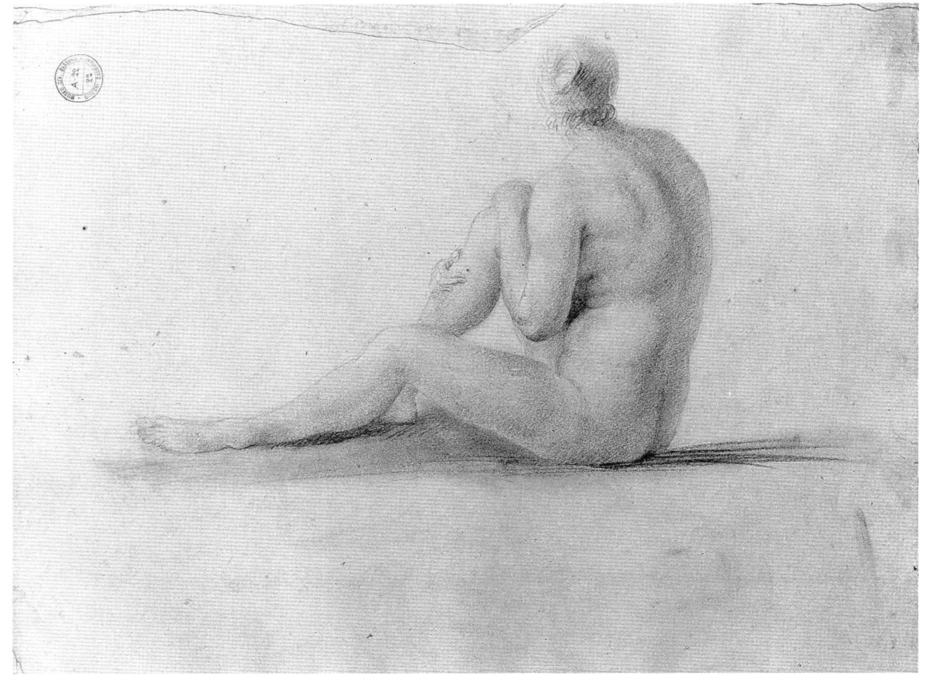

CATALOGUE NO. 83

Antonio Canova
Male Nude with Sword and Shield
1794

84
Graphite, pen, and brown ink on cream laid paper
Watermark: *H. BLAU*
46 x 32 cm (18 1/8 x 12 5/8 in.)
Inscribed at upper left in pen and brown ink: *No. 48.*; at lower right in pencil: *27 Xbre 1794*
Museo Civico di Bassano del Grappa (inv. no. D.I.48.617)
(Minneapolis only)

PROVENANCE
The artist.

EXHIBITED
Paris 1983, 78, no. 84.

LITERATURE
Bassi 1959, no. D.I.48.617.

Canova's study of a male nude armed with a Roman *gladius* (sword) and *clipeatus* (shield) was drawn from a live studio model on October 27, 1794. The aggressive pose derives from ancient prototypes, for example, the Naples Gladiator (Reinach 1897–1910, vol. 1, 530) and the Borghese Gladiator (Haskell/Penny 1981, 221–24, no. 43, fig. 115). Canova maintained albums of his academic studies for reference in future projects. The pose of the model in the Bassano sheet was adapted for the figure of Socrates in Canova's bas-relief *Socrates Rescuing Alcibiades at the Battle of Potidea,* executed in 1797. The relief was presented by the artist to the Accademia di San Luca (Licht 1983, 256, 259, fig. 267).

In its brutally expressive power Canova's study transcends the typical academic exercise and can be viewed as protoromantic in conception. The artist's bold, layered, staccato strokes of pen and ink hatching evoke the graphic technique of Henry Fuseli's figure studies (see, for example, Schiff 1973, vol. 2, 203, no. 793, and a corpus of figures from the recently auctioned Moore Album [Christie's, London, April 14, 1992, lots 43, 45, 46]). RJC

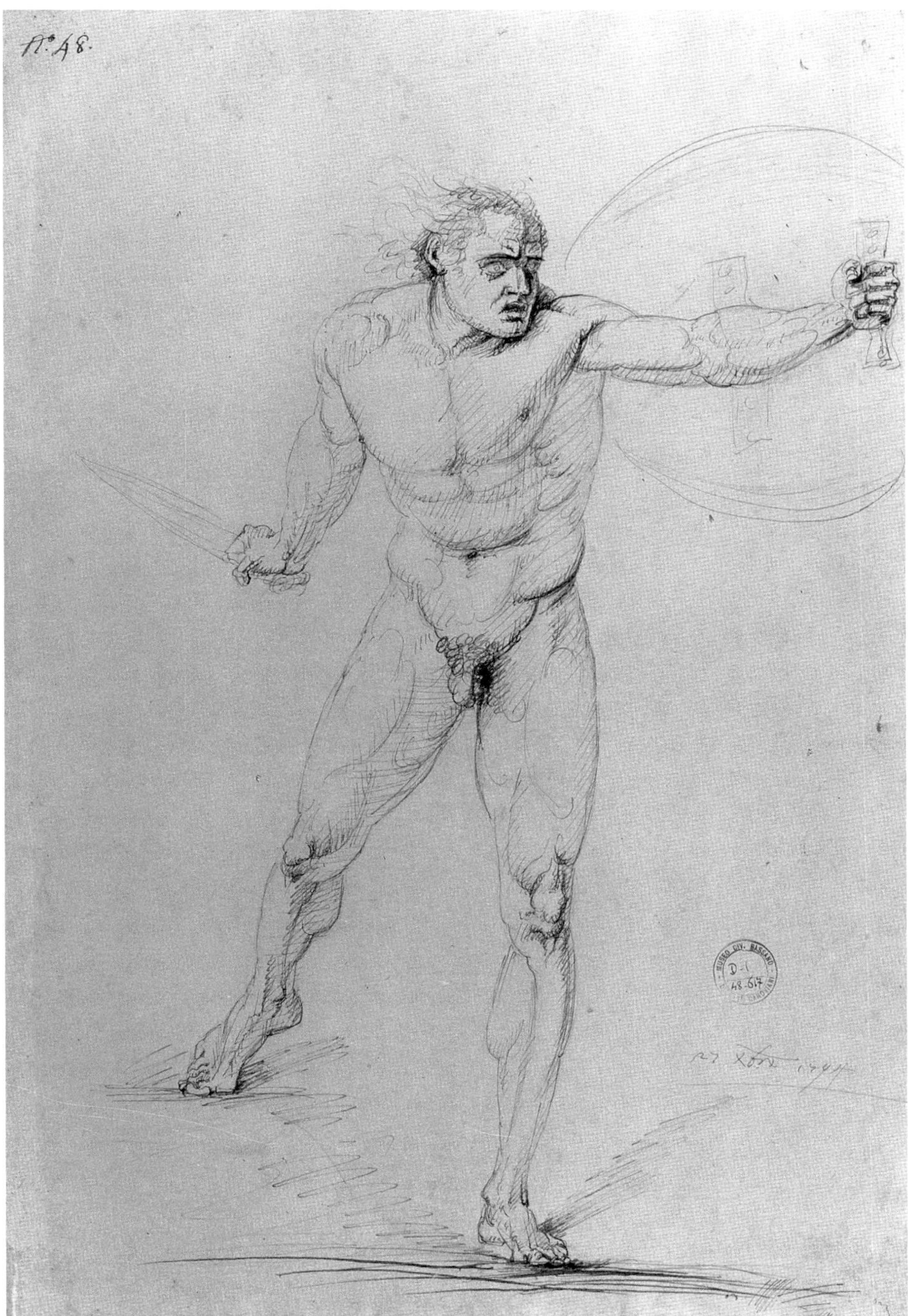

CATALOGUE NO. 84

Antonio Canova
Male Nude (Pointing Rightward), with Sketches of Another Male Nude (Leaning on a Staff) and a Dancing Faun
1807

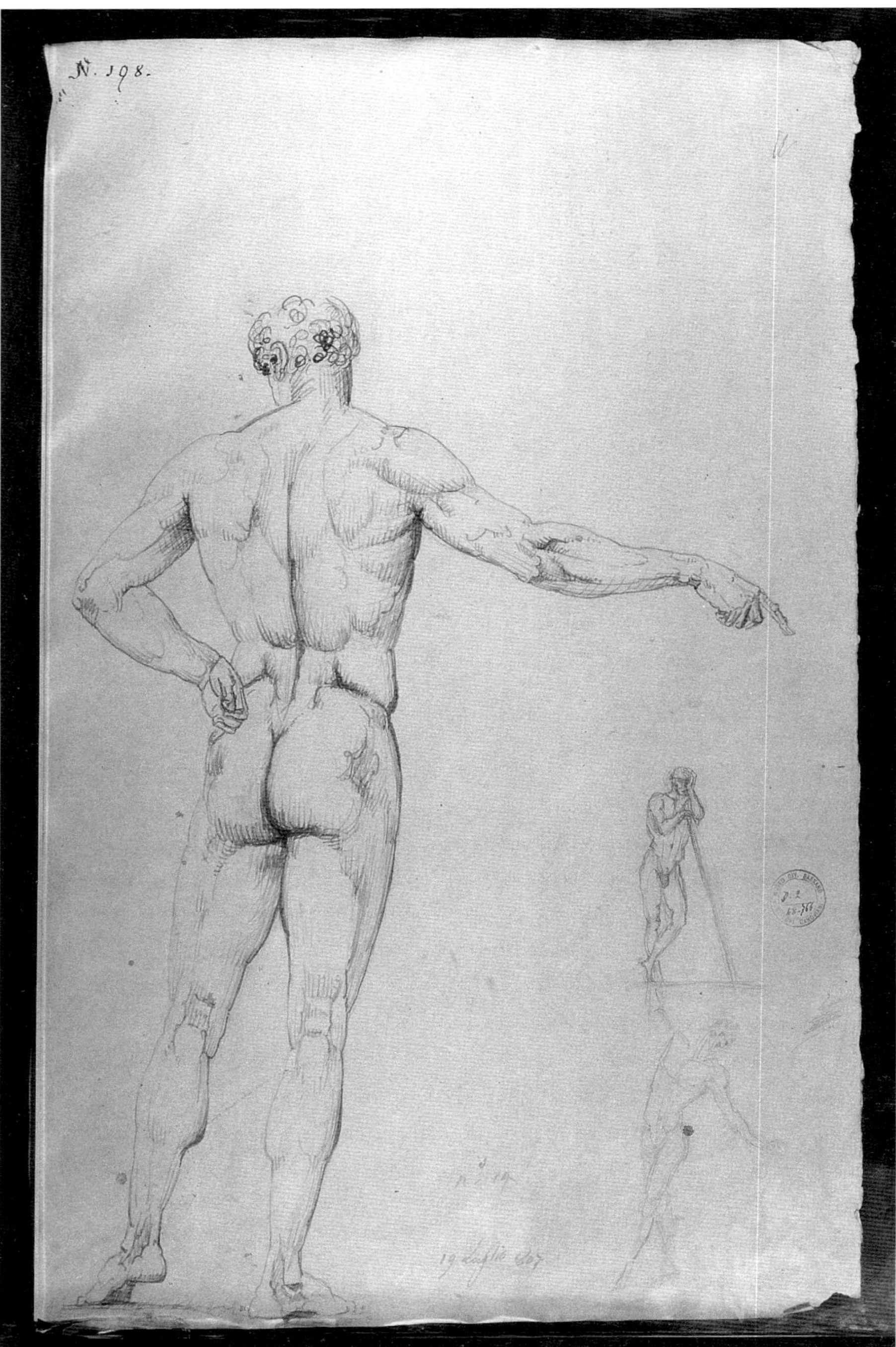

CATALOGUE NO. 85

85
Black chalk, pen, and brown ink on white laid paper
53 x 34.4 cm (20 7/8 x 13 9/16 in.)
Inscribed at upper left in pen and brown ink: *N. 198.*; at bottom center in graphite: *n°. 14/19 Luglio 807*
Museo Civico di Bassano del Grappa (inv. no. D.2.48.766)
(Philadelphia only)

PROVENANCE
The artist.

EXHIBITED
Paris 1983, 87, no. 98.

LITERATURE
Bassi 1959, no. D.2.48.766.

Canova's study and sketches of three male nudes were executed after a live model on July 19, 1807. The poses of the drawings on the sheet, however, were inspired by Graeco-Roman statuary. The large figure on the left is a variation of a Faun, with hand on hip and left foot extended, that is now at the Glyptothek, Munich (Reinach 1897–1910, vol. 1, 398, no. 1727). The sketch of the figure in the lower right corner of the sheet derives from poses of Dancing Fauns in Paris and Naples (Reinach 1897–1910, vol. 1, 407–8, nos. 1715a, 1715d; Haskell/Penny 1981, 208, no. 35, fig. 107); Canova visited the latter city in 1807. The pose of the small figure above the dancing nude is based on that of an Endymion leaning on a staff with legs crossed on a relief now at the Musée du Louvre, Paris (Reinach 1897–1910, vol. 1, 61, no. 73).

It was not uncommon for Canova to have his models pose in imitation of ancient sculptures. There exists at the Museo Civico, Bassano, a study of a live model in the stance of the Borghese Gladiator (Haskell/Penny 1981, 221–24, no. 43, fig. 115), dated November 30, 1797, on which Canova inscribed: "This is Giacomo de Rossi and not the gladiator." Rossi repeatedly served as a model for Canova (Bassi 1959, 77, no. D.1.42.611; Honour 1968, 116). RJC

Antonio Canova
Male Nude (Raised Fist)
c. 1794–1801

86
Charcoal and white chalk on cream laid paper
Watermark: Three circles (fragment)
56.5 x 40.1 cm (22 1/4 x 15 3/4 in.)
Museo Civico di Bassano del Grappa (inv. no. E.39.908)
(Los Angeles only)

PROVENANCE
The artist.

EXHIBITED
Paris 1983, 102, no. 120b.

LITERATURE
Bassi 1959, no. E.39.908.

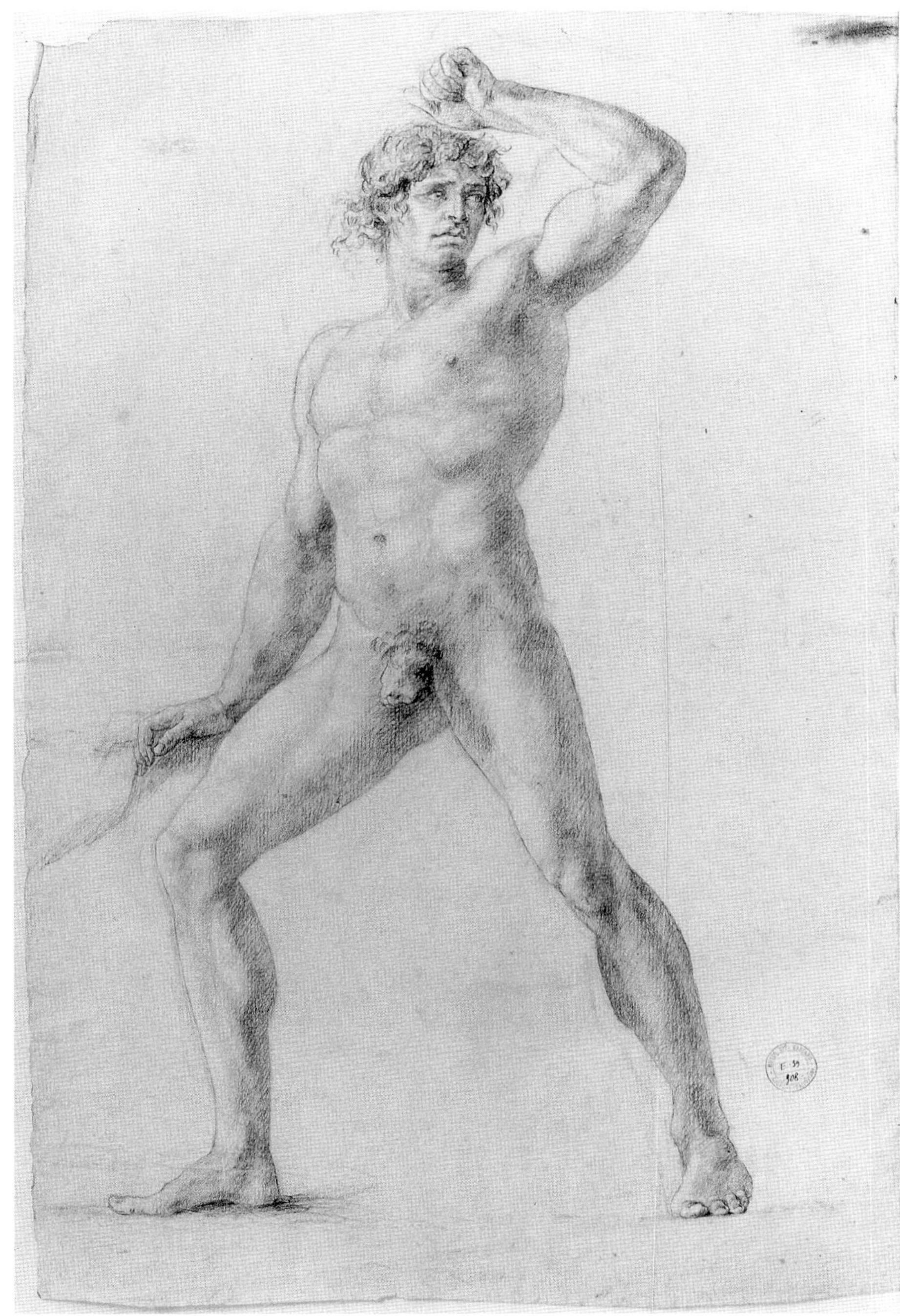

CATALOGUE NO. 86

Canova's vigorous male nude academy can be related to his marble sculpture of the ancient pugilist Creugas (Musei Vaticani, Rome), executed between 1795 and 1801. Its pendant, *Damoxenos*, completed in 1806, is also in the collection of the Vatican (Licht 1983, 187). Following the critical successes of his *Theseus and the Minotaur*, the papal tombs, and *Cupid and Psyche*, Canova tried his hand at a brutal subject—a fight to the death at the Nemean Games. After boxing to a draw, Creugas and Damoxenos were given the opportunity to strike one blow each to establish the victor of the contest. After being struck on the head by Creugas, Damoxenos penetrated the abdomen of his opponent with a thrust of his hand and pulled out his entrails (the story is told in Pausanias, *Description of Greece* 8.40).

Canova rendered six additional full-length studies of pugilists, and there also exist four sheets with multiple sketches including pugilists, all of these drawings executed between 1794 and 1807 (Bassi 1959, 75–76, 78–79, 86, 89, 91–92, 94, 129, 179, 206). Damoxenos had demanded that Creugas raise his arm prior to his dealing the fatal blow, and Canova's studies for *Creugas* typically show the pugilist with his left arm raised (Bassi 1959, 76, 598, nos. D.1.29, D.1.53.622). As noted by Licht (1983, 187), Canova was influenced by the Tyrannicides (Museo Archeologico Nazionale, Naples; Franciscis n.d., 7) as ancient prototypes for his Creugas and Damoxenos. RJC

Antonio Canova
Sketch of Two Female Dancers
c. 1797–99

87
Black chalk on cream laid paper
Watermark: Coat of arms with three beehives
19.7 x 12.8 cm (7 3/4 x 5 in.)
Inscribed at upper left in black chalk: *17*; at upper right: *14*
Museo Civico di Bassano del Grappa (inv. no. F.8.19.1741)
(Philadelphia only)

PROVENANCE
The artist.

EXHIBITED
Florence 1952, no. 8.
Copenhagen 1969, no. 110.
Paris 1983, 152, no. 211.

LITERATURE
Bassi 1959, 269, no. F.8.19.1741.

Canova's charming, vibrant sketch is related to a bas-relief, *Venus and the Graces Dancing before Mars* (Gipsoteca, Possagno), executed in 1797 (Bassi 1943, 50). The composition was duplicated by Canova about 1799 in a dark-ground tempera painting of the same title (Casa Canova, Possagno; Bassi 1972, fig. 98).

In both works two Graces crown Venus in an elegant ballet performed before the enthroned god of war to the tune of the third Grace, who plays the lyre. Roman wall painting was the ancient source for Canova's dancers (Antichità di Ercolano 1755–92, vol. 1, 95, pl. XVII). There exist in the Bassano collection six additional sketches and four grisailles that relate to the Possagno relief and painting (Bassi 1959, 111, 266, 271, nos. E.a.42.955, F.8.3.1725, .1731, .1737, .1747, .1764, .1765, .1785; monocrimi nos. 10, 12–14).
RJC

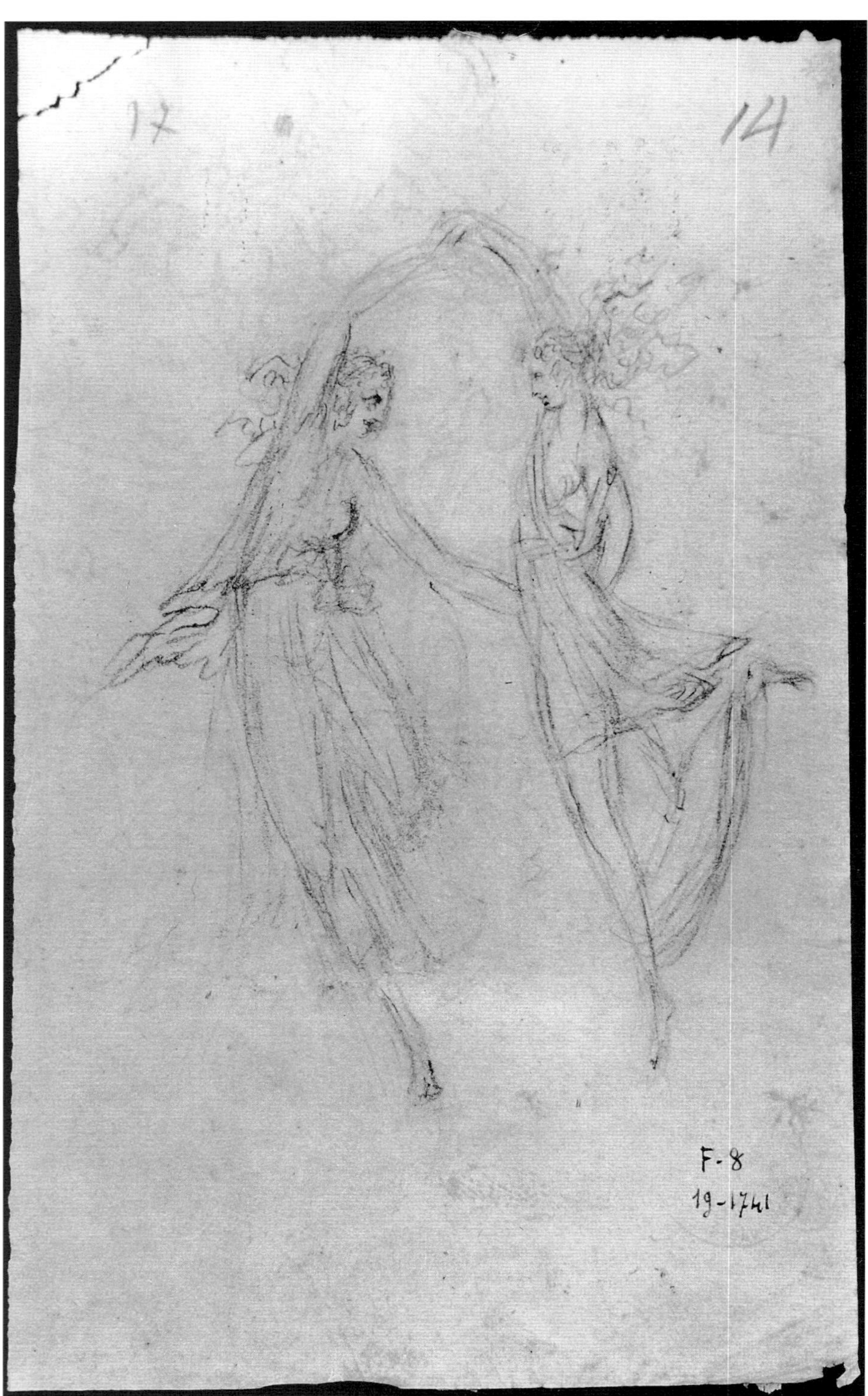

CATALOGUE NO. 87

Antonio Canova

Two Female Nudes, One Seated and Seen from Behind; One Standing in Right Profile with Arms Crossed over Her Chest

Before 1804–12

88

Black chalk on off-white laid paper

46 x 35.8 cm (18 1/8 x 14 1/16 in.)

Museo Civico di Bassano del Grappa (inv. no. A.9.9)

(Los Angeles only)

PROVENANCE

The artist.

LITERATURE

Bassi 1959, 26–27, no. A.9.9.

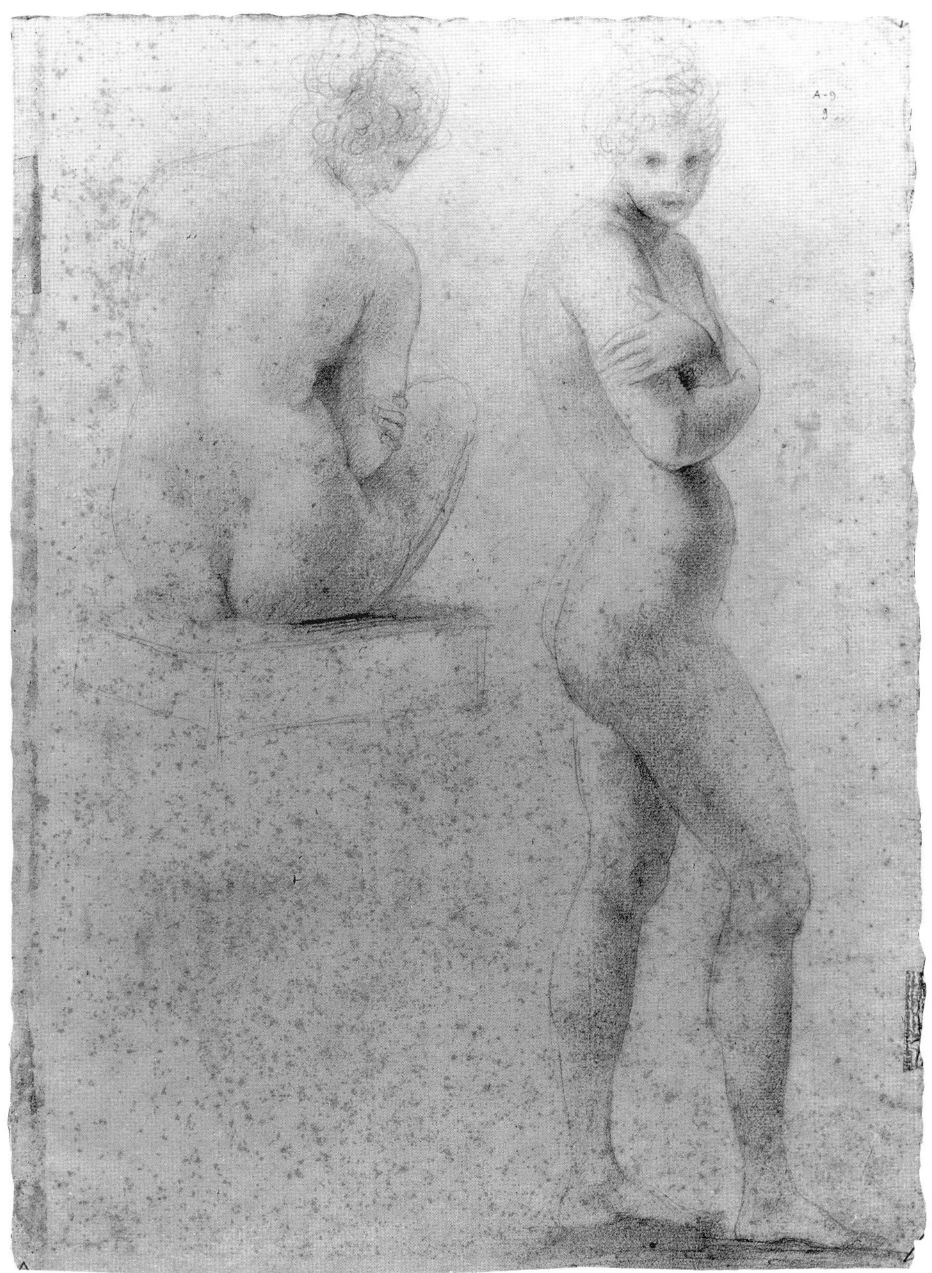

CATALOGUE NO. 88

The female nude studies on the Bassano sheet were drawn from the live model. The standing figure, with arms clasped around her breasts and right foot extended, anticipates the pose of Canova's *Venus Italica* (Galleria Pallatina, Florence), executed 1804–12, for the grand duke of Tuscany. Originally, the duke had commissioned Canova to execute a copy of the Graeco-Roman Medici Venus, which the French had seized from the Uffizi (Honour 1972a, 658–70; see also Bassi 1959, 26; Pavanello/Praz 1976, no. 168; and Licht 1983, 190–93).

There exist several other female nude studies in Canova's so-called Album A in Bassano with figures in similar poses (Bassi 1959, 27, 29, nos. A.1.1, A.8.8, A.16.16). Stylistically and technically, the handling of Canova's chalk studies resemble those of Pierre-Paul Prud'hon, although the elongated proportions of the figures anticipate Jean-Auguste-Dominique Ingres (see CATALOGUE NO. 75).

Canova maintained a repertory of academic studies for future reference. In subsequent sketches, preserved in Albums E and F, Canova refined the pose of his *Venus Italica*, seen from various angles (Bassi 1959, 109, 158, 226, nos. E.a.34.947, E.b.163.1174, F.3.14.1522, F.3.17.1525).

Although it was formally inspired by the Medici Venus, Canova's *Venus Italica* was celebrated for its realistic carnal aspects that unquestionably derived from the sculptor's studies of the live nude model (Honour 1972a, 69–70). RJC

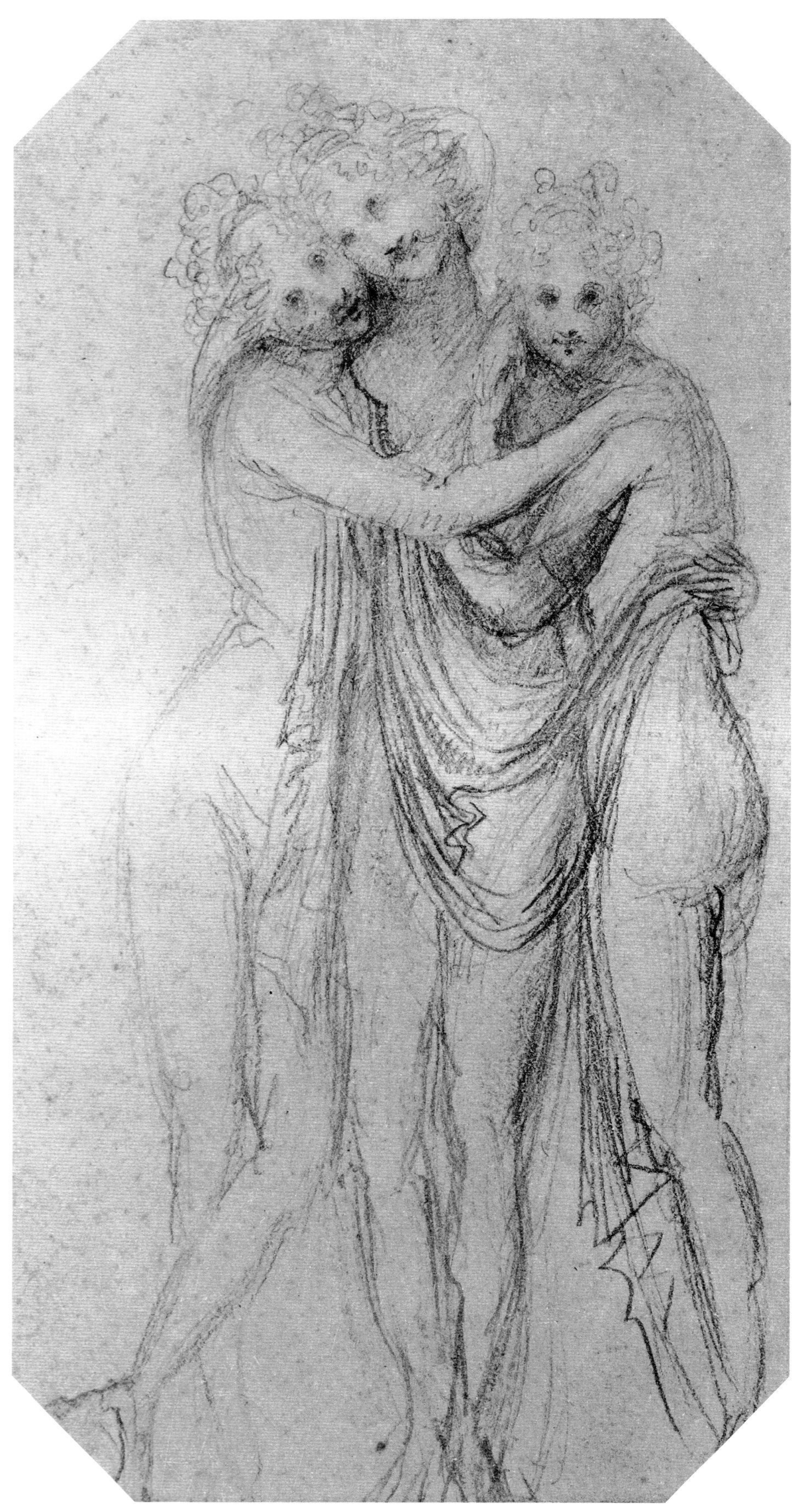

CATALOGUE NO. 89

Antonio Canova
Study for The Graces
Before 1815

89
Black chalk on white paper
20 x 11.1 cm (7 7/8 x 4 3/8 in.)
Biblioteca Correr, Venice (inv. no. 74, no. 7)
(Philadelphia and Minneapolis only)

PROVENANCE
Bartolomeo Gamba.

EXHIBITED
Venice 1978, no. 141.
New York 1985b, 128, no. 105.
Venice 1985–86, no. 105.

LITERATURE
Pavanello/Praz 1976, no. 270(4).
Rigon 1982, no. 200.

The Museo Correr drawing is one of at least five preliminary sketches for Canova's marble masterpiece, *The Three Graces* (Hermitage Museum, Saint Petersburg), 1815–16, originally commissioned by Josephine Bonaparte (Pavanello/Praz 1976, no. 270; New York 1985b, 128). For a prospective sculptural project Canova would typically render several graphite sketches on paper, followed by a series of clay *bozzetti*—all executed with the utmost freedom—prior to the completion of the plaster cast. The final marble version would be executed only on commission by a patron (Honour 1972b, 146, 214).

As noted by Hugh Honour, Canova seemed to have adhered to Johann Joachim Winckelmann's maxim, "Sketch with fire and execute with phlegm" (Honour 1968, 101). On a single sheet in Bassano, Canova represents a pair of "first thoughts" for the theme. In the foreground group the right and central figures embrace as the head of the former tilts backward; the left figure, who stands cross-legged, looks away from her sisters. In the background group the faces of the right and central figure are aligned. Both groups are rendered in highly schematic shorthand (Bassi 1959, 244, no. F.5.25.1648; see also F.5.26.1649).

On a second sheet in the Museo Correr, Canova depicts the right Grace in right profile cut off at the shoulder; immediately above, the entire group is represented in miniature. Here, the left and central Graces embrace with faces aligned and with hands poised on heads; the right figure looks outward at the spectator; the group is united by the extended right arm of the figure on the left, which rests on the shoulder of her sister at the far right (New York 1985b, 129, no. 106).

In the present sheet Canova envelops the central Grace with the respective concave configuration of the poses of her sisters. The left elbow of the right figure bends to a more acute angle, akin to the final group in marble. In the sculpture, however, the Graces do not look out at the spectator. The bodies of the two outer figures are rotated inward in profile. Canova's sketching technique has strong, stylistic affinities with that of Pierre-Paul Prud'hon in, for example, the softness of modeling (*morbidezza*) with fine, diagonally hatched strokes and the schematic dots and dashes to suggest hollow eyes and delicate mouths and noses—all executed with a marvelous spontaneity (Bassi 1959, 25; for similar examples by Prud'hon see Guiffrey 1924, figs. 37, 858, 1012). (It should be noted that Canova had visited Paris in 1802 and 1810, when he may have seen Prud'hon's graphic style.)

Canova departed radically from ancient prototypes of the Graces, most notably the groups at the Vatican and in Siena, in which the sisters were represented frontally (Reinach 1897–1910, vol. 1, 340, 346). The Venice and Bassano sketches afford a fascinating perspective of the evolution of Canova's highly original conception of the theme. Importantly, as observed by Canova's early biographer, Antoine-Chrysostome Quatremère de Quincy, the infinitely subtle variety of forms, contours, and poses and the ingenious disposition of the figures were intended to convey the nuances of the ideal of grace in three aspects. In essence, Canova created a modern sculpture in the spirit rather than the letter of ancient art (Quatremère de Quincy 1834, 249–52; Licht 1983, 203–11). RJC

Felice Giani

❧

1758 San Sebastiano (Genoa)–Rome 1823

GIANI WORKED IN many Italian cities throughout his long career. He was trained by Carlo Bianchi and Antonio Galli Bibiena in Pavia and in 1778 moved to Bologna to study with Domenico Pedrini and Ubaldo Gandolfi. He spent the years between 1780 and 1786 in Rome studying with Pompeo Batoni, Giuseppe Antolini, and Christoph Unterberger at the Accademia di San Luca. During this time he won a prize for painting at the Accademia and a second prize from the Accademia di Belle Arti di Parma for his *Samson and Delilah*.

Giani established himself as an important decorative painter; he contributed to projects in Forlì, Venice, Ravenna, Ariccia, Bologna, Faenza, and Rome. He had an international clientele and worked for Catherine II of Russia in 1788 and in Paris for Napoleon at the Tuilleries and Malmaison in 1803. In 1805 he settled more or less permanently in Rome and contributed to the decoration of the Palazzo di Spagna in 1806 and the Palazzo Quirinale in 1812–13. He was elected a member of the Accademia di San Luca in 1811 and to the Congregazione dei Virtuosi of the Pantheon in 1819. His last large decorative project was the Teatro della Valle in Rome in 1821. LDM

Felice Giani
Iris Encourages Priam to Beg the Body of Hector from Achilles
1810–20

90
Pen and brown ink, brush and brown wash over black chalk on off-white wove paper
47 x 73.6 cm (18 1/2 x 29 in.)
Inscribed by the artist on the lower margin in pen and brown ink: *Iride consola Priamo*
Cooper-Hewitt, National Museum of Design, Smithsonian Institution, purchase, Friends of the Museum Fund (inv. no. 1901-39-600)
(Los Angeles only)

PROVENANCE
Giovanni Piancastelli, Rome.

EXHIBITED
London 1973b, 41, no. 94.
Faenza 1979, 75, no. 168, fig. 142.

Giani's drawing represents an episode from the concluding book of Homer's *Iliad* (24.169–80). After the Greek warrior Achilles had slain Hector in combat, he defiled his corpse by dragging it from a chariot around the walls of Troy for twelve days. At the behest of Zeus, Iris, messenger of the gods, instructs the grieving King Priam of Troy to go to Achilles and retrieve the body of his son. In Giani's composition Iris descends from her symbolic rainbow in billowing clouds before the startled Priam, who raises his arms in fright. In the left background the artist depicts Priam's daughters and daughters-in-law "wailing through the house, thinking of the many splendid men who had lost their lives at Argive hands and now lay dead." Iris simultaneously points upward to the heavens with her right hand and gestures with her left arm to the corpse of Hector, lying behind Achilles's chariot, visible in the background, through the portico of Priam's palace, beneath a moonlit sky. She thus delivers her message, "And I am sent to you by Zeus, who far off as he is, is much concerned on your behalf and pities you. The Olympian bids you ransom Prince Hector by taking presents to Achilles which will melt his heart" (Homer 1969, 441–42, book 24, lines 173–76). In the background Thetis, also at Zeus's command, informs her son Achilles that the gods are displeased with him and that he must release Hector's body for a ransom.

Giani turned to the standard repertory of ancient sculpted prototypes for his figures: Dacian or barbarian captives constitute the source for Priam, who is garbed in a cloak, pantaloons, and slippers; Iris's pose is derived from statues of Diana the Huntress, whose arm is upraised as she withdraws arrows from a quiver strapped on her back; and the poses of Priam's daughters are based on Roman bas-reliefs depicting scenes of mourning (Reinach 1897–1910, vol. 1, 518, 304–6, 48–49, respectively). Giani's composition is enlivened, however, by his characteristically rapid "shorthand" strokes in pen and ink and his bravura wash passages.

The Cooper-Hewitt drawing is a study for a gouache painting now in the Pinacoteca, Bologna (Faenza 1979, 75, no. 169; Milan 1992, 122, 292) that has been dated 1810–20. In the latter work Giani does not differentiate the bands of the rainbow, which merge into the cloud; he also adds a ewer and basin at the lower-right corner. RJC

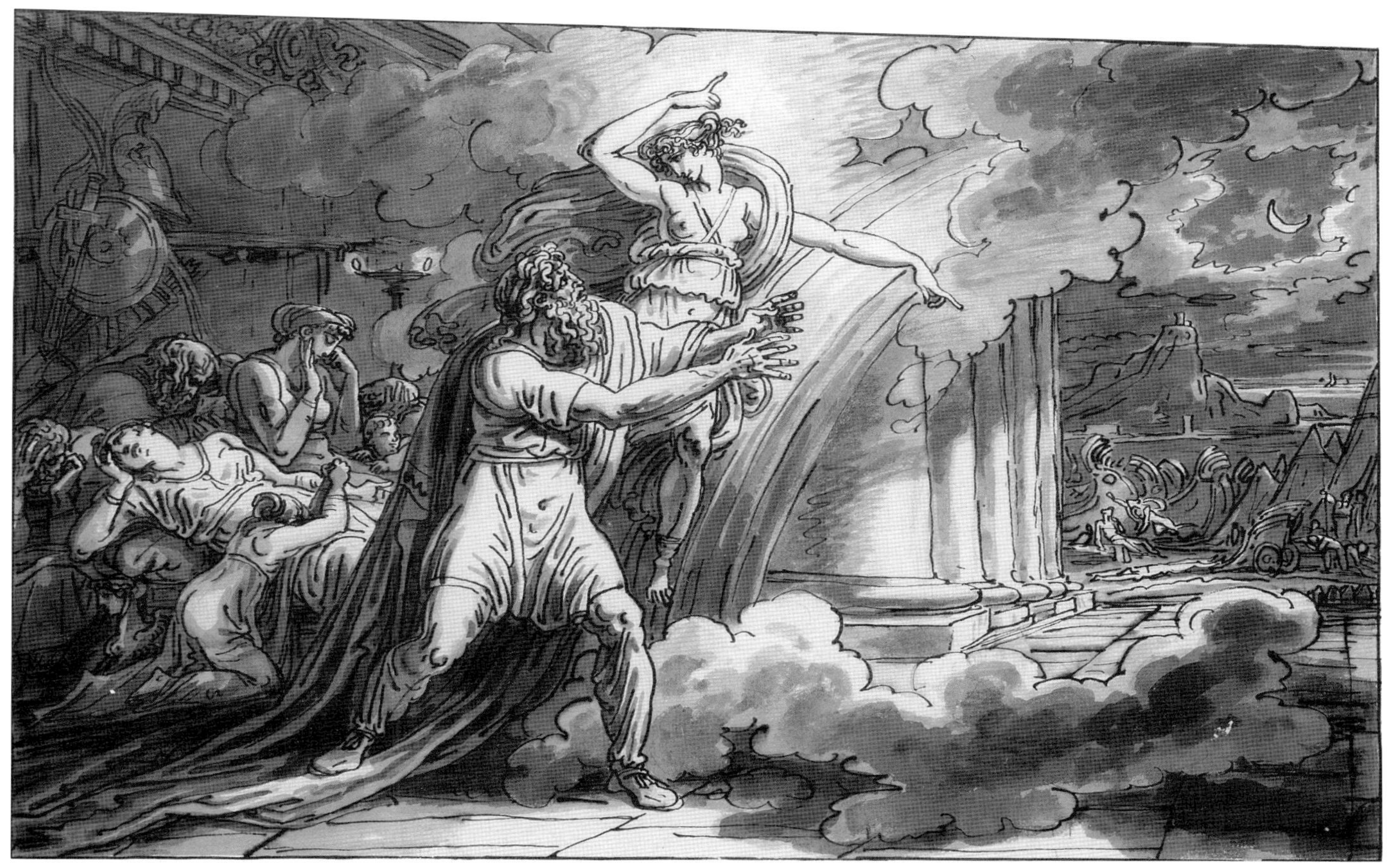

CATALOGUE NO. 90

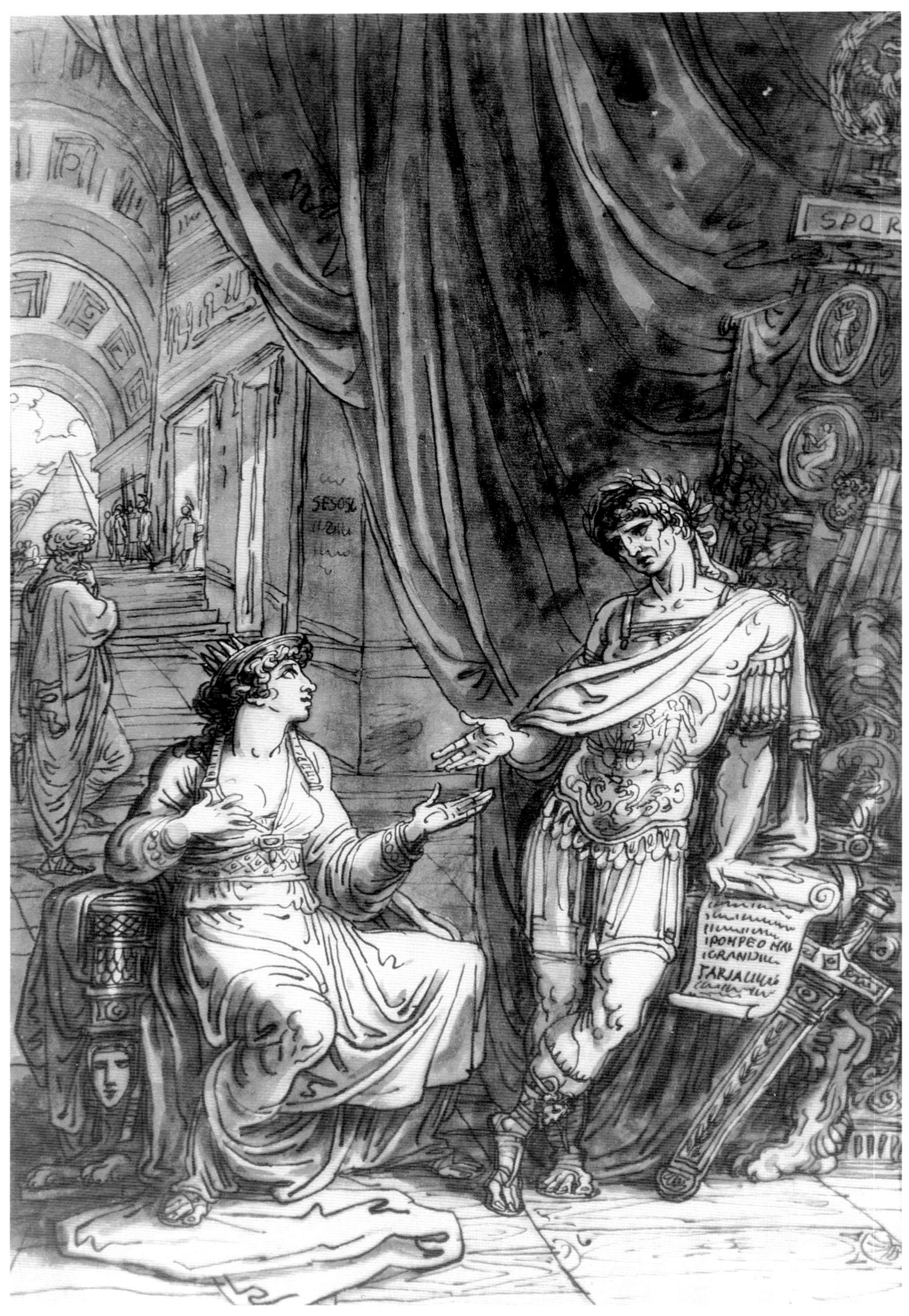

CATALOGUE NO. 91

Felice Giani
Cleopatra Pleading with Octavian

91
Pen and brown ink, brush and brown wash over black chalk on off-white laid paper
53.5 x 37.5 cm (21 1/16 x 14 3/4 in.)
Cooper-Hewitt, National Museum of Design, Smithsonian Institution, purchase, Friends of the Museum Fund (inv. no. 1901-39-1928)
(Philadelphia and Minneapolis only)

PROVENANCE
Giovanni Piancastelli, Rome.

EXHIBITED
London 1973b, 41, no. 93.

Giani depicts the first encounter between Cleopatra and Octavian, later the emperor Augustus Caesar, following the death of Marc Antony. The incident is recorded in book 51 of the *Roman History* of Cassius Dio. Cleopatra requested a meeting with Octavian to plead for pardon and to retain the crown of Egypt. To ingratiate herself with Octavian, she tucked into her bosom letters that she had received from his granduncle, Julius Caesar, which she presented to him, proclaiming: "You have heard people tell how [Caesar] honored me in various ways and made me queen of the Egyptians. That you may, however, learn something about me from him himself, take and read the letters which he wrote me with his own hand." Octavian remained impervious to her ploy, however, looked away and merely replied, "Be of good cheer, woman, and keep a stout heart; for you shall suffer no harm." Cleopatra feigned friendship for Octavian and his family but secretly resolved to commit suicide rather than be brought back to Rome for the victor's triumph (Dio 1914–27, vol. 6, 33–39; Volkmann/Cadoux 1958, 202–5).

In Giani's composition Octavian stands in front of a Roman eagle standard, fasces, helmet, and sword. He leans on an elaborately carved table upon which he has placed Caesar's correspondence and gestures at Cleopatra. The queen, seated upon a throne adorned with a sphinx, gazes imploringly at Octavian and extends her left palm in supplication. Octavian's freedman Epaphroditus intently observes the meeting from a distance. Assigned to guard Cleopatra, he appears to suspect her true motives.

Giani's Roman master, Pompeo Batoni, had painted a *Cleopatra before Augustus* (Musée des Beaux-Arts, Dijon) in the early 1760s, in which the queen is represented gesturing toward a bust of Julius Caesar, which, according to Cassius Dio, she had installed in her chamber; Batoni's source was an engraving after Hubert-François Gravelot published in Charles Rollin's *Histoire Romaine* (Clark/Bowron 1985, 287–88, no. 252, pl. 233). However, Giani was more probably influenced by Sebastiano Conca's *Cleopatra Offering Octavius Inventories of Her Treasures*, painted for Cardinal Acquaviva in the early 1720s (present location unknown; see Clark 1981, 4, pl. 5). Conca's painting is based on Plutarch's account of the encounter of Cleopatra and Octavian in his *Life of Antony*; the laurel-crowned Octavian is flanked by Roman legionaries bearing standards and by Epaphroditus with his hand raised to his chin in grave contemplation of the scene.

Giani turned to the Capitoline Augustus for Octavian's costume and to Trajanic reliefs for the other accoutrements (Reinach 1897–1910, vol. 1, 560). The drapery and pyramid are conventional props, while the sphinx-throne and the architecture with vaguely rendered hieroglyphic reliefs are products of his own invention. Anton Raphael Mengs had concocted similar Egyptian fantasies in his two painted versions of *Augustus and Cleopatra*, executed about 1759–60 (Pelzel 1979, 91–107).

The emphasis on staccato pen-and-ink line in combination with bold wash passages and a distinct formal shorthand typify Giani's protoromantic style of drawing.

The Cooper-Hewitt drawing does not relate to a specific painted commission. Like Giuseppe Cades and Bartolomeo Pinelli, Giani produced a vast corpus of drawings that were conceived as autonomous works of art. RJC

Pelagio Palagi

1775 Bologna–Turin 1860

PALAGI BEGAN HIS STUDIES under Andrea Appiani at the Accademia Clementina in Bologna. He relocated to Rome in 1806, worked with Felice Giani in 1812 on the decoration of Palazzo del Quirinale, Napoleon's residence in Rome, and in 1813 completed a fresco cycle of *The Exploits of Theseus* (*Le gesta di Teseo*) in the gallery of Palazzo Torlonia. He moved to Milan in 1818 and taught portraiture and history painting. Palagi was also an important designer and was called by King Carlo Alberto of Sardinia to supervise the decoration of the royal palaces in Turin in 1831 and direct the royal school of ornamental design of the Accademia Albertina. LDM

Pelagio Palagi
Medea Killing Jason's Children
c. 1810–15 (?)

92
Black, red, and white chalks, charcoal on white paper
157.7 x 116.9 cm (62 1/16 x 46 in.)
The Art Museum, Princeton University, museum purchase, Laura P. Hall Memorial Fund (inv. no. x1987-75)

PROVENANCE
Old Masters (Paintings and Sculptures) Ltd., London.

LITERATURE
Record of The Art Museum, Princeton University 87, no. 1 (1988): 35–36.

The Princeton cartoon cannot at present be related to a specific painted commission executed by Pelagio Palagi. The attribution is based on its stylistic affinities with a corpus of Palagi drawings conserved at the Biblioteca dell'Archiginnasio in Bologna (Matteucci 1974, 92), such as a charcoal and white-chalk *Tragic Scene* (*Scena tragica*; Bologna 1976, no. 70).[†] Moreover, the emphatic disposition of figures in the front plane corresponds to the compositional format of several paintings by Palagi, for example, *Marius at Minturnae*, 1809, which was exhibited at the Paris Salon of 1810 (Janson 1977, 77, no. 617).

The drawing probably dates from about 1810–15, when the artist was working in his purest neoclassical manner. In 1813 he painted a fresco cycle, *The Exploits of Theseus*, for the gallery in the Palazzo Torlonia (now destroyed; see Gregori 1973, 500, 503; Milan 1992, 274–75). A contemporary critic, Giuseppe Tambroni, claimed in 1816 that the *Theseus* cycle was "among the noblest and most impressive paintings ever done in this manner in our time." Significantly, Tambroni also observed, "The battle is depicted very ingeniously by the artist in such restricted space; and there are so many different types of men, ferocity and ways of violently injuring each other" (Tambroni 1816, 26–28).

In *Medea Killing Jason's Children* Palagi depicts an equally violent theme. Relative to the Torlonia commission, it is pertinent to note that Theseus was to be Medea's next victim after the slaughter of Jason's sons. Palagi's conception of the theme adheres to the text of the tragedy *Medea* by Seneca, who explicitly describes the murder, as opposed to the accounts by Euripides and Ovid.

After a decade of marriage to the enchantress Medea, Jason divorced his wife to wed Creusa, daughter of Creon, king of Corinth. Medea was to be exiled from Corinth and her sons raised by Creusa. In revenge, Medea destroyed Creusa and Creon with a poisoned, incendiary bridal gown conveyed as a gift by her sons, Mermerus and Phares. Medea next plotted to take revenge on Jason, for whom she had betrayed her father and brother to aid him in his escape with the Golden Fleece. Tormented by rage and guilt, Medea decided to slay Jason's beloved children. Haunted by the avenging furies and the shade of her brother, Medea struck down her first son and, carrying his body, led the other by the hand to the rooms above.

Jason arrives with troops and sees her: "Behold, there she is, leaning over a precipitous projection of the roof." She replies to his threats by showing him that one child "has met his fate already, and this one, in thy very own sight, shall receive a similar end." Jason pleads with Medea to spare the remaining boy and let him perish instead, but she strikes the child down, mounts her griffin-drawn chariot, and flies away to Athens (Seneca 1902, 456–68). Palagi depicts the poignant moment when Medea glances at

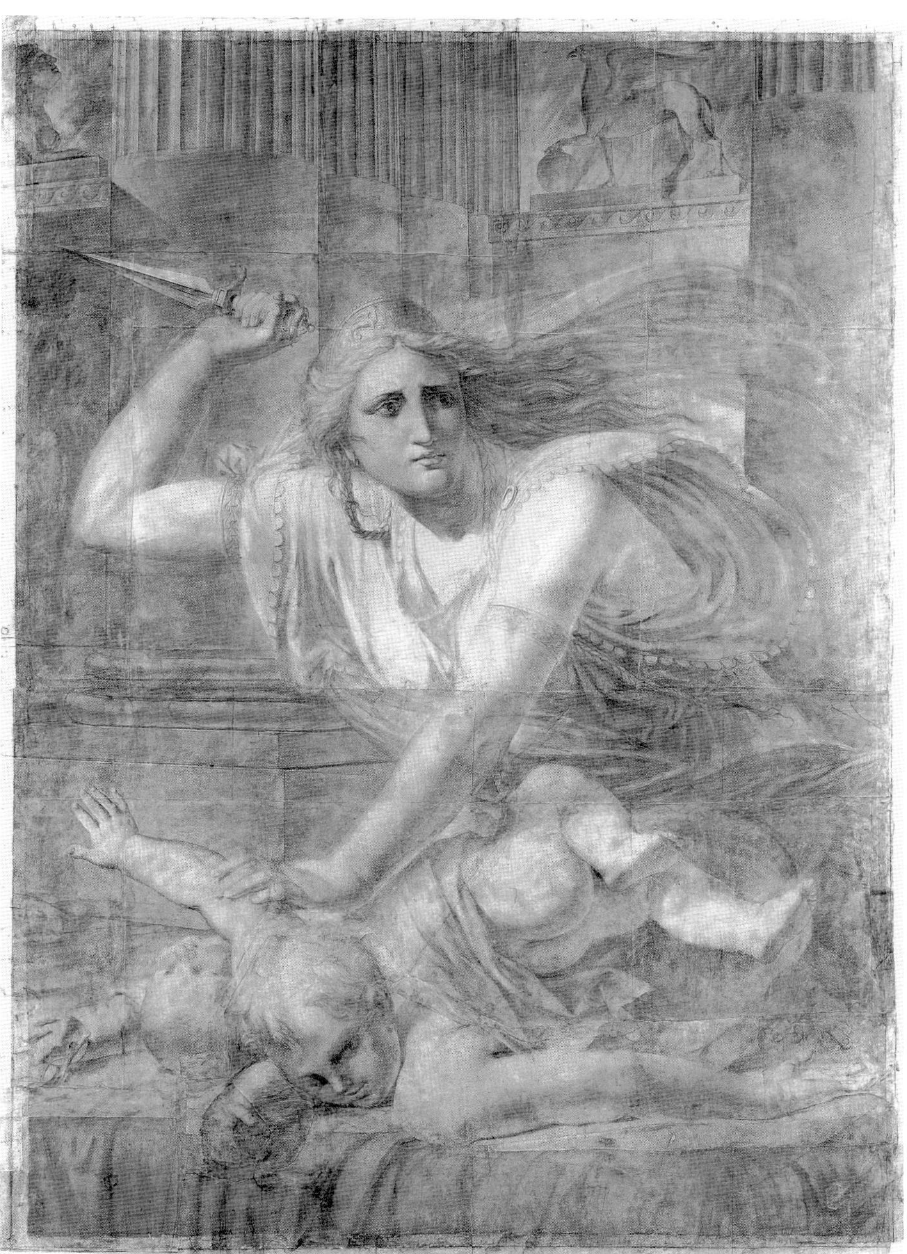

CATALOGUE NO. 92

Jason prior to stabbing their second son on the ledge atop the palace. Medea's expression subtly conveys both her bitterness and remorse.

The infanticide of Medea is not a common theme in European art. Interestingly, Gotthold Ephraim Lessing, in his treatise *Laocoön* discussed a depiction of the subject by the ancient Greek painter Timomachus (Lessing 1968, 18–19):

> *But from the descriptions we have . . . it is clear that he had rare skill in selecting that point which leads the observer to imagine crisis without actually showing it, and in uniting with this an appearance not so essentially transitory as to become offensive through the continuity conferred by art. He did not paint Medea actually murdering her children, but just before, when motherly love is still struggling with jealousy. We anticipate the result and tremble at the idea of soon seeing Medea in her unmitigated ferocity, our imagination far outstripping anything the painter could have shown us of that terrible moment.*

A copy of Timomachus's painting, discovered at Pompeii, exists in the Museo Archeologico Nazionale in Naples and was reproduced in *L'antichità di Ercolano* (pt. 1, vol. 13, 73). A second ancient prototype existed for Palagi: the *Vengeance of Medea* bas-relief, formerly at the Lateran, in which Medea similarly contemplated her sons, who appeared oblivious to her intentions (Bober/Rubinstein 1986, no. 110). It is evident, however, that Palagi chose to exploit the "neoclassic-horrific" aspects of the theme.

The Jason and Medea theme proliferated in French art toward the middle of the eighteenth century, probably attributable to the revival of Pierre Corneille's tragedy *Médée.* The painters Jean-Baptiste Pierre, Jean-François de Troy, and Carle Van Loo exhibited *Medea Stabbing Her Children* (*Médée poignarde ses enfants*), *The Story of Medea* (*Histoire de Médée*), a series of seven canvases, and *Mademoiselle Clairon as Medea* (*Mlle Clairon en Médée*) at the Salons of 1746, 1748, and 1759, respectively (Janson 1977, Salon of 1746, 15, no. 60; Salon of 1748, 25–26, nos. 1–7; Salon of 1759, 7, no. 7).

The violence and expression of Palagi's protoromantic *Medea Killing Jason's Children* eclipse the feeble efforts of his mid-eighteenth-century predecessors. This cartoon foreshadows his later work influenced by Felice Giani, which establishes him as a key transitional figure between neoclassicism and romanticism (Gregori 1973, 500; Olson 1990, 77–81). RJC

†My sincere thanks go to Dr. Renzo Grandi for sharing his opinion on the attribution of the drawing to Palagi, which he accepts with reservations, due to the lack of archival documentation. He questions the "hard execution" of the drawing but attests to the "high quality of the invention," which makes the attribution plausible (written communication, June 6, 1992).

Bartolomeo Pinelli

1781 Rome 1835

PINELLI PRODUCED PRINTS, drawings, oils, and terra-cottas. He was a pupil at the Accademia di San Luca, and his early work was influenced by Felice Giani and the Roman *veduta* painters. Pinelli was most famous for his numerous illustrations and genre scenes. His series of caricaturelike engravings called *Costumi romanae*, 1809, illustrated the views, customs, and costumes of the people of Rome and Naples. Because of their popularity with tourists, other editions of this type followed until 1828. He also created a series about a group of bandits, 1818–19, and their leader Massaroni, 1823, as well as *A History of Greece*, 1821, inspired by the writings of Winckelmann. Pinelli illustrated Italian editions of Virgil's *Aeneid*, 1811, Dante's *Divina Commedia*, 1825, Cervantes's *Don Quixote*, 1834, Fénelon's *Telemachus*, 1808, and a mythology. LDM

Bartolomeo Pinelli
Telemachus Consoled by Termosiris
1808

93
Pen and brown ink, brush and brown and gray washes over graphite on ivory laid paper
47.6 x 59 cm (18 3/4 x 23 1/4 in.)
Inscribed below the image in black ink: *Mentre Telemaco era immerso nella più cupa,/ viene consolato da Termosiri Sacerdote di Appollo.* (While Telemachus was sunk in despair, he was consoled by Termosiris, priest of Apollo)
Signed below the inscription in black ink: *Pinelli f. Romae*
The Art Institute of Chicago, Wirt D. Walker Fund (inv. no. 1963.564)
(Minneapolis only)

Bartolomeo Pinelli
The Dream of Telemachus
1808

94
Pen and brown ink, brush and brown and gray washes on ivory laid paper
45.8 x 57.9 cm (18 x 22 13/16 in.)
Inscribed below the image in black ink: *Sogno di Telemaco, mentre era trasportato nell/vascello dei Cipri.* (Dream of Telemachus, when he was transported in the ship of the Cypriots)
Signed below the inscription in black ink: *Pinelli f. Roma*
The Art Institute of Chicago, Wirt D. Walker Fund (inv. no. 1963.566)
(Philadelphia only)

Pinelli's drawings illustrate two scenes from the epic novel *Les Aventures de Télémaque* (*The adventures of Telemachus*), 1699, by François de Salignac de La Mothe-Fénelon. This book was composed in imitation of Homer's *Odyssey* and proved to be a major source of themes for European artists, from Angelica Kauffmann and Jacques-Louis-Michel Grandin to Michele Sangiorgi (Janson 1977, Salon of 1806, 42, no. 230; Faenza 1979, no. 259, fig. 225; Clark 1981, 165–66).

The Art Institute of Chicago owns twelve drawings in the Telemachus series, which was executed in Rome in 1808 (Cleveland 1964, no. 165). *Telemachus Consoled by Termosiris* is taken from book 2 of the novel. En route to the city of Tyre in search of his father, Ulysses, Telemachus was seized by Egyptians, who enslaved him and dispatched him to the desert of Oasis to tend flocks. The gods communicated to the disconsolate Telemachus that he would one day be a great ruler but that he must first acquire patience and wisdom. Toward this end, Termosiris, priest of Apollo, approached Telemachus in a forest, consoled him, and presented him with books to help him pass the time in captivity (Fénelon 1805, 28–29).

Pinelli was highly attentive to Fénelon's text in his faithful rendering of the sylvan setting and his portrayal of Termosiris as a man of majestic stature, with bald head and long white beard and bearing a scroll. The figure derives from ancient prototypes of philosophers portrayed clutching scrolls (Reinach 1897–1910, vol. 1, 512). The figure of Telemachus is based on statues of Paris as Shepherd, standing with legs crossed and holding a staff (Reinach 1897–1910, vol. 1, 502–3, nos. 2077a, 2081b).

The second drawing, *The Dream of Telemachus*, represents a scene from book 4, as Telemachus was recounting for Calypso his sea voyage to Cyprus. During the trip Telemachus was overcome by sleep. In his dream Venus descended from the clouds in her dove-drawn chariot and beckoned Telemachus to her sacred island, where he would bask in pleasure and burn perfume as a sacrifice on her altars. Cupid appeared in the chariot and shot an arrow at the somnolent youth, but Minerva, Telemachus's protector, intervened, deflecting the arrow and warding off Cupid. Venus then remounted her chariot and flew away in the moonlit sky. At the stern of the vessel the Cypriot sailors became intoxicated with wine and chanted bawdy songs to Venus, heedless of the approaching storm (Fénelon 1805, 62–64).

Again, Pinelli interprets the text literally. Cupid's errant arrow lies at Minerva's feet. The nude, sensual goddess of love is contrasted with the chaste goddess of reason, clad in armor. The vessel's pilot, his head crowned with flowers, reclines in a stupor—all as described by Fénelon.

Pinelli again gleaned the standard repertory of antique statuary for his figures: a relief of Achilles and Priam for the figure of Telemachus, the Capitoline Athena, Venus Victrix, and a Seated Bacchus with a Panther for the pilot (Reinach 1897–1910, vol. 1, 1, 229, 318, 383). In this composition Pinelli seized the opportunity to show off his mastery of the nude. In the preceding year the young artist had obtained the first prize at the Accademia del Nudo in Rome for his anatomical study of a male nude (Olson 1980, 75).

In general, the *Telemachus* series represents Pinelli's most self-consciously neoclassical manner. The drawings do not relate to a painted composition but are fully independent works of art. In 1827, however, Pinelli produced an album of etchings entitled *Avventure di Telemaco* with variant compositions conceived in a bolder, protoromantic vein that reflects the influence of Giuseppe Cades and Felice Giani. RJC

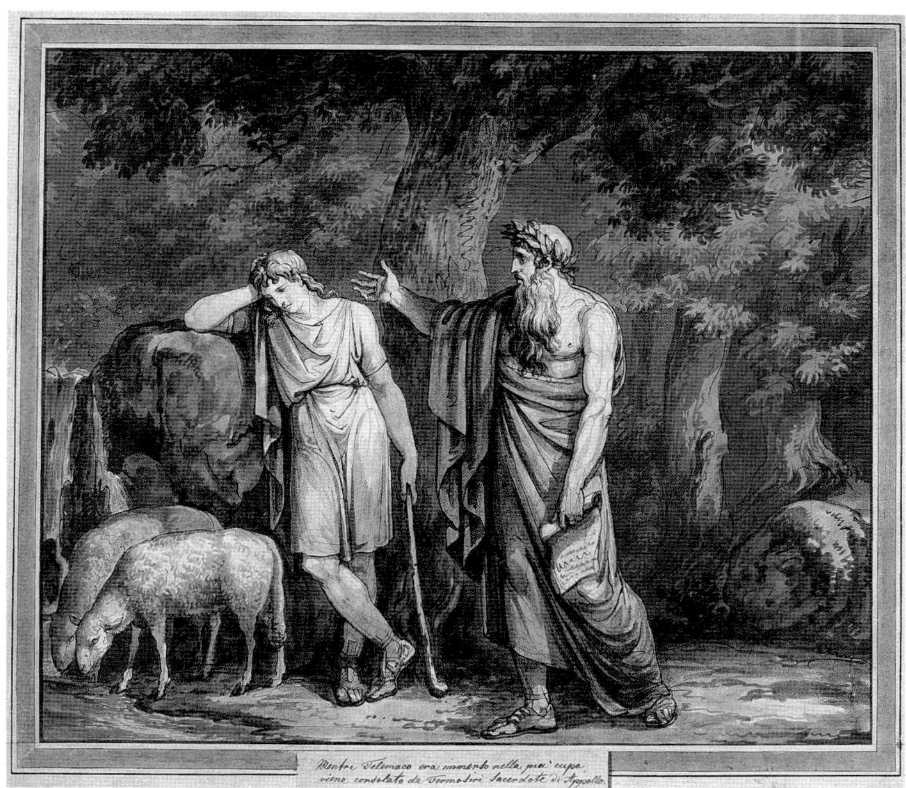

CATALOGUE NO. 93

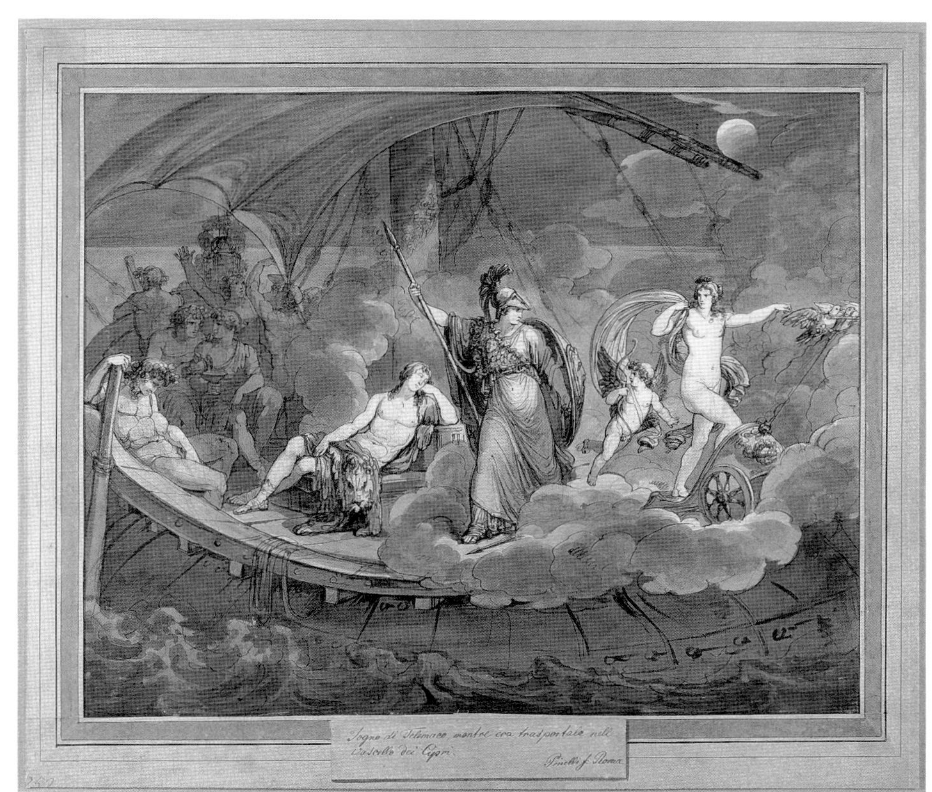

CATALOGUE NO. 94

Northern Drawings

Anton Raphael Mengs

ꕥ

1728 Aussig (Bohemia)–Rome 1779

MENGS WAS STRONGLY encouraged by his father to become an artist, even to the point of being locked in the Vatican Stanze to copy Raphael's paintings. Mengs had accompanied his father to Rome in 1741, where he began his studies of the nude with Marco Benefial and his studies of the antique with Sebastiano Conca. In 1746 he returned to Dresden and became court painter to Augustus III of Saxony. He was back in Rome by 1748, at this time converting to Catholicism, but he returned again to Dresden for the years 1749–52 as first painter to the court of Saxony.

When Mengs moved back to Italy in 1752, he became good friends with Johann Joachim Winckelmann, who arrived in Rome in 1755. The artist's fresco of *The Apotheosis of Saint Eusebius*, 1757, for the church of Sant'Eusebio in Rome so impressed Charles III of Spain that he appointed Mengs painter of the court of Spain in 1760. Before he left for Spain, Mengs painted the seminal *Parnassus* (see FIGURE 3) on a ceiling in Cardinal Alessandro Albani's villa in Rome; this work helped to inform his writings in *Betrachtungen über die Schönheit und den guten Geschmack in der Malerei* (Thoughts on beauty and taste in painting) of 1762.

Mengs worked at the Spanish court for four years before he returned to Rome, where he was elected to the Accademia di San Luca in 1771 and, during the next year, executed the decorations for the Camera dei Papiri in the Vatican Library. After three more years in Madrid, he returned to Rome in 1776 and remained there until his death in 1779. LDM

Anton Raphael Mengs
Male Nude
1778

95
Graphite and chalk on blue laid paper
52.1 x 34.5 cm (20 1/2 x 13 9/16 in.)
Signed and dated at lower right in graphite:
Antonio Rafael Mengs año 1778
National Gallery of Art, gift of Howard Sturges
(inv. no. 1956.9.12)

PROVENANCE
Howard Sturges.

LITERATURE
Princeton 1989, 154 n. 1.

Mengs enjoyed a long, distinguished pedagogic career ranging from his early teaching at the Accademia Capitolina (or del Nudo), Rome, and his advisory role at the Real Academia de San Fernando, Madrid, to his tenure as *principe* (president) of the Accademia di San Luca, Rome, and as master of students in his own studio in the Villa Barberini, near the Vatican. In addition, he was the author of several treatises on the instruction of artists, most notably, *Lezioni pratiche di pittura* (Practical lessons in painting), 1780. Included among Mengs's most illustrious students were his brother-in-law Anton von Maron, Friedrich Heinrich Füger, Nicolas Guibal, and Giovanni Casanova—all of whom became professors or directors at the academies in Dresden (Casanova), Ludwigsburg (Guibal), and Vienna (Füger and von Maron) (Pelzel 1979, 173–175, 182, 189).

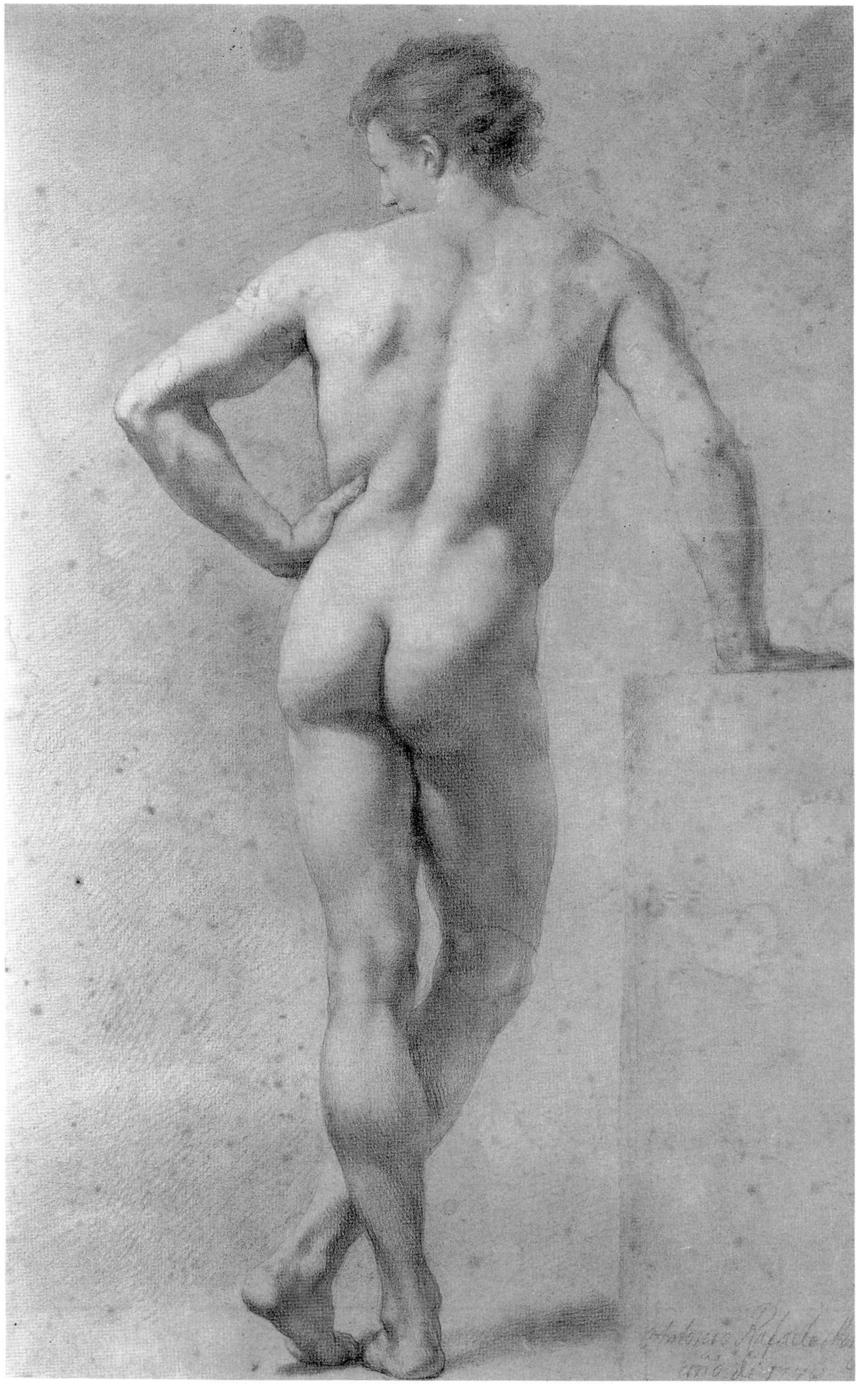

CATALOGUE NO. 95

The National Gallery's academy of a male nude seen from the rear was undoubtedly executed as a model to be copied by pupils (there exists in the same collection a frontal view of a male nude by Mengs; see Princeton 1989, 154–55, no. 55). In 1778, the date of the drawing, Mengs mounted an exhibition of his most recent masterpiece, *Perseus and Andromeda* (Hermitage Museum, Saint Petersburg), in his Villa Barberini atelier, and a contemporary visitor remarked on the horde of young students in the studio busily engaged in copying both drawings and statuary (Jones 1951, 68; Pelzel 1979, 176). Stylistically, Mengs's sheet compares to similar academic nudes by Pompeo Batoni (see CATALOGUE NO. 79; see FIGURE 40) and Benjamin West (see CATALOGUE NO. 4; see also FIGURE 41 for another example of an academic nude by Mengs). RJC

Johan Tobias Sergel

1740 Stockholm 1814

SERGEL FIRST STUDIED with Jean Eric Rehn and Jacques Adrien Masreliez in Stockholm. The French sculptor Pierre-Hubert L'Archevêque became his teacher in 1756 and accompanied him on a seven-month trip to Paris in 1758, where Sergel studied at the Académie. After his return to Stockholm he received royal commissions and, in 1760, a gold medal at the Kunglig Akademien för de Fria Konsterna (The Royal Academy of Fine Arts). On a royal stipend he left for Italy in 1767, visiting Naples, Florence, Pompeii, and Herculaneum, settling in Rome, studying at the Académie de France, and moving in the circle of Henry Fuseli and Nikolai Abraham Abildgaard. He began work on *The Faun* in 1770, which established his international reputation as a sculptor. It was also during this period in Rome that Sergel completed most of his original mythological works.

Despite his protest Sergel was recalled to Stockholm after eleven years in Rome and appointed court sculptor to King Gustavus III. His time was taken up with portrait sculpture and his duties as a professor at the Kunglig Akademien för de Fria Konsterna. When Gustavus traveled to Rome in 1783–84, Sergel was in his entourage as the royal advisor on the arts. He worked for the king until the latter's assassination in 1792. Sergel became Surveyor of the Royal Works of Art in 1803 and director of the Kunglig Akademien in 1810 but always regretted having to leave Rome. LDM

Johan Tobias Sergel
Chiron Teaching Achilles to Throw a Javelin
c. 1770–71

96
Pen and black ink, brush and brown wash on white laid paper
27.8 x 19.4 cm (10 15/16 x 7 5/8 in.)
Kongelige Kobberstiksamling, Statens Museum for Kunst, Copenhagen (inv. no. Tu.128.27)

PROVENANCE
Carl August Ehrensvärd, Stockholm; Dr. Karl Asplund, Stockholm, 1922.

LITERATURE
Josephson 1956, vol. 1, 172, fig. 233; vol. 2, 662, no. 233.

The centaur Chiron's instruction of the young Achilles is mentioned or alluded to by Homer, Apollodorus, Ovid, and Statius, but Achilles's prowess with the javelin is most specifically cited by Pindar in the third of his *Nemean Odes* (Pindar 1972, 180–82):

Fair-haired Achilles dwelling in Philyra's halls
While yet a child made mighty deeds his play;
Many a time his hand brandished the short tipped javelin,
Like to the wind in speed, and with wild lions
He fought, and dealt them death.
Boars too he slew,
Whose panting frames,
The first in his sixth year
And then through all his days,
He brought to the centaur, Cronos' son.

Sergel's selection of the relatively obscure theme of Chiron and Achilles may possibly stem from the counsel of his erudite friends in Rome, Henry Fuseli and Jean-Antoine Julien, called Julien of Parma (Josephson 1956, vol. 1, 110–14, 234–46).

The present drawing, *Chiron Teaching Achilles to Throw a Javelin*, was executed during Sergel's sojourn in Rome. It relates thematically to a terra-cotta group, dating about 1770–71, in the Nationalmuseum, Stockholm (inv. no. NM SK 486; Josephson 1956, vol. 1, 175, 242; Stockholm 1990, 190, fig. 198). There also exist an ink sketch and an ink wash drawing similar to the Copenhagen sheet and depicting the same subject, also in the collection of the Nationalmuseum (sketch: inv. no. NM 1008/1875; Josephson 1956, vol. 1, 172, fig. 235; drawing: inv. no. NMH 893/1875; Josephson 1956, vol. 1, 172, fig. 234; Stockholm 1990, 190, fig. 199).

The Copenhagen sheet appears to constitute Sergel's first conception of the subject. Achilles stands almost upright in left profile with the javelin raised in his right hand. He is flanked by Chiron, whose head and torso are to the left, paralleling those of Achilles; the centaur raises his pupil's right arm and straightens his left arm.

In the Stockholm pen, ink, and wash drawing, the stance of Achilles is more animated, with knees bent and left leg stretched back as he prepares to hurl the javelin, and he faces his mentor. Chiron is seen entirely in left profile; he straightens the extended left arm of Achilles and guides the javelin clasped in the hero's right hand.

The pen and ink sketch in Stockholm most closely resembles Sergel's terracotta in composition. Here, both Achilles and Chiron are shown in right profile; their arms are raised and posed to create a strong diagonal line of movement toward the right. (The sheet also shows a study of the right leg of Achilles from the rear and a sketch of Chiron's face.) The terracotta, however, is more static in concept.

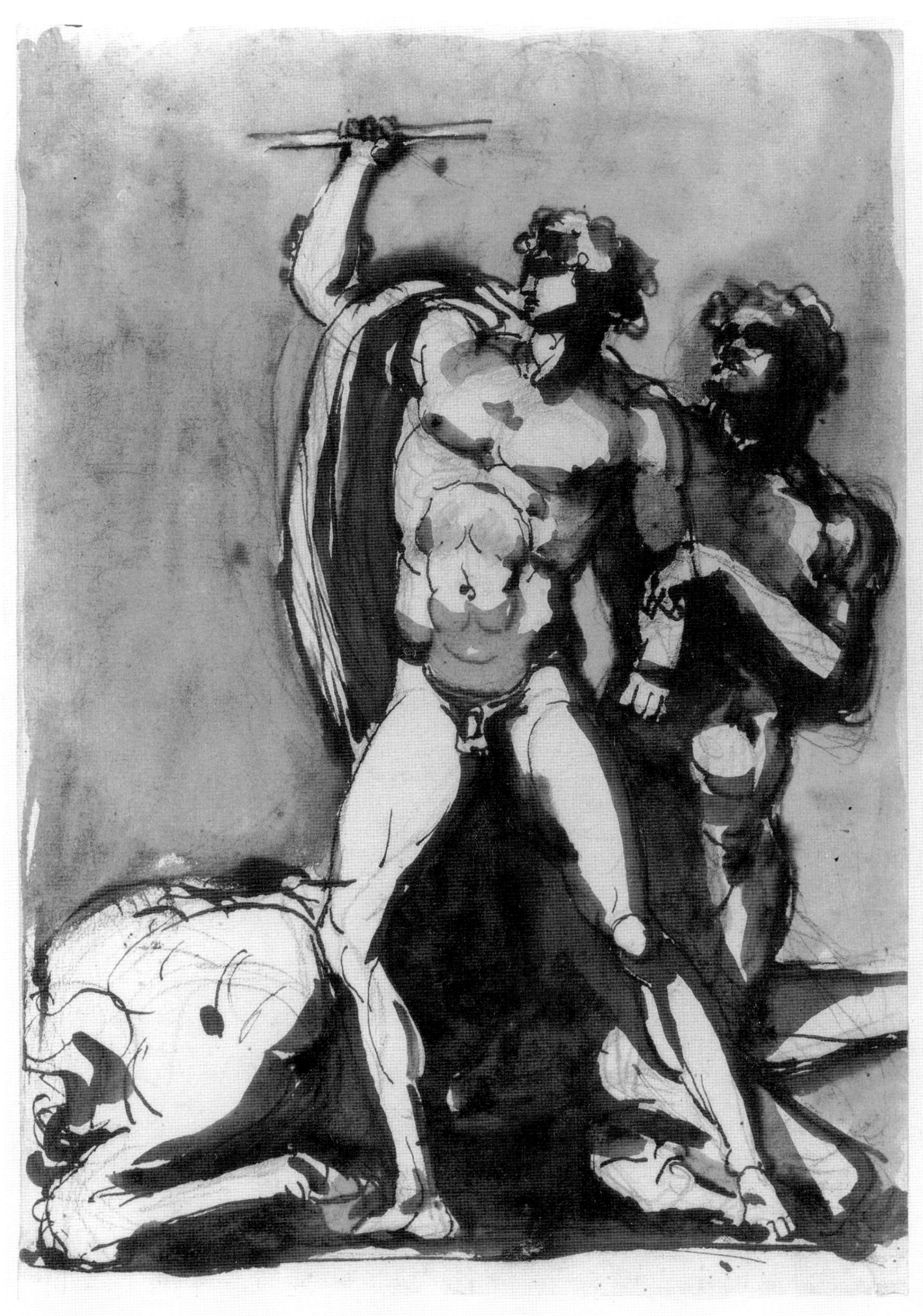

CATALOGUE NO. 96

Chiron's torso is turned toward Achilles, and his left arm presses the latter's chest. The diagonal thrust of the sketch is thus replaced by a horizontal created by the parallel placement of the left arms of the figures.

As noted by Per Bjurström (1976, n.p.), Sergel's drawings were not strictly studies for sculptures. A prolific draftsman, Sergel gave free reign to his imagination in his drawings, which are highly pictorial in conception, especially during his Roman period. The Copenhagen sheet is a consummate example, with its "painterly" wash passages and bold chiaroscuro.

The figure of Chiron was inspired by Roman wall paintings of centaurs published in *Le pitture antiche d'Ercolano* (Naples, 1755–92, vol. 5, pl. 50) and by the sculpture of an old centaur, discovered by Monsignor Furietti, now in the Museo Capitolino (Reinach 1897–1910, vol. 1, 426, no. 1781; Haskell/Penny 1981, no. 20, fig. 91). In the Copenhagen drawing Sergel quoted the figure of Alexander from one of the Alexander and Bucephalus marble groups in the Piazza del Quirinale, Rome, for his Achilles (Haskell/Penny 1981, no. 3, fig. 72). RJC

Johan Tobias Sergel
The Vestal Virgins Rescuing the Statue of Minerva from the Burning Temple of Vesta
Probably c. 1780s

97
Pen and black ink, brush and gray wash on white laid paper
35 x 80.4 cm (13 3/4 x 31 11/16 in.)
Signed at lower right in pen and ink: *Sergel*
Kongelige Kobberstiksamling, Statens Museum for Kunst, Copenhagen (inv. no. Tu.131.a.2a)

LITERATURE
Josephson 1956, vol. 2, 573–77, fig. 744.

The Vestal Virgins Rescuing the Statue of Minerva from the Burning Temple of Vesta illustrates a passage from the *History of the Empire from the Time of Marcus Aurelius* (1.14.1–6) by Herodian, a third-century A.D. Greek historian living in Rome. His works had been available in French since the mid-sixteenth century, and a Danish edition appeared in 1753 (Josephson 1956, vol. 2, 568).

In A.D. 192 the city of Rome was ravaged by a disastrous conflagration of unknown origin that destroyed many buildings (Herodian 1969, 91–93):

> *The temple of Vesta, too, went up in flames on this occasion, exposing the statue of Pallas to view. The image, reputedly brought from Troy by the Romans, is venerated and kept concealed. Our generation were the first ones to see it since it had been brought to Italy from Troy. For the Vestal Virgins snatched up the image and carried it along the Sacred Way from the temple to the palace of the emperor.*

The holocaust was interpreted as a divine omen of the downfall of the emperor Commodus as retribution for his decadence and a portent of the subsequent civil wars. (About 1800 Sergel rendered a series of drawings that illustrate the plot to assassinate Commodus [Nationalmuseum, Stockholm; Josephson 1956, vol. 2, 574–77, figs. 749–52].)

Stylistically the Copenhagen drawing was undoubtedly inspired by Sergel's colleague, the architect Louis-Jean Desprez, who popularized imaginary views of smoky temple interiors in his stage-set designs, prints, and drawings. Sergel had first become acquainted with Desprez during his Roman sojourn, and the latter later settled in Stockholm and was appointed architect to King Gustav III in 1788 (Paris 1974b).

Based on stylistic criteria, Sergel's drawing appears to date from the 1780s. The wash passages lack the brio and exaggerated chiaroscuro that had distinguished his *Sturm und Drang* compositions of the preceding decade. Given the dramatic potential of the subject, Sergel's composition is remarkably restrained: the desperate exodus of the Vestals resembles more closely a stately procession. The proportions of the figures are attenuated, and they are modeled in flickering light and dark washes.

At the end of his career Sergel executed a second, smaller version of the theme in a drawing now in the Nationalmuseum, Stockholm (Josephson 1956, vol. 2, 615, fig. 795, 672). The conception is highly schematic and even more static in effect. The temples, basilica, and column in the background dissolve in an arabesque of pen and ink flourishes. The forms of the Vestals, attendants, and onlookers are rendered with broad blobs of wash atop a web of pen and ink lines. Ironically, in a letter of 1813 (cited in Josephson 1956, vol. 2, 614–16) Sergel, whose eyesight was now failing, spoke of a new "correction of style" and a *"belle manière,"* which is reflected in the Stockholm sheet. RJC

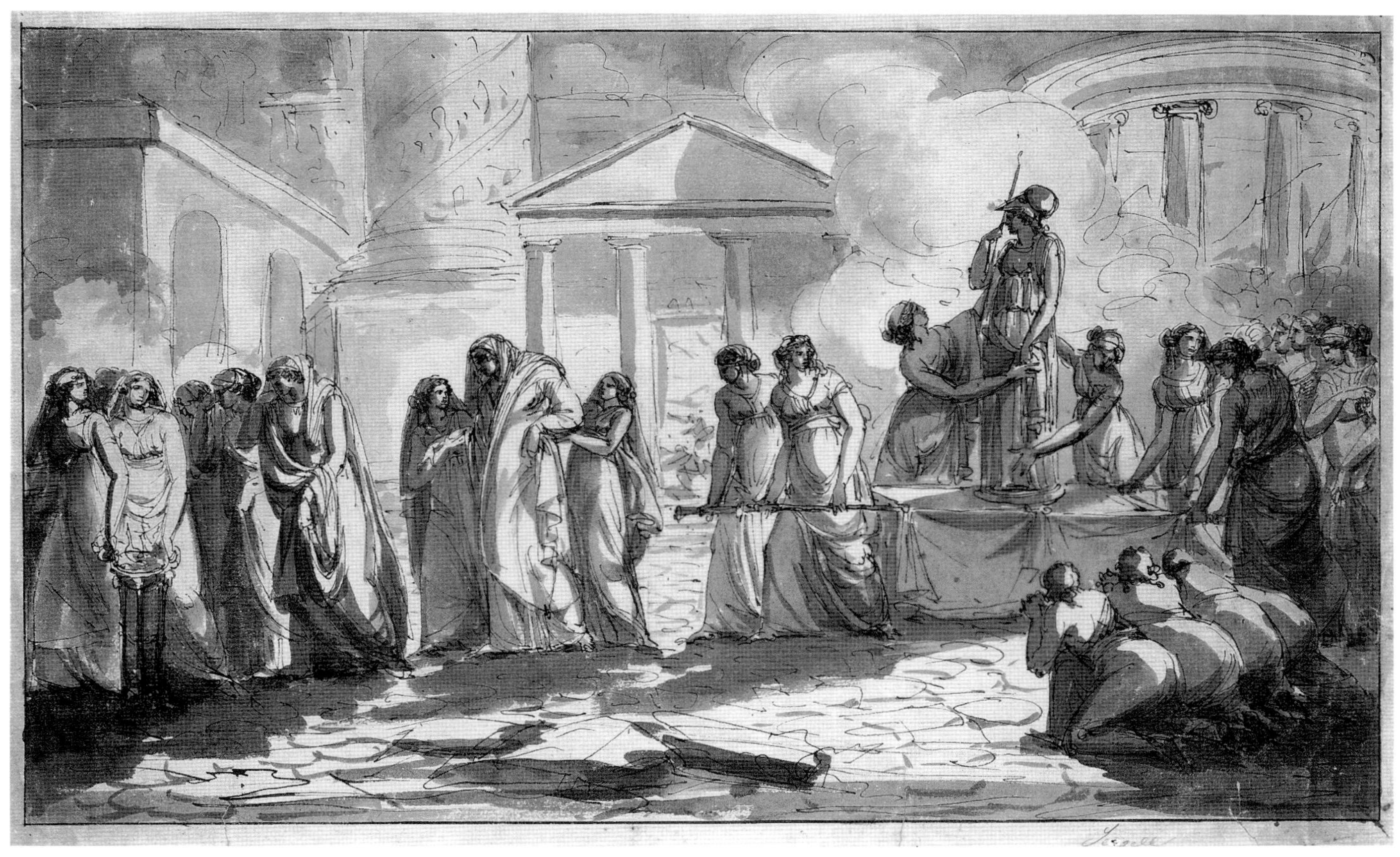

CATALOGUE NO. 97

Henry Fuseli (born Johann Heinrich Füssli)

1741 Zurich–Putney 1825

ALTHOUGH FUSELI came from a family of artists, his father would not allow him to pursue a career in the arts, and he was ordained as a minister of the Zwinglian church in 1761. His unique training familiarized him with the writings of Homer, Dante, Shakespeare, and Milton, and he became fluent in eight languages. Soon after his ordination Fuseli was forced to leave the country because of a controversial political pamphlet he published with Johann Kaspar Lavater. Fuseli relocated to London, where he moved in literary circles and translated books. In 1768, with the encouragement of Sir Joshua Reynolds, he decided to devote himself fully to the visual arts.

Fuseli lived in Rome from 1770 to 1778 while he trained as a painter, developing the style he would keep his entire life. He became the leader of a group of artists living in Rome that included John Brown, George Romney, Nikolai Abraham Abildgaard, and Johan Tobias Sergel. His works from this period depict scenes from the Greek tragedies and the works of Homer, Dante, and Shakespeare.

On his return to London Fuseli stopped in Zurich to execute *Oath on the Rüttli* for the town hall. In 1782 he exhibited *The Nightmare* at the Royal Academy, where it caused a scandal and established his reputation. He illustrated the successful French edition of Lavater's *Physiognomische Fragmente* (Physiognomical fragments). He worked for John Boydell's Shakespeare Gallery and in 1799 opened his own Milton Gallery with forty of his paintings. In 1790 Fuseli was elected to the Royal Academy and became a professor there in 1799. LDM

Henry Fuseli
Psychostasy
c. 1800–1802

98

Pen and ink, brush and gray-brown and gray-blue washes on white paper
47.6 x 33 cm (18 3/4 x 13 in.)
Inscribed at upper right in brown ink: *Febr. 1800*; at lower right in brown ink: *Willm Blake* and *πεφυε στραταρχον Αιϑιοπων αφοβον—Μεμνονα* ([who] killed the fearless general of the Ethiopians—Memnon); at lower left: *ΨΥΧΟΣΤΑΣΙΑ* (Psychostasie)
The Pierpont Morgan Library, New York, gift of Miss Louise Crane in memory of her mother, Mrs. W. Murray Crane (inv. no. 1974.44)
(Philadelphia and Minneapolis only)

PROVENANCE
Mrs. W. Murray Crane, New York.

EXHIBITED
Northampton 1947, no. 18.

LITERATURE
Schiff 1973, vol. 1, 134, 277, 308, 584, no. 1365; vol. 2, 433.

Psychostasy (weighing of souls) typifies the arcane themes that appealed to the erudite Fuseli. The subject is based on two ancient sources, Pindar and Plutarch. In three of his *Odes* (Nemean 3, 6; Isthmian 5) Pindar alluded to the combat between Achilles and the Ethiopian king Memnon, son of Aurora and nephew of King Priam, during the Trojan War:

Great Achilles stepped down
From his chariot to the ground,
And slew the son of shining Dawn
With his fell-pointed spear
(Pindar 1972, 199).

Jupiter weighed on a scale the souls of warriors engaged in battle, and victory was granted to the heavier soul (Homer, *Iliad* 19.224–25). The psychostasy of Achilles and Memnon was described by Plutarch, who based the theme on a lost tragedy by Aeschylus (Plutarch 1802, vol. 1, 75–76). As recounted by Plutarch, Thetis and Aurora, the mothers of Achilles and Memnon, respectively, stand by Jupiter's scales and plead for their sons (Aurora's plea can be found in Ovid's *Metamorphoses* 13.578–618).

In Fuseli's composition Memnon's corpse lies prone atop his shield in the foreground. Jupiter is depicted enthroned above with his eagle and presides at the scales. He gestures and turns toward Thetis, who implores him with upturned palms. To the right the grieving Aurora is seen with eyes cast downward and clasped hands. In the center of the sheet the triumphant Achilles brandishes his spear and mounts his chariot as he looks upward at Jupiter; behind him the battle between the Greeks and Trojans still rages furiously.

Fuseli incorporated an eclectic combination of visual sources in his composition. The pose of the figure of Achilles is based on Alexander from the Alexander and Bucephalus marble group in the Piazza del Quirinale in Rome (Haskell/Penny 1981, 136–39, no. 3, fig. 72). Gert Schiff cites an engraving by Cornelis II Bloemart after a figure of Eurydice by Abraham van Diepenbeck for Fuseli's Thetis (Schiff 1973, vol. 1, 134, 661, no. 2; the engraving was published in Michel Marolles, *Tableaux du temple des muses* [Paris, 1655], opp. 411). He also indicates that the figure of Memnon derives from that of Hector in Gavin Hamilton's *Achilles Vents His Rage on Hector* (Schiff 1973, vol. 1, 308, 676, no. 20; the work was known to Fuseli in an engraving by Domenico Cunego); although ancient statuary representing dying gladiators was the ultimate source for the latter figure (Reinach 1897–1910,

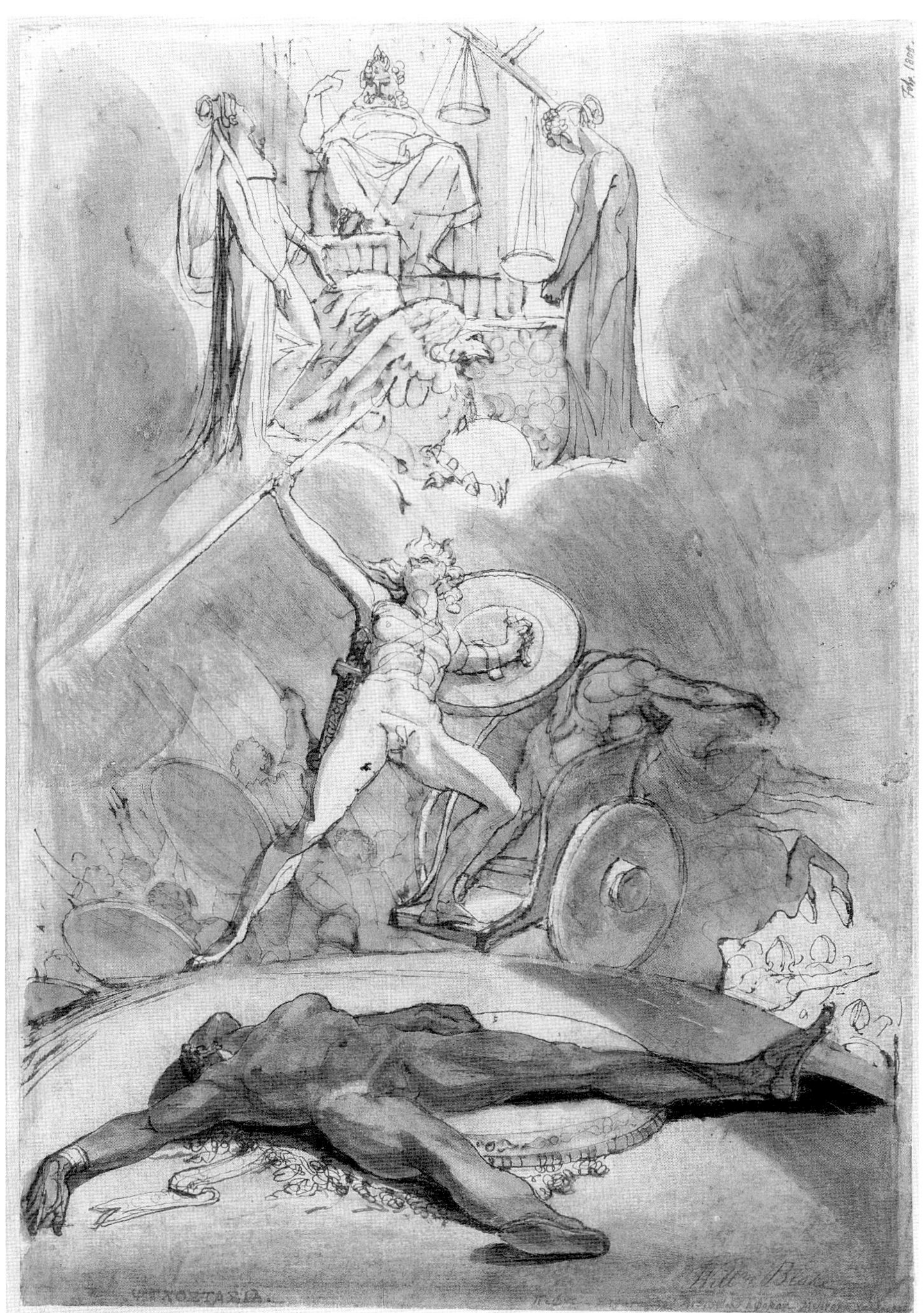

CATALOGUE NO. 98 (see color plate on page 110)

vol. 1, 531). Finally, Schiff views Raphael's painting *The Transfiguration* (Musei Vaticani, Rome) as a precedent for the spatial organization of Fuseli's design (Schiff 1973, vol. 1, 308).

The New York drawing is a study for a painting commissioned from Fuseli by Thomas Lawrence. The canvas, which is now lost, was exhibited at the Royal Academy in London, in 1803 (Schiff 1973, vol. 1, 277, 652, no. 64). Fuseli again treated the *Psychostasy* theme in a pencil drawing of 1813, with a simpler composition and a reduced format (31.7 x 21.6 cm; Cecil Higgins Museum, Bedford Castle Close; Schiff 1973, vol. 1, 606, no. 1521; vol. 2, 504). RJC

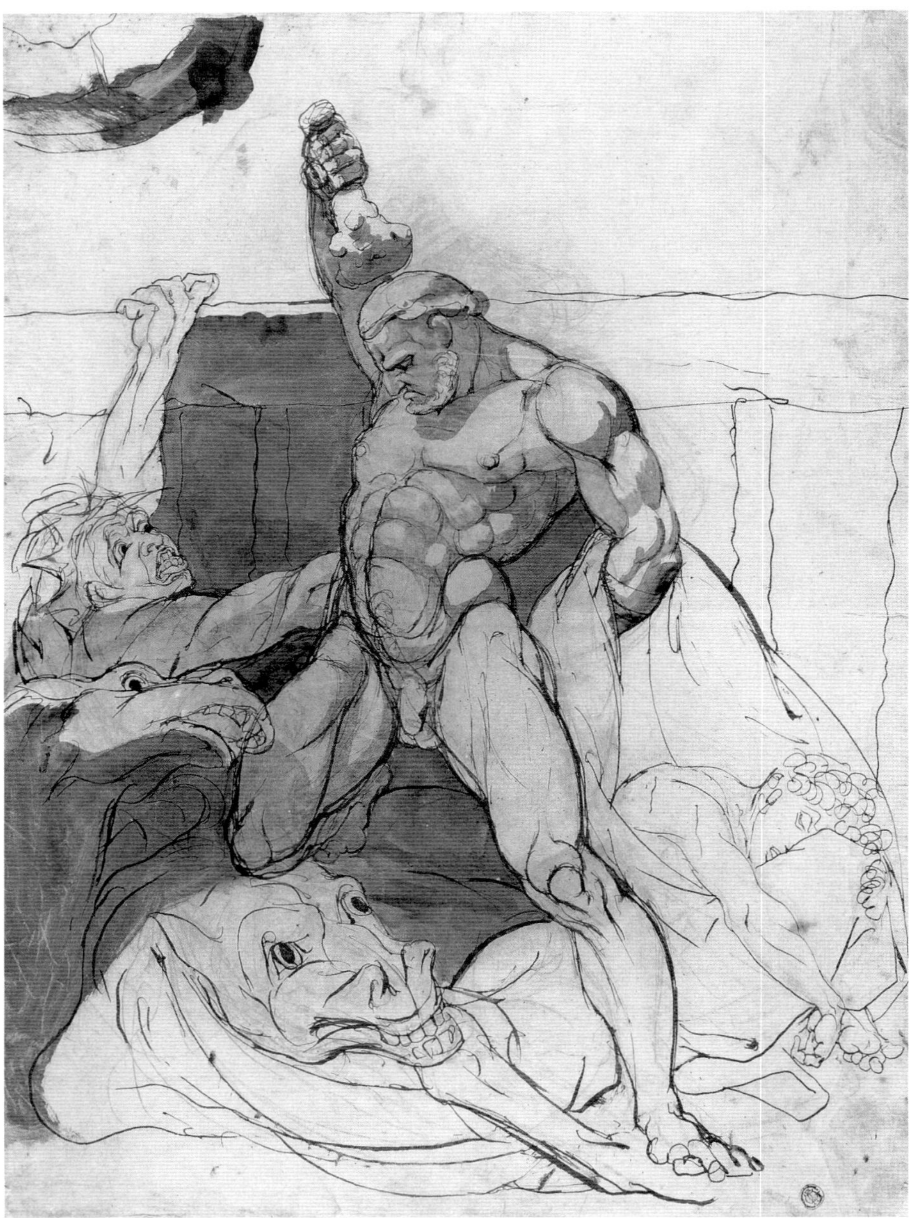

CATALOGUE NO. 99

Henry Fuseli
Hercules Killing the Flesh-Eating Mares of Diomedes
c. 1800–1805

99
Graphite, pen and ink, brush and wash on white paper
50.5 x 38.3 cm (19 7/8 in. x 15 1/16 in.)
The Art Institute of Chicago, the Leonora Hall Gurley Memorial Collection (inv. no. 1922.2152)
(Los Angeles only)

EXHIBITED
Chicago 1946, no. 15.

LITERATURE
Nüscheler 1807–9, 6–7.
Federmann 1927, 74.
Ganz 1947, no. 67.
Lankheit 1951, 179.
Schiff 1973, vol. 1, 312, 585, no. 1371; vol. 2, 437.

The Chicago drawing illustrates the eighth Labor of Hercules. Fuseli's interpretation of the episode is based on two classical sources—Apollodorus and Quintus Smyrnaeus. Diomedes, son of Ares and Cyrene, was the king of a warlike Thracian tribe, the Bistones, and the owner of a stable of flesh-eating mares. In the narrative of Apollodorus (*Bibiothēkē* 2.96–97), Hercules traveled to Thrace with his armor-bearer and companion, Abderus. After subduing Diomedes's grooms, he seized the horses and handed them over to Abderus for safekeeping. Hercules then engaged and slew Diomedes on the seashore and drove away his Bistone cohorts. In the meantime, however, the mares broke loose and killed Abderus by dragging him along the shore.

In the succinct account of Quintus Smyrnaeus (*The Fall of Troy* 6.240–50; Smyrnaeus 1962, 273):

There in the Thracian land
Were Diomedes' grim man-eating steeds:
These at their gruesome mangers had he slain,
And dead they lay with their fiend-hearted lord.

Fuseli sets his composition within the stable cited by Quintus. Hercules raises his club to smite Diomedes and a mare and pins down a second mare beneath his right knee and left foot. The hero wraps his left arm in a fold of the shroud containing the corpse of Abderus, which is visible behind him on the floor of the stable. The grimacing Diomedes clings to the side of the stall and attempts to ward off the menacing blow of Hercules.

Fuseli's drawing may well have been inspired by a statuette discovered at Ostia, which represents Hercules, flanked by two mares, raising his club to strike the crouching Diomedes; the latter wears the garb of a Dacian or barbarian (Museo Pio-Clementino, Rome; Reinach 1897–1910, vol. 1, 470, no. 2001). However, as observed by Schiff, the drawings Fuseli executed about 1800–1805 were far removed in conception from the "neo-classical" norm. Fuseli's Hercules and Diomedes even exceeds the violence of Antonio Canova's statue of *Hercules and Lichas* (Galleria d'Arte Moderna, Rome) and John Flaxman's *Fury of Athamas* (National Trust, Ickworth). Schiff contrasts Fuseli's bold wash drawings of this period with the exactly contemporary and stylistically conservative entries in the Weimar *Preisaufgabe*, the open competition sponsored by Goethe and Schiller to encourage artists to depict themes from classical literature (Schiff 1973, vol. 1, 312).

Fuseli's brutish Hercules derives from the figure of a soldier in the left foreground of Daniele da Volterra's painting *The Massacre of the Innocents* (Galleria degli Uffizi, Florence) and reaffirms the artist's indebtedness to Italian sixteenth-century mannerism (Schiff 1973, vol. 1, 312).

Fuseli had treated the Hercules and Diomedes theme in a pen, sepia, and wash drawing of 1798, now in a Swiss private collection. In this sheet Hercules tramples two mares and prepares to strike with his club the prone figure of Diomedes, who brandishes a staff in self-defense; the hero grasps the nude corpse of Abderus in his right arm (Schiff 1973, vol. 1, 535, no. 989; vol. 2, 289). As noted by Schiff, the figure of Hercules, seen from behind, is quoted from the executioner in Andrea del Sarto's *Beheading of John the Baptist* (Monasterio dello Scalzo, Florence; Schiff 1973, vol. 1, 185, 734).

Schiff (1973, vol. 1, 585, no. 1372) cites a pen, ink, and wash "outline" drawing of Hercules and Diomedes based on the Chicago sheet, now in the collection of the Öffentliche Kunstsammlung, Basel (inv. no. U.1.217). Ostensibly, Fuseli executed this version for the engraving by Heinrich Lips, published by Felix Nüscheler 1807–9. RJC

Nikolai Abraham Abildgaard

1743 Copenhagen 1809

ABILDGAARD STUDIED under J. E. Mandeberg at the Kunstakademiet in Copenhagen from 1764 to 1767. In his last year at the Kunstakademiet he won a gold medal for *David Anointed by Samuel*, and in 1771 he was awarded a travel stipend. He arrived in Rome in 1772 and moved in the circle of Johan Tobias Sergel and Henry Fuseli. He studied the works of Raphael, Michelangelo, and the Carracci as well as classical antiquities in Rome and Naples. His *Philoctetes* of 1774–75 was well received when it was sent to Copenhagen.

Abildgaard left Rome in 1777 and returned to Copenhagen by way of Paris. His first major project upon his return was the decoration of the Palace of Charlottenburg, 1780–92. In 1778 he became a professor of painting at the Kunstakademiet and its director in 1789–91 and again from 1801 until his death in 1809. LDM

Nikolai Abraham Abildgaard
Claudius Discovered by a Soldier
c. 1780

100
Pen and brown ink, brush and gray wash heightened with white over graphite on off-white laid paper
21.8 x 23.4 cm (8 9/16 x 9 3/16 in.)
Kongelige Kobberstiksamling, Statens Museum for Kunst, Copenhagen (Td.536.45)

EXHIBITED
Munich 1985, 32, no. 9, pl. 8.
Berlin 1989, 32–33, no. 9.

The discovery of Claudius (Tiberius Claudius Nero Germanicus) by a Roman soldier is related in book 10 of Suetonius's *De vita Caesarum* (Lives of the Caesars). From his youth Claudius was hampered by a physical disability and the belief, shared even by his mother, that he was in some respect mentally deficient. Consequently Claudius led a retired life, devoted largely to writing. After the emperor Gaius (Caligula) was murdered, a soldier passing by the balcony of Claudius's apartment noticed a pair of feet sticking out below a curtain covering a doorway. When the soldier pulled the drapery aside, he recognized Claudius and hailed him as emperor, the moment Abildgaard chose to represent in this drawing. Following his discovery Claudius was brought before the senate, but that body could not agree on whom to elect as emperor. The populace looking on, however, called for Claudius to fill the position. When the army swore allegiance to him, Claudius secured their fidelity with a bribe of money. He became emperor in 41 A.D.

In Abildgaard's drawing Claudius appears as a craven victim, kneeling on the ground and attempting to fend off the warrior with the futile gesture of an upraised arm. This pathetic figure, although he was soon to rule the Roman empire, could not embody any of the virtues of moral rectitude or magnanimity that artists usually chose, or were commissioned, to represent from classical history. In fact, many of Abildgaard's works, whether or not they refer to classical subject matter, emphasize extremes of emotion and anatomical distortion for expressive purposes. The excited movement of the artist's pencil or brush, evident here, enhances the tension of the event being represented. Drawings such as the present sheet surely reflect the impact of Henry Fuseli's art on the Danish student, who knew the Swiss artist during his years of study in Rome (1772–77; for a study of their relationship see New Haven 1979, 64–70). Abildgaard, like Fuseli, often chose obscure incidents from antiquity that allowed him to exercise his imaginative fancy, particularly in the representation of highly pitched emotions. In this respect Abildgaard and Fuseli, together with their mutual friend Johan Tobias Sergel, deliberately rejected the viewpoint of Johann Joachim Winckelmann and Gotthold Ephraim Lessing that emotional calm was an essential component of ideal beauty. VC

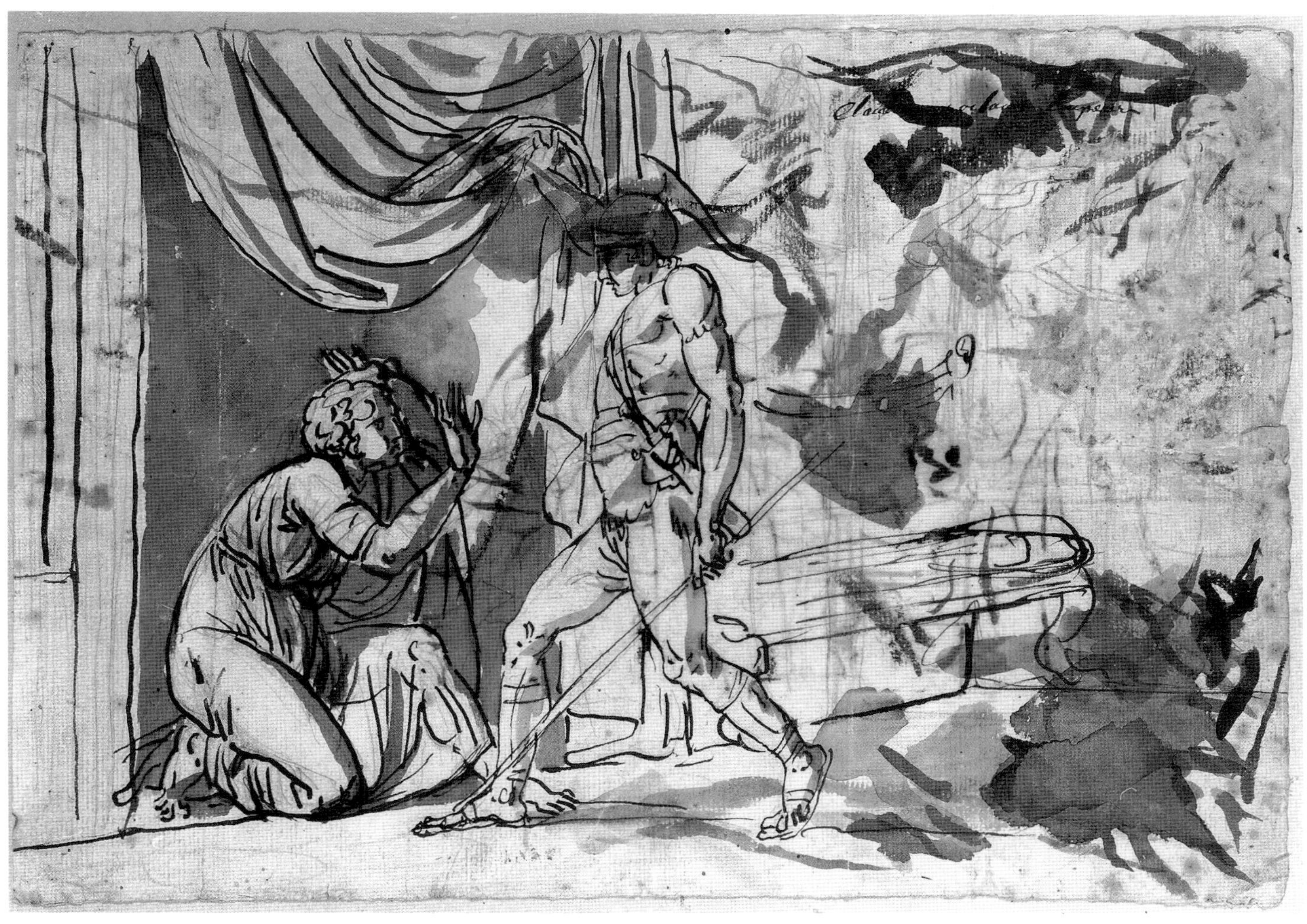

CATALOGUE NO. 100

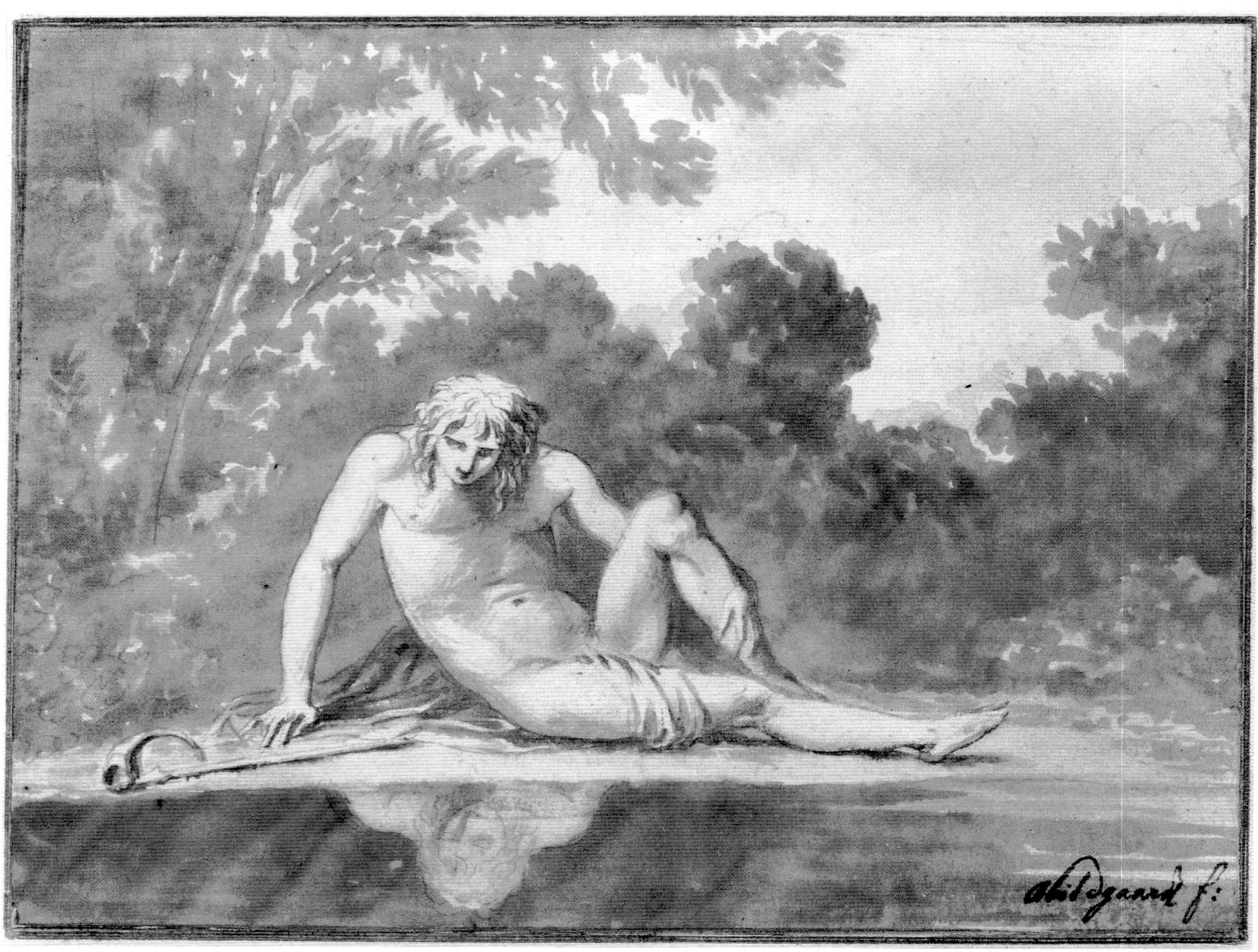

CATALOGUE NO. 101

Nikolai Abraham Abildgaard
Narcissus
c. 1790–1800

101
Brush and brown wash, over a faint sketch in black chalk on white laid paper
10.9 x 14.7 cm (4 5/16 x 5 13/16 in.)
Signed at lower right with pen and dark brown ink: *Abildgaard f.*
Crocker Art Museum, Sacramento, California: E. B. Crocker Collection (inv. no. 1871.486)
(Los Angeles and Philadelphia only)

PROVENANCE
Dr. Ambrigen (oval stamp on verso).
Edwin Bryant Crocker, Sacramento.

EXHIBITED
Davis/Sacramento 1971, 54, no. 28.

Narcissus's legend is related in book 3 of Ovid's *Metamorphoses*, which tells how this son of a nymph and a water god was given at birth the gift of great beauty. A prophet told him that he would have a long life only if he never saw himself. As a youth Narcissus was much admired but rejected all offers of love. Finally, Aphrodite and Nemesis condemned him to suffer from eternal self-pride as penance for his conceit. One day while hunting, Narcissus paused beside a pool and caught sight of his reflection, thus fulfilling the prophecy that sealed his fate—he remained transfixed by the reflection until his death.

Abildgaard's *Narcissus* is one of the few drawings by a Danish neoclassical artist to be found in a museum in the United States. A study of this sheet permits a fascinating insight into the process of an artist's making a replica of one of his drawings. Another version of this composition is known, in pen and brown ink with brown wash over graphite (15.2 x 10.5 cm; Kongelige Kobberstiksamling, Statens Museum for Kunst, Copenhagen; Berlin 1989, no. 10), in which the pose of the figure is identical, but there is considerably more space at the top of the composition. The verso of the Copenhagen drawing is partially covered with black chalk, while the contours of Narcissus's figure are outlined in pencil, clearly visible over the ink wash. If an artist wants to transfer a design onto another surface, one of the easiest procedures is to cover the back of the first drawing with chalk. The sheet is then placed face up on another sheet of paper, the main features of the original drawing are drawn over with a stylus (which leaves only a faintly visible indentation) or a hard pencil. Whatever the medium, a pale outline will be transferred onto the sheet of paper underneath, which can then serve the artist as a guide. The dimensions of the figure of Narcissus are the same in both drawings (9 centimeters from finger to toe), and the fact that in the Copenhagen version the figure is outlined in pencil on top of the ink wash indicates that this drawing was executed prior to the Crocker version. The only change worthy of note that the artist made in the composition of the Crocker drawing is the addition of a spear and horn to one side of Narcissus's right hand. In this replica the figure is modeled with very delicate brush strokes, the refinement of which gives Narcissus a rather flaccid, almost effeminate character in comparison to the brisk, decisive draftsmanship of the Copenhagen version.

A signed preliminary sketch for a slightly different composition of the Narcissus legend is in Stockholm (Nationalmuseum; inv. no. NM H8/1882). In this rapidly drawn study in pen, brush, and brown ink over graphite, Narcissus is shown leaning forward with one hand raised, as if surprised by the sight of his reflection. No evidence exists to establish a chronology for the three drawings, although the Copenhagen work is customarily thought to have been done during the 1790s.

Abildgaard's figure surely reflects his knowledge of one of the most celebrated of all antique statues, the Dying Gladiator, then as now in the Musei Capitolini, Rome (Haskell/Penny 1981, 224–27, no. 44, fig. 116). The artist certainly would have seen the Gladiator during his years of study in Rome, while innumerable engravings and copies of the antiquity spread its fame throughout every country and art academy in Europe. It is somewhat ironic that the Roman statue, so admired for its nobility and pathos, should have been adapted by Abildgaard for his Narcissus, whose story is a denial of the virtues embodied by the Gladiator.
VC

Friedrich Heinrich Füger

1751 Heilbron–Vienna 1818

FÜGER BEGAN AS A PUPIL of Nicolas Guibal in Stuttgart, but he soon abandoned the visual arts for a career in law and enrolled at the University of Halle in 1768. Two years later he returned to his art studies under the supervision of Adam Friedrich Oeser in Leipzig and eventually of Guibal once again. Füger gained fame as a portrait miniaturist in Dresden and was so esteemed at the imperial court in Vienna that in 1774 he was awarded a scholarship for study in Rome. There he trained as a history painter, encouraged by Anton Raphael Mengs and Alexander Trippel, from 1776 until 1781. During a stay in Naples (1781–83) he was patronized by Queen Maria Carolina and received an important commission to decorate the royal library of the Palazzo Reale in Caserta. Füger returned to Vienna in 1783, and two years later he became director of the Vienna Akademie. A successful portraitist, he was named director of the Kaiserlich Gemäldegalerie in 1805. LDM

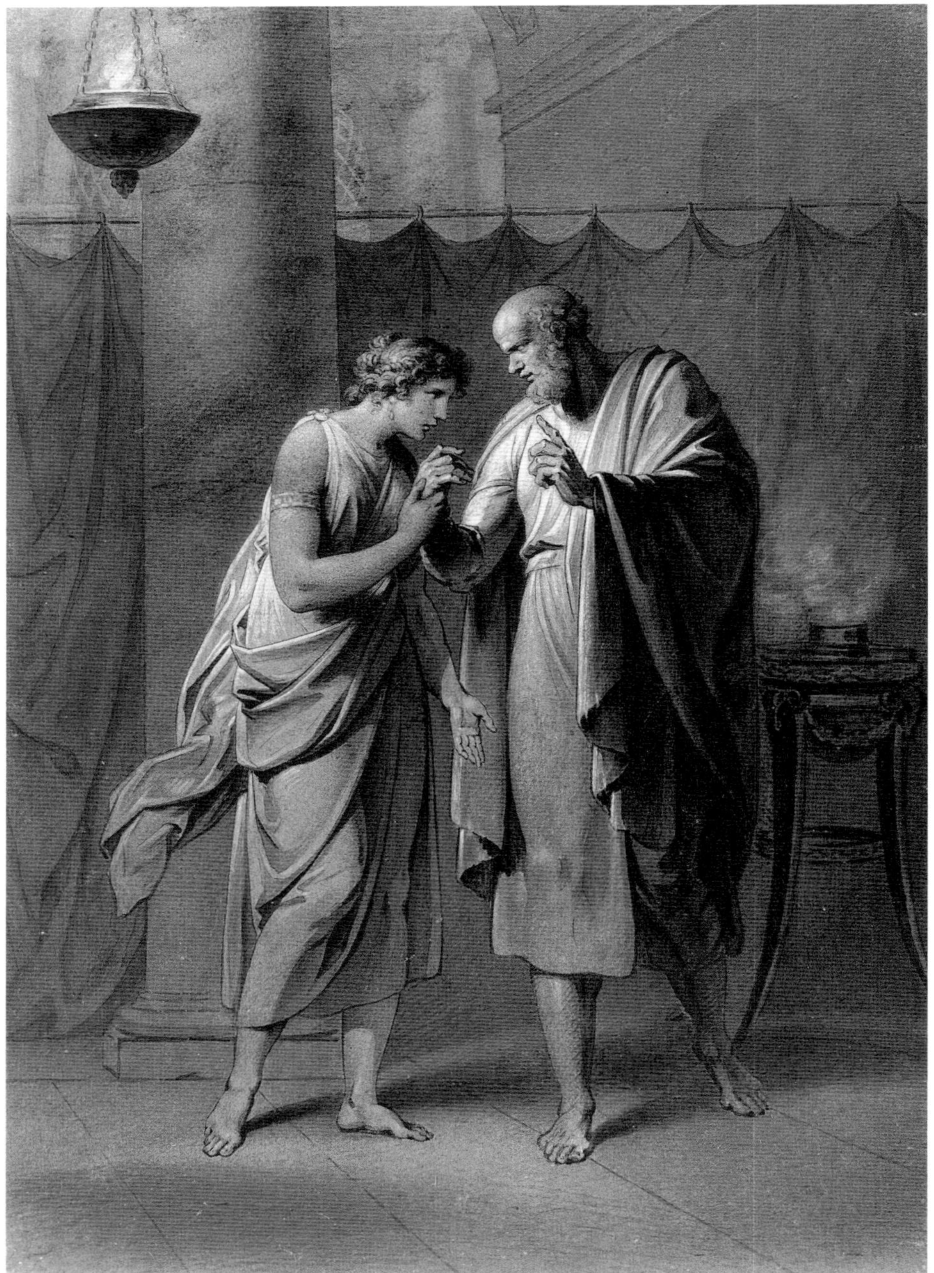

CATALOGUE NO. 102

Friedrich Heinrich Füger
Socrates and Aspasia
1802–3

102
Pen and black ink, gray washes, and white heightening over black chalk on light blue paper
45.8 x 33.2 cm (18 x 13 1/16 in.)
Signed and dated in the lower left in black ink:
H. Füger 1803
Crocker Art Museum, Sacramento, California:
E. B. Crocker Collection (inv. no. 1871.82)

PROVENANCE
Edwin Bryant Crocker; Mrs. E. B. Crocker, 1885.

EXHIBITED
Sacramento 1939, no. 69.
Sacramento 1971, 152.
Sacramento 1972, 39, 59, no. 38.
Princeton 1989, 136–37, no. 48.

LITERATURE
Scheyer 1949, 235, no. 19.

Although the subject of Füger's drawing is traditionally identified as a debate between Socrates and the courtesan Aspasia (Sacramento 1972, 39; Princeton 1989, 136), this interpretation of the subject matter remains problematic. The identity of Socrates can be ascertained from an extensive, unbroken iconographical repertoire, based on carved gems and busts that date from antiquity through the eighteenth century (Sauvage 1960, 168–69). Socrates's bald pate, unkempt beard, and crude features are recognizable in contemporary paintings, such as Jacques-Louis David's *Death of Socrates* (*Socrate au moment de prendre la ciguë*; the Metropolitan Museum of Art, New York) and Étienne-Barthélémy Garnier's *Socrates and Alcibiades* (see CATALOGUE NO 50). Füger himself executed an undated pen and ink drawing representing a man contemplating a bust of Socrates, now in the collection of the Graphische Sammlung Albertina, Vienna (inv. no. O.XIX, 2 [30]).

Although Aspasia's physical appearance was never described, her wisdom, political acumen, and rhetorical gifts were extolled by Plato, Plutarch, and Xenophon. She was greatly admired by Socrates, who with his disciples attended her brilliant discourses, but a specific debate between them is not cited in the literature. At the Paris Salon of 1806 Nicholas-André Monsiau exhibited the painting *Aspasia Conversing with the Most Illustrious Men of Athens* (Musée du Louvre, Paris), in which he depicted Pericles, Socrates, Alcibiades, Plato, Xenophon, Sophocles, Phidias, Euripides, Parrhasias, and Isocrates (Janson 1977, 77, no. 391).

Xenophon (*Memoirs of Socrates* 3.12) recounts an amusing dialogue between Socrates and another Athenian courtesan, Theodota, concerning the meaning of friendship. Renowned for her beauty, Theodota attracted artists from all regions, and through the generosity of her numerous lovers she was sumptuously clothed and occupied luxurious quarters, appointed with elegant and costly furniture. To assess her legendary beauty Socrates visited Theodota in person, demanding to know the source of her apparent wealth. She responded, "From my friends." In a drawn-out conversation Socrates cleverly indicated that he possessed charms and incantations that would enable Theodota to ensnare more friends, that is, clients, but that she must first persuade Socrates to reveal them to her. "Communicate these charms to me," Theodota says, "and the first proof of their power shall be upon you." Socrates replies, "But I would not be attracted to you, Theodota; I would rather you should come to me." "Give me but a favorable reception and I will certainly come," she retorts. Socrates then proclaims triumphantly, "So I will provided I have then no-one with me whom I love better."

In Füger's scenario the woman grasps Socrates's right arm and raises her left palm in an attitude of supplication, as the philosopher gestures with his left hand. In effect, Socrates appears to be teaching the young woman a lesson rather than engaging her in debate. The encounter between Socrates and Theodota is thus more likely the subject of the drawing.

Füger's composition—with its distinctly Roman architecture and background drapery—and figure types are dependant on "neo-Poussinists" such as David, Gavin Hamilton, and Jean-François-Pierre Peyron, whose work would have been familiar to him from his seven-year Italian sojourn. RJC

Johann Heinrich Wilhelm Tischbein

ꕥ

1751 Hayna–Eutin 1829

TISCHBEIN WAS A STUDENT of his uncles, Johann Heinrich Tischbein the Elder in Kassel and Jacob Tischbein in Hamburg. He returned to Kassel in 1773 and visited Dresden and Berlin in 1777. In 1779 he made the trip to Rome as a pensioner of the court of Hesse and spent much of his time studying antiquities and the works of Raphael. Tischbein traveled in 1781 to Switzerland, where he made illustrations for the scientist Johann Kaspar Lavater, who greatly admired his work. In 1782 he received funds for a second trip to Italy. He became good friends with Johann Wolfgang von Goethe and painted his well-known *Goethe in the Roman Campagna* in 1787. That year he accompanied Goethe to Naples, where he was made director of the Accademia di Belle Arti in 1789. After the fall of Naples in 1799 he returned to Germany, traveling widely before entering the service of the duke of Oldenburg in Eutin as court painter and supervisor of the ducal galleries. LDM

Johann Heinrich Wilhelm Tischbein
The Power of Man

103
Pen and black ink, watercolor over black chalk on white laid paper
34.9 x 44.3 cm (13 3/4 x 17 7/16 in.)
Inscribed and dated at lower left on the verso in pencil: *12 Septbr 1820/Das bild aufgezeichnet/ Wilhelm Tischbein*
The Pierpont Morgan Library, New York, a gift of Mrs. Christian H. Aall in honor of Cara Dufour Denison (inv. no. 1988.11)
(Philadelphia and Minneapolis only)

PROVENANCE
A. Glüenstein (Lugt 1921, no. 123).
Dr. Grosse.
Private collection, Switzerland.
Thomas Le Claire, Hamburg.
Mrs. Christian H. Aall, New York.

EXHIBITED
Hamburg 1987.

LITERATURE
Berlin 1949, 16. pl. 10.
Hamburg 1987, 92–93, no. 45.
New York 1988b, 63–64.

Tischbein's watercolor relates to an oil painting completed in 1821 for the Weisser Saal in the castle of his patron, Duke Peter Friedrich Ludwig von Oldenburg, which formed part of a larger painted cycle commissioned by the duke (Keiser 1973, 3, 16, 36; Mildenberger 1986, 65–68; Hamburg 1987, 92; New York 1988b, 64).

The generation of the peculiar theme, which is entirely Tischbein's invention, is well documented. In Johann Wolfgang Goethe's diary of his Italian travels, much of which were made in Tischbein's company, he observed on November 7, 1786 (Goethe 1962, 121–22):

> *I am coming to appreciate Tischbein more and more, his talents, his ideas on art and his aims as a painter. . . . His stay with* [Swiss scholar Johann Jakob] *Bodmer has turned his thoughts towards the earliest ages of man when he found himself on earth and was expected to solve the problem of becoming the lord of creation. . . . He has made one curious drawing showing man as the tamer of horses, superior not in strength but in cunning to all the beasts of the field, the air and the waters. This composition is of extraordinary beauty and should look most effective when done in oils. We must certainly acquire a drawing of it for Weimar.*

A more highly finished watercolor depicting *The Power of Man*, signed and dated *W. Tischbein Rom 1786* (Berlin, Nationalgalerie) is most likely the drawing described by Goethe (New York 1988b, 63, no. 1). There exist several other watercolors and a small-scale version in oil (Hamburg 1987, 92).
As Tischbein indicated in his memoirs, *Aus meinem Leben* (From my life), "Since connoisseurs praised the composition and amateurs made frequent requests, however, it appeared many times in small format before the full-scale production" (Tischbein 1922, 239–40).

Tischbein himself explained the genesis and meaning of the theme in his memoirs. In Sicily the artist's imagination had been stimulated by the approach of a horse and rider in a "blue morning fog," which rendered them larger than life in appearance. Tischbein began to muse "about man and how he rules exalted over all creatures" (cited in New York 1988b, 64):

> *He subjugates them, uses them for his purposes, brings them from the forest, and from the heights, captures them on the open plains. None can escape him; he lays claim to one, slaughters it, removes its skin and clothes himself; he prepares small delicacies from its flesh, loads them on another animal, seats himself on it, and lets himself be carried wherever it pleases him to eat. . . . It occurred to me that this was a subject for a painting, but that I would have to ennoble*

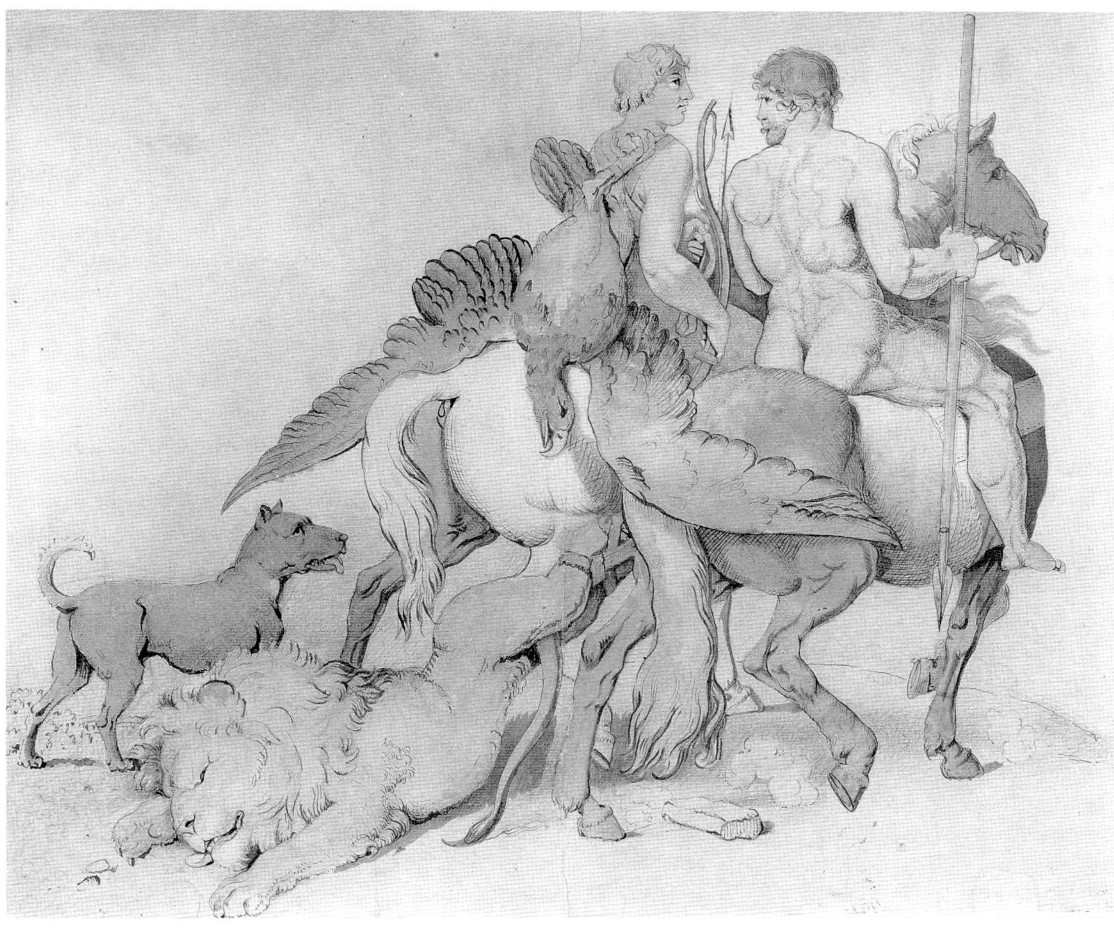

CATALOGUE NO. 103

it, since sheep hanging on a horse are a pitiful sight. . . . I thought of more beautiful creatures to include: man, horse, dog, lion and . . . the eagle.

Tischbein continued to be obsessed with the theme of the power of man and elaborated upon it further in an unpublished novel of 1812, *Die Eselsgeschichte; oder, Der Schwachmatikus und seine vier Brüder, der Sanguinikus, Cholerikus, Melancholikus und Phlegmatikus* (The story of a fool, or the ignoramus and his four brothers, the sanguine, the choleric, the melancholic and the phlegmatic) (cited in New York 1988b, 64):

Two hunters with a great entourage emerged from the forest . . . one was in the full bloom of youth, the other in his vigorous maturity. Both bore the imprint of nobility on their brows, and desperate fear had never paled their countenances. . . . They sat on splendid horses and engaged in earnest conversation. The man seemed to be instructing the boy, their quivers rattled on their shoulders; one hand grasped the powerful bow, the other held the reins tightly. A mighty lion that the strong man had felled was tied to this horse and he dragged it along behind him; even in death it seemed menacing to me. The boy bore a great eagle behind him, the tips of its wings touching the earth. A large hunting dog followed the lion. . . . "Who are these mighty heroes?" I asked the lad. "It is Nimrod, the divine hunter," he answered, "the embodiment of heroic strength." "How wonderful to be here, where the deeds of antiquity pass before me in living form and illuminate my obscure thoughts with clarity."

For the final version (1821) of *The Power of Man*, painted for the duke of Oldenburg, Tischbein coined the term *Vernunft-Bild* (reason-image) to describe his composition in that man was, by virtue of his reason, master of nature (New York 1988b, 63).

Tischbein's outline engravings illustrating Sir William Hamilton's collection of ancient vases, published in 1791–95, are acknowledged as a key influence in the genesis of the "primitivist" phase of neoclassical art occurring about 1800. Yet, by the mid-1780s Tischbein's own original compositions had already revealed aspects of Greek primitivism derived from fifth-century B.C. relief sculptures. *The Power of Man*, first conceived in 1786, is a consummate example of "primitivism," both thematically and formally. The subject evokes the most remote epoch of antiquity. Tischbein's nude hunters anticipate the warriors in Jacques-Louis David's "purely Greek" *The Sabine Women* (see FIGURE 13) by more than a decade.

Tischbein's various drawings of *The Power of Man* are distinguished by emphatic lines of contour that merge the hunters and animals in a friezelike format. The interior modeling of man and beast is achieved by infinitely subtle stippling and cross-hatching in pen and ink comparable to an engraving. With respect to technique, Tischbein's sheet heralds the graphic manner of the Nazarenes, in particular, Julius Schnorr von Carolsfeld (see CATALOGUE NO. 116). RJC

Jean-Pierre Saint-Ours

1752 Geneva 1809

SAINT-OURS WAS A PUPIL of Joseph-Marie Vien at the Académie in Paris at the same time as Jacques-Louis David. Saint-Ours won the Grand Prix de Rome in 1780 but did not receive a royal pension since he was both a foreigner and a Protestant. He nevertheless left that year for Rome, where he became well established. He was the protégé of Cardinal de Bernis and painted *The Choice of the Children of Sparta* (*Le Choix des enfants de Sparte*), 1786, which was exhibited at the Salon de la Liberté in Paris in 1791. Saint-Ours returned to Geneva in 1792 and changed his focus from history painting to portraiture. He became a member of the Institut de France in 1803. LDM

Jean-Pierre Saint-Ours
Titus Quincticus Flaminius Granting Liberty to Greece at the Isthmian Games
1780

104
Pen and ink, brush and brown wash, heightened with white ink, over black chalk on yellow-tan paper, on original blue mount covering the edges of the sheet
35.4 x 72 cm (13 15/16 x 28 5/16 in.)
Signed at lower center in brush and brown ink: *a Paris St. Ours ft/1780*
Los Angeles County Museum of Art, gift of Mr. and Mrs. Guy Stair Sainty (inv. no. M.86.65)

PROVENANCE
Private collection, Paris.
Stair Sainty Matthiesen, New York.

LITERATURE
Untitled catalogue (New York: Stair Sainty Matthiesen, n.d.), 11.

This drawing, and a version of the composition now in the Musée d'Art et d'Histoire, Geneva, very probably illustrate an incident from Plutarch's *Lives*. On the original mount of the Geneva drawing are the remains of a once longer inscription: . . . *Grecq assemblés dans le Cirque après les avoir vincus* (. . . Greek assembled in the Circus after having vanquished them). The standing figure addressing the crowd is a Roman general, identified as such by the lictors carrying fasces behind him at the right. These details suggest that Saint-Ours may have based his drawing on an episode in Plutarch's account of the Roman general Titus Quincticus Flaminius, who defeated the Greeks at the battle of Cynoscephlae at the beginning of the second century B.C. The conqueror displayed his magnanimity by restoring their liberty at the Isthmian Games in Corinth in 196 B.C. (Geneva/Dijon 1984, 112). The artist chose the climactic moment of this event, when the assembled Greeks rose up in jubilation upon hearing the news of their freedom. Saint-Ours shows several figures running forward to prostrate themselves at the general's feet in gratitude for their release.

Subjects such as the benefits of wise government, the generosity of monarchs, and the obligations of the citizen to the state were increasingly popular themes for artists during the 1770s and 1780s. At times these lessons in morality had an overtly propagandistic intent, for example, to glorify the reign of a monarch or to exemplify the virtue of individual sacrifice for the greater good of the state. As a native of Geneva, Saint-Ours may have found this lesson from classical history extolling the generous act of granting liberty to the oppressed to be of immediate significance: at this time the stable government of the city was disturbed by disenfranchised members of society demanding a greater voice in political affairs, which were largely controlled by a few aristocratic families; these agitations finally erupted into actual revolt in 1782.

In comparison with the version in Geneva, Saint-Ours made several major changes in the composition of the present drawing. Most obviously, for this work he adopted an elongated format that necessitated several compositional adjustments. Horsemen appear behind the general in the Los Angeles drawing to reinforce his commanding presence, whereas in the Geneva version the mounted soldiers, gesturing dramatically, dominate the center of the scene. In their place in this drawing the artist added an inscribed pillar and in front of it a group of men praising Flaminius. There are a number of minor differences among the

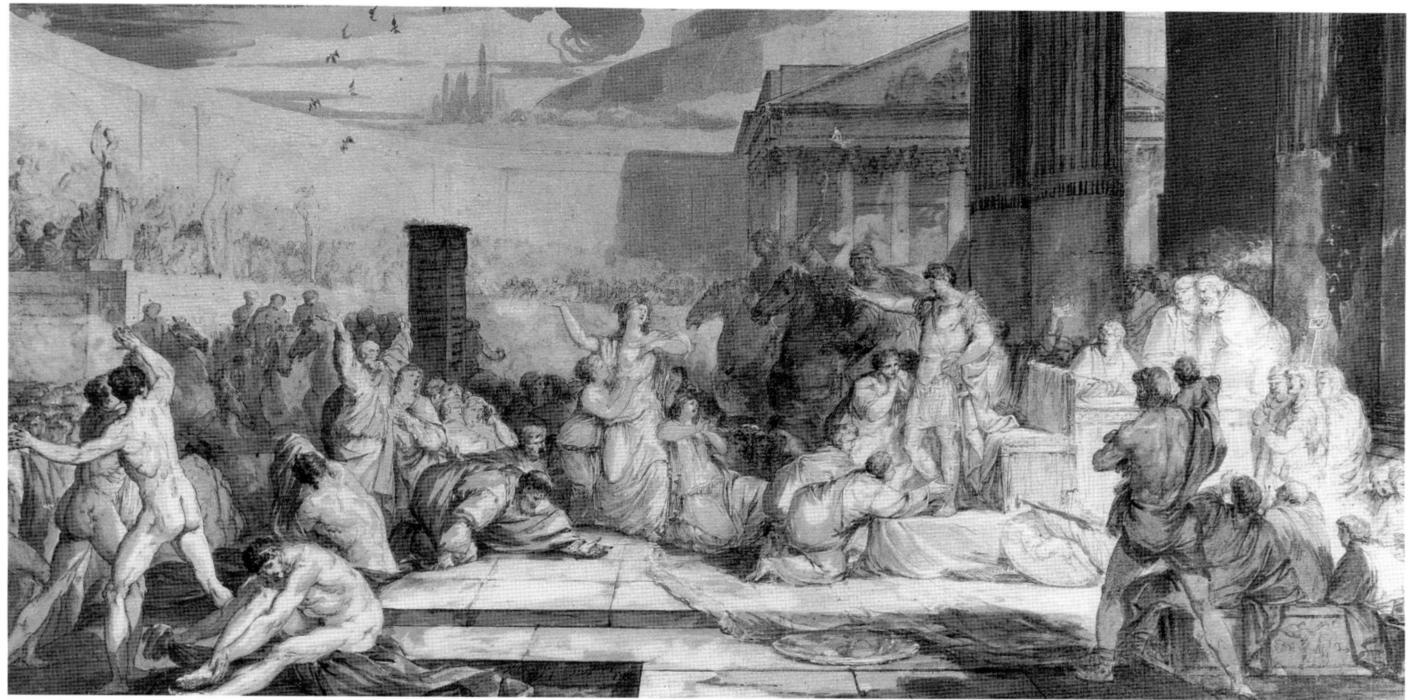

CATALOGUE NO. 104

figures in each drawing but no changes that would modify the content of the story. The architectural background is certainly imaginary, since examples of Greek architecture were scarcely known at this time, and is essentially the same in the two drawings, although Saint-Ours omitted the theatrical swag of drapery that appears in the upper-right corner of the Geneva version. His most significant revision is the pose of Flaminius, who here is in profile with his right arm outstretched, posed to suggest a classical Roman sculpture. It is not known whether Saint-Ours had in mind a specific antique model, however, he might well have consulted Bernard de Montfaucon's lavishly illustrated *L'Antiquité expliquée et representée en figures* (Paris, 1719–24), where in plate 2 of volume 4 there is in the upper-right corner an engraving of a sculpture then in the Mattei Collection that has the same general pose as Saint-Ours's figure, although the latter does not wear a decorated cuirass as shown in the print. Montfaucon notes in his text that when these Roman figures wear a plain cuirass, as in this drawing, it is then carefully modeled to reveal the musculature underneath, a small point that does correspond to Saint-Ours's representation. One cannot help but speculate whether the Swiss artist read Montfaucon before going to Italy or wonder whether he was fortunate enough to find in Paris originals, or modern replicas, that could inform him of such details.

Saint-Ours created a somewhat more restrained, dignified composition by suppressing several of the agitated poses of figures in the Geneva drawing and eliminating the bathetic gesture of Flaminius receiving homage in favor of a more austere pose with an unmistakable classical reference. There is nothing to indicate which drawing the artist made first, although this work may have followed the one in Geneva, if one assumes that an increasing use of classical motifs is a guide to Saint-Ours's chronology. At any event, the artist's inscription on this drawing notes that he executed it in Paris, just prior to his departure for Rome in 1780.

Both drawings are fully resolved works, carried to a high degree of finish more readily associated with painting, although Saint-Ours used conventional draftsman's materials. The artist displayed a genuine appreciation for the potential of brush and ink to create clearly defined figures and to evoke atmospheric effects. He often extended the tonal range of ink washes with the addition of white highlights and frequently drew on a colored or tinted paper. Such finished drawings, which the artist called "compositions dessinés," were sold with success to collectors throughout Europe. Generally, drawings worked up to a high degree of finish became an important type favored by neoclassical artists throughout Europe. Occasionally, rapidly executed preparatory sketches exist for the compositions of these finished drawings, as well as for individual figures (de Herdt 1978, 240, 252, 270, nos. 17j, 18j, 44i); undoubtedly, many other such preliminary studies will be identified as the drawings of this period receive further study and attention. VC

Asmus Jacob Carstens

1754 St. Jürgen (Schleswig)–Rome 1798

NEVER ONE TO COMPROMISE, Carstens declined an apprenticeship with Johann Heinrich Wilhelm Tischbein as too traditional a training. Instead, he worked as a cooper for seven years before enrolling in classes at the Copenhagen Kunstakademiet as a pupil of Nikolai Abraham Abildgaard. He left for Italy at his own expense in 1783 but only got as far as Mantua before his funds ran out; he spent his time there studying Giulio Romano's frescoes in the Palazzo del Te before he relocated to Germany. Carstens worked in Lübeck as a portrait painter until 1788, when he moved to Berlin, received a position as a professor in the Akademie, and had a successful exhibition of his painting *The Fall of the Angels* in 1790.

Carstens received a stipend from the Prussian government and left for Rome in 1792. He was recalled to Berlin two years later but refused to go, a move that resulted in the loss of his position. The one-man exhibition of his works at the Studio Buttoni in 1795 established his reputation with such works as *Night with Her Children Sleep and Death* (*Die Nacht mit ihren Kindern Schlaf und Tod*) and *The Battle between the Titans and Gods*, both 1795. He developed a following of young German and Nordic artists and was especially influential in the development of the talents of Joseph Anton Koch and Bertel Thorvaldsen. LDM

Asmus Jacob Carstens
Calais and Zetes Deliver Phineas from the Torments of the Harpies
1797

105
Graphite and traces of red chalk on white paper
19.2 x 24.3 cm (7 9/16 x 9 9/16 in.)
Kongelige Kobberstiksamling, Statens Museum for Kunst, Copenhagen (inv. no. Td.562.19)

PROVENANCE
Joseph Anton Koch.
Bertel Thorvaldsen.
Count Adam Moltke.

LITERATURE
Fernow 1867, 382.
Heine 1928, 154.
Einem 1935, 222, 224, fig. 28.
Kamphausen 1941, 228–31.
Neuwirth 1989, 47, 124, fig. 28.

In 1797, at the twilight of his career, Carstens executed twenty-four preliminary drawings for a prospective portfolio of engravings entitled *The Argonauts*. The drawing *Calais and Zetes* belongs to this series, all of which are preserved in Copenhagen (inv. nos. Td.562.7–.30.a; Neuwirth 1989, 22–69, figs. 4–50 [even numbers]). The drawings were discovered in Carstens's estate after his death in 1798 and were acquired by his friend and former pupil Joseph Anton Koch (Neuwirth 1989, 85). He later gave them to his friend, the sculptor Bertel Thorvaldsen.

In recognition of his debt to his master, Koch engraved Carstens's designs, which he published in Rome in 1799 with abbreviated French texts as *Les Argonautes selon Pindare, Orphée, et Apollonius de Rhodes en vingt-quatre planches inventées et dessinées par Asmus Jacques Carstens et gravées par Joseph Koch* (The Argonauts according to Pindar, Orpheus, and Apollonius of Rhodes in twenty-four plates invented and drawn by Asmus Jacob Carstens and engraved by Joseph Koch). Between 1807 and 1810 Koch sold the plates to the engraver Tommaso Piroli, whose name appears on the title plate of subsequent editions (Neuwirth 1989, 18, 71–77, 84–89, figs. 1, 51). Neuwirth (1989, 139–43, fig. 61) cited a Parisian edition with copies of Koch's engravings executed by Louis-François Charon (1783–about 1831).

Carstens's portfolio was undoubtedly inspired by the extraordinary international popularity of John Flaxman's designs for outline engravings illustrating the *Iliad* and the *Odyssey* of Homer and the tragedies of Aeschylus, dating 1793–95 (London 1979b, 178, 184–85; see also CATALOGUE NO. 8). The actual stylistic influence on Carstens's designs is controversial, however. Koch had enhanced Carstens's sketches for the engravings, particularly in the landscape passages (Neuwirth 1989, 126–28). Carl Ludwig Fernow, Carstens's panegyrist and first biographer, complained that Koch's engravings too closely resembled Flaxman's outlines. He contended that Carstens had wanted his designs "etched in copper with indications of light and shade," and that they were considered by the artist as a means to "painterly execution" (London 1979b, 178; Neuwirth 1989, 107–13). In a letter of March 21, 1807, to Karl Friedrich von Uexküll, Koch responded to Fernow's adverse criticism, protesting that Carstens's sketches were executed on his deathbed and were scarcely complete (Neuwirth 1989, 110–12).

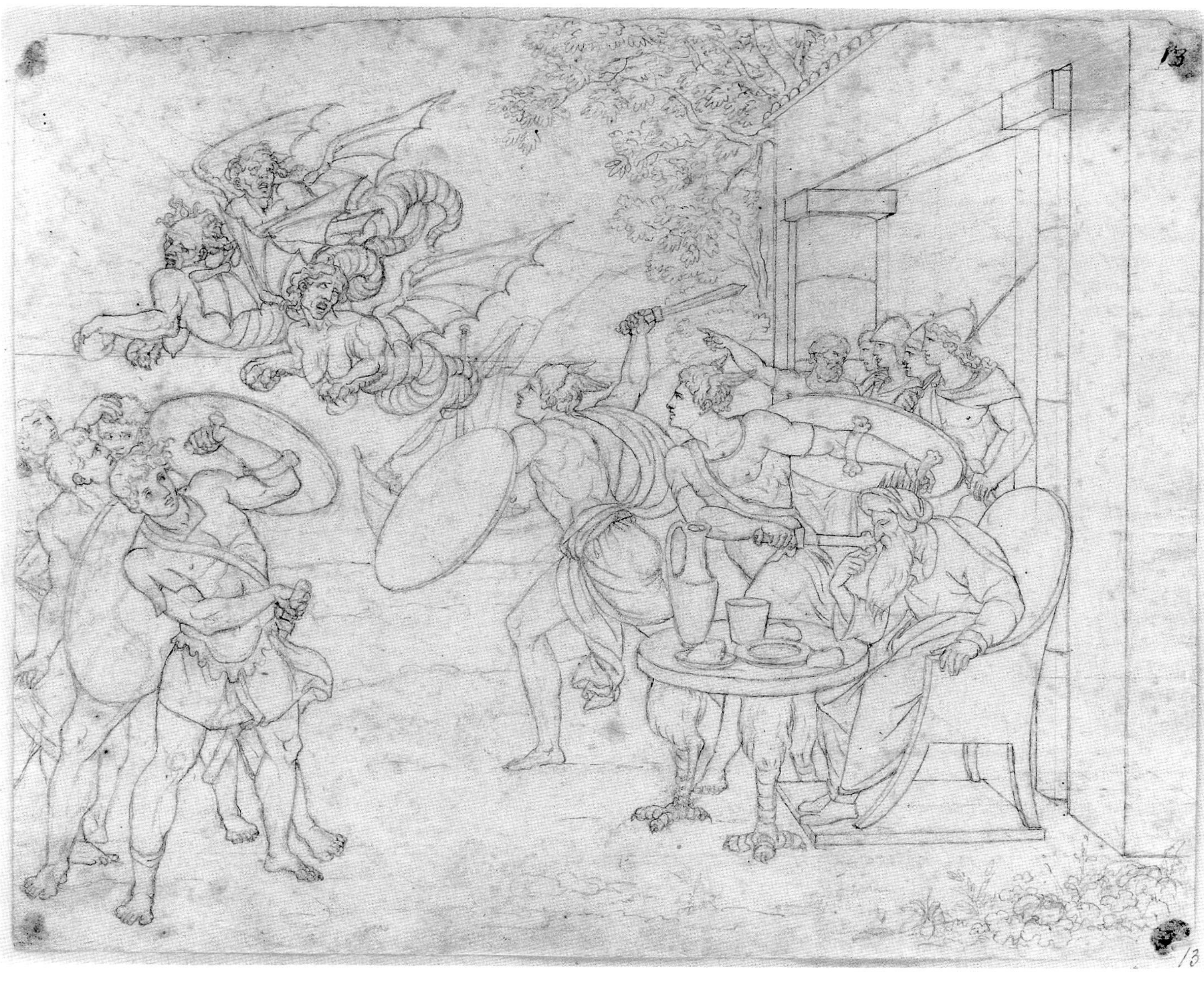

CATALOGUE NO. 105

As demonstrated by the Copenhagen *Calais and Zetes*, Carstens does stress the outline of his figures, which reveal slimmer proportions than the weighty, volumetric beings that populate his earlier drawings (see FIGURES 29, 31). Nevertheless, the depth of Carstens's composition is firmly established by the architecture, which differs from the deliberate "flatness" of Flaxman's designs. In realization, the *Argonaut* engravings occupy a middle ground between Flaxman's outline and the highly finished engraved illustrations after Chaudet, Gérard, Girodet, Guérin, Moitte, and Prud'hon for Didot's celebrated editions of the works of Apuleius, Virgil, Longus, and Jean Racine, published between 1797 and 1802.

The Copenhagen drawing illustrates an episode from book 2 of the *Argonautica* of Apollonius of Rhodes (2.170–350). The Argonauts Calais and Zetes, twin sons of the god Boreas, come to the aid of their brother-in-law, King Phineus of Bythnia. Although endowed with the gift of prophecy by Apollo, Phineus failed to respect the gods. Zeus punished him with blindness, a lingering old age, and when Phineus sat down to dine, his food was snatched away and befouled by marauding harpies. Calais and Zetes prepared a great feast for the king, which immediately attracted the harpies. The winged heroes drove away the monsters with their swords and pursued them to the Floating Islands. There the goddess Iris intervened to save the harpies from the Argonauts on the condition that they would never again torment Phineus. In return, Phineus instructed Jason and his Argonauts how to pass safely through the Clashing Cliffs (the Symplegades) on route to find the Golden Fleece. RJC

Josef Abel

1764 Aschach–Vienna 1818

JOSEF ABEL ENTERED the Vienna Akademie in 1782 under the supervision of Heinrich Füger and was recognized as a star pupil. One of his earliest commissions was for the Czartoryski family in Poland in 1795. He was an early recipient of a scholarship to study in Rome and left in 1802 for that city, where he painted *Hector's Departure* and *Andromache on Hector's Corpse*. In Rome he also executed what he considered his masterpiece, *Klopstock in Elysium*, 1803–7, with his friend Johann Christian Reinhart, and while there he was influenced by the work of Antonio Canova and the Germans Albert Christophe Dies, Joseph Anton Koch, and Gottlieb Schick. Abel returned to Vienna in 1808, where he painted portraits and large historical compositions as well as set designs for the theater. LDM

Josef Abel
Klopstock, Conducted by a Muse, Is Received by Homer on the Poet's Mountain in Elysium
c. 1803–7

106
Pen and brown ink, brush and brown wash, heightened with white and brown body color on blue-gray paper
47.5 x 62 cm (18 11/16 x 24 3/8 in.)
Private collection

Abel's painting *Klopstock in Elysium*, his masterpiece, was carried out in Rome between 1803 and 1807, when the grant that had made it possible for him to travel to Italy ran out (Aurenhammer 1966, 11 nn. 28–29, 23, fig. 9; London 1972, no. 1). A preparatory drawing in the Graphische Sammlung Albertina, Vienna, and an oil sketch in the Národni Galeri, Prague, were until now the only works known to have been made in the course of the four years the artist was occupied with the allegory. The present drawing must have been executed at the moment when Abel's plans had finally resolved themselves because in comparison with the canvas there are no significant changes. Each of the major figures seen here is repeated with only slight modifications of costume in the oil. In describing his program for the composition, Abel wrote: "Religion leads Klopstock into the circle of the most famous of the epic poets. Homer welcomes him; around are the Graces with the Muse, Clio. Behind are Virgil, Orpheus, Horace, Pindar, Sappho and the blind Milton led by his daughter. The second group consists of Petrarch and Laura, surrounded by Dante, Ariosto, Boccaccio, Metastasio, Alfieri and Tasso" (London 1972, no. 1).

Friedrich Gottlieb Klopstock is remembered today as one of the predecessors of the *Sturm und Drang* (Storm and stress) movement, because he began to question Johann Joachim Winckelmann's claims for the preeminence of Hellenistic culture. Klopstock proposed instead that the two great traditions of the modern world are Christianity and nationalism (Hatfield 1943, 80–83). This philosophy had important repercussions for German painters such as Philipp Otto Runge, who abandoned his neoclassic orientation to embrace this point of view. By honoring Klopstock, a recently deceased national figure, Abel endorsed at least one of the poet's tenets, that national history can provide heroes to rival the fame of the antique gods.

Interestingly enough, Abel's painting is not a visual paraphrase of the poet's ideals. The artist used a traditional format for a Parnassus or Elysium that would have been acceptable to Nicolas Poussin or Anton Raphael Mengs. Because Homer presided over Abel's Parnassus, the artist must have felt constrained to represent the other poets of this Elysium by references to the classical past, even if the result was a scene peopled by antique Roman statues. Ironically, these references were contravened by Klopstock's philosophy that Christianity and nationalism could provide modern equivalents to the ancients' mythology. In this sense, Abel's *Klopstock* imagery is a more bizarre example of historicism than Fulchran-Jean Harriet's near-contemporary *The Death of Raphael* (see CATALOGUE NO. 69), because the Renaissance artist who was the subject of Harriet's composition admired the classical past and was touched by such examples of its heritage as he knew. VC

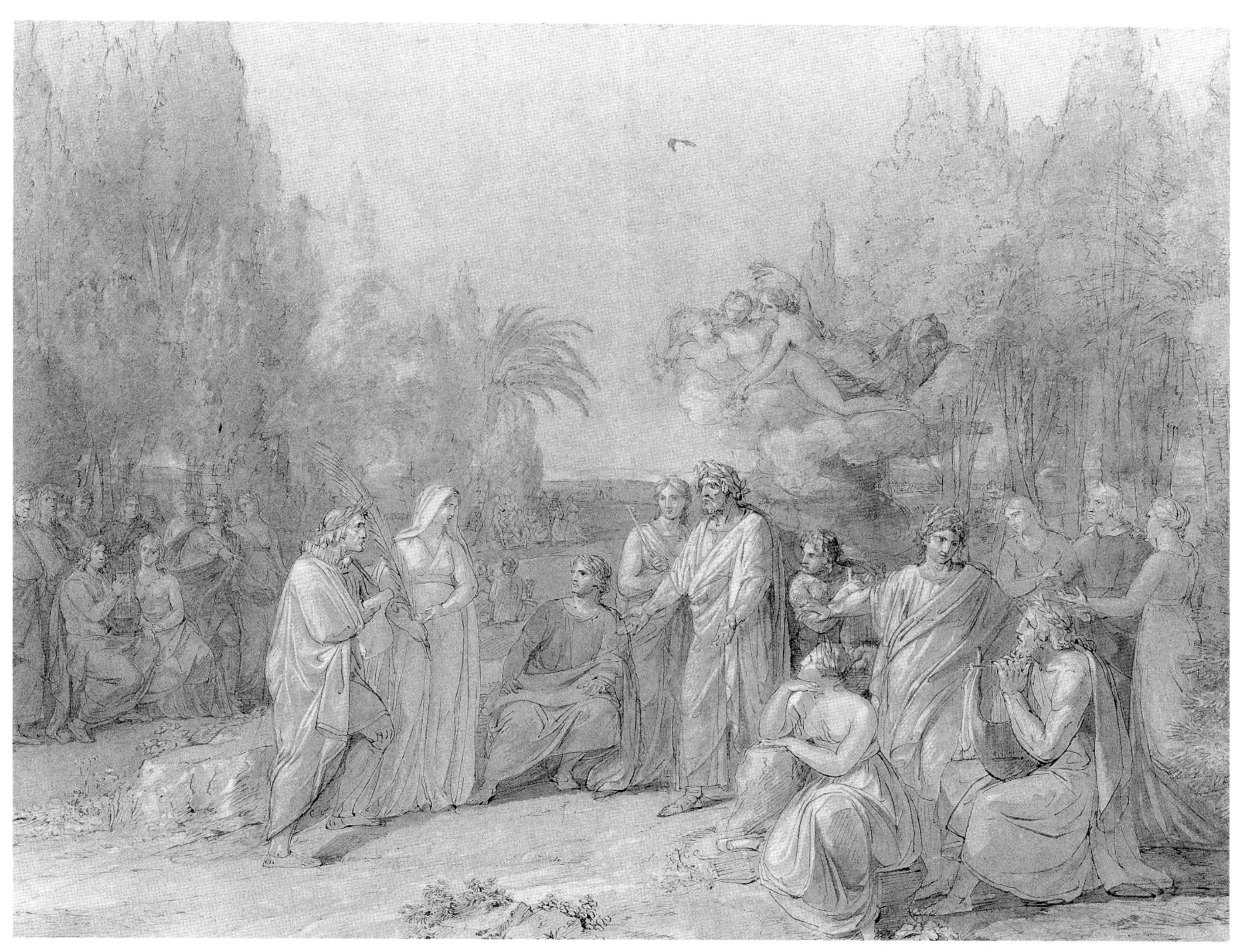

CATALOGUE NO. 106

Joseph Anton Koch

1768 Obergibeln (Tirol)–Rome 1839

KOCH BEGAN HIS TRAINING in 1785 at the Hohe Karlsschule in Stuttgart with Adolf Friedrich Harper and Philipp Friedrich Hetsch. He rebelled against academic discipline and in 1791 left for France and Switzerland, where he studied and painted the alpine landscapes. Assisted by a stipend from an Englishman named Nott, Koch spent part of 1794 traveling in Italy, visiting Naples and Florence. He settled in Rome in 1795, where he stayed until his death, with the exception of three fruitful years spent in Vienna (1812–15). During his first years in Rome Koch moved in the circle of his teacher, Asmus Jacob Carstens, and became friends with Johann Christian Reinhart and Bertel Thorvaldsen. Koch was best known for "heroic" classical landscapes, such as *Schmadribach Falls*, 1811, as well as for his association with the Nazarenes. He joined this group in executing fresco decorations for the Casino Massimo in Rome, for which he painted scenes from Dante's *Divina Commedia* in 1825–28. LDM

Joseph Anton Koch
(after Asmus Jacob Carstens)
Paolo and Francesca in the Whirlwind
1823

107
Pen and brown ink, watercolor on four sheets of white cardboard pasted together
76.5 x 100.5 cm (30 1/16 x 39 9/16 in.)
Signed and dated at lower right in brown ink: *A. I. Karstens./inv. 1797/I. Koch exe./1823*
Thorvaldsens Museum, Copenhagen (inv. no. D684)

PROVENANCE
Acquired from the artist by Bertel Thorvaldsen in Rome.

EXHIBITED
Hamburg/Copenhagen/London 1979, no. 216.
Berlin 1989–90, no. 53.

LITERATURE
Lutterotti 1985, 346, no. Z443.

In 1796–97 Asmus Jacob Carstens worked on a composition representing the second circle of Hell from Dante's *Divina Commedia*, with its whirlwind of doomed lovers, and executed both a large outline drawing and a series of studies for separate figures (all now in the Weimar Kunstsammlungen). These drawings were part of Carstens's estate, of which Koch, Bertel Thorvaldsen, and the art critic Carl Ludwig Fernow were executors. The majority of Carstens's drawings were transferred to Weimar through Fernow in 1803 (Schleswig 1992), but before this date the two young artists copied a large number of them. Thorvaldsen acquired both a series of original drawings by Carstens, among them the sketches for his series on Jason and the Argonauts (see CATALOGUE NO. 105)—which later came to the Kongelige Kobberstiksamling in Copenhagen—and some copies by Koch after Carstens's compositions. Thorvaldsen also executed for himself some carefully finished drawings copying such famous compositions as *Night with Her Children Sleep and Death* (*Die Nacht mit ihren Kindern Schlaf und Tod*; see FIGURE 31), *The Blind Homer Reciting His Verses* (*Der blinde Homer, seine Verse vortragend*), and *The Golden Age* (*Das goldene Zeitalter*).

Both Thorvaldsen and Koch, who in 1801–3 had shared lodgings in the via Sistina in Rome, worked during the first decade of the nineteenth century in a manner strongly influenced by Carstens in both form and content. Among their collaborations can be found motifs completely in the spirit of Carstens, such as Dante and Virgil on the back of Geryon (Holst 1980). Thorvaldsen's earliest sketches of this subject are from around 1802, while his more finished drawings can be dated as late as 1810. Among Koch's versions are a painting of the heads of Dante and Virgil (Staatsgalerie, Stuttgart), which can be dated about 1802–4, and a watercolor of the entire composition (Thorvaldsens Museum, Copenhagen), executed at the beginning of the 1820s. The present drawing is dated 1823; twenty-five years after Carstens's death his art was still valid for his friends and imitators.

The *Divina Commedia* was an important source for artists around 1800, from John Flaxman's outline illustrations of 1792 to Koch's Casino Massimo frescoes of 1825–28. In the latter, Koch's Carstens-inspired manner culminates in scenes from Hell and Purgatory, while Paradise, painted in 1819–24 by Philipp Veit, is on the vaulted ceiling. In Koch's fresco of Hell can be recognized two subjects that he had already rendered several times: Dante and Virgil on the back of Geryon and the lovers Paolo and Francesca da Rimini.

In the fifth canto of the *Inferno* Dante recounted the true story of the ill-fated love of Francesca, the wife of the

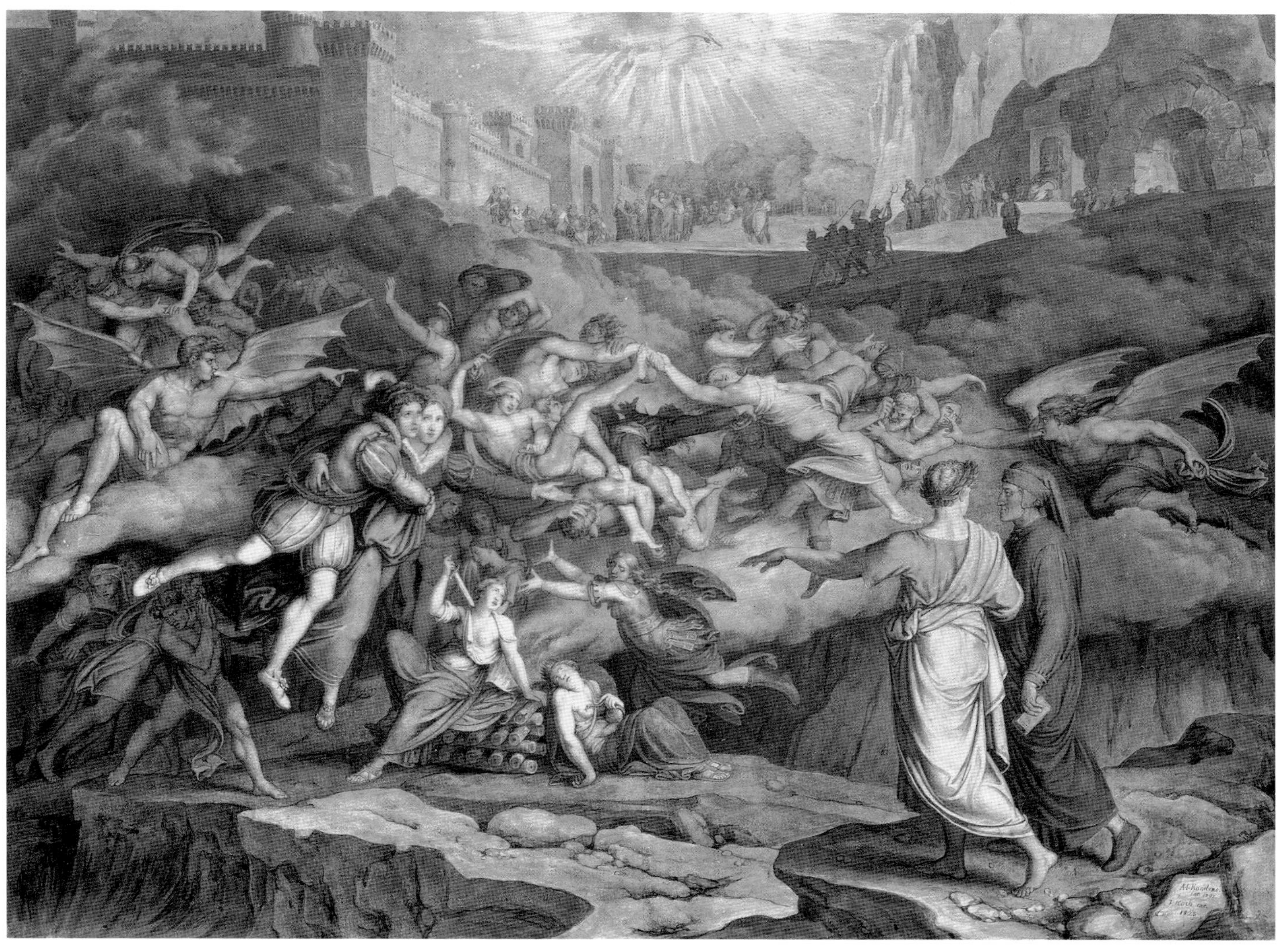

CATALOGUE NO. 107

deformed Gianciotto da Rimini, and her young brother-in-law, Paolo, whom Dante knew. The lovers, stabbed to death by Gianciotto when he found them together, were consigned by Dante to the second circle of Hell, where they were swept in a ceaseless wind.

In this watercolor the laurel-crowned poet Virgil indicates to Dante the whirl of twisted bodies, sped on their way by demons at left and right. Paolo and Francesca, dressed in Renaissance costume, can be seen to the left; among the other doomed lovers are, in a group at lower center, the deserted Dido seated on her pyre, Cleopatra and the fleeing Mark Antony, and Paris and Helen of Troy.

In the background is the first circle of Hell, where, at right, souls are presented for judgment to Minos, those condemned being carried down the slope by a band of demons. At the left is Limbo, where virtuous pagans reside. BJ

Bertel Thorvaldsen

1770 Copenhagen 1844

THE SON OF A WOOD-CARVER, Thorvaldsen began his training as a pupil of Nikolai Abraham Abildgaard at the Kunstakademiet in Copenhagen in 1781, winning the major gold medal in 1793 and the Kunstakademiet's traveling scholarship in 1795. He left for Italy in 1796 and remained there until 1838, except for a brief return to Denmark in 1819–20. During his early years in Rome Thorvaldsen was influenced by Asmus Jacob Carstens and supported financially by Thomas Hope, whose advance on a marble version of *Jason with the Golden Fleece* (see FIGURE 15), 1802–3, enabled him to remain in Italy. He modeled *Ganymede Offering the Cup*, 1804, and in 1807 was commissioned to execute four reliefs for Christian Frederik Hansen's Christiansborg Slot (palace) in Copenhagen. His equestrian monument to Jozef Poniatowski in Warsaw was commissioned in 1817, the same year he began *The Three Graces and Cupid*.

Thorvaldsen returned from his visit to Copenhagen in 1820 with many commissions on behalf of the city, the greatest of these being the statues of Christ and his apostles for the Vor Frue Kirke (Church of Our Lady) of Copenhagen. He became a member of the Accademia di San Luca in 1808 and was president of the organization in 1827–28. The sculptor's tomb for Pope Pius VII was unveiled in the basilica of San Pietro in 1831. In 1837 he made the decision to give his works, collections, and fortune to his native city to establish a museum; he returned to Denmark the next year, accompanied by a frigate full of his work. Thorvaldsen was occupied with his duties as director and professor of the Kunstakademiet in Copenhagen, various sculptural commissions, and the completion of his museum until his death in 1844. His body was laid in a tomb in the courtyard of the Thorvaldsen Museum when it was completed in 1848. LDM

Bertel Thorvaldsen
Hector
c. 1804

108
Graphite, black and white chalks on gray paper
42.5 x 25.5 cm (16 3/4 x 10 1/16 in.)
Thorvaldsens Museum, Copenhagen
(inv. no. c80).

PROVENANCE
Found in Thorvaldsen's lodgings, Casa Buti, via Sistina, Rome, 1844.

LITERATURE
Thiele 1851–54, vol. 2, 100, 136.
London 1973a, 17.

Throughout his career Thorvaldsen was occupied with themes from Homer's *Iliad*, from 1791 in his student work at the Kunstakademiet in Copenhagen to 1837, when he was commissioned to execute a statue of Achilles for Sir Henry Labouchère. In a number of drawings dated around 1804 and later, Thorvaldsen depicted the incident from the first canto of the *Iliad*, in which Prince Hector, commander of the Trojan army, comes to the chamber of his brother Paris to persuade him to leave the beautiful Helen and come out to the battlefield to fight the Greeks.

In this drawing Hector is shown alone, scowling and gesticulating as he urges Paris to fight. Thorvaldsen experiments in this sheet, as he often did, with different positions, here of the head, arms, spear, and legs. Furthermore, he has—somewhat atypically for him in such a preliminary drawing—made some effort to depict details in the musculature, helmet, and costume, using shading and light to accentuate the volumes.

Thorvaldsen's biographer, J. M. Thiele, recorded that in 1808 the sculptor was given a commission by a Russian nobleman, Pierre de Balck, to execute a relief of the subject of Phaedra and Hippolytus (Thiele 1851–54, vol. 2, 100). The commission, however, was given instead to the sculptor Daniel Rauch, and Thorvaldsen contracted with de Balck for a relief of Hector, Paris, and Helen, thus being able to put to use the general concept he had developed in the earlier drawings. A precise date for the drawings, including the present sheet, cannot be established; they are tentatively dated to about 1804 only because one of them is drawn on the verso of a printed sonnet dated 1804. The drawings could actually have been executed about the time the artist began to work on the 1809 relief. The relief depicts the figures in reverse, as does a later relief, of 1837, in which the three protagonists are accompanied by two maids (the original plaster models for both reliefs, as well as the marble version of the 1809 relief are in the Thorvaldsen Museum).

This sheet was among the many drawings found after Thorvaldsen's death in the artist's Roman lodgings in Casa Buti in via Sistina; it was part of the original collection of the Thorvaldsens Museum, founded in 1848. SM

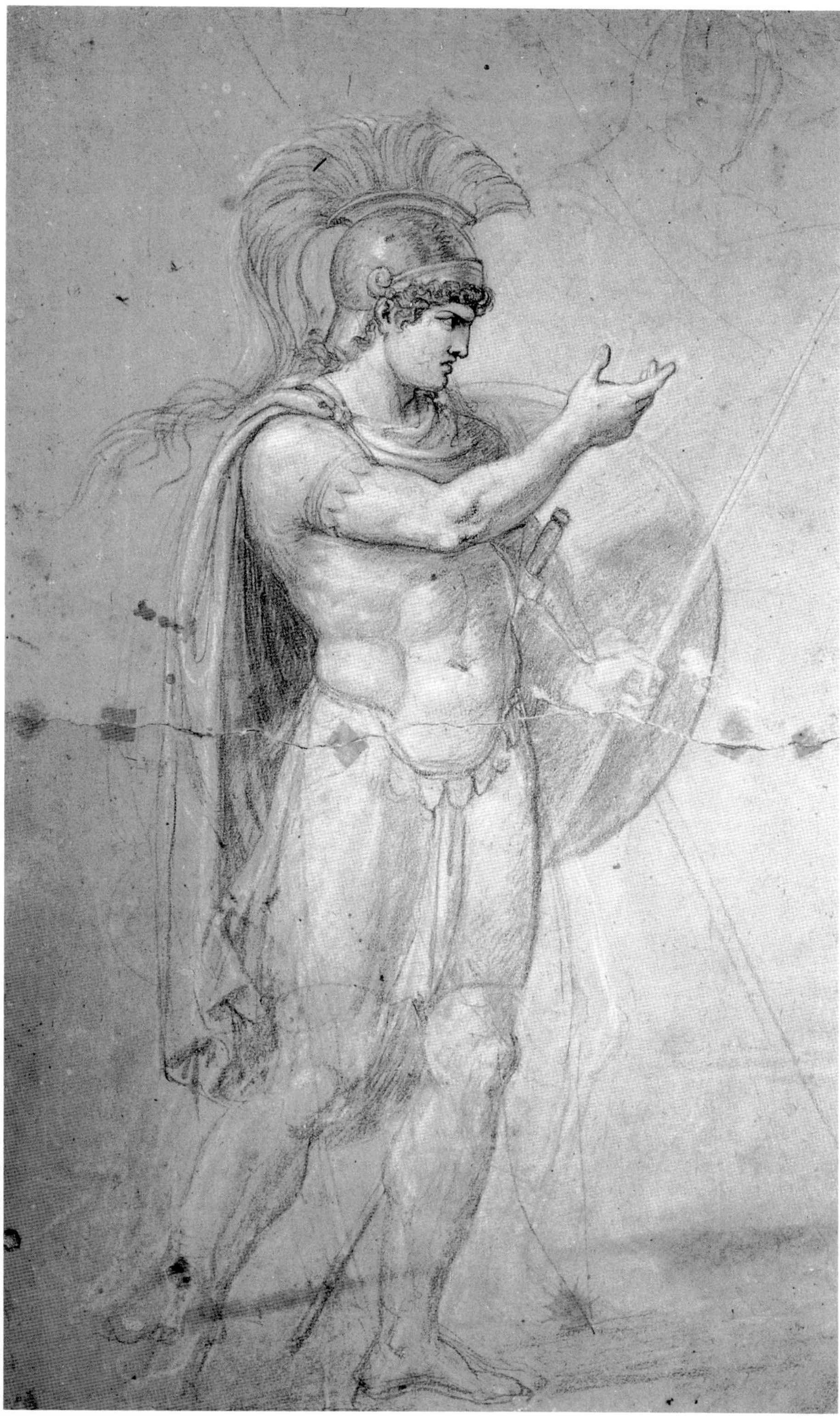

CATALOGUE NO. 108

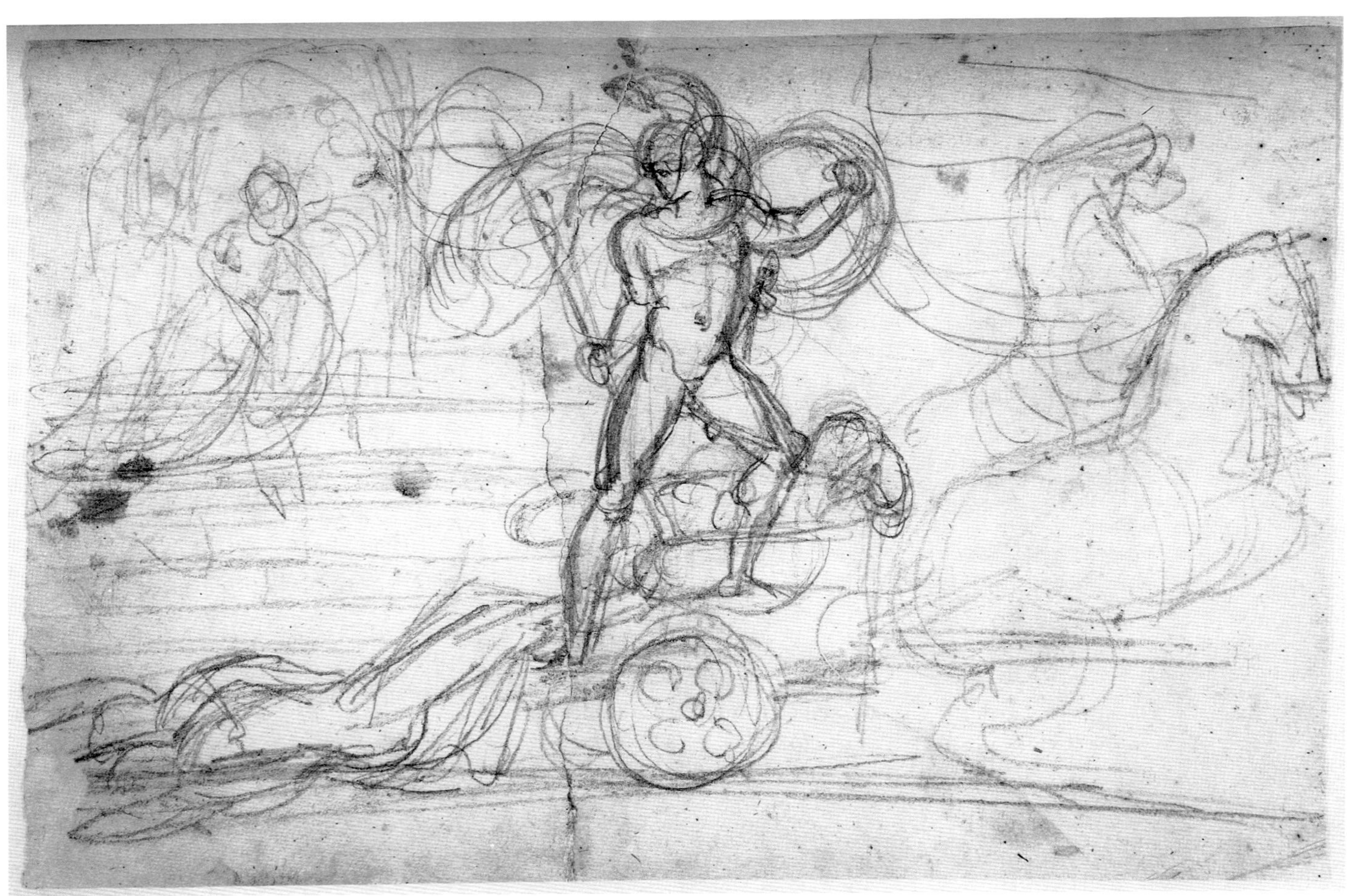

CATALOGUE NO. 109

Bertel Thorvaldsen
Achilles Dragging the Body of Hector around the Walls of Troy
c. 1804

109
Black chalk on white laid paper
22.1 x 34 cm (8 11/16 x 13 3/8 in.)
Watermark: *BRACCIANO*
Thorvaldsens Museum, Copenhagen
(inv. no. C26)

PROVENANCE
Found in Thorvaldsen's lodgings, Casa Buti, via Sistina, Rome, 1844.

EXHIBITED
London 1973a, no. 12.
Hamburg/Copenhagen/London 1979, no. 237b.

LITERATURE
Thiele 1851–54, vol. 1, 250.
Johansen 1923, 247–49.

This chalk study represents the revenge of the Greek warrior Achilles on the dead body of the Trojan prince Hector, who had killed Achilles's friend Patroclus in battle, an episode described by Homer in the *Iliad* (22.395–515). After killing Hector in single combat, the enraged Achilles tied the body to his chariot by the heels and dragged it around the walls of the besieged city of Troy.

Two British works of art are sources for this composition. The pose of Achilles—essentially nude, but with indications of the formfitting armor forged for him by Hephaestus—was derived from that of the clothed figure in a painting of the same subject by Gavin Hamilton, which would have been known to Thorvaldsen through an engraving of 1766 by Domenico Cunego. The composition of Thorvaldsen's drawing, however, is even closer to John Flaxman's rendering of the scene from his illustrations to the *Iliad*, engraved in 1793 by Tommaso Piroli. Thorvaldsen had acquired an early edition of Flaxman's *Iliad* and traced some of the engravings on semitransparent paper, among them the motif of Achilles with Hector's body. Both Flaxman and Thorvaldsen employed a friezelike arrangement of the elements of the composition; Thorvaldsen's figure of the flying Apollo at the left is specifically taken from Flaxman's illustration.

According to his biographer, J. M. Thiele (1851–54, vol. 1, 250), Thorvaldsen worked with Homeric themes in a series of drawings around 1804, after having modeled a relief of *Briseis Led Away from Achilles by Agamemnon's Heralds* (Thorvaldsens Museum, Copenhagen) the previous year. Among his drawings from this period, besides the present work, are several related to it, representing King Priam of Troy pleading with Achilles for Hector's mutilated body, the episode that succeeds the incident depicted in this drawing. Thorvaldsen's inspiration for the representation of Priam and Achilles was Asmus Jacob Carstens's rendering of the subject in a drawing, now in the Nationalgalerie, Berlin. In 1791, while at the Kunstakademiet, Thorvaldsen had modeled a relief representing Priam pleading with Achilles (Thorvaldsens Museum, Copenhagen); in 1815 he executed the motif again as a relief, when the duke of Bedford commissioned a pendant to the *Briseis* (Woburn Abbey, Bedfordshire).

Achilles Dragging the Body of Hector around the Walls of Troy was never executed as a relief, but Thorvaldsen used a similar vigorous figure of a hero mounted on a *biga*, a two-horse chariot, in his *Alexander* frieze, which he executed in plaster in 1812 for the Palazzo del Quirinale in Rome as an homage to Napoleon, whose visit to Rome was expected in that year. BJ

Bertel Thorvaldsen
Theseus Slaying the Minotaur
c. 1805

110
Pen, wash, and graphite on grayish paper
49 x 61.3 cm (19 5/16 x 24 1/8 in.)
Thorvaldsens Museum, Copenhagen
(inv. no. C10b)

PROVENANCE
Found in Thorvaldsen's lodgings, Casa Buti, via Sistina, Rome, 1844.

EXHIBITED
London 1973a, no. 16.
Cologne 1977, no. B14.
Rome 1989, no. D83.

LITERATURE
Schlegel 1846, vol. 9, 241.
Thiele 1851–54, vol. 2, 47.
Gerlach 1970, 77.

In 1805 Thorvaldsen received a major commission from Marchese Giovanni Raimondo Torlonia for a large sculpture that was to be a pendant to the *Hercules and Lichas* executed by Antonio Canova, which was commissioned in marble to stand in the marchese's palace in Piazza Venezia (now in the Galleria Nazionale d'Arte Moderna, Rome).

According to Thorvaldsen's biographer, J. M. Thiele, Thorvaldsen was permitted to choose the subject himself, but for some time he remained undecided (Thiele 1851–54, vol. 2, 47). He considered *Achilles and Penthesilea*, a *Centauromachia*, and *Mars and Venus*—in fact, the last was actually begun but never completed in the intended form. A letter from the philosopher August Wilhelm von Schlegel to Goethe (Schlegel 1846, vol. 9, 241) seems to confirm that the subject of *Theseus Slaying the Minotaur* was also among the subjects Thorvaldsen considered for the Torlonia commission.

An incitement for the sculptor to create a major sculpture of Theseus fighting the Minotaur was undoubtedly provided by

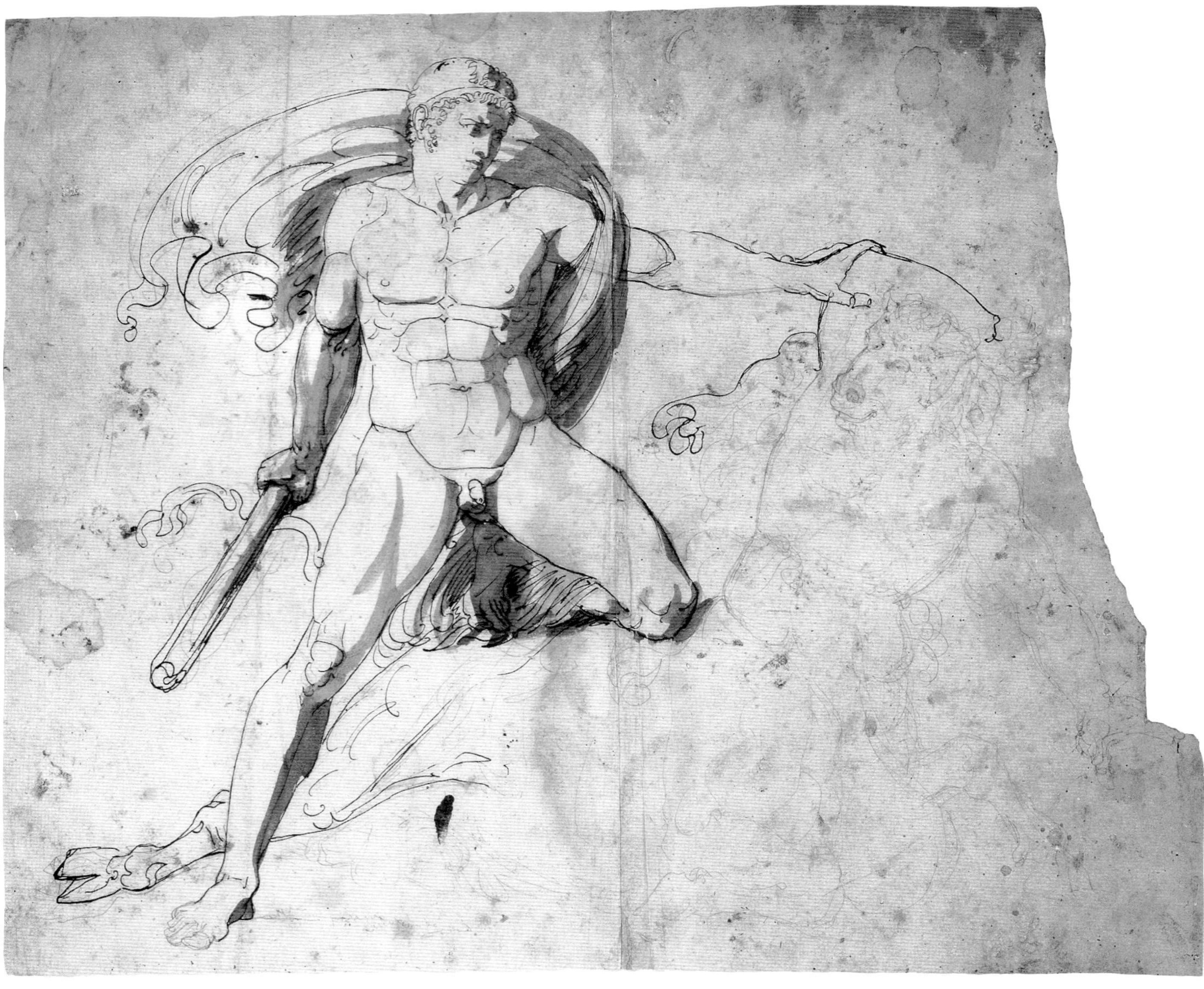

CATALOGUE NO. 110

the fact that Canova had recently finished the model for a sculpture of *Theseus Slaying a Centaur* (the marble version of the group is now in the Kunsthistorisches Museum in Vienna). Thorvaldsen had openly expressed several times his eagerness to compete with Canova by depicting the same subjects as the Italian artist. While Thorvaldsen may have been inspired in this drawing by Canova's group, the composition is also reminiscent, as Peter Gerlach has pointed out (1970, 77), of the ancient emblem of the Persian god Mithras killing a bull, a familiar emblem on antique altars throughout the city of Rome and its former empire, where the cult of Mithras was promoted and spread by the Roman army.

A series of drawings of Theseus, son of the king of Athens, in combat with either a centaur or the bull-headed Minotaur reflects Thorvaldsen's formative processes. The nature of the present drawing, with its exact rendering in outline of the body of Theseus, suggests that Thorvaldsen has ceased to experiment and has now decided how the sculptural group must be realized.

The drawing, which was never to be realized as a sculpture, is exceptional among Thorvaldsen's drawings not only for its size but also as evidence of the artist's mastery of heroic classicism just two years after the sculpture *Jason with the Golden Fleece* (see FIGURE 15) had made him known in Rome. As with so many of his drawings, this sheet was found in his Roman lodgings, Casa Buti, after his death in 1844 and was part of the original collection in the Thorvaldsen Museum at its opening in 1848. SM

Bertel Thorvaldsen
Cupid Playing with a Butterfly
Probably 1805–10

111
Black and white chalks on brown prepared paper
42 x 33.2 cm (16 1/2 x 13 1/16 in.)
Signed at lower right in black chalk: *Thorwaldsen*
Watermark: *BRACCIANO*
Kongelige Kobberstiksamling, on deposit in the Thorvaldsens Museum, Copenhagen

PROVENANCE
Possibly Friederike Brun.
The Brun family.

LITERATURE
Thiele 1851–54, vol. 2, 135.
Bobé 1938, 145.
Jørnæs 1978, 298–300.

The subject of Cupid playing with a butterfly was probably drawn the first time by Thorvaldsen near the end of 1805 as a birthday gift to his patron Baron Herman Schubart, who was living in Pisa or on Montenero outside Livorno. The artist sent the drawing from Rome to the baroness so that she could present it to her husband on his actual birthday, January 14, 1806. In a letter of February 3 she thanked Thorvaldsen in Italian: "That adorable Cupid was received with the greatest of pleasure. He could not hope to find a haven more secure, more loving, or more constant." Schubart's letter of thanks dates from February 14 and mentions that he finds the drawing so beautiful that he has to look at it every day.

In this context the butterfly symbolizes the human soul, here being totally ensnared by the power of love. The motif was known from antiquity and also took the form of Cupid chasing or burning a butterfly. It was found on antique carved gems, examples of which were to be found in Thorvaldsen's own collection of antiquities (Fossing 1929, nos. 745–51).

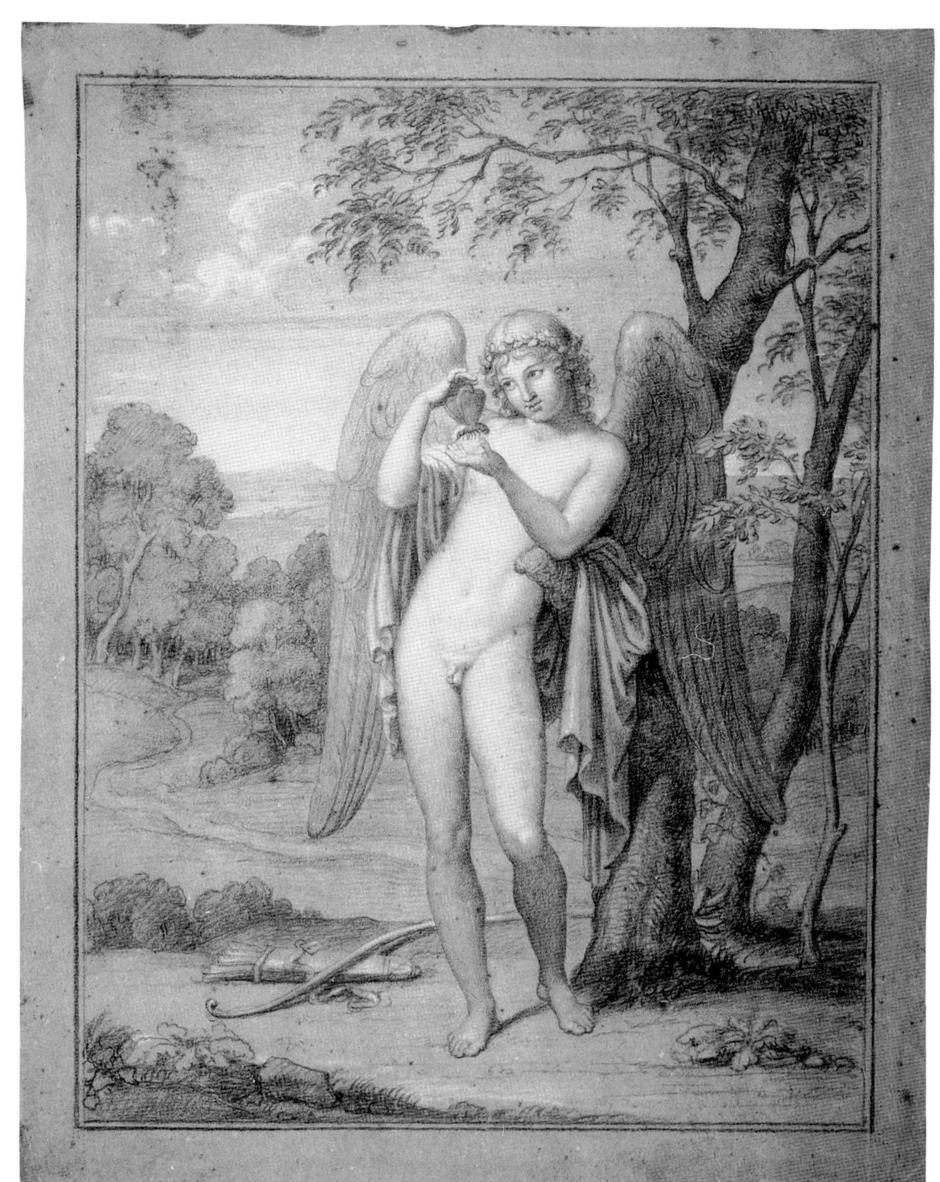

CATALOGUE NO. 111

Unfortunately, the Schubart drawing cannot now be identified among the extant versions of the subject. During the first two decades of the nineteenth century Thorvaldsen made a series of highly finished drawings of subjects such as *Cupid Playing with a Butterfly*, *Cupid and Bacchus*, *Caritas*, *Mary with Christ and John the Baptist as Children*, and *Dante and Virgil on the Back of Geryon*. Several of them were gifts to the Schubarts, but replicas were also executed for other friends or patrons. Drawings of *Cupid Playing with a Butterfly* exist in several versions now in the Thorvaldsen Museum, Kunsthalle Hamburg, and private collections. One was given by the artist to the Austrian Fanny Caspers, with whom he had an affair at the beginning of 1819. The exhibited drawing might have been in the possession of the poetess Friederike Brun, who visited Rome several times and was one of the first to write about Thorvaldsen. She may have acquired the drawing or received it as a gift during her Roman stay of 1807–10.

Between 1809 and 1811 Thorvaldsen executed a statue, now lost, representing Cupid holding a butterfly; the contract for the work was signed on August 20, 1809, by Thorvaldsen and Baron Theodor de Hahn. It was described by J. M. Thiele as "the God of Love holding a butterfly by the wings in order to hurt it with his arrow" (Thiele 1851–54, vol. 2, 135). The statue is reproduced in an engraving in the earliest publication of Thorvaldsen's works by Ferdinando Mori in 1811 (pl. 28). In both the drawing and the statue Cupid gently holds the butterfly with the fingers of his right hand, but in the latter version he has an arrow in his left hand, intending to hurt the small insect—an allegory of love being forced upon the human soul.

A friend of Thorvaldsen, the Danish painter Christian Gottlieb Kratzenstein Stub, copied one of the sculptor's *Cupid* drawings in a painting (now in a private collection) during his stay in Rome in 1810–11 and exhibited it in the Kunstakademiet's annual exhibition in Copenhagen in 1812. The landscape behind Cupid in Thorvaldsen's drawing is idealized in the manner of Thorvaldsen's friends Joseph Anton Koch and Johann Christian Reinhart. He was acquainted with this landscape style through his collaboration with George Augustus Wallis, for whom he executed staffage figures around 1800. BJ

Bertel Thorvaldsen
Sheet of Studies
c. 1823

112
Pen and brown ink, black chalk on yellowed paper
34.1 x 22 cm (13 7/16 x 8 11/16 in.)
Thorvaldsens Museum, Copenhagen
(inv. no. C261)

PROVENANCE
Found in Thorvaldsen's lodgings, Casa Buti, via Sistina, Rome, 1844.

LITERATURE
Thiele 1851–54, vol. 3, 185.
Bott 1989, 97.
Helsted/Henschen/Jørnæs 1990, 94.

In this sheet of studies Thorvaldsen has let his hand be guided by the thoughts and images rushing through his mind. The subjects on the sheet reflect reliefs by the sculptor spanning a period of fourteen years. Scattered among the sketches and notations are more than a dozen signatures as *A Thorvaldsen* and several as *Alberto*—an Italianization of his first name, written without any obvious practical purpose. In psychological terms this action suggests concern with one's own identity; an introverted and somewhat melancholic state of mind is reflected by the sentiment of a number of the drawings, which have as their theme the inevitability of old age.

Two sketches of a solitary old man with his chin in his hand, rendered both clothed and, in profile, nude, is probably a study for the relief *The Ages of Love* (the original plaster model and a marble version are in the Thorvaldsen Museum), which Thorvaldsen executed in a few days' time during Easter of 1824, when most studios were closed for the holiday and the rain was pouring outside. Part of the relief is derived from the famous ancient Roman wall painting at Stabiae depicting *The Merchant of Cupids*, but Thorvaldsen continues to chart the course of love as man ages. Old age, represented in this sketch, feels love as a burden and Cupid flies away.

That love has no respect for age is the theme behind the figures of Cupid and Anacreon drawn twice on the recto of the sheet and five times on the verso. The subject is taken from the *Anacreontea*, a collection of poems by the Greek poet Anacreon and his followers. In the third song the old Anacreon lets a freezing, wet boy come into his dwelling, but as soon as the boy is warm, he reveals himself as Cupid and sticks an arrow into the heart of the poet. The studies were used for a relief of this theme commissioned by the German count Franz Erwein von Schönborn in 1823. The relief, with its references to old age and cold weather, was meant to be an allegory of winter and was thus related to two reliefs already modeled by Thorvaldsen in 1810: *Cupid with a Swan and Boys Picking Fruit*, symbolizing summer, and *Cupid and the Young Bacchus Treading Grapes*, symbolizing autumn (Schönborn also ordered marble versions of these two reliefs in 1823). *Cupid with a Swan* is reflected in two sketches of boys playing with swans in the present drawing.

Hans Christian Andersen saw the relief *Cupid and Anacreon* in Thorvaldsen's studio in 1833, and this inspired him to write the fairy tale *The Naughty Boy*, published in 1835. SM

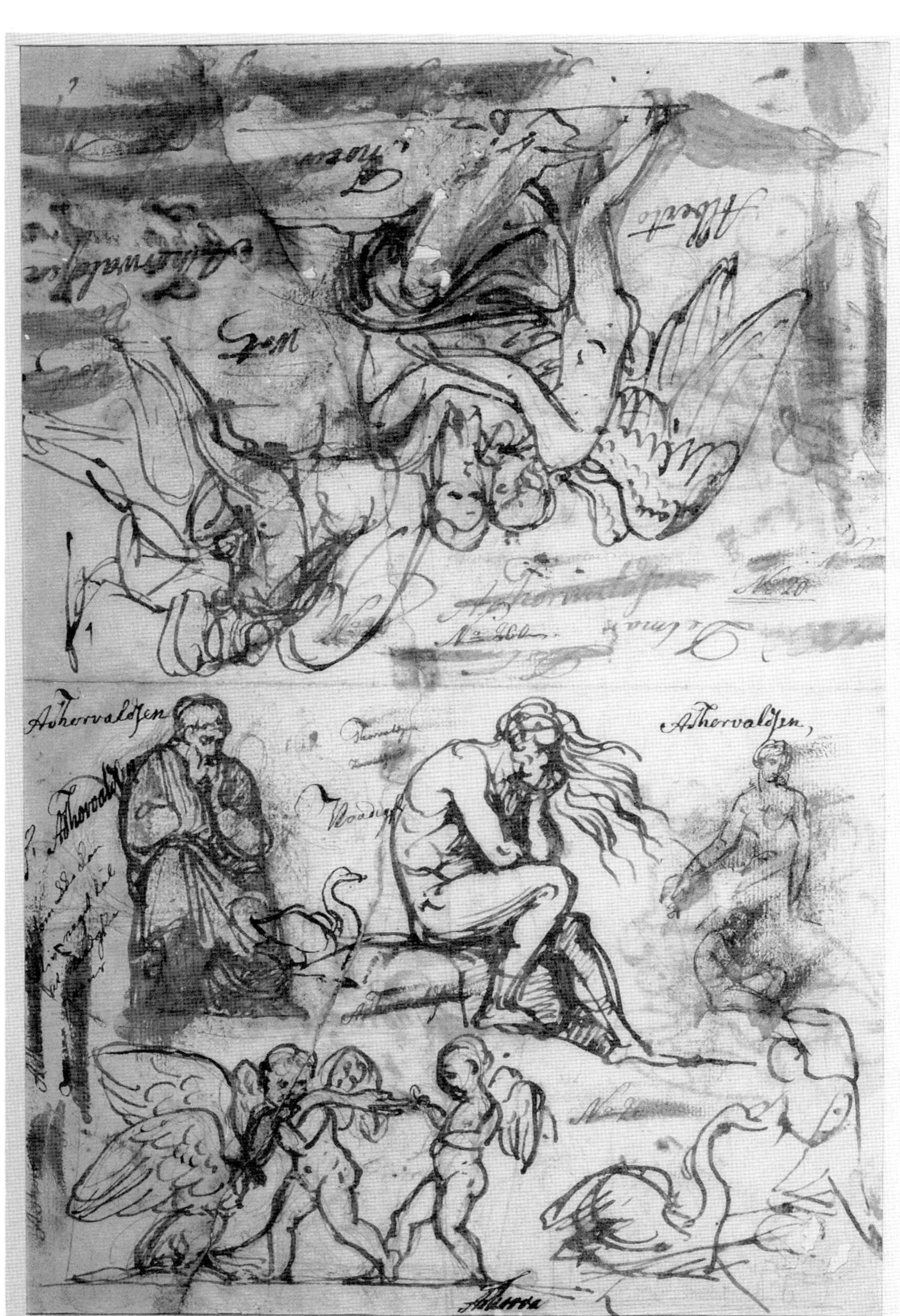

CATALOGUE NO. 112

Johann Peter Krafft

1780 Hanau–Vienna 1856

KRAFFT BEGAN HIS STUDIES in 1790 in Vienna, as the pupil of Anton Wilhelm Tischbein and Friedrich Heinrich Füger. In 1801 he moved to Paris and worked in the studios of Jacques-Louis David and Antoine-Jean Gros. After four years Krafft returned to Vienna and then traveled to Rome and painted portraits of Napoleon's generals. He returned to Vienna in 1808 and brought to Austria the influence of David and Jean-Baptiste Greuze. He became a member of the Vienna Akademie in 1815 and a professor there in 1823. He painted more than two thousand portraits during his career and was made director of the Kaiserlich Galerie im Belvedere in 1829. LDM

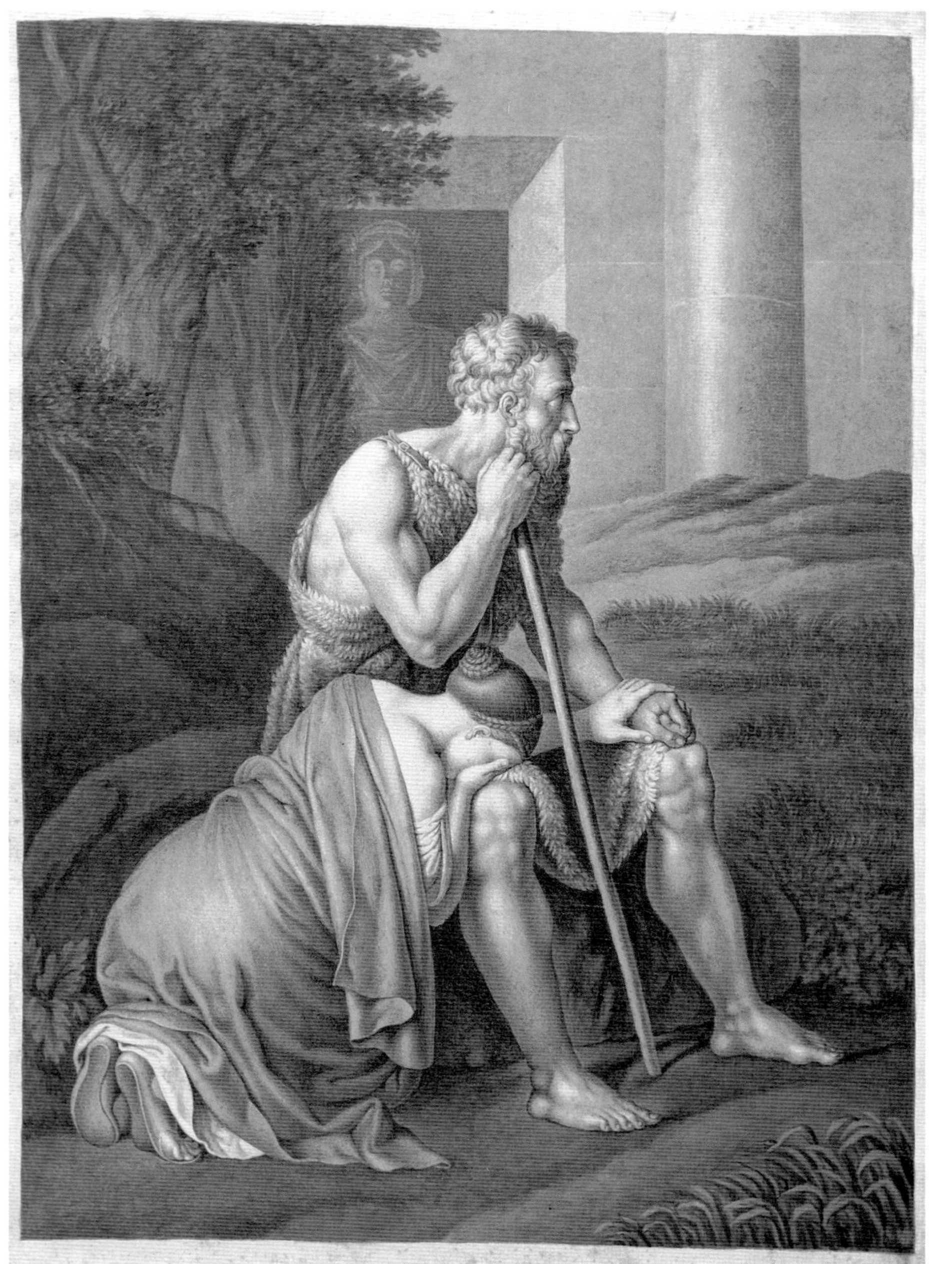

CATALOGUE NO. 113 (see color plate on page 111)

Johann Peter Krafft
Oedipus and Antigone at Colonus
c. 1814

113
Pen and brown ink, brush and brown wash over graphite on off-white wove paper
Watermark: *WHATMAN 1813*
46.5 x 34.6 cm (18 5/16 x 13 5/8 in.)
The Minneapolis Institute of Arts, the Richard Lewis Hillstrom Fund, 1989 (inv. no. 89.65)

PROVENANCE
Friedrich Schlosser, "Stift Neuburg" (Lugt 1921, no. 1940c).
Heinz Fein.

LITERATURE
Frodl-Schneemann 1984, 137, no. 64.

Krafft executed three paintings depicting the theme of Oedipus and Antigone at Colonus. During his Paris sojourn in the atelier of Jacques-Louis David, Krafft exhibited the first version at the Salon of 1802. The work was commissioned by Count Antoine-François Andréossy; its present whereabouts is unknown, but its appearance is recorded in a signed outline drawing undoubtedly a preparatory study for a line engraving, now in a private collection (Frodl-Schneemann 1984, 19, 127, no. 18; Janson 1977, Salon of 1802, 99, no. 745). After his return to Vienna, Krafft painted in 1809 a replica of the Andréossy picture, which is now in the Musée du Louvre, Paris (*Revue du Louvre*, no. 2, 1986, 140).

Krafft executed a third, slightly modified version in Vienna in 1815, which was auctioned in 1906 (ex-collection Dr. Alois Spitzer; sold Wawra, Vienna, January 24, lot 46; Frodl-Schneemann 1984, 137, no. 64), but whose present location is unknown. Fortunately, the composition is documented in an 1816 stipple engraving by Friedrich John published in *Aglaja*, 1816 (Frodl-Schneemann 1984, 137). The Minneapolis sheet is a highly finished study for the painting of 1815, in which Krafft employed a new, more elderly model for the figure of Oedipus. He also modified the tree in the upper-left corner of the composition; in the previous works a branch of the tree was broken. In addition, the delineation of the blocks in the architecture of the temple has been minutely altered. Otherwise, the composition remains essentially unchanged.

Krafft's composition is based on Sophocles's tragedy *Oedipus at Colonus*. Having unknowingly killed his father, Laius, and married his mother, Jocasta, the cursed King Oedipus blinded himself and was later exiled from Thebes. Guided by his devoted daughter Antigone, Oedipus wandered until he arrived at Colonus, near Athens, in the sacred grove of the avenging Furies. After their long journey Oedipus desperately sought a place to rest. Antigone informed him that they were now on "holy ground" and bid him to "rest thy limbs on this unpolished stone." Shortly thereafter a stranger from Athens approached and warned the father and daughter that they were trespassing on the domain of "the terrible goddesses" (the Furies). Apollo had previously informed the remorseful Oedipus, however, that he would finally find rest at the shrine of the Eumenides. Upon the departure of the stranger Oedipus exclaimed, "Oh grant me, goddesses, according to Apollo's word, some passage now from life to death, some end to my career; unless haply, I seem to come short in suffering, albeit I am sorrow's slave for evermore, beyond all mortal men" (Sophocles 1892, 11–14). Krafft represents Antigone kneeling by her father and grieving at his impending death. A statue of a Fury looms within the confines of the temple immediately behind Oedipus and gives an air of foreboding to the scenario.

Paintings depicting Oedipus and his children Antigone and Polynices were to proliferate at the Paris Salons about 1800. Fulchran-Jean Harriet, Charles Thévenin, Georges Rouget, Jean-François Peyron, and Jacques-Augustin Pajou—to name a few—all represented Oedipus and Antigone in canvases executed between 1796 and 1804 (Rubin 1973, 142–46). The impetus for these works has been attributed to the influence of Jean-François Ducis's play and Nicolas-François Guillard's libretto for the opera *Oedipe à Colone*, which depart significantly from Sophocles's text (Rubin 1973, 141–42, 148). It has been further suggested that the figure of the exiled King Oedipus alluded to the fate of the French royal and aristocratic *emigrés* in the course of the Revolution, the Consulate, and the Empire (Rubin 1973, 142). Krafft adheres more closely to Sophocles's description of the harmonious setting—"a holy ground all thickly grown with olive, bay and vine," as opposed to the windswept, arid, craggy desert landscapes depicted by his contemporaries (Rubin 1973, 145). In general, Krafft's conception of the theme is more restrained. The figure of Oedipus derives from classical prototypes of seated philosophers (Reinach 1897–1910, vol. 1, 510–15). The influence of Carstens, however, is clearly evident in the volumetric figures and the architectural setting (see Neuwirth 1989, 40, 50). In 1796 Carstens had executed a red-chalk drawing, *Oedipus and His Daughters Greeted by Theseus* now in the collection of the Kunstsammlungen zu Weimar (inv. no. KK651; Copenhagen 1990, 132–33, no. 59). RJC

Christoffer Wilhelm Eckersberg

1783 Sundeved–Copenhagen 1853

ECKERSBERG BEGAN HIS STUDIES under Nikolai Abraham Abildgaard at the Kunstakademiet in Copenhagen in 1803. He won the gold medal for *The Death of Jacob* (*La Mort de Jacob*) in 1809 and traveled to Paris the next year. From 1811 until 1813 he worked in the studio of Jacques-Louis David; he then moved to Rome, where he stayed until 1816. When Eckersberg returned to Copenhagen, he was accepted into the Kunstakademiet in 1817. He became a professor the next year and taught two generations of students. LDM

Christoffer Wilhelm Eckersberg
Odysseus Fleeing from Polyphemus
1812

114
Graphite, pen and black ink, brush and gray and brown washes on white paper
22 x 33.1 cm (8 11/16 x 13 in.)
Signed and dated at upper right in ink: *Eckersberg. 1812. Paris*
Kongelige Kobberstiksamling, Statens Museum for Kunst, Copenhagen (inv. no. Td.582.3)

PROVENANCE
The artist; sale, Copenhagen, January, 17, 1854, lot 220.

EXHIBITED
Aarhus 1983, no. 130.
Copenhagen 1983a, 172, no. 82.

Eckersberg's drawing *Odysseus Fleeing from Polyphemus* was executed in 1812, during the artist's sojourn in Paris as a student in the atelier of Jacques-Louis David. It is a study for a painting that was last documented in 1927, when it was sold at auction (Winkel & Magnussen, Copenhagen, May 10, lot 19; Bramsen 1947, 99, 136; Copenhagen 1983a, 172). The drawing illustrates a horrific episode from Homer's *Odyssey* (9.427–94). Odysseus and his companions became trapped in the mountain lair of the cyclops Polyphemus. The cannibalistic monster spurned Odysseus's plea for hospitality and devoured random captives. With a brew of nectar and ambrosia, Odysseus succeeded in intoxicating the cyclops. While Polyphemus slept, the hero blinded him by plunging a smoldering six-foot shaft into his single eye. Odysseus then tied his comrades to the bellies of braces of three rams from Polyphemus's great flock and secured himself beneath the cyclops's lead ram. At dawn the maimed giant was in the habit of removing the massive boulder that sealed the entrance to his cave to let his flock out to graze. On this occasion, seated near the entrance, Polyphemus stroked each ram as it exited, yet failed to detect the fugitives below. Eckersberg represents the climactic moment, when Odysseus "dropped and rolled clear of the ram's belly," and rushed off to untie his companions (Homer 1963, 158–59).

The figure of Polyphemus is derived from the Belvedere Torso (Musei Vaticani, Rome), which was then in the collection of the Musée Napoléon. The pose of Odysseus was inspired by ancient prototypes of fallen gladiators or other combatants (see Reinach 1897–1910, vol. 1, 522–23, 529–31). Eckersberg's composition, however, was most likely based on posed models, as is suggested by the patently unidealized physiognomies. It is known that the artist applied himself assiduously to sketching live models as a pupil of David (Bramsen 1947, 66, 92; London 1984, 27).

Stylistically, the Copenhagen sheet typifies Eckersberg's pre-Roman draftsmanship, characterized by heavy, emphatic contours and passages of fussy, stippled brush and wash strokes to achieve the interior modeling of his figures.

Between 1812 and 1814 Eckersberg depicted several other scenes from the *Odyssey*: *Odysseus and Calypso*, *The Return of Odysseus*, and *Odysseus Slaying the Suitors of Penelope* (Hannover 1898, 66, 98, 326, 331, nos. 111–12, 143, fig. 47; Copenhagen 1990, 108, no. 14). There also exist in Copenhagen three other drawings, representing *Odysseus in the Hut of the Swineherd Eumaios*, *Telemachus and Eumaios*, and *Odysseus Recounting His Adventures for Alcinous* (Copenhagen 1983a, 175–76, nos. 91–93). RJC

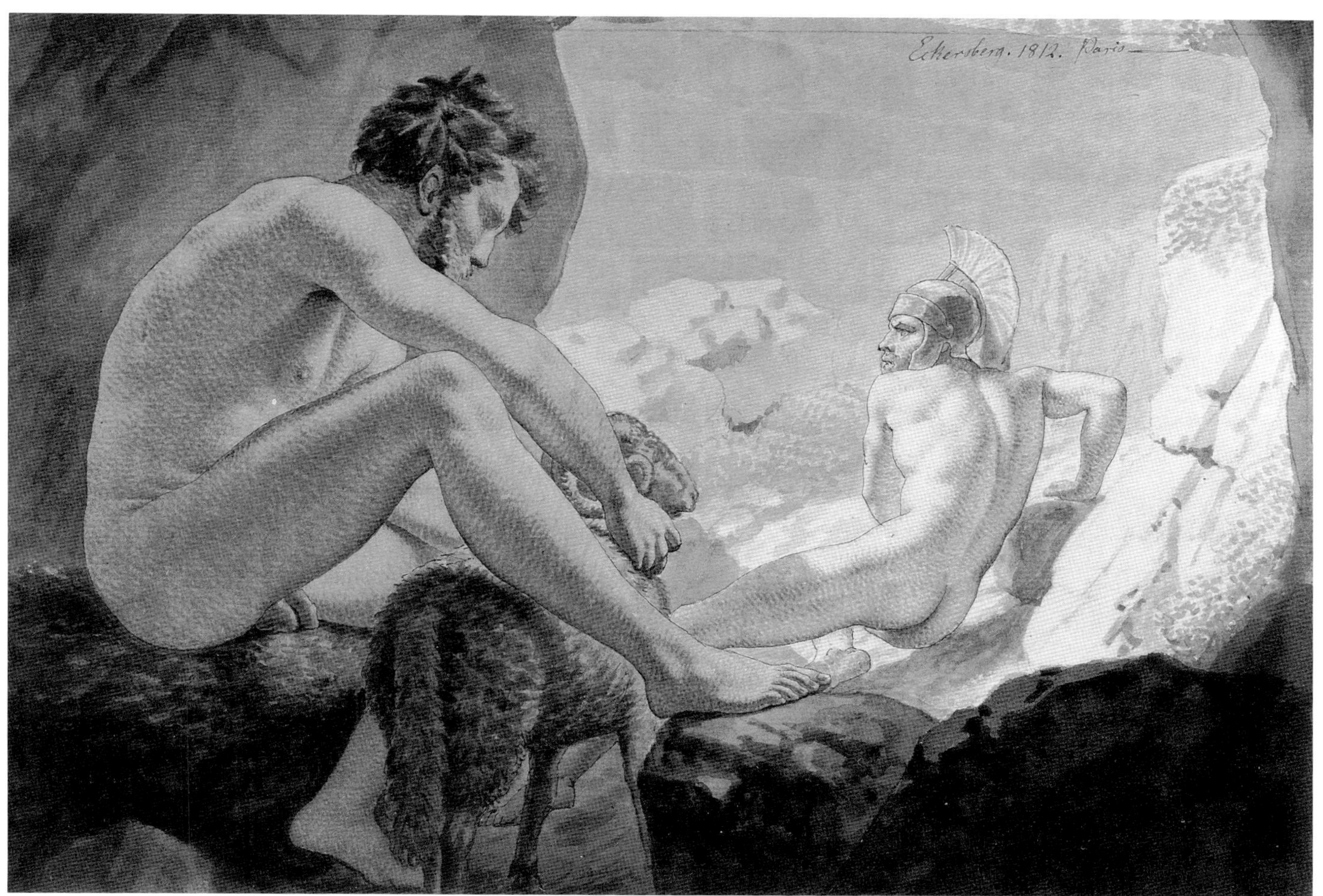

CATALOGUE NO. 114

Christoffer Wilhelm Eckersberg
The Dream of Halcyone
1813

115
Graphite, pen and brown ink, brush and brown and gray washes, blue watercolor on white paper
47.5 x 64.8 cm (18 11/16 x 25 1/2 in.)
Kongelige Kobberstiksamling, Statens Museum for Kunst, Copenhagen (inv. no. 01.28)

PROVENANCE
The artist; sale, Copenhagen, January 17, 1854, lot 6.

EXHIBITED
Copenhagen 1983a, 172–73, no. 83.
Paris 1984, 132, no. 35.
Munich 1985, 52, no. 52, fig. 46.

Eckersberg's study of the somnolent Halcyone is related to an uncompleted canvas, *The Dream of Halcyone*, of 1813 (collection of Johan Ludwig Lund; Hannover 1898, 329, no. 135; Copenhagen 1990, 81, 160, no. 101); it has been suggested that the painting is a copy by a pupil of Eckersberg (Copenhagen 1983b, 49, 51 n. 6, fig. 17). It is a pendant to *Halcyone by the Sea* of the same year (Hannover 1898, 87, 329, no. 136, fig. 43; Copenhagen 1983a, 23, 75, no. 20). Both works were executed early in the artist's Roman sojourn, ostensibly for the Danish patron Kaufmann Mendel Levin Nathanson (Munich 1985, 52, no. 52).

The subject of the devoted spouses Ceyx and Halcyone is taken from Ovid's *Metamorphoses* (11.633–75). Despite Halcyone's premonitions of disaster, Ceyx, the virtuous king of Thessaly, set out by ship to consult the oracle of Apollo at Claros. Ceyx's ship was lost at sea, and the king was drowned. Meanwhile, Halcyone continued to beseech Juno for her husband's safety and fidelity to her. When Juno could not withstand Halcyone's entreaties on behalf of a dead man, however, she ordered Iris to implore the god of Sleep to communicate in a dream to Halcyone the fact of the death of Ceyx. Sleep, in turn, ordered his son Morpheus, skilled in imitating human forms, to appear to Halcyone in the guise of her departed husband—pale, naked, weeping, and dripping with water—to communicate his fate and to implore her to mourn for him prior to his entrance into Tartarus. Eckersberg depicts Ovid's text quite literally: "As he spoke, Morpheus seemed to Halcyone to be weeping real tears: moreover, she could easily believe that the voice was that of her husband, and he had Ceyx's gestures, too. She moaned and began to cry in her sleep, raising her arms and trying to touch his body—but she embraced only empty air" (Ovid 1970, 262–63).

Eckersberg's composition was undoubtedly inspired by a painting of the same title by Louis Prot, a pupil of David, which was exhibited at the Paris Salon of 1806 (Janson 1977, 83, no. 427); Prot's painting was reproduced in a line engraving, which was in turn published in Charles-Paul Landon's *Annales du Musée et de l'École Moderne des Beaux-Arts* of 1807 (vol. 15, pl. 63). The Danish painter Christian Gottlieb Kratzenstein Stub executed a graphite drawing of *The Dream of Halcyone* in 1810, and in the same year he painted canvases depicting *Halcyone Waiting in Vain for Her Husband Ceyx* and *Halcyone Finding the Body of Her Husband Ceyx* (Copenhagen 1990, 78–79, 158–60). Eckersberg was the sole artist to represent the figure of a servant in a composition of *The Dream of Halcyone* (Munich 1985, 53). There exists in the collection of the Thorvaldsen Museum, Copenhagen (inv. no. B.209), an oil sketch for the sleeping woman at the bedside of Halcyone, which is signed and dated by Eckersberg in 1813 (Copenhagen 1990, 25, 109, no. 15); the figure derives from that of Camilla in David's *The Oath of the Horatii* (see FIGURE 9).

The Copenhagen drawing reveals the stylistic influence of Eckersberg's contemporaries in Rome, especially in the delicate sfumato modeling of the figures. The influence of Ingres's graphic technique, with its infinitely subtle gradations of light and shade, is recognizable (see CATALOGUE NO. 75). It has been suggested that Eckersberg derived the placement of the legs and feet of the reclining Halcyone from the graphite studies by Ingres for his *Grand Odalisque*; however, this painting was not even commissioned until 1813 (Copenhagen 1983a, 173). Eckersberg may well have been inspired, however, by the drawings of Antonio Canova with respect to the modeling (see CATALOGUE NOS. 83, 88). At any rate, a bold stylistic progression is clearly discernible in the refined modeling of the anatomy and drapery. As in the Paris drawing, Eckersberg based his figure of Halcyone on a Roman studio model. He rendered a graphite, sepia, and wash study of the same model for his painting *Halcyone by the Sea*; the study is now in the Kunstmuseet, Søro (Copenhagen 1983a, 75, 139, no. 19). RJC

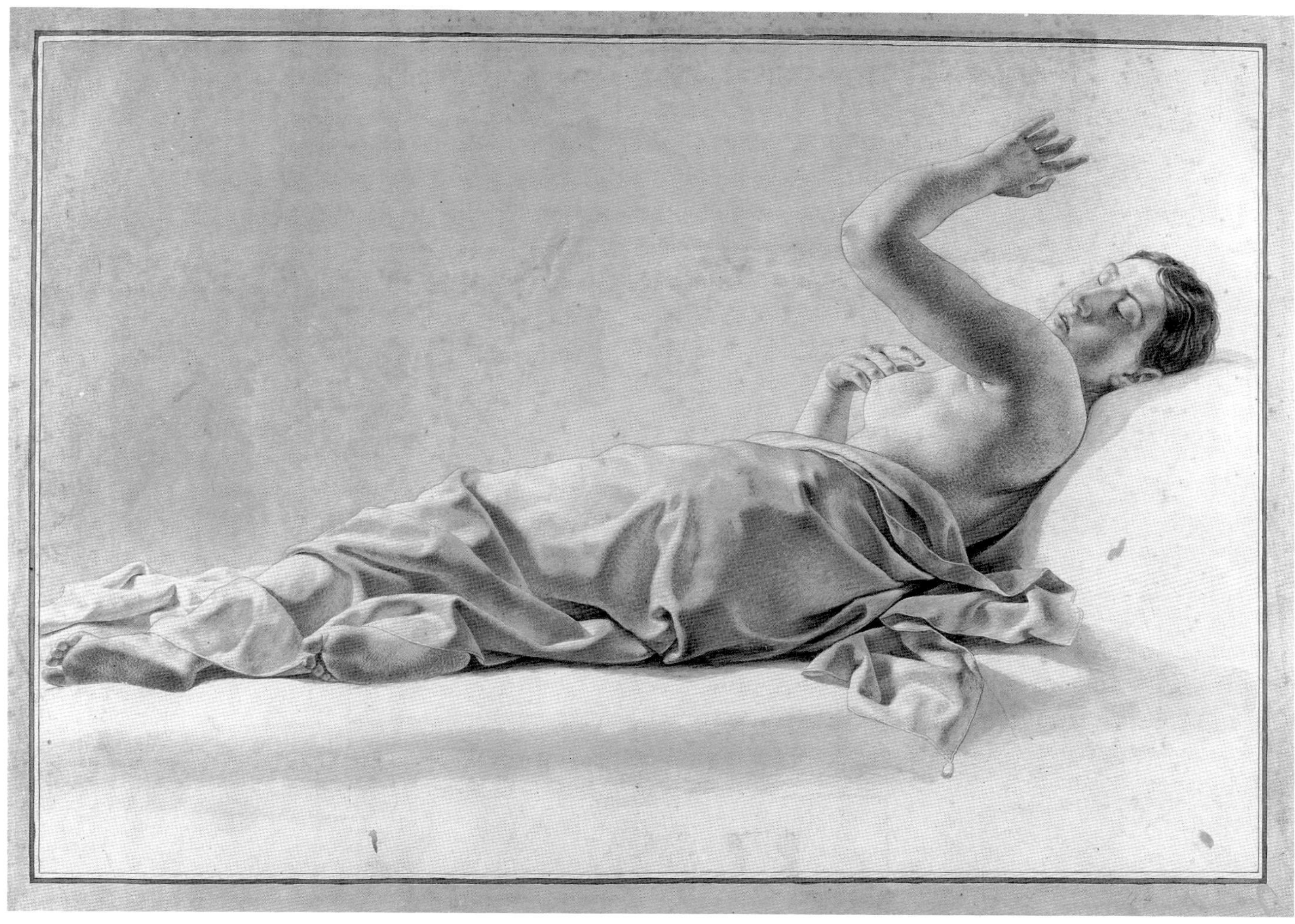

CATALOGUE NO. 115 (see color plate on page 112)

Julius Schnorr von Carolsfeld

1794 Leipzig–Dresden 1872

SCHNORR BEGAN HIS STUDIES at the Vienna Akademie in 1811 and studied with Joseph Anton Koch when the latter was a visiting professor in 1812–15. He was also a pupil of Ferdinand Olivier, with whom he lived from 1814 to 1817. Schnorr went to Rome in 1818 and joined the artistic circle known as the Nazarenes. His most important work with this group was the decoration in the Ariosto room of the Casino Massimo, 1822–26. In 1827 he was in Munich to paint historical frescoes for King Ludwig of Bavaria. In 1846 Schnorr became a professor at the Dresden Akademie as well as director of the Gemäldegalerie. Late in his career he received much acclaim for his *Bible in Pictures* (*Bibelbilder*), which he illustrated with 240 drawings executed over the span of several years. LDM

Julius Schnorr von Carolsfeld
Life Study of a Female Nude
1825–26

116
Graphite with brush and brown ink and wash on wove paper
37.9 x 20.9 cm (15 x 9 1/2 in.)
National Gallery of Canada, Ottawa (inv. no. 18769)

PROVENANCE
Alexander Flinsch, Berlin.
Sale, C. G. Boerner, Leipzig, Auction 3, November 29–30, 1912, lot 533.
Heinrich Stinnes, Cologne.
C. G. Boerner, Düsseldorf, 1977.

EXHIBITED
Düsseldorf 1976, no. 104.
Washington 1988, 147, no. 45.

LITERATURE
Gerstenberg/Rave 1934, 159–63.
Andrews 1964, 43–54.

Schnorr's vigorous study of a female nude relates to a fresco, *The Army of Charlemagne in Paris*, painted in 1826 for the Ariosto room of the Casino Massimo in Rome (Gerstenberg/Rave 1934, pls. 48, 56; Andrews 1964, 119, pl. 54; Washington 1988, 147–49, no. 5). The work is a pendant to the fresco *The Army of the Saracen King Agramante at the Gates of Paris*, painted on the same wall to the left of the central doorway (Gerstenberg/Rave 1934, pls. 47, 55; Andrews 1964, pl. 53b). The Casino Massimo commission employed for a decade the talents of Peter Cornelius, Friedrich Overbeck, Philipp Veit, Joseph Anton Koch, and Joseph Führich, as well as Schnorr. It is acclaimed as the paradigm of the artistic production of the Nazarene school in Rome (Andrews 1964, 54).

The theme of Schnorr's fresco is based on an episode in the epic poem *Orlando Furioso*, by Ludovico Ariosto (15.8–9). Having defeated the army of Charlemagne, the Saracen forces under King Agramante besieged Paris. Schnorr's fresco represents the final assault of Agramante's horde (Ariosto 1981, 448–49):

But the resistance at the gate was more
Than had been looked for by the Africans,
For there, in person, stood the Emperor,
Ugier, the Dane, among his paladins,
King Salamone of the Breton shore,
The Guidos, Gano, both the Angelins,
Duke Namo and his sons: Avolio,
Otto, Avino, Berlingier, who go
Together everywhere; of less account,
Innumerable Germans, Lombards, Franks,
Who, in the presence of their monarch, count
To earn his commendation and his thanks.

The figure depicted in the Ottawa study is seen in a loggia at the right edge of the fresco. She and three other figures lean over a ledge to catch a glimpse of the emperor Charlemagne and his retinue. A young boy appears between her arms. Schnorr's conception of the figure evolved dramatically, as is documented by two compositional studies and three sketches, all rendered in pen and ink, in the collection of the Museum in Leipzig (Gerstenberg/Rave 1934, 159, 161–62, 182, nos. 60, 62–64, 66; figs. 146, 149–50, 152–53). In the first compositional study (inv. no. 930,8) the woman and child appear in the right foreground peering over a rampart at the besieging Saracens;

the pair is embraced by a second female figure. In a subsequent sketch (inv. no. 930, 10) Schnorr introduces the loggia as a *repoussoir* element, and the shoulder of the woman rests against a column as she grasps the boy with her left hand; the attendant figure crouches upon a ledge of the balcony—the group is thus reoriented toward Charlemagne. In another, very free sketch (inv. no. 930, 12) the crouching figure embraces the woman and child. In a third sketch (inv. no. 930, 11) Schnorr places the attendant figure behind the woman, who now restrains the boy with her right arm. In the second compositional study (inv. no. 930, 16), which is dated February 4, 1825, the woman's right hand rests on the boy's shoulder. The Ottawa study postdates the latter drawing since both of the woman's hands are firmly planted on the ledge. This configuration is retained in the cartoon (Gerstenberg/Rave 1934, 129, 182, no. 55, fig. 106) and fresco (Gerstenberg/Rave 1934, pls. 48, 56).

Schnorr's development of his composition through an extensive series of sketches and studies is typical of the Nazarene school. Technically, the sheet has affinities with the drawing manner of Schnorr's great German predecessor in Rome, Johann Heinrich Wilhelm Tischbein, especially in the passages of cross-hatching in pen and ink along the contours of the figure. RJC

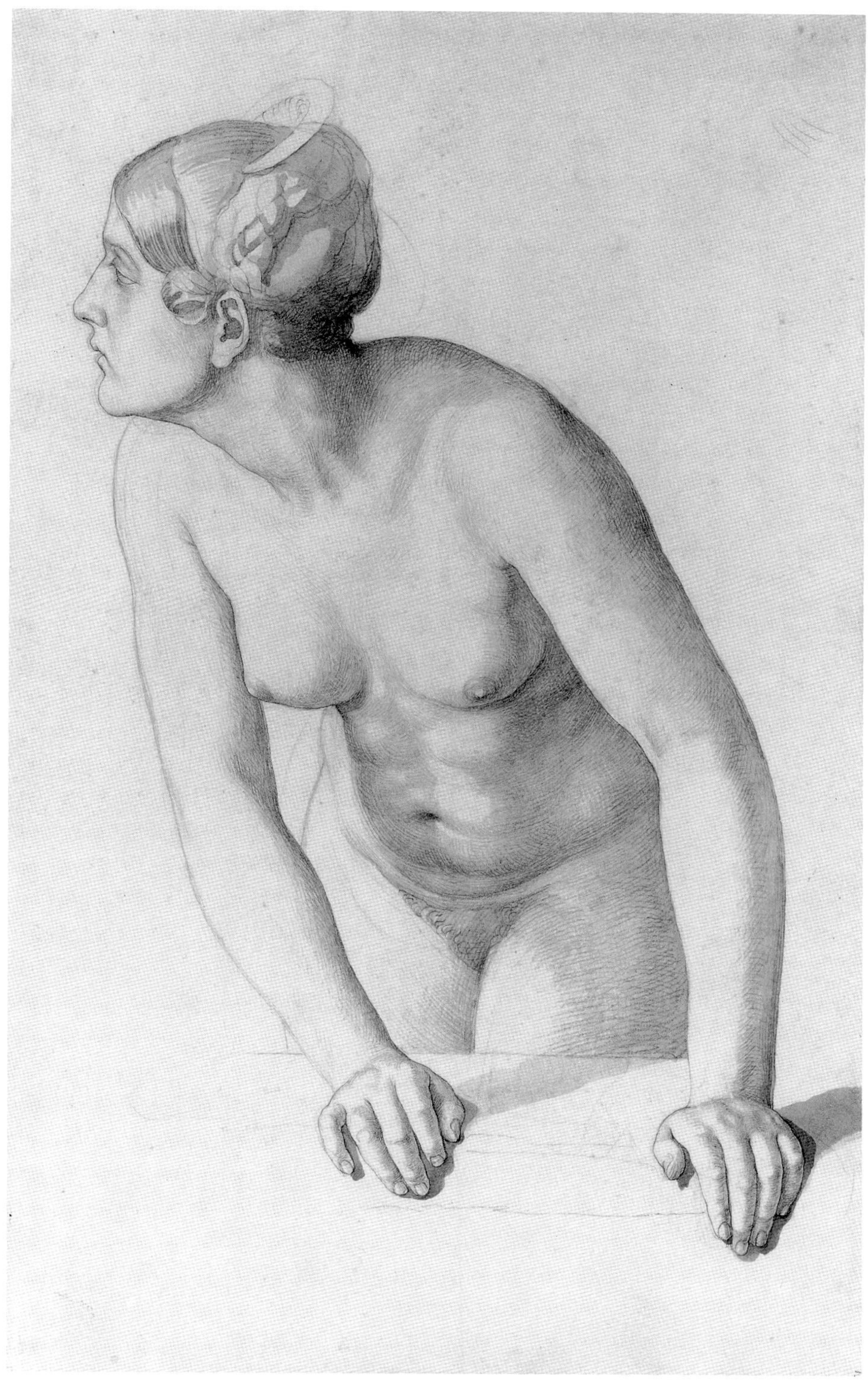

CATALOGUE NO. 116

Bibliography

AARHUS 1983
Aarhus: Kunstmuseum. *C. W. Eckersberg.* Exh. cat., 1983.

ALAZARD 1950
Jean Alazard. *Ingres et l'ingrisme.* Paris: Michel, 1950.

ALLENTOWN 1977
Allentown: Allentown Art Museum. *French Masterpieces of the 19th Century from the Henry P. McIlhenny Collection.* Exh. cat., 1977.

ANANOFF 1961–70
Alexandre Ananoff. *L'Oeuvre dessiné de Jean-Honoré Fragonard, 1732–1806.* 4 vols. Paris: F. de Nobèle, 1961–70.

ANANOFF 1984
Alexandre Ananoff. "Fragonard: Quelques dessins d'une collection." *L'Estampille,* no. 165 (January 1984): 10–17.

ANDREWS 1964
Keith Andrews. *The Nazarenes: A Brotherhood of German Painters in Rome.* Oxford: Clarendon Press, 1964.

ANN ARBOR 1969
Ann Arbor: University of Michigan Museum of Art. *The World of Voltaire.* Exh. cat., 1969.

ANTICHITÀ DI ERCOLANO 1755–92
Antichità di Ercolano. Naples: Accademia Ercolanense, 1755–92.

APPIANUS 1911
Appian's Roman History. Translated by Horace White. London: William Heinemann/New York: Macmillan, 1911.

ARIOSTO 1981
Ludovico Ariosto. *Orlando Furioso.* Translated by Barbara Reynolds. Harmondsworth, Middlesex/New York: Penguin Books, 1981.

ARNASON 1975
H. Harvard Arnason. *The Sculptures of Houdon.* New York: Oxford University Press, 1975.

ATLANTA 1984
Atlanta: High Museum of Art. *The Henry P. McIlhenny Collection: Nineteenth-Century French and English Masterpieces.* Exh. cat., 1984.

AULUS GELLIUS 1970
Aulus Gellius. *The Attic Nights.* Translated by John C. Rolfe. 3 vols. London: William Heinemann/Cambridge: Harvard University Press, 1970.

AURENHAMMER 1966
Hans Aurenhammer. "Joseph Abel (1764–1818)." *Mitteilungen der Österreichisches Galerie* 10, no. 54 (1966): 3–26.

AUZAS/TERNOIS 1973
Jacqueline Auzas and Daniel Ternois. "Dessins de Girodet à sujets ossianiques." *Revue du Louvre,* nos. 4/5 (1973): 261–70.

BALTIMORE/LOS ANGELES/FORT WORTH 1986–87
Baltimore: The Baltimore Museum of Art/Los Angeles: Los Angeles County Museum of Art/Fort Worth: Kimbell Art Museum. *Nineteenth-Century French Drawings from the Museum Boymans-van Beuningen.* Exh. cat., 1986–87.

BANKS 1931
M. A. Banks. "The Radeke Collection of Drawings." *Bulletin of the Rhode Island School of Design* 19, no. 4 (October 1931): 62–72.

BANKS 1979
Ada Shadmi Banks. "Two Letters from Girodet to Flaxman." *The Art Bulletin* 61, no. 1 (March 1979): 100–101.

BARDON 1963
Henry Bardon. "Les Peintures à sujets antiques au XVIIIe siècle d'après les livrets de Salons." *Gazette des Beaux-Arts* ser. 6, 61 (April 1963): 217–50.

BARTSCH 1978–
The Illustrated Bartsch. Edited by Walter L. Strauss (1978–88) and John T. Spike (1988–present). 80 vols. (to date). New York: Abaris Books, 1978– .

BASSI 1943
Elena Bassi. *Canova.* Bergamo/Milan/Rome: Istituto Italiano d'Arti Grafiche, 1943.

BASSI 1959
Elena Bassi. *Il Museo Civico di Bassano: I disegni di Antonio Canova.* Venice: Neri Pozza Editore, 1959.

BASSI 1972
Elena Bassi. *Antonio Canova a Possagno.* Treviso: Edizioni Canova, 1972.

BAUDI DI VESME 1963–68
Alessandro Baudi di Vesme. *Schede Vesme: L'arte in Piemonte dal XVI al XVIII secolo.* 3 vols. Turin: Società Piemontese di Archeologia e Belle Arti, 1963–68.

BEAN 1962
Jacob Bean. "The Drawings Collection." *The Metropolitan Museum of Art Bulletin* 20, no. 5 (January 1962): 157–75.

BEAN 1964
Jacob Bean. *100 European Drawings in the Metropolitan Museum of Art.* New York: The Metropolitan Museum of Art, 1964.

BEAN 1986
Jacob Bean with Lawrence Turčić. *15th–18th-Century French Drawings in the Metropolitan Museum of Art.* New York: The Metropolitan Museum of Art, 1986.

BENISOVICH 1953
Michel N. Benisovich. "Drawings of the Sculptor Augustin Pajou in the United States." *The Art Bulletin* 35, no. 4 (December 1953): 295–98.

BENISOVICH 1959
Michel N. Benisovich. "Some Drawings by European Masters in United States Museum Collections." *The Art Quarterly* 22, no. 1 (Spring 1959): 56–62.

BÉRALDI 1874
Béraldi (Henri Draibel). *L'Oeuvre de Moreau le jeune: Notice & catalogue.* Paris: P. Rouquette, 1874.

BERLIN 1949
Berlin: Freie Universität. *Goethe und seine Zeit.* Exh. cat., 1949.

BERLIN 1989
Berlin: Nationalgalerie, Staatliche Museen zu Berlin. *Zeichnungen aus Dänemark, von Abildgaard, Juel, Eckersberg, Købke, Lundbye und Marstrand.* Exh. cat., 1989.

BERLIN 1989–90
Berlin: Nationalgalerie, Staatliche Museen zu Berlin. *Asmus Jakob Carstens und Joseph Anton Koch: Zwei Zeitgenossen der Französischen Revolution: Zeichnungen.* Exh. cat., 1989–90.

BERNIER 1975
Georges Bernier. *Anne-Louis Girodet Prix de Rome 1789.* Paris/Brussels: Jacques Damase, 1975.

BERTRAND 1897
Alexandre Bertrand. *La Religion des gaulois: Les Druides et le druidisme.* Paris: Leroux, 1897.

BINDMAN 1977
David Bindman. *Blake as an Artist.* Oxford: Oxford University Press, 1977.

BINDMAN 1978
David Bindman assisted by Deirdre Toomey. *The Complete Graphic Works of William Blake.* New York: G. P. Putnam's Sons, 1978.

BINDMAN 1982
David Bindman. *William Blake: His Art and Times.* Yale Center for British Art/Art Gallery of Ontario. Exh. cat., 1982.

BINGHAMTON 1970
Binghamton: University Art Gallery, State University of New York/Williamstown: Williams College Museum of Art/Houston: Museum of Fine Arts/Chapel Hill: Ackland Memorial Art Center, University of North Carolina/Notre Dame: Art Gallery, University of Notre Dame/Oberlin: Allen Memorial Art Museum, Oberlin College/Poughkeepsie: Vassar College Art Gallery. *Loan Exhibition: Selections from the Drawing Collection of Mr. and Mrs. Julius S. Held.* Exh. cat., 1970.

BINYON 1900
Laurence Binyon. *Catalogue of Drawings by British Artists and Artists of Foreign Origin Working in Great Britain, Preserved in the Department of Prints and Drawings in the British Museum.* 2 vols. London: Trustees of the British Museum, 1900.

BINYON 1922
Laurence Binyon. *The Drawings and Engravings of William Blake.* London: The Studio, 1922.

BJURSTRÖM 1976
Per Bjurström. *Sergel Tecknar.* Stockholm: Nationalmuseum och Liberförlag, 1976.

BLUNT 1943
Anthony Blunt. "Blake's Pictorial Imagination." *Journal of the Warburg and Courtauld Institutes* 6 (1943): 190–212.

BLUNT 1959
Anthony Blunt. *The Art of William Blake.* New York: Columbia University Press, 1959.

BLUNT 1967
Anthony Blunt. *Nicolas Poussin.* 2 vols. New York: Bollingen Foundation, 1967.

BOBÉ 1938
Louis Bobé. *Thorvaldsen i Kærlighedens Aldre.* Copenhagen: Berlingske Forlag, 1938.

BOBER/RUBINSTEIN 1986
Phyllis Pray Bober and Ruth Rubinstein. *Renaissance Artists and Antique Sculpture.* Oxford: Oxford University Press/New York: Harvey Miller Publishers, 1986.

BOIME 1987
Albert Boime. *Art in an Age of Revolution, 1750–1800.* Chicago: Chicago University Press, 1987.

BOLOGNA 1976
Bologna: Museo Civico. *Pelagio Palagi, artista e collezionista.* Exh. cat., 1976.

BONNARDET 1938
E. Bonnardet. "Comment un Oratorien vint en aide à un grand peintre." *Gazette des Beaux-Arts,* ser. 6, 19 (May/June 1938): 311–15.

BORDEAUX 1989
Bordeaux: Musée des Beaux-Arts. *Le Port des lumières: La Peinture à Bordeaux, 1750–1800.* Exh. cat., 1989.

BOTT 1989
Katharina Bott. "Un illustre viaggiatore e collezionista a Roma: Franz Erwein von Schönborn." In Rome: Galleria Nazionale d'Arte Moderna. *Bertel Thorvaldsen.* Exh. cat., 1989.

BOTTINEAU 1989
Josette Bottineau. "La Jeunesse de Pierre Guérin: Étude de quelques dessins." *Revue du Louvre* 39, nos. 5/6 (1989): 300–309.

BOUCHER 1952
François Boucher, ed. *Le Dessin français du XVIIIe siècle.* Lausanne: Mermod, 1952.

BOURNEMOUTH 1949
Bournemouth: College of Art. *Original Works by William Blake from the Graham Robertson Collection.* Exh. cat., 1949.

BRAMSEN 1947
Henrik Bramsen. *C. W. Eckersberg i Paris: Dagbog og Breve 1810–13.* Copenhagen: Thaning & Appels Forlag, 1947.

BREAZEALE 1980
Mary K. Breazeale. "The Art of Joseph-Marie Vien." Ph.D. diss., University of Chicago, 1980.

BREGENZ/VIENNA 1968–69
Bregenz: Vorarlberger Landesmuseum/Vienna: Österreichisches Museum für Angewandte Kunst. *Angelika Kauffmann und ihre Zeitgenossen.* Exh. cat., 1968–69.

BRUSSELS 1985–86
Brussels: Musée communal des Beaux-Arts d'Ixelles. *1770–1830: Autour du néo-classicisme en Belgique.* Exh. cat., 1985–86.

BRUUN NEERGAARD 1801
T. C. Bruun Neergaard. *Sur la situation des beaux-arts en France, ou Lettres d'un danois à son ami.* Paris: Dupont, 1801.

BRYAN 1904
Michael Bryan. *Bryan's Dictionary of Painters and Engravers.* Edited by George C. Williamson. Rev. and enl. ed. 5 vols. New York: Macmillan, 1904.

BURKE 1970
J. T. Burke. *The Iconography of the Enlightenment in English Art.* Sydney: Sydney University Press, 1970.

BURROUGHS 1919
Bryson Burroughs. "Recent Accessions: Drawings by Ingres." *The Metropolitan Museum of Art Bulletin* 14, no. 11 (November 1919): 246–47.

BUTLIN 1978
Martin Butlin. *William Blake.* London: Tate Gallery, 1978.

BUTLIN 1981
Martin Butlin. *The Paintings and Drawings of William Blake.* 2 vols. New Haven: Paul Mellon Center/Yale University Press, 1981.

BUZZONI 1985
Andrea Buzzoni et al. *Torquato Tasso tra letteratura, musica, teatro e arti figurative.* Bologna: Nuova Alfa Editoriale, 1985.

CAMBRIDGE 1910
Cambridge, England: Fitzwilliam Museum. *Loan Exhibition of Works by Blake from the W. Graham Robertson Collection.* Exh. cat., 1910.

CAMBRIDGE 1929
Cambridge: Fogg Art Museum, Harvard University. *French Painting of the Nineteenth and Twentieth Centuries.* Exh. cat., 1929.

CAMBRIDGE 1958
Cambridge: Fogg Art Museum, Harvard University. *Class of 1933 Exhibition.* Exh. cat., 1958.

CAMBRIDGE 1967
Cambridge: Fogg Art Museum, Harvard University. *Ingres Centennial Exhibition, 1867–1967: Drawings, Watercolors, and Oil Sketches from American Collections*. Exh. cat. by Agnes Mongan and Hans Naef, 1967.

CAMBRIDGE 1973
Cambridge: Fogg Art Museum, Harvard University. *Ingres' Sculptural Style: A Group of Unknown Drawings*. Exh. cat. by Phyllis Hattis, 1973.

CAMBRIDGE 1980
Cambridge: Houghton Library, Harvard University. *Drawings for Book Illustration: The Hofer Collection*. Exh. cat. by David P. Becker, 1980.

CAMBRIDGE/NEW YORK 1965–67
Cambridge: Fogg Art Museum, Harvard University/New York: Museum of Modern Art. *Memorial Exhibition: Works of Art from the Collection of Paul J. Sachs, 1878–1965*. Exh. cat. compiled by Agnes Mongan, 1965–67.

CAMPBELL 1981–82
Richard J. Campbell. "The Sculptor as Draftsman: Three French Neoclassical Drawings." *The Minneapolis Institute of Arts Bulletin* 65 (1981–82): 94–110.

CAMPBELL 1982
Richard J. Campbell. "Jean-Guillaume Moitte: The Sculpture and Graphic Art, 1785–99." Ph.D. diss., Brown University, 1982.

CAMPBELL 1983–86
Richard J. Campbell. "*The Sacrifice of the Rose* by Jean-Honoré Fragonard: A Late Eighteenth-Century Inflection of a Traditional Erotic Symbol." *The Minneapolis Institute of Arts Bulletin* 66 (1983–86, published 1991): 18–47.

CANADAY 1959
John Canaday. *Mainstreams of Modern Art*. New York: Simon and Schuster, 1959.

CARACCIOLO ARIZZOLI 1977
Maria Teresa Caracciolo Arizzoli. "L'ispirazione letteraria di Giuseppe Cades." *Antologia di belle arti* 1, no. 3 (September 1977): 246–65.

CHAPEL HILL 1969
Chapel Hill: W. H. Ackland Memorial Art Center, University of North Carolina. *First Decade of Collecting*. Exh. cat., 1969.

CHAPEL HILL 1975
Chapel Hill: W. H. Ackland Memorial Art Center, University of North Carolina. *English Watercolors and Drawings, 1700–1900*. Exh. cat., 1975.

CHAPEL HILL 1976
Chapel Hill: W. H. Ackland Memorial Art Center, University of North Carolina. *Six Centuries of Drawings in the Ackland Collection*. Exh. cat., 1976

CHAPEL HILL 1982
Chapel Hill: W. H. Ackland Memorial Art Center, University of North Carolina. *100 Master Drawings from the Ackland Collection*. Exh. cat., 1982.

CHAPEL HILL 1984
Chapel Hill: W. H. Ackland Memorial Art Center, University of North Carolina. *Aspects of Blake and the Art of His Time*. Exh. cat., 1984.

CHAPEL HILL 1990–91
Chapel Hill: W. H. Ackland Memorial Art Center, University of North Carolina. *Highlights from the Drawing Collection*. Exh. cat., 1990–91.

CHARLOTTE 1963
Charlotte: Mint Museum. *A University Collects*. Exh. cat., 1963.

CHAUDONNERET 1977
Marie-Claude Chaudonneret. "À propos des tableaux détruits au Musée Saint-Pierre." *Bulletin des musées et monuments lyonnais*, no. 1 (1977), 16–17.

CHAUDONNERET 1980
Marie-Claude Chaudonneret. *Fleury-Richard et Pierre Révoil: La Peinture troubadour*. Paris: Arthena, 1980.

CHICAGO 1946
Chicago: David and Alfred Smart Art Gallery, University of Chicago. *An Exhibition of Drawings and Prints by English Artists of the Eighteenth and Nineteenth Centuries*. Exh. cat., 1946.

CHICAGO 1982
Chicago: David and Alfred Smart Gallery, University of Chicago. *Alumni Who Collect: 1. Drawings from the 16th Century to the Present*. Exh. cat., 1982.

CHOIX DE DESSINS 1926
Un Choix de dessins de Jean-Auguste-Dominique Ingres. Paris: Braun et Cie, 1926.

CLARAC 1826–53
Comte de Clarac. *Musée de sculpture antique et moderne; ou Description historique et graphique du Louvre* . . . . 6 text vols., 6 pl. vols. Paris: Imprimerie Royale, 1826–53.

CLARK 1981
Anthony M. Clark. "An Introduction to the Drawings of Giuseppe Cades." In *Studies in Roman Eighteenth-Century Painting*, 150–54. Edited by Edgar Peters Bowron. Washington, D.C.: Decatur House Press, 1981. (Originally published in *Master Drawings* 2, no. 1 [1964]: 18–26.)

CLARK/BOWRON 1985
Anthony M. Clark. *Pompeo Batoni: A Complete Catalogue of His Works, with an Introductory Text*. Edited and prepared for publication by Edgar Peters Bowron. Oxford: Phaidon/New York: New York University Press, 1985.

CLÉMENT 1872
Charles Clément. *Prud'hon*. Paris: Didier, 1872.

CLÉMENT 1879
Charles Clément. *Géricault: Étude biographique et critique*. 3d ed. Paris, 1879.

CLEVELAND 1964
Cleveland: The Cleveland Museum of Art. *Neo-Classicism: Style and Motif*. Exh. cat. by Henry Hawley, 1964.

COLOGNE 1977
Cologne: Wallraf-Richartz-Museum in der Kunsthalle Köln. *Bertel Thorvaldsen*. Exh. cat., 1977.

COLOGNE 1987
Cologne: Museen der Stadt Köln. *Triumph und Tod des Helden*. Exh. cat. by Ekkehard Mai and Anke Repp-Eckert, 1987.

COOPER-HEWITT 1991–92
The Cooper-Hewitt Collections: A Design Resource. New York: Cooper-Hewitt Museum, 1991–92.

COPENHAGEN 1969
Copenhagen: Thorvaldsens Museum. *Antonio Canova: Tegninger fra Museet i Bassano*. Exh. cat., 1969.

COPENHAGEN 1975
Copenhagen: Thorvaldsens Museum. *Fransk Nyklassicisme*. Exh. cat., 1975.

COPENHAGEN 1983A
Copenhagen: Statens Museum for Kunst. *Tegninger af C. W. Eckersberg*. Exh. cat., 1983.

COPENHAGEN 1983B
Copenhagen: Thorvaldsens Museum. *C. W. Eckersberg i Rom 1813–16*. Exh. cat., 1983.

COPENHAGEN 1990
Copenhagen: Statens Museum for Kunst. *Mellem guder og helte: Historiemaleriet i Rom, Paris og København 1770–1820*. Exh. cat., 1990.

COUPIN 1829
P. A. Coupin. *Oeuvres posthumes d'Anne-Louis Girodet-Trioson peintre d'histoire, suivies par sa correspondance . . . .* 2 vols. Paris: J. Renouard, 1829.

COUSIN 1872
Ambroise-Firmin Didot. *Jean Cousin.* Paris: Librarie de Firmin-Didot, 1872.

CROW 1985
Thomas E. Crow. *Painters and Public Life in Eighteenth-Century Paris.* New Haven: Yale University Press, 1985.

CUZIN 1987
Jean-Pierre Cuzin. *Jean-Honoré Fragonard: Vie et oeuvre. Catalogue complet des peintures.* Fribourg: Office du Livre, 1987.

CUZIN N.D. [1988?]
Jean-Pierre Cuzin. *François-André Vincent, 1746–1816. Cahiers du dessin français, no. 4.* Paris: Galerie de Bayser, n.d. [1988?].

DACIER 1929–31
Émile Dacier. *Gabriel de Saint-Aubin: Peintre, dessinateur et graveur, 1724–1780.* 2 vols. Paris: G. van Oest, 1929–31.

DAVID 1880
J.-L.-Jules David. *Le Peintre Louis David, 1748–1825.* Vol. 1, *Souvenirs et documents inédits.* Paris: Havard, 1880.

DAVIS/SACRAMENTO 1971
Davis: University of California at Davis/ Sacramento: E. B. Crocker Art Gallery. *Classical Narrative in Master Drawings Selected from the Collections of the E. B. Crocker Art Gallery.* Exh. cat., 1971.

DELABORDE 1870
Henri Delaborde. *Ingres, sa vie et ses travaux, sa doctrine, d'après les notes manuscrits et les lettres du maître.* Paris: Plon, 1870.

DELÉCLUZE 1855
Étienne-Jean Delécluze. *Louis David, son école, et son temps: Souvenirs.* Paris: Didier, 1855.

DETROIT 1951
Detroit: The Detroit Institute of Arts. *French Drawings of Five Centuries from the Collection of the Fogg Art Museum.* Exh. cat., 1951.

DETROIT 1962
Detroit: The Detroit Institute of Arts. *French Drawings and Water Colors from Michigan Collections.* Exh. cat., 1962.

DETROIT/PHILADELPHIA 1968
Detroit: The Detroit Institute of Arts/ Philadelphia: Philadelphia Museum of Art. *Romantic Art in Britain: Paintings and Drawings 1760–1860.* Exh. cat. by Frederick Cummings and Allen Staley, 1968.

DIDEROT 1957–67
Denis Diderot. *Salons.* Edited by Jean Seznec and Jean Adhémar. 4 vols. Oxford: Clarendon, 1957–67.

DIDOT 1810
Firmin Didot. *Catalogues des livres rares, précieux, et tres-bien conditionnés du cabinet de M. Didot.* Paris: Firmin Didot, 1810.

DIJON 1938
Dijon: Musée Magnin. *Peintures et dessins de l'école français.* Cat., 1938.

DIJON 1959
Dijon: Musée des Beaux-Arts. *P.-P. Prud'hon, 1758–1823: Les Premiers Étapes de sa carrière.* Exh. cat., 1959.

DIO 1914–27
Cassius Dio Cocceianus. *Dio's Roman History.* Translated by Earnest Cary. 9 vols. London: William Heinemann/Cambridge: Harvard University Press, 1914–27.

DÜSSELDORF 1976
Düsseldorf: C. G. Boerner. *Ausgewählte Graphik und Zeichnungen aus sechs Jahrhunderten.* Exh. cat., 1976.

EASSON/ESSICK 1979
Roger R. Easson and Robert N. Essick. *William Blake: Book Illustrator; A Bibliography and Catalogue of the Commercial Engravings.* 2 vols. Memphis: American Blake Foundation/Memphis State University, 1979.

EINEM 1935
Herbert von Einem. *Carl Ludwig Fernow: Eine Studie zum deutschen Klassizismus.* Berlin: Deutscher Verein für Kunstwissenschaft, 1935.

EISLER 1981
Colin Eisler. "Entre vision et réalité." *Connaissance des arts,* no. 353 (July 1981): 64–71.

EITNER 1963
Lorenz Eitner. "Géricault's 'Dying Paris' and the Meaning of His Romantic Classicism." *Master Drawings* 1 (1963): 21–34.

EITNER 1970
Lorenz E. A. Eitner. *Neoclassicism and Romanticism 1750–1850: Sources and Documents.* 2 vols. Englewood Cliffs, New Jersey: Prentice-Hall, 1970.

EITNER 1983
Lorenz E. A. Eitner. *Géricault: His Life and Work.* London: Orbis, 1983.

ERDMAN 1969
David V. Erdman. *Blake, Prophet against Empire: A Poet's Interpretation of the History of His Time.* Rev. ed. Princeton: Princeton University Press, 1969.

VON ERFFA/STALEY 1986
Helmut von Erffa and Allen Staley. *The Paintings of Benjamin West.* New Haven: Barra Foundation/ Yale University Press, 1986.

ESCHOLIER 1926–29
Raymond Escholier. *Delacroix: Peintre, graveur, écrivain.* Paris: H. Floury, 1926–29.

ESSICK 1983
Robert N. Essick. *The Separate Plates of William Blake: A Catalogue.* Princeton: Princeton University Press, 1983.

ESSICK/LA BELLE 1977
Robert N. Essick and Jenijoy La Belle, eds. *Flaxman's Illustrations to Homer.* New York: Dover Publications, 1977.

FAENZA 1979
Faenza: Palazzo Milzetti. *L'età neoclassica a Faenza, 1780–1820.* Exh. cat., 1979.

FEDERMANN 1927
Arnold Federmann. *Johann Heinrich Füssli: Dichter und Maler, 1741–1825.* Zurich/Leipzig: Orell Füssli Verlag, 1927.

FÉNELON 1805
François de Salignac de La Mothe-Fénelon. *Les Aventures de Télémaque.* New York: W. A. Davis, 1805.

FERNOW 1867
Carl Ludwig Fernow. *Carstens Leben und Werke.* Edited by Hermann Riegel. Hannover: Carl Rümpler, 1867.

FLEMING 1962
John Fleming. *Robert Adam and His Circle in Edinburgh and Rome.* Cambridge: Harvard University Press, 1962.

FLORENCE 1952
Florence: La Strozzina. *Antonio Canova: Monocromi e disegni.* Exh. cat., 1952.

FOSSING 1929
Poul Fossing. *Catalogue of the Antique Engraved Gems and Cameos, Thorvaldsens Museum.* Copenhagen: G.E.C. Gad, 1929.

FRANCIS 1945
H. S. Francis. "A Drawing by Jean-Honoré Fragonard." *The Bulletin of The Cleveland Museum of Art* 32, no. 5 (June 1945): 88.

FRANCISCIS N.D.
Alfonso de Franciscis. *The National Archaeological Museum of Naples*. Naples: Interdipress, n.d.

FRODL-SCHNEEMANN 1984
Marianne Frodl-Schneemann. *Johann Peter Krafft 1780–1856: Monographie und Verzeichnis der Gemälde*. Munich/Vienna: Herold Verlag, 1984.

GAEHTGENS/LUGAND 1988
Thomas W. Gaehtgens and Jacques Lugand. *Joseph-Marie Vien, peintre du roi (1716–1809)*. Paris: Arthena, 1988.

GALT 1820
John Galt. *The Life, Studies, and Works of Benjamin West, Esq*. London, 1820.

GANZ 1947
Paul Ganz. *Die Zeichnungen Hans* [Johann] *Heinrich Füsslis*. Bern: Olten, 1947.

GATTEAUX 1875
Édouard Gatteaux. *Collection de 120 dessins, croquis et peintures de M. Ingres*. 2 vols. Paris, n.d. [1875].

GENEVA/DIJON 1984
Geneva: Musée Rath/Dijon: Musée des Beaux-Arts. *Dessins genevois de Liotard à Hodler*. Exh. cat. by Anne de Herdt, 1984.

GERLACH 1970
Peter Gerlach. "Johan Nepomuk Schaller: Bellerophon und die Chimaira." *Mitteilungen der Österreichischen Galerie*, no. 58 (1970): 75–98.

GERSTENBERG/RAVE 1934
Kurt Gerstenberg and Paul Ortwin Rave. *Die Wandgemälde der Deutschen Romantiker im Casino Massimo zu Rom*. Berlin: Deutscher Verein für Kunstwissenschaft, 1934.

GILCHRIST 1907
Alexander Gilchrist. *Life of William Blake*. Edited by W. Graham Robertson. London: John Lane, 1907.

GIRODET 1807
Anne-Louis Girodet de Roussy-Trioson. *La Critique des critiques du salon de 1806: Étrennes aux connoisseurs*. Paris, 1807.

GOETHE 1962
Johann Wolfgang Goethe. *Italian Journey, 1786–1788*. Translated by W. H. Auden and Elizabeth Mayer. London: Collins, 1962.

GOLDNER 1988
George R. Goldner. *European Drawings 1, Catalogue of the Collections*. Malibu: The J. Paul Getty Museum, 1988.

GOLDNER/HENDRIX 1992
George R. Goldner and Lee Hendrix. *European Drawings 2, Catalogue of the Collections*. Malibu: The J. Paul Getty Museum, 1992.

GONCOURT 1876
Edmond de Goncourt. *Catalogue raisonné de l'oeuvre . . . de Pierre-Paul Prud'hon*. Paris: Rapilly, 1876.

GONCOURT 1981
Edmond and Jules de Goncourt. *French Eighteenth-Century Painters*. Translated by Robin Ironside. Ithaca: Cornell University Press, 1981.

GOULD 1976
Cecil Gould. *The Paintings of Correggio*. London: Faber and Faber, 1976.

GRADMANN 1949
Erwin Gradmann. *French Master Drawings of the Eighteenth Century*. New York: Harper and Brothers, 1949.

GRAMACCINI 1989
Gisela Gramaccini. "Jean-Guillaume Moitte et la revolution française." *Revue de l'art*, no. 83 (1989): 61–70.

GREENHALGH 1978
Michael Greenhalgh. *The Classical Tradition in Art*. London: Duckworth, 1978.

GREGORI 1973
Luisa Bandera Gregori. "Filippo Pelagio Palagi, an Artist between Neo-Classicism and Romanticism." *Apollo* 97, no. 135 (May 1973): 500–509.

GRUNCHEC 1979
Philippe Grunchec. "Géricault: Problèmes de méthodes." *Revue de l'art* 43 (1979), 37–58.

GRUNCHEC 1983
Philippe Grunchec. *Le Grand Prix de peinture: Les Concours des Prix de Rome de 1797 à 1863*. Paris: École Nationale Supérieure des Beaux-Arts, 1983.

GRUNCHEC 1986
Philippe Grunchec. *Les Concours des Prix de Rome, 1797–1863*. 2 vols. Paris: École Nationale Supérieure des Beaux-Arts, 1986.

GUÉRINET N.D.
Armand Guérinet. *Décorations du XVIIIe siècle, V^e série: Ruines par Hubert Robert, etc.* Paris: Union Centrale des Arts Décoratifs, n.d.

GUEULLETTE 1879
Charles Gueullette. "Mademoiselle Constance Mayer et Prud'hon." *Gazette des Beaux-Arts*, ser. 2, 19 (May 1879): 476–90; 20 (October 1879): 337–57, 525–38.

GUIFFREY 1924
Jean Guiffrey. *L'Oeuvre de P.-P. Prud'hon*. Paris: Librairie Armand Colin, 1924.

HAMBURG 1974
Hamburg: Kunsthalle. *Ossian und die Kunst um 1800*. Exh. cat., 1974.

HAMBURG 1977–78
Hamburg: Kunsthalle. *Runge in seiner Zeit*. Exh. cat. by Werner Hofmann et al., 1977–78.

HAMBURG 1987
Hamburg: Thomas Le Claire Kunsthandel IV. *Handzeichnungen und Aquarelle, 1500–1900*. Cat., 1987.

HAMBURG 1989
Hamburg: Kunsthalle. *Europa 1789: Aufklärung—Verklärung—Verfall*. Exh. cat., 1989.

HAMBURG/COPENHAGEN/LONDON 1979
Hamburg: Kunsthalle/Copenhagen: Thorvaldsens Museum/London: Royal Academy. *John Flaxman, R.A.* Exh. cat. edited by David Bindman, 1979.

HANNOVER 1898
Emil Hannover. *Maleren C. W. Eckersberg*. Copenhagen: Thieles Bogtrykkeri, 1898.

HARDIE 1967
Martin Hardie. *Water-Colour Painting in Britain*. Vol. 2, *The Romantic Period*. Edited by Dudley Snelgrove with Jonathan Mayne and Basil Taylor. New York: Barnes and Noble, 1967.

HARTFORD/HANOVER/BOSTON 1973
Hartford: Wadsworth Atheneum/Hanover, New Hampshire: Hopkins Center Art Galleries, Dartmouth College/Boston: Museum of Fine Arts. *One Hundred Master Drawings from New England Private Collections*. Exh. cat. by Franklin W. Robinson, 1973.

HARTFORD/SAN FRANCISCO/DIJON 1976–77
Hartford: Wadsworth Atheneum/San Francisco: California Palace of the Legion of Honor/Dijon: Musée des Beaux-Arts. *Jean-Baptiste Greuze, 1725–1805*. Exh. cat. by Edgar Munhall, 1976–77.

HASKELL 1980
Francis Haskell. *Patrons and Painters: A Study in the Relations between Italian Art and Society in the Age of the Baroque*. New Haven: Yale University Press, 1980.

HASKELL/PENNY 1981
Francis Haskell and Nicholas Penny. *Taste and the Antique: The Lure of Classical Sculpture 1500–1900*. New Haven: Yale University Press, 1981.

HATFIELD 1943
Henry C. Hatfield. *Winckelmann and His German Critics, 1755–1781: A Prelude to the Classical Age*. New York: King's Crown Press, 1943.

HAYLEY 1809
William Hayley. *The Life of George Romney, Esq*. London: T. Payne, 1809.

HEIM/BÉRAUD/HEIM 1989
Jean-François Heim, Claire Béraud, and Philippe Heim. *Les Salons de peinture de la révolution française 1789–1799*. Paris: C.A.C. Édition, 1989.

HEINE 1928
Albrecht-Friedrich Heine. *Asmus Jakob Carstens und die Entwicklung des Figurenbildes*. Straussburg: J. H. Ed. Heitz, 1928.

HELSTED/HENSCHEN/JØRNÆS 1990
Dyveke Helsted, Eva Henschen, and Bjarne Jørnæs. *Thorvaldsen*. Copenhagen: Thorvaldsens Museum, 1990.

DE HERDT 1978
Anne de Herdt. "Rousseau illustré par Saint-Ours, suivi du catalogue des peintures et dessins pour 'Le Lévite d'Éphraim.' " *Geneva*, n.s., 26 (1978): 229–72.

HERODIAN 1969
Herodian. Translated by C. R. Whittaker. Cambridge: Harvard University Press, 1969.

HOLST 1980
Christian von Holst. *Dante—Vergil—Geryon*. Stuttgart: Staatsgalerie, 1980.

HOMER 1963
Homer. *The Odyssey*. Translated by Robert Fitzgerald. Garden City, New York: Anchor Books/Doubleday and Company, 1963.

HOMER 1969
Homer. *The Iliad*. Translated by E. V. Rieu. Harmondsworth, Middlesex/Baltimore: Penguin Books, 1969.

HONOUR 1960
Hugh Honour. "Antonio Canova and the Anglo-Romans: Part 2, The First Year in Rome." *The Connoisseur* 144 (January 1960): 225–31.

HONOUR 1968
Hugh Honour. *Neo-classicism*. Harmondsworth, Middlesex/Baltimore: Penguin Books, 1968.

HONOUR 1972A
Hugh Honour. "Canova's Statues of Venus." *The Burlington Magazine* 114, no. 835 (October 1972): 658–70.

HONOUR 1972B
Hugh Honour. "Canova's Studio Practice." *The Burlington Magazine* 114, nos. 828–29 (March–April 1972): 146–59 (March), 214–29 (April).

HOUSTON 1981
Houston: Museum of Fine Arts. *Drawing into Sculpture 1400–1980*. Exh. cat. by Colin Eisler, 1981.

INVENTAIRE 1907–75
Archives des Musées Nationaux et de l'École du Louvre: Inventaire général des dessins du Musée du Louvre et du Musée de Versailles. 12 vols. Paris: Librairie Centrale d'Art et d'Architecture, 1907–75.

INVENTAIRE 1930–85
Bibliothèque Nationale, Département des Estampes: Inventaire du fonds français après 1800. 15 vols. Paris: Maurice Le Garrec/Bibliothèque Nationale, 1930–85.

IRWIN 1966
David Irwin. *English Neoclassical Art: Studies in Inspiration and Taste*. London: Faber and Faber, 1966.

IRWIN 1980
David Irwin. *John Flaxman, 1755–1826: Sculptor, Illustrator, Designer*. New York: Rizzoli, 1980.

ITHACA 1978
Ithaca: Herbert F. Johnson Museum of Art, Cornell University. *The Linear Tradition: Selected Drawings from the Eighteenth to the Twentieth Century*. Exh. cat., 1978.

JANSON 1977
H. W. Janson, comp. *Catalogues of the Paris Salon 1673–1881*. New York: Garland Publishing, 1977.

JOANNIDES/SELLS 1974
Paul Joannides and Christopher Sells. "Ossian at the Grand Palais." *The Burlington Magazine* 116, no. 855 (June 1974): 358–62.

JOHANSEN 1923
K. Friis Johansen. "Om Thorvaldsens 'Priamos og Achilleus.' " *Kunst og Kultur* 4 (1923): 240–52.

JONES 1951
"Memoirs of Thomas Jones." *The Walpole Society* 32 (1946–48; published 1951): 1–142.

JØRNÆS 1978
Bjarne Jørnæs. "Thorvaldsen-malernes ven." In *En bog om kunst til Else Kai Sass*, 290–308. Copenhagen: Forum, 1978.

JOSEPHSON 1956
Ragnar Josephson. *Sergels Fantasi*. 2 vols. Stockholm: Bokförlaget Natur och Kultur, 1956.

JOUIN 1889
Henry Jouin. *Charles Le Brun et les arts sous Louis XIV*. Paris: Imprimerie Nationale, 1889.

KAMPHAUSEN 1941
Alfred Kamphausen. *Asmus Jakob Carstens*. Neumünster in Holstein: Karl Wachholtz, 1941.

KEISER 1973
Herbert Wolfgang Keiser. *Des Mannes Stärke und andere Bilder für das Schloss zu Oldenburg von J. W. Tischbein*. Oldenburg: Landesmuseum, 1973.

KENWOOD 1972
Kenwood: Iveagh Bequest. *Lady Hamilton in Relation to the Art of Her Time*. Exh. cat., 1972.

KORSHAK 1987
Yvonne Korshak. "*Paris and Helen* by Jacques-Louis David: Choice and Judgment on the Eve of the French Revolution." *The Art Bulletin* 69, no. 1 (March 1987): 102–16.

KRAEMER 1975
Ruth S. Kraemer. *Drawings by Benjamin West and His Son Raphael Lamar West*. New York: David R. Godine/The Pierpont Morgan Library, 1975.

LACAMBRE 1975
Geneviève and Jean Lacambre. "La Galerie de Diane aux Tuileries sous la restauration." *Revue du Louvre* 25, no. 1 (1975), 39–50.

LANDON 1809
Charles Paul Landon. *Annales du Musée de l'Ecole Moderne des Beaux-Arts, premiere collection, tome complémentaire*. Paris: Charles Paul Landon, 1809, xvi *bis*, 71, pl. 45.

LANDON 1820
Charles Paul Landon. *Annales du Musée et de l'École Moderne des Beaux Arts. Salon de 1819: Receuil de morceaux choisi* . . . . Paris: Imprimerie Royale, 1820.

LANKHEIT 1951
Klaus Lankheit. "Zur Füssliforschung: Gedanken im Anschluss an Paul Ganz, *Die Zeichnungen Hans Heinrich Füsslis*." *Zeitschrift für Kunstgeschichte* 14 (1951): 175–80.

LAUNAY 1991
Elisabeth Launay. *Les Frères Goncourt, collectionneurs de dessins*. Paris: Arthena, 1991.

LAVEISSIÈRE 1988
Sylvain Laveissière. "Prud'hon à l'Hôtel de Lannoy: La Salon de la richesse." *Antologia di belle arti*, nos. 33/34 (1988): 2–23.

LE BRETON 1812
Joachim Le Breton. "Notice historique sur la vie et les ouvrages de M. Moitte." *Magasin encyclopédique* 6 (1812): 46–50.

LEE 1967
Rensselaer W. Lee. *Ut Pictura Poesis: The Humanistic Theory of Painting*. New York: Norton and Company, 1967.

LEONARD 1951
H. Stewart Leonard. "Benjamin West's *Antiochus and Stratonice*." *Bulletin of the City Art Museum of Saint Louis* 36, no. 3 (1951): 48–50.

LESSING 1968
Gotthold Ephraim Lessing. *Laocoön*. Translated by Ellen Frothingham. New York: Noonday Press, 1968.

LETTRES 1819
Lettres à David sur le Salon de 1819, par quelques élèves de son école. Paris: Pillet, 1819.

LEVITINE 1954
Georges Levitine. "The Influence of Lavater on Girodet's *Expression des sentiments de l'âme*." *The Art Bulletin* 36, no. 1 (March 1954): 32–44.

LEVITINE 1978
Georges Levitine. *The Dawn of Bohemianism, the Barbu Rebellion, and Primitivism in Neoclassical France*. State College: Pennsylvania State University Press, 1978.

LEXINGTON 1967
Lexington: University of Kentucky Art Gallery. *Masterpieces from University Collections*. Exh. cat., 1967.

LICHT 1980
Fred Licht. "Tomb Sculpture." In *The Romantics to Rodin*, 96–108. Exh. cat. edited by Peter Fusco and H. W. Janson, Los Angeles: Los Angeles County Museum of Art, 1980.

LICHT 1983
Fred Licht. *Canova*. New York: Abbeville Press, 1983.

LILLE 1983
Lille: Musée des Beaux-Arts. *Autour de David: Dessins néo-classiques du Musée des Beaux-Arts de Lille*. Exh. cat., 1983.

LOCQUIN 1912
Jean Locquin. *La Peinture d'histoire en France de 1747 à 1785: Étude sur l'évolution des idées artistiques dans la seconde moitié du XVIIIe siècle*. Paris: Henri Laurens, 1912. Reprint, Paris: Arthena, 1978.

LOCQUIN 1921
Jean Locquin. "La Part de l'influence anglaise dans l'orientation néo-classique de la peinture française entre 1750 et 1780." *Actes du Congrès d'histoire de l'art* 2, pt. 1, 391–99. Paris, September 26–October 5, 1921. Reprint, Nendeln, Liechtenstein: Kraus, 1979.

LONDON 1876
London: Burlington Fine Arts Club. *The Works of William Blake*. Exh. cat., 1876.

LONDON 1906
London: Carfax and Company. *Frescoes, Prints and Drawings by William Blake*. Exh. cat., 1906.

LONDON 1932
London: Royal Academy. *Exhibition of French Art, 1200–1900*. Exh. cat., 1932.

LONDON 1934
London: Wildenstein Galleries. *French Drawings from Clouet to Ingres*. Exh. cat., 1934.

LONDON 1947
London: Tate Gallery. *William Blake (1757–1827)*. Exh. cat., 1947.

LONDON 1948
London: Tate Gallery. *David, 1748–1825*. Exh. cat., 1948.

LONDON 1950–51
London: Royal Academy. *Winter Exhibition*. Exh. cat., 1950–51.

LONDON 1951–52
London: Royal Academy. *The First Hundred Years of the Royal Academy, 1768–1868*. Exh. cat., 1951–52.

LONDON 1968
London: Royal Academy. *France in the Eighteenth Century*. Exh. cat., 1968.

LONDON 1972
London: Royal Academy/Victoria and Albert Museum. *The Age of Neo-Classicism*. Exh. cat., 1972.

LONDON 1973A
London: Heim Gallery. *Thorvaldsen: Drawings and Bozzetti*. Exh. cat. by Dyveke Helsted, 1973.

LONDON 1973B
London: Victoria and Albert Museum. *An American Museum of Art and Design: Designs from the Cooper-Hewitt Collection, New York*. Exh. cat., 1973.

LONDON 1975
London: Heim Gallery. *Exhibition of French Drawings: Neo-Classicism*. Exh. cat. by Philip Conisbee, 1975.

LONDON 1979A
London: Arts Council of Great Britain. *Ingres: Drawings from the Musée Ingres at Montauban and Other Collections*. Exh. cat., 1979.

LONDON 1979B
London: Royal Academy of Arts. *John Flaxman, R.A.* Exh. cat. edited by David Bindman, 1979.

LONDON 1981
London: Wildenstein Galleries. *Consulat, Empire, Restauration: Art in Early XIX-Century France*. Exh. cat. by G. Bernier, 1981.

LONDON 1982
London: Hazlitt Gallery. Untitled catalogue. 1982.

LONDON 1983
London: Tate Gallery. *James Barry: The Artist as Hero*. Exh. cat. by William L. Pressly, 1983.

LONDON 1984
London: National Gallery. *Danish Painting: The Golden Age*. Exh. cat., 1984.

LONDON 1985
London: Colnaghi. *Old Master Drawings*. Exh. cat., 1985.

LOS ANGELES 1961
Los Angeles: University of California. *French Masters, Rococo to Romanticism*. Exh. cat., 1961.

LOS ANGELES 1971
Los Angeles: Los Angeles County Museum of Art. *Géricault*. Exh. cat., 1971.

LOS ANGELES 1988
Los Angeles: Grunwald Center for the Graphic Arts, Wight Art Gallery, University of California. *French Caricature and the French Revolution, 1789–1799*. Exh. cat., 1988.

LOSSKY 1938
Boris Lossky. "Tableaux de Ménageot et de Vincent en Tchécoslovaquie." *Gazette des Beaux-Arts*, ser. 6, 19 (January 1938): 47–53.

LOUISVILLE/FORT WORTH 1983–84
Louisville: J. B. Speed Art Museum/Fort Worth: Kimbell Art Museum. *In Pursuit of Perfection: The Art of J.-A.-D. Ingres*. Exh. cat. by Patricia Condon, M. B. Cohn, and Agnes Mongan, 1983–84.

LUGT 1921
Frits Lugt. *Les Marques de collections de dessins & d'estampes . . . .* Amsterdam: Vereenigde Drukkerijen, 1921.

LUGT 1956
Frits Lugt. *Les Marques de collections de dessins & d'estampes . . . : Supplément*. The Hague: Martinus Nijhoff, 1956.

LUTTEROTTI 1985
Otto R. von Lutterotti. *Joseph Anton Koch 1768–1839: Leben und Werk*. Vienna/Munich: Herold Verlag, 1985.

LYONS 1989–90
Lyons: Musée des Beaux-Arts. *Les Muses de Messidor: Peintres et sculpteurs lyonnais de la Révolution à l'Empire*. Exh. cat., 1989–90.

MANNERS/WILLIAMSON 1924
Victoria Manners and George C. Williamson. *Angelica Kauffmann, R.A.: Her Life and Her Works*. London: John Lane, 1924.

MARTIN/MASSON 1908
C. Martin and C. Masson. *Catalogue raisonné de l'oeuvre peint et dessiné de J.-B. Greuze*. Paris, 1908.

MARTINE/MAROTTE 1923
Charles Martine and Léon Marotte. *Pierre-Paul Prud'hon: Soixante-douze reproductions . . . accompagnées d'une vie du peintre . . . .* Vol. 3 of *Dessins des maîtres français.* Paris: Helleu et Sergent, 1923.

MASSAR 1976
Phyllis Dearborn Massar. "Felice Giani Drawings at the Cooper-Hewitt Museum." *Master Drawings* 14, no. 4 (1976): 396–420.

MATHEY N.D.
Jacques Mathey. *Ingres: Dessins.* Paris: O. Lesourd, n.d.

MATTEUCCI 1974
Anna Maria Matteucci. "Carlo Filippo Aldrovandi e Pelagio Palagi." *Atti e memorie dell'Accadèmia Clementina di Bologna* 11 (1974): 87–98.

MAYER 1972
Dorothy Moulton Mayer. *Angelica Kauffmann, R.A. 1741–1807.* Gerrards Cross: Colin Smythe, 1972.

MAYNARD 1991
Marie-Noëlle Maynard. "Acquisitions." *Revue du Louvre* 41, nos. 5/6 (1991): 105.

MAYOR 1980
Susan Mayor. *Collecting Fans.* Christie's International Collectors Series. New York: Mayflower Books, 1980.

MELLOR 1974
Anne Kostelanetz Mellor. *Blake's Human Form Divine.* Berkeley: University of California Press, 1974.

MICHEL 1984
Christian Michel. "Les Peintures d'Herculanum et la querelle des anciens et des modernes (1740–1760)." *Bulletin de la société de l'histoire de l'art français* (1984): 105–17.

MILAN 1992
Milan: Palazzo Reale. *Il primo '800 italiano: La pittura tra passato e futuro.* Exh. cat., 1992.

MILDENBERGER 1986
Hermann Mildenberger. *Johann Heinrich Wilhelm Tischbein: Goethes Maler und Freund.* Neumünster: Karl Wachholtz, 1986.

MILLIER 1955
Arthur Millier. *The Drawings of Ingres.* Los Angeles: Borden Publishing Company, 1955.

MILWAUKEE 1977
Milwaukee: Milwaukee Art Museum. *Collecting the Masters.* Exh. cat., 1977.

MINNEAPOLIS 1960
Minneapolis: The Minneapolis Institute of Arts. *Drawings, Paintings and Sculpture from Three Private Collections.* Exh. cat., 1960.

MINNEAPOLIS 1967
Minneapolis: The Minneapolis Institute of Arts. *Roman Eighteenth-Century Drawings from a Private Collection.* Exh. cat., 1967.

MINNEAPOLIS 1971
Minneapolis: The Minneapolis Institute of Arts. *A Loan Exhibition of Drawings and Watercolors from Minnesota Private Collections.* Exh. cat., 1971.

MINNEAPOLIS 1984
Minneapolis: The Minneapolis Institute of Arts. *Regency to Empire French Printmaking 1715–1814.* Exh. cat. edited by Victor I. Carlson and John W. Ittmann, 1984.

MINNEAPOLIS 1986
Minneapolis: The Minneapolis Institute of Arts. *The Art of Collecting: Acquisitions at the Minneapolis Institute of Arts, 1980–1985.* Exh. cat., 1986.

MINNEAPOLIS/CHICAGO/KANSAS CITY/CAMBRIDGE 1968
Minneapolis: The Minneapolis Institute of Arts/ Chicago: The Art Institute of Chicago/Kansas City: Nelson-Atkins Museum/Cambridge: Fogg Art Museum, Harvard University. *Loan Exhibition Selections from the Drawing Collection of David Daniels.* Exh. cat., 1968.

MINNEAPOLIS/NEW YORK 1962
Minneapolis: University Gallery, University of Minnesota/New York: Solomon R. Guggenheim Museum. *The Nineteenth Century: One Hundred Twenty-Five Master Drawings.* Exh. cat., 1962.

MIREUR 1911–12
Hippolyte Mireur. *Dictionnaire des ventes d'art faites en France et à l'étranger pendant les XVIIIme & XIXme siècles.* 7 vols. Paris: Maison d'éditions d'oeuvres artistiques, 1911–12.

MONGAN 1962
Agnes Mongan. *Great Drawings of All Time, Vol. 3 (French).* New York: Shorewood Publishers, 1962.

MONGAN FORTHCOMING
Agnes Mongan et al. *David to Corot: French Drawings in the Fogg Art Museum.* Cambridge: Harvard University Press, forthcoming.

MONGAN/SACHS 1940
Agnes Mongan and Paul J. Sachs. *Drawings in the Fogg Museum of Art.* Cambridge: Harvard University Press, 1940.

MONTAGU 1986
Jennifer Montagu. "Quand un musée s'expose." *Connaissance des arts,* no. 416 (October 1986): 88–93.

MONTAIGLON 1858–60
Anatole de Montaiglon. "Projet de colonne monumental à la glorie des armées français." *Archives de l'art français* 6 (1858–60): 344–45.

MONTARGIS 1864
Montargis: Musée de Montargis. *Catalogue des tableaux, dessins, gravures, sculptures et objets d'art appartenant au Musée de Montargis.* Cat. by Alexandre Levain, 1864.

MONTARGIS 1874
Montargis: Musée de Montargis. *Catalogue des tableaux, dessins, gravures et sculptures appartenant au Musée de Montargis.* Cat. by Alexandre Levain, 1874.

MONTARGIS 1885
Montargis: Musée Girodet. *Catalogue des tableaux, dessins, gravures, sculptures et objets d'art appartenant au Musée de Montargis,* 1885.

MONTARGIS 1937
Montargis: Musée Girodet. *Catalogue des tableaux, dessins, gravures, sculptures et objets d'art appartenant au Musée de Montargis,* 1937.

MONTARGIS 1967
Montargis: Musée Girodet. *Girodet: Exposition du deuxième centenaire.* Exh. cat. by Jacqueline Auzas, 1967.

MONTARGIS 1983
Montargis: Musée Girodet. *Girodet dessins du musée.* Exh. cat. by Jacqueline Boutet-Loyer, 1983.

MONTARGIS 1989A
Montargis: Musée Girodet. *La Légende d'Ossian, illustrée par Girodet.* Exh. cat., 1989.

MONTARGIS 1989B
Montargis: Musée Girodet. *Un Peintre sous la révolution: Jean Charles-Nicaise Perrin (1754–1831).* Exh. cat., 1989.

MONTAUBAN/REUILLY 1991
Montauban: Musée Ingres/Reuilly: Château de Malmaison. *Ingres, prix de Rome.* Exh. cat., 1991.

MONTFAUCON 1976
Bernard de Montfaucon. *Antiquity Explained and Represented in Sculptures.* Translated by David Humphreys. 5 vols. London: J. Tonson and J. Watts, 1721–24. Reprinted in 2 vols., New York: Garland Publishing, 1976.

MONTREAL 1950
Montreal: Montreal Museum of Fine Arts. *Eighteenth-Century Art of France and England.* Exh. cat., 1950.

MORI 1811
Ferdinando Mori. *Le statue e li bassirelievi inventati e scolpiti in marmo dal Cavaliere Alberto Thorwaldsen . . . .* Rome, 1811.

MOUILLESEAUX 1974
Jean-Pierre Mouilleseaux. "'Léandre et Héro' de Taillasson, à propos d'un thème iconographique et littéraire." *Revue du Louvre* 24, no. 6 (1974): 411–16.

MRÁZ 1983
Bohumír Mráz. *Ingres Zeichnungen*. Honau: Werner Dausien, 1983.

MUNICH 1985
Munich: Neue Pinakothek (Staatliche Graphische Sammlung). *Von Abildgaard bis Marstrand: Meisterzeichnungen der Kopenhagener Schule aus dem Besitz der Königlichen Kupferstichsammlung Kopenhagen*. Exh. cat., 1985.

MUSEO VATICANO 1908
Guida del Museo Vaticano di Scultori. Rome: Tipografia Vaticana, 1908.

NEUWIRTH 1989
Markus Neuwirth. *J. A. Koch—A. J. Carstens: Die Argonauten*. Graz: Akademische Druck- und Verlagsanstalt, 1989.

NEW HAVEN 1979
New Haven: Yale Center for British Art. *The Fuseli Circle in Rome: Early Romantic Art of the 1770s*. Exh. cat. by Nancy L. Pressly, 1979.

NEW YORK 1922
New York: Wildenstein Galleries. *Exhibition Prud'hon*. Exh. cat., 1922.

NEW YORK 1942–43
European Drawings from the Collections of the Metropolitan Museum of Art, Vol. II: Flemish, Dutch, German, Spanish, French, and British Drawings. New York: The Metropolitan Museum of Art, 1942–43.

NEW YORK 1947–48
New York: Wildenstein Galleries. *French XIX-Century Drawings*. Exh. cat., 1947–48.

NEW YORK 1959
New York: Jacques Seligmann and Company. *Master Drawings*. Exh. cat., 1959.

NEW YORK 1962
New York: Lambert-Spector. *Extravagant Drawings of the Eighteenth Century from the Collection of the Cooper Union Museum*. Exh. cat. by Richard P. Wunder, 1962

NEW YORK 1965
New York: Jacques Seligmann Galleries. *Master Drawings*. Exh. cat., 1965.

NEW YORK 1972
New York: The Pierpont Morgan Library. *English Drawing and Watercolors 1550–1850 in the Collection of Mr. and Mrs. Paul Mellon*. Exh. cat. by John Baskett, 1972.

NEW YORK 1976
New York: Wildenstein Galleries. *French Neoclassicism*. Exh. cat., 1976.

NEW YORK 1977
New York: Shepherd Gallery. *French Nineteenth-Century Drawings*. Exh. cat., 1977.

NEW YORK 1981
New York: Drawing Center. *Sculptors' Drawings over Six Centuries, 1400–1950*. Exh. cat. by Colin Eisler, 1981.

NEW YORK 1982A
New York: Colnaghi/F. A. den Broeder. *Aspects of Neoclassicism: Drawings and Watercolors 1760–1840*. Exh. cat., 1982.

NEW YORK 1982B
New York: Wildenstein Galleries. *Consulat, Empire, Restauration: Art in Early XIX-Century France*. Exh. cat. by G. Bernier, 1982.

NEW YORK 1985A
New York: Colnaghi. *French Drawings 1760–1880*. Exh. cat., 1985.

NEW YORK 1985B
New York: Drawing Center. *Drawings from Venice: Masterworks from the Museo Correr, Venice*. Exh. cat., 1985.

NEW YORK 1985–86
New York: Frick Collection. *Ingres and the Comtesse d'Haussonville*. Exh. cat. by Edgar Munhall, 1985–86.

NEW YORK 1986A
New York: Shepherd Gallery. *French Nineteenth-Century Watercolors, Drawings, Pastels, Paintings, and Sculpture*. Exh. cat., 1986.

NEW YORK 1986B
New York: Zangrilli, Brady and Company, Ltd. *French and English Drawings 1700–1875*. Exh. cat., 1986.

NEW YORK 1988A
New York: W. M. Brady and Company. *French Drawings and Watercolors*. Exh. cat., 1988.

NEW YORK 1988B
New York: The Pierpont Morgan Library. *The Romantic Spirit: German Drawings, 1750–1850*. Exh. cat., 1988.

NEW YORK 1989A
New York: W. M. Brady and Company. *Master Drawings, 1700–1890*. Exh. cat., 1989.

NEW YORK 1989B
New York: Colnaghi. *1789: French Art during the Revolution*. Exh. cat., 1989.

NEW YORK 1990
New York: W. M. Brady and Company. *Master Drawings 1760–1880*. Exh. cat., 1990.

NEW YORK 1991
New York: W. M. Brady and Company. *19th-Century French Drawings and Oil Sketches*. Exh. cat., 1991.

NEW YORK/FORT WORTH/OTTAWA 1990–91
New York: National Academy of Design/Fort Worth: Kimbell Art Museum/Ottawa: National Gallery of Canada. *Masterful Studies: Three Centuries of French Drawings from the Prat Collection*. Exh. cat., 1990–91.

NEW YORK/SAN DIEGO/HOUSTON 1985–86
New York: The Pierpont Morgan Library/San Diego: San Diego Museum of Art/Houston: Museum of Fine Arts. *Master Drawings by Géricault*. Exh. cat., 1985–86.

NEW YORK/WASHINGTON 1984
New York: Shepherd Gallery/Washington, D.C.: Ossuna Gallery. *The French Neoclassic and Academic Traditions, 1800–1900*. Exh. cat., 1984.

NISHINOMIYA 1978
Nishinomiya: Otani Museum of Fine Arts. *Exposition Rococo: Poésie et rêve de la peinture française au XVIIIe siècle*. Exh. cat., 1978.

NODET 1921
Victor Nodet. "Les Sympathies artistiques de P.-P. Prud'hon en 1801: Prud'hon et Corrège." In *Actes du Congrès d'histoire de l'art*. Paris, 1921, 408–16.

NORTHAMPTON 1947
Northampton: Smith College Museum of Art. *The Art of Eighteenth-Century England*. Exh. cat., 1947.

NORTHAMPTON 1962
Northampton: Smith College Museum of Art. *The Drawings of George Romney*. Exh. cat., 1962.

NOTRE DAME 1987
Notre Dame: Snite Museum of Art, University of Notre Dame. *Selected Works from the Snite Museum of Art*. Exh. cat., 1987.

NOTTINGHAM/KENWOOD 1991
Nottingham: University Art Gallery/Kenwood: Iveagh Bequest. *The Artist's Model: Its Role in British Art from Lely to Etty*. Exh. cat. by Ilaria Bignamini and Martin Postle, 1991.

NÜSCHELER 1807–9
[Felix Nüscheler]. *Heinrich Fuessli's Sämmtliche Werke: Nebst einem Versuche seiner Biographie*. 2 vols. Zurich: Fuessli und Compagnie, 1807–9.

OLSON 1974
Roberta J. M. Olson. "Selected Drawings at Wildenstein." *Arts Magazine* 48, no. 6 (March 1974): 74.

OLSON 1980
Roberta J. M. Olson. "Bartolemeo Pinelli: An Underestimated Ottocento Master." *Drawing* 11, no. 4 (November–December 1980): 73–78.

OLSON 1990
Roberta J. M. Olson. "Pelagio Palagi's Works on the Theme of Charles VIII and Gian Galeazzo Sforza at Pavia." *Antologia di belle arti* 5, nos. 35–38 (1990): 77–81.

OSBORNE 1985
Carol Osborne. *Pierre Didot the Elder and French Book Illustration, 1789–1822*. New York: Garland Publishing, 1985.

OTTAWA 1976
Ottawa: National Gallery of Canada/Galerie nationale du Canada. *European Drawings from Canadian Collections, 1500–1900/Dessins européens des collections canadiennes, 1500–1900*. Exh. cat. by Mary Cazort Taylor, 1976.

OVID 1970
Ovid (Publius Ovidius Naso). *The Metamorphoses*. Translated by Mary M. Innes. Harmondsworth, Middlesex: Penguin Books, 1970.

PARIS 1860
Paris: 26 boulevard des Italiens. *Tableaux et dessins de l'école française, principalement du XVIIIe siècle, tirés de collections d'amateurs et exposés au profit de la Caisse de Secours des Artistes*. Exh. cat., 1860.

PARIS 1867
Paris: École Impériales des Beaux-Arts. *Tableaux, études, peintures, dessins et croquis de J.-A.-D. Ingres*. Exh. cat., 1867.

PARIS 1874
Paris: École des Beaux-Arts. *Exposition des oeuvres de Prud'hon au profit de sa fille*. Exh. cat., 1874.

PARIS 1911
Paris: Galerie Georges Petit. *Exposition Ingres*. Exh. cat., 1911.

PARIS 1913
Paris: Palais des Beaux-Arts. *David et ses élèves*. Exh. cat., 1913.

PARIS 1922
Paris: Palais des Beaux-Arts. *Exposition Pierre-Paul Prud'hon*. Exh. cat., 1922.

PARIS 1928
Paris: Galerie Buvelot. *Exposition du centenaire de Houdon*. Exh. cat., 1928.

PARIS 1937
Paris: Palais National des Arts. *Chefs-d'oeuvre de l'art français*. Exh. cat., 1937.

PARIS 1948
Paris: Musée de l'Orangerie. *David: Exposition en l'honneur du deuxième centenaire de sa naissance*. Exh. cat., 1948.

PARIS 1950
Paris: Musée Carnavalet. *Chefs-d'oeuvre des collections parisiennes*. Exh. cat., 1950.

PARIS 1958
Paris: Musée Jacquemart-André. *Prud'hon*. Exh. cat., 1958.

PARIS 1968
Paris: Petit Palais. *Ingres*. Exh. cat., 1968.

PARIS 1973–74
Paris: Musée du Louvre. *Dessins français du Metropolitan Museum of Art, New York, de David à Picasso*. Exh. cat., 1973–74.

PARIS 1974A
Paris: Centre Culturel Suédois. *Louis-Jean Desprez, 1743–1804: Peintre, graveur, architecte et décorateur de théâtre en Italie et en Suède*. Exh. cat., 1974.

PARIS 1974B
Paris: Grand Palais. *Ossian*. Exh. cat., 1974.

PARIS 1974–75
Paris: Grand Palais. *Le Néo-Classicisme français: Dessins des musées de province*. Exh. cat., 1974–75.

PARIS 1979
Paris: Musée du Louvre. *Dessins français du XIXe siècle du Musée Bonnat à Bayonne*. Exh. cat., 1979.

PARIS 1983
Paris: Mairie du IVe Arrondissement. *Dessins de Canova du Musée de Bassano*. Exh. cat., 1983.

PARIS 1983–84
Paris: Grand Palais. *Raphaël et l'art français*. Exh. cat., 1983–84.

PARIS 1984
Paris: Grand Palais. *L'Age d'or de la peinture danoise, 1800–1850*. Exh. cat., 1984.

PARIS 1984–85
Paris: Hôtel de la Monnaie. *Diderot & l'art de Boucher à David: Les Salons 1759–1781*. Exh. cat., 1984–85.

PARIS 1986
Paris: Musée du Louvre. *Prud'hon: "La Justice et la vengeance poursuivant le crime."* Exh. cat. by Sylvain Laveissière, 1986.

PARIS 1987–88
Paris: Grand Palais. *Fragonard*. Exh. cat. by Pierre Rosenberg, 1987–88.

PARIS 1989A
Paris: Grand Palais. *La Révolution française et l'Europe 1789–1799*. 3 vols. Exh. cat., 1989.

PARIS 1989B
Paris: Musée du Louvre, Cabinet des dessins. *Le Beau Idéal, ou L'Art du concept*. Exh. cat. by Régis Michel, 1989.

PARIS 1991
Paris: Grand Palais. *Les Amours des dieux: La Peinture mythologique de Watteau à David*. Exh. cat. by Colin Bailey, 1991.

PARIS 1991–92
Paris: Grand Palais. *Géricault*. Exh. cat., 1991–92.

PARIS N.D.
Paris: Patrick Perrin. *De Lebrun à Rodin*. Exh. cat., n.d.

PARIS/DETROIT/NEW YORK 1974–75
Paris: Grand Palais/Detroit: The Detroit Institute of Arts/New York: The Metropolitan Museum of Art. *French Painting 1774–1830: The Age of Revolution*. Exh. cat., 1974–75.

PARIS/ROTTERDAM/NEW YORK 1958–59
Paris: Musée de l'Orangerie/Rotterdam: Museum Boymans/New York: The Metropolitan Museum of Art. *French Drawings from American Collections, Clouet to Matisse*. Exh. cat., 1958–59.

PARIS/VERSAILLES 1989–90
Paris: Musée du Louvre/Versailles: Musée National du Château. *Jacques-Louis David, 1748–1825*. Exh. cat. by Antoine Schnapper, Arlette Sérullaz, et al., 1989–90.

PARKER 1930
R. A. Parker. "Notes on Drawings at the Fogg Museum." *International Studio* 95, no. 392 (January 1930): 36–40.

PAVENELLO/PRAZ 1976
Giuseppe Pavanello and Mario Praz. *L'opera completa del Canova*. Milan: Rizzoli, 1976.

PELZEL 1979
Thomas Pelzel. *Anton Raphael Mengs*. New York: Garland Publishing, 1979.

PHILADELPHIA 1947
Philadelphia: Philadelphia Museum of Art. *Masterpieces of Philadelphia Private Collections*. Exh. cat., 1947.

PHILADELPHIA 1949
Philadelphia: Philadelphia Museum of Art. *The Henry P. McIlhenny Collection*, 1949.

PHILADELPHIA 1980–81
Philadelphia: Philadelphia Museum of Art. *A Scholar Collects: Selections from the Anthony Morris Clark Bequest*. Exh. cat. edited by Ulrich W. Hiesinger and Ann Percy, 1980–81.

PIGLER 1956
A. Pigler. *Barockthemen: Eine Auswahl von Verzeichnissen zur Ikonographie des 17. und 18. Jahrhunderts.* 2 vols. Budapest: Verlag der Ungarischen Akademie der Wissenschaften, 1956.

PINDAR 1972
Pindar. *The Odes of Pindar.* Translated by Geoffrey S. Conway. London: J. M. Dent and Sons, 1972.

PITTSBURGH 1951
Pittsburgh: Carnegie Institute. *French Paintings, 1100–1900.* Exh. cat., 1951.

PITTSBURGH 1979
Pittsburgh: Carnegie Institute. *French Masterpieces of the 19th Century from the Henry P. McIlhenny Collection,* 1979.

PITTSBURGH 1992
Pittsburgh: Frick Art Museum. *The Real and the Spiritual: Nineteenth-Century French Drawings from the Musée des Beaux-Arts du Lyon.* Exh. cat., 1992.

PLUTARCH 1802
Oeuvres morales de Plutarque. Translated by Jacques Amyot. 4 vols. Paris: Cussac, 1802.

PLUTARCH 1821
Plutarch's Lives. Translated by John Langhorne and William Langhorne. 8 vols. London: Richardson, 1821.

PORÉE 1907
A. Porée. "Quelques Lettres de peintres français." In *La Correspondance historique et archéologique.* Paris, 1907, 285.

PORTALIS 1877
Baron Roger Portalis. *Les Dessinateurs d'illustrations au dix- huitième siècle.* 2 vols. Paris: Damascène Morgand et Charles Fatout, 1877.

PORTALIS 1880
Baron Roger Portalis. "La Collection Walferdin et ses Fragonards." *Gazette des Beaux-Arts,* ser. 2, 21 (April 1880): 297–322.

PORTALIS 1889
Baron Roger Portalis. *Honoré Fragonard: Sa Vie et son oeuvre.* Paris: J. Rothschild, 1889.

POSNER 1971
Donald Posner. *Annibale Carracci: A Study in the Reform of Italian Painting around 1590.* 2 vols. London: Phaidon, 1971.

POWELL 1952
Nicolas Powell. "Brown and the Women of Rome." *Signature,* n.s., no. 14 (1952): 40–50.

PRESTON 1952
Kerrison Preston, ed. *The Blake Collection of W. Graham Robertson, Described by the Collector.* London: Faber and Faber, 1952.

PRESTON 1960
Stuart Preston. "Current and Forthcoming Exhibitions, New York." *The Burlington Magazine* 102, no. 682 (January 1960): 47–48.

PRINCETON 1977
Princeton: The Art Museum, Princeton University. *Eighteenth-Century Life-Drawing.* Exh. cat., 1977.

PRINCETON 1981
Princeton: The Art Museum, Princeton University. *Princeton Alumni Collections: Works on Paper.* Exh. cat. by Allen Rosenbaum, 1981.

PRINCETON 1983
Princeton: The Art Museum, Princeton University. *Sixteenth- to Eighteenth-Century French Drawings from the Permanent Collection.* Exh. cat., 1983.

PRINCETON 1989
Princeton: The Art Museum, Princeton University. *Central European Drawings 1680–1800: A Selection from American Collections.* Exh. cat., 1989.

PROVIDENCE 1957
Providence: Museum of Art, Rhode Island School of Design. *The Age of Canova.* Exh. cat., 1957.

PROVIDENCE 1975
Providence: Museum of Art, Rhode Island School of Design. *Rubenism.* Exh. cat., 1975.

PROVIDENCE 1983
Providence: Museum of Art, Rhode Island School of Design. *Old Master Drawings from the Museum of Art, Rhode Island School of Design.* Exh. cat., 1983.

PRUD'HON 1857–58
Pierre-Paul Prud'hon. "Lettres écrites par Pierre-Paul Prud'hon à MM. Devosge et Fauconnier pendant son voyage d'Italie." Edited by Frédéric Villot. *Archives de l'art français* 5 (1857–58): 97–170.

QUATREMÈRE DE QUINCY 1834
Antoine-Chrysostome Quatremère de Quincy. *Canova et ses ouvrages, ou Mémoires historiques sur la vie et les travaux de ce célèbre artiste.* Paris: Adrien Le Clere et Cie, 1834.

RACINE 1801
Jean Racine. *Oeuvres de Racine.* Paris: Pierre Didot l'Aîné, 1801.

RACINE 1813
Jean Racine. *Théatre de Jean Racine, orné de cinquante-sept estampes d'apres les dessins de MM. Prud'hon, Gérard, Girodet, Chaudet, Serangeli et Peyron.* Paris: Pierre Didot l'Aîné, 1813.

RALEIGH 1967
Raleigh: North Carolina Museum of Art. *North Carolina Collects.* Exh. cat., 1967.

RAY 1982
Gordon N. Ray. *The Art of the French Illustrated Book, 1700 to 1914.* New York: The Pierpont Morgan Library, 1982. Reprint, New York: Dover Publications, 1986.

RÉAU 1956
Louis Réau. *Fragonard: Sa Vie et son oeuvre.* Brussels: Elzevier, 1956.

REGNAULT 1808
F.-L. Regnault. *Catalogue de tableaux, gouaches et dessins de différens maîtres . . . Estampes anciennes et modernes encadrées et en feuilles . . . après le décès de Mr. Guyot, graveur et marchand d'estampes.* Paris, 1808.

REINACH 1897–1910
Salomon Reinach. *Répertoire de la statuaire grecque et romaine.* 4 vols. Paris: Ernest Leroux, 1897–1910.

REINACH 1909–12
Salomon Reinach. *Répertoire de reliefs grecs et romains.* 3 vols. Paris: Ernest Leroux, 1909–12.

REINACH 1922–24
Salomon Reinach. *Répertoire des vases peint, grecs et étrusques.* 2 vols. 2d ed. Paris: Ernest Leroux, 1924.

RICHTER 1906
Helene Richter. *William Blake.* Strasbourg: J. H. Ed. Heitz, 1906.

RIGON 1982
Fernando Rigon. *Disegni di Canova al Museo di Bassano.* Milan: Electa, 1982.

ROLAND MICHEL 1987
Marianne Roland Michel. *Le Dessin français au dix-huitième siècle.* Fribourg: Office du Livre, 1987.

ROME 1968
Rome: Villa Medici (Académie de France). *Ingres in Italia (1806–1824/1835–1841).* Exh. cat., 1968.

ROME 1981–82
Rome: Villa Medici (Académie de France). *David et Rome/David e Roma.* Exh. cat., 1981–82.

ROME 1986
Rome: École Française de Rome. *Annibale Carracci e i suoi incisori.* Exh. cat., 1986.

ROME 1989
Rome: Galleria Nazionale d'Arte Moderna. *Bertel Thorvaldsen.* Exh. cat., 1989.

ROME 1990–91
Rome: Villa Medici (Académie de France). *Fragonard e Hubert Robert a Roma.* Exh. cat., 1990–91.

ROME/DIJON 1983
Rome: Villa Medici (Académie de France)/Dijon: Musée des Beaux-Arts. *Bénigne Gagnereaux (1756–1795): Un Peintre bourguignon dans la Rome néo-classique*. Exh. cat., 1983.

ROMNEY 1830
John Romney. *Memoirs of the Life and Works of George Romney* . . . . London: Baldwin and Cradock, 1830.

ROSCHACH 1920
Ernest Roschach. *Catalogue des collections de peinture du Musée de Toulouse*. Toulouse: Édouard Privat, 1920.

ROSENBERG/REYNAUD/COMPIN 1974
Pierre Rosenberg, Nicole Reynaud, and Isabelle Compin. *Musée du Louvre, catalogue illustré des peintures: École française XVIIe et XVIIIe siècles*. 2 vols. Paris: Éditions des musées nationaux, 1974.

ROSENBERG/VAN DE SANDT 1983
Pierre Rosenberg and Udolpho van de Sandt. *Pierre Peyron, 1744–1814*. Neuilly-sur-Seine: Arthena, 1983.

ROSENBLUM 1957
Robert Rosenblum. "The Origin of Painting: A Problem in the Iconography of Romantic Classicism." *The Art Bulletin* 39, no. 4 (December 1957): 279–90.

ROSENBLUM 1967A
Robert Rosenblum. *Jean-Auguste-Dominique Ingres*. London: Thames and Hudson, 1967.

ROSENBLUM 1967B
Robert Rosenblum. *Transformations in Late Eighteenth-Century Art*. Princeton: Princeton University Press, 1967.

ROSENBLUM 1976
Robert Rosenblum. *The International Style of 1800: A Study in Linear Abstraction*. New York: Garland Publishing, 1976.

ROSS 1983
Barbara T. Ross. "Notes on Selected French Old Master Drawings from the Permanent Collection." *Record of The Art Museum, Princeton University* 42, no. 1 (1983): 4–42.

ROSSETTI 1880
William Rossetti. "Annotated Catalogue of Blake's Pictures and Drawings." In Alexander Gilchrist, *Life of William Blake*. London: Macmillan, 1880.

ROTTERDAM/PARIS/NEW YORK 1958–59
Rotterdam: Museum Boymans-van Beuningen/ Paris: Musée de l'Orangerie/New York: The Metropolitan Museum of Art. *French Drawings from American Collections, Clouet to Matisse*. Exh. cat., 1958–59.

ROUEN 1970
Rouen: Bibliothèque Municipale. *Choix de dessins anciens, Bibliothèque Municipale de Rouen*. Exh. cat. by Pierre Rosenberg and Antoine Schnapper, 1970.

RUBIN 1972
James Henry Rubin. "An Early Romantic Polemic: Girodet and Milton." *The Art Quarterly* 35, no. 3 (Autumn 1972): 211–37.

RUBIN 1973
James Henry Rubin. "Oedipus, Antigone and Exiles in Post-Revolutionary French Painting." *The Art Quarterly* 36, no. 3 (Autumn 1973): 141–71.

RUBIN 1979
James Henry Rubin. "Gros and Girodet." *The Burlington Magazine* 121, no. 920 (November 1979): 716–21.

RUBIN 1980
James Henry Rubin. "Aesthetic Subversion of Politics in Girodet's Riot of Cairo." *Proceedings of the Consortium of Revolutionary Europe, 1750–1850*, no. 2 (1980): 95–105.

SACRAMENTO 1939
Sacramento: E. B. Crocker Art Gallery. *Old Master Drawings from the E. B. Crocker Collection: The German Masters, 15th to 19th Centuries*. Exh. cat., 1939.

SACRAMENTO 1971
Sacramento: E. B. Crocker Art Gallery. *Master Drawings from Sacramento*. Exh. cat., 1971.

SACRAMENTO 1972
Sacramento: E. B. Crocker Art Gallery. *Classical Narrative in Master Drawings Selected from the Collection of the E. B. Crocker Art Gallery*. Exh. cat., 1972.

SANDOZ 1960
Marc Sandoz. "Nicolas-Guy Brenet, peintre d'histoire (1728–1792)." *Bulletin de la société de l'histoire de l'art français* (1960): 33.

SANDOZ 1983
Marc Sandoz. *Les Lagrenée: I. Louis-Jean-François Lagrenée 1725–1805*. Paris: Éditart/Les Quatre Chemins, 1983.

SANDOZ 1988
Marc Sandoz. *Les Lagrenée: II. Jean-Jacques Lagrenée 1739–1821*. Paris: Éditart/Les Quatre Chemins, 1988.

SAN FRANCISCO 1962
San Francisco: California Palace of the Legion of Honor. *The Henry P. McIlhenny Collection*. Exh. cat., 1962.

SAN FRANCISCO 1989–90
San Francisco: The Fine Arts Museums of San Francisco, California Palace of the Legion of Honor. *Works of Art from the Collection of Mr. & Mrs. John Jay Ide*. Exh. cat., 1989–90.

SANTA BARBARA 1976
Santa Barbara: University Art Galleries, University of California Santa Barbara. *William Blake in the Art of His Time*. Exh. cat., 1976.

SAUVAGE 1960
Micheline Sauvage. *Socrates and the Human Conscience*. New York: Harper, 1960.

SCHEYER 1941
Ernst Scheyer. "French Drawings of the Great Revolution and the Napoleonic Era." *The Art Quarterly* 4, no. 3 (Summer 1941): 187–204.

SCHEYER 1949
Ernst Scheyer. "German Paintings and Drawings from the Time of Goethe in American Collections." *The Art Quarterly* 12, no. 3 (Summer 1949): 231–56.

SCHIFF 1973
Gert Schiff. *Johann Heinrich Füssli 1741–1825*. 2 vols. Zurich: Berichthaus/Munich: Prestel, 1973.

SCHLEGEL 1846
A. W. von Schlegel. "Schreiben an Goethe über einige Arbeiten in Rom lebender Künstler im Sommer 1805." In *Sämmtliche Werke*, vol. 9. Leipzig: Weidmannsche Buchhandlung, 1846.

SCHLESWIG 1992
Schloss Gottorf, Schleswig: Schleswig-Holsteinisches Landesmuseum. *Asmus Jakob Carstens: Goethes Erwerbungen für Weimar*. Cat. by Renate Barth, 1992.

SCHLUMBERGER 1972
Eveline Schlumberger. "Le Néo-classicisme regardé de plus près." *Connaissance des arts*, no. 247 (September 1972): 78–89.

SCHNAPPER 1982
Antoine Schnapper. *David*. Translated by Helga Harrison. New York: Alpine Fine Arts Collection, 1982.

SEELIG 1990
Lorenz Seelig. "Tableaux des néo-classicismes français et belge de la Résidence de Coblence." *Revue de l'art*, no. 87 (1990): 52–58.

SELLS 1977
Christopher Sells. "Socrate et Alcibiade de J.-B. Regnault au Louvre." *Revue du Louvre* 27, nos. 5/6 (1977): 354–57.

SENECA 1902
Lucius Annaeus Seneca. *The Ten Tragedies*. Translated by Watson Bradshaw. London: Swan Sonnenschein and Company, 1902.

SÉRULLAZ 1976
Arlette Sérullaz. "À Propos d'un album de dessins de Jean-Germain Drouais au Musée de Rennes." *Revue du Louvre* 26, nos. 5/6 (1976): 380–87.

SÉRULLAZ 1991
Arlette Sérullaz. *Inventaire général des dessins: École française, dessins de Jacques-Louis David, 1748–1825*. Paris: Réunion des Musées Nationaux, 1991.

SHOOLMAN/SLATKIN 1950
Regina Shoolman and Charles E. Slatkin. *Six Centuries of French Master Drawings in America*. New York: Oxford University Press, 1950.

SIMONS 1985
Katrin Simons. *Jacques Réattu, 1760–1833: Peintre de la révolution française*. Neuilly-sur-Seine: Arthena, 1985.

SLAYMAN 1970
James Hugus Slayman. "The Drawings of Pierre-Paul Prud'hon: A Critical Study." Ph.D. diss., University of Wisconsin, 1970.

SMYRNAEUS 1962
Quintus Smyrnaeus. *The Fall of Troy*. Translated by Arthur S. Way. London: William Heinemann/ Cambridge: Harvard University Press, 1962.

SNODIN/BAKER 1980
Michael Snodin and Malcolm Baker. "William Beckford's Silver." *The Burlington Magazine* 122, nos. 932–33 (November–December 1980): 735–48 (November), 830–34 (December).

SOPHOCLES 1892
Sophocles. *The Oedipus at Colonus of Sophocles*. Translated by Edward P. Coleridge. London/New York: George Bell and Sons, 1892.

SPENCE 1949
Lewis Spence. *The History and Origins of Druidism*. London: Rider and Company, 1949.

STAATLICHE MUSEEN ZU BERLIN 1980
Kunst der Welt in den Berliner Museen. Kunstbibliothek und Museum für Architektur, Modebild und Grafik-Design. Stuttgart: Belser, 1980.

STECHOW 1945
Wolfgang Stechow. "The Love of Antiochus with Faire Stratonica." *The Art Bulletin* 27, no. 4 (December 1945): 221–37.

STEIN 1912
Henri Stein. *Augustin Pajou*. Paris: Librairie Central des Beaux-Arts, 1912.

STOCKHOLM 1990
Stockholm: Nationalmuseum. *Sergel*. Exh. cat., 1990.

STRONG 1976
Donald Strong. *Roman Art*. Harmondsworth, Middlesex: Penguin Books, 1976.

SUNDERLAND 1988
John Sunderland. *John Hamilton Mortimer: His Life and Works*. London: Walpole Society, 1988.

SWARZENSKI 1921
Georg Swarzenski. *Franzöische Meister der Achtzehnten Jahrhunderts, Facsimiles nach Zeichnungen und Aquarellen*. Munich: Verlag der Marées-Gesellschaft, R. Piper and Co., 1921.

SYMMONS 1984
Sarah Symmons. *Flaxman and Europe: The Outline Illustrations and Their Influence*. New York: Garland Publishing, 1984.

TAMBRONI 1816
Giuseppe Tambroni. *Descrizione dei dipinti a buon fresco eseguiti in una galleria del palazzo del Sig. Duca di Bracciano in Roma dal Pelagio Palagi*. Rome: Nella Stamperia de Romanis, 1816.

TASSO 1852
Torquato Tasso. *The Jerusalem Delivered*. Translated by J. H. Wiffen. New York: D. Appleton and Co., 1852.

TERNOIS 1970
Daniel Ternois. "Napoléon et la décoration du Palais Impérial de Monte Cavallo en 1811–1813." *Revue de l'art*, no. 7 (1970): 68–89.

TERNOIS 1980
Daniel Ternois. *Ingres*. Paris: Nathan, 1980.

THIELE 1851–54
J. M. Thiele. *Thorvaldsens Biographi*. 3 vols. Copenhagen: C. A. Reitzel, 1851–54.

THOMÉ 1826
A. Thomé. *Vie de David, premier peintre de Napoléon*. Brussels: H. Tarlier et Grignon, Maison Baudoin Frères, 1826.

THUCYDIDES 1934
The Complete Writings of Thucydides. Translated by R. Crawley. New York: Modern Library, 1934.

THUILLIER 1967
Jacques Thuillier. *Fragonard*. Geneva: Skira, 1967.

TILLY 1986
Andrew Tilly. *Erotic Drawings*. New York: Rizzoli, 1986.

TILLYARD 1987
Virginia Tillyard. "New York, Nineteenth-Century Works on Paper." *The Burlington Magazine* 129, no. 1010 (May 1987): 350–51.

TINTI 1936
Mario Tinti. *Lorenzo Bartolini*. Rome: Reale Accadèmia d'Italia, 1936.

TISCHBEIN 1922
Johann Heinrich Tischbein. Edited by Lothar Brieger. *Aus meinem Leben*. Berlin: Propyläen-Verlag, 1922.

TOKYO/KYOTO 1980
Tokyo: National Museum of Western Art/Kyoto: Kyoto Municipal Museum. *Fragonard*. Exh. cat. by Denys Sutton, 1980.

TORONTO 1962
Toronto: Art Gallery. *Héritage de France*. Exh. cat., 1962.

TORONTO/OTTAWA/SAN FRANCISCO/NEW YORK 1972–73
Toronto: Art Gallery of Ontario/Ottawa: National Gallery of Canada/San Francisco: California Palace of the Legion of Honor/New York: New York Cultural Center. *French Master Drawings of the 17th and 18th Centuries in North American Collections*. Exh. cat. by Pierre Rosenberg; translated by Catherine Johnston, 1972–73.

TOUSSAINT 1974
Hélène Toussaint. "Ossian." *Le Petit Journal des grandes expositions* (February 16–April 15, 1974): 4.

VAISSE 1974
Pierre Vaisse. "Ossian et les peintres du XIXe siècle: Notes à propos d'une exposition." *L'Information d'histoire de l'art* (March/April 1974): 82.

VASARI 1897
Giorgio Vasari. *Lives of Seventy Painters, Sculptors and Architects*. Translated, edited, and annotated by E. H. and E. W. Blashfield and A. A. Hopkins. 4 vols. New York: Scribner, 1897.

VENICE 1978
Venice: Museo Correr. *Venezia dell età di Canova, 1780–1830*. Exh. cat. by Elena Bassi et al., 1978.

VENICE 1985–86
Venice: Museo Correr. *Disegni dalle collezioni del Museo Correr: XV–XIX Secolo*. Exh. cat., 1985–86.

VERDI 1982
Richard Verdi. "London: Summer Exhibitions." *The Burlington Magazine* 124, no. 953 (August 1982): 518–21.

VERMEULE 1964
Cornelius C. Vermeule. *European Art and the Classical Past*. Cambridge: Harvard University Press, 1964.

VERSAILLES 1928
Versailles: Bibliothèque. *Exposition du centenaire de Houdon*. Exh. cat., 1928.

VIRCH 1962
Claus Virch. *Master Drawings in the Collection of Walter C. Baker*. New York: The Metropolitan Museum of Art, 1962.

VITRY 1928A
Paul Vitry. "Le Centenaire de Houdon." *La Revue de l'art ancien et moderne* 54 (June–August 1928): 9–21 (June), 57–70 (July/August).

VITRY 1928B
Paul Vitry. "Houdon dessinateur." *Beaux-Arts*, no. 7 (April 1, 1928): 100–101.

VITRY/BRIÈRE 1969
Paul Vitry and Gaston Brière. *Documents de sculpture française*. New York: Arno Press, 1969.

VOLKMANN/CADOUX 1958
Hans Volkmann and T. J. Cadoux. *Cleopatra*. London: Elek Books, 1958.

WALCH 1967
Peter Walch. "Charles Rollin and Early Neoclassicism." *The Art Bulletin* 49, no. 2 (June 1967): 226–27.

WALDEMAR GEORGE 1967
Waldemar George. *Dessins d'Ingres*. Paris: Éditions du Colombier, 1967.

WALLACE COLLECTION 1968
London: Wallace Collection. *Wallace Collection Catalogues: Pictures and Drawings*, 1968.

WARK 1970
Robert R. Wark. *Drawings by John Flaxman in the Huntington Collection*. San Marino: Henry E. Huntington Library and Art Gallery, 1970.

WASHINGTON 1967
Washington, D.C.: National Collections of Fine Arts. *Treasures from the Cooper Union Museum*. Exh. cat., 1967.

WASHINGTON 1974
Washington, D.C.: National Gallery of Art. *Recent Accessions and Promised Gifts: Sculpture, Drawings, Prints*. Exh. cat., 1974.

WASHINGTON 1978
Washington, D.C.: National Gallery of Art. *Drawings by Fragonard in North American Collections*. Exh. cat. by Eunice Williams, 1978.

WASHINGTON 1983
Washington, D.C.: National Gallery of Art. *Piazzetta: A Tercentenary Exhibition of Drawings, Prints, and Books*. Exh. cat., 1983.

WASHINGTON 1988
Washington, D.C.: National Gallery of Art. *Master Drawings from the National Gallery of Art of Canada*. Exh. cat., 1988.

WESTON 1981
Helen Weston. "London: Prud'hon at Wildenstein's and the Heim Gallery." *The Burlington Magazine* 123, no. 941 (August 1981): 501.

WESTON 1984
Helen Weston. "Prud'hon in Rome—Pages from an Unpublished Sketchbook." *The Burlington Magazine* 126, no. 970 (January 1984): 6–19.

WILDENSTEIN 1973
Daniel and Georges Wildenstein. *Documents complémentaires au catalogue de l'oeuvre de Louis David*. Paris: Fondation Wildenstein/La Bibliothèque des arts, 1973.

WILLIAMS 1979
Eunice Williams. "Rescuing Fragonard from a Kind of Limbo." *Art News* 78, no. 5 (May 1979): 74–78.

WILLIAMSTOWN 1979
Williamstown, Massachusetts: Sterling and Francine Clark Art Institute. *Master Drawings from the Collection of Ingrid and Julius S. Held*. Exh. cat. by Laura Giles, Elizabeth Milroy, and Gwendolyn Owens, 1979.

WINCKELMANN 1872
John [Johann Joachim] Winckelmann. *The History of Ancient Art*. Translated by G. Henry Lodge. 4 vols. in 2. Boston and New York: Houghton, Mifflin and Company, 1872.

WINCKELMANN 1972
Johann Joachim Winckelmann. *Winckelmann: Writings on Art*. Ed. David Irwin. London: Phaidon, 1972.

WISNER 1990
David A. Wisner. "Une Esquisse peinte de J.-J.-F. Le Barbier: 'Lycurgue présantant aux Spartiates leur nouveau Roi' (1791)." *Gazette des Beaux-Arts*, ser. 6, 116 (October 1990): 129–36.

WITTKOWER 1973
Rudolf Wittkower. *Art and Architecture in Italy, 1600–1750*. 3d ed. Harmondsworth, Middlesex: Penguin Books, 1973.

WOOD 1978
William P. Wood. "Annual Report." *Philadelphia Museum of Art Bulletin* 74, no. 323 (December 1978): 2–8.

ZIESENISS 1966
Charles Otto Zieseniss. "Le Décor de la galerie de Diane aux Tuileries sous le premier Empire." *Bulletin de la Société de l'Histoire de l'Art Français*, 1966 (published 1967): 199–235.

Index

References to black-and-white illustrations are in *italics*, color plates in ***bold italics***.